About This Book

This book is designed to help you teach yourself the new and necessary aspects of programming with Turbo C++ 4.5. In 21 days, you'll learn about such fundamentals as the Turbo C++ 4.5 environment, managing I/O, loops and arrays, object-oriented programming, game programming OLE2, VBX creation, and creating basic OWL applications—all in well-structured and easy-to-follow lessons. Each lesson provides a sample listing—complete with sample output and an analysis of the code—to illustrate the topics of the day. Syntax examples are clearly marked for handy reference.

To help you become more proficient, each lesson ends with a set of common questions and answers, exercises, and a quiz. You can check your progress by examining the quiz answers provided in the book's appendix.

Who Should Read This Book

You don't need any previous experience in programming to learn Turbo C++ with this book. You'll find the numerous examples of syntax and detailed analysis of code an excellent guide as you begin your journey into this rewarding environment. If you have programmed before or have some familiarity with C++, you will see that this book treats many important new features of the Turbo product. Whether you are just beginning or need only to learn the latest about Turbo C++ 4.5, this book's clear organization makes doing so fast and easy.

Conventions

 Note: These boxes highlight information that can make your Turbo C++ 4.5 programming more efficient and effective.

 Warning: These boxes focus your attention on problems or side effects that can occur in specific situations.

NEW TERM These boxes provide clear definitions of essential terms.

DO DON'T **DO** use the "Do/Don't" boxes to find a quick summary of a fundamental principle in a lesson.

DON'T overlook the useful information offered in these boxes.

This book uses various typefaces to help you distinguish C++ code from regular English. Actual C++ code is typeset is a special `monospace` font. Placeholders—words or characters used to represent the real words or characters you would type in code—are typeset in *`italic monospace`*. New or important terms are typeset in *italic*.

In the listings in this book, each real code line is numbered. If you see an unnumbered line in a listing, you'll know that the unnumbered line is really a continuation of the preceding numbered code line (some code lines are too long for the width of the book).

Teach Yourself
Turbo C++ 4.5
for Windows
in 21 Days

Teach Yourself
Turbo C++ 4.5
for Windows
in 21 Days

Craig Arnush

SAMS
PUBLISHING

201 West 103rd Street
Indianapolis, Indiana 46290

This book is dedicated to René for her patience and support.

Copyright © 1995 by Sams Publishing

International Standard Book Number: 0-672-30727-8

Library of Congress Catalog Card Number: 95-67646

98   97   96   95   4   3   2   1

Interpretation of the printing code: the rightmost double-digit number is the year of the book's printing; the rightmost single-digit, the number of the book's printing. For example, a printing code of 95-1 shows that the first printing of the book occurred in 1995.

Composed in AGaramond and MCPdigital by Macmillan Computer Publishing

Printed in the United States of America

Trademarks

Overview

Appendix

Contents

Appendix

Acknowledgments

I would like to thank Grace Buechlein at Sams Publishing for having the patience to deal with the likes of me. Also, thanks to Dean Miller, who listened to my suggestions and even liked my bugs; and Jill Bond, who had some insightful comments on my prose. My thanks go out to all those at Sams who participated in putting this book together.

Another hearty thank you goes out to Bruneau Babet's diligence in picking up on all the twiddly bits I had missed. He must surely have been more awake than I.

A very special dedication to Ian Spencer who appeared in a crisis, waved his wand, and made the problems disappear. Thanks, Ian. I needed that.

Last but by *absolutely no means* least, super-special thanks with sugar on top go out to all the people who took the time to contact me and let me know where I had screwed up in earlier incarnations of this book: Greg Bowerbank, Matt Clayton, Manuel Derieux, John Fischer, Huy Viet Le, Aaron Moy, Brian Poff, and Jim Willeke.

About the Author

Craig Arnush is an independent software consultant in San Diego and is an expert on Windows. He volunteers his time answering technical questions on the Borland CompuServe forums as a member of Team Borland. Craig can be reached via his CompuServe account at 71333,3052 or via the Internet at craiga@netcom.com.

Introduction

This book has three major goals: to teach you to program in C++, teach you to create Windows applications using Turbo C++, and teach you the new features of Turbo C++ 4.5. No prior programming experience is required. However, knowing how to program in other languages, such as BASIC or Pascal, certainly helps. This book is not for the faint-hearted, because becoming familiar with the new features of a new compiler is hard enough, but also learning to program in C++ and learning to write Windows applications in C++ are two nontrivial tasks!

The book contains 21 chapters, one for each study day. The material is somewhat fast-paced in order to meet the goals of the book. Each chapter contains a Q&A section, a Quiz section, and an Exercise section. Appendix A provides the answers to the quizzes and to many of the exercises.

Day 1 gives you a brief tour of the Turbo C++ IDE, the Windows environment that you use to develop C++ programs. This chapter also presents your first C++ program to demonstrate the basic components of a non-Windows C++ program.

Day 2 looks at C++ program components in more detail. This chapter discusses the preprocessor as well as naming and declaring variables, constants, and functions. This book also provides an early focus on C++ functions because they are important program building blocks.

Day 3 covers C++ decision-making constructs and loops. The constructs include the various types of if statements as well as the switch statement, while loops include the for, while, and do-while loops. The chapter demonstrates how to use the for loop as an open loop. In addition, the chapter discusses skipping loop iterations, exiting loops, and nesting loops.

Day 4 covers user-defined types and pointers. This chapter discusses enumerated data types, structures, unions, reference variables, and pointers. The text demonstrates how to declare and use pointers with simple variables, arrays, structures, and dynamic memory.

Day 5 examines functions and how they are constructed. This chapter discusses the differences between preprocessor macros, regular functions, and inline functions.

Day 6 presents arrays in C++. This chapter covers both single-dimensional and multidimensional arrays and discusses how to declare them and initialize them. In addition, this chapter discusses sorting and searching single-dimensional arrays.

Day 7 focuses on strings and the STRING.H library, which is inherited from C. The chapter covers topics such as assigning, concatenating, comparing, converting, and reversing strings. In addition, this chapter discusses searching for characters and substrings in strings before moving on to formatted stream input and output, as well the famous printf function. The latter function supports versatile formatted output.

Day 8 introduces you to the world of object-oriented programming (OOP). This chapter covers the basics of OOP and presents C++ classes. The text discusses the basic components of a C++ class and the rules related to using these components.

Day 9 discusses the basic stream file I/O, which is supported by the C++ stream library. This chapter covers common stream functions, sequential text stream I/O, sequential binary stream I/O, and random-access stream I/O.

Day 10 covers the string class, an alternative to strings, and the functions in STRING.H that work with them. This class conforms to the preliminary strings class from the ANSI C++ committee and is prototyped in the header file CSTRING.H. This chapter then goes on to discuss templates and the Borland Class Library.

Day 11 presents very simple OWL-based Windows applications. Object Windows Library version 2.5, or OWL 2.5, is included with Turbo C++ 4.5. It is a C++ library for use in Windows programming, and using it shortens the time and effort in developing a Windows program.

Day 12 focuses on drawing text in a window. This chapter presents both nonscrolling and scrolling windows and illustrates how to draw text (as graphics) in these windows.

Day 13 presents the OWL library classes, which model static text controls, edit controls, and pushbutton controls. This chapter also presents a nontrivial command-oriented line calculator as an example that uses these controls.

Day 14 focuses on creating and using dialog boxes. This chapter shows you how to use resource files to define modal and modeless dialog boxes. In addition, this chapter discusses data transfer between a dialog box and its parent window.

Day 15 presents the OWL library classes that model the check box control, the radio button control, and the group control.

Day 16 covers the OWL library class that models list box controls. This chapter discusses both single-selection and multiple-selection list boxes. The programs in the chapter illustrate both types of list boxes.

Day 17 presents the OWL library classes, which model the scroll bar control and the combo box control. This chapter also discusses how to create history boxes using combo boxes. In addition, the chapter presents a version of the calculator program that uses the combo boxes. Finally, VBXs are introduced and explained.

Day 18 looks at Multiple Document Interface (MDI) windows. The chapter presents the classes that support MDI-compliant applications and illustrates how to manage MDI-child windows.

Day 19 shows how to use the Application and Class Experts to automatically generate the skeleton of your Windows applications, then modify them in a browser-like atmosphere.

Day 20 describes OLE2 and how it's implemented by Borland's ObjectComponents Framework (OCF). This chapter concentrates on how OCF is integrated into OWL.

Day 21 gives a quick tutorial on some simple debugging techniques. No program is perfect, but this chapter will help you get as close to perfect as possible.

The book contains Windows programs that illustrate aspects of programming that go beyond the trivial aspects of using various visual controls. Study these programs, as they contain techniques and tricks that can enrich your Windows programming. We all learn to program by looking at examples (including nontrivial ones) and by asking friends questions.

> **Note:** You can obtain the source code and the project files presented in this book by downloading the files from CompuServe; type **GO SAMS**. The files can be found in the Sams Programming Library 9.
>
> The files are also available via anonymous FTP to `ftp.netcom.com` in the `pub/cr/craiga` directory.

Happy programming!

About This Book

This book is designed to help you teach yourself the new and necessary aspects of programming with Turbo C++ 4.5. In 21 days, you'll learn about such fundamentals as the Turbo C++ 4.5 environment, managing I/O, loops and arrays, object-oriented programming, creating basic OWL applications, and using OLE2—all in well-structured and easy-to-follow lessons. Each lesson provides a sample listing—complete with sample output and an analysis of the code—to illustrate the topics of the day. Syntax examples are clearly marked for handy reference.

To help you become more proficient, each lesson ends with a set of common questions and answers, exercises, and a quiz. You can check your progress by examining the quiz answers provided in the book's appendix.

Who Should Read This Book

You don't need any previous experience in programming to learn Turbo C++ with this book. You'll find the numerous examples of syntax and detailed analysis of code an excellent guide as you begin your journey into this rewarding environment. If you have programmed before or have some familiarity with C++, you will see that this book treats many important new features of the Borland product. Whether you are just beginning or need only to learn the latest about Turbo C++ 4.5, this book's clear organization makes doing so fast and easy.

Conventions Used in This Book

Note: These boxes highlight information that can make your Turbo C++ 4.5 programming more efficient and effective.

Warning: These boxes focus your attention on problems or side effects that can occur in specific situations.

NEW☞ TERM This icon indicates clear definitions of essential terms.

DO	DON'T

DO use the "Do/Don't" boxes to find a quick summary of a fundamental principle in a lesson.
DON'T overlook the useful information offered in these boxes.

The type icon denotes a new program for you to enter into your editor.

The output icon highlights the results of compiling and executing the program.

Analysis of the program reveals insights and information about key lines of the listing.

This book uses various typefaces to help you distinguish C++ code from regular English. Actual C++ code is typeset is a special `monospace` font. Placeholders—words or characters used to represent the real words or characters you would type in code—are typeset in *`italic monospace`*. New or important terms are typeset in *italic*.

In the listings in this book, each real code line is numbered. If you see an unnumbered line in a listing, you'll know that the unnumbered line is really a continuation of the preceding numbered code line (some code lines are too long for the width of the book).

1

1
2
3
4
5
6
7

The first week of your journey into learning to write Windows applications starts with an introduction to the Turbo C++ 4.5 environment—the IDE (integrated development environment). The remaining days in this week present the basics of the C++ language itself. You learn about the following:

- ☐ Predefined data types
- ☐ Naming constants, variables, and functions
- ☐ C++ operators and expressions
- ☐ Managing basic input and output
- ☐ Making decisions
- ☐ Writing loops
- ☐ Declaring and using arrays

You also will learn about simple user-defined types and pointers along with basic string operations. Thus, this week covers the basic components of the C++ language.

You might be interested to note that the topics covered this week are all the components included in the C language. Starting with the second week, you will be introduced to the portions of the language that are new with C++ along with the basics of Windows programming.

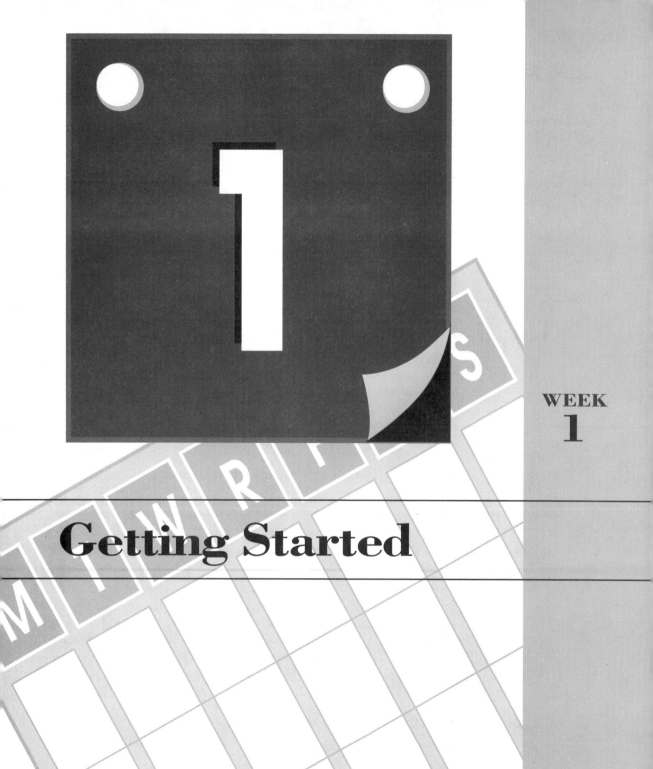

WEEK
1

Getting Started

Welcome to the world of C++ and Windows programming. Your journey into this exciting world begins today. Most of the information in today's lesson familiarizes you with the Turbo C++ Integrated Development Environment (IDE). You will learn about the following topics:

- [ ] The basics and history of C++ programs
- [ ] Reading the Turbo C++ documentation
- [ ] Loading and using the Turbo C++ IDE
- [ ] EasyWin applications
- [ ] Projects and nodes
- [ ] Typing and running your first C++ program

The Basics of C++ Programs

You don't need any previous experience in programming to learn Turbo C++ with this book; but if you have programmed before, things will be easier. As with other languages, C++ is made up of declarations and statements that specify exact instructions to be executed when the program runs.

C++ was developed by Bjarne Stroustrup at Bell Labs. The language is meant to supersede and build on the popular C language, mainly by adding object-oriented language extensions.

NEW☞
TERM An *object-oriented language* represents the attributes and operations of objects.

In addition, C++ offers a number of enhancements to C that are not object-oriented. Thus, learning C++ gives you the bonus of becoming very familiar with C. However, unlike C, which has been standardized, C++ is still undergoing the standardization process by the ANSI/ISO committee. As of this writing, it looks like a standard for C++ will be finalized and ratified by the end of 1996.

Programming in C++ requires that you become aware of the supporting libraries, which perform various tasks such as input/output, text manipulation, math operations, file I/O (input/output), and so on. In languages such as BASIC, support for such operations is transparent to programs, meaning that it is automatically available to these programs. As a result, many programs come across as single components that are independent of any other programming components. By contrast, programming in C++ makes you more aware of a program's dependency on various libraries. The advantage of this language feature is that you are able to select between similar libraries, including ones that you develop. Thus, C++ programs are modular. C++ compilers, including Turbo C++, use project files and program files. The Turbo C++ IDE uses project files to manage the creation and updating of a program.

NEW **TERM** *Project files* specify the library. *Program files* create an application.

Reading the Documentation

While this book makes a good learning tool, it always will be necessary to refer back to the original Borland-supplied documentation from time to time. There you will find reference manuals containing all the functions and all the classes provided by Turbo C++, as well as tutorials for subjects that are beyond the scope of this book.

Starting with version 4.5, Turbo C++ no longer comes automatically with printed manuals. Instead, the CD-ROM version has all the manuals available on the CD itself, and they can be read or printed directly from Windows. You can, however, order printed documentation from Borland for an additional fee.

The Acrobat Reader

All the documentation on the CD-ROM is in the Acrobat format and can be read with the Acrobat Reader v2.0, included with the Turbo C++ package. Table 1.1 lists the books available with Turbo C++ and what is in them.

Table 1.1. List of Turbo C++ Books

Book Title	Contents
Turbo C++ Programmer's Guide	A guide to the Turbo C++ compiler
Turbo C++ User's Guide	A guide to the Turbo C++ IDE and its various supporting tools
ObjectWindows Programmer's Guide	A guide to the OWL classes
ObjectWindows Tutorial	A step-by-step guide to using OWL

The Acrobat Reader is a simple application to use. Access it by double-clicking on the Turbo C++ 4.5 Online Books icon in the Turbo C++ 4.5 Program Manager group. You should see the screen as shown in Figure 1.1 which shows the various books you can select to read. There also is a button here that will lead you to some easy instructions on using the Acrobat Reader, mostly just a list of what the buttons on the toolbar do. You should probably take some time to study this help screen and experiment with the toolbar buttons.

Upon selecting one of the books by double-clicking on the appropriate button, a new window will open up to display the beginning of that book, such as in Figure 1.2.

Figure 1.1.
The Acrobat Reader Book List.

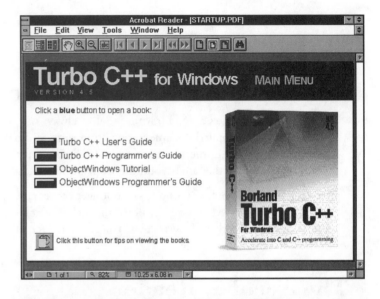

Figure 1.2.
The Turbo C++ User's Guide.

Here, you see a window containing two separate sections. The left side of the window shows all the sections in the chapter, while the right side shows the actual text of the book. At the bottom of the window is a status bar in which the separate sections can be used as buttons to provide extra functionality to the reader. Following is a description of the various buttons:

- The first button looks like a pair of arrows separated by a vertical line. By clicking on this and then moving the mouse, you can adjust the various sizes of the two main sections of the view window.

- The next button shows the current page number and the total page count of the document you are viewing. When you click on this button you will be presented with a dialog asking you to select a page number. This enables you to instantly jump to any page in the document.

- Next is a button that shows the current magnification level. You can manipulate this to better view the document in the main window. Clicking the button pops up a menu that enables you to select from various magnification levels.

- The last button before the horizontal scroll bar is one that displays the size of the page you are viewing. You can't click on this button for any sort of functionality, but you can consult it to determine the size of the page if you decide to print it.

I advise you to take some time now and explore the Acrobat Reader to find out what it can do. The Find function can be extremely useful in locating various topics in the supplied books.

Reference Information and Help Files

It is important to note that not all information can be obtained via the online manuals. There is a large amount of reference information covering details of the C++ language itself that are contained in various help files. The files are integrated into the Turbo C++ IDE in several ways. You can either select one of the Help menu items that will be described later this chapter, or you can click the right mouse button while in the IDE's editor window. Also, pressing the F1 key will access the help system.

From the Turbo C++ help window, you can click any one of a number of buttons that will enable you to change to specific reference help files. These buttons are shown in Table 1.2.

Table 1.2. List of Turbo C++ References in Help

Button Label	Reference Manual
Class Ref	The Class Library is a group of classes and functions you can use to hold collections of other objects. This is described later in Day 10.
OWL	The ObjectWindows Library (OWL) is a system whereby the large complexity of writing to the Windows operating system can be concealed behind easy-to-use classes. OWL is described starting on Day 11 and its description will continue through the rest of the book.

continues

Table 1.2. continued

Button Label	Reference Manual
OCF	The ObjectComponents Framework (OCF) is Borland's solution to building complex OLE2 applications with relatively little work. OCF, while it doesn't depend upon OWL, can be combined seamlessly with it. OCF is described on Day 20.
Win16	The Windows 16-bit Reference describes the Application Program Interface (API) for the direct Windows system calls available in the 16-bit version of Windows (Windows 3.1 and Windows for Workgroups 3.11). While OWL makes it easy for you to ignore the actual Windows functions, you will find yourself needing to bypass OWL occasionally, and this reference will be invaluable.

One of the most important methods of reaching the reference manual help you will use is when you're editing a file. By placing the editing cursor over a keyword in the file and pressing F1, you can tell Turbo C++ to search the manuals for the entry that describes the particular keyword. It's immensely useful for getting quick help on keywords, including all the information describing their precise usage and limitations.

Loading the Turbo C++ IDE

The Turbo C++ IDE is the visual interface for the C++ compiler, linker, debugger, and other tools that are used to create, manage, and maintain C++ programs. You can load the IDE by simply clicking the Turbo C++ icon or by double-clicking the TCW.EXE program from the File Manager. (The file TCW.EXE is located in the directory \TCWIN45\BIN.)

An Overview of the Turbo C++ IDE

The Turbo C++ IDE is an MDI-compliant application with the following main components:

- ☐ The frame window with the menu system, minimize, and maximize icons. You can resize, move, maximize, and minimize the main Turbo C++ IDE window.
- ☐ The system menu, which offers numerous options
- ☐ The speed bar, which contains special bitmapped buttons that offer shortcuts to specific commands. The IDE enables you to customize the bitmapped buttons on the speed bar. In addition, these buttons are context sensitive. Their number and type can change, depending on the current task or active window. The IDE supports a nice feature that displays what a bitmapped button does (the text appears in the status line) when you move the mouse over that button.

☐ The client area, which contains various windows, such as the source-code editing window, the message window, the variable watch window, and so on

☐ The status line located at the bottom of the IDE window. This line displays brief online help as you move the mouse over the buttons in the speed bar, offers a brief explanation for the various menu items, displays the cursor location, and shows the status of the insert/overwrite mode.

Figure 1.3 shows a sample session with the Turbo C++ IDE.

Figure 1.3.
The Turbo C++ IDE.

Note: Because the IDE is meant to accommodate software developers, many of the options will seem advanced to you if you are a novice programmer. However, you only need to be familiar with the options and their related terms. As you become more experienced, these options and terms will become part of your knowledge as a Turbo C++ programmer.

The File Menu

The File menu provides options that enable you to manage files, print text, and exit the IDE. Table 1.3 summarizes the options on the File menu. The File menu also includes a dynamic list of the most recently opened source-code files.

Table 1.3. Summary of the options in the File menu.

Command	Shortcut Keys	Function
New		Opens a new edit window
Open...		Loads an existing source-code file into a new edit window
Save	Ctrl+K S	Saves the contents of the active edit window
Save as...		Saves the contents of the active edit window using a new filename
Save all		Saves all the opened source-code windows in their respective files
Print...		Prints the contents of a source code window
Print setup...		Sets up the printer
Exit		Exits the IDE

The New Command

The New option opens a new edit window (also known as a source-code window) and assigns it a default associated filename. The default filename of the first new window you open is NONAME00.CPP. Likewise, the default filename of the second new window is NONAME01.CPP, and so on. The newly opened window initially is empty.

The Open... Option

The Open... option enables you to load the contents of an existing source code file into a new edit window. In fact, the IDE is capable of loading multiple files. The option invokes the Open a File dialog box, shown in Figure 1.4. The dialog box contains several list box and combo box controls that enable you to locate the source-code file and then select it. These controls permit you to choose the drive, directory, and filename wildcards that help you locate the source-code file you seek.

The Save Option

The Save option assists you in saving the contents of the active edit window to its associated file. If you invoke this option with a new edit window, the Save option invokes the Save File As dialog box, shown in Figure 1.5. This dialog box enables you to optionally specify the nondefault filename, as well as the destination drive and directory. The shortcut keys for the Save option are normally Ctrl+K, S; note, however, that they can change if you modify the key mappings (in the Options|Environment menu).

Figure 1.4.
The Open a File dialog box.

Figure 1.5.
The Save File As dialog box.

The Save As... Option

The Save **As**... option enables you to save the contents of the active edit window in a file that is different from the currently associated file. In fact, the new filename becomes the new associated file for the active edit window. The Save **As**... option invokes the Save File As dialog box, shown in Figure 1.5. If you select an existing file, the option displays a message dialog box that asks you whether you want to overwrite the contents of the existing file with those of the active edit window.

The Save All Option

The Save All option writes the contents of all the modified edit windows to their associated files. If the IDE contains new edit windows, this option invokes the Save File As dialog box to save these new windows.

The Print... Option

The Print... option enables you to print the contents of the active edit window. The option displays the Print Options dialog box, shown in Figure 1.6. This dialog box contains check boxes for the following options:

☐ Print a header and page numbers

☐ Print line numbers

☐ Highlight syntax keywords by printing them in bold characters

☐ Use color (if your printer supports colors)

☐ Wrap lines

☐ Left margin edit box option

Figure 1.6.
The Print Options dialog box.

The Print Setup... Option

The Print Setup... option enables you to set up your printer using the Print... option before you print. The printer setup option displays the Setup dialog. This is the same dialog box that will appear whenever you select Print Setup... from any program.

The Exit Option

The Exit option enables you to exit altogether the Turbo C++ IDE. The IDE prompts you for any modified edit window that has not been saved.

The Edit Menu

The Edit menu contains options that enable you to edit the text in the edit windows. Table 1.4 summarizes the options in the Edit menu.

Table 1.4. Summary of the options in the Edit menu.

Command	Shortcut Keys	Function
Undo	Ctrl+Z	Undoes the last editing action
Redo	Shift+Ctrl+Z	Reverses the action of the last Undo option
Cut	Ctrl+X	Deletes the selected text and copies it to the Clipboard. The previous contents of the Clipboard are lost.
Copy	Ctrl+C	Copies the selected text to the Clipboard. The previous contents of the Clipboard are lost.
Paste	Ctrl+V	Inserts the contents of the Clipboard at the current cursor location
Clear	Ctrl+Delete	Deletes selected text but does not write it to the Clipboard
Select all		Selects all the text in the active edit window
Buffer list...		Displays the Buffer List dialog box

The Undo Option

The Undo option enables you to reverse the effect of the last editing task and restore the contents of the active edit window. The shortcut keys for this option are Ctrl+Z. This option enables you to quickly and efficiently deal with editing errors—especially after working long hours.

The Redo Option

The Redo option enables you to reverse the action of the Undo option. The shortcut keys for the Redo option are Shift+Ctrl+Z. The Redo option enables you to switch between two versions of edited source code. This option is beneficial to the truly exhausted programmer who cannot make up his mind about how the source code should look!

The Cut Option

The Cut option deletes selected text and places it in the Clipboard. The previous contents of the Clipboard are lost. The shortcut keys for the Cut option are Ctrl+X.

The Copy Option

The Copy option copies the selected text into the Clipboard. The previous contents of the Clipboard are lost. The shortcut keys for the Copy option are Ctrl+C.

The Paste Option

The Paste option inserts the contents of the Clipboard at the current insertion point. The contents of the Clipboard remain unaffected. Thus, you can use the Cut and Paste options to move text in the same edit window or across different edit windows. You also can use the Copy and Paste options to duplicate blocks of text in the same edit window or across different edit windows. The shortcut keys for the Paste option are Ctrl+V.

The Clear Option

The Clear option clears the selected text without copying it to the Clipboard. This does not mean that the deleted text is irreversibly lost, because you can use the Undo option to undelete that text. The shortcut keys for the Clear option are Ctrl+Delete.

The Select All Option

The Select All option selects all the text in the active edit window. You can copy this text to the Clipboard by using the Copy option. You then can write the contents of the Clipboard to another edit window using the Paste option.

The Buffer List... Option

The Buffer List... option enables you to examine the list of buffers used with the various edit windows. This option displays the Buffer List dialog box. This dialog box enables you to load a buffer into an edit window. The dialog box contains the list of buffers; those that have changed since they were last loaded have the word MODIFIED (placed in parentheses) after them.

The dialog box is a feature borrowed from the BRIEF editor. In that, you have a list of buffers and a single window; you switch between the different files, changing the currently viewed buffer in the edit window. The IDE's buffer list dialog box enables you to replace the contents of the current edit window without closing the associated file. If the replaced file is not loaded into another edit window, it is hidden. You may use the buffer list later in order to load the hidden buffer into an edit window.

You can use the Save pushbutton of the Buffer List dialog box to update the file associated with the selected buffer. This action causes the word MODIFIED to disappear from the selected buffer entry. You also can use the Delete pushbutton to remove the selected buffer from memory, if that buffer is not in an Edit window.

The Search Menu

The Search menu contains options that enable you to locate various types of information, such as text, symbol definitions, function declarations, and program-building errors. Table 1.5 summarizes the options in the Search menu.

Table 1.5. Summary of the options in the Search menu.

Command	Shortcut Keys	Function
Find...	Ctrl+Q F	Searches for text in the active edit window
Replace...	Ctrl+Q A	Replaces text in the active source-code window
Search again	F3	Repeats the last Find or Replace operation
Browse symbol...		Locates a symbol in any source code that is part of the current project
Locate function...		Locates a function
Previous message	Alt+F7	Selects the previous program-building message and places the cursor at the offending line in an edit window
Next message	Alt+F8	Selects the next program-building message and places the cursor at the offending line in an edit window

The Find... Option

The **Find...** option supports searches for text in the active edit window. This option, which has the shortcut keys Ctrl+Q F, displays the Find Text dialog box, shown in Figure 1.7. This dialog box has the following controls:

☐ The **Text** to find combo box control, which enables you to type in the search text or to recall recently searched text.

☐ The Options check boxes, which include

   ☐ The Case sensitive check box, which enables you to select case-sensitive or case-insensitive text search.

☐ The Whole words only check box, which enables you to choose between matching entire words or matching any text.

☐ The Regular expression check box, which turns on or off the use of the BRIEF editor's regular expressions feature. Such expressions result in using the text in the Text to find control as the text pattern.

☐ The Direction diamond-shaped radio button controls. These controls enable you to choose between Forward and Backward search.

☐ The Scope diamond-shaped radio button controls. These controls enable you to choose between searching the entire text and limiting the search to the Selected text.

☐ The Origin diamond-shaped radio button controls. These controls enable you to choose between searching the Entire edit window and searching From the cursor position.

☐ The OK, Cancel, and Help buttons.

Figure 1.7.
The Find Text dialog box.

The Replace... Option

The Replace... option supports replacing text in the active edit window and has the shortcut keys Ctrl+Q A. This option displays the Replace Text dialog box, which looks exactly like the Find... dialog box, except for a few additions. There's a single edit field into which you can enter the text that will be used to replace the found text, and there's a Change All button that will make changes to all occurrences instead of simply the next one.

The Search Again Option

The Search Again option enables you to repeat the last Find... or Replace... option. The shortcut key for this option is the F3 function key.

The Browse Symbol... Option

The Browse Symbol... option enables you to browse the makeup of a symbol, including classes, functions, and variables. These symbols need not be defined in the active edit window, as long as they are defined in one of the current project's source-code files (your files or the library's included files); the symbols depend upon the symbolic information produced by a compile with debugging on. Figure 1.8 shows a sample symbol-browsing dialog box.

Figure 1.8.
A sample symbol-browsing dialog box.

The Locate Function... Option

The Locate Function... option enables you to find the definition of a function. This option displays the Locate Function dialog box which prompts you to enter the name of the function you want to find. The IDE responds by moving to it in an existing edit window or by displaying the function definition in a new edit window, if necessary.

The Previous Message Option

The Previous Message option enables you to zoom in on the offending source-code line that is associated with the previous message in the Message window. The IDE responds to this option by displaying the edit window that contains the offending source-code line. The shortcut keys for this option are Alt+F7.

The Next Message Option

The Next Message option enables you to zoom in on the offending source-code line that is associated with the next message in the Message window. The IDE responds to this option by displaying the edit window which contains the offending source-code line. The shortcut keys for this option are Alt+F8.

The View Menu

The View menu contains options that enable you to view and browse through a wide variety of information. This information goes beyond the declarations in the source-code files of your own project. Table 1.6 summarizes the options in the View menu.

Table 1.6. Summary of the options in the View menu.

Command	Shortcut Keys	Function
ClassExpert		Invokes the ClassExpert utility, which works with project files generated by AppExpert
Project		Displays the Project window
Message		Displays the Message window
Classes		Browses through the classes
Globals		Browses through global data types, constants, and variables
Watch		Selects or opens the Watch window
Breakpoint		Selects or opens the Breakpoints window
Call stack		Selects or opens the Call Stack window
Register		Selects or opens the Registers window
Event log		Selects or opens the Event Log window
Information...		Displays system or status information

The ClassExpert Option

The ClassExpert option invokes the ClassExpert utility, which works only with project files created by the AppExpert (both of these topics are discussed on Day 19). This option invokes the ClassExpert window, which has three panes, as follows:

☐ The Classes pane lists the classes involved in the project created using AppExpert. The information in the other two panes is related to the currently selected class in this pane.

☐ The Events pane lists the command notification, control notifications, virtual functions, Windows messages, and other events related to the class selected in the Classes pane.

☐ The source-code window, in which the selected class is defined.

The Project Option

The **P**roject option selects or opens the Project window, which lists the targets in the nodes in the current .IDE file. The Project window displays the files of a target in the form of a tree-like outline. The outline is made up of nodes that you can expand and collapse (if they have child nodes). Each node has a bitmap to its left. If the bitmap graphic has a + sign, then the node has child nodes that are currently hidden. If you click the + sign, you expand that node, and the IDE replaces the + sign with a – sign. The child nodes without + or – signs have no child nodes of their own.

If you click the right mouse button on a node in the Project window, the IDE displays a floating menu that enables you to view various components of the project, manage nodes, and edit project-related components.

The project window is discussed in more detail later on today.

The Message Option

The **M**essage option displays, selects, or opens the Message window, which contains the source-code compiler, resource compiler, and linker messages. These messages inform you of the progress of building the .EXE program file. In addition, the Message window contains any warning or error messages generated by the compilers or by the linker.

The Classes Option

The **C**lasses option displays the Browsing Objects window, showing a graph of the various classes in the current project and how they are interlinked. Typically, the Browsing Objects window has a vertical and horizontal scroll bar to enable you to scroll through the various classes involved in the current project. This topic is covered a little later, when there are some classes to browse.

The Globals Option

The **G**lobals option displays the Browsing Globals window, which shows the global data types, constants, variables, and functions. Figure 1.9 shows a sample Browsing Globals window. The window identifies each item by using the following special bitmaps:

☐ The bitmap T indicates that the symbol is a data type.

☐ The bitmap C signals that the symbol is a constant.

☐ The bitmap F signifies that the symbol is a function.

☐ The bitmap V indicates that the symbol is a variable.

The Browsing Globals window contains switches that enable you to filter the viewing of certain global symbols. The window also contains an edit box control that enables you to type in the name of the symbol you want to find. The edit box control filters the symbols with every keystroke you enter.

Figure 1.9.
A sample Browsing Globals window.

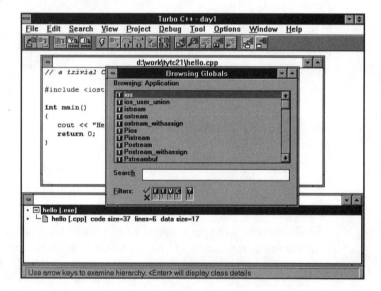

The Watch Option

The **W**atch option selects or opens the Watch window. This window lists the currently watched variables in your program during debugging. The window displays a check box to the left of each variable. The check box is checked by default to display and update the value in the associated variable. You can uncheck the control to temporarily disable displaying the value of a variable. This task especially is meaningful when the watched variable is not defined in the currently traced function. The Watch window is discussed on Day 21.

The Breakpoint Option

The **B**reakpoint option displays the Breakpoints window, which lists the location and type of breakpoints. A *breakpoint* is a program statement at which the program stops to enable you to inspect its variables. The Breakpoints window displays the following information:

☐ The filename that contains the breakpoint

- [ ] The line number where the breakpoint is located
- [ ] The state of the breakpoint
- [ ] The number of passes (that is, the number of times the statement is executed before the program stops at the breakpoint)

If you double-click any entry in the Breakpoints window, the IDE displays the Breakpoints Properties dialog box. This dialog box enables you to edit the breakpoint's data. This dialog box is discussed on Day 21.

The Call Stack Option

The Call Stack option displays the Call Stack window, which lists the pending program and the DLL functions that were called (and not yet returned) when the program reached the current breakpoint or the current single-stepped line. The DLL functions are referenced by the name of the DLL library, followed by the address of the function. Again, this is a debugging-related function and will be covered on Day 21.

The Register Option

The Register option displays the Registers window, which reveals the current values in CPU registers. The information in this window helps you perform a low-level debug and trace of a program, and it requires some knowledge of assembly language and how C++ is translated into it.

The Event Log Option

The Event Log option displays the Event Log window, which lists the sequence of breakpoint events that have occurred. Each log entry includes the breakpoint address, followed by text that identifies the related Windows messages, output messages, or exceptions.

The Information... Option

The Information... option displays the Information dialog box. This dialog box contains the following information:

- [ ] The current directory
- [ ] The Windows version and mode
- [ ] The MS-DOS version
- [ ] The total free memory space
- [ ] The largest free memory block
- [ ] The percent of USER, GDI, and total free heap space

This information can be useful when mysterious problems start showing up in Windows. It lets you know just how much memory is available and how much is free, and informs you of just how many resources are available. If any of these numbers get too low, things can start to get rather weird in Windows.

The Project Menu

The Project menu offers options that manage a project to build an executable program or a library. Table 1.7 summarizes the options in the Project menu.

Table 1.7. Summary of the options in the Project menu.

Command	Shortcut Keys	Function
AppExpert...		Invokes the AppExpert utility to generate the files of a project
New project...		Creates a new project
Open project...		Opens an existing project and closes the current project
Close project		Closes the current project
New target...		Creates a new target in the current project
Compile	Alt+F9	Compiles the file in the active edit window
Make all		Updates the project files by compiling and linking the necessary source-code files
Build all		Unconditionally compiles and links all of the project source-code files

The AppExpert... Option

The AppExpert... option invokes the AppExpert utility, which is a valuable and sophisticated tool for rapid program development. Day 19 discusses using the AppExpert.

The New Project... Option

The New project... option triggers the process that enables you to create a new project without involving the AppExpert utility. This option displays the New Project dialog box, shown in Figure 1.10. The dialog box enables you to specify the following information:

☐ The path and name of the new project

☐ The target name (that is, the name of the .EXE file)

- ☐ The target type, which can be one of the following:
  - ☐ A Windows .EXE application
  - ☐ A Windows .DLL dynamic library
  - ☐ An EasyWin .EXE program.
  - ☐ A .LIB static library
  - ☐ A .LIB import library
  - ☐ A Windows .HLP help file
- ☐ The application's platform, which must be 16-bit Windows 3.*x*. In order to develop for other platforms, such as Win32 or MS-DOS, you will need to upgrade to the full Borland C++ product.
- ☐ The target's memory model, which can be small, compact, medium, or large
- ☐ A variety of choices related to the libraries included; these are sensitive to the target type and change correspondingly.
- ☐ The options to specify child node files with .C or .CPP extension along with an optional .RC resource file and a .DEF definition file. The Advanced pushbutton control in the dialog box offers these options through a special dialog box.
- ☐ The option to select the path for the project. The Browse pushbutton control in the dialog box offers this option.

This is discussed a little bit later in this chapter when projects are introduced.

Figure 1.10.
A sample New Project dialog box.

The Open Project... Option

The **O**pen Project... option enables you to open a new project and automatically close the current one. This option displays the Open Project File dialog box, which resembles the File Open dialog box. The Project File dialog box enables you to specify the drive, directory, and filename wildcards involved in selecting the .IDE or .PRJ project files. The .PRJ project files from previous versions of Turbo C++ can still be loaded for backward compatibility; they are converted automatically to .IDE files. Project files from the full Borland C++ product also can be loaded, but if they contain any options that aren't supported in Turbo C++, the options will be ignored unless they conflict. If you load a project that targets Win32, for example, then the option will be changed to Win16 as that is the only platform supported.

The Close Project Option

The **C**lose Project option closes the current project and its edit windows.

The New Target... Option

The New **T**arget... option enables you to add another target to the project. The option first displays the New Target dialog box, which enables you to enter the name and type of the target. The target type may be AppExpert, Standard, and SourcePool. If you choose the AppExpert target type, the IDE invokes the AppExpert once you close the New Target dialog box. If you select the Standard target type, the IDE invokes the Add Project dialog box. If you choose the SourcePool target type, the IDE quietly adds a SourcePool target node. The Project window reflects the addition of the new target and indicates its type.

A source pool target contains a set of nodes that are not built in the project. Instead, source pools play the role of templates for creating reference copies, which allow different targets to employ common source code.

The Compile Option

The **C**ompile option compiles the source code in the active edit window. The option displays the Compile Status dialog box, which informs you of the files being compiled, the number of lines, the number of warnings, and the number of errors. When the compilation process ends, the Message window displays general messages for the compilation steps and includes warning and error messages generated by the compiler, linker, and other tools. The shortcut key for this option is Alt+F9.

The Make All Option

The **M**ake All option updates the project's target by compiling and linking only those files that have been changed since the previous program make or build operations. The option also uses the Compile Status dialog box to display the progress of the compilation and linking steps. Once this process is terminated, the Message window displays messages that reflect the progress of compiling and linking, along with any warning and error messages.

The Build All Option

The Build All option is similar to the Make All option, except that it systematically recompiles and links all of the project's files.

The Debug Menu

The Debug menu provides you with options that enable you to manage debugging and executing your C or C++ source code. Table 1.8 summarizes the options in the Debug menu. Day 21 offers a short tutorial on some simple debugging techniques.

Table 1.8. Summary of the options in the Debug menu.

Command	Shortcut Keys	Function
Run	Ctrl+F9	Runs the program of the current target. If necessary, this option also compiles and links the project source-code files.
Step over	F8	Runs the next statement without tracing into the parts that make it up. Contrast this with tracing into a function, the next command.
Trace into	F7	Single-steps through the next statement and also traces the statements of functions that are called in the next statement. This is a way of following the contents of a function.
Toggle breakpoint	F5	Toggles making the line at the current cursor location an unconditional breakpoint
Find execution point		Shows the source code at the point of execution
Pause program		Pauses the program and switches to the debugger
Terminate program	Ctrl+F2	Stops the program. If you start or step into the program again, it will restart at the beginning as if you never had run it before.

Table 1.8. continued

Command	Shortcut Keys	Function
Add **w**atch...	Ctrl+F5	Opens the Watch Properties dialog box to add a variable to watch
Add **b**reakpoint...		Opens the Breakpoint Properties dialog box to add a breakpoint
Evaluate/Modify...		Evaluates an expression and modifies the value in a variable
Inspect...	Alt+F5	Inspects the contents of a variable.
Load symbol table...		Loads DLL symbol table

The Tool Menu

The Tool menu provides you with access to several programming utilities. The IDE **T**ools... option in the Options menu enables you to customize the list of programming tools that appear in the Tool menu. Table 1.9 summarizes the default options in the Tool menu.

Table 1.9. Summary of the default options in the Tool menu.

Command	Shortcut Keys	Function
Resource Workshop		Invokes the Resource Workshop utility
Grep		Runs the Grep utility on the currently selected nodes
WinSight		Invokes the WinSight utility to monitor Windows messages
WinSpector		Runs the WinSpector utility to perform postmortem analysis
Key map compiler		Compiles the IDE key map file

The Options Menu

The Options menu enables you to fine-tune the operations of the compiler, linker, editor, and all the other components of the IDE. Table 1.10 summarizes the options in the Options menu.

Table 1.10. Summary of the options in the Options menu.

Command	Shortcut Keys	Function
Project...		Inspects and edits the setting of the current project
Target...		Allows you to use the TargetExpert to modify the build options of the current project's targets
Environment...		Views and edits the setting of the environment.
Tools...		Adds or deletes (or both) tools in the Tool commands
Sty**l**e Sheets...		Edits the options style sheets
Save...		Configures to save the project, desktop, and environment

The Project... Option

The **P**roject... option displays the dialog box with the title Project Options, as shown in Figure 1.11. The Project Option dialog box contains a list of topics on the left side and a set of controls on the right. Those controls are changed according to the topic selected in the left list. Following are the Project Options topics:

- ☐ The Directories topic enables you to specify the directories for the include, library, and source code files, as well as to specify the paths for intermediate and final files.

- ☐ The Compiler topic enables you to fine-tune the compiling of C and C++ source code, specify the preprocessor definitions, manage the inclusion of debug information, and manage precompiled header files.

- ☐ The Advanced Compiler topic enables you to manage compiling for 16-bit Windows 3.x applications, select the processor type, and choose the memory model for the compiled files.

- ☐ The C++ Options topic assists you in determining how the C++ compiler interprets your source code to manage new and old C++ language features.

- ☐ The Messages topic enables you to determine the type of messages emitted during the creation of the program. The options in the Message topic enables you to choose anything from a very strict to a very relaxed level of warnings and errors.

- ☐ The Linker topic enables you to control the creation of .OBJ, and .LIB files, which are united into the executable .EXE files.

- ☐ The Librarian section enables you to combine a set of .OBJ files into a .LIB file and control this process.

☐ The Resources section enables you to specify the target Windows version in order to create the right type of .RES compiled resource file and how it is bound to the .EXE.

☐ The Make section offers options that control the integrated make process.

Figure 1.11.

A sample session with the Project Options dialog box.

The Target... Option

The Target... option displays a small dialog box that contains a list of the top-level targets in the current project. These targets then can be selected and edited in order to change such things as their target type, platform, memory model, and standard libraries.

The Environment... Option

The Environment... option displays the Environment Options dialog box, shown in Figure 1.12, which enables you to customize various aspects of the IDE. These aspects are organized and controlled by the following sections that appear in the dialog box:

☐ The Editor topic controls the operations of the IDE's text editor. The Editor's subtopics enable you to select the default text editor (which is similar to WordStar), select the IDE classical text editor, emulate the BRIEF editor, emulate the Epsilon editor, or customize various aspects of the current text editor.

☐ The Syntax Highlighting topic enables you to determine both the color and style used by the editor to display the source code. The syntax topic offers a few predefined sets of colors and styles.

☐ The Browser topic enables you to determine the default filters for the Browser. In addition, the topic enables you to request the creation of new windows as you traverse through the hierarchy of classes.

☐ The Debugger topic enables you to select between hard mode and soft mode debugging and to select smart mode debugging. (The hard and soft debugging modes determine how the Windows messages are intercepted by the debugger.) In addition, this topic enables you to select the capture of Windows messages, output messages, and breakpoints.

☐ The Speedbar section enables you to customize the location and contents of the speed bar.

☐ The Preferences section provides options related to saving various IDE components, such as the editor files, the environment, the desktop, and the project. The section also provides options to specify which parts of the desktop to save.

☐ The Project View section provides options that determine the type of information to include in the Project window—code size, data size, location, name, number of lines, node type, and so on.

Figure 1.12.
A sample session with the Environment Options dialog box.

The Tools... Option

The Tools... option enables you to add new menu items to the Tool menu and to delete items from that menu. Figure 1.13 shows the Tools dialog box, which contains a Tools list box that shows you the available tools. If you click the Edit pushbutton, the dialog box displays the Tools Options dialog box, as shown in Figure 1.14. The latter dialog box enables you to specify the name of the tool, along with its path, command line, menu text, and help hint (which appears in the status line).

Note that most of the tools displayed in the list actually are internal tools and don't appear in the Tool menu. Some of the listed tools can be added to the menu if desired; however, many wouldn't make sense there.

Figure 1.13.
The Tools dialog box.

Figure 1.14.
The Tools Options dialog box.

The Style Sheets... Option

The Style Sheets... option displays the Style Sheet dialog box, shown in Figure 1.15, which enables you to select a configuration for the compile and runtime settings for a project. Each style sheet is a predefined collection of settings that can be affiliated with a node.

Figure 1.15.
The Style Sheet dialog box.

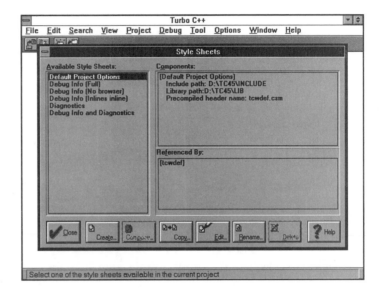

The Save... Option

The **Save...** option enables you to specify to automatically save the desktop, environment, and project file. This option invokes the Save Options dialog box, which offers check boxes for saving these three IDE components.

The Window Menu

The Window menu offers options to manage windows in the IDE client area. These options, which are summarized in Table 1.11, enable you to arrange, close, minimize, and restore some or all the windows. In addition to the standard options, the Window menu also lists the current windows.

Table 1.11. Summary of the options in the Window menu.

Command	Shortcut Keys	Function
Cascade	Shift+F5	Cascades the windows in the client area of the IDE.

continues

Table 1.11. continued

Command	Shortcut Keys	Function
Tile **h**orizontal	Shift+F4	Tiles the windows horizontally on the client area of the IDE
Tile vertical		Tiles the windows vertically on the client area of the IDE
Arrange **i**cons		Arranges the icons in the client area of the IDE
Close **a**ll		Closes all windows—debugger windows, browser windows, or editor windows
Mi**n**imize all		Minimizes all windows, debugger windows, browser windows, or editor windows
Restore all		Restores all windows, debugger windows, browser windows, or editor windows

The Help Menu

The Help menu provides you with the kind of online help you may have gotten from other software. Table 1.12 summarizes the options in the Help menu.

Table 1.12. Summary of the options in the Help menu.

Command	Shortcut Keys	Function
Contents		Displays the table of contents for the online help system
Keyword **s**earch	F1	Displays help regarding the keyword on which the cursor is situated
Keyboard		Displays information about the mapping of the keyboard.
Using **h**elp		Displays information to assist you in using the online help system
Quick Tour		This offers a tutorial-like tour through Turbo C++.
Tips		Displays a list of special tips for using Turbo C++. Clicking on these tips displays a help screen with the appropriate information.
Windows API		Takes you to the Win16 API reference mentioned earlier

Command	Shortcut Keys	Function
OWL API		Opens up the OWL reference mentioned earlier
About...		Displays information regarding the software version and copyright

The EasyWin Applications

Microsoft Windows is a complicated environment. Applications are responsible for creating windows, providing support for mouse events, and all sorts of other things. Before windowing environments came about, programs ran in simple console environments like that found in standard MS-DOS. When a program is run, it has simple input from the keyboard and simple output directly to the screen on a character-by-character basis. Although the interface isn't very pretty, it's good for writing simple programs without having to worry about all the many features required for a full windowed program.

The Turbo C++ IDE enables you to build a special kind of program called an EasyWin application that provides a simple window that acts like an old-style console program. The programs in Days 1 through 10 of this book are EasyWin applications that enable you to focus on learning C++ using a console interface and input/output procedure. The EasyWin window is the standard input and output for C++ programs (compiled as EasyWin applications). The EasyWin window has a simple menu with few options and a few selections.

To create an EasyWin application, perform the following steps:

1. Load the Turbo C++ IDE.
2. Choose the Project menu from the menu bar.
3. Select the **N**ew Project command to invoke the New Project dialog box.
4. Enter the path and name of the .IDE project file in the topmost edit box. The dialog box echoes the pathname (as you type it) in the Target name edit box (that is, it makes the program name match the name of the project). You need to edit the target name if the name of the program does not match the name of the .IDE project file. You can use the Browse pushbutton to select the directory that will contain the project files.
5. Click the Advanced pushbutton to invoke the Advanced Options dialog box. Select the check box labeled .cpp node. This selection causes the IDE to insert the .CPP node for the EasyWin source-code file. This dialog also enables you to add or remove an .RC or .DEF module. Because these are useful only for real Windows applications and not for EasyWin, make sure these two options are unchecked. Close the Advanced Options dialog box by clicking on the OK button.

6. Select the EasyWin [.exe] item in the Target type list box.

7. Click the OK pushbutton to create the new project file.

8. The IDE displays the Project window, which lists the nodes for the various programs. When you first create a project file, the Project window will have only one node.

9. Click the main node to view the files contained in that node. The nodes of EasyWin programs contain only one file, a .CPP file, which has the source code. Double-click the .CPP file to request editing the file. Initially, the source window for the .CPP file is empty.

10. Enter the source code for the EasyWin program.

11. Press the Ctrl+F9 keys to compile, link, and run the EasyWin program. The compiler flags any errors and lists them in the Message window. If the EasyWin program is correct, the IDE will launch it.

Introduction to Projects and Nodes

When you create a new project or load an old one from disk, the Turbo C++ IDE creates a Projects window at the bottom of the IDE. This window contains all the nodes and sub-nodes needed for the application.

NEW☞   A *node* is the term used to describe the various items found in the project window. These
TERM   nodes each have specific rules associated with them that the IDE uses to decide how to build applications. Furthermore, each node may, in turn, depend on one or more nodes for compilation. This means that before any particular node can be dealt with, the nodes on which it depends must already have been dealt with successfully.

You can add more than one program to an .IDE file. I suggest that you group the separate programs of each of the first twelve days in .IDE files named for their respective days, such as DAY1.IDE, DAY2.IDE, and so on. Grouping related program files in a single IDE saves space because the .IDE files are not small.

To add another target to an existing .IDE file, follow these steps:

1. Load the Turbo C++ IDE.

2. Choose the Project menu from the menu bar.

3. Select the New Target command to invoke the New Target dialog box.

4. Enter the name of the new program and click the OK pushbutton.

5. The IDE displays the New Project dialog box. Simply click the OK pushbutton to add a new program node in the Project window. All the changes you made earlier, including those made in the Advanced dialog, are remembered from last time.

6. The IDE displays the Project window, which lists the new nodes for the new program.

This last step just adds a new top-level target to the project with a single .CPP file for its main source code. You can add more nodes as dependencies to any target by selecting that node, clicking the right mouse button, and selecting the Add Node option from the resulting pop-up menu. A dialog box entitled Add to Project List appears and enables you to set the filename of the new node.

You also should note that some nodes have either a plus or a minus sign in their bitmaps. This operates in much the same way as the File Manager's folder bitmaps. A plus sign means there are node dependencies that have been hidden in order to help clean up the display. By clicking on the bitmap, the plus sign will change to a minus sign, and the node will expand to show its dependencies. Clicking on the node's bitmap again will collapse the display and change the minus back into a plus.

It can be extremely useful to have multiple files in conjunction with a single application. Eventually, when you start writing full-fledged Windows applications in Day 11, you're going to start seeing some rather large programs. Putting all the source code for the program in a single file can get extremely unwieldy, so splitting up that source code into multiple files can make life for the programmer much easier. You can find more about this on Day 11, which also discusses the AppExpert and its output.

Your First C++ Program

The first C++ program presented in this book displays a one-line greeting message. This simple program enables you to see the very basic components of a C++ program.

Listing 1.1 contains the source code for the program HELLO.CPP with numbered lines. *Do not* enter the line numbers when you type the program. These line numbers serve as reference only. This simple program displays the string `Hello Programmer!` Carry out the following steps to create and run this first C++ program. (Note that, with minor modifications, the line numbers can be used for all the program examples in the book that you type in yourself; the IDEs all are provided for you if you obtain the source disk):

1. Load the Turbo C++ IDE if it is not already loaded.
2. Choose the Project menu from the menu bar.
3. Select the **N**ew Project command to invoke the New Project dialog box.
4. Type **tcwin45\\tc21day\\day1\\hello.ide** in the edit box requesting the Project path and name. The dialog box also shows the name **"hello"** in the Target name edit box.
5. Click the Advanced pushbutton to invoke the Advanced Options dialog box. Select the check box labeled .cpp Node and turn off the RC and DEF options. Close the Advanced Options dialog box.
6. Select the EasyWin [.exe] item in the Target type list box.
7. Click the OK pushbutton to create the new project file.

The IDE displays the Project window, which lists the node for the hello program.

8. Click the hello.exe node to view the hello.cpp node. Double-click the hello.cpp node to invoke the IDE editor.

9. Enter in the new window the program shown in Listing 1.1.

10. Choose the **S**ave command in the File menu.

11. Press the Ctrl+F9 keys to compile, link, and run the HELLO.EXE program.

When an EasyWin program ends, the runtime system alters the title of the program's window to include the word Inactive. To close the program's window, select the **C**lose command from the system menu, or simply press Alt+F4.

Listing 1.1. Source code for the program HELLO.CPP.

```
1: // a trivial C++ program that says hello
2:
3: #include <iostream.h>
4:
5: int main()
6: {
7:   cout << "Hello Programmer!";
8:   return 0;
9: }
```

The output of the program appears in Figure 1.16. Notice that the caption of the output window starts with the word Inactive to indicate that the program has terminated.

Figure 1.16.
The output of the
HELLO.EXE program.

Analysis Examine the short code of the C++ program and notice the following characteristics:

☐ C++ uses the // characters for comments that go to the end of the line. C++ also supports the C-style comments that begin with the /* characters and end with the */ characters. Line 1 contains a comment that briefly describes the program.

NEW☛ TERM *Comments* are remarks that you put in the program to explain or clarify certain parts of the program. The compiler ignores comments but the programmer relies on them to figure out what is meant in a program, especially if the code hasn't been looked at in a long time.

☐ The C++ program has no reserved keywords that declare the end of a program. In fact, C++ uses a rather simple scheme for organizing a program. This scheme supports two levels of code: global and single-level functions. In addition, the function main, which starts on line 5, plays a very special role because runtime execution begins with this function. Therefore, there can be only a single function main in a C++ program. You can place the function main anywhere in the code.

☐ The C++ strings and characters are enclosed in double and single quotes, respectively. Thus, 'A' is a single character, whereas, "A" is a single-character string. Mixing C++ single-character strings and characters is not allowed.

NEW☛ TERM Strings can have any number of characters, including no characters. A string without any characters is called the *empty string*.

☐ C++ defines blocks using the { and } characters. See examples in lines 6 and 9, respectively.

☐ Every statement in a C++ program must end with a semicolon (;). When looking at other code, it might appear that there are exceptions to this rule, but there really isn't, and this will be discussed later on.

☐ C++ contains the #include compiler preprocessor directive. An example of this is in line 3, instructing the Turbo C++ compiler to include the IOSTREAM.H header file. C++ extends the notion of streams, which already exists in C. IOSTREAM.H provides the operations that support basic stream input and output. The C++ language does not include built-in I/O routines. Instead, the language relies on libraries specializing in various types of I/O.

NEW☛ TERM A *compiler directive* is a special instruction for the compiler and will be described under the Preprocessor heading in Day 2.

A *header file* contains the declarations of constants, data types, variables, and function prototypes.

A *stream* is a sequence of data flowing from one part of a computer to another.

☐ The C++ program outputs the string Hello Programmer! to the standard output stream cout, which is the EasyWin window. In addition, the program uses the output operator, <<, to send the emitted string to the output stream.

☐ The function `main` must return a value that reflects the error status of the C++ program. Returning the value `0` signals to the operating system that the program terminated normally.

Exiting the IDE

To exit the IDE, choose the Exit command from the File menu.

Summary

Today's lesson introduced you to a tremendous amount of material about the Turbo C++ IDE and presented you with the first C++ program. You learned these basics:

☐ C++ programs are modular and rely on standard and custom libraries.

☐ The DynaText documentation reader can be used to access the manuals that come with Turbo C++ on the CD-ROM.

☐ Reference information is available via the help system, which is available via the top menu; pop-up menus when the right mouse button is clicked; and by pressing either F1 or Ctrl+F1.

☐ The two ways to load the Turbo C++ IDE are by clicking the Turbo C++ icon or double-clicking the TCW.EXE file when using the File Manager (or any similar utility).

☐ The Turbo C++ IDE is a versatile environment for developing, maintaining, and debugging C and C++ programs and libraries for Windows applications.

☐ The File menu manages the creation of new files, the opening of files, the saving of files, printing, and exiting the IDE.

☐ The Edit menu offers options to perform popular editing operations (such as undo, cut, copy, paste, and delete).

☐ The Search menu enables you to find and replace text, as well as to browse through symbols, locate functions, and visit the offending source-code lines.

☐ The View menu enables you to view a wide variety of information. Among the viewable information are the project nodes, compiler and linker messages, the hierarchy of the project classes, global symbols, watched variables, the stack of called functions, and the CPU registers.

☐ The Project menu provides options to create, open, close and manage a project. The project options enable you to compile and link related source code files.

☐ The Debug menu offers options that enable you to debug and single-step in the source code from within the IDE and watch the values of variables in the Watch window.

- [ ] The Tool menu enables quick access to a variety of Windows programming tools, such as the Turbo Debugger for Windows, the message-tracing WinSight utility, the postmortem WinSpector utility, and your own tools.
- [ ] The Options menu enables you to fine-tune various aspects of your project—environment, tools, and project style sheets.
- [ ] The Window menu is for managing, arranging, closing, and restoring the windows in the IDE desktop.
- [ ] The Help menu provides you with the online help.
- [ ] EasyWin applications are Windows applications providing special windows that act as standard input and output devices. EasyWin applications enable you to write DOS-like programs.
- [ ] New projects are easy to create by setting certain options on a simple dialog box.
- [ ] Turbo C++ Project files enable you to create multiple targets and to have these targets contain multiple files.
- [ ] The first C++ program in this book is a simple greeting program that illustrates the basic components of a C++ program. These components include comments, the `#include` directive, and the `main` function.
- [ ] You exit the IDE through the Exit selection on the File menu.

Q&A

Q Does C++ use line numbers?

A No. We are using line numbers in the listings in this book only for the sake of reference.

Q Does the IDE's editor monitor what I type?

A Yes, it does. In fact, when you type a C++ keyword, the IDE quickly colors that keyword.

Q What happens if I forget to type the second double quote in the first program?

A The compiler tells you that there is an error in the program. You need to add the second double quote and build the project.

Q How do I delete all occurrences of some text in the currently edited window?

A Use the Replace selection in the Edit option and specify nothing for the replacement string, or use the Edit menu's Cut and Clear commands.

Workshop

The Workshop provides quiz questions to help you solidify your understanding of the material covered and exercises to provide you with experience in using what you've learned. Try to understand the quiz and exercise answers before continuing on to the next day's lesson. (Answers are provided in Appendix A.)

Quiz

1. What is the output of the following program?

```
1: // quiz program #1
2:
3: #include <iostream.h>
4:
5: main()
6: {
7:   cout << "C++ in 21 Days?";
8:   return 0;
9: }
```

2. What is the output of the following program?

```
1: // quiz program #2
2:
3: #include <iostream.h>
4:
5: main()
6: {
7:   // cout << "C++ in 21 Days?";
8:   return 0;
9: }
```

3. What is wrong with the following program?

```
1: // quiz program #3
2:
3: #include <iostream.h>
4:
5: main()
6: {
7:   cout << "C++ in 21 Days?"
8:   return 0;
9: }
```

Exercise

Write a program that displays the message I am a C++ Programmer.

C++ The Preprocessor, Variables, and Operators

Day 1 presented the Borland IDE and a simple C++ program. Today you will focus on the basic components of C++ programs, including data types, variables, constants, and functions. You will learn about the following topics:

- The predefined data types in Turbo C++ 4.5
- Naming items in Turbo C++ 4.5
- The `#include` directive
- Declaring variables
- Declaring constants
- Arithmetic operators and expressions
- Increment operators
- Arithmetic assignment operators
- Typecasting and data conversion
- Relational operators and conditional expressions
- Bit-manipulating operators
- The comma operator

Predefined Data Types in Turbo C++ 4.5

Turbo C++ 4.5 offers the `bool`, `int`, `char`, `float`, `double`, and `void` data types to represent booleans, integers, characters, single-precision floating-point numbers, double-precision floating-point numbers, and valueless data, respectively. C++ uses the `void` type with a function's returned values to indicate that the function does not yield a significant result—that is, the function acts as a procedure. Functions are described in more detail on Day 5.

C++ adds more flexibility to data types by supporting data type modifiers. The type modifiers are as follows: `signed`, `unsigned`, `short`, and `long`. Table 2.1 shows the predefined data types in C++ (and includes the type modifiers), along with their sizes and ranges. Notice that `int` and `unsigned int` are system-dependent.

NEW☞
TERM   *Data type modifiers* alter the precision and the range of values.

Table 2.1. Predefined data types in C++.

Data Type	Byte Size	Range	Examples
bool	1	false to true	true, false
char	1	−128 to 127	'A','!'
wchar_t	2	−32768 to 32767	L'A', L'!'

Data Type	Byte Size	Range	Examples
signed char	1	–128 to 127	23
unsigned char	1	0 to 255	200,0x1a
int	2	Depends on system –32768 to 32767 for 16-bit	3000
unsigned int	2	Depends on system 0 to 65535 for 16-bit	0xffff, 65535
short int	2	–32768 to 32767	100
unsigned short int	2	0 to 65535	0xff, 40000
long int	4	–2147483648L to 2147483647L	0xfffffL, -123456L
unsigned long int	4	0L to 4294967295L	123456L
float	4	3.4E–38 to 3.4E+38 and –3.4E–38 to –3.4E+38	2.35, -52.354 1.3e+10
double	8	1.7E–308 to 1.7E+308 and –1.7E–308 to –1.7E+308	12.354 -2.5e+100 -78.32544
long double	10	3.4E–4932 to 1.1E+4932 and –1.1E–4932 to –3.4E+4932	8.5e-3000

NEW☞ TERM C++ supports *hexadecimal numbers.* Such numbers begin with the characters 0x, followed by the hexadecimal value. For example, the number 0xff is the hexadecimal equivalent of the decimal number 255.

Note: Although I've listed bool here, and although some of the libraries supplied with Turbo C++ make use of it (particularly OWL), it hasn't quite made it into the language proper as of yet. When the appropriate header file (classlib\defs.h) is included, a special version of the bool type is set up to "fake it" until the compiler is outfitted with the proper equipment. This header file is included automatically whenever you make use of the Class Libraries or OWL, or you can add #include <classlib\defs.h> to your program manually.

Also note that C++ regards 0 as false and any nonzero value as true. The "faked" bool type in classlib\defs.h sets up false to be 0 and true to be 1. In previous versions of the Turbo C++ compiler, (and in the standard Windows header files) TRUE and FALSE (in all capitals) were used.

Naming Items in Turbo C++ 4.5

Turbo C++ 4.5 requires you to observe the following rules with identifiers:

- ☐ The first character must be a letter or an underscore (_).
- ☐ Subsequent characters can be letters, digits, or underscores.
- ☐ The maximum length of an identifier is 32 characters by default (that can be changed in the compiler options).
- ☐ Identifiers are case-sensitive in C++. Thus, the names rate, RATE, and Rate refer to three different identifiers.
- ☐ Identifiers cannot be reserved words, such as int, double, or static to name just a few.

The following are examples of valid identifiers:

```
X
x
aString
DAYS_IN_WEEK
BinNumber0
bin_number_0
bin0Number2
_length
```

And here are some invalid ones.

```
123aNumber
const
NoSpaces Allowed
NorAre*Most+Symbols
```

DO	**DON'T**

DO use descriptive names that have a reasonable length.

DON'T use identifier names that are too short or too long. Short names yield poor readability, and long names are prone to typographical errors. Some notable exceptions would be with iterators used in loops (to be explained on Day 3). In those cases, a simple i or ix often is used.

The Preprocessor

A long time ago, on a computer far, far away, compilers were a lot simpler than they are today. Back then, compilers required multiple passes through the source code in order to successfully create the machine code that could run on the computer. In those days, the preprocessor was an integral part of the compiling process. The preprocessor would do a quick run through the code in order to bring extra files together and to process macros.

The instructions that were meant for the preprocessor alone were called *directives*, and while the preprocessor as a separate entity doesn't really exist in the same way today, the terminology has. In C and C++, all directives must begin with a number sign (sometimes called sharp or pound—#) on the far left of a line followed by the directive name. There are a number of directives, most of them meant to control how the compiler operates, but the most important ones are `#include` and `#define`.

The *#include* Directive

The C++ program in Day 1 contains an `#include` directive. This directive tells the compiler to include the text of a file as if you have typed that text yourself. Thus, the `#include` directive is a better alternative than cutting text from one file and pasting in another file. Instead, one can create a header file that includes the common code and then simply include it in all the relevant programs.

It is vitally important, however, to recognize the difference between including a header file and separating code out into separate source files that all combine later into the target. Once a variable is created in memory, another creation is illegal. Therefore, if you actually create a variable in a header file, then include it in two different source files that combine into a single target, you will get compiler errors informing you of duplicate symbols. Typically, the only things that get placed in a header file are macro definitions, structure definitions, type definitions, and function prototypes. All of these will be described in time.

Syntax

The *#include* Directive

The general syntax for the `#include` directive is

```
#include <filename>
#include "filename"
```

The filename represents the name of the included file. The two forms differ in how the `#include` directive searches for the included file. The first form searches for the file in the special directory for included files. The second form extends the search to involve the current directory before searching the include directory.

Examples

```
#include <iostream.h>
#include "string.h"
```

The *#define* Directive

The #define directive is what creates macro definitions. The most common of these is a simple substitution-type of macro: you tell the preprocessor to substitute every occurrence of a particular text pattern with another. In these cases, the compiler proper never really sees what you originally typed into the source code, but rather its substitution.

The other, slightly less common usage for the #define directive is to create macros that involve some sort of substitution via parameters. This is similar to functions that will be described on Day 5, except, again, the compiler proper never even sees the original source code, but rather is shown only the substitution. Because of that similarity, they will be described then.

Syntax

The *#define* Directive

The general syntax for the #define directive is

```
#define constantName constantValue
```

The #define directive causes the preprocessor to perform text substitution to replace the macro-based constants with their values. This text replacement step occurs before the compiler processes the statements in the source file. Consequently, the compiler never sees the macro-based constants themselves, only what they expand to.

Examples

```
#define ASCII_A 65
#define DAYS_IN_WEEK 7
```

Note the tendency for macros to be in all uppercase. This merely is a convention that has survived from the original C macros, but it helps to keep the macros separate from other parts of the program, and makes them easier to pick out from all the other code.

Declaring Variables

Declaring variables requires you to state the data type of the variable and the name of the variable. The word *variable* indicates that you can alter the data of these data containers.

NEW☞
TERM   *Variables* are identifiers used to store and recall information.

In order to help in understanding variables, imagine that there are a number of cardboard boxes, and they are each made to hold only a certain type of object. These objects are called `ints` and `chars`, and so on. You can have any number of any type of box, but you need to have one for each object you want to store; you cannot store an object without a box. So, for example, if you wanted to hold on to an int, you would need to have the appropriate type of variable into which you could store the number. Then, when you want to use that number later on, you can just refer to the box to find out what's in it.

Declaring Variables

Syntax

The general syntax for declaring variables is

```
type variableName;
type variableName = initialValue;
type var1 [= initVal1], var2 [= initVal2], ...;
```

Examples

```
int j;
double z = 32.314;
long fileSize, diskSize, totalFileSize = 0;
```

C++ enables you to declare a list of variables (that have the same types) in a declarative statement, such as the following:

```
int j, i = 2, k = 3;
double x = 3.12;
double y = 2 * x, z = 4.5, a = 45.7;
```

The initializing values may contain other variables defined earlier.

DO	DON'T

DO resist using global variables. It's considered to be very bad form, especially in object-oriented languages like C++.

DON'T declare variables within the same program unit with names that are different in character case (such as `rate` and `Rate`).

Look at a simple example that uses variables. Listing 2.1 shows the source code for the program VAR1.CPP. The program declares four variables, two of which are initialized during their declarations. The program then assigns values to the uninitialized variables and displays the contents of all four variables. Create the project DAY2.IDE (in the directory \TCWIN45\TC21DAY) and include the VAR1.CPP file as a node. Compile and run the VAR1.EXE program.

Type Listing 2.1. Source code for the program VAR1.CPP.

```
1:  // C++ program that illustrates simple variables
2:
3:  #include <iostream.h>
4:
5:  main()
6:  {
7:    int i, j = 2;
8:    double x, y = 355.0 / 113;
9:
10:   i = 3 * j;
11:   cout << "i = " << i << "\n"
12:        << "j = " << j << "\n";
13:
14:   x = 2 * y;
15:   x = x * x;
16:   cout << "y = " << y << "\n"
17:        << "x = " << x << "\n";
18:   return 0;
19:
20: }
```

Here is a sample session with the program in Listing 2.1.

```
i = 6
j = 2
y = 3.14159
x = 39.4784
```

The program uses the #include directive in line 3 to include the stream I/O header file IOSTREAM.H; it is this header file that defines the code necessary for output. The function main appears in line 5. The function contains the declarations of the int-typed variables i, j in line 7, and the double-typed variables x and y in line 8. The declarations initialize the variable j and y. The statement in line 10 multiplies the value in variable j (which is 2) by 3 and stores the result in variable x. The stream output statement in lines 11 and 12 displays the values of variables i and j. The statement includes strings that label the output.

The statement in line 14 doubles the value in variable y and stores it in variable x. The statement in line 15 squares the value in variable x and assigns the result back to variable x. This statement uses the variable x on both sides of the equal sign. The stream output statement in lines 16 and 17 displays the values in variable x and y. The statement in line 18 returns 0 as the result of function main.

Declaring Constants

Many languages, such as BASIC (the more recent implementations), Modula-2, Ada, C, Pascal, and C++, support constants. No one can deny that constants enhance the readability of a program by replacing numeric constants with identifiers that are more descriptive. Moreover, using constants enables you to change the value of a program parameter by merely changing the value of that parameter in one location. This capability is more convenient and less prone to generate the errors that may occur when you employ your text editor to replace certain numbers with other numbers.

NEW☞ *Constants* are identifiers that are associated with fixed values. C++ offers constants in two **TERM** varieties: *macro-based* and *formal.* The macro-based constants are inherited from C and use the #define compiler directive.

The Formal Constant

The general syntax for the formal constant is

```
const dataType constantName = constantValue;
```

The dataType item is an optional item that specifies the data type of the constant values. If you omit the data type, the C++ compiler assumes the int type.

Examples

```
const unsigned char ASCII_A = 65;
const DAYS_IN_WEEK = 7;
const char FIRST_DISK_DRIVE = 'A';
```

DO	DON'T

DO use uppercase names for constants. This naming style enables you to determine quickly if an identifier is a constant.

DON'T assume that other people who read your code will know what embedded numbers mean. Use declared constants to enhance the readability of your programs.

Using Macro-Based Constants

Now consider an example that uses macro-based constants. Listing 2.2 shows the source code for the program CONST1.CPP. The program prompts you to enter the number of hours, minutes, and seconds since midnight. The program then calculates and displays the total number of seconds since midnight. Add the CONST1.CPP file as a node in the project file DAY2.IDE, and then compile and run the CONST1.EXE program.

Type

Listing 2.2. Source code for the program CONST1.CPP.

```
1:  // C++ program that illustrates constants
2:
3:  #include <iostream.h>
4:
```

Listing 2.2. continued

```
5:  #define SEC_IN_MIN 60
6:  #define MIN_IN_HOUR 60
7:
8:  main()
9:  {
10:   long hours, minutes, seconds;
11:   long totalSec;
12:
13:   cout << "Enter hours: ";
14:   cin >> hours;
15:   cout << "Enter minutes: ";
16:   cin >> minutes;
17:   cout << "Enter seconds: ";
18:   cin >> seconds;
19:
20:   totalSec = ((hours * MIN_IN_HOUR + minutes) *
21:               SEC_IN_MIN) + seconds;
22:
23:   cout <<"\n\n" << totalSec << " seconds since midnight";
24:   return 0;
25: }
```

Here is a sample session with the program in Listing 2.2.

```
Enter hours: 10
Enter minutes: 0
Enter seconds: 0
```

```
36000 seconds since midnight
```

The program uses the #include directive in line 3 to include the header file IOSTREAM.H; in addition to providing the definitions necessary for output, IOSTREAM.H also is required for input. Lines 5 and 6 contain the #define directive that declares the macro-based constants SEC_IN_MIN and MIN_IN_HOUR. Both constants have the value 60, but each value has a different meaning. The function main, which starts at line 8, declares 4 long-typed variables: hours, minutes, seconds, and totalSec.

The function uses pairs of statements to output the prompting messages and receive input. Line 13 contains the stream output statement that prompts you for the number of hours. Line 14 contains the stream input statement. The identifier cin is the name of the standard input stream and uses the input operator >> to read data from the keyboard and to store it in the variable hours. The input and output statements in lines 15 through 18 perform a similar task of prompting for input and obtaining keyboard input.

Line 20 contains a statement that calculates the total number of seconds since midnight and stores the result in the variable totalSec. The statement uses the macro-based constants MIN_IN_HOUR and SEC_IN_MIN. As you can see, using these constants enhances the readability of the statement, compared to using the number 60 in place of both constants. Line 23 contains a stream output statement that displays the total number of seconds since midnight (stored in the variable totalSec), followed by qualifying text to clarify the output.

Using Formal Constants

Now look at a new version of the program—one that uses the formal C++ constants. Listing 2.3 shows the source code for the program CONST2.CPP. This program works like the CONST1.CPP program. Add the CONST2.CPP file as a node in the project file DAY2.IDE. Compile and run the CONST2.EXE program.

> **Note:** At this point, we assume that you are familiar with the process of creating the .CPP source file, creating the .IDE project file, and adding .CPP files as nodes in the project file. From now on we will not mention creating these files, unless there is a special set of source files in a project.

Listing 2.3. Source code for the program CONST2.CPP.

```
1:  // C++ program that illustrates constants
2:
3:  #include <iostream.h>
4:
5:  const SEC_IN_MIN = 60; // global constant
6:
7:  main()
8:  {
9:    const MIN_IN_HOUR = 60; // local constant
10:
11:    long hours, minutes, seconds;
12:    long totalSec;
13:
14:    cout << "Enter hours: ";
15:    cin >> hours;
16:    cout << "Enter minutes: ";
17:    cin >> minutes;
18:    cout << "Enter seconds: ";
19:    cin >> seconds;
20:
21:    totalSec = ((hours * MIN_IN_HOUR + minutes) *
22:                SEC_IN_MIN) + seconds;
23:
24:    cout <<"\n\n" << totalSec << " seconds since midnight";
25:    return 0;
26: }
```

Here is a sample session with the program in Listing 2.3.

```
Enter hours: 1
Enter minutes: 10
Enter seconds: 20

4220 seconds since midnight
```

The programs in Listings 2.2 and 2.3 are similar. The difference between them is how they declare their constants. In Listing 2.3, the formal C++ constant syntax is used to declare the constants. In addition, the constant SEC_IN_MIN in line 5 is declared, outside the function main. This type of declaration makes the constant global. That is, if there were another function in the program, it would be able to use the constant SEC_IN_MIN. By contrast, the constant MIN_IN_SEC is declared inside the function main. Thus, the constant MIN_IN_SEC is local to the function main.

Operators and Expressions

The manipulation of data involves expressions made up of operands and operators. C++ supports several kinds of operators and expressions.

NEW☞ TERM Operators are special symbols that take the values of operands and produce a new value.

If you've taken any simple algebra in school, you will recognize the types of things that are described in this section. They're mostly extensions of the familiar equations you were taught.

Arithmetic Operators

Table 2.2 shows the C++ arithmetic operators. The compiler carries out floating-point or integer division, depending on the operands. If both operands are integer expressions, the compiler yields the code for an integer division. If either or both operands are floating-point expressions, the compiler generates code for floating-point division.

Table 2.2. C++ arithmetic operators.

C++ Operator	Purpose	Data Type	Example
+	Unary plus	Numeric	x = +y + 3;
-	Unary minus	Numeric	x = -y;
+	Add	Numeric	z = y + x;
-	Subtract	Numeric	z = y - x;
*	Multiply	Numeric	z = y * x;
/	Divide	Numeric	z = y / x;
%	Modulus	Integers	z = y % x;

Look at an example that uses the mathematical operators with integers and floating-point numbers. Listing 2.4 shows the source code for program OPER1.CPP. The program performs the following tasks:

☐ Prompts you to enter two integers (one integer per prompt).

☐ Applies the +, -, *, /, and % operators to the two integers, storing the results in separate variables.

☐ Displays the results of the integer operations.

☐ Prompts you to enter two floating-point numbers (one number per prompt).

☐ Applies the +, -, *, and / operators to the two numbers, storing the results in separate variables.

☐ Displays the result of the floating-point operations.

Type

Listing 2.4. Source code for the program OPER1.CPP.

```
1:  // simple C++ program to illustrate simple math operations
2:
3:  #include <iostream.h>
4:
5:  main()
6:  {
7:
8:      int int1, int2;
9:      long long1, long2, long3, long4, long5;
10:     float x, y, real1, real2, real3, real4;
11:
12:     cout << "\nType first  integer : ";
13:     cin >> int1;
14:     cout << "Type second integer : ";
15:     cin >> int2;
16:     cout << "\n";
17:     long1 = int1 + int2;
18:     long2 = int1 - int2;
19:     long3 = int1 * int2;
20:     long4 = int1 / int2;
21:     long5 = int1 % int2;
22:     cout << int1 << " + " << int2 << " = " << long1 << '\n';
23:     cout << int1 << " - " << int2 << " = " << long2 << '\n';
24:     cout << int1 << " * " << int2 << " = " << long3 << '\n';
25:     cout << int1 << " / " << int2 << " = " << long4 << '\n';
26:     cout << int1 << " mod " << int2 << " = " << long5 << '\n';
27:     cout << "\n\n";
28:     cout << "Type first  real number : ";
29:     cin >> x;
30:     cout << "Type second real number : ";
31:     cin >> y;
32:     cout << "\n";
33:     real1 = x + y;
34:     real2 = x - y;
35:     real3 = x * y;
36:     real4 = x / y;
```

Listing 2.4. continued

```
37:     cout << x << " + " << y << " = " << real1 << '\n';
38:     cout << x << " - " << y << " = " << real2 << '\n';
39:     cout << x << " * " << y << " = " << real3 << '\n';
40:     cout << x << " / " << y << " = " << real4 << '\n';
41:     cout << "\n\n";
42:     return 0;
43: }
```

Here is a sample session with the program in Listing 2.4.

```
Type first  integer : 10
Type second integer : 5

10 + 5 = 15
10 - 5 = 5
10 * 5 = 50
10 / 5 = 2
10 mod 5 = 0


Type first  real number : 1.25
Type second real number : 2.58

1.25 + 2.58 = 3.83
1.25 - 2.58 = -1.33
1.25 * 2.58 = 3.225
1.25 / 2.58 = 0.484496
```

The program in Listing 2.4 declares a set of int-typed, long-typed, and float-typed variables in the function main. Some of these variables store your input, and others store the results of the mathematical operations. The output statement in line 12 prompts you to enter the first integer. The input statement in line 13 obtains your input and stores it in the variable int1. Lines 14 and 15 perform a similar operation to prompt you for the second integer and store it in variable int2.

The program performs the integer math operation in lines 17 through 21 and stores the results of these operations in variables long1 through long5. These variables were declared as long-typed to guard against possible numeric overflow. The output statements in lines 22 through 26 display the integer operands, the operators used, and the results.

The output statement in line 28 prompts you to enter the first floating-point number. The input statement in line 29 obtains your input and stores it in the variable x. Lines 30 and 31 perform a similar operation to prompt you for the second floating-point number and to store it in variable y.

NEW☞
TERM   A floating-point number also is known as a *real number*.

The program performs the floating-point math operation in lines 33 through 36 and stores the results of these operations in variables real1 through real4. The output statements in lines 37 through 40 display the operands, the operators used, and the results.

Arithmetic Expressions

The simplest types of expressions are the ones that contain literals, such as

```
-12
34.45
'A'
"Hello"
```

NEW☞
TERM In general terms, an *arithmetic expression* is part of a program statement that contains a value.

The literal constants -12 and 35.45 are the simplest arithmetic expressions. The next level of arithmetic expressions includes single variables or constants, such as

```
DAYS_IN_WEEK // a constant
i
x
```

Yet another level of arithmetic expressions contains a single operator with numbers, constants, and variables as operands. Following are a few examples:

```
355 / 113
4 * i
45.67 + x
```

More advanced arithmetic expressions contain multiple operators, parentheses, and even functions, such as

```
(355 / 113) * square(radius)
PIE * square(radius)
((2 * x - 3) * x + 2) * x - 5
(1 + x) / (3 - x)
```

The order of executing the operators are discussed at the end of today's lesson, after other types of operators are introduced.

Increment Operators

C++ supports the special increment and decrement operators.

NEW☞
TERM *Increment* (++) and *decrement* (–) *operators* enable you to increment and decrement, respectively, the value stored in a variable by 1.

Syntax

Increment Operators

The general syntax for the increment operators is

```
variable++  // post-increment
++variable  // pre-increment
```

Examples

```
lineNumber++;
++index;
```

Decrement Operators

The general syntax for the decrement operators is

```
variable // post-decrement
variable // pre-decrement
```

Examples

```
lineNumber;
index
```

This general syntax demonstrates that there are two ways to apply the ++ and – operators. Placing these operators to the left of their operand changes the value of the operand *before* the operand contributes its value in an expression. Likewise, placing these operators to the right of their operands alters the value of the operand *after* the operand contributes its value in an expression. If the ++ or – operators are the only operators in a statement, there is no practical distinction between using the pre- or post-forms.

Following are a few simple examples:

```
int n, m, t = 5;

t++; // t is now 6, same effect as ++t
-t; // t is now 5, same effect as t-
t = 5;
n = 4 * t++; // t is now 6 and[]is 20
t = 5;
m = 4 * ++m; // m is now 6 and[]is 24
```

The first statement uses the post-increment ++ operator to increment the value of variable t. If you write ++t instead, you get the same result when the statement finishes executing. The second statement uses the pre-decrement operator. Again, if you write t instead, you get the same result. The next two statements assign 5 to variable t and then use the post-increment ++ operator in a simple math expression. This statement multiplies 4 by the current value of t (that is, 5), assigns the result of 20 to the variable n, and then increments the values in variable t to 6. The last two statements show a different outcome. The statement first increments the value in variable t (the value in variable t becomes 6), and then performs the multiplication, and finally assigns the result of 24 to the variable n.

Look at a simple program that illustrates the feature of the increment operator. Listing 2.5 shows the source code for the program OPER2.CPP. The program requires no input from you. It simply displays two integers whose values were obtained using the increment operator.

Type

Listing 2.5. Source code for the program OPER2.CPP.

```
1:  /*
2:      C++ program to illustrate the feature of the increment operator.
3:      The ++ or  may be included in an expression.  The value
4:      of the associated variable is altered after the expression
5:      is evaluated if the var++ (or var) is used, or before
6:      when ++var (or var) is used.
```

```
 7:   */
 8:
 9:   #include <iostream.h>
10:
11:   main()
12:   {
13:      int i, k = 5;
14:
15:      // use post-incrementing
16:      i = 10 * (k++); // k contributes 5 to the expression
17:      cout << "i = " << i << "\n\n"; // displays 50 (= 10 * 5)
18:
19:      k; // restores the value of k to 5
20:
21:      // use pre-incrementing
22:      i = 10 * (++k); // k contributes 6 to the expression
23:      cout << "i = " << i << "\n\n"; // displays 60 (= 10 * 6)
24:      return 0;
25:   }
```

Here is a sample session with the program in Listing 2.5.

```
i = 50

i = 60
```

The program in Listing 2.5 has the function main, which declares 2 int-typed variables, i and k. The function initializes the variable k by assigning it the value 5. Line 16 contains a statement that applies the post-increment operator to the variable k. Consequently, the statement multiplies 10 by the initial value in k, 5, and assigns the product, 50, to variable i. After assigning the result to variable i, the program increments the value in variable k. The output statement in line 17 displays the value in variable i. The statement in line 19 decrements the value in variable k back to 5. The statement in line 22 applies the pre-increment operator to the variable k. Therefore, the program first increments the value in variable k (from 5 to 6) and then multiplies 10 by the updated value in k. The program assigns the result of the multiplication, 60, to the variable i. The output statement in line 23 displays the current value of variable i.

Assignment Operators

As a programmer, you often may come across statements that look similar to the following:

```
IndexOfFirstElement = IndexOfFirstElement + 4;
GraphicsScaleRatio = GraphicsScaleRatio * 3;
CurrentRateOfReturn = CurrentRateOfReturn / 4;
DOSfileListSize = DOSfileListSize - 10;
```

The variable that receives the result of an expression also is the first operand. (Of course, the addition and multiplication are commutative operations. Therefore, the assigned variable can be either operand with these operations.) Notice that we chose relatively long names to remind you of your need to shorten the expression without making the names of the variables shorter.

C++ offers *assignment operators* that merge with simple math operators.

You can write the following statements:

```
IndexOfFirstElement += 4;
GraphicsScaleRatio *= 3;
CurrentRateOfReturn /= 4;
DOSfileListSize -= 10;
```

Notice that the name of the variable appears only once. In addition, notice that the statements use the operators +=, *=, /=, and -=. Table 2.3 shows the arithmetic assignment operators. C++ supports other types of assignment operators.

Table 2.3. Arithmetic assignment operators.

Assignment Operator	Long Form	Example
x += y	x = x + y	x += 12;
x -= y	x = x - y	x -= 34 + y;
x *= y	x = x * y	scale *= 10;
x /= y	x = x / y	z /= 34 * y;
x %= y	x = x % y	z %= 2;

Look at a program that applies the assignment operators to integers and floating-point numbers. Listing 2.6 shows the source code for the program OPER3.CPP. The program performs the following tasks:

☐ Prompts you to enter two integers (one integer per prompt).

☐ Applies a set of assignment and increment operators to the two integers.

☐ Displays the new values of the integers.

☐ Prompts you to enter two floating-point numbers (one number per prompt).

☐ Applies a set of assignment and increment operators to the two numbers.

☐ Displays the new values of the floating-point numbers.

Listing 2.6. Source code for the program OPER3.CPP.

```
1:  // C++ program to illustrate math assignment operators
2:
3:  #include <iostream.h>
4:
5:  main()
6:  {
7:      int i, j;
8:      double x, y;
9:
```

```
10:      cout << "Type first  integer : ";
11:      cin >> i;
12:      cout << "Type second integer : ";
13:      cin >> j;
14:      i += j;
15:      j -= 6;
16:      i *= 4;
17:      j /= 3;
18:      i++;
19:      j;
20:      cout << "i = " << i << "\n";
21:      cout << "j = " << j << "\n";
22:
23:      cout << "Type first  real number : ";
24:      cin >> x;
25:      cout << "Type second real number : ";
26:      cin >> y;
27:      // abbreviated assignments also work with doubles in C++
28:      x += y;
29:      y -= 4.0;
30:      x *= 4.0;
31:      y /=  3.0;
32:      x++;
33:      y;
34:      cout << "x = " << x << "\n";
35:      cout << "y = " << y << "\n";
36:      return 0;
37: }
```

Here is a sample session with the program in Listing 2.6.

```
Type first  integer : 55
Type second integer : 66
i = 485
j = 19
Type first  real number : 2.5
Type second real number : 4.58
x = 29.32
y = -0.806667
```

The program in Listing 2.6 contains the function main, which declares two int-typed variables (i and j) and two double-typed variables (x and y) in lines 7 and 8, respectively. The output statement in line 10 prompts you to enter the first integer. The input statement in line 11 receives your input and stores it in the variable i. Lines 12 and 13 are similar to lines 10 and 11—they prompt you for the second integer and store it in variable j.

The program manipulates the values in variables i and j using the statements in lines 14 through 19. In line 14, the program uses the += operator to increment the value in variable i by the value in variable j. Line 15 uses the -= operator to decrement the value in variable j by 6. Line 16 applies the *= operator to multiply the value in variable i by 4 and to assign the result back to variable i. Line 17 utilizes the /= operator to divide the value in variable j by 3 and to store the result in j. Lines 18 and 19 apply the increment and decrement operators to variables i and j, respectively. The output statements in lines 20 and 21 display the contents of variables i and j, respectively.

The output statement in line 23 prompts you to enter the first floating-point number. The input statement in line 24 receives your input and saves it in the variable x. Lines 25 and 26 are similar to lines 23 and 24; they prompt you for the second floating-point number and store it in variable y.

The program manipulates the values in variable x and y using the statements in lines 28 through 33. In line 28, the program uses the += operator to increment the value in variable x by the value in variable y. Line 29 uses the -= operator to decrement the value in variable y by 4. Line 30 applies the *= operator to multiply the value in variable x by 4 and to save the result back to x. Line 31 utilizes the /= operator to divide the value in variable y by 3 and to store the result in y. Lines 32 and 33 apply the increment and decrement operators to variable x and y, respectively. The output statements in lines 34 and 35 display the contents of variables x and y, respectively.

The *sizeof* Operator

Frequently, your programs need to know the byte size of a data type or of a variable. C++ provides the sizeof operator, which takes an argument of either a data type or the name of a variable (scalar, array, structure, and so on).

The *sizeof* Operator

The general syntax for the sizeof operator is

```
sizeof({variable_name ¦ data_type})
sizeof {variable_name ¦ data_type}
```

Examples

```
int sizeDifference = sizeof(double) - sizeof(float);
int intSize = sizeof int;
```

DO	DON'T

DO use sizeof with the name of the variable rather than its data type. This approach is safer because if you alter the data type of the variable, the sizeof operator still returns the correct answer. By contrast, if you use the sizeof operator with the data type of the variable and later alter the variable's type, you create a bug if you do not update the argument of the sizeof operator.

DON'T use numbers to represent the size of a variable. This approach often causes errors.

Look at an example that uses the sizeof operator with variables and data types. Listing 2.7 contains the source code for the program SIZEOF1.CPP. The program displays two similar tables that indicate the sizes of the short int, int, long int, char, and float data types. The program displays the first table by applying the sizeof operators to variables of these types. The program displays the second table by directly applying the sizeof operator to the data types.

Listing 2.7. Source code for the program SIZEOF1.CPP.

```
1:  /*
2:    simple program that returns the data sizes using the sizeof()
3:    operator with variables and data types.
4:  */
5:
6:  #include <iostream.h>
7:
8:  main()
9:
10: {
11:     short int aShort;
12:     int anInt;
13:     long aLong;
14:     char aChar;
15:     float aReal;
16:
17:     cout << "Table 1. Data sizes using sizeof(variable)\n\n";
18:     cout << "    Data type         Memory used\n";
19:     cout << "                        (bytes)\n";
20:     cout << "    ";
21:     cout << "\n      short int           " << sizeof(aShort);
22:     cout << "\n       integer            " << sizeof(anInt);
23:     cout << "\n    long integer          " << sizeof(aLong);
24:     cout << "\n      character           " << sizeof(aChar);
25:     cout << "\n        float             " << sizeof(aReal);
26:     cout << "\n\n\n\n";
27:
28:     cout << "Table 2. Data sizes using sizeof(dataType)\n\n";
29:     cout << "    Data type         Memory used\n";
30:     cout << "                        (bytes)\n";
31:     cout << "    ";
32:     cout << "\n      short int           " << sizeof(short int);
33:     cout << "\n       integer            " << sizeof(int);
34:     cout << "\n    long integer          " << sizeof(long);
35:     cout << "\n      character           " << sizeof(char);
36:     cout << "\n        float             " << sizeof(float);
37:     cout << "\n\n\n\n";
38:
39:     return 0;
40: }
```

Here is a sample session with the program in Listing 2.7.

```
Table 1. Data sizes using sizeof(variable)

Data type          Memory used
(bytes)
--------          -----------
short int              2
integer               2
```

```
long integer        4
character         1
float             4
```

```
Table 2. Data sizes using sizeof(dataType)

Data type         Memory used
(bytes)
..........        ............
short int         2
integer           2
long integer        4
character         1
float             4
```

Analysis

The program in Listing 2.7 declares five variables in the function `main`. Each variable has a different data type and derives its name from its data type. For example, the variable `anInt` is an `int`-typed variable, the variable `aLong` is a `long`-typed variable, and so on.

The statements in lines 17 through 25 display the table of data sizes. The output statements in lines 21 through 25 use the `sizeof` operator with the variables.

The statements in lines 28 through 36 also display the table of data sizes. The output statements in lines 32 through 36 use the `sizeof` operator with the data-type identifiers.

Typecasting

Automatic data conversion of a value from one data type to another compatible data type is one of the duties of a compiler. This data conversion simplifies expressions and eases the frustration of both novice and veteran programmers. With behind-the-scenes data conversion, you do not need to examine every expression that mixes compatible data types in your program. For example, the compiler handles most expressions that mix various types of integers or mix integers and floating-point types. You get a compile-time error if you attempt to do something illegal.

NEW☞ TERM *Typecasting* is a language feature that enables you to specify explicitly how to convert a value from its original data type into a compatible data type. Thus, typecasting instructs the compiler to perform the conversion you want and not the one the compiler thinks is needed.

Syntax

Typecasting

C++ supports the following forms of typecasting:

```
type_cast(expression)
```

and

```
(type_cast) expression
```

Examples

```
int i = 2;
float a, b;
a = float(i);
b = (float) i;
```

Look at an example that illustrates implicit data conversion and typecasting. Listing 2.8 shows the source code for the program TYPCAST1.CPP. The program declares variables that have the character, integer, and floating-point data types. Then the program performs two sets of similar mathematical operations. The first set relies on the automatic conversions of data types, performed by the compiler. The second set of operations uses typecasting to explicitly instruct the compiler on how to convert the data types. The program requires no input—it provides its own data—and it displays the output values for both sets of operations. The program illustrates that the compiler succeeds in generating the same output for both sets of operations.

Listing 2.8. Source code for the program TYPCAST1.CPP.

```
1:   // simple C++ program that demonstrates typecasting
2:
3:   #include <iostream.h>
4:
5:   main()
6:   {
7:       short shortInt1, shortInt2;
8:       unsigned short uShort;
9:       int anInt;
10:      long aLong;
11:      char aChar;
12:      float aReal;
13:
14:      // assign values
15:      shortInt1 = 10;
16:      shortInt2 = 6;
17:      // perform operations without typecasting
18:      uShort = shortInt1 + shortInt2;
19:      anInt = shortInt1 - shortInt2;
20:      aLong = shortInt1 * shortInt2;
21:      aChar = aLong + 5; // conversion is automatic to character
22:      aReal = shortInt1 * shortInt2 + 0.5;
23:
24:      cout << "shortInt1 = " << shortInt1 << '\n'
25:          << "shortInt2 = " << shortInt2 << '\n'
26:          << "uShort = " << uShort << '\n'
27:          << "anInt = " << anInt << '\n'
28:          << "aLong = " << aLong << '\n'
29:          << "aChar is " << aChar << '\n'
30:          << "aReal = " << aReal << "\n\n\n";
31:
32:      // perform operations with typecasting
33:      uShort = (unsigned short) (shortInt1 + shortInt2);
34:      anInt = (int) (shortInt1 - shortInt2);
```

continues

Listing 2.8. continued

```
35:     aLong = (long) (shortInt1 * shortInt2);
36:     aChar = (unsigned char) (aLong + 5);
37:     aReal = (float) (shortInt1 * shortInt2 + 0.5);
38:
39:     cout << "shortInt1 = " << shortInt1 << '\n'
40:          << "shortInt2 = " << shortInt2 << '\n'
41:          << "uShort = " << uShort << '\n'
42:          << "anInt = " << anInt << '\n'
43:          << "aLong = " << aLong << '\n'
44:          << "aChar is " << aChar << '\n'
45:          << "aReal = " << aReal << "\n\n\n";
46:     return 0;
47: }
```

Here is a sample session with the program in Listing 2.8.

```
shortInt1 = 10
shortInt2 = 6
aByte = 16
anInt = 4
aLong = 60
aChar is A
aReal = 60.5


shortInt1 = 10
shortInt2 = 6
aByte = 16
anInt = 4
aLong = 60
aChar is A
aReal = 60.5
```

The program in Listing 2.8 declares the following variables in the function `main`:

- ☐ The `short`-typed variables `shortInt1` and `shortInt2`
- ☐ The `unsigned short`-typed variable `uShort`
- ☐ The `int`-typed variable `anInt`
- ☐ The `long`-typed variable `aLong`
- ☐ The `char`-typed variable `aChar`
- ☐ The `float`-typed variable `aReal`

Lines 15 and 16 assign the integers 10 and 6 to variable `shortInt1` and `shortIn2`, respectively. Lines 18 through 22 perform various mathematical operations and assign the results to variables `uShort`, `anInt`, `aLong`, `aChar`, and `aReal`.

Note: C and C++ treat the char type as a special integer. Each char-type literal (such as 'A'), constant, or variable has an integer value that is equal to its ASCII representation. This language feature enables you to store an integer in a char-type variable and treat a char-type data item as an integer. The statement in line 21 adds the integer 5 to the value of the variable aLong and assigns the result, an integer, to the variable aChar. The value of the assigned integer, 65, represents the ASCII code for the letter A.

The output statement in lines 24 through 30 displays the values stored in the variables. Notice that the output for variable aChar is the letter A. If you write the output term for variable aChar as << (int) aChar, you get 65, the ASCII code of the character stored in aChar.

The statements in lines 32 through 37 perform similar operations to the statements in lines 18 through 22. The main difference is that the statements in lines 32 through 37 use typecasting to explicitly instruct the compiler on how to convert the result. The output statement in lines 39 through 45 displays the contents of the variables.

Relational and Logical Operators

Table 2.4 shows the C++ relational and logical operators. Notice that C++ does not spell out the operators AND, OR, and NOT. Rather, it uses single- and dual-character symbols. Also notice that C++ does not support the relational XOR operator.

NEW TERM The *relational operators* (less than, greater than, and equal to) and the *logical operators* (AND, OR, and NOT) are the basic building blocks of decision-making constructs in any programming language.

Table 2.4. C++ relational and logical operators.

C++ Operator	Meaning	Example
&&	Logical AND	if (i > 1 && i < 10)
||	Logical OR	if (c==0 || c==9)
!	Logical NOT	if (!(c>1 && c<9))
<	Less than	if (i < 0)
<=	Less than or equal to	if (i <= 0)
>	Greater than	if (j > 10)
>=	Greater than or equal to	if (x >= 8.2)

continues

Table 2.4. continued

C++ Operator	Meaning	Example
==	Equal to	`if (c == '\0')`
!=	Not equal to	`if (c != '\n')`
? :	Conditional assignment	`k = (i<1) ? 1 : i;`

Although these macros are permissible in C++, you might get a negative reaction from veteran C++ programmers who read your code. Who says that programming is always objective?

Warning: Do *not* use the = operator as the equality relational operator. This common error is a source of logical bugs in a C++ program. You may be accustomed to using the = operator in other languages to test the equality of two data items. In C++, you *must* use the == operator. What happens if you employ the = operator in C++? Do you get a compiler error? The answer is that you may get a compiler warning. Other than that, your C++ program should run. When the program reaches the expression that it is supposed to test for equality, it actually attempts to assign the operand on the right of the = sign to the operand on the left of the = sign. Of course, a session with such a program most likely leads to weird program behavior or even a system hang.

Notice that the last operator in Table 3.3 is the ?: operator. This special operator supports what is known as the conditional expression.

NEW The *conditional expression* is a shorthand for a dual-alternative simple if-else statement.
TERM (See Day 3 for more information about the if statement.)

For example, the following is an if-else statement that can be compressed into a conditional expression:

```
if (condition)
variable = expression1;
else
variable = expression2;
```

The equivalent conditional expression is as follows:

```
variable = (condition) ? expression1 : expression2;
```

The conditional expression tests the condition. If that condition is true, it assigns expression1 to the target variable. Otherwise, it assigns expression2 to the target variable.

Boolean Expressions

Often, you need to use a collection of relational and logical operators to formulate a nontrivial condition. Here are examples of such conditions.

```
x < 0 || x > 11
(i != 0 || i > 100) && (j != i || j > 0)
x != 0 && x != 10 && x != 100
```

NEW *Boolean* (also called *logical*) *expressions* are expressions that involve logical operators
TERM and/or relational operators.

DO	DON'T

DO double-check to avoid Boolean expressions that are either always true or always false. For example, the expression (x < 0 && x > 10) is always false, because no value of x can be negative and greater than 10 at the same time.

DON'T use the = operator to test for equality.

Consider now an example that uses relational and logical operators and expressions. Listing 2.9 shows the source code for the program RELOP1.CPP. The program prompts you to enter three integers and then proceeds to perform a battery of tests. The program displays the relational and logical operations, their operands, and their results.

 Listing 2.9. Source code for the program RELOP1.CPP.

```
1:  /*
2:      simple C++ program that uses logical expressions
3:      this program uses the conditional expression to display
4:      TRUE or FALSE messages, since C++ does not support the
5:      BOOLEAN data type.
6:  */
7:
8:  #include <iostream.h>
9:
10: const MIN_NUM = 30;
11: const MAX_NUM = 199;
12: const int TRUE = 1;
13: const int FALSE = 0;
14:
15: main()
16: {
17:     int i, j, k;
18:     int flag1, flag2, in_range,
19:         same_int, xor_flag;
20:
21:     cout << "Type first  integer : "; cin >> i;
```

continues

Listing 2.9. continued

```
22:     cout << "Type second integer : "; cin >> j;
23:     cout << "Type third   integer : "; cin >> k;
24:
25:     // test for range [MIN_NUM...MAX_NUM]
26:     flag1 = i >= MIN_NUM;
27:     flag2 = i <= MAX_NUM;
28:     in_range = flag1 && flag2;
29:     cout << "\n" << i << " is in the range "
30:          << MIN_NUM << " to " << MAX_NUM << " : "
31:          << ((in_range) ? "TRUE" : "FALSE");
32:
33:     // test if two or more entered numbers are equal
34:     same_int = i == j || i == k || j == k;
35:     cout << "\nat least two integers you typed are equal : "
36:          << ((same_int) ? "TRUE" : "FALSE");
37:
38:     // miscellaneous tests
39:     cout << "\n" << i << " != " << j << " : "
40:          << ((i != j) ? "TRUE" : "FALSE");
41:     cout << "\nNOT (" << i << " < " << j << ") : "
42:          << ((!(i < j)) ? "TRUE" : "FALSE");
43:     cout << "\n" << i << " <= " << j << " : "
44:          << ((i <= j) ? "TRUE" : "FALSE");
45:     cout << "\n" << k << " > " << j << " : "
46:          << ((k > j) ? "TRUE" : "FALSE");
47:     cout << "\n(" << k << " = " << i << ") AND ("
48:          << j << " != " << k << ") : "
49:          << ((k == i && j != k) ? "TRUE" : "FALSE");
50:
51:     // NOTE: C++ does NOT support the logical XOR operator for
52:     // boolean expressions.
53:     // add numeric results of logical tests.  Value is in 0...2
54:     xor_flag = (k <= i) + (j >= k);
55:     // if xor_flag is either 0 or 2 (i.e. not = 1), it is
56:     // FALSE therefore interpret 0 or 2 as false.
57:     xor_flag = (xor_flag == 1) ? TRUE : FALSE;
58:     cout << "\n(" << k << " <= " << i << ") XOR ("
59:          << j << " >= " << k << ") : "
60:          << ((xor_flag) ? "TRUE" : "FALSE");
61:     cout << "\n(" << k << " > " << i << ") AND("
62:          << j << " <= " << k << ") : "
63:          << ((k > i && j <= k) ? "TRUE" : "FALSE");
64:     cout << "\n\n";
65:     return 0;
66: }
```

Here is a sample session with the program in Listing 2.9.

```
Type first  integer : 55
Type second integer : 64
Type third  integer : 87

55 is in the range 30 to 199 : TRUE
at least two integers you typed are equal : FALSE
55 != 64 : TRUE
```

```
NOT (55 < 64) : FALSE
55 <= 64 : TRUE
87 > 64 : TRUE
(87 = 55) AND (64 != 87) : FALSE
(87 <= 55) XOR (64 >= 87) : FALSE
(87 > 55) AND(64 <= 87) : TRUE
```

The program in Listing 2.9 declares 4 global constants. The constants MIN_NUM and MAX_NUM define a range of numbers used in the logical tests. The constants TRUE and FALSE represent the Boolean values. The function main declares a number of int variables that are used for input and various testing. The statements in lines 21 through 23 prompt you for 3 integers and store them in the variables i, j, and k, respectively.

The statements in lines 26 through 31 involve testing whether the value in variable i lies in the range of MIN_NUM and MAX_NUM. The statement in line 26 tests if the value in i is greater than or equal to the constant MIN_NUM. The program assigns the Boolean result to the variable flag1. The statement in line 27 tests whether the value in i is less than or equal to the constant MAX_NUM. The program assigns the Boolean result to the variable flag2. The statement in line 28 applies the && operator to the variable flag1 and flag2, and it assigns the Boolean result to the variable in_range. The output statement in lines 29 through 31 states what the test is and displays TRUE or FALSE depending on the value in the variable in_range. The statement uses the conditional operator ?: to display the string TRUE if in_range has a nonzero value and to display the string FALSE if otherwise.

The statements in lines 34 through 36 determine whether at least two of the three integers you entered are equal. The statement in line 34 uses a Boolean expression that applies the == relational operators and the || logical operators. The statement assigns the Boolean result to the variable same_int. The output statement in lines 35 and 36 states the test and displays the TRUE/FALSE outcome. The output statement uses the conditional operator to display the strings TRUE or FALSE depending on the value in variable same_int.

The statements in lines 39 through 49 perform miscellaneous tests that involve the input values, and they display both the test and the results. Please feel free to alter these statements to conduct different tests.

Note: The statements in lines 54 through 60 perform an XOR test and display the outcome. The program uses a simple programming trick to implement the XOR operator. The statement in line 54 adds the Boolean value of the subexpressions (k <= i) and (j >= k). The result is 0 if both subexpressions are false, 1 if only one of the subexpressions is true, and 2 if both subexpressions are true. Because the XOR operator is true only if either subexpression is true, the statement in line 57 assigns TRUE to the variable xor_flag if the previous value is 1. Otherwise, the statement assigns FALSE to xor_flag. The statements in lines 61 through 63 perform another miscellaneous test.

Bit-Manipulation Operators

C++ is a programming language that is suitable for system development. System development requires bit-manipulating operators.

NEW☞ TERM *Bit-manipulating operators* toggle, set, query, and shift the bits of a byte or a word.

Table 2.5 shows the bit-manipulating operators. Notice that C++ uses the symbols & and ¦ to represent the bitwise AND and OR, respectively. Recall that the && and ¦¦ characters represent the logical AND and OR operators, respectively. In addition to the bit-manipulating operators, C++ supports the bit-manipulating assignment operators, shown in Table 2.6. (Using bit-manipulating operators is a part of advanced programming that involves fiddling with single bits. As a novice C++ programmer, you most likely will not use these operators in the near future.)

Table 2.5. C++ bit-manipulating operators.

C++ Operator	Meaning	Example
&	Bitwise AND	i & 128
¦	Bitwise OR	j ¦ 64
^	Bitwise XOR	j ^ 12
~	Bitwise NOT	~j
<<	Bitwise shift left	i << 2
>>	Bitwise shift right	j >> 3

Table 2.6. C++ bit-manipulating assignment operators.

C++ Operator	Long Form	Example
x &= y	x = x & y	i &= 128
x ¦= y	x = x ¦ y	j ¦= 64
x ^= y	x = x ^ y	k ^= 15
x <<= y	x = x << y	j <<= 2
x >>= y	x = x >> y	k >>= 3

Let us present a C++ program that performs simple bit manipulation. Listing 2.10 contains the source code for the program BITS1.CPP. The program requires no input, because it uses internal data. The program applies the ¦, &, ^, >>, and << bitwise operators and displays the results of the bitwise manipulation.

Type

Listing 2.10. Source code for the program BITS1.CPP.

```cpp
 1:  // C++ program to perform bit manipulations
 2:
 3:  #include <iostream.h>
 4:
 5:  main()
 6:  {
 7:
 8:      int i, j, k;
 9:
10:      // assign values to i and j
11:      i = 0xF0;
12:      j = 0x1A;
13:
14:      k = j & i;
15:      cout << j << " AND " << i << " = " << k << "\n";
16:
17:      k = j ¦ i;
18:      cout << j << " OR " << i << " = " << k << "\n";
19:
20:      k = j ^ 0x1C;
21:      cout << j << " XOR " << 0x1C << " = " << k << "\n";
22:
23:      k = i << 2;
24:      cout << i << " shifted left by 2 bits = " << k << "\n";
25:
26:      k = i >> 2;
27:      cout << i << " shifted right by 2 bits = " << k << "\n";
28:      return 0;
29:  }
```

Output

Here is a sample session with the program in Listing 2.10.

```
26 AND 240 = 16
26 OR 240 = 250
26 XOR 28 = 6
240 shifted left by 2 bits = 960
240 shifted right by 2 bits = 60
```

Analysis

The program in Listing 2.10 declares three int-typed variables, i, j, and k. The statements in lines 11 and 12 assign hexadecimal numbers to the variables i and j, respectively. The statement in line 14 applies the bitwise AND operator to the variables i and j, and it stores the result in variable k. The output statement in line 15 displays the operands, the bitwise operator, and the results. The statement in line 17 applies the bitwise OR operator to the variable i and j, and it saves the result to variable k. The output statement in line 18 displays the operands, the bitwise operator, and the results. The statement in line 20 applies the bitwise XOR operator using the variable j and the hexadecimal integer 0x1C. The output statement in line 21 displays the operands, the bitwise operator, and the results.

The statements in lines 23 through 27 apply the shift-left and shift-right operators to variable i. These operators shift the bits of the variable i by two bits and assign the result to variable k. The effect of the left-shift operator is the same as multiplying the value in the variable i by 4. Similarly, the effect of the right-shift operator is the same as dividing the value in the variable i by 4.

The Comma Operator

The comma operator requires that the program completely evaluate the first expression before evaluating the second expression. Both expressions are located in the same C++ statement. What does located in the same C++ statement mean exactly? Why use this rather unusual operator in the first place? Because the comma operator with its peculiar role does serve a specific and very important purpose in the for loop.

NEW *Loops* are powerful language constructs that enable computers to excel in achieving
TERM repetitive tasks. The *comma operator* enables you to create multiple expressions that initialize multiple loop-related variables.

Syntax

The Comma Operator

The general syntax for the comma operator is

```
expression1, expression2
```

Example

```
for (i = 0, j = 0; i < 10; i++, j++)
```

You will learn more about the for loop in Day 3. For now, this example shows you how to apply the comma operator.

Operator Precedence and Evaluation Direction

Now that you are familiar with most of the C++ operators (there are a few more operators that deal with pointers and addresses), you need to know two related aspects: first, the precedence of the C++ operators; and second, the direction (or sequence) of evaluation. Table 2.7 shows the C++ precedence of the C++ operators covered so far and also indicates the evaluation direction.

Table 2.7. C++ operators and their precedence.

Category	Name	Symbol	Evaluation Direction	Precedence
Monadic				
	Post-increment	++	Left to right	2
	Post-decrement	–	Left to right	2
	Address	&	Right to left	2
	Bitwise NOT	~	Right to left	2
	Typecast	(type)	Right to left	2
	Logical NOT	!	Right to left	2
	Negation	-	Right to left	2
	Plus sign	+	Right to left	2
	Pre-increment	++	Right to left	2
	Pre-decrement	–	Right to left	2
	Size of data	sizeof	Right to left	2
Multiplicative				
	Modulus	%	Left to right	3
	Multiply	*	Left to right	3
	Divide	/	Left to right	3
Additive				
	Add	+	Left to right	4
	Subtract	-	Left to right	4
Bitwise Shift				
	Shift left	<<	Left to right	5
	Shift right	>>	Left to right	5
Relational				
	Less than	<	Left to right	6
	Less or equal	<=	Left to right	6
	Greater than	>	Left to right	6
	Greater or equal	>=	Left to right	6
	Equal	==	Left to right	7
	Not equal	!=	Left to right	7

continued

Table 2.7. continued

Category	Name	Symbol	Evaluation Direction	Precedence
Bitwise				
	AND	&	Left to right	8
	XOR	^	Left to right	9
	OR	¦	Left to right	10
Logical				
	AND	&&	Left to right	11
	OR	¦¦	Left to right	12
Ternary				
	Cond. express.	?:	Right to left	13
Assignment				
	Arithmetic	=	Right to left	14
		+=	Right to left	14
		-=	Right to left	14
		*=	Right to left	14
		/=	Right to left	14
		%=	Right to left	14
	Shift	>>=	Right to left	14
		<<=	Right to left	14
	Bitwise	&=	Right to left	14
		¦=	Right to left	14
		^=	Right to left	14
	Comma	,	Left to right	15

Summary

Today's lesson presented the basic components of C++ programs. These components include data types, variables, constants, and expressions. You learned the following basics:

☐ The predefined data types in Turbo C++ 4.5 include the `bool`, `int`, `char`, `float`, `double`, and `void` data types. C++ adds more flexibility to data types by supporting data-type modifiers. These modifiers alter the precision and the range of values. The type modifiers are `signed`, `unsigned`, `short`, and `long`.

- [ ] Turbo C++ 4.5 identifiers can be up to 32 characters long and must begin with a letter or an underscore. The subsequent characters of an identifier may be a letter, digit, or underscore. C++ identifiers are case-sensitive.

- [ ] The `#include` directive is a special instruction to the compiler. The directive tells the compiler to include the contents of the specified file as though you typed it in the currently scanned source file.

- [ ] Declaring constants involves using the `#define` directive to declare macro-based constants or using the `const` keyword to declare formal constants. The formal constants require that you specify the constant's type (the default is `int`, when omitted), the name of the constants, and the associated value.

- [ ] Declaring variables requires you to state the data type of the variable and the name of the variable. C++ enables you to initialize a variable when you declare it. You can declare multiple variables in a single declarative statement.

- [ ] The arithmetic operators include +, -, *, /, and % (modulus).

- [ ] The arithmetic expressions vary in complexity. The simplest expression contains a single data item (literal, constant, or variable). Complex expressions include multiple operators, functions, literals, constants, and variables.

- [ ] The increment and decrement operators come in the pre- and post-forms. C++ enables you to apply these operators to variables that store characters, integers, and even floating-point numbers.

- [ ] The arithmetic assignment operators enable you to write shorter arithmetic expressions in which the primary operand also is the variable receiving the result of the expression.

- [ ] The `sizeof` operator returns the byte size of either a data type or a variable.

- [ ] Typecasting enables you to force the type conversion of an expression.

- [ ] Relational and logical operators enable you to build logical expressions. C++ does not support a predefined Boolean type and instead considers `0` as false and any nonzero value as true.

- [ ] Boolean expressions combine relational and logical operators to formulate nontrivial conditions. These expressions allow a program to make sophisticated decisions.

- [ ] The conditional expression offers you a short form for the simple dual-alternative `if-else` statement.

- [ ] The bit-manipulation operators perform bitwise AND, OR, XOR, and NOT operations. In addition, C++ supports the << and >> bitwise shift operators.

- [ ] The bit-manipulation assignment operators offer short forms for simple bit-manipulation statements.

Q&A

Q Is there a specific style for naming identifiers?

A There are a few styles that have become popular in recent years. The one we use has the identifier begin with a lowercase character. If the identifier contains multiple words, such as `numberOfElements`, make the first character of each subsequent word an uppercase letter.

Q How does the compiler react when you declare a variable in a function but never assign a value to it?

A The compiler issues a warning that the variable is unreferenced.

Q What is the Boolean expression for checking that the value of a variable, `i`, is in the range of values (for example, defined by variables `lowVal` and `hiVal`)?

A The expression that determines whether the value in variable `i` is located in a range is

```
(i >= lowVal && i <= hiVal)
```

Workshop

The Workshop provides quiz questions to help you solidify your understanding of the material covered and exercises to provide you with experience in using what you've learned. Try to understand the quiz and exercise answers before continuing on to the next day's lesson. Answers are provided in Appendix A.

Quiz

1. Which of the following variables are valid, and which are not? Why?

```
numFiles
n0Distance_02_Line
0Weight
Bin Number
static
Static
```

2. What is the output of the following program?

```
    #include <iostream.h>

main()
{
  int i = 3;
  int j = 5;
  double x = 33.5;
  double y = 10.0;
```

```
      cout << 10 + j % i << "\n";
      cout << i * i - 2 * i + 5 << "\n";
      cout << (19 + i + j) / (2 * j + 2) << "\n";
       cout << x / y + y / x << "\n";
      cout << i * x + j * y << "\n";
      return 0;
    }
```

3. What is the output of the following program?

```
        #include <iostream.h>

main()
{
  int i = 3;
  int j = 5;

  cout << 10 + j % i++ << "\n";
  cout << -i * i - 2 * i + 5 << "\n";
  cout << (19 + ++i + ++j) / (2 * j + 2) << "\n";
  return 0;
}
```

4. What is the output of the following program?

```
#include <iostream.h>

main()
{
  int i = 3;
  int j = 5;

  i += j;
  j *= 2;
  cout << 10 + j % i << "\n";
  i -= 2;
  j /= 3;
  cout << i * i - 2 * i + j << "\n";
  return 0;
}
```

5. What is the output of the following program?

```
#include <iostream.h>

main()
{
  int i = 5;
  int j = 10;

  cout << ((i < j) ? "TRUE" : "FALSE") << "\n";
  cout << ((i > 0 && j < 100) ? "TRUE" : "FALSE") << "\n";
  cout << ((i > 0 && i < 10) ? "TRUE" : "FALSE") << "\n";
  cout << ((i == 5 && i == j) ? "TRUE" : "FALSE") << "\n";
  return 0;
}
```

Exercises

1. Use the conditional operator to write the function max, which returns the greater of two integers.

2. Use the conditional operator to write the function min, which returns the smaller of two integers.

3. Use the conditional operator to write the function abs, which returns the absolute value of an integer.

4. Use the conditional operator to write the function isOdd, which returns 0 if its integer argument is an odd number and yields 1 if otherwise.

The Decision-Making Constructs and Loops

Different programming languages offer varying support for decision-making constructs. Some languages provide only simple decision-making constructs, whereas others offer more sophisticated constructs.

NEW   *Decision-making constructs* allow your applications to examine conditions and choose
TERM   courses of action.

Another facet of the decision-making constructs in C++ are the loops that improve the processing of repetitive tasks. They allow the computer to take over the job of doing something repeatedly without forcing the programmer to type the same stuff in over and over, changing things only slightly for each version.

Today's lesson looks at the decision-making constructs and loops in C++ and covers the following topics:

- ☐ The single-alternative `if` statement
- ☐ The dual-alternative `if-else` statement
- ☐ The multiple-alternative `if-else` statement
- ☐ The multiple-alternative `switch` statement
- ☐ Nested decision-making constructs
- ☐ The `try`, `catch`, and `throw` statements
- ☐ The `for` loop statement
- ☐ The `do-while` loop statement
- ☐ The `while` loop statement
- ☐ Skipping iterations
- ☐ Exiting loops
- ☐ Nested loops

Decision-Making Constructs

Today's lesson starts with decision-making constructs. These are methods by which an application can perform different tasks based on differing conditions. For example, if a program asks the user whether to continue an action, the program needs to be able to actually continue (or not continue) based on the user's input. These are the first of the decision-making constructs.

The Single-Alternative *if* Statement

Unlike many programming languages, C++ does not have the keyword `then` in any form of the `if` statement. This language feature may lead you to ask how the `if` statement separates the tested condition from the executable statements. The answer is that C++ dictates that you enclose the tested condition in parentheses.

NEW An `if` statement is a *single-alternative* statement.
TERM

The Single-Alternative *if* Statement

The general syntax for the single-alternative `if` statement is

```
if (condition)
   statement;
```

for a single executable statement, and

```
if (condition) {
   <sequence of statements>
}
```

for a sequence of executable statements.

Examples

```
if (numberOfLines < 0)
   numberOfLines = 0;

if ((height - 54) < 3) {
   area = length * width;
   volume = area * height;
}
```

C++ uses the open and close braces {} to define a block of statements. Figure 3.1 shows the flow in a single-alternative `if` statement.

Figure 3.1.
The program flow in the single-alternative if *statement.*

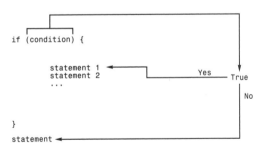

Look at an example. Listing 3.1 shows a program with a single-alternative `if` statement. The program prompts you to enter a nonzero number and stores the input in the variable x. If the value in x is not zero, the program displays the reciprocal of x.

Type **Listing 3.1. Source code for the program IF1.CPP.**

```
1: // Program that demonstrates the single-alternative if statement
2:
3: #include <iostream.h>
4:
5: main()
```

continues 81

Listing 3.1. continued

```
6:  {
7:    double x;
8:    cout << "Enter a non—zero number : ";
9:    cin >> x;
10:   if (x != 0)
11:     cout << "The reciprocal of " << x
12:           << " is " << (1/x) << endl;
13:   return 0;
14: }
```

Here is a sample session with the program in Listing 3.1.

```
Enter a non-zero number : 25
The reciprocal of 25 is 0.04
```

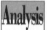

The program in Listing 3.1 declares the double-typed variable x in the function main. The output statement in line 8 prompts you to enter a nonzero number. The input statement in line 9 stores your input in variable x. The if statement in line 10 determines whether x does not equal zero. If this condition is true, the program executes the output statement in lines 11 and 12. This statement displays the value of x and its reciprocal, 1/x. If the tested condition is false, the program skips the statements in lines 11 and 12 and resumes at the statement in line 13.

The Dual-Alternative *if-else* Statement

In the *dual-alternative* form of the if statement, the else keyword separates the statements that are used to execute each alternative.

NEW☞ The *dual-alternative* if-else statement provides two alternate courses of action based on
TERM the Boolean value of the tested condition.

The Dual-Alternative *if-else* Statement

The general syntax for the dual-alternative if-else statement is

```
if (condition)
    statement1;
else
    statement2;
```

for a single executable statement in each clause, and

```
if (condition) {
    <sequence #1 of statements>
}
else {
    <sequence #2 of statements>
}
```

for a sequence of executable statements in both clauses.

Example

```
if (moneyInAccount > withdraw) {
   moneyInAccount -= withdraw;
   cout << "You withdrew $" << withdraw << endl;
   cout << "Balance is $" << moneyInAccount << endl;
}
else {
   cout << "Cannot withdraw $" << withdraw << endl;
   cout << "Account has $" << moneyInAccount << endl;
}
```

Figure 3.2. shows the program flow in the dual-alternative if-else statement.

Figure 3.2.
The program flow in the dual-alternative if-else statement.

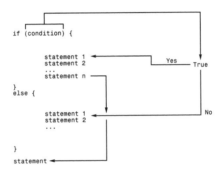

Look at an example that uses the dual-alternative if-else statement. Listing 3.2 contains the source code for the program IF2.CPP. The program prompts you to enter a character and then determines whether you entered a letter. The program output classifies your input as either a letter or a nonletter character.

Type   **Listing 3.2. Source code for the program IF2.CPP.**

```
1:  // Program that demonstrates the dual-alternative if statement
2:
3:  #include <iostream.h>
4:  #include <ctype.h>
5:
6:  main()
7:  {
8:    char c;
9:    cout << "Enter a letter : ";
10:   cin >> c;
11:   // convert to uppercase
12:   c = toupper;
13:   if (c >= 'A' && c <= 'Z')
14:     cout << "You entered a letter\n";
15:   else
16:     cout << "Your input was not a letter\n";
17:   return 0;
18: }
```

Here is a sample session with the program in Listing 3.2.

```
Enter a character : g
You entered a letter
```

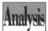

The program in Listing 3.2 declares the char-typed variable c in line 8. The output statement in line 9 prompts you to enter a letter. The input statement in line 10 obtains your input and stores it in variable c. The statement in line 12 converts the value in the variable to uppercase by calling the function toupper (prototyped in the CTYPE.H header file). This character case conversion simplifies the tested condition in the if-else statement at line 13. The if-else statement determines if the variable c contains a character in the range of A to Z. If this condition is true, the program executes the output statement in line 14. This statement displays a message stating that you have entered a letter. Alternatively, if the tested condition is false, the program executes the else clause statement in line 16. This statement displays a message stating that your input was not a letter.

Potential Problems with the *if* Statement

There is a potential problem with the dual-alternative if statement. This problem occurs when the if clause includes another single-alternative if statement. In this case, the compiler considers that the else clause pertains to the nested if statement. (A nested if statement is one that contains another if statement in the if and/or else clauses. You learn more about nesting in the next section.) Here is an example.

```
if (i > 0)
   if (i = 10)
      cout << "You guessed the magic number";
else
   cout << "Number is out of range";
```

In this code fragment, when the variable i is a positive number other than 10, the code displays the message Number is out of range. The compiler treats these statements as though the code fragment meant

```
if (i > 0)
   if (i = 10)
      cout << "You guessed the magic number";
   else
      cout << "Number is out of range";
```

To correct this problem, enclose the nested if statement in a statement block.

```
if (i > 0) {
   if (i = 10)
      cout << "You guessed the magic number";
}
else
   cout << "Number is out of range";
```

The Multiple-Alternative *if-else* Statement

C++ enables you to nest `if-else` statements to create a multiple-alternative form. This alternative gives a lot of power and flexibility to your applications.

NEW◆ The *multiple-alternative* `if-else` statement contains nested `if-else` statements.
TERM

Syntax

The Multiple-Alternative *if-else* Statement

The general syntax for the multiple-alternative `if-else` statement is

```
if (tested_condition1)
    statement1; ¦ { <sequence #1 of statement> }
else if (tested_condition2)
    statement2; ¦ { <sequence #2 of statement> }
...
else if (tested_conditionN)
    statementN; ¦ { <sequence #N of statement> }
[else
    statementN+1; ¦ { <sequence #N+1 of statement> }]
```

Example

```
char op;

int opOk = 1;
double x, y, z;
cout << "Enter operand1 operator operand2: ";
cin >> x >> op >> y;
if (op == '+')
    z = x + y;
else if (op == '-')
    z = x - y;
else if (op == '*')
    z = x * y;
else if (op == '/' && y != 0)
    z = x / y;
else
    opOk = 0;
```

The multiple-alternative `if-else` statement performs a series of cascaded tests until one of the following occurs:

☐ One of the conditions in the `if` clause or in the `else if` clauses is true. In this case, the accompanying statements are executed.

☐ None of the tested conditions are true. The program executes the statements in the catch-all `else` clause (if there is an `else` clause).

Figure 3.3 shows the program flow in the multiple-alternative `if-else` statement.

Figure 3.3.

The program flow in the multiple-alternative if-else *statement.*

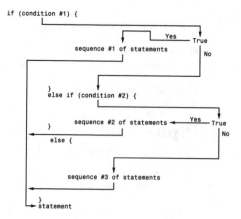

Consider the following example. Listing 3.3 shows the source code for the program IF3.CPP. The program prompts you to enter a character and uses the multiple—alternative if-else statement to determine whether your input is one of the following:

- ☐ An uppercase letter
- ☐ A lowercase letter
- ☐ A digit
- ☐ A non-alphanumeric character

Listing 3.3. Source code for the IF3.CPP program.

```
1: // Program that demonstrates the multiple-alternative if statement
2:
3: #include <iostream.h>
4:
5: main()
6: {
7:    char c;
8:    cout << "Enter a character : ";
9:    cin >> c;
10:    if (c >= 'A' && c <= 'Z')
11:      cout << "You entered an uppercase letter\n";
12:    else if (c >= 'a' && c <= 'z')
13:      cout << "You entered a lowercase letter\n";
14:    else if (c >= '0' && c <= '9')
15:      cout << "You entered a digit\n";
16:    else
17:      cout << "You entered a non-alphanumeric character\n";
18:    return 0;
19: }
```

Here is a sample session with the program in Listing 3.3.

```
Enter a character : !
You entered a non—alphanumeric character
```

Analysis The program in Listing 3.3 declares the char-typed variable c in line 7. The output statement in line 8 prompts you to enter a letter. The input statement in line 9 obtains your input and stores it in variable c. The multi-alternative if-else statement tests the following conditions:

☐ In line 10, the if statement determines whether the variable c contains a letter in the range of A to Z. If this condition is true, the program executes the output statement in line 11. This statement confirms that you entered an uppercase letter. The program then resumes at line 18.

☐ If the condition in line 10 is false, the program jumps to the first else if clause, in line 12. There the program determines whether the variable c contains a letter in the range of a to z. If this condition is true, the program executes the output statement in line 13. This statement confirms that you entered a lowercase letter. The program then resumes at line 18.

☐ If the condition in line 12 is false, the program jumps to the second else if clause, in line 14. There the program determines whether the variable c contains a digit. If this condition is true, the program executes the output statement in line 15. This statement confirms that you entered a digit. The program then resumes at line 18.

☐ If the condition in line 14 is false, the program jumps to the catch-all else clause in line 16 and executes the output statement in line 17. This statement displays a message telling you that your input was neither a letter nor a digit.

The *switch* Statement

The switch statement offers a special form of multiple-alternative decision-making. It enables you to examine the various values of an integer-compatible expression and choose the appropriate course of action.

Syntax

The *switch* Statement

The general syntax for the switch statement is

```
switch (expression) {
  case constant1_1:
  [    case constant1_2: ...]
     <one or more statements>
     break;
  case constant2_1:
  [    case constant2_2: ...]
     <one or more statements>
     break;
...
  case constantN_1:
  [    case constantN_2: ...]
     <one or more statements>
```

```
        break;
    default:
        <one or more statements>
}
```

Example

```
OK = 1;
switch (op) {
    case '+':
        z = x + y;
        break;
    case '-':
        z = x - y;
        break;
    case '*':
        z = x * y;
        break;
    case '/':
        if (y != 0)
            z = x / y;
        else
            OK = 0;
        break;
    default:
        Ok = 0;
}
```

Following are the rules for using a switch statement:

1. The switch requires an integer-compatible value. This value may be a constant, variable, function call, or expression. The switch statement does not work with floating-point data types.

2. The value after each case label *must* be a constant.

3. C++ does not support case labels with ranges of values. Instead, each value must appear in a separate case label.

4. You need to use a break statement after each set of executable statements. The break statement causes program execution to resume after the end of the current switch statement. If you do not use the break statement, the program execution resumes at the subsequent case labels.

5. The default clause is a catch-all clause.

6. The set of statements in each case label or grouped case labels need not be enclosed in open and close braces.

Note: The lack of single case labels with ranges of values makes it more appealing to use a multiple-alternative if-else statement if you have a large contiguous range of values.

Figure 3.4 shows the program flow in the multiple-alternative switch statement.

Look at an example that uses the switch statement. Listing 3.4 contains the source code for the program SWITCH1.CPP that you obtained by editing Listing 3.3. The new program performs the same task of classifying your character input, this time using a switch statement.

Figure 3.4.

The program flow in the multiple-alternative switch *statement.*

  Listing 3.4. Source code for the SWITCH1.CPP program.

```
1:  // Program that demonstrates the multiple-alternative switch statement
2:
3:  #include <iostream.h>
4:
5:  main()
6:  {
7:    char c;
8:    cout << "Enter a character : ";
9:    cin >> c;
10:   switch  {
11:     case 'A':
12:     case 'B':
13:     case 'C':
14:     case 'D':
15:     // other case labels
16:       cout << "You entered an uppercase letter\n";
17:       break;
18:     case 'a':
19:     case 'b':
20:     case 'c':
21:     case 'd':
22:     // other case labels
23:       cout << "You entered a lowercase letter\n";
24:       break;
25:     case '0':
26:     case '1':
27:     case '2':
28:     case '3':
```

continues

Listing 3.4. continued

```
29:    // other case labels
30:      cout << "You entered a digit\n";
31:      break;
32:    default:
33:      cout << "You entered a non-alphanumeric character\n";
34:   }
35:   return 0;
36: }
```

Here is a sample session with the program in Listing 3.4.

```
Enter a character : 2
You entered a digit
```

The program in Listing 3.4 declares the char-typed variable c. The output statement in line 8 prompts you to enter a character. The statement in line 9 stores your input in variable c. The switch statement starts at line 10. Lines 11 through 14 contain the case labels for the letters A through D. You omitted the case labels for the rest of the uppercase letters to keep the program short. If the character in variable c matches any value in lines 11 through 14, the program executes the output statement in line 16. This statement confirms that you entered an uppercase letter. (Because you reduced the number of case labels, the program executes the statement in line 16 only if you enter one of the letters A through D.) The break statement in line 17 causes the program flow to jump to line 35, past the end of the switch statement.

If the character in variable c does not match any of the case labels in lines 11 through 14, the program resumes at line 18 where it encounters another set of case labels. These labels are supposed to represent lowercase characters. As you can see, you reduced the number of labels to shorten the program. If the character in variable c matches any value in lines 18 through 21, the program executes the output statement in line 23. This statement confirms that you entered a lowercase letter. (Because you reduced the number of case labels, the program executes the statement in line 23 only if you enter one of the letters a through d.) The break statement in line 24 causes the program flow to jump to line 35, past the end of the switch statement.

If the character in variable c does not match any of the case labels in lines 18 through 21, the program resumes at line 25, where it encounters another set of case labels. These labels are supposed to represent digits. Again, you can see that you reduced the number of labels to shorten the program. If the character in variable c matches any value in lines 25 through 28, the program executes the output statement in line 30. This statement confirms that you entered a digit. (Because you reduced the number of case labels, the program executes the statement in line 30 only if you enter one of the digits 0 to 3.) The break statement in line 31 causes the program flow to jump to line 35, past the end of the switch statement.

If the character in variable c does not match any case label in lines 25 through 28, the program jumps to the catch-all clause in line 32. The program executes the output statement in line 33. This statement tells you that you entered a non-alphanumeric character.

Nested Decision-Making Constructs

Often you need to use nested decision-making constructs to manage nontrivial conditions. Nesting decision-making constructs enables you to deal with complicated conditions using a divide-and-conquer approach. The outer-level constructs help you to test preliminary or more general conditions. The inner-level constructs help you deal with more specific conditions.

Look at an example. Listing 3.5 shows the source code for the program IF4.CPP. The program prompts you to enter a character. Then the program determines if your input is an uppercase letter, a lowercase letter, or a character that is not a letter. The program displays a message that classifies your input.

Listing 3.5. Source code for the program IF4.CPP.

```
1:  // Program that demonstrates the nested if statements
2:
3:  #include <iostream.h>
4:
5:  main()
6:  {
7:    char c;
8:    cout << "Enter a character : ";
9:    cin >> c;
10:   if ((c >= 'A' && c <= 'Z') || (c >= 'a' && c <= 'z'))
11:     if (c >= 'A' && c <= 'Z')
12:       cout << "You entered an uppercase letter\n";
13:     else
14:       cout << "You entered a lowercase letter\n";
15:   else
16:     cout << "You entered a non-letter character\n";
17:   return 0;
18: }
```

Here is a sample session with the program in Listing 3.5.

```
Enter a character : a
You entered a lowercase letter
```

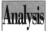

The program in Listing 3.5 declares the char-typed variable c. The output statement in line 8 prompts you to enter a character. The statement in line 9 stores your input in variable c. The program uses nested if-else statements that begin at lines 10 and 11. The outer if-else statement determines whether the variable c contains a letter. If the tested condition is true, the program executes the inner if-else statement in line 11. Otherwise, the program resumes at the else clause of the outer if-else statement and executes the output statement in line 16. This statement tells you that your input was not a letter.

The program uses the inner if-else statement to further examine the condition of the outer if-else statement. The if-else statement in line 11 determines whether the variable c contains an uppercase letter. If this condition is true, the program executes the output statement in line 12. Otherwise, the program executes the `else` clause statement in line 14. These output statements tell you whether you entered an uppercase or a lowercase letter. After executing the inner `if-else` statement, the program jumps to line 17, past the end of the outer `if-else` statement.

Exception Handling

Exception handling was introduced into the ANSI/ISO C++ standard as a way of letting a program deal with unexpected problems that might occur, and also as a means of presenting a universal method of specifying errors. Before exceptions, it sometimes was difficult to tell when something was supposed to be an error and when something was supposed to be a valid number. This especially was true with the return values from functions, which is discussed on Day 6, and with class constructors, which is discussed on Day 9.

The exception mechanism revolves around placing the statements that might generate a runtime error in a special block—the `try` block. This block is followed by one or more `catch` blocks that identify and handle the errors generated in the `try` block.

The *try* and *catch* Blocks

The syntax for the try and `catch` blocks is

```
try {
    // place code that may generate an exception
}
catch(T1 [X1]) {
    // handle exception type T1
}
[catch(T2 [X2]) {
    // handle exception type T2
}]
[other catch blocks]
[catch(...) {
    // handle remaining types of exceptions
}]
```

The types T1 and T2 are structures or classes that support user-defined exceptions. The parameter X1 can have the type T1, T1&, const T1, and const T1&. The parameter X2 can have the same variations for type T2. The last `catch` block uses the ellipsis (three dots) to indicate that it is a catch-all block.

```
try {
    // Do something to a file
    DoSomething("filename.ext");
}
catch(char* str) {
    cout << "Couldn't " << str << endl;
}
```

```
catch(...) {
   cout << "Unknown exception\n"
}
```

The preceding example has a try block that attempts to call a function to manipulate a file called FILENAME.TXT (functions are discussed on Day 6). This function *throws* (that is, generates) an exception. The catch block handles the xmsg exception type by displaying an error message that contains the message generated by the exception. The last catch block uses an ellipsis (...) rather than actually specifying a type to handle. This enables you to handle exceptions you didn't expect; any exception for which you don't actually specify the type gets handled in this all-encompassing block.

NEW☞ An *exception* is runtime error. To *throw* an exception means to generate a runtime error.
TERM

3

C++ enables you to define your own exception types, using structures or classes (discussed on Day 4). An exception type can be an empty structure or object if you only need the name of the structure or object type. If you want to provide more information related to the nature of the exception, the exception type can include data members and member functions that support manipulating the exception state.

The last component of handling exceptions deals with throwing them. C++ supplies the keyword throw, which throws an exception.

The *throw* Keyword

Syntax

The syntax for the throw keyword is

```
throw(exceptionInstance);
```

The exceptionInstance is an instance of an exception structure or class.

Example

```
try {
   int rslt;
   if (!(rslt = DoSomething(filename)))
      throw "do something";
   if (!UseRslt(rslt))
      throw "use rslt";
   if (rslt >= 100)
      throw rslt;
}
catch(char* str) {
   cout << "Couldn't " << str << endl;
}
catch(int i) {
```

```
    cout << "Result was too high: " << i << endl;
}
```

The preceding function throws the exception instances whenever it encounters an error. Note the use of the `char*` type. This is a pointer to a character which is one of the ways that C++ can handle strings. Pointers are discussed in more detail on Day 4, and strings are discussed in depth on Day 8.

Loops

Loops are employed in order to get C++ to do things repeatedly. Rather than have the programmer type in the same code over and over again, each time modifying it slightly so that it will perform actions in sequence, you can use a loop to perform the repetition automatically.

The *for* Loop

The `for` loop in C++ is a versatile loop because it offers both fixed and conditional iterations. The latter feature of the `for` loop deviates from the typical use of the `for` loop in other programming languages, such as Pascal and BASIC.

The *for* Loop

The general syntax for the `for` loop statement is

```
for (<initialization of loop control variables>;
    <loop continuation test>;
    <modification of loop control variables, often an increment or decrement>)
```

Example

```
for (i = 0; i < 10; i++)
    cout << "The cube of " << i << " = " << i * i * i << endl;
```

The `for` loop statement has three components, each of which is optional. The first component initializes the loop control variables. (C++ enables you to use more than one loop control variable.) The second part of the loop is the condition that determines whether the loop makes another iteration (sort of like an `if` statement without the actual `if` keyword). The last part of the `for` loop is the clause that modifies the loop control variables; often this simply is an increment and/or decrement operation.

> **Note:** The C++ `for` loop enables you to declare the loop control variables. Such variables exist in the scope of the loop and also immediately outside in the containing scope. This scope is defined by the block of statements that contains the loop.

So, for example, the following is possible:

```cpp
for (int i = 0; i < 10; ++i)

    cout << "Hello" << endl;

cout << "i is still accessible: " << i << endl;
```

Look at an example. Listing 3.6 contains the source code for the program FOR1.CPP. The program prompts you to define a range of integers by specifying the lower- and upper-bounds. The program then calculates the sum of the integers, as well as the average value, in the range you specify.

 Listing 3.6. Source code for the program FOR1.CPP.

3

```cpp
 1:  // Program that calculates a sum and average of a range of
 2:  // integers using a for loop
 3:
 4:  #include <iostream.h>
 5:
 6:  main()
 7:  {
 8:      double sum = 0;
 9:      double sumx = 0.0;
10:      int first, last, temp;
11:
12:      cout << "Enter the first integer : ";
13:      cin >> first;
14:      cout << "Enter the last integer : ";
15:      cin >> last;
16:      if (first > last) {
17:        temp = first;
18:        first = last;
19:        last = temp;
20:      }
21:      for (int i = first; i <= last; i++) {
22:        sum++;
23:        sumx += (double)i;
24:      }
25:      cout << "Sum of integers from "
26:           << first << " to " << last << " = "
27:           << sumx << endl;
28:      cout << "Average value = " << sumx / sum;
29:      return 0;
30:  }
```

 Here is a sample session with the program in Listing 3.6.

```
Enter the first integer : 1
Enter the last integer : 100
Sum of integers from 1 to 100 = 5050
Average value = 50.5
```

The program in Listing 3.6 declares a collection of `int`-typed and `double`-typed variables in function `main`. The function initializes the summation variables, `sum` and `sumx`, to `0`. The input and output statements in lines 12 through 15 prompt you to enter the integers that define a range of values. The program stores these integers in the variables `first` and `last`. The `if` statement in line 16 determines whether the value in variable `first` is greater than the value in variable `last`. If this condition is true, the program executes the block of statements in lines 17 through 19. These statements swap the values in variables `first` and `last`, using the variable `temp` as a swap buffer. Thus, the `if` statement ensures that the integer in variable `first` is less than or equal to the integer in variable `last`.

The program carries out the summation using the `for` loop in line 21. The loop declares its own control variable, `i`, and initializes it with the value in the variable `first`. The loop continuation condition is `i <= last`. This condition indicates that the loop iterates as long as `i` is less than or equal to the value in the variable `last`. The loop increment component is `i++`, which increments the loop control variable by 1 for every iteration. The loop contains two statements. The first statement increments the value in the variable `sum`. The second statement adds the value of `i` (after typecasting it to `double`) to the variable `sumx`.

Note: You can rewrite the `for` loop to move the first loop statement to the loop increment component.

```
for (int i = first; i <= last; i++, sum++)
    sumx += (double)i;
```

The output statement in lines 25 through 27 displays the sum and average of integers in the range you specified.

To illustrate the flexibility of the `for` loop, we created the program FOR2.CPP, shown in Listing 3.7, by editing the program FOR1.CPP.

Listing 3.7. Source code for the program FOR2.CPP.

```
1:  // Program that calculates a sum and average of a range of
2:  // integers using a for loop
3:
4:  #include <iostream.h>
5:
6:  main()
7:  {
8:      double sum = 0;
9:      double sumx = 0.0;
10:     int first, last, temp, i;
11:
12:     cout << "Enter the first integer : ";
```

```
13:     cin >> first;
14:     cout << "Enter the last integer : ";
15:     cin >> last;
16:     if (first > last) {
17:       temp= first;
18:       first = last;
19:       last = temp;
20:     }
21:     i = first;
22:     for (; i <= last; ) {
23:       sum++;
24:       sumx += (double)i++;
25:     }
26:     cout << "Sum of integers from "
27:          << first << " to " << last << " = "
28:          << sumx << endl;
29:     cout << "Average value = " << sumx / sum;
30:     return 0;
31: }
```

Output

Here is a sample session with the program in Listing 3.7.

```
Enter the first integer : 10
Enter the last integer : 100
Sum of integers from 10 to 100 = 5005
Average value = 55
```

The FOR1.CPP and FOR2.CPP programs perform the same tasks and interact identically with the user. The changes we made are in line 10 and lines 21 through 25. Line 10 declares the loop control variable. In line 21, we initialize the variable i using the value in the variable first. The for loop is located at line 22. The loop has no initialization part, because we took care of that in line 21. In addition, we removed the loop increment component and compensated for it by applying the post-increment operator to the variable i in line 24.

Open Loops Using the *for* Loops

When we introduced you to the C++ for loop, we stated that the three components of the for loop are optional. In fact, C++ permits you to leave these three components empty.

NEW ☛ When you leave the three components of a loop empty, the result is an *open loop*.
TERM

It is worthwhile to point out that other languages, such as ADA and Modula-2, do support formal open loops and provide mechanisms to exit these loops. C++ permits you to exit from a loop in the following two ways:

☐ The break statement causes the program execution to resume after the end of the current loop. Use the break statement when you want to exit a for loop and resume with the remaining parts of the program.

☐ The `return` statement will return from the current function (including `main`). You'll learn more about `return` and functions on Day 5.

☐ The `throw` statement causes an exception to be thrown. This is used when an error has occurred and you can't continue with the rest of the program without some sort of error handler. You'll learn more about exceptions later today.

☐ In very extreme cases, the `exit` function (declared in the STDLIB.H header file) enables you to exit the program. Use the `exit` function in dire emergencies when there isn't even any hope of recovering from an error. This will stop iteration and exit the program.

Consider the following example. Listing 3.8 contains the source code for the program FOR3.CPP. The program uses an open loop to prompt you repeatedly for a number. The program takes your input and displays it along with its reciprocal value. Then the program asks you whether you want to calculate the reciprocal of another number. If you type in the letter **Y** or **y**, the program performs another iteration. Otherwise, the program ends. If you continue to type **Y** or **y** for the latter prompt, the program keeps running—at least until the computer breaks down!

 Listing 3.8. Source code for the program FOR3.CPP.

```
1:  // Program that demonstrates using the
2:  // for loop to emulate an infinite loop.
3:
4:  #include <iostream.h>
5:  #include <ctype.h>
6:
7:  main()
8:  {
9:      char ch;
10:     double x, y;
11:
12:     // for loop with empty parts
13:     for (;;) {
14:         cout << "\nEnter a number : ";
15:         cin >> x;
16:         // process number if non-zero
17:         if (x != 0) {
18:             y = 1/ x;
19:             cout << "1/(" << x << ") = " << y << endl;
20:             cout << "More calculations? (Y/N) ";
21:             cin >> ch;
22:             ch = toupper(ch);
23:             if (ch != 'Y')
24:                 break;
25:         }
26:         else
27:             // display error message
28:             cout << "Error: cannot accept 0\n";
29:     }
```

```
30:    return 0;
31: }
```

Here is a sample session with the program in Listing 3.8.

```
Enter a number : 5
1/(5) = 0.2
More calculations? (Y/N) y

Enter a number : 12
1/(12) = 0.0833333
More calculations? (Y/N) y

Enter a number : 16
1/(16) = 0.0625
More calculations? (Y/N) n
```

The program in Listing 3.8 declares the char-typed variable ch and two double-typed variables, x and y. The function main uses the for loop, in line 13, as an open loop by eliminating all three loop components. The output statement in line 14 prompts you to enter a number. The input statement in line 15 obtains your input and stores it in variable x. The if-else statement in line 17 determines if the value in variable x is not zero. If this condition is true, then the program executes the block of statements in lines 18 through 24. Otherwise, the program executes the else clause statement in line 28. This statement displays an error message.

The statement in line 18 assigns the reciprocal of the value in variable x to variable y. The output statement in line 19 displays the values in variables x and y. The output statement in line 20 prompts you for more calculations, and requires a Y/N (in either uppercase or lowercase) type of answer. The input statement in line 21 stores your single-character input in variable c. The statement in line 22 converts your input into uppercase, using the function toupper. (This function is prototyped in the CTYPE.H header file.) The if statement in line 23 determines whether the character in variable c is not the letter Y. If this condition is true, the program executes the break statement in line 24. This statement causes the program execution to exit the open loop and to resume at line 30.

The *do-while* Loop

The do-while loop in C++ is a conditional loop that tests the iteration condition at the end of the loop. Therefore, the do-while loop iterates at least once.

NEW☛ TERM A *conditional loop* iterates as long as a condition is true. This condition is tested at the end of the loop.

99

The *do-while* Loop

The general syntax for the do-while loop is

```
do {
    <sequence of statements>
} while (condition);
```

Example

The following loop displays the squares of 2 to 10:

```
int i = 2;
do {
    cout << i << "^2 = " << i * i << endl;
} while (++i < 11);
```

Look at an example. Listing 3.9 shows the source code for the program DOWHILE1.CPP, which essentially calculates square root values. The program performs the following tasks:

☐ Prompts you to enter a number. (If you enter a negative number, the program reprompts you for a number.)

☐ Calculates and displays the square root of the number you entered.

☐ Prompts you to enter another number. (If you enter the letter Y or y, the program resumes at step number 1; otherwise, the program ends.)

Type

Listing 3.9. Source code for the program DOWHILE1.CPP.

```
1:  // Program that demonstrates the do-while loop
2:
3:  #include <iostream.h>
4:
5:  const double TOLERANCE = 1.0e-7;
6:
7:  double abs(double x)
8:  {
9:    return (x >= 0) ? x : -x;
10: }
11:
12: double sqroot(double x)
13: {
14:   double guess = x / 2;
15:   do {
16:     guess = (guess + x / guess) / 2;
17:   } while (abs(guess * guess - x) > TOLERANCE);
18:   return guess;
19: }
20:
21: double getNumber()
22: {
23:   double x;
24:   do {
25:     cout << "Enter a number: ";
26:     cin >> x;
```

```
27:     } while (x < 0);
28:     return x;
29: }
30:
31: main()
32: {
33:     char c;
34:     double x, y;
35:
36:     do {
37:         x = getNumber();
38:         y = sqroot(x);
39:         cout << "Sqrt(" << x << ") = " << y << endl
40:             << "Enter another number? (Y/N) ";
41:         cin >> c;
42:         cout << endl;
43:     } while (c == 'Y' || c == 'y');
44:     return 0;
45: }
```

3

Here is a sample session with the program in Listing 3.9.

```
Enter a number: 25
Sqrt(25) = 5
Enter another number? (Y/N) y

Enter a number: 144
Sqrt(144) = 12
Enter another number? (Y/N) n
```

The program in Listing 3.9 declares the global constant TOLERANCE and the functions abs, sqroot, getNumber, and main. The function abs, located in line 7, returns the absolute value of double-typed arguments. Note that, even though functions have not yet been introduced, you should have relatively little trouble understanding their use in the preceding listing. Functions are discussed formally on Day 6.

The function sqroot, located in line 12, returns the square root of the parameter x. The function sets the initial guess for the square root to x / 2 in line 14. Then the function uses a do-while loop to refine iteratively the guess for the square root. The condition in the while clause determines whether the absolute difference between the square of the current guess and the parameter x is greater than the allowable error (represented by the constant TOLERANCE). The loop iterates as long as this condition is true. The function returns the guess for the square root in line 18. The function sqroot implements Newton's method for iteratively obtaining the square root of a number.

The function getNumber, located in line 21, prompts you for a number and stores your input in the local variable x. The function uses a do-while loop to ensure that you enter a non-negative number. The while clause in line 27 determines if the value in variable x is negative. As long as this condition is true, the do-while loop iterates. In line 28, the return statement yields the value of x.

The function `main`, located in line 31, uses a `do-while` loop to perform the following tasks:

☐ Prompts you for a number by calling function `getNumber`. (The statement in line 37 contains the function call and assigns the result to the local variable x.)

☐ Calculates the square root of x by calling function `sqroot`, and assigns the result to the variable y. (The statement that contains this function call is in line 38.)

☐ Displays the values in variables x and y.

☐ Prompts you to enter another number. (The input statement in line 41 takes your single-character Y/N input and stores it in variable c.)

The `while` clause, located in line 43, determines whether the variable c contains either the letter Y or y. The `do-while` loop iterates as long as this condition is true.

The program in Listing 3.9 illustrates the following uses for the `do-while` loop:

1. *Iterative calculations.* The loop in function `sqroot` demonstrates this aspect.

2. *Data validation.* The loop in function `getNumber` demonstrates this aspect.

3. *Program continuation.* The loop in function `main` demonstrates this aspect.

The *while* Loop

The `while` loop in C++ is another conditional loop that iterates as long as a condition is true. Thus, the `while` loop may not iterate if the tested condition is initially false.

Syntax

The *while* Loop

The general syntax of the `while` loop is

```
while (condition)
    statement; ¦ { sequence of statements }
```

Example

```
double power(double x, int n)
{
    double pwr = 1;
    while (n— > 0)
        pwr *= x;
    return pwr;
}
```

Look at the next example. Listing 3.10 shows the source code for the program WHILE1.CPP. This program performs the same operations as the program FOR1.CPP, in Listing 3.6. The two programs interact with the user in the same way and yield the same results.

Listing 3.10. Source code for the program WHILE1.CPP.

```
 1:  // Program that demonstrates the while loop
 2:
 3:  #include <iostream.h>
 4:
 5:  main()
 6:  {
 7:      double sum = 0;
 8:      double sumx = 0.0;
 9:      int first, last, temp, i;
10:
11:      cout << "Enter the first integer : ";
12:      cin >> first;
13:      cout << "Enter the last integer : ";
14:      cin >> last;
15:      if (first > last) {
16:        temp= first;
17:        first = last;
18:        last = temp;
19:      }
20:      i = first;
21:      while (i <= last) {
22:        sum++;
23:        sumx += (double)i++;
24:      }
25:      cout << "Sum of integers from "
26:           << first << " to " << last << " = "
27:           << sumx << endl;
28:      cout << "Average value = " << sumx / sum;
29:      return 0;
30: }
```

Here is a sample session with the program in Listing 3.10.

```
Enter the first integer : 1
Enter the last integer : 100
Sum of integers from 1 to 100 = 5050
Average value = 50.5
```

Because the programs in Listings 3.10 and 3.6 are similar, we focus here on lines 20 through 24, where lies the main difference between the two programs. The statement in line 20 assigns the value of the variable first to the variable i. The while loop starts at line 21. The loop iterates as long as the value in the variable i is less than or equal to the value in the variable last. The variable i plays the role of the loop control variable. The statement in line 22 increments the value in the variable sum. The statement in line 23 adds the value in variable i to the variable sumx and also increments the variable i. The statement performs the latter task by applying the post-increment operator to the variable i.

Skipping Loop Iterations

C++ enables you to jump to the end of a loop and resume the next iteration using the continue statement. This programming feature permits your loop to skip iteration for special values that may cause runtime errors.

The *continue* Statement

The general form for using the continue statement is

```
<loop-start clause> {
    // sequence #1 of statements
    if (skipCondition)
        continue;
    // sequence #2 of statements
} <loop-end clause>
```

Example

```
double x, y;
for (int i = -10; i < 11; i++) {
    x = i;
    if (i == 1)
        continue;
    y = 1/sqrt(x * x - 1);
    cout << "1/sqrt(" << (x*x-1) << ") = " << y << endl;
}
```

This form shows that the evaluation of the first sequence of statements in the for loop gives rise to a condition tested in the if statement. If that condition is true, then the if statement invokes the continue statement to skip the second sequence of statements in the for loop.

Look at an example. Listing 3.11 shows the source code for the program FOR4.CPP. The program displays the table of values for the function $f(X) = =(X^2-9)$ at integer values between -10 and 10. Because the integers between -2 and 2 yield complex results, which the program avoids, the table does not display the complex values for $f(X)$ between -2 and 2.

Listing 3.11. Source code for the program FOR4.CPP.

```
1:  // Program that demonstrates using the continue statement
2:  // to skip iterations.
3:
4:  #include <iostream.h>
5:  #include <math.h>
6:
7:
8:  double f(double x)
9:  {
10:    return sqrt(x * x - 9);
11: }
12:
13: main()
```

```
14: {
15:     double x, y;
16:
17:     cout << "          X";
18:     cout << "                  f(X)\n";
19:     cout << "_____\n\n";
20:     // for loop with empty parts
21:     for (int i = =10; i <= 10; i++) {
22:       if (i > =3 && i < 3)
23:         continue;
24:       x = (double)i;
25:       y = f(x);
26:       cout << "        ";
27:       cout.width(3);
28:       cout << x << "        ";
29:       cout.width(7);
30:       cout << y << endl;
31:     }
32:     return 0;
33: }
```

Here is a sample session with the program in Listing 3.11.

```
X              f(X)
_____

-10            9.53939
 -9            8.48528
 -8            7.4162
 -7            6.32456
 -6            5.19615
 -5               4
 -4            2.64575
 -3               0
  3               0
  4            2.64575
  5               4
  6            5.19615
  7            6.32456
  8            7.4162
  9            8.48528
 10            9.53939
```

The program in Listing 3.11 declares the function f to represent the mathematical function f(X). The function main declares the double-typed variables x and y in line 15. The output statements in lines 17 through 19 display the table's heading. The for loop in line 21 declares its own control variable and iterates between -10 and 10, in increments of 1. The first statement inside the loop is the if statement located at line 22. This statement determines if the value in variable i is greater than -3 and less than 3. If this condition is true, then the program executes the continue statement in line 23. Thus, the if statement enables the for loop to skip error-generating iterations and resume with the next iteration. The statement in line 24 assigns the value in variable i to variable x. The statement in line 25 calls the function f and supplies it with the argument x. The statement then assigns the result to variable y. The output statements in lines 25 through 30 display the values of the variables x and y. The statements use the function width for simple formatting.

Exiting Loops

C++ supports the break statement to exit a loop. The break statement makes the program resume after the end of the current loop.

The *break* Statement

The general form for using the break statement in a loop is

```
<start-loop clause> {
    // sequence #1 of statements
    if (exitLoopCondition)
        break;
    // sequence #2 of statements
} <end-loop clause>
// sequence #3 of statements
```

Example

```
// calculate the factorial of n
factorial = 1;
for (int i = 1; ; i++) {
    if (i > n)
        break;
    factorial *= (double)i;
}
```

This form shows that the evaluation of the first sequence of statements in the for loop gives rise to a condition tested in the if statement. If that condition is true, then the if statement invokes the break statement to exit the loop altogether. The program execution resumes at the third sequence of statements.

For a good example that uses the break statement, we recommend that you reexamine the FOR3.CPP program in Listing 3.8.

Nested Loops

Nested loops enable you to contain repetitive tasks as part of other repetitive tasks. C++ enables you to nest any type of loop to just about any level needed. Nested loops frequently are used to process arrays (which are covered in Day 5).

Following is an example that uses nested loops. Listing 3.12 shows the source code for the program NESTFOR1.CPP. The program displays a table for square roots for whole numbers in the range of 1 to 10. The program uses an outer loop to iterate over this range of numbers and employs an inner loop to iteratively calculate the square root.

 Listing 3.12. Source code for the program NESTFOR1.CPP.

```
1:  // Program that demonstrates nested loops
2:
3:  #include <stdio.h>
4:
5:  const double TOLERANCE = 1.0e-7;
6:  const int MIN_NUM = 1;
7:  const int MAX_NUM = 10;
8:
9:  double abs(double x)
10: {
11:   return (x >= 0) ? x : -x;
12: }
13:
14: main()
15: {
16:    double x, sqrt;
17:
18:    printf("  X        Sqrt(X)\n");
19:    printf("_____\n\n");
20:    // outer loop
21:    for (int i = MIN_NUM; i <= MAX_NUM; i++) {
22:      x = (double)i;
23:      sqrt = x /2;
24:      // inner loop
25:      do {
26:        sqrt = (sqrt + x / sqrt) / 2;
27:      } while (abs(sqrt * sqrt - x) > TOLERANCE);
28:      printf("%4.1f     %8.6lf\n", x, sqrt);
29:    }
30:    return 0;
31: }
```

Here is a sample session with the program in Listing 3.12.

```
X        Sqrt(X)
_____

1.0      1.000000
2.0      1.414214
3.0      1.732051
4.0      2.000000
5.0      2.236068
6.0      2.449490
7.0      2.645751
8.0      2.828427
9.0      3.000000
10.0      3.162278
```

The program in Listing 3.12 includes the header file STDIO.H in order to use the `printf` output function with its powerful formatting capabilities. Lines 5 through 7 define the constants TOLERANCE, MIN_NUM, and MAX_NUM to represent, respectively, the tolerance in square root values, the first number in the output table, and the last number in the output table. The program defines the function abs to return the absolute number of a double-typed number.

The function main declares the double-typed variables x and sqrt. The output statements in lines 18 and 19 display the table's heading. Line 21 contains the outer loop—a for loop. This loop declares its control variable, i, and iterates from MIN_NUM to MAX_NUM in increments of 1. Line 22 stores the typecast value of i in variable x. The statement in line 23 obtains the initial guess for the square root and stores it in variable sqrt. Line 25 contains the inner loop, a do-while loop that iterates to refine the guess for the square root. The statement in line 26 refines the guess for the square root. The while clause in line 27 determines whether the refined guess is adequate. The output statement in line 28 displays the formatted values for the variables x and sqrt.

Summary

Today's lesson presented the various decision-making constructs and loops in C++, including the following:

☐ The single-alternative if statement, such as

```
if (tested_condition)
    statement; ¦ {    <sequence of statements> }
```
☐ The dual-alternative if-else statement, such as

```
if (tested_condition)
    statement1; { <sequence #1 of statements> }
else
    statement1; { <sequence #1 of statements> }
```
☐ The multiple-alternative if-else statement, such as

```
if (tested_condition1)
    statement1; ¦ { <sequence #1 of statement> }
else if (tested_condition2)
    statement2; ¦ { <sequence #2 of statement> }
...
else if (tested_conditionN)
    statementN; ¦ { <sequence #N of statement> }
[else
    statementN+1; ¦ { <sequence #N+1 of statement> }]
```

☐ The multiple-alternative `switch` statement, such as

```
switch (caseVar) {
    case constant1_1:
    case constant1_2:
    <other case labels>
        <one or more statements>
        break;
    case constant2_1:
    case constant2_2:
    <other case labels>
        <one or more statements>
        break;
    ...
    case constantN_1:
    case constantN_2:
    <other case labels>
        <one or more statements>
        break;

    default:
        <one or more statements>
        break;
}
```

You also learned about the following topics:

☐ The `if` statements require you to observe the following two rules:

    ☐ The tested condition must be enclosed in parentheses.

    ☐ Blocks of statements are enclosed in pairs of open and close braces.

☐ Nested decision-making constructs enable you to deal with complex conditions using a divide-and-conquer approach. The outer-level constructs help you in testing preliminary or more general conditions. The inner-level constructs assist in handling more specific conditions.

☐ The `try`, `catch`, and `throw` statements enable you to use exception handling for error control.

☐ The `for` loop in C++ has the following general syntax:

```
for (<initialization of loop control variables>;
    <loop continuation test>;
    <increment/decrement of loop control variables>)
```

The `for` loop contains three components: the loop initialization, loop continuation condition, and the increment/decrement of the loop variables.

☐ The conditional loop `do-while` has the following general syntax:

```
do {
    sequence of statements
} while (condition);
```

The `do-while` loop iterates at least once.

☐ The conditional `while` loop has the following general syntax:

```
while (condition)
    statement; ¦ { sequence of statements }
```

The `while` loop might not iterate if its tested condition is initially false.

☐ The `continue` statement enables you to jump to the end of the loop and resume with the next iteration. The advantage of the `continue` statement is that it uses no labels to direct the jump.

☐ Open loops are `for` loops with empty components. The `break` statement enables you to exit the current loop and resume program execution at the first statement that comes after the loop. The `exit` function (declared in STDLIB.H) enables you to make a critical loop exit by halting the C++ program altogether.

☐ Nested loops enable you to contain repetitive tasks as part of other repetitive tasks. C++ enables you to nest any kind of loops to just about any level needed.

Q&A

Q Does C++ impose any rules for indenting statements in the clauses of an `if` statement?

A No. The indentation purely is up to you. Typical indentations range from two to four spaces. Using indentations makes your listings much more readable. Following is the case of an `if` statement with unindented clause statements:

```
if (i > 0)
    j = i * i;
    else
    j = 10 - i;
```

Compare the readability of that listing with this indented version.

```
if (i > 0)
  j = i * i;
else
  j = 10 - i;
```

The indented version is much easier to read.

Q What are the rules for writing the condition of an `if-else` statement?

A There are two schools of thought. The first recommends that you write the condition so that it is more often true than not. The second school recommends avoiding negative expressions (those that use the relational operator `!=` and the Boolean operator `!`). Programmers in this camp translate this `if` statement,

```
if (i != 0)
    j = 100 / i;
else
    j = 1;
```

into the following equivalent form,

```
if (i == 0)
    j = 1;
else
    j = 100 \ i;
```

even though the likelihood of variable `i` storing 0 might be very low.

Q How do I handle a condition such as the following, which divides by a variable that can possibly be zero?

```
if (i != 0 && 1/i > 1)
    j = i * i;
```

A C++ does not always evaluate the entire tested condition. This partial evaluation occurs when a term in the Boolean expression renders the entire expression false or true, regardless of the values of the other terms. In this case, if variable `i` is `0`—the runtime system does not evaluate the term `1/i > 1`. This is because the term `i != 0` is false and would render the entire expression false, regardless of what the second term yields.

Q Is it really necessary to include an else or default clause in multi-alternative `if-else` and `switch` statements?

A Programmers highly recommend the inclusion of these catch-all clauses to ensure that the multiple-alternative statements handle all conditions. However, they are not technically required for a program to compile.

Q How can a `while` loop simulate a `for` loop?

A Here is a simple example.

```
int i;                          int i = 1;
for (i = 1; i <= 10; i +=2){    while (i <= 10) {
   cout << i << endl;              cout << i << endl;
}                                  i += 2;
                                   }
```

The while loop needs a leading statement that initializes the loop control variable. Also notice that the while loop uses a statement inside it to alter the value of the loop control variable.

Q How can a while loop simulate a do-while loop?

A Here is a simple example.

```
i = 1;                      i = 1;
do {                        while (i <= 10) {
   cout << i << endl;          cout << i << endl;
   i += 2;                     i += 2;
} while (i <= 10);          }
```

The two loops have the same condition in their while clauses. Note, however, that if the loop is designed in such a way that it doesn't necessarily know the initial value of i, it could have different effects if, for example, i starts out as 10. The loop on the left would run through once while the loop on the right would never make it through a single iteration.

Q How can the open for loop emulate the while and do-while loops?

A The open for loop emulates the other C++ loops by placing the loop-escape if statement near the beginning or end of the loop. Here is how the open for loop emulates a sample while loop.

```
i = 1;                      i = 1;
while (i <= 10) {           for (;;) {
                               if(i > 10) break;
   cout << i << endl;          cout << i << endl;
   i += 2;                     i += 2;
}                           }
```

Notice that the open for loop uses a loop-escape if statement as the first statement inside the loop. The condition tested by the if statement is the logical reverse of the while loop condition. Here is a simple example showing the emulation of the do-while loop.

```
i = 1;                      i = 1;
do {                        for (;;) {
   cout << i << endl;          cout << i << endl;
   i += 2;                     i += 2;
                               if (i > 10) break;
} while (i <= 10);          }
```

The open for loop uses a loop-escape if statement right before the end of the loop. The if statement tests the reverse condition as the do-while loop.

Please take note, however, that these examples are rather crude and inelegant. One would never use an open for loop in this manner. Rather, one might skip one of the three clauses inside the for loop's parentheses (like the initialization clause if the control variable already has been initialized). Open for loops are more often used in cases where exiting the loop would be a rare occurrence, such as if one were accepting and processing a user's keystrokes, but exiting when the Esc key is encountered.

Q In nested for loops, can I use the loop control variable of the outer loops as part of the range of values for the inner loops?

A Yes. Not only does C++ not prohibit such use, it actually is rather quite common. Here is a simple example.

```
for (int i = 1; i <= 100; i += 5)
    for (int j = i; j <= 100; j++)
        cout << i * j << endl;
```

Q Does C++ restrict nesting of the various types of loops?

A No. You can nest any combination of loops in a C++ program.

Workshop

The Workshop provides quiz questions to help you solidify your understanding of the material covered and exercises to provide you with experience in using what you've learned. Try to understand the quiz and exercise answers before continuing on to the next day's lesson. (Answers are provided in Appendix A.)

Quiz

1. Simplify the following nested if statements by replacing them with a single if statement:

```
if (i > 0)
  if (i < 10)
     cout << "i = " << i << endl;
```

2. Simplify the following if statements by replacing them with a single if statement:

```
if (i > 0) {
    j = i * i;
    cout << "j = " << j << endl;
}
if (i < 0) {
    j = 4 * i;
    cout << "j = " << j << endl;
```

```
    }
    if (i == 0) {
        j = 10 + i
        cout << "j = " << j << endl;
    }
```

3. True or false? The following if statements perform the same tasks as the subsequent if-else statement:

```
if (i < 0) {
    i = 10 + i;
    j = i * i;
    cout << "i = " << i << endl;
    cout << "j = " << j << endl;
}
if (i >= 0) {
    k = 4 * i + 1;
    cout << "k = " << k << endl;
}


if (i < 0) {
    i = 10 - i;
    j = i * i;
    cout << "i = " << i << endl;
    cout << "j = " << j << endl;
}
else {
    k = 4 * i + 1;
    cout << "k = " << k << endl;
}
```

4. Simplify the following if-else statement:

```
if (i > 0 && i < 100)
    j = i * i;
else if (i > 10 && i < 50)
    j = 10 + i;
else if (i >= 100)
    j = i;
else
    j = 1;
```

5. What is wrong with the following if statement?

```
if (i > (1 + i * i)) {
```

```
    j = i * i
    cout << "i = " << i << " and j = " << j << endl;
}
```

6. What is wrong with the following loop?

```
i = 1;
while (i < 10) {
  j = i * i - 1;
  k = 2 * j - i;
  cout << "i = " << i << endl;
  cout << "j = " <<   j << endl;
  cout << "k = " << k << endl;
}
```

7. What is the output of the following for loop?

```
for (int i = 5; i < 10; i + 2)
    cout << i - 2 << endl;
```

8. What is the output of the following for loop?

```
for (int i = 5; i < 10; )
    cout << i - 2 << endl;
```

9. What is wrong with the following code?

```
for (int i = 1; i <= 10; i++)
    for (i = 8; i <= 12; i++)
        cout << i << endl;
```

10. Where is the error in the following nested loops?

```
for (int i = 1; i <= 10; i++)
  cout << i * i << endl;
for (int i = 1; i <= 10; i++)
  cout << i * i * i << endl;
```

11. Where is the error in the following loop?

```
i = 1;
while (i > 0) {
  cout << i << endl;
  i++;
}
```

12. The factorial of a number is the product of the sequence of integers from 1 to that number. The following general equation defines the factorial (which uses the symbol !):

```
n! = 1 * 2 * 3 * ... * n
```

Following is a C++ program that calculates the factorial of a number. The problem is that for whatever positive value you enter, the program displays a 0 value for the factorial. Where is the error in the program?

```
int n;
double factorial;
cout << "Enter positive integer : ";
cin >> n;
for (int i = 1; i <= n; i++)
   factorial *= i;
cout << i << "! = " << factorial;
```

Exercises

1. Write the program IF5.CPP to solve for the roots of a quadratic equation. The quadratic equation is

   $Ax^2 + Bx + C = 0$

   The roots of the quadratic equation are

   $root1 = (-B + \sqrt{B^2 - 4AC})\ /\ (2A)$
   $root1 = (-B - \sqrt{B^2 - 4AC})\ /\ (2A)$

   If the term in the square root is negative, then the roots are complex. If the term in the square root term is zero, then the two roots are the same and are equal to $-B/(2A)$.

2. Write the program SWITCH2.CPP, which implements a simple four-function calculator. The program should prompt you for the operand and the operator, and display both the input and the result. Include error checking for bad operators and for the attempt to divide by zero.

3. Write the program FOR5.CPP, which uses a for loop to obtain and display the sum of odd integers in the range of 11 to 121.

4. Write the program WHILE2.CPP, which uses a while loop to obtain and display the sum of the squared odd integers in the range of 11 to 121.

5. Write the program DOWHILE2.CPP, which uses a do-while loop to obtain and display the sum of the squared odd integers in the range of 11 to 121.

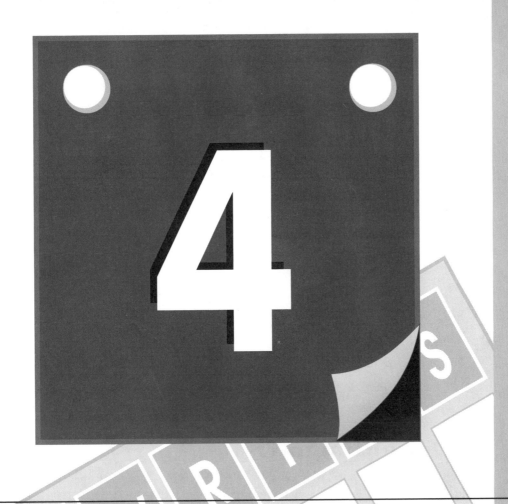

4

User-Defined
Types and Pointers

Creating user-defined data types is one of the necessary features of a modern programming language. Today's lesson looks at the enumerated data types and structures that enable you to better organize your data. In addition, this lesson discusses using pointers with simple variables, arrays, structures, and dynamic data. Today, you will learn about the following topics:

- The type definition using `typedef`
- Enumerated data types
- Structures
- Unions
- Reference variables
- Pointers to existing variables
- Simple arrays
- Pointers to arrays
- Pointers to structures
- Using pointers to access and manage dynamic data
- Far pointers

Type Definition in C++

C++ offers the `typedef` keyword, which enables you to define new data type names as aliases of existing types.

Syntax

The *typedef* Keyword

The general syntax for using `typedef` is

```
typedef knownType newType;
```

Examples

```
typedef unsigned word;
typedef unsigned char byte;
typedef unsigned char boolean;
```

The `typedef` keyword defines a new type from a known one. You can use `typedef` to create aliases that shorten the names of existing data types or to define names of data types that are more familiar to you. (See the second of the preceding examples, which `typedef`s a byte type). In addition, the `typedef` statement can define a new type name that better describes how the data type is used. The third of the preceding examples illustrates this use of `typedef`. You also can use `typedef` to define the name of an array type.

An Array Type Name

The general syntax for defining the name of an array type is

```
typedef baseType arrayTypeName[arraySize];
```

The `typedef` statement defines the `arrayTypeName`, whose basic type and size are `baseType` and `arraySize`, respectively.

Examples

```
typedef double vector[10];
typedef double matrix[10][30];
```

Thus, the identifiers `vector` and `matrix` are names of data types.

Enumerated Data Types

The rule to follow with enumerated data types is that although the enumerated identifiers must be unique, the values assigned to them need not be unique.

NEW☞ TERM An *enumerated type* defines a list of unique identifiers and associates values with these identifiers.

An Enumerated Type

The general syntax for declaring an enumerated type is

```
enum enumType { <list of enumerated identifiers> };
```

Examples

```
enum Boolean { false, true };
enum YesNo { no, yes, dontCare, maybe };
enum weekday { Sunday, Monday, Tuesday,
               Wednesday, Thursday, Friday, Saturday };
```

Following is an example of declaring an enumerated type:

```
enum CPUtype { i8088, i80286, i80386DX, i80386SX,
               i80486DX, i80486SX };
```

C++ associates integer values with the enumerated identifiers. For example, in this type, the compiler assigns 0 to i8088, 1 to i80286, and so on.

C++ is very flexible in declaring an enumerated type. First, the language enables you to explicitly assign a value to an enumerated identifier. Following is an example:

```
enum weekday { Sunday = 1, Monday, Tuesday, Wednesday,
               Thursday, Friday, Saturday };
```

This declaration explicitly assigns 1 to the enumerated identifier Sunday. The compiler then assigns the next integer, 2, to the next identifier, Monday, and so on. C++ enables you to explicitly assign a value to each member of the enumerated list. Moreover, these values need not be unique. Following are some examples of the flexibility in declaring enumerated types in C++:

```
// explicit value assignment for every list member
enum colors { black = 1, red = 2, blue = 3, green = 5,
              yellow = 7, white = 11 };

// intermittent value assignment
enum colors { black = 1, red, blue, green = 5,
              yellow = 7, white = 11 };

// duplicate values
enum CPUtype { i8088 = 1, i80286 = 2,
               i80386DX = 3, i80386SX = 3,
               i80486DX = 4, i80486SX = 4 };

enum choiceType { false, true, dontCare = 0 };
```

In the last example, the compiler associates the identifier false with 0 by default. However, the compiler also associates the value 0 with dontCare because of the explicit assignment.

C++ enables you to declare variables that have enumerated types in the following ways:

☐ The declaration of the enumerated type may include the declaration of the variables of that type. The general syntax is

```
enum enumType { <list of enumerated identifiers> }
            <list of variables>;
```

Following is an example.

```
enum weekDay { Sun = 1, Mon, Tue, Wed, Thu, Fri, Sat }
          recycleDay, payDay, movieDay;
```

☐ The separate declaration of the enumerated type and its variables includes multiple statements to declare the type and the associated variables separately. The general syntax is

```
enum enumType { <list of enumerated identifiers> };
enumType var1, var2, ..., varN;
```

Look at an example. Listing 4.1 shows the source code for the program ENUM1.CPP. The program implements a simple one-line, four-function calculator that performs the following tasks:

☐ Prompts you to enter a number, an operator (+, −, *, or /), and a number.

☐ Performs the requested operation, if valid.

☐ Displays the operands, the operator, and the result, if the operation was valid; otherwise, displays an error message that indicates the type of error. (You either entered a bad operator or attempted to divide by 0.)

Listing 4.1. Source code for the program ENUM1.CPP.

```
1:  /*
2:  C++ program that demonstrates enumerated types
3:  */
4:
5:  #include <iostream.h>
6:
7:  enum mathError { noError, badOperator, divideByZero };
8:
9:  void sayError(mathError err)
10: {
11:    switch (err) {
12:      case noError:
13:        cout << "No error";
14:        break;
15:      case badOperator:
16:        cout << "Error: invalid operator";
17:        break;
18:      case divideByZero:
19:        cout << "Error: attempt to divide by zero";
20:    }
21: }
22:
23: main()
24: {
25:    double x, y, z;
26:    char op;
27:    mathError error = noError;
28:
29:    cout << "Enter a number, an operator, and a number : ";
30:    cin >> x >> op >> y;
31:
32:    switch (op) {
33:      case '+':
34:        z = x + y;
35:        break;
36:      case '--':
37:        z = x -- y;
38:        break;
39:      case '*':
40:        z = x * y;
41:        break;
42:      case '/':
43:        if (y != 0)
44:          z = x / y;
45:        else
46:          error = divideByZero;
47:        break;
48:      default:
49:        error = badOperator;
50:    }
51:
52:    if (error == noError)
```

continues

Listing 4.1. continued

```
53:    cout << x << " " << op << " " << y << " = " << z;
54:  else
55:    sayError(error);
56:  return 0;
57: }
```

Here is a sample session with the program in Listing 4.1.

```
Enter a number, an operator, and a number : 355 / 113
355 / 113 = 3.14159
```

The program in Listing 4.1 declares the enumerated type mathError in line 7. This data type has three enumerated values: noError, badOperator, and divideByZero.

The program also defines the function sayError in lines 9 through 21 to display a message based on the value of the enumerated parameter err. The function uses the switch statement in line 11 to display messages that correspond to the various enumerated values.

The function main declares the double-typed variables x, y, and z to represent the operands and the result, respectively. In addition, the function declares the char-typed variable op to store the requested operation, and the enumerated variable error to store the error status. The function initializes the variable error with the enumerated value noError.

The output statement in line 29 prompts you to enter the operands and the operator. The statement in line 30 stores your input in variables x, op, and y, in that order. The function uses the switch statement in line 32 to examine the value in variable op and perform the requested operation. The case labels in lines 33, 36, 39, and 42 provide the values for the four supported math operations. The last case label contains an if statement that detects the attempt to divide by zero. If this is true, then the else clause statement assigns the enumerated value divideByZero to the variable error.

The catch-all default clause in line 48 handles invalid operators. The statement in line 49 assigns the enumerated value badOperator to the variable error.

The if statement in line 52 determines whether the variable error contains the enumerated value noError. If this condition is true, then the program executes the output statement in line 53. This statement displays the operands, the operator, and the result. Otherwise, the program executes the else clause statement that calls the function sayError and passes it the argument error. This function call displays a message that identifies the error.

Structures

C++ supports structures, and these members can be predefined types or other structures.

NEW☞
TERM *Structures* enable you to define a new type that logically groups several fields or members.

A Structure

Syntax

The general syntax for declaring a structure is

```
struct structTag {
  < list of members >
};
```

Examples

```
struct point {
    double x;
    double y;
};

struct rectangle {
    point upperLeftCorner;
    point lowerRightCorner;
    double area;
};

struct circle {
    point center;
    double radius;
    double area;
};
```

4

Once you define a struct type, you can use that type to declare variables. Following are examples of declarations that use structures that we declared in the syntax box:

```
point p1, p2, p3;
```

You also can declare structured variables when you define the structure itself.

```
struct point {
double x;
double y;
} p1, p2, p3;
```

NEW☞
TERM *Untagged structures* enable you to declare structure variables without defining a name for their structures.

Note: Interestingly, C++ permits you to declare untagged structures. For example, the following structure definition declares the variables p1, p2, and p3 but omits the name of the structure:

```
struct {
    double x;
    double y;
} p1, p2, p3;
```

123

C++ enables you to declare and initialize a structured variable. Here is an example:

```
point pt = { 1.0, -8.3 };
```

Accessing the members of a structure uses the dot operator. Following are a few examples:

```
p1.x = 12.45;
p1.y = 34.56;
p2.x = 23.4 / p1.x;
p2.y = 0.98 * p1.y;
```

Note: This method of initializing a struct is the old C way of doing things. C++ has a better way: by using a constructor. This can work because structs are actually just special forms of classes. The class is covered on Day 8.

Consider an example. Listing 4.2 shows the source code for the program STRUCT1.CPP. The program prompts you for four sets of coordinates that define four rectangles. Each rectangle is defined by the x and y coordinates of the upper-left and lower-right corners. The program calculates the areas of each rectangle, sorts the rectangles by area, and displays the rectangles in the order of their areas.

Listing 4.2. Source code for the program STRUCT1.CPP.

```
 1:  /*
 2:    C++ program that demonstrates structured types
 3:  */
 4:
 5:  #include <iostream.h>
 6:  #include <stdio.h>
 7:  #include <math.h>
 8:
 9:  const MAX_RECT = 4;
10:
11:  struct point {
12:    double x;
13:    double y;
14:  };
15:
16:  struct rect {
17:    point ulc; // upper left corner
18:    point lrc; // lower right corner
19:    double area;
20:    int id;
21:  };
22:
23:  typedef rect rectArr[MAX_RECT];
24:
25:  main()
26:  {
```

```
27:    rectArr r;
28:    rect temp;
29:    double length, width;
30:
31:    for (int i = 0; i < MAX_RECT; i++) {
32:      cout << "Enter (X,Y) coord. for ULC of rect. # "
33:           << i << " : ";
34:      cin >> r[i].ulc.x >> r[i].ulc.y;
35:      cout << "Enter (X,Y) coord. for LRC of rect. # "
36:           << i << " : ";
37:      cin >> r[i].lrc.x >> r[i].lrc.y;
38:      r[i].id = i;
39:      length = fabs(r[i].ulc.x -- r[i].lrc.x);
40:      width = fabs(r[i].ulc.y -- r[i].lrc.y);
41:      r[i].area = length * width;
42:    }
43:
44:    // sort the rectangles by areas
45:    for (i = 0; i < (MAX_RECT -- 1); i++)
46:      for (int j = i + 1; j < MAX_RECT; j++)
47:        if (r[i].area > r[j].area) {
48:          temp = r[i];
49:          r[i] = r[j];
50:          r[j] = temp;
51:        }
52:
53:    // display rectangles sorted by area
54:    for (i = 0; i < MAX_RECT; i++)
55:      printf("Rect # %d has area %5.4lf\n", r[i].id, r[i].area);
56:    return 0;
57: }
```

Here is a sample session with the program in Listing 4.2.

```
Enter (X,Y) coord. for ULC of rect. # 0 : 1 1
Enter (X,Y) coord. for LRC of rect. # 0 : 2 2
Enter (X,Y) coord. for ULC of rect. # 1 : 1.5 1.5
Enter (X,Y) coord. for LRC of rect. # 1 : 3 4
Enter (X,Y) coord. for ULC of rect. # 2 : 1 2
Enter (X,Y) coord. for LRC of rect. # 2 : 5 8
Enter (X,Y) coord. for ULC of rect. # 3 : 4 6
Enter (X,Y) coord. for LRC of rect. # 3 : 8 4
Rect # 0 has area 1.0000
Rect # 1 has area 3.7500
Rect # 3 has area 8.0000
Rect # 2 has area 24.0000
```

The program in Listing 4.2 includes the header files IOSTREAM. MATH.H, and STDIO.H. The program declares the global constant MAX_RECT to specify the maximum number of rectangles. Line 11 contains the declaration of structure point, which is made up of two double-typed members: x and y. This structure models a two-dimensional point. Line 16 contains the declaration of structure rect, which models a rectangle. The structure contains two point-typed members, ulc and lrc, the double-typed member area, and the int-typed member id. The members ulc and lrc represent the coordinates for the upper-left and lower-right corners that define a rectangle. The member area stores the area of the rectangle. The member id stores a numeric identification number.

The typedef statement in line 23 defines the type recArr as an array of MAX_RECT elements of structure rect.

The function main declares the rectArr-typed array r, the rect-typed structure temp, and the double-typed variables length and width.

The function main uses the for loop in lines 31 through 42 to prompt you for the coordinates of the rectangles, calculate their areas, and assign their id numbers. The output statements in lines 32 and 33, and in lines 35 and 36, prompt you for the x and y coordinates of the upper-left and lower-right corners, respectively. The input statements in lines 34 and 37 store the coordinates you enter in members r[i].ulc.x, r[i].ulc.y, r[i].lrc.x, and r[i].lrc.y, respectively. The statement in line 38 stores the value of the loop control variable i in member r[i].id. The statement in line 39 calculates the length of a rectangle using the x members of the ulc and lrc members in the element r[i]. The statement in line 40 calculates the width of a rectangle using the y members of the ulc and lrc members in the element r[i]. The statement in line 41 calculates the area of the rectangle and stores it in member r[i].area.

The nested loops in lines 44 through 51 sort the elements of array r using the member area. The loops implement the simple bubble sort method (which is useful for very small arrays). The if statement in line 47 compares the areas of elements r[i] and r[j]. If the area of rectangle r[i] is larger than that of rectangle r[j], the statements in lines 48 through 50 swap all the members of r[i] and r[j]. The swap uses the structure temp. This task illustrates that you can assign all the members of a structure to another structure in one statement.

The for loop in lines 54 and 55 displays the rectangles sorted according to their areas. The output statement in line 55 uses the printf function to display the rectangle id numbers and areas.

Unions

The size of a union is equal to the size of its largest member.

NEW☞ TERM   *Unions* are special structures that store members with shared address spaces.

Syntax

Unions

The general syntax for unions is

```
union unionTag {
    type1 member1;
    type2 member2;
    ...
    typeN memberN;
};
```

Example

```
union Long {
   unsigned mWord[2];
   long mLong;
};
```

The union Long stores either two unsigned integers (each requiring two bytes) or a four-byte long integer. In addition, the union Long enables you to access the lower or higher words (two-byte integers) of a long integer.

Unions offer an easy alternative for quick data conversion. Unions were more significant in the recent past, when the price of computer memory was much higher and it was feasible to use unions to consolidate memory. Accessing union members involves the dot access operators, just as in structures.

Reference Variables

In Day 2, you learned that you declare reference parameters by placing the & symbol after the parameter's type. Recall that a reference parameter becomes an alias to its arguments. In addition, any changes made to the reference parameter affect its argument. In addition to reference parameters, C++ supports *reference variables*. You can manipulate the referenced variable by using its alias. As a novice C++ programmer, your initial use of reference variables will most likely be limited. On the other hand, you probably are using reference parameters more frequently. As you advance in using C++, you will discover how reference variables can implement programming tricks that deal with advanced class design. This book discusses only the basics of reference variables.

NEW☞ TERM   Like reference parameters, *reference variables* become aliases to the variables they access.

A Reference Variable

The general syntax for declaring a reference variable is

```
type& refVar = Var;
type& refVar = aVar;
```

The refVar is the reference variable that can be initialized when declared. You must ensure that a reference variable is initialized or assigned a referenced variable before using the reference variable.

Examples

```
int x = 10, y = 3;
int& rx = x;
int& ry = y; // take the reference
```

Here is a simple example that shows a reference variable at work. Listing 4.3 shows the source code for the program REFVAR1.CPP. The program displays and alters the values of a variable using either the variable itself or its reference. The program requires no input.

Listing 4.3. Source code for the program REFVAR1.CPP.

```
 1: /*
 2:    C++ program that demonstrates reference variables
 3: */
 4:
 5: #include <iostream.h>
 6:
 7: main()
 8: {
 9:    int x = 10;
10:    int& rx = x;
11:    // display x using x and rx
12:    cout << "x contains " << x << "\n";
13:    cout << "x contains (using the reference rx) "
14:         << rx << "\n";
15:    // alter x and display its value using rx
16:    x *= 2;
17:    cout << "x contains (using the reference rx) "
18:         << rx << "\n";
19:    // alter rx and display value using x
20:    rx *= 2;
21:    cout << "x contains " << x << "\n";
22:    return 0;
23: }
```

Here is a sample session with the program in Listing 4.3.

```
x contains 10
x contains (using the reference rx) 10
x contains (using the reference rx) 20
x contains 40
```

The program in Listing 4.3 declares the int-typed variable x and the int-typed reference variable rx. The program initializes the variable x with 10 and the reference variable rx with the variable x.

The output statement in line 12 displays the value in variable x using the variable x itself. By contrast, the output statement in lines 13 and 14 displays the value in variable x using the reference variable rx.

The statement in line 16 doubles the integer in variable x. The output statement in lines 17 and 18 displays the new value in variable x using the reference variable rx. As the output shows, the reference variable accurately displays the updated value in variable x.

The statement in line 20 doubles the value in variable x by using the reference variable rx. The output statement in line 21 displays the updated value in variable x using variable x. Again, the output shows that the variable x and the reference variable rx are synchronized.

Overview of Pointers

Each piece of information, both code and data, in the computer's memory resides at a specific address and occupies a specific number of bytes. When you run a program, your variables reside at specific *addresses*. With a high-level language such as C++, you are not concerned about the actual address of every variable. That task is handled transparently by the compiler and the runtime system. Conceptually, each variable in your program is a *tag* for a memory address. Manipulating the data using the tag is much easier than dealing with actual numerical addresses, such as 0F64:01AF4.

NEW☞
TERM   An *address* is a memory location. A *tag* is the variable's name.

Going back to the box analogy (in Day 3), imagine that your computer's memory is just a large number of tiny boxes. Now, imagine that when you declare a variable, you're really just setting aside a box to hold the value of that variable. But what if you weren't so much interested in what that box contained, but rather you wanted to know just where that box was in memory? You would create a pointer to that box. Creating a pointer is just declaring another variable, but the value that can be found in the pointer's box really is just the address of another variable's box. Regard Figure 4.1 as it relates to the following code snippet:

```
int myInt = 42;
int *pInt = &myInt;
```

Figure 4.1.
Memory depicted by boxes.

The variable myInt has been declared, which created a box for it, and the value 42 has been placed into it. That box happens to be at memory address 8076. When the pointer pInt was declared, another box was created at another memory address. In this particular case, that memory happens to be 8094. It's important to note that the memory addresses will not necessarily be next to each other, as in this case. When pInt was declared, it was initialized with the address (that's what the & means) of myInt. So, the memory address at which myInt resides was placed inside of pInt's box. pInt is a variable of its own, but its value just happens to be the address of another variable. Note that it is entirely possible, at this point, to declare yet another box, and have that be a pointer to pInt; this would be called a *pointer to a pointer*.

C++ and its parent C are programming languages that also are used for low-level systems programming. In fact, many programmers regard C as a high-level assembler. Low-level system programming requires that you work frequently with the address of data. This is where pointers, in general, come into play. Knowing the address of a piece of data enables you to set and query its value.

NEW☞ TERM   A *pointer* is a special variable that stores the address of another variable or information.

> **Warning:** Pointers are very powerful language components. They also can be dangerous if used carelessly, because they may hang your system. This malfunction occurs when the pointer hasn't been set up yet. Don't forget that simply declaring something doesn't automatically give it any value. Until you've set the value of a pointer (with the address of another variable), that pointer is just referring to something random in memory, and if you use that pointer, you could get some really weird results.

Pointers to Existing Variables

In this section, you learn how to use pointers to access the values in existing variables. C++ requires that you associate a data type (including void) with a declared pointer. The associated data type may be a predefined type or a user-defined structure.

A Pointer

The general syntax for declaring a pointer is

```
type* pointerName;
type* pointerName = pointerVariable;
type* pointerName = &variable;
```

The & operator is the address-of operator (this is not the reference operator, which also uses the & symbol) and is used to take the address of a variable. The address-of operator returns the address of a variable, structure, function, and so on. By contrast, the reference operator creates an alias to a variable using another variable.

Example

```
int *intPtr; // pointer to an int
double *realPtr; // pointer to a double
char *aString; // pointer to a character
long lv;
long* lp = &lv;
```

You also can declare nonpointers in the same lines that declare pointers.

```
int *intPtr, anInt;
double *realPtr, x;
char *aString, aKey;
```

Note: C++ allows you to place the asterisk character right after the associated data type. You should not interpret this type of syntax to mean that every other identifier appearing in the same declaration is automatically a pointer.

```
int* intPtr; // pointer to an int

double* realPtr; // pointer to a double

char* aString; // pointer to a character

int *intP, j; // intP is a pointer to int, j is an int

double *realPtr, *doublePtr;  // both identifiers

                             // are pointers to a double
```

DO	DON'T

DO initialize a pointer before you use it, just as you do with ordinary variables. In fact, the need to initialize pointers is even more pressing—using uninitialized pointers invites trouble that can lead to unpredictable program behavior or a system hang. Whenever you see a General Protection Fault (a GPF) in a program, it usually is caused by using a pointer that has not been initialized properly.

DON'T assume that uninitialized pointers are harmless.

Once a pointer contains the address of a variable, you can access the value in that variable using the * operator followed by the name of the pointer. For example, if px is a pointer to the variable x, then you can use *px to access the value in variable x.

DO	DON'T

DO include the * operator to the left of a pointer to access the variable whose address is stored in the pointer.

DON'T forget to use the * operator. Without it, a statement ends up manipulating the address in the pointer instead of the data at that address.

Following is a simple example that shows a pointer at work. Listing 4.4 shows the source code for the program PTR1.CPP. The program displays and alters the values of a variable using either the variable itself or its pointer. The program requires no input.

Listing 4.4. Source code for the program PTR1.CPP.

```
1:  /*
2:    C++ program that demonstrates pointers to existing variables
3:  */
4:
5:  #include <iostream.h>
6:
7:  main()
8:  {
9:    int x = 10;
10:   int* px = &x;
11:   // display x using x and rx
12:   cout << "x contains " << x << "\n";
13:   cout << "x contains (using the pointer px) "
14:        << *px << "\n";
15:   // alter x and display its value using *px
16:   x *= 2;
17:   cout << "x contains (using the pointer px) "
18:        << *px << "\n";
19:   // alter *px and display value using x
20:   *px *= 2;
21:   cout << "x contains " << x << "\n";
22:   return 0;
23: }
```

Here is a sample session with the program in Listing 4.4.

```
x contains 10
x contains (using the pointer px) 10
x contains (using the pointer px) 20
x contains 40
```

The program in Listing 4.4 declares the int-typed variable x and the int-typed pointer px. The program initializes the variable x with 10 and the pointer px with the address of variable x.

The output statement in line 12 displays the value in variable x using the variable x. By contrast, the output statement in lines 13 and 14 displays the value in variable x using the pointer px. Notice that the statement uses *px to access the value in variable x.

The statement in line 16 doubles the integer in variable x. The output statement in lines 17 and 18 displays the new value in variable x using the pointer px. As the output shows, the pointer accurately displays the updated value in variable x.

The statement in line 20 doubles the value in variable x by using the pointer px. Notice that the assignment statement uses *px on the left side of the = operator to access the variable x. The output statement in line 21 displays the updated value in variable x using variable x. Again, the output shows that the variable x and the pointer px are synchronized.

A Short Introduction to Arrays

An *array* is one of the most useful components in a programming language. It enables the programmer to store a number of data items in a single location. The single-dimensional array is the simplest kind of array. In a single-dimensional array, each variable is individually accessed using a single index.

NEW☞ TERM An *array* is a group of variables that share the same name (the name of the array).

A Single-Dimensional Array

The general syntax for declaring a single-dimensional array is

```
type arrayName[numberOfElements];
```

C++ requires you to observe the following rules in declaring single-dimensional arrays:

☐ The lower bound of a C++ array is set at 0. C++ does not allow you to override or alter this lower bound.

☐ Declaring a C++ array entails specifying the number of members. Keep in mind that the number of members is equal to the upper bound plus one.

The valid range of indices for this form extends between `0` and `numberOfElements - 1`.

Examples

```
int intArray[10];
char name[31];
double x[100];
```

Using a single-dimensional array involves stating both its name and the valid index in order to access one of its members. Depending on where the reference to an array element occurs, it can either store or recall a value. Following are the simple rules to remember:

☐ Assign a value to an array element before accessing that element to recall data. Otherwise, you get garbage data.

☐ Use a valid index. This is of paramount importance, because trying to access an array with an invalid index is like using an uninitialized pointer; it can lead to strange behavior in your program and GPFs in Windows.

DO	DON'T
DO make reasonable checks for the indices that access the arrays. **DON'T** assume that indices are always valid.	

4

The following is a simple example of accessing arrays:

```
double nums[5];
for (int i = 0; i < 5; ++i)
    {
    cout << "Enter number " << i << ": ";
    cin >> nums[i];
    }
cout << "You entered the following numbers: ";
for (i = 0; i < 5; ++i)
    cout << "nums[" << i << "] is " << nums[i];
cout << endl;
```

Pointers to Arrays

C++ and its parent language, C, support a special use for the names of arrays. The compiler interprets the name of an array as the address of its first element. Thus, if x is an array, the expressions &x[0] and x are equivalent. In the case of a matrix—call it mat—the expressions &mat[0][0] and mat also are equivalent. This aspect of C++ and C makes them work as high-level assembly languages. Once you have the address of a data item, you've got its number, so to speak. Your knowledge of the memory address of a variable or an array enables you to manipulate its contents using pointers.

NEW☛
TERM A *program variable* is a label that tags a memory address. Using a variable in a program means accessing the associated memory location by specifying its name (or tag, if you prefer). In this sense, a variable becomes a name that points to a memory location—a pointer.

C++ enables you to use a pointer to access the various elements of an array. When you access the element x[i] of array x, the compiled code performs two tasks. First, it obtains the base address of the array x (that is, where the first array element is located). Second, it uses the index i to calculate the offset from the base address of the array. This offset equals i multiplied by the size of the basic array type.

```
address of element x[i] = address of x + i * sizeof(basicType)
```

Looking at the preceding equation, assume that you have a pointer ptr that takes the base address of array x.

```
ptr = x; // pointer ptr points to address of x[0]
```

You now can substitute x with ptr in the equation and come up with the following:

```
address of element x[i] = ptr + i * sizeof(basicType)
```

In order for C++ and C to be high-level assemblers, they simplify the use of this equation by absolving it from having to explicitly state the size of the basic array type. Thus, you can write the following:

```
address of element x[i] = p + i
```

This equation states that the address of element x[i] is the expression (p + i).

The PTR 2.CPP program in Listing 4.5 illustrates the use of pointers to access one-dimensional arrays. This program is a modified version of the program ARRAY1.CPP that calculates the average value for data in an array. The program begins by prompting you to enter the number of data points and the data itself. The program then calculates the average of the data in the array and displays the average value.

 Listing 4.5. Source code for the program PTR2.CPP.

```
1:  /*
2:      C++ program that demonstrates the use of pointers with
3:      one-dimension arrays.  Program calculates the average
4:      value of the data found in the array.
5:  */
6:
7:  #include <iostream.h>
8:
9:  const int MAX = 30;
10:
11: main()
12: {
13:
14:      double x[MAX];
15:      // declare pointer and initialize with base
16:      // address of array x
17:      double *realPtr = x; // same as = &x[0]
18:      double sum, sumx = 0.0, mean;
19:      int n;
20:      // obtain the number of data points
21:      do {
22:          cout << "Enter number of data points [2 to "
23:               << MAX << "] : ";
24:          cin >> n;
25:          cout << "\n";
26:      } while (n < 2 ||[]> MAX);
27:
28:      // prompt for the data
29:      for (int i = 0; i < n; i++) {
30:          cout << "X[" << i << "] : ";
31:          // use the form *(x+i) to store data in x[i]
32:          cin >> *(x + i);
33:      }
34:
35:      sum = n;
36:      for (i = 0; i < n; i++)
37:      // use the form *(realPtr + i) to access x[i]
38:          sumx += *(realPtr + i);
39:      mean = sumx / sum;
40:      cout << "\nMean = " << mean << "\n\n";
41:      return 0;
42: }
```

135

Here is a sample session with the program in Listing 4.5.

```
Enter number of data points [2 to 30] : 5

X[0] : 1
X[1] : 2
X[2] : 3
X[3] : 4
X[4] : 5

Mean = 3
```

The program in Listing 4.5 declares the double-typed array x to have MAX elements. In addition, the program declares the pointer realPtr and initializes it using the array x. Thus, the pointer realPtr stores the address of x[0], which is the first element in array x.

The program uses the pointer for `*(x + i)` in the input statement at line 32. Thus, the identifier x works as a pointer to the array x. Using the expression `*(x + i)` accesses the element number i of array x, just as does using the expression `x[i]`.

The program uses the pointer realPtr in the for loop at lines 37 and 38. The expression `*(realPtr + i)` is the equivalent of `*(x + i)`, which in turn is equivalent to `x[i]`. Thus, the for loop uses the pointer realPtr with an offset value, i, to access the elements of array x.

The Pointer Increment/Decrement Method

The preceding C++ program maintains the same address in the pointer realPtr. Employing pointer arithmetic with the for loop index i, you can write a new program version that increments the offset to access the elements of array x. C++ provides you with another choice that enables you to access sequentially the elements of an array without the help of an explicit offset value. The method merely involves using the increment or decrement operator with a pointer. You still need to initialize the pointer to the base address of an array and then use the ++ operator to access the next array element. Following is a modified version of the preceding program, a version that uses the pointer increment method. Listing 4.6 shows the source code for the PTR3.CPP program.

Listing 4.6. Source code for the program PTR3.CPP.

```
1:  /*
2:      C++ program that demonstrates the use of pointers with
3:      one-dimension arrays.  The average value of the array
4:      is calculated.  This program modifies the previous version
5:      in the following way:  the realPtr is used to access the
6:      array without any help from any loop control variable.
7:      This is accomplished by 'incrementing' the pointer, and
8:      consequently incrementing its address.  This program
```

```
9:     illustrates pointer arithmetic that alters the pointer's
10:    address.
11:
12: */
13:
14: #include <iostream.h>
15:
16: const int MAX = 30;
17:
18: main()
19: {
20:
21:     double x[MAX];
22:     double *realPtr = x;
23:     double sum, sumx = 0.0, mean;
24:     int i, n;
25:
26:     do {
27:         cout << "Enter number of data points [2 to "
28:             << MAX << "] : ";
29:         cin >> n;
30:         cout << "\n";
31:     } while (n < 2 || n > MAX);
32:
33:     // loop variable i is not directly involved in accessing
34:     //   the elements of array x
35:     for (i = 0; i < n; i++) {
36:         cout << "X[" << i << "] : ";
37:         // increment pointer realPtr after taking its reference
38:         cin >> *realPtr++;
39:     }
40:
41:     // restore original address by using pointer arithmetic
42:     realPtr -= n;
43:     sum = n;
44:     // loop variable i serves as a simple counter
45:     for (i = 0; i < n; i++)
46:         // increment pointer realPtr after taking a reference
47:         sumx += *(realPtr++);
48:     mean = sumx / sum;
49:     cout << "\nMean = " << mean << "\n\n";
50:     return 0;
51:
52: }
```

Here is a sample session with the program in Listing 4.6.

```
Enter number of data points [2 to 30] : 5

X[0] : 10
X[1] : 20
X[2] : 30
X[3] : 40
X[4] : 50

Mean = 30
```

The program in Listing 4.6 initializes the realPtr pointer to the base address of array x, in line 22. The program uses the realPtr pointer in the keyboard input statement in line 38. This statement uses *realPtr++ to store your input in the currently accessed element of array x and then to increment the pointer to the next element of array x. When the input loop terminates, the pointer realPtr points past the tail of array x. To reset the pointer to the base address of array x, the program uses the assignment statement in line 42. This statement uses pointer arithmetic to decrease the current address in pointer realPtr by n times sizeof(real). The statement resets the address in the pointer realPtr to access the array element x[0]. The program uses the same incrementing method to calculate the sum of data in the second for loop in line 47.

Pointers to Structures

C++ supports declaring and using pointers to structures. Assigning the address of a structured variable to a pointer of the same type uses the same syntax as with simple variables. Once the pointer has the address of the structured variable, it needs to use the -> operator to access the members of the structure.

Accessing Structure Members

The general syntax for a pointer to access the members of a structure is

```
structPtr->aMember
```

Example

```
struct point {
    double x;
    double y;
};

point p;
point* ptr = &p;

ptr->x = 23.3;
ptr->y = ptr->x + 12.3;
```

Here is a sample program that uses pointers to structures. Listing 4.7 shows the source code for the program PTR4.CPP. This program is the version of program STRUCT1.CPP that uses pointers. The program prompts you for four sets of coordinates that define four rectangles. Each rectangle is defined by the x and y coordinates of the upper-left and lower-right corners. The program calculates the area of each rectangle, sorts the rectangles by area, and displays the rectangles in the order of their areas.

Listing 4.7. Source code for the program PTR4.CPP.

```
1:  /*
2:     C++ program that demonstrates pointers to structured types
3:  */
4:
5:  #include <iostream.h>
6:  #include <stdio.h>
7:  #include <math.h>
8:
9:  const MAX_RECT = 4;
10:
11: struct point {
12:   double x;
13:   double y;
14: };
15:
16: struct rect {
17:   point ulc; // upper left corner
18:   point lrc; // lower right corner
19:   double area;
20:   int id;
21: };
22:
23: typedef rect rectArr[MAX_RECT];
24:
25: main()
26: {
27:   rectArr r;
28:   rect temp;
29:   rect* pr = r;
30:   rect* pr2;
31:   double length, width;
32:
33:   for (int i = 0; i < MAX_RECT; i++, pr++) {
34:     cout << "Enter (X,Y) coord. for ULC of rect. # "
35:          << i << " : ";
36:     cin >> pr-->ulc.x >> pr-->ulc.y;
37:     cout << "Enter (X,Y) coord. for LRC of rect. # "
38:          << i << " : ";
39:     cin >> pr-->lrc.x >> pr-->lrc.y;
40:     pr-->id = i;
41:     length = fabs(pr-->ulc.x -- pr-->lrc.x);
42:     width = fabs(pr-->ulc.y -- pr-->lrc.y);
43:     pr-->area = length * width;
44:   }
45:
46:   pr --= MAX_RECT; // reset pointer
47:   // sort the rectangles by areas
48:   for (i = 0; i < (MAX_RECT -- 1); i++, pr++) {
49:     pr2 = pr + 1; // reset pointer pr2
50:     for (int j = i + 1; j < MAX_RECT; j++, pr2++)
51:       if (pr—>area > pr2—>area) {
52:         temp = *pr;
```

continued

Listing 4.7. continued

```
53:        *pr = *pr2;
54:        *pr2 = temp;
55:      }
56:   }
57:
58:   pr --= MAX_RECT -- 1; // reset pointer
59:   // display rectangles sorted by area
60:   for (i = 0; i < MAX_RECT; i++, pr++)
61:     printf("Rect # %d has area %5.4lf\n", pr-->id, pr-->area);
62:   return 0;
63: }
```

Here is a sample session with the program in Listing 4.7.

```
Enter (X,Y) coord. for ULC of rect. # 0 : 1 1
Enter (X,Y) coord. for LRC of rect. # 0 : 2 2
Enter (X,Y) coord. for ULC of rect. # 1 : 1.5 1.5
Enter (X,Y) coord. for LRC of rect. # 1 : 3 4
Enter (X,Y) coord. for ULC of rect. # 2 : 1 2
Enter (X,Y) coord. for LRC of rect. # 2 : 5 8
Enter (X,Y) coord. for ULC of rect. # 3 : 4 6
Enter (X,Y) coord. for LRC of rect. # 3 : 8 4
Rect # 0 has area 1.0000
Rect # 1 has area 3.7500
Rect # 3 has area 8.0000
Rect # 2 has area 24.0000
```

The program in Listing 4.7 declares the pointers pr and pr2 in lines 29 and 30, respectively. These pointers access the structure of type rect. The program initializes the pointer pr with the base address of array r.

The first for loop, which begins at line 33, uses the pointer pr to access the elements of array r. The loop increment part contains the expression pr++, which uses pointer arithmetic to make the pointer pr access the next element in array r. The input statements in lines 36 and 39 use the pointer pr to access the members ulc and lrc. Notice that the statements use the pointer access operator -> to allow pointer pr to access the members ulc and lrc. The statements in lines 40 through 43 also use the pointer pr to access the members id, ulc, lrc, and area, using the -> operator.

The statement in line 46 resets the address stored in pointer pr by MAX_RECT units (that is MAX_RECT * sizeof(double) bytes). The nested loops in lines 48 through 56 use the pointers pr and pr2. The outer for loop increments the address in pointer pr by one before the next iteration. The statement in line 49 assigns pr + 1 to the pointer pr2. This statement gives the pointer pr2 the initial access to the element i + 1 in array r. The inner for loop increments the pointer pr2 by 1 before the next iteration. Thus, the nested for loops use the pointers pr and pr2 to access the elements of array r. The if statement in line 51 uses the pointers pr and pr2 to access the area member in comparing the areas of various rectangles. The statements in line 52 through 54 swap the elements of array r, which are accessed by pointers pr and pr2. Notice that the statements use *pr and *pr2 to access an entire element of array r.

The statement in line 58 resets the address in the pointer pr by subtracting MAX_RECT - 1. The last for loop also uses the pointer pr to access and display the members id and area of the various elements in array r.

This program illustrates that you can completely manipulate an array using pointers only. They are powerful and versatile.

Pointers and Dynamic Memory

The programs presented thus far create the space for their variables at compile-time. When the programs start running, the variables have their memory spaces preassigned. There are many applications in which you need to create new variables during the program execution. You need to allocate the memory space dynamically for these new variables at runtime. The designers of C++ have chosen to introduce new operators, which are not found in C, to handle the dynamic allocation and de-allocation of memory. These new C++ operators are new and delete. While the C-style dynamic memory functions malloc, calloc, and free are still available, you should use the operators new and delete. These operators are more aware of the type of dynamic data that is created than are functions malloc, calloc, and free. Also, the standard C functions for creating and deleting dynamic memory won't handle class constructors and destructors (which are discussed on Day 8).

The *new* and *delete* Operators

The general syntax for using the new and delete operators in creating dynamic scalar variables is

```
pointer = new type;
delete pointer;
```

The operator new returns the address of the dynamically allocated variable. The operator delete removes the dynamically allocated memory accessed by a pointer. If the dynamic allocation of operator new fails, it throws an exception of type xalloc (declared in the EXCEPT.H header file). Therefore, you should make sure that you enclose your dynamic memory allocations in try blocks if you suspect trouble.

Example

```
try {
    int *pint;
    pint = new int;
    *pint = 33;
    cout << "Pointer pint stores " << *pint;
    delete pint;
}
catch(xalloc)
{
    cout <<< "Couldn't allocate memory." << endl;
}
```

141

A Dynamic Array

To allocate and de-allocate a dynamic array, use the following general syntax:

```
arrayPointer = new type[arraySize];
delete[] arrayPointer;
```

The operator new returns the address of the dynamically allocated array. If the allocation fails, the operator throws an xalloc exception. The operator delete removes the dynamically allocated array that is accessed by a pointer.

Example

```
try {
   const int MAX = 10;
   int* pint;
   pint = new int[MAX];
   for (int i = 0; i < MAX; i++)
      pint[i] = i * i;
   for (i = 0; i < MAX; i++)
      cout << *(pint + i) << endl;
   delete [] pint;
}
catch(xalloc)
{
   cout << "Couldn't allocate memory." << endl;
}
```

DO   DON'T

DO maintain access to dynamic variables and arrays at all times. Such access does not need the original pointers that were used to create these dynamic variables and arrays. Here is an example.

```
int* p = new int;
int* q;
*p = 123;
q = p; // q now also points to 123
p = new int; // create another dynamic variable
*p = 345; // p points to 345 whereas q points to 123
cout << *p << " " << *q << " " << (*p + *q) << "\n";
delete p;
delete q;
```

DON'T forget to delete dynamic variables and arrays at the end of their scope. If you do, there is the potential of a "memory leak." This is the condition when memory seems to keep getting lower in your system for no apparent reason. It means that something has allocated memory without freeing it.

Using pointers to create and access dynamic data can be illustrated with the next program, PTR5.CPP (Listing 4.8). This program is a modified version of program ARRAY1.CPP that calculates the average value for data in an array. The program begins by prompting you to enter the actual number of data and validates your input. Then the program prompts you for the data and calculates the average of the data in the array. Next, the program displays the average value.

 Listing 4.8. Source code for the program PTR5.CPP.

```
1:  /*
2:     C++ program that demonstrates the pointers to manage
3:     dynamic data
4:  */
5:  #include <iostream.h>
6:  #include <except.h>
7:
8:  const int MAX = 30;
9:
10: main()
11: {
12:
13:     double* x;
14:     double sum, sumx = 0, mean;
15:     int *n;
16:
17:     try { n = new int; }
18:     catch {xalloc&) { return 1; }
19:
20:     do { // obtain number of data points
21:         cout << "Enter number of data points [2 to "
22:             << MAX << "] : ";
23:         cin >> *n;
24:         cout << "\n";
25:     } while (*n < 2 || *n > MAX);
26:     // create tailor-fit dynamic array
27:     try { x = new double[*n]; }
28:     catch (xalloc&) {
29:       delete n;
30:       return 1;
31:     }
32:     // prompt user for data
33:     for (int i = 0; i < *n; i++) {
34:         cout << "X[" << i << "] : ";
35:         cin >> x[i];
36:     }
37:
38:     // initialize summations
39:     sum = *n;
40:     // calculate sum of observations
41:     for (i = 0; i < *n; i++)
42:         sumx += *(x + i);
43:
44:     mean = sumx / sum; // calculate the mean value
45:     cout << "\nMean = " << mean << "\n\n";
```

continued

Listing 4.8. continued

```
46:    // deallocate dynamic memory
47:    delete n;
48:    delete [] x;
49:    return 0;
50: }
```

Here is a sample session with the program in Listing 4.8.

```
Enter number of data points [2 to 30] : 5

X[0] : 1
X[1] : 2
X[2] : 3
X[3] : 4
X[4] : 5

Mean = 3
```

The program in Listing 4.8 uses two pointers for dynamic allocations. Line 13 declares the first pointer, which is used to allocate and access the dynamic array. Line 15 declares the pointer to create a dynamic variable.

The statement in line 17 uses the operator new to allocate the space for a dynamic int variable. The statement returns the address of the dynamic data to the pointer n. The catch statement in line 18 determines whether the dynamic allocation failed. If so, the function main exits and returns an exit code of 1 (to flag an error).

The do-while loop in lines 20 through 25 prompts you to enter the number of data points. The statement in line 23 stores your input in the dynamic variable accessed by pointer n. The statement uses the pointer reference *n for this access. The while clause also uses *n to access the value in the dynamic variable. In fact, all the statements in the program access the number of data points using the pointer reference *n.

The statement in line 27 creates a dynamic array using the operator new. The statement creates a dynamic double-typed array with the number of elements that you specify. This feature demonstrates the advantage of using dynamic allocation to create custom-fit arrays. The catch statement in line 28 determines whether the allocation of the dynamic array was successful. If not, the statements in lines 29 and 30 de-allocate the dynamic variable accessed by pointer[ ] and exit the function with a return value of 1.

The for loop in lines 33 through 36 prompts you to enter values for the dynamic array. The statement in line 35 stores your input to the element i of the dynamic array. Notice that the statement uses the expression x[i] to access the targeted element. This form resembles that of static arrays. C++ treats the expression x[i] as equivalent to *(x + i). In fact , the program uses the latter form in the second for loop in lines 41 and 42. The statement in line 42 accesses the elements in the dynamic array using the form *(x + i).

The last statements in function `main` delete the dynamic variable and array. The statement in line 47 de-allocates the space for the dynamic variable accessed by pointer `n`. The statement in line 48 deletes the dynamic array accessed by pointer `x`.

Far Pointers

The architecture of processors, such as the family of Intel 80×86, features segmented memory. Each segment is 64 kilobytes (KB) in size. Using segments has advantages and disadvantages. This storage scheme supports two types of pointers: *near pointers* and *far pointers.*

NEW☞
TERM Within a segment you can use near pointers to access data in the same segment. The pointers only store the offset address in the segment and, thus, require fewer bytes to store their address. By contrast, far pointers store the segment and offset addresses and, thus, they require more space. Windows applications use far pointers.

To declare far pointers, insert the keyword `__far` (or sometimes `_far`) between the type and the name of the pointer.

It's important to note that far pointers are extremely non-portable. That is, they only apply to applications written for the IBM PC and compatible computers, and only then when in a 16-bit mode, such as MS-DOS or Windows 3.1. If you upgrade to the full Borland C++ compiler and write for Windows NT or any other 32-bit version of Windows, you will be able to ignore far pointers completely.

You also should note that far pointers really only make sense when compiling in something other than the large memory model (changeable in the Project dialog box accessible from the Options menu in the IDE). I strongly recommend that you always compile in large model and never leave it. The memory savings you get from using other memory models is minimal compared to the potential for bugs and consternation in mixing and matching far and near pointers.

Summary

Today's lesson introduced you to user-defined data types and covered the following topics:

☐ You can use the `typedef` statements to create alias types of existing types and define array types. The general syntax for using `typedef` is

```
typedef knownType newType;
```

☐ Enumerated data types enable you to declare unique identifiers that represent a collection of logically related constants. The general syntax for declaring an enumerated type is

```
enum enumType { <list of enumerated identifiers> };
```

☐ Structures enable you to define a new type that logically groups several fields or members. These members can be predefined types or other structures. The general syntax for declaring a structure is

```
struct structTag {
< list of members >
};
```

☐ Unions are a form of variant structures. The general syntax for unions is

```
union unionTag {
type1 member1;
type2 member2;
  ...
typeN memberN;
};
```

☐ Reference variables are aliases of the variables that they reference. To declare a reference variable, place the & after the data type of the reference variable or to the left of the variable's name.

☐ Pointers are variables that store the addresses of other variables or data. C++ uses pointers to offer flexible and efficient manipulation of data and system resources.

☐ Pointers to existing variables use the & operator to obtain the addresses of these variables. Armed with these addresses, pointers offer access to the data in their associated variables. To access the value by using a pointer, use the * operator followed by the name of the pointer.

☐ Arrays are groups of variables stored in a list with the same name, and they're useful for holding on to collections of the same type of data.

☐ Pointers access the elements of arrays by being assigned the base address of a class. C++ considers the name of an array as equivalent to the pointer of the base address. For example, the name of the array X is treated as &X[0]. Pointers can be used to sequentially traverse the elements of an array to store and/or recall values from these elements.

☐ Pointers to structures manipulate structures and access their members. C++ provides the -> operator in order to allow a pointer access to the members of a structure.

☐ Pointers can create and access dynamic data by using the operators new and delete. These operators enable you to create dynamic variables and arrays. The new operator assigns the address of the dynamic data to the pointer used in creating and accessing the data. The operator delete assists in recuperating the space of dynamic data when that information is no longer needed.

☐ Far pointers are pointers that store both the segment and the offset addresses of an item. Near pointers only store the offset address of an item. Far pointers require more storage than near pointers.

Q&A

Q Does C++ support pointers to the predefined type `void`?

A Yes, `void*` pointers are considered typeless pointers and can be used to copy arbitrary data.

Q Because C++ pointers (including `void*` pointers) have types, can I use typecasting to translate the data accessed by the general-purpose `void*` pointers to non-`void*` pointers?

A Yes. C++ enables you to typecast pointer references, such as

```
void* p = data;
long *lp = (long*) p;
```

The pointer `lp` uses the typecast to translate the data it accesses.

Q What happens if I delete a dynamic array by using the `delete` operator without following it with the empty brackets?

A The effect of deleting an array with a plain `delete` operator is undefined. Expect the plain `delete` operator to leave orphaned dynamic memory and cause memory leaks.

Q Can a structure contain a pointer to itself?

A Yes. Many structures that model dynamic data structures use this type of declaration. For example, the following structure models the nodes of a dynamic list with pointer-based links:

```
struct listNode {
dataType data;
listNode *next;
};
```

Q Does C++ allow the declaration of a pointer-to-structure type before declaring the structure?

A Yes. This feature makes declaring nodes of dynamic data structures possible.

Q Does C++ allow pointers that access the addresses of other pointers?

A Yes. C++ supports pointers-to-pointers (also called *double pointers*). To declare such pointers, use two `*` characters, as shown in the following example, which declares the double pointer `p`:

```
int x;
int *px = &x;
int **p = &px;
```

The expression `*p` accesses the pointer `px`, and the expression `**p` accesses the variable `x`.

Workshop

The Workshop provides quiz questions to help you solidify your understanding of the material covered and exercises to provide you with experience in using what you've learned. Try to understand the quiz and exercise answers before continuing on to the next day's lesson. Answers are provided in Appendix A.

Quiz

1. What is the error in the following statements?

```
enum Boolean { false, true };
enum State { on, off };
enum YesNo { yes, no };
enum DiskDriveStatus { on , off };
```

2. True or false? The declaration of the following enumerated type is incorrect.

```
enum YesNo ( no = 0, No = 0, yes = 1, Yes = 1 };
```

3. What is the problem with the following program?

```
#include <iostream.h>
int main()
{
  int *p = new int;
  cout << "Enter a number : ";
  cin >> *p;
  cout << "The square of " << *p << " = " << (*p * *p);
  return 0;
}
```

Exercises

1. Modify the program PTR4.CPP to create the program PTR6.CPP, which uses the Comb sort method to sort the array of rectangles.

2. Define a structure that can be used to model a dynamic array of integers. The structure should have a member to access the dynamic data and a member to store the size of the dynamic array. Call the structure intArrStruct.

3. Define a structure that can be used to model a dynamic matrix. The structure should have a member to access the dynamic data and two members to store the number of rows and columns. Call the structure matStruct.

Functions

Today you will be introduced to a vital aspect of C++: functions. Functions provide a way of compartmentalizing parts of a program into more easily accessible pieces.

☐ Declaring and prototyping functions

☐ Local variables in functions

☐ Static variables in functions

☐ Macro expansion

☐ Inline functions

☐ Exiting functions

☐ Default arguments

☐ Passing arguments by reference

☐ Recursive functions

☐ Function overloading

Declaring and Prototyping Functions

Most programming languages use functions and procedures. C++ does not support formal procedures. Instead, all C++ routines are functions.

NEW ☞   *Functions* are the primary building blocks that conceptually extend the C++ language to
TERM   fit your custom programs. One could think of each function as a small routine that gets a small, very specific piece of a job done.

Syntax

Declaring Functions

The general form for the ANSI C style of declaring functions (which is maintained by C++) is

```
returnType functionName(typedParameterList)
```

Examples

```
double sqr(double y)
{ return y * y; }

char prevChar(char c)
{ return c - 1; }
```

Remember the following rules when declaring C++ functions:

☐ The return type of the C++ function appears before the function's name.

☐ If the parameter list is empty, you still use empty parentheses. C++ also allows you the option of using the void keyword to explicitly state that there are no parameters, but this is a throwback to the C language. I only mention the void keyword here so that you can recognize old code you might encounter that has been updated from C.

☐ The typed parameter list consists of a list of typed parameters that use the following general format:

```
[const] type1 parameter1, [const] type2 parameter2, ...
```

This format shows that the individual parameter is declared like a variable—you state the type first and then the parameter's identifier. The list of parameters in C++ is comma-delimited. In addition, you cannot group a sequence of parameters that have exactly the same data type. You must declare each parameter explicitly. If a parameter has the const clause, the compiler makes sure that the function does *not* alter the arguments of that parameter.

☐ The body of a C++ function is enclosed in braces ({}). There is no semicolon after the closing brace.

☐ C++ supports passing arguments either by value or by reference. By default, parameters pass their arguments by value. Consequently, the functions work with a copy of the data, preserving the original data. To declare a reference parameter, insert the & character after the data type of the parameter. A reference parameter becomes an alias to its arguments. Any changes made to the reference parameter also affect the original variable used as the argument. The general form for reference parameters is

```
[const] type1& parameter1, [const] type2& parameter2, ...
```

If a parameter has the const clause, the compiler makes sure that the function does not alter the arguments of that parameter. (Yes, there are good reasons for passing arguments by const reference, and they are discussed later in this chapter.)

☐ C++ supports local constants, data types, and variables. Although these data items can appear in nested block statements, C++ does not support nested functions.

☐ The return keyword returns the function's value.

☐ If the function's return type is void, you do not have to use the return keyword, unless you need to provide an exit route in the middle of the function.

NEW 🖝 C++ dictates that you either declare or define a function before you use it. Declaring a
TERM function, commonly called *prototyping*, lists the function name, return type, and the number and type of its parameters. Including the name of the parameter is optional. You also need to place a semicolon after the close parenthesis. C++ requires that you declare a function if you call it before you define it.

The following is a simple example of prototyping:

```
// prototype the function square
double sqr(double);

main()
{
    cout << "5^2 = " << sqr(5) << "\n";
    return 0;
}
```

```
double sqr(double z)
{ return z * z; }
```

Notice that the declaration of function sqr only contains the type of its single parameter. This is a common practice; however, I discourage it. By placing the name of parameters in prototypes, it makes figuring out the purpose of a function easier, especially if it's been a while since you wrote the function and can't remember exactly what it's supposed to do.

Typically, the declaration of a function is global. You still may prototype a function within its client function. This technique conceals the prototype from other functions.

Calling a function requires you to supply its parameter with arguments. The arguments are mapped onto the parameter by the sequence in which the parameters are declared. The arguments must be data types that match or are compatible with those of the parameters. For example, you may have a function volume, defined as follows:

```
double volume(double length, double width, double height)
{
    return length * width * height;
}
```

To call the function volume, you need to supply double-typed arguments or arguments with compatible types (which, in this case, are all of numeric data types). Here are a number of sample calls to the function volume.

```
double len = 34, width = 55, ht = 100;
int i = 3;
long j = 44;
unsigned k = 33;

cout << volume(len, width, ht) << endl;
cout << volume(1, 2, 3) << endl;
cout << volume(i, j, k) << endl;
cout << volume(len, j, 22.3) << endl;
```

Note: C++ enables you to discard the result of a function. This type of function call is used when the focus is on what the function does rather than its return value.

The Declaration of Exceptions Thrown by a Function

The syntax for declaring functions that can or cannot throw exceptions is

```
[returnType] functionName([parameterList]);
```

The preceding syntax declares that the function functionName can throw any type of exception.

```
[returnType] functionName([parameterList]) throw();
```

The preceding syntax declares that the function `functionName` should *not* throw an exception.

```
 [returnType] functionName([parameterList])
throw(exceptionTypeList)
```

The preceding syntax declares that the function `functionName` can only throw an exception in the comma-delimited exception type list, `exceptionTypeList`.

Examples

```
void parse();
void calc() throw();
void input() throw(TFileErr, TMemoryErr);
```

The declaration of function `parse` states that the function can throw any type of exception. By contrast, the declaration of function `calc` states that the function cannot throw any type of exception. The declaration of function `input` states that the function can only throw the exceptions of type `TFileErr`, `TMemoryErr`, or their descendant classes. This function `throws` an exception of type `TFileError` (a user-defined exception type). The catch block handles the `TFileError` exception type by displaying an error message.

Turbo C++ requires that you declare the `throw` clause in both the declaration and the definition of a function.

Local Variables in Functions

5

Good structured-programming techniques foster the notion that functions should be as independent and as reusable as possible. Consequently, functions can have their own data types, constants, and variables to give them this independence.

NEW☞   The *local variable* in a function exists only when that function is called. Once the
TERM   function terminates, the runtime system removes the local variables. Consequently, local variables lose their data between function calls. In addition, the runtime system applies any initialization to local variables every time the host function is called.

DO	**DON'T**

DO use local variables to store and alter the values of parameters that are declared with the const clause.

DON'T declare a local variable to have the same name as a global variable that you need to access in the function.

Look at an example. Listing 5.1 displays the value of the mathematical function

```
f(X) = X2 - 5 X + 10
```

and its slope at the argument 3.5. The program calculates the slope using the approximation

```
f'(X) = (f(X + h) - f(X - h)) / 2h
```

where *h* is a small increment.

Listing 5.1. Source code for the program VAR2.CPP.

```
1:  // C++ program that illustrates local variables in a function
2:
3:  #include <iostream.h>
4:
5:  double f(double x)
6:  {
7:    return x * x — 5 * x + 10;
8:  }
9:
10: double slope(double x)
11: {
12:   double f1, f2, incrim = 0.01 * x;
13:   f1 = f(x + incrim);
14:   f2 = f(x — incrim);
15:   return (f1 — f2) / 2 / incrim;
16: }
17:
18: main()
19: {
20:   double x = 3.5;
21:
22:   cout << "f(" << x << ") = " << f(x) << "\n"
23:        << "f'(" << x << ") = " << slope(x) << "\n";
24:
25:   return 0;
26: }
```

Here is a sample session with the program in Listing 5.1.

```
f(3.5) = 4.75
f'(3.5) = 2
```

The program in Listing 5.1 declares three functions, namely f (in line 5), slope (in line 10), and main (in line 18). The function f is simple and returns the value of the mathematical function. The function f is void of local variables. By contrast, the function slope declares the local variables f1, f2, and incrim. This function also initializes the latter variable. Line 13 assigns the value of f(x + incrim) to the local variable f1. Line 14 assigns the value of f(x - incrim) to the local variable f2. Line 15 returns the value for function slope using the local variables f1, f2, and incrim. The function main simply displays the values of the mathematical function and its slope when x = 3.5.

Static Variables in Functions

In Listing 5.1, the local variables in the function `slope` lose their values once the function terminates. C++ enables you to declare a local variable as static simply by placing the `static` keyword to the left of its data type. Static variables usually are initialized. This initialization is performed once, when the host function is called for the first time.

 NEW There are a number of programming techniques that require maintaining the values of
TERM local variables between function calls. These special local variables are called *static variables*. They're sort of like global variables, in that they are always around, but they can only be accessed from within the function in which they're declared—they are local to that function.

When the host function terminates, the static variables maintain their values. The compiler supports this language feature by storing static variables in a separate memory location that is maintained while the program is running. You can use the same names for static variables in different functions. This duplication does not confuse the compiler because it keeps track of which function owns which static variables.

Look at a simple program. Listing 5.2 uses a function with static variables to maintain a moving average. The program supplies its own data and calls that function several times in order to obtain and display the current value of the moving average.

Type **Listing 5.2. Source code for the program STATIC1.CPP.**

```
1:  // C++ program that illustrates static local variables
2:
3:  #include <iostream.h>
4:
5:  double mean(double x)
6:  {
7:    static double sum = 0;
8:    static double sumx = 0;
9:
10:   sum = sum + 1;
11:   sumx = sumx + x;
12:   return sumx / sum;
13: }
14:
15: main()
16: {
17:   cout << "mean = " << mean(1) << "\n";
18:   cout << "mean = " << mean(2) << "\n";
19:   cout << "mean = " << mean(4) << "\n";
20:   cout << "mean = " << mean(10) << "\n";
21:   cout << "mean = " << mean(11) << "\n";
22:   return 0;
23: }
```

Here is a sample session with the program in Listing 5.2.

```
mean = 1
mean = 1.5
mean = 2.33333
mean = 4.25
mean = 5.6
```

The program in Listing 5.2 declares the function `mean`, which contains static local variables. Lines 7 and 8 declare the static variables `sum` and `sumx`, respectively. The function initializes both static variables with 0. The statement in line 10 increments the variable `sum` by 1. The statement in line 11 increments the variable `sumx` by the value of parameter x. Line 12 returns the updated moving average, obtained by dividing `sumx` by `sum`.

The function `main` issues a series of calls to function `mean`. The stream output statements in lines 17 through 21 display the updated moving average. These results are possible thanks to the static local variables `sum` and `sumx` in function `mean`. If static variables were not supported by C++, you would need to resort to using global variables—a highly questionable programming choice.

The *#define* Statement Revisited

It now is time to come back to the `#define` statement. It was mentioned on Day 2 that the `#define` statement really was creating macros, and then I went over the simple macro substitution in which a single identifier was replaced with another. Actually, macros also can take parameters in much the same way as regular functions, but you first must take a little care.

Parameters in the *#define* Macro

Syntax

The parameterized syntax for the `#define` function is

```
#define macroName(arg1, arg2, ..., argN) substitution
```

The `substitution` expression can be anything, and doesn't even need to make use of the parameters given to the macro name (it's common to turn off a macro simply by defining it as blank, with no `substitution` expression). It also is important to note that there are no types involved here; the parameters are just names that are to be used in the `substitution` expression. Furthermore, be very careful to not put a semicolon on the end of the `substitution` expression. The following is an example of how to use a macro to figure out the smallest (`min`) and greatest (`max`) of two variables:

```
#define min(n1, n2) (((n1) < (n2)) ? (n1) : (n2))
#define max(n1, n2) (((n1) > (n2)) ? (n1) : (n2))
```

Note all the parentheses used in that last example. In order to help explain that, I'm going to digress slightly from the topic and discuss how arguments are passed to functions.

When a parameter is sent to a function, a brand new variable is declared (the one inside the function definition's parentheses) and the passed argument is copied into this new declaration. When you use the variable inside the function, you really are using the copy of the original value. This actually explains why actions taken on the parameter inside the function don't affect the originally passed value: you're not even using it. References are a slightly different case, and I'll explain why when I describe passing pointers to functions later on today.

Getting back to the macro's parameters, you might begin to understand a little more about just how different they are from functions. Their arguments really are just substitutions; no new declarations are made and no variables are copied. To expand on the previous example, regard the following which shows a before and after picture, comparing the original source code to what the preprocessor produces for the compiler to use:

```
#define min(n1, n2) (((n1) < (n2)) ? (n1) : (n2))
double num1 = 50, num2 = 5, rslt;
rslt = min(num1 / 2, num2 * 2);
```

Now take a look at that last line when the preprocessor is done with it.

```
rslt = (((50 / 2) < (5 * 2)) ? (50 / 2) : (5 * 2));
```

First note that if there had been a semicolon at the end of the first line, there would have been two at the end of the final result, because the last line of the original source line that calls min has a semicolon at its end.

Finally, to explain about all the parentheses, look at what that expression would have looked like without all the parentheses in the original macro definition.

```
rslt = 50 / 2 < 5 * 2 ? 50 / 2 : 5 * 2;
```

What operator is doing what to what else? By placing the parentheses, you ensure that if an expression is used as an argument (rather than just a simple variable or constant), it won't confuse the compiler when the preprocessor is done with the substitutions.

Inline Functions

Using functions requires the overhead of calling them, passing their arguments, and returning their results. While macros get around this problem, they have the added problem of being only macros, and they lose all the advantages of local variables, and so on, that are available in full-fledged functions. C++ enables you to use *inline functions* that expand into their statements. Thus, inline functions offer faster execution time—especially helpful where speed is critical—at the cost of expanding the code.

Syntax

The *inline* Function

The general syntax for the inline function is

```
inline returnType functionName(typedParameterList)
```

Examples

```
inline double cube(double x)
{ return x * x * x; }

inline char nextChar(char c)
{ return c + 1; }
```

The alternative to using inline functions is the use of the #define directive to create macro-based pseudo-functions. Many C++ programmers strongly recommend foregoing this method in favor of inline functions. The justification for this is that inline functions provide type checking. Macros created with the #define directive do not. However, this lack of type checking is exactly what makes macros so appealing: one can write a single macro that will act on many different types of data by expanding the same code in place for each instance.

Also, because the parameters to an inline function are used as if they were sent into a real function, rather than expanded in a macro, there is less risk of side effects. Regard the min macro, again, and a dangerous use of it.

```
#define min(n1, n2) (((n1) < (n2)) ? (n1) : (n2))
int num1 = 5, num2 = 10;
rslt = min(++num1, num2);
```

The last line expands to the following:

```
rslt = (((++num1) < (num2)) ? (++num1) : (num2);
```

Note that both rslt and num1 will end up with the value of 7. This is because num1 is incremented twice: once in the comparison and once in the result portion of the ?: operator. An inline function would only increment num1 once before executing the contents of the function.

There is a middle ground that allows for macro-like expansion of full-fledged functions. These are called templates and are explained on Day 10.

DO	DON'T
DO start by declaring inline functions as ordinary functions when you develop your programs. Non-inline functions are easier to debug. Once your program is working, insert the inline keyword where needed. **DON'T** use inline functions on anything really large. Again, it's important to stress that inline functions are expanded as if they were typed directly at the location from where they are called. There also are some restrictions on what the compiler will let	

you do within an inline function; but, if you put the inline keyword on something the compiler doesn't like, it will just give you a warning and ignore the inline keyword. Your program still will compile and run just fine.

DON'T declare inline functions with many statements. The increase in .EXE program size may not be acceptable.

Here is a simple example of a program that uses inline functions. Listing 5.3 contains the source code for the program INLINE1.CPP. This program prompts you for a number, and then calculates and displays the square and cube values for your input.

 Listing 5.3. Source code for the program INLINE1.CPP.

```
1:  // C++ program that illustrates inline functions
2:
3:  #include <iostream.h>
4:
5:  inline double sqr(double x)
6:  {
7:     return x * x;
8:  }
9:
10: inline double cube(double x)
11: {
12:    return x * x * x;
13: }
14:
15: main()
16: {
17:    double x;
18:
19:    cout << "Enter a number: ";
20:    cin >> x;
21:
22:    cout << "square of "  << x << " = " << sqr(x) << "\n"
23:         << "cube of " << x << " = " << cube(x) << "\n";
24:
25:    return 0;
26: }
```

5

 Here is a sample session with the program in Listing 5.3.

```
Enter a number: 2.5
square of 2.5 = 6.25
cube of 2.5 = 15.625
```

 The program in Listing 5.3 declares the inline functions sqr and cube on lines 5 and 10, respectively. Each function heading starts with the keyword inline. The other aspects of the inline functions resemble short normal functions. The function main calls the functions sqr and cube on lines 22 and 23 to display the square and cube values, respectively.

Exiting Functions Prematurely

Usually you make an early exit from a function because particular conditions do not allow you to proceed with executing the statements in that function. C++ provides the return statement to exit from a function. If the function has the void type, you then employ the statement return and include no expression after the return. By contrast, if you exit a non-void function, the return statement should produce a value that indicates the purpose for exiting the function.

Default Arguments

Default arguments are a language feature that is quite simple and yet very powerful. When you omit the argument of a parameter that has a default argument, that argument is used automatically.

> **Note:** C++ permits you to assign default arguments to the parameters of a function.

Using default arguments requires that you follow these rules:

- ☐ Once you assign a default argument to a parameter, you must do so for all subsequent parameters in the same parameter list. You cannot randomly assign default arguments to parameters. This rule means that the parameter list can be divided into two sublists: the leading parameters, which do not have default arguments, and the trailing parameters, which do.

- ☐ The caller of the function must provide an argument for every parameter that has no default argument.

- ☐ The caller may omit the argument for a parameter that has a default argument.

- ☐ Once you omit the argument for a parameter with a default argument, the arguments for all subsequent parameters also must be omitted.

> **Note:** The best way to list the parameters with default arguments is to locate them according to the likelihood of using their default arguments. Place the least-likely-to-be-used arguments first and the most-likely-to-be-used arguments last.

Look at a simple example that uses a function with default arguments. Listing 5.4 shows the source code for the program DEFARGS1.CPP. The program prompts you to enter the x and y coordinates of two points. The program then calculates and displays the distance between the two points and between each point and the origin (0, 0).

Listing 5.4. Source code for the program DEFARGS1.CPP.

```
1:  // C++ program that illustrates default arguments
2:
3:  #include <iostream.h>
4:  #include <math.h>
5:
6:  inline double sqr(double x)
7:  { return x * x; }
8:
9:  double distance(double x2, double y2,
10:                   double x1 = 0, double y1 = 0)
11: {
12:    return sqrt(sqr(x2 — x1) + sqr(y2 — y1));
13: }
14:
15: main()
16: {
17:    double x1, y1, x2, y2;
18:
19:    cout << "Enter x coordinate for point 1: ";
20:    cin >> x1;
21:    cout << "Enter y coordinate for point 1: ";
22:    cin >> y1;
23:    cout << "Enter x coordinate for point 2: ";
24:    cin >> x2;
25:    cout << "Enter y coordinate for point 2: ";
26:    cin >> y2;
27:
28:    cout << "distance between points = "
29:         << distance(x1, y1, x2, y2) << "\n";
30:    cout << "distance between point 1 and (0,0) = "
31:         << distance(x1, y1, 0) << "\n";
32:    cout << "distance between point 2 and (0,0) = "
33:         << distance(x2, y2) << "\n";
34:
35:    return 0;
36: }
```

5

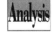

Here is a sample session with the program in Listing 5.4.

```
Enter x coordinate for point 1: 1
Enter y coordinate for point 1: 1
Enter x coordinate for point 2: --1
Enter y coordinate for point 2: 1
distance between points = 2
distance between point 1 and (0,0) = 1.41421
distance between point 2 and (0,0) = 1.41421
```

The program in Listing 5.4 includes not one but two header files. Line 4 uses the #include directive to include the MATH.H header file, which declares the square-root math function, sqrt. The program declares the inline sqr function in line 6. This function returns the square value of the arguments for parameter x. The program also declares the function distance with four double-typed parameters. The parameters x2 and y2 represent the

161

x and y coordinates, respectively, for the second point, whereas the parameters x1 and y1 represent the x and y coordinates, respectively, for the first point. Both parameters x1 and y1 have the default argument of 0. The function returns the distance between the two points. If you omit the arguments for x1 and y1, the function returns the distance between the point (x2, y2) and the origin (0, 0). If you omit only the argument for the last parameter, the function yields the distance between the points (x2, y2) and (x1, 0).

The function main prompts you to enter the x and y coordinates for two points, using the statements in lines 19 through 26. The output statement in lines 28 and 29 calls the function distance, providing it with 4 arguments, namely, x1, y1, x2, and y2. Therefore, this call to the function distance uses no default arguments. By contrast, the statement in lines 30 and 31 calls the function distance, supplying it with only three arguments. This call to the function distance uses the default argument for the last parameter. The statement in lines 32 and 33 calls the function distance, providing it with only two arguments. This call to the function distance uses the two default arguments for the third and fourth parameters. You can omit the third argument in the second call to the function distance and still compile and run the program.

Passing Arguments by Reference

It's time to talk a little more about how arguments are passed by reference. You already have learned about pointers in general and how they hold the addresses of other variables. References are very similar, except that all the pointer stuff is hidden from you. When you make a reference to another variable, somewhere deep in the compiler is a pointer that is pointing at the original variable, and the reference just hides that fact by allowing you to use the reference as if it were a regular variable, only it continues to modify the original.

Remember that, when it comes to passing arguments to a function, the contents of the original variable is copied into the function's newly declared version of the variable, and it then can be used throughout the life of the function. If you want to modify the original version, you can pass it by reference. At this point, you really are only copying a pointer to the original variable rather than the entire contents of the original. While inside the function, you can use the variable as normal— it's just that you're really modifying the original.

Now, when you're copying the contents of something such as an int or a pointer, which are only going to be a few bytes, there's no problem with copying their contents. When it comes to passing something such as a structure, however, you could start copying a tremendous amount of data. Some structures can be in the kilobyte range or larger. If you were to copy its contents every time you passed it to a function, it is conceivably possible that you could slow down your system enough that you would even notice it in realtime.

The solution, of course, is to pass the structure by reference. Now, rather than copying the entire contents of the structure, you are only copying a few bytes to create the reference to the original structure, which is much more manageable.

The problem, of course, is that the function now is capable of modifying the original structure, and that's not always a good thing.

Using *const* in Arguments

The const type modifier comes to the rescue here. So far, we've only really discussed it with respect to creating constant variables. It's best to use it as a modifier of such types as pointers and references. By specifying a function's argument as a const reference, not only are you preventing the copying of a potentially huge structure, you also are preventing the function from modifying the contents of that structure. The function can look at the structure and use anything inside of it; it's just not allowed to modify any part of it.

The *const* argument modifier

The general syntax for using the const modifier in function parameters is

```
returnType functionName(const argType &arg)
```

Example

```
struct userInfo {
   int age;
   char name[150];    // Should be big enough for most names
}

void processUserInfo(const userInfo& ui)
{
   if (ui.age < 18) {
      cout << "You're too young to be using this function." << endl;
      return;
   }
   if (ui.age < 21)
      ui.age = 21;        // -=*> !!!ERROR!!! <*=-
}
```

Note the line with the comment about the error. Whereas the compiler will have absolutely no problems with processUserInfo checking to make sure the passed user is old enough, the compiler will stop with an error when it encounters this rogue function trying to arbitrarily change the person's age. So much for getting a fake ID.

Now, after all this argument for passing structures by reference rather than by value, let me just say that there's nothing wrong with passing a smaller structure by value. If there are only a few members in it and it doesn't take up much memory on its own, then there's no reason why you shouldn't just pass it right on in. It can be good, however, to get into the habit of just passing structures by reference all the time.

Recursive Functions

There are many problems that can be solved by breaking them down into simpler and similar problems. Such problems are solved using recursion.

NEW☞
TERM *Recursive functions* are functions that obtain a result and/or perform a task by calling themselves. These recursive calls must be limited in order to avoid exhausting the memory resources of the computer. Consequently, every recursive function must examine a condition that determines the end of the recursion.

NEW☞
TERM A common example of a recursive function is the *factorial function*. A factorial of a number is the product of all the integers from 1 to N, with the exclamation point (!) as the mathematical symbol for the factorial function.

The mathematical equation for a factorial is

N! = 1 * 2 * 3 * ... * (N-2) * (N-1) * N

The recursive version of this equation is

N! =N * (N-1)!
(N-1)! = (N-1) * (N-2)!
(N-2)! = (N-2) * (N-3)!
...
2! = 2 * 1!
1! = 1

Recursion entails looping to obtain a result. Most recursive solutions have alternate non-recursive solutions. In some cases, the recursive solutions are more elegant than the non-recursive ones. The factorial function is an example of a mathematical function that can be implemented using either recursion or a non-recursive straightforward loop.

DO	DON'T
DO include a decision-making statement in a recursive function to end the recursion. **DON'T** use recursion unless its advantages significantly outweigh the alternate non-recursive solution.	

Look at an example that implements the recursive factorial function. Listing 5.5 shows the source code for the program ADVFUN6.CPP. The program prompts you to enter two positive integers; the first one must be greater than or equal to the second one. The program displays the number of combinations and permutations obtained from the two integers. The number of combinations is given by the following equation:

$$_mC_n = m! / ((m - n)! * n!)$$

The number of permutations is given by the following equation:

$$_mP_n = m! / (m - n)!$$

Listing 5.5. Source code for the program ADVFUN6.CPP.

```cpp
1:  // C++ program that uses a recursive function
2:
3:  #include <iostream.h>
4:
5:  const int MIN = 4;
6:  const int MAX = 30;
7:
8:  double factorial(int i)
9:  {
10:   if (i > 1)
11:     return double(i) * factorial(i - 1);
12:   else
13:     return 1;
14: }
15:
16: double permutation(int m, int n)
17: {
18:   return factorial(m) / factorial(m - n);
19: }
20:
21: double combination(int m, int n)
22: {
23:   return permutation(m, n) / factorial(n);
24: }
25:
26: main()
27: {
28:   int m, n;
29:
30:   do {
31:     cout << "Enter an integer between "
32:          << MIN << " and " << MAX << " : ";
33:     cin >> m;
34:   } while (m < MIN || m > MAX);
35:
36:   do {
37:     cout << "Enter an integer between "
38:          << MIN << " and " << m << ": ";
39:     cin >> n;
40:   } while (n < MIN ||[]> m);
41:
42:   cout << "Permutations(" << m << ", " << n
43:        << ") = " << permutation(m, n) << "\n";
44:   cout << "Combinations(" << m << ", " << n
45:        << ") = " << combination(m, n) << "\n";
46:
47:   return 0;
48: }
```

Here is a sample session with the program in Listing 5.5.

```
Enter an integer between 4 and 30 : 10
Enter an integer between 4 and 10 : 5
Permutations(10, 5) = 30240
Combinations(10, 5) = 252
```

The program in Listing 5.5 declares the recursive function `factorial` and the functions `permutation`, `combination`, and `main`. The program also declares the global constants `MIN` and `MAX`, which specify the limits of the first integer you enter.

The function `factorial` has a single parameter—the `int`-typed parameter `i`. The function returns a `double`-typed value. The `if` statement in line 10 compares the value of parameter `i` with 1. This comparison determines whether to make a recursive call, in line 11, or to return the value 1, in line 13. The recursive call in line 11 invokes the function `factorial` with the argument `i - 1`. Thus, the recursive call supplies the function with a smaller (or simpler) argument.

The function `permutation` takes two `int`-typed parameters: `m` and `n`. The function calls the recursive function `factorial` twice—once with the argument `m` and once with the argument `m - n`. The function `permutation` returns the ratio of the two calls to the function `factorial`.

The function `combination` also takes two `int`-typed parameters: `m` and `n`. The function calls the function `permutation` and passes it the arguments `m` and `n`. The function also calls the function `factorial` and passes it the argument `n`. The function `combination` returns the ratio of the values returned by the functions `permutation` and `factorial`.

The function `main` declares the `int`-typed variable `m` and `n`. The function uses two `do-while` loops to prompt you for integer values. The output statement in the first loop prompts you to enter an integer between `MIN` and `MAX`. The statement in line 33 stores your input in variable `m`. The `while` clause of the `do-while` loop validates your input. The clause determines whether your input is less than `MIN` or greater than `MAX`. If this condition is true, then the loop iterates again.

The output statement in the second `do-while` loop prompts you to enter an integer between `m` and `MAX`. The statement in line 39 saves your input in variable `n`. The `while` clause validates your input. The clause determines if your input is less than `MIN` or greater than `m`. If this condition is true, then the loop iterates again.

The output statement in lines 42 and 43 displays the permutations of the values in variables `m` and `n`. The statement calls the function `permutation` and passes it the argument `m` and `n`. The output statement in lines 44 and 45 displays the combinations of the values in variables `m` and `n`. The statement calls function `combination` and passes it the argument `m` and `n`.

Function Overloading

Function overloading is a language feature in C++ that has no parallel in C, Pascal, or BASIC. This new feature enables you to declare multiple functions that have the same name but different parameter lists. The function's return type is not part of the function signature, because C++ enables you to discard the result type. Consequently, the compiler cannot distinguish between two functions with the same parameters and different return type when these return types are omitted.

NEW A parameter list also is called the *function signature*.
TERM

> **Warning:** Using default arguments with overloaded functions may duplicate the signature for some of the functions (when the default arguments are used). The C++ compiler can detect this ambiguity and generate a compile-time error.

DO	DON'T

DO use default arguments to reduce the number of overloaded functions.
DON'T use overloaded functions to implement different operations.

The real power of overloaded functions is in the capability to define several versions of the same routine that is capable of acting with different types of data. Look at a simple program that uses overloaded functions. Listing 5.6 contains the source code for the program OVERLOAD.CPP. The program performs the following tasks:

☐ Declares variables that have the char, int, and double types, and initializes them with values

☐ Displays the initial values

☐ Invokes overloaded functions that increment the variables

☐ Displays the updated values stored in the variables

Listing 5.6. Source code for the program OVERLOAD.CPP.

```
1:  // C++ program that illustrates function overloading
2:
3:  #include <iostream.h>
4:
5:  // inc version for int types
6:  void inc(int& i)
7:  {
8:    i = i + 1;
9:  }
```

continues

Listing 5.6. continued

```
10:
11: // inc version for double types
12: void inc(double& x)
13: {
14:   x = x + 1;
15: }
16:
17: // inc version for char types
18: void inc(char& c)
19: {
20:   c = c + 1;
21: }
22:
23: main()
24: {
25:   char c = 'A';
26:   int i = 10;
27:   double x = 10.2;
28:
29:   // display initial values
30:   cout << "c = " << c << "\n"
31:        << "i = " << i << "\n"
32:        << "x = " << x << "\n";
33:   // invoke the inc functions
34:   inc(c);
35:   inc(i);
36:   inc(x);
37:   // display updated values
38:   cout << "After using the overloaded inc function\n";
39:   cout << "c = " << c << "\n"
40:        << "i = " << i << "\n"
41:        << "x = " << x << "\n";
42:
43:   return 0;
44: }
```

Here is a sample session with the program in Listing 5.6.

```
c = A
i = 10
x = 10.2
After using the overloaded inc function
c = B
i = 11
x = 11.2
```

The program in Listing 5.6 declares three versions of the overloaded void function inc. The first version of function inc has an int-typed reference parameter, i. The function increments the parameter i by 1. Because the parameter i is a reference to its arguments, the action of function inc(int&) affects the argument outside the scope of the function. The second version of function inc has a double-typed reference parameter, x. The function increments the parameter x by 1. Because the parameter x is a reference to its arguments, the action of function inc(double&) affects the argument beyond the scope of the function. The second version of function inc has a char-typed reference parameter, c. The function increments the parameter c by 1. The reference parameter affects its arguments outside the scope of the function.

The function main declares the variables c, i, and x to have the char, int, and double types, respectively. The function also initializes the variables c, i, and x using the values 'A', 10, and 10.2, respectively. The statement in lines 30 through 32 displays the initial values in variables c, i, and x. The function main invokes the overloaded function inc in lines 34 through 36. The call to function inc in line 34 ends up calling the function inc(char&) because the argument used is a char-typed variable. The call to function inc in line 35 results in calling the function inc(int&) because the argument used is an int-typed variable. The call to function inc in line 36 invokes the function inc(double&) because the argument used is a double-typed variable. The output statement in lines 39 through 41 displays the updated values in variable c, i, and x.

Summary

Today's lesson presented the various C++ operators and discussed how to use these operators to manipulate data. You learned the following:

☐ The general form for defining functions is

```
returnType functionName(parameterList)
{
    <declarations of data items>

    <function body>
    return returnValue;
}
```

You need to prototype a function if it is used by a client function before the prototyped function is defined. The general form for prototyping functions is

```
returnType functionName(parameterList);
```

You can omit the name of the parameters from the parameter list.

☐ Local variables in a function support the implementation of highly independent functions. Declaring local variables is similar to declaring global variables.

☐ Static variables in functions are declared by placing the keyword static before the data type of the variables. Static variables retain their values between function calls. In most cases, you need to initialize static variables. These initial values are assigned to the static variables the first time the program calls the host function.

☐ Macros enable you to create simple expressions that are capable of working on many different types of data because of their independence from the actual type-checking parts of the C++ compiler.

☐ Inline functions enable you to expand their statements in place, similar to macro-based pseudo-functions. Unlike these pseudo-functions, however, inline functions perform type checking.

☐ You exit functions with the `return` statement. `void` functions do not need to include an expression after the `return` keyword.

☐ Default arguments enable you to assign default values to the parameters of a function. When you omit the argument of a parameter that has a default argument, that argument is used automatically.

☐ Passing arguments with references can allow the function to modify the original variables, and it also can allow for smaller amounts of memory to be copied when a structure is passed as an argument.

☐ The `const` type modifier can be extremely useful in preventing arguments that have been passed by reference from being accidentally modified by a function.

☐ Recursive functions are functions that obtain a result and/or perform a task by calling themselves. These recursive calls must be limited to avoid exhausting the memory resources of the computer. Consequently, every recursive function must examine a condition that determines the end of the recursion.

☐ Function overloading enables you to declare multiple functions that have the same name but different parameter lists (the parameter list also is called the function signature). The function's return type is not part of the function signature, because C++ enables you to discard the result type.

Q&A

Q Can C++ functions declare nested functions?

A No. Nested functions actually add a lot of overhead at runtime.

Q When can I use static global variables?

A You can use them whenever you want. When the `static` keyword is applied to a global variable (although I still recommend that you never have any global variables in the first place), it tells the compiler to not make it visible to any other source file. This prevents the same variable from being accessed from different nodes of the same project.

Q What is the memory resource used in managing calls to recursive functions?

A The runtime system uses the stack to store intermediate values, including the ones generated by calls to recursive functions. As with other memory resources, stacks have a limited space. Consequently, recursive calls with long sequence or memory-consuming arguments drain the stack space and cause runtime errors.

NEW☛ A *stack* is a memory location where information is inserted and removed on a last-in-first-
TERM out (LIFO) priority.

Workshop

The Workshop provides quiz questions to help you solidify your understanding of the material covered and exercises to provide you with experience in using what you've learned. Try to understand the quiz and exercise answers before continuing on to the next day's lesson. Answers are provided in Appendix A.

Quiz

1. What is the output of the following program? What can you say about the function swap?

```
#include <iostream.h>

void swap(int i, int j)
{
  int temp = i;
  i = j;
  j = temp;
}

int main()
{
  int a = 10, b = 3;
  swap(a, b);
  cout << "a = " << a << " and b = " << b;
  return 0;
}
```

2. What is the output of the following program? What can you say about the function swap?

```
#include <iostream.h>

void swap(int& i, int& j)
{
  int temp = i;
  i = j;
  j = temp;
}

int main()
{
```

```
      int a = 10, b = 3;
      swap(a, b);
      cout << "a = " << a << " and b = " << b;
      return 0;
   }
```

3. What is the problem with the following overloaded functions?

```
   void inc(int& i)
   {
     i = i + 1;
   }

   void inc(int& i, int diff = 1)
   {
     i = i + diff;
   }
```

4. Where is the error in the following function?

```
   double volume(double length, double width = 1, double
   height)
   {
     return length * width * height
   }
```

5. Where is the error in the following function?

```
   void inc(int& i, int diff = 1)
   {
     i = I + diff;
   }
```

6. What is the error in the following program, and how can you correct it?

```
   #include <iostream.h>

   int main()
   {
     double x = 5.2;

     cout << x << "^2 = " << sqr(x);
     return 0;
   }

   double sqr(double x)
   { return x * x ; }
```

7. Can you use the conditional operator to write the recursive factorial function?

Exercise

Create the program OVERLOD2.CPP by adding a second parameter with default arguments to the overloaded inc functions in the program OVERLOAD.CPP. The new parameter should represent the increment value, with a default argument of 1.

6

Arrays

Arrays are among the most utilized data structures. They enable programs to store data for later processing. Most popular programming languages support static arrays. Many languages also support dynamic arrays.

Today, you will learn about the following topics related to static arrays:

- ☐ Using single-dimensional arrays
- ☐ Initializing single-dimensional arrays
- ☐ Declaring single-dimensional arrays as function parameters
- ☐ Sorting arrays
- ☐ Searching arrays
- ☐ Declaring multidimensional arrays
- ☐ Using multidimensional arrays
- ☐ Initializing multidimensional arrays
- ☐ Declaring multidimensional arrays as function parameters

Using Single-Dimensional Arrays

On Day 4, I provided a very simple example of using a single-dimensional array. Today let's look at a slightly more involved example. Listing 6.1 shows the source code for the program ARRAY1.CPP. The program uses a 30-element numeric array to calculate the average for the data in a numeric array. The program performs the following tasks:

- ☐ Prompts you to enter the number of actual data points. (This value must lie in the range of valid numbers indicated by the prompting message.)
- ☐ Prompts you to enter the data for the array elements
- ☐ Calculates the average of the data in the array
- ☐ Displays the average value

Listing 6.1. Source code for the program ARRAY1.CPP.

```
1:  /*
2:    C++ program that demonstrates the use of one-dimensional
3:    arrays.  The average value of the array is calculated.
4:  */
5:
6:  #include <iostream.h>
7:
8:  const int MAX = 30;
9:
10: main()
11: {
12:
```

```
13:      double x[MAX];
14:      double sum, sumx = 0.0, mean;
15:      int i, n;
16:
17:      do { // obtain number of data points
18:          cout << "Enter number of data points [2 to "
19:                  << MAX << "] : ";
20:          cin >> n;
21:          cout << "\n";
22:      } while (n < 2 || n > MAX);
23:
24:      // prompt user for data
25:      for (i = 0; i < n; i++) {
26:          cout << "X[" << i << "] : ";
27:          cin >> x[i];
28:      }
29:
30:      // initialize summations
31:      sum = n;
32:
33:      // calculate sum of observations
34:      for (i = 0; i < n; i++)
35:          sumx += x[i];
36:
37:      mean = sumx / sum; // calculate the mean value
38:      cout << "\nMean = " << mean << "\n\n";
39:      return 0;
40: }
```

Output

Here is a sample session with the program in Listing 6.1.

```
Enter number of data points [2 to 30] : 5

X[0] : 12.5
X[1] : 45.7
X[2] : 25.6
X[3] : 14.1
X[4] : 68.4

Mean = 33.26
```

6

Analysis

The program in Listing 6.1 declares the global constant MAX as the size of the array used in the program. The function main declares the double-typed array x, in line 13, to have MAX elements. The function also declares other nonarray variables in lines 14 and 15.

The do-while loop, located in lines 17 through 22, obtains the number of data points that you want to store in the array x. The output statement in lines 18 and 19 prompts you to enter the number of data points. The output indicates the range of valid numbers, which is 2 to MAX. The statement in line 20 obtains your input and stores it in the variable n. The while clause validates your input. The clause determines if the value in variable n is less than 2 or is greater than MAX. If this condition is true, the do-while loop iterates again to obtain a correct input value.

The for loop statement, in lines 25 through 28, prompts you to enter the data. The loop uses the control variable i and iterates from 0 to n-1, in increments of 1. The output statement in line 26 prompts you to enter the value for the indicated array element. The input statement in line 27 obtains your input and stores it in the element x[i].

The statement in line 31 assigns the integer in variable n to the double-typed variable sum. The for loop in lines 34 and 35 adds the values in array x to the variable sumx. The loop uses the control variable i and iterates from 0 to n-1, in increments of 1. The statement in line 35 uses the increment assignment operator to add the value in element x[i] to the variable sumx.

The statement in line 37 calculates the mean value and stores it in variable mean. The output statement in line 38 displays the mean value.

Note: The program in Listing 6.1 shows how to use a for loop to process the elements of an array. The loop-continuation test uses the < operator and the value beyond the last valid index. You can use the <= operator followed by the last index. For example, we can write the data-input loop as

```
24:     // prompt user for data
25:     for (i = 0; i <= (n - 1); i++) {
26:         cout << "X[" << i << "] : ";
27:         cin >> x[i];
28:     }
```

This form is not popular, however, because it requires an additional operator, whereas the condition i < n does not.

DO	DON'T

DO write the loop-continuation expression so that it uses the minimum number of operators. This approach reduces the code size and speeds up loop execution.

DON'T use the <= operator in the loop-continuation condition, unless using the operator helps you write an expression that minimizes the number of operations.

Initializing Single-Dimensional Arrays

C++ enables you to initialize arrays and is flexible about the initialization. You need to enclose the list of initializing values in a pair of open and close braces ({ }). The list is comma-delimited and may continue on multiple lines. If there are fewer items in the initializing list than there are array elements, the compiler assigns 0 to balance the array elements. By contrast, if the list of initializing values has more items than the number of array elements, the compiler flags a compile-time error.

The next program, Listing 6.2, modifies the last program to supply data internally. Consequently, we eliminate the steps that prompt you for the number of data points and the data itself. The program simply displays the array elements (obtained from the initialization list) and the average value for the data. Although this program does not interact with the user, it offers a version that stores data in the source code. You can edit the program periodically to add, edit, and delete data before recalculating a new average value.

Listing 6.2. Source code for the program ARRAY2.CPP.

```
1:  /*
2:     C++ program that demonstrates the use of single-dimensional
3:     arrays.  The average value of the array is calculated.
4:     The array has its values preassigned internally.
5:  */
6:
7:  #include <iostream.h>
8:
9:  const int MAX = 10;
10:
11: main()
12: {
13:
14:     double x[MAX] = { 12.2, 45.4, 67.2, 12.2, 34.6, 87.4,
15:                       83.6, 12.3, 14.8, 55.5 };
16:     double sum = MAX, sumx = 0.0, mean;
17:     int n = MAX;
18:
19:     // calculate sum of observations
20:     cout << "Array is:\n";
21:     for (int i = 0; i < n; i++) {
22:         sumx += x[i];
23:         cout << "x[" << i << "] = " << x[i] << "\n";
24:     }
25:
26:     mean = sumx / sum; // calculate the mean value
27:     cout << "\nMean = " << mean << "\n\n";
28:     return 0;
29: }
```

Here is a sample session with the program in Listing 6.2.

```
Array is:
x[0] = 12.2
x[1] = 45.4
x[2] = 67.2
x[3] = 12.2
x[4] = 34.6
x[5] = 87.4
x[6] = 83.6
x[7] = 12.3
```

```
x[8] = 14.8
x[9] = 55.5

Mean = 42.52
```

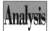

Now we will focus on the initialization of the array x in Listing 6.2. Line 14 contains the declaration of array x and its initialization. The initializing list, which runs to line 15, is enclosed in a pair of braces and has comma-delimited values. The statement in line 16 declares the variables sum and sumx and initializes these variables to MAX and 0, respectively. The statement in line 17 declares the int-typed variable n and initializes it with the value MAX. The rest of the program resembles parts of the program in Listing 6.1.

If you are somewhat dismayed by the fact that you have to count the exact number of initializing values, then we have some good news for you: C++ enables you to size an array automatically by using the number of items in the corresponding initializing list. Consequently, you don't need to place a number in the square brackets of the array, and you can let the compiler do the work for you.

DO	DON'T

DO include dummy values in the initializing list, if the initialized array needs to expand later.

DON'T rely on counting the number of items in the initializing list to provide the data for the number of array elements.

Listing 6.3 shows the source code for the program ARRAY3.CPP. This new version uses the feature of automatic array sizing.

Listing 6.3. Source code for the program ARRAY3.CPP.

```
1:  /*
2:    C++ program that demonstrates the use of single-dimensional
3:    arrays.  The average value of the array is calculated.
4:    The array has its values preassigned internally.
5:  */
6:
7:  #include <iostream.h>
8:
9:  main()
10: {
11:
12:     double x[] = { 12.2, 45.4, 67.2, 12.2, 34.6, 87.4,
13:                     83.6, 12.3, 14.8, 55.5 };
14:     double sum,  sumx = 0.0, mean;
15:     int n;
16:
```

```
17:     n = sizeof(x) / sizeof(x[0]);
18:     sum = n;
19:
20:     // calculate sum of observations
21:     cout << "Array is:\n";
22:     for (int i = 0; i < n; i++) {
23:         sumx += x[i];
24:         cout << "x[" << i << "] = " << x[i] << "\n";
25:     }
26:
27:     mean = sumx / sum; // calculate the mean value
28:     cout << "\nNumber of data points = " << n << "\n"
29:          << "Mean = " << mean << "\n";
30:     return 0;
31: }
```

Here is a sample session with the program in Listing 6.3.

```
Array is:
x[0] = 12.2
x[1] = 45.4
x[2] = 67.2
x[3] = 12.2
x[4] = 34.6
x[5] = 87.4
x[6] = 83.6
x[7] = 12.3
x[8] = 14.8
x[9] = 55.5

Number of data points = 10
Mean = 42.52
```

Notice that the program in Listing 6.3 does not declare the constant MAX, which appears in the previous version (shown in Listing 6.2). How does the program determine the number of array elements? Line 17 shows that the program calculates the number of elements in array x by dividing the size of the array x (obtained by using sizeof(x)) by the size of the first element (obtained by using sizeof(x[0])). You can use this method to obtain the size of any array of any data type.

Array Parameters in Functions

C++ enables you to declare function parameters that are arrays. In fact, C++ permits you to be either specific or general about the size of the array parameter. You can specify the size of the array in the parameter declaration or you can use empty brackets with the array parameter.

A Fixed-Array Parameter

The general syntax for declaring a fixed-array parameter is

```
type parameterName[arraySize]
```

Examples

```
int minArray(int arr[100], int n);
void sort(unsigned dayNum[7]);
```

An Open-Array Parameter

The general syntax for declaring an open-array parameter is

```
type parameterName[]
```

Examples

```
int minArray(int arr[], int n);
void sort(unsigned dayNum[]);
```

DO	DON'T

DO use open-array parameters in functions.

DON'T forget to check the upper bounds of an open-array parameter in general-purpose functions.

Look at a simple example. Listing 6.4 shows the source code for the program ARRAY4.CPP. The program performs the following tasks:

☐ Prompts you to enter the number of data points, which ranges from 2 to 10

☐ Prompts you to enter the integer values for the arrays

☐ Displays the smallest value in the array

☐ Displays the largest value in the array

Listing 6.4. Source code for the program ARRAY4.CPP.

```
1:  // C++ program that passes arrays as arguments of functions
2:
3:  #include <iostream.h>
4:
5:  const int MAX = 10;
6:
7:  main()
8:  {
9:    int arr[MAX];
10:   int n;
11:
12:   // declare prototypes of functions
```

```
13:    int getMin(int a[MAX], int size);
14:    int getMax(int a[], int size);
15:
16:    do { // obtain number of data points
17:      cout << "Enter number of data points [2 to "
18:          << MAX << "] : ";
19:      cin >> n;
20:      cout << "\n";
21:    } while (n < 2 || n > MAX);
22:
23:    // prompt user for data
24:    for (int i = 0; i < n; i++) {
25:      cout << "arr[" << i << "] : ";
26:      cin >> arr[i];
27:    }
28:
29:    cout << "Smallest value in array is "
30:        << getMin(arr, n) << "\n"
31:        << "Biggest value in array is "
32:        << getMax(arr, n) << "\n";
33:    return 0;
34: }
35:
36:
37: int getMin(int a[MAX], int size)
38: {
39:   int small = a[0];
40:   // search for the smallest value in the
41:   // remaining array elements
42:   for (int i = 1; i < size; i++)
43:     if (small > a[i])
44:       small = a[i];
45:   return small;
46: }
47:
48: int getMax(int a[], int size)
49: {
50:   int big = a[0];
51:   // search for the biggest value in the
52:   // remaining array elements
53:   for (int i = 1; i < size; i++)
54:     if (big < a[i])
55:       big = a[i];
56:   return big;
57: }
```

Here is a sample session with the program in Listing 6.4.

```
Enter number of data points [2 to 10] : 5

arr[0] : 55
arr[1] : 69
arr[2] : 47
arr[3] : 85
arr[4] : 14
Smallest value in array is 14
Biggest value in array is 85
```

The program in Listing 6.4 declares the global constant MAX, in line 5, to size up the array of data. The function main declares the int-typed array arr in line 9. Line 10 contains the declaration of the int-typed variable n. Lines 13 and 14 declare the prototypes for the functions getMin and getMax, which return the smallest and largest values in an int-typed array, respectively. The prototype of the function getMin indicates that it uses a fixed-array parameter. By contrast, the prototype of the function getMax indicates that it uses an open-array parameter. We use both types of array parameters for the sake of demonstration.

The do-while loop, located in lines 16 through 21, obtains the number of data points you want to store in the array arr. The output statement in lines 17 and 18 prompts you to enter the number of data points. The output indicates the range of valid numbers, which runs between 2 and MAX. The statement in line 19 obtains your input and stores it in variable n. The while clause validates your input. The clause determines if the value in variable n is less than 2 or is greater than MAX. If this condition is true, the do-while loop iterates again to obtain a correct input value.

The for loop statement in lines 24 through 27 prompts you to enter the data. The loop uses the control variable i and iterates from 0 to n-1, in increments of 1. The output statement in line 25 prompts you to enter the value for the indicated array element. The statement in line 26 obtains your input and stores it in the element arr[i].

The output statement in lines 29 through 32 displays the smallest and biggest integers in array arr. The statement invokes the functions getMin and getMax, supplying each one of them with the arguments arr and n.

The program defines the function getMin in lines 37 through 46. The function has 2 parameters: the int-typed, fixed-array parameter a, and the int-typed parameter size. The function declares the local variable small and initializes it with a[0], the first element of parameter a. The function searches for the smallest value in the parameter a using the for loop in line 42. This loop declares the control variable i, and iterates from 1 to size-1, in increments of 1. The loop contains an if statement that assigns the value in element a[i] to variable small, if the latter is greater than element a[i]. The function returns the value in variable small. The function getMin only accepts int-typed arrays that have MAX elements.

The program defines the function getMax in lines 48 through 57. This function, which is similar to the function getMin, has 2 parameters: the int-typed, open-array parameter a, and the int-typed parameter size. The function declares the local variable big and initializes it with a[0], the first element of parameter a. The function searches for the smallest value in the parameter a, using the for loop in line 53. This loop declares the control variable i, and iterates from 1 to size-1, in increments of 1. The loop contains an if statement that assigns the value in element a[i] to the variable big, if the latter is less than element a[i]. The function returns the value in the variable big. The function getMax accepts int-typed arrays of any size.

Sorting Arrays

Sorting and searching are the most common nonnumerical operations for arrays. Sorting an array typically arranges its elements in ascending order. The process uses parts of or all the value in each element to determine the precedence of the elements in the array. Searching for data in sorted arrays is much easier than in unordered arrays.

Computer scientists have spent much time and effort studying and creating methods for sorting arrays. A comprehensive discussion of these methods is beyond the scope of this book. We only mention that some favorite array-sorting methods include the QuickSort, Shell-Metzner sort, heap sort, and the new Comb sort. The QuickSort method is the fastest method, in general, but requires some operational overhead. The Shell-Metzner and Comb sort methods do not require similar overhead. The example in this section uses the new Comb sort method, which is more efficient than the Shell-Metzner method.

The Comb sort method uses the following steps, given an array, A, with N elements:

1. Initializes the Offset value, used in comparing elements, to N.
2. Sets the Offset value to either 8*Offset/11 or 1, whichever is larger.
3. Sets the InOrder flag to true.
4. Loops for values 0 to N-Offset, using the loop control variable i:
    □ Assigns I + Offset to J
    □ If A[I] is greater than A[J], swaps A[I] with A[J] and sets the InOrder flag to false
5. Resumes at step 2 if Offset is not 1 and InOrder is false.

Look at a program that sorts an array of integers. Listing 6.5 shows the source code for the program ARRAY5.CPP. The program performs the following tasks:

□ Prompts you to enter the number of data points
□ Prompts you to enter the integer values for the array
□ Displays the elements of the unordered array
□ Displays the elements of the sorted array

Listing 6.5. Source code for the program ARRAY5.CPP.

```
1:  // C++ program that sorts arrays using the Comb sort method
2:
3:  #include <iostream.h>
4:
5:  const int MAX = 10;
6:  const int TRUE = 1;
7:  const int FALSE = 0;
8:
```

continues   183

Listing 6.5. continued

```
 9:  int obtainNumData()
10:  {
11:    int m;
12:    do { // obtain number of data points
13:      cout << "Enter number of data points [2 to "
14:           << MAX << "] : ";
15:      cin >> m;
16:      cout << "\n";
17:    } while (m < 2 || m > MAX);
18:    return m;
19:  }
20:
21: void inputArray(int intArr[], int n)
22: {
23:   // prompt user for data
24:   for (int i = 0; i < n; i++) {
25:     cout << "arr[" << i << "] : ";
26:     cin >> intArr[i];
27:   }
28: }
29:
30: void showArray(int intArr[], int n)
31: {
32:   for (int i = 0; i < n; i++) {
33:     cout.width(5);
34:     cout << intArr[i] << " ";
35:   }
36:   cout << "\n";
37: }
38:
39: void sortArray(int intArr[], int n)
40: {
41:   int offset, temp, inOrder;
42:
43:   offset = n;
44:   do {
45:     offset = (8 * offset) / 11;
46:     offset = (offset == 0) ? 1 : offset;
47:     inOrder = TRUE;
48:     for (int i = 0, j = offset; i < (n -- offset); i++, j++) {
49:       if (intArr[i] > intArr[j]) {
50:         inOrder = FALSE;
51:         temp = intArr[i];
52:         intArr[i] = intArr[j];
53:         intArr[j] = temp;
54:       }
55:     }
56:   } while (!(offset = 1 && inOrder == TRUE));
57: }
58:
59: main()
60: {
61:   int arr[MAX];
62:   int n;
63:
64:   n = obtainNumData();
```

```
65:    inputArray(arr, n);
66:    cout << "Unordered array is:\n";
67:    showArray(arr, n);
68:    sortArray(arr, n);
69:    cout << "\nSorted array is:\n";
70:    showArray(arr, n);
71:    return 0;
72: }
```

Here is a sample session with the program in Listing 6.5.

```
Enter number of data points [2 to 10] : 10
arr[0] : 55
arr[1] : 68
arr[2] : 74
arr[3] : 15
arr[4] : 28
arr[5] : 23
arr[6] : 69
arr[7] : 95
arr[8] : 22
arr[9] : 33
Unordered array is:
55     68     74     15     28     23     69     95     22     33

Sorted array is:
15     22     23     28     33     55     68     69     74     95
```

The program in Listing 6.5 declares the constants MAX, TRUE, and FALSE in lines 5 through 7. The constant MAX defines the size of the array used in the program. The constants TRUE and FALSE define the Boolean values. The program also defines the functions obtainNumData, inputArray, showArray, sortArray, and main.

The parameterless function obtainNumData, defined in lines 9 through 19, prompts you to enter the number of values. The output statement in lines 13 and 14 also specifies the valid range for your input. The statement in line 15 stores your input in the local variable m. The function uses a do-while loop to ensure that it returns a valid number. The loop iterates as long as the value in variable m is less than 2 or greater than MAX. The function returns the value in variable m.

The function inputArray, defined in lines 21 through 28, obtains the data for the tested array. The function has two parameters. The open-array parameter intArr passes the input values back to the caller of the function. The parameter n specifies how many values to obtain for parameter intArr. The function uses a for loop, which iterates from 0 to n-1, in increments of 1. Each loop iteration prompts you for a value and stores that value in an element of the array intArr.

Note: The function inputArray illustrates that C++ functions treat array parameters as if they were references to their arguments because these parameters affect the values in the arguments beyond the scope of the functions. In reality, the C++ compiler passes a copy of the address of the array argument to the function when dealing with an array parameter. Armed with the address of the array, C++ functions then can alter the values of the array beyond the scope of these functions. This feature is possible because the function is working with the original array and not a copy.

The function showArray, defined in lines 30 through 37, displays the meaningful data in an array. The function has two parameters. The open-array parameter intArr passes the array values to be displayed by the function. The parameter n specifies how many elements of array intArr to display. (Remember that not all the array elements are used to store your data.) The function uses a for loop, which iterates from 0 to n-1, in increments of 1. Each loop iteration displays the value in an array element. The array elements appear on the same line.

The function sortArray, defined in lines 39 through 57, sorts the elements of an array using the Comb sort method. The function has two parameters. The open-array parameter intArr passes the array values to be sorted by the function. The parameter n specifies how many array elements to sort. The statements in the function sortArray implement the Comb sort method outlined earlier.

Note: The function sortArray illustrates how array parameters can pass data to and from a function. The function sortArray receives an unordered array, sorts it, and passes the ordered array to the function's caller. The compiler supports this feature by passing a copy of the address of the array to the function. Thus, the function need not explicitly return the array because it is working with the original data and not a copy.

The function main performs the various program tasks by calling the functions mentioned earlier. The function declares the array arr and the simple variable n in lines 61 and 62, respectively. The statement in line 64 calls function obtainNumData to obtain the number of data points you want to store in the array. The statement assigns the result of the function obtainNumData to variable n. The statement in line 65 calls the function inputArray to prompt you for the data. The function call passes the arguments arr and n. The output statement in line 66 displays a message indicating that the program is about to display the elements of the unordered array. The statement in line 67 calls showArray and passes it the arguments arr and n. This function call displays the elements of the array arr on one line. The statement in line 68 calls the function sortArray to sort the first n elements in array arr. The output statement in line 69 displays a message indicating that the program is about to display the elements of the sorted array. The statement in line 70 calls showArray and passes the arguments arr and n. This function call displays the elements of the ordered array arr on one line.

Searching Arrays

Searching arrays is another important nonnumerical operation. Because arrays can be sorted or unordered, there is a general category of search methods for each. The simplest search method for unordered arrays is the *linear search method*. The simplest search method for sorted arrays is the versatile *binary search method*. The search methods for unordered arrays also can be applied to sorted arrays; however, they do not take advantage of the array order.

NEW☞
TERM The *linear search method* sequentially examines the array elements, looking for an element that matches the search value. If the sought value is not in the array, the linear search method examines the entire array's elements.

NEW☞
TERM The *binary search method* takes advantage of the order in the array. The method searches for a matching value by using the shrinking intervals approach. The initial search interval includes all the array elements (which contain meaningful data). The method compares the median element of the interval with the search value. If the two match, the search stops. Otherwise, the method determines which sub-interval to use as the next search interval. Consequently, each search interval is half the size of the previous one. If the search value has no match in the examined array, the binary method makes far fewer examinations than the linear search method. The binary search method is the most efficient general-purpose search method for sorted arrays.

DO	DON'T

DO use the unordered-array search method when you are not sure that the array is sorted.

DON'T use sorted-array search methods with unordered arrays. The results of such searches are not reliable.

Look at a program that sorts an array of integers. Listing 6.6 shows the source code for the program ARRAY6.CPP. We created this program by adding functions and operations to the program ARRAY5.CPP. The program performs the following tasks:

☐ Prompts you to enter the number of data points

☐ Prompts you to enter the integer values for the array

☐ Displays the elements of the unordered array

☐ Asks you if you want to search for data in the unordered array. (If you type characters other than **Y** or **y**, the program resumes at step 8.)

☐ Prompts you for a search value

- Displays the search outcome. (If the program finds a matching element, it displays the index of that element; otherwise, the program tells you that it found no match for the search value.)

- Resumes at step 4

- Displays the elements of the sorted array

- Asks you if you want to search for data in the unordered array. (If you type characters other than **Y** or **y** the program ends.)

- Prompts you for a search value

- Displays the search outcome. (If the program finds a matching element, it displays the index of that element; otherwise, the program tells you that it found no match for the search value.)

- Resumes at step 9

Listing 6.6. Source code for the program ARRAY6.CPP.

```
 1:  // C++ program that searches arrays using the linear
 2:  // and binary searches methods
 3:
 4:  #include <iostream.h>
 5:
 6:  const int MAX = 10;
 7:  const int TRUE = 1;
 8:  const int FALSE = 0;
 9:  const int NOT_FOUND = --1;
10:
11:  int obtainNumData()
12:  {
13:    int m;
14:    do { // obtain number of data points
15:      cout << "Enter number of data points [2 to "
16:          << MAX << "] : ";
17:      cin >> m;
18:      cout << "\n";
19:    } while (m < 2 || m > MAX);
20:    return m;
21:  }
22:
23:  void inputArray(int intArr[], int n)
24:  {
25:    // prompt user for data
26:    for (int i = 0; i < n; i++) {
27:      cout << "arr[" << i << "] : ";
28:      cin >> intArr[i];
29:    }
30:  }
31:
32:  void showArray(int intArr[], int n)
33:  {
34:    for (int i = 0; i < n; i++) {
35:      cout.width(5);
36:      cout << intArr[i] << " ";
```

```
37:   }
38:   cout << "\n";
39: }
40:
41: void sortArray(int intArr[], int n)
42: // sort the first n elements of array intArr
43: // using the Comb sort method
44: {
45:   int offset, temp, inOrder;
46:
47:   offset = n;
48:   do {
49:     offset = (8 * offset) / 11;
50:     offset = (offset == 0) ? 1 : offset;
51:     inOrder = TRUE;
52:     for (int i = 0, j = offset; i < (n -- offset); i++, j++) {
53:       if (intArr[i] > intArr[j]) {
54:         inOrder = FALSE;
55:         temp = intArr[i];
56:         intArr[i] = intArr[j];
57:         intArr[j] = temp;
58:       }
59:     }
60:   } while (!(offset = 1 && inOrder == TRUE));
61: }
62:
63: int linearSearch(int searchVal, int intArr[], int n)
64: // perform linear search to locate the first
65: // element in array intArr that matches the value
66: // of searchVal
67: {
68:   int notFound = TRUE;
69:   int i = 0;
70:   // search through the array elements
71:   while (i < n && notFound)
72:     // no match?
73:     if (searchVal != intArr[i])
74:       i++; // increment index to compare the next element
75:     else
76:       notFound = FALSE; // found a match
77:   // return search outcome
78:   return (notFound == FALSE) ? i : NOT_FOUND;
79: }
80:
81: int binarySearch(int searchVal, int intArr[], int n)
82: // perform binary search to locate the first
83: // element in array intArr that matches the value
84: // of searchVal
85: {
86:   int median, low, high;
87:
88:   // initialize the search range
89:   low = 0;
90:   high = n - 1;
91:   // search in array
92:   do {
93:     // obtain the median index of the current search range
94:     median = (low + high) / 2;
```

Listing 6.6. continued

```
95:      // update search range
96:      if (searchVal > intArr[median])
97:        low = median + 1;
98:      else
99:        high = median -- 1;
100:   } while (!(searchVal == intArr[median] || low > high));
101:   // return search outcome
102:   return (searchVal == intArr[median]) ? median : NOT_FOUND;
103: }
104:
105: void searchInUnorderedArray(int intArr[], int n)
106: // manage the linear search test
107: {
108:   int x, i;
109:   char c;
110:   // perform linear search
111:   cout << "Search in unordered array? (Y/N) ";
112:   cin >> c;
113:   while (c == 'Y' || c == 'y') {
114:     cout << "Enter search value : ";
115:     cin >> x;
116:     i = linearSearch(x, intArr, n);
117:     if (i != NOT_FOUND)
118:       cout << "Found matching element at index " << i << "\n";
119:     else
120:       cout << "No match found\n";
121:     cout << "Search in unordered array? (Y/N) ";
122:     cin >> c;
123:   }
124: }
125:
126: void searchInSortedArray(int intArr[], int n)
127: // manage the binary search test
128: {
129:   int x, i;
130:   char c;
131:   // perform binary search
132:   cout << "Search in sorted array? (Y/N) ";
133:   cin >> c;
134:   while (c == 'Y' || c == 'y') {
135:     cout << "Enter search value : ";
136:     cin >> x;
137:     i = binarySearch(x, intArr, n);
138:     if (i != NOT_FOUND)
139:       cout << "Found matching element at index " << i << "\n";
140:     else
141:       cout << "No match found\n";
142:     cout << "Search in sorted array? (Y/N) ";
143:     cin >> c;
144:   }
145: }
146:
147: main()
148: {
149:   int arr[MAX];
150:   int n;
```

```
151:
152:    n = obtainNumData();
153:    inputArray(arr, n);
154:    cout << "Unordered array is:\n";
155:    showArray(arr, n);
156:    searchInUnorderedArray(arr, n);
157:    sortArray(arr, n);
158:    cout << "\nSorted array is:\n";
159:    showArray(arr, n);
160:    searchInSortedArray(arr, n);
161:    return 0;
162: }
```

Here is a sample session with the program in Listing 6.6.

```
Enter number of data points [2 to 10] : 5

arr[0] : 85
arr[1] : 41
arr[2] : 55
arr[3] : 67
arr[4] : 48
Unordered array is:
85      41      55      67      48
Search in unordered array? (Y/N) y
Enter search value : 55
Found matching element at index 2
Search in unordered array? (Y/N) y
Enter search value : 41
Found matching element at index 1
Search in unordered array? (Y/N) n

Sorted array is:
41      48      55      67      85
Search in sorted array? (Y/N) y
Enter search value : 55
Found matching element at index 2
Search in sorted array? (Y/N) y
Enter search value : 67
Found matching element at index 3
Search in sorted array? (Y/N) n
```

The program in Listing 6.6 declares the functions obtainNumData, inputArray, sortArray, linearSearch, binarySearch, searchInUnorderedArray, searchInSortedArray, and main. Because the first three functions are identical to those in Listing 6.5, only the remaining functions are discussed.

The linearSearch function performs a linear search to find the first element in array intArr with a value that matches the one in parameter searchVal. The function searches the first n elements in array intArr. The linearSearch function returns the index of the matching element in array intArr or yields the value of the global constant NOT_FOUND if no match is found. The function uses a while loop to examine the elements in array intArr. The search loop iterates while the value in variable i is less than that in variable n and while the local variable notFound stores TRUE. The statement in line 78 returns the function result using the conditional operator.

The `binarySearch` function has the same parameters as the `linearSearch` function and returns the same type of value. The function uses the local variables `low` and `high` to store the current search interval. The function initializes the variables `low` and `high` using the values 0 and n-1, respectively. The `do-while` loop in lines 92 through 100 calculates the index of the median element and compares the median element with the search value. The `if` statement in line 96 performs this comparison, and its clauses update the value of either variable `low` or variable `high`, depending on the outcome of the comparison. The update in either variable shrinks the search interval. The return statement in line 102 yields the function's value based on one last comparison between the search value and the median element of the current search interval.

The function `searchInUnorderedArray` manages the search in the unordered array. The function accesses the unordered array using the open-array parameter `intArr`. The function declares local variables that are used to prompt you for and store the search value. The statement in line 116 calls the function `linearSearch` and passes the argument `x` (the local variable that stores the search value), `intArr`, and `n`. The statement assigns the result of function `linearSearch` to the local variable `i`. The `if` statement in line 117 determines whether the value in variable `i` is not `NOT_FOUND`. If this condition is true, then the output statement in line 118 shows the index of the matching element. Otherwise, the output statement in line 120 displays a `no-match-found` message.

The function `searchInSortedArray` is very similar to the function `searchInUnorderedArray`. The main difference is that the function `searchInSortedArray` deals with ordered arrays and, therefore, calls the `binarySearch` function to conduct a binary search on the ordered array `intArr`.

The function `main` invokes these functions to support the program tasks described earlier.

Multidimensional Arrays

In a *multidimensional array*, each additional dimension provides an additional access attribute. Two-dimensional arrays (or matrices, if you prefer) are the most popular type of multidimensional array. Three-dimensional arrays are used less frequently than matrices, and so on.

NEW *Multidimensional arrays* are supersets of the single-dimensional arrays.
TERM

Two-Dimensional and Three-Dimensional Arrays

The general syntax for declaring two-dimensional and three-dimensional arrays is

```
type array [size1][size2];
type array [size1][size2][size3];
```

As with simple arrays, each dimension has a lower bound index of 0, and the declaration defines the number of elements in each dimension.

Examples

```
double matrixA[100][10];
char table[41][22][3];
int index[7][12];
```

It is important to understand how C++ stores the elements of a multidimensional array. Most compilers store the elements of a multidimensional array in a contiguous fashion (that is, as one long array). The runtime code calculates where a sought element is located in that long array. To explain the storage scheme of multidimensional arrays, we'll start by employing a convention for referencing the indices of the different dimensions. The following schema specifies the dimension numbering and the concept of high- and low-order dimensions. Following is a six-dimensional array—an extreme case that is a good example:

```
1    2    3    4    5    6   <— dimension number
M [20]  [7]  [5]  [3]  [2]  [2]
higher dimension order —>
```

The first element of the array M is M[0][0][0][0][0][0] and is stored at the first memory location of array M. The array M is stored in a contiguous block of 8,400 elements. The location in that contiguous block stores the element at index 1 in the highest dimension number, dimension 6 (that is, M[0][0][0][0][0][1]). The location of the next elements in the contiguous block stores the subsequent elements in dimension 6 until the upper limit of dimension 6 is reached. Reaching this limit bumps the index of dimension 5 by 1 and resets the index of dimension 6 to 0. This process is repeated until every element in a multidimensional array is accessed. You can compare this storage scheme to looking at a gasoline pump meter when refueling your car: the right digits turn the fastest, the left digits turn the slowest.

Here is another example that uses a three-dimensional array, M[3][2][2].

```
M[0][0][0]      <— the starting memory address
M[0][0][1]      <— 3rd dimension is filled
M[0][1][0]
M[0][1][1]      <— 2nd and 3rd dimensions are filled
M[1][0][0]
M[1][0][1]      <— 3rd dimension is filled
M[1][1][0]
M[1][1][1]      <— 2nd and 3rd dimensions are filled
M[2][0][0]
M[2][0][1]      <— 3rd dimension is filled
M[2][1][0]
M[2][1][1]      <— all dimensions are filled
```

Consider an example that illustrates basic matrix manipulation. Listing 6.7 shows the source code for the MAT1.CPP program. The program manages a matrix that contains up to 10 columns and 30 rows and performs the following tasks:

- ☐ Prompts you to enter the number of rows; the program validates your input
- ☐ Prompts you to enter the number of columns; the program validates your input
- ☐ Prompts you to enter the matrix elements
- ☐ Calculates and displays the average for each column in the matrix

6

Listing 6.7. Source code for the program MAT1.CPP.

```
1:  /*
2:    C++ program that demonstrates the use of two-dimensional arrays.
3:    The average value of each matrix column is calculated.
4:  */
5:
6:  #include <iostream.h>
7:
8:  const int MAX_COL = 10;
9:  const int MAX_ROW = 30;
10:
11: main()
12: {
13:     double x[MAX_ROW][MAX_COL];
14:     double sum, sumx, mean;
15:     int rows, columns;
16:
17:     // get the number of rows
18:     do {
19:       cout << "Enter number of rows [2 to "
20:            << MAX_ROW << "] : ";
21:       cin >> rows;
22:     } while (rows < 2 ¦¦ rows > MAX_ROW);
23:
24:     // get the number of columns
25:     do {
26:       cout << "Enter number of columns [1 to "
27:            << MAX_COL << "] : ";
28:       cin >> columns;
29:     } while (columns < 1 ¦¦ columns > MAX_COL);
30:
31:     // get the matrix elements
32:     for (int i = 0; i < rows; i++)  {
33:       for (int j = 0; j < columns; j++) {
34:           cout << "X[" << i << "][" << j << "] : ";
35:           cin >> x[i][j];
36:       }
37:       cout << "\n";
38:     }
39:
40:     sum = rows;
41:     // obtain the sum of each column
42:     for (int j = 0; j < columns; j++)  {
43:       // initialize summations
44:       sumx = 0.0;
45:       for (i = 0; i < rows; i++)
46:         sumx += x[i][j];
47:       mean = sumx / sum;
48:       cout << "Mean for column " << j
49:            << " = " << mean << "\n";
50:     }
51:     return 0;
52: }
```

Here is a sample session with the program in Listing 6.7.

```
Enter number of rows [2 to 30] : 3
Enter number of columns [1 to 10] : 3
X[0][0] : 1
X[0][1] : 2
X[0][2] : 3

X[1][0] : 4
X[1][1] : 5
X[1][2] : 6

X[2][0] : 7
X[2][1] : 8
X[2][2] : 9

Mean for column 0 = 4
Mean for column 1 = 5
Mean for column 2 = 6
```

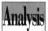

The program in Listing 6.7 declares the global constants MAX_COL and MAX_ROW in lines 8 and 9, respectively. These constants define the dimensions of the matrix that is created in the program. The function main declares the matrix x to have MAX_ROW rows and MAX_COL columns. The function also declares other nonarray variables.

The do-while loop, in lines 18 through 22, prompts you to enter the number of rows of matrix x that will contain your data. The output statement in lines 19 and 20 indicates the range of the valid number of rows. The statement in line 21 stores your input in the variable rows.

The second do-while loop, in lines 25 through 29, prompts you to enter the number of columns of matrix x that will contain your data. The output statement in lines 26 and 27 indicates the range of the valid number of columns. The statement in line 28 saves your input in the variable columns.

The nested for loops, in lines 32 through 38, prompt you for the matrix elements. The outer for loop uses the control variable i and iterates from 0 to rows-1, in increments of 1. The inner for loop uses the control variable j and iterates from 0 to columns-1, in increments of 1. The output statement in line 34 displays the index of the matrix element that will receive your input. The statement in line 35 stores your input in the matrix element x[i][j].

The process of obtaining the average of each matrix column starts at line 40. The statement in that line assigns the integer in variable rows to the double-typed variable sum. The program uses another pair of nested for loops in lines 42 through 50. The outer for loop uses the control variable j and iterates from 0 to columns-1, in increments of 1. This loop processes each column. The first statement inside the outer for loop assigns 0 to the variable sumx. The inner for loop is located at line 45. This loop uses the control variable i and iterates from 0 to rows-1, in increments of 1. The inner loop uses the statement in line 46 to add the values of elements x[i][j] to the variable sumx. The statement in line 47 (which is outside the inner for loop) calculates the column average and assigns it to the variable mean. The output statement in lines 48 and 49 displays the column number and its average value.

Note: The for loop in line 42 redeclares its control variable j. (This is not the case with the for loop in line 45.) Why? The for loop in line 33 also declares the control variable j. However, the scope of that loop is limited to the scope of the outer for loop. Once the first pair of nested loops finishes executing, the loop control variable j is removed by the runtime system.

Initializing Multidimensional Arrays

C++ enables you to initialize a multidimensional array in a manner similar to single-dimensional arrays. You need to use a list of values that appear in the same sequence in which the elements of the initialized multidimensional array are stored. Now you realize the importance of understanding how C++ stores the elements of a multidimensional array. We modified the previous C++ program to use an initializing list that internally supplies the program with data. Consequently, the program does not prompt you for any data. Rather, the program displays the values of the matrix and the average for its columns. Listing 6.8. shows the source code for the MAT2.CPP program.

 Listing 6.8. Source code for the program MAT2.CPP.

```
 1:  /*
 2:    C++ program that demonstrates the use of two-dimensional arrays.
 3:    The average value of each matrix column is calculated.
 4:  */
 5:
 6:  #include <iostream.h>
 7:
 8:  const int MAX_COL = 3;
 9:  const int MAX_ROW = 3;
10:
11:  main()
12:  {
13:      double x[MAX_ROW][MAX_COL] = {
14:                                    { 1, 2, 3 }, // row # 1
15:                                    { 4, 5, 6 }, // row # 2
16:                                    { 7, 8, 9 }  // row # 3
17:                                    };
18:      double sum, sumx, mean;
19:      int rows = MAX_ROW, columns = MAX_COL;
20:
21:      cout << "Matrix is:\n";
22:      // display the matrix elements
23:      for (int i = 0; i < rows; i++)  {
24:        for (int j = 0; j < columns; j++)  {
25:            cout.width(4);
26:            cout.precision(1);
27:            cout << x[i][j] << " ";
```

```
28:       }
29:       cout << "\n";
30:     }
31:     cout << "\n";
32:
33:     sum = rows;
34:     // obtain the sum of each column
35:     for (int j = 0; j < columns; j++)  {
36:       // initialize summations
37:       sumx = 0.0;
38:       for (i = 0; i < rows; i++)
39:         sumx += x[i][j];
40:       mean = sumx / sum;
41:       cout << "Mean for column " << j
42:            << " = " << mean << "\n";
43:     }
44:     return 0;
45: }
```

Here is a sample session with the program in Listing 6.8.

```
Matrix is:
1    2    3
4    5    6
7    8    9

Mean for column 0 = 4
Mean for column 1 = 5
Mean for column 2 = 6
```

The program in Listing 6.8 declares the matrix x and initializes its elements with a list of values. Notice that the program declares the constants MAX_COL and MAX_ROW with values that match the size of the initialized matrix. The declaration statement in lines 13 through 17 shows the elements assigned to each row. The function main also initializes the variables rows and columns with the constants MAX_ROW and MAX_COL, respectively. The function performs this initialization for two reasons. First, the program no longer prompts you to enter values for the variables rows and columns. Second, the program is working with a custom-fit size for matrix x.

The program uses the nested for loops in lines 21 through 30 to display the elements of the matrix x. The second pair of nested for loops calculates the average for each matrix column. This nested for loop is identical to the one in Listing 6.7.

Multidimensional Array Parameters

C++ enables you to declare function parameters that are multidimensional arrays. As with single-dimensional arrays, C++ enables you either to be specific or general about the size of the array parameter. In the latter case, however, you can only generalize the first dimension of the array. If you want an array parameter to accept arrays of a fixed dimension, you can specify the size of each dimension of the array in the parameter declaration.

6

A Fixed-Array Parameter

The general syntax for declaring a fixed-array parameter is

```
type parameterName[dim1Size][dim2Size]...
```

Examples

```
int minMatrix(int intMat[100][20], int rows, int cols);
void sort(unsigned mat[23][55],
int rows, int cols, int colIndex);
```

An Open-Array Parameter

The general syntax for declaring an open-array parameter is

```
type parameterName[][dim2Size]...
```

Examples

```
int minMat(int intMat[][100], int rows, int cols);
void sort(unsigned mat[][55],
int rows, int cols, int colIndex);
```

Look at an example. Listing 6.9 shows the source code for the program MAT3.CPP. The program performs the same tasks as program MAT1.CPP in Listing 6.7. We created program MAT3.CPP by editing program MAT1.CPP and placing each program task in a separate function. Thus, program MAT3.CPP is a highly structured version of program MAT1.CPP.

Type

Listing 6.9. Source code for the program MAT3.CPP.

```
1:  /*
2:    C++ program that demonstrates the use of two-dimensional arrays.
3:    The average value of each matrix column is calculated.
4:  */
5:
6:  #include <iostream.h>
7:
8:  const int MAX_COL = 10;
9:  const int MAX_ROW = 30;
10:
11: int getRows()
12: {
13:   int n;
14:   // get the number of rows
15:   do {
16:     cout << "Enter number of rows [2 to "
17:          << MAX_ROW << "] : ";
18:     cin >> n;
19:   } while (n < 2 || n > MAX_ROW);
20:   return n;
21: }
22:
```

```
23: int getColumns()
24: {
25:   int n;
26:   // get the number of columns
27:   do {
28:     cout << "Enter number of columns [1 to "
29:          << MAX_COL << "] : ";
30:     cin >> n;
31:   } while (n < 1 || n > MAX_COL);
32:   return n;
33: }
34:
35: void inputMatrix(double mat[][MAX_COL],
36:                  int rows, int columns)
37: {
38:   // get the matrix elements
39:   for (int i = 0; i < rows; i++)  {
40:     for (int j = 0; j < columns; j++)  {
41:       cout << "X[" << i << "][" << j << "] : ";
42:       cin >> mat[i][j];
43:     }
44:     cout << "\n";
45:   }
46: }
47:
48: void showColumnAverage(double mat[][MAX_COL],
49:                        int rows, int columns)
50: {
51:   double sum, sumx, mean;
52:   sum = rows;
53:   // obtain the sum of each column
54:   for (int j = 0; j < columns; j++)  {
55:     // initialize summations
56:     sumx = 0.0;
57:     for (int i = 0; i < rows; i++)
58:       sumx += mat[i][j];
59:     mean = sumx / sum;
60:     cout << "Mean for column " << j
61:          << " = " << mean << "\n";
62:   }
63: }
64:
65: main()
66: {
67:     double x[MAX_ROW][MAX_COL];
68:     int rows, columns;
69:     // get matrix dimensions
70:     rows = getRows();
71:     columns = getColumns();
72:     // get matrix data
73:     inputMatrix(x, rows, columns);
74:     // show results
75:     showColumnAverage(x, rows, columns);
76:     return 0;
77: }
```

6

this is a comic for kids

Here is a sample session with the program in Listing 6.9.

```
Enter number of rows [2 to 30] : 3
Enter number of columns [1 to 10] : 3
X[0][0] : 10
X[0][1] : 20
X[0][2] : 30

X[1][0] : 40
X[1][1] : 50
X[1][2] : 60

X[2][0] : 70
X[2][1] : 80
X[2][2] : 90

Mean for column 0 = 40
Mean for column 1 = 50
Mean for column 2 = 60
```

The program in Listing 6.9 declares the functions getRows, getColumns, inputMatrix, showColumnAverage, and main. The function getRows prompts you for the number of matrix rows that you will be using. The function returns your validated input. Similarly, the function getColumns returns the validated number of matrix columns.

The function inputMatrix obtains the data for the matrix. The function has three parameters. The parameter mat specifies the matrix parameter (with an open first dimension). The parameters rows and columns specify the number of rows and the number of columns of matrix mat that will receive input data.

The function showColumnAverage calculates and displays the column averages for the matrix parameter mat. The parameters rows and columns specify the number of rows and the number of columns of matrix mat that contain meaningful data.

This function contains the same statements that appeared in the program MAT1.CPP. Program MAT3.CPP uses these functions as shells or wrappers for the statements that perform the various tasks. From a structured programming point of view, program MAT3.CPP is superior to program MAT1.CPP.

The function main declares the matrix x with MAX_ROW rows and MAX_COL columns. The function calls the functions getRows and getColumns to obtain the number of working rows and columns, respectively. The statement in line 73 invokes the function inputMatrix and supplies it with the arguments x, rows, and columns. The statement in line 75 calls function showColumnAverage and passes it the arguments x, rows, and columns.

Summary

Today's lesson covered various topics related to arrays, including single-dimensional and multidimensional arrays. You learned the following:

- The initializing of single-dimensional arrays can be carried out while declaring them. The initializing list of data is enclosed in braces and contains comma-delimited data. C++ enables you to include fewer data than the size of the array. In this case, the compiler automatically assigns zeros to the elements that you do not explicitly initialize. In addition, C++ enables you to omit the explicit size of the initialized array and instead use the number of initializing items as the number of array elements.

- Declaring single-dimensional arrays as function parameters takes two forms. The first one deals with fixed-array parameters, whereas the second one handles open-array parameters. Fixed-array parameters include the size of the array in the parameter. Arguments for this type of parameter must match the type and size of the parameter. Open-array parameters use empty brackets to indicate that the arguments for the parameters can be of any size.

- Sorting arrays is an important nonnumerical array operation. Sorting arranges the elements of an array in either ascending or descending order. Sorted arrays are much easier to search. For sorting arrays, the new Comb sort method is very efficient.

- Searching arrays involves locating an array element that contains the same data as the search value. Searching methods either are geared toward unordered or ordered arrays. The linear search method is used for unordered arrays, and the binary search method is used for sorted arrays.

- Declaring multidimensional arrays requires you to state the data type of the array elements, the name of the array, and the size of each dimension (enclosed in separate brackets). The lower index of each dimension is 0. The upper bound of each dimension in an array is equal to the dimension size minus one.

- Using multidimensional arrays requires you to state the array's name and to include valid indices. Each index must be enclosed in a separate set of brackets.

- The initializing of multidimensional arrays can be carried out while declaring them. The initializing list of data is enclosed in braces and contains comma-delimited data. C++ enables you to include fewer data than the total size of the array. In this case, the compiler automatically assigns zeros to the elements that you do not explicitly initialize.

- Declaring multidimensional arrays as function parameters take two forms. The first one deals with fixed-array parameters, whereas, the second one handles parameters with an open first dimension. Fixed-array parameters include the size of each dimension in the array parameter. Arguments for this type of parameter must match the type and sizes of the parameter. Open-array parameters use empty brackets for only the first dimension to indicate that the arguments for the parameters have varying sizes for the first dimensions. The other dimensions of the arguments must match those of the array parameter.

6

Q&A

Q Does C++ permit me to alter the size of an array?

A No. C++ does not allow you to redimension arrays.

Q Can I declare arrays with the basic type `void` (for example, `void array[81];`) to create buffers?

A No. C++ does not allow you to use the `void` type with an array, because the `void` type has no defined size. Use the `char` or `unsigned char` type to create an array that works as a buffer.

Q Does C++ allow me to redeclare an array?

A Not really, but C++ enables you to declare a new version of the array in a new statement block in order to change its basic type, the number of dimensions, and its size. Here is an example.

```
#include <iostream.h>
const MAX = 100;
const MAX_ROWS = 100;
const MAX_COLS = 20;

main()
{
  // declare variables here?
  {
    double x[MAX];
    // declare other variables?
    // statements to manipulate the single-dimensional
       array x
  }
  {
    double x[MAX_ROWS][MAX_COLS];
    // declare other variables?
    // statements to manipulate the matrix x
  }
  return 0;
}
```

The function `main` declares the array `x` in the first nested statement block. When program execution reaches the end of that block, the runtime system removes the array `x` and all other variables declared in that block. Then the function redeclares `x` as a matrix in the second block. When program execution reaches the end of the second block, the runtime system removes the matrix `x` and all other variables declared in that block.

Q Are arrays limited to the predefined types?

A Not at all. C++ enables you to create arrays using user-defined types.

Workshop

The Workshop provides quiz questions to help you solidify your understanding of the material covered and exercises to provide you with experience in using what you've learned. Try to understand the quiz and exercise answers before continuing on to the next day's lesson. Answers are provided in Appendix A.

Quiz

1. What is the output of the following program?

```cpp
#include <iostream.h>
const int MAX = 5;
main()
{
  double x[MAX];
  x[0] = 1;
  for (int i = 1; i < MAX; i++)
    x[i] = i * x[i-1];
  for (i = 0; i < MAX; i++)
    cout << "x[" << i << "] = " << x[i] << "\n";
  return 0;
}
```

2. What is the output of the following program?

```cpp
#include <iostream.h>
#include <math.h>
const int MAX = 5;
main()
{
  double x[MAX];
  for (int i = 0; i < MAX; i++)
    x[i] = sqrt(double(i));
  for (i = 0; i < MAX; i++)
    cout << "x[" << i << "] = " << x[i] << "\n";
  return 0;
}
```

3. Where is the error in the following program?

```cpp
#include <iostream.h>
const int MAX = 5;
main()
{
  double x[MAX];
  x[0] = 1;
  for (int i = 0; i < MAX; i++)
    x[i] = i * x[i-1];
  for (i = 0; i < MAX; i++)
    cout << "x[" << i << "] = " << x[i] << "\n";
  return 0;
}
```

6

Exercise

Write the program ARRAY7.CPP by editing program ARRAY6.CPP and replacing the Comb sort method in the function sortArray with an implementation of the Shell-Metzner method.

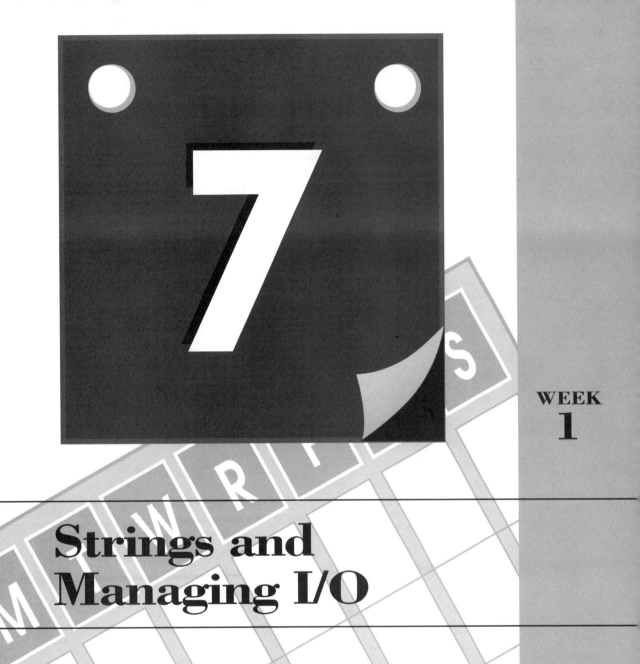

7

Strings and
Managing I/O

Today you will learn about basic console input/output (I/O). C++, like its parent language C, does not define I/O operations that are part of the core language. Instead, C++ and C rely on I/O libraries to provide the needed console I/O support. Such libraries mainly are aimed at non-GUI (graphical user interface) environments such as MS-DOS. These libraries usually work with EasyWin applications, which is why they are of interest in this book. Because our primary goal here is to teach you how to write Windows programs, however, the discussion of these console I/O libraries are kept to a minimum. Today's lesson looks at a small selection of input and output operations and functions that are supported by the STDIO.H and IOSTREAM.H header files.

The examples presented so far have been predominantly numeric, with a few that involve character manipulation. You may have grown suspicious about the absence of strings in all of these examples. On Day 10 you will learn about the special C++ string class that makes strings into a more usable type. Today's lesson discusses C++ strings as they are inherited from C.

You will learn about the following topics:

- ☐ Formatted stream output
- ☐ Stream input
- ☐ The printf function
- ☐ Strings in C++
- ☐ String input
- ☐ Using the standard string library
- ☐ Assigning strings
- ☐ Obtaining the length of strings
- ☐ Concatenating strings
- ☐ Comparing strings
- ☐ Converting strings
- ☐ Reversing the characters in a string
- ☐ Locating characters
- ☐ Locating substrings

Formatted Stream Output

C++ brings with it a family of extendable I/O libraries. The language designers recognized that the I/O functions in STDIO.H, inherited from C, have their limitations when dealing with classes. (You learn more about classes in Day 8.) Consequently, C++ extends the notion of streams. Recall that streams, which already exist in C, are a sequence of data flowing from part of a computer to another. In the programs presented thus far, you have seen the extractor operator << working with the standard output stream, cout. You also saw the inserter operator >> and the standard input stream, cin. In this section, you are introduced to the stream functions width and precision, which help in formatting the output. The C++ stream libraries have many more functions to additionally fine-tune the output. The width function specifies the width of the output. The general form for using this function with the cout stream is

```
cout.width(widthOfOutput);
```

The precision function specifies the number of digits for floating-point numbers. The general form for using this function with the cout stream is

```
cout.precision(numberOfDigits);
```

Look at an example. Listing 7.1 contains the source code for the program OUT1.CPP. (We suggest that you place all of today's programs in the DAY4.IDE project file.) The program, which requires no input, displays formatted integers, floating-point numbers, and characters using the width and precision stream functions.

Listing 7.1. Source code for the program OUT1.CPP.

```
1: // Program that illustrates C++ formatted stream output
2: // using the width and precision functions
3:
4: #include <iostream.h>
5:
6: main()
7: {
8:    short     aShort    = 4;
9:    int       anInt     = 67;
10:   unsigned char aByte = 128;
11:   char      aChar     = '@';
12:   float     aSingle   = 355.0;
13:   double    aDouble    = 1.130e+002;
14:   // display sample expressions
15:   cout.width(3); cout << int(aByte) << " + ";
16:   cout.width(3); cout << anInt << " = ";
17:   cout.width(3); cout << (aByte + anInt) << '\n';
18:
19:   cout.precision(4); cout << aSingle << " / ";
20:   cout << aDouble << " = ";
21:   cout.precision(5); cout << (aSingle / aDouble) << '\n';
22:
23:   cout << "The character in variable aChar is "
24:        << aChar << '\n';
25:   return 0;
26: }
```

7

Here is a sample session with the program in Listing 7.1.

```
128 +  67 = 195
355 / 113 = 3.1416
The character in variable aChar is @
```

Analysis The program in Listing 7.1 declares a set of variables that have different data types. The statements in lines 15 through 17 use the stream function width to specify the output width for the next item displayed by a cout statement. Notice that it takes six statements to display three integers. In addition, notice that in line 15 the program uses the expression int(aByte) to typecast the unsigned char type into an int. Without this type conversion, the contents of the variable aByte appear as a character rather than a number. If you use the stream output to display integers that have default widths, you indeed can replace the six stream-output statements with a single one. Note that the width automatically is reset after each output, which is why you need to set it to the same value multiple times.

Lines 19 through 21 contain the second set of stream-output statements for the floating-point numbers. The statements in these lines contain the stream function precision to specify the total number of digits to display. It takes five C++ statements to output three floating-point numbers. Once more, if you use the stream output to display numbers that have default widths, you can replace the five stream-output statements with a single one. Note that the precision is *not* reset after each output, so the output on line 20 is still using a precision of 4.

Stream Input

Like the standard output stream, C++ offers the standard input stream, cin. This input stream can read predefined data types, such as int, unsigned, long, and char. Typically, you use the inserter operator >> to obtain input for the predefined data types. The programs presented so far use the >> operator to enter a single item. C++ streams enable you to chain the >> operator to enter multiple items. In the case of multiple items, you need to observe the following rules:

1. Enter a space between two consecutive numbers to separate them.

2. Entering a space between two consecutive chars is optional.

3. Entering a space between a char and a number (or vice versa) is necessary only if the char is a digit.

4. The input stream ignores spaces.

5. You can enter multiple items on different lines. The stream-input statements are not fully executed until they obtain all the specified input.

Look at a program that illustrates both the input of multiple items and different combinations of data types. Listing 7.2 shows the source code for the program IN1.CPP. The program performs the following tasks:

☐ Prompts you to enter three numbers

☐ Calculates the sum of the three numbers

☐ Displays the sum and the average of the three numbers you entered

☐ Prompts you to type in three characters

☐ Displays your input

☐ Prompts you to enter a number, a character, and a number

☐ Displays your input

☐ Prompts you to enter a character, a number, and a character

☐ Displays your input

Listing 7.2. Source code for the program IN1.CPP.

```
1:  // Program that illustrates standard stream input
2:
3:  #include <iostream.h>
4:
5:  main()
6:  {
7:    double x, y, z, sum;
8:    char c1, c2, c3;
9:
10:   cout << "Enter three numbers separated by a space : ";
11:   cin >> x >> y >> z;
12:   sum = x + y + z;
13:   cout << "Sum of numbers = " << sum
14:        << "\nAverage of numbers = " << sum / 2 << "\n";
15:   cout << "Enter three characters : ";
16:   cin >> c1 >> c2 >> c3;
17:   cout << "You entered characters '" << c1
18:        << "', '" << c2 << "', and '"
19:        << c3 << "'\n";
20:   cout << "Enter a number, a character, and a number : ";
21:   cin >> x >> c1 >> y;
22:   cout << "You entered " << x << " " << c1 << " " << y << "\n";
23:   cout << "Enter a character, a number, and a character : ";
24:   cin >> c1 >> x >> c2;
25:   cout << "You entered " << c1 << " " << x << " " << c2 << "\n";
26:
27:   return 0;
28: }
```

Here is a sample session with the program in Listing 7.2.

```
Enter three numbers separated by a space : 1 2 3
Sum of numbers = 6
Average of numbers = 3
Enter three characters : ABC
You entered characters 'A', 'B', and 'C'
Enter a number, a character, and a number : 12A34.4
You entered 12 A 34.4
Enter a character, a number, and a character : A3.14Z
You entered A 3.14 Z
```

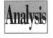

The program in Listing 7.2 declares four double-typed variables and three char-typed variables. The output statement in line 10 prompts you to enter three numbers. The input statement in line 11 obtains your input and stores the numbers in variables x, y, and z. You need to enter a space character between any two numbers. You also can enter each number on a separate line. The statement stores the first number you enter in variable x, the second number

209

in variable y, and the third one in variable z. This sequence is determined by the sequence in which these variables appear in line 11. The statement in line 12 calculates the sum of the values in variables x, y, and z. The output statement in lines 13 and 14 displays the sum and average of the numbers that you entered.

The output statement in line 15 prompts you to enter three characters. The input statement in line 16 obtains your input and sequentially stores the characters in variables c1, c2, and c3. Your input need not separate the characters with a space. Thus, you can type in characters such as 1A2, Bob, and 1   D   d. The output statement in lines 17 through 19 displays the characters that you type, separated by spaces.

The output statement in line 20 prompts you to enter a number, a character, and a number. The input statement in line 21 sequentially stores your input in variables x, c1, and y. You need to type a space between the character and either of the numbers only if the character can be interpreted as part of either number. For example, if you want to enter the number 12, the dot character, and the number 55, type 12 . 55. The spaces around the dot ensure that the input stream does not consider it as a decimal part of either floating-point number. The output statement in line 22 displays the values you entered, separated by spaces.

The output statement in line 23 prompts you to enter a character, a number, and a character. The input statement in line 24 sequentially stores your input in variables c1, x, and c2. You need to enter a space between the characters and the number only if the characters can be interpreted as part of the number. For example, if you want to enter the character -, the number 12, and the digit 0, type - 12 0. The output statement in line 25 displays the values you entered, separated by spaces.

The *printf* Function

As a novice C++ programmer, you have a wealth of I/O functions from which to choose. This section discusses the formatting features of the function printf, which is part of the standard I/O of C. The function is prototyped in the header file STDIO.H.

The printf function offers much power and presents formatted controls. The general syntax for the individual formatting instruction is

```
% [flags] [width] [.precision] [F ¦[]¦ h ¦ l] <type character>
```

The *flags* options indicate the output justification, numeric signs, decimal points, and trailing zeros. In addition, these flags also specify the octal and hexadecimal prefixes. Table 7.1 shows the options for the flags in the format string of the printf function.

The *width* option indicates the minimum number of displayed characters. The printf function uses zeros and blanks to pad the output if needed. When the width number begins with a 0, the printf function uses leading zeros, instead of spaces, for padding. When the * character appears instead of a width number, the printf function obtains the actual width number from the function's argument list. The argument that specifies the required width must come before the argument that actually is being formatted. The following is an example that displays the integer 3 using 2 characters, as specified by the third argument of printf:

```
printf("%*d", 3, 2);
```

The *precision* option specifies the maximum number of displayed characters. If you include an integer, the precision option defines the minimum number of displayed digits. When the * character is used in place of a precision number, the printf function obtains the actual precision from the argument list. The argument that specifies the required precision must come before the argument that is actually being formatted. The following is an example that displays the floating-point number 3.3244 using 10 characters, as specified by the third argument of printf:

```
printf("%7.*f", 10, 3.3244);
```

The F, N, h, and l options are sized options used to overrule the argument's default size. The F and [ ] options are used in conjunction with far and near pointers, respectively. The h and l options are used to indicate short int or long, respectively.

Table 7.1. The escape sequence.

Sequence	Decimal Value	Hex Value	Task
\a	7	0×07	Bell
\b	8	0×08	Backspace
\f	12	0×0C	Formfeed
\n	10	0×0A	New line
\r	13	0×0D	Carriage return
\t	9	0×09	Horizontal tab
\v	11	0×0B	Vertical tab
\\	92	0×5C	Backslash
\'	44	0×2C	Single quote
\"	34	0×22	Double quote
\?	63	0×3F	Question mark
\000			1 to 3 digits for octal value
\Xhhh and \xhhh		0×hhh	Hexadecimal value

The printf function requires that you specify a data type character with each % format code. Table 7.2 shows the options for the flags in the format string of printf. Table 7.3 shows the data type characters used in the format string of printf.

7

Table 7.2. Options for the flags in the format string of the `printf` function.

Format Option	Outcome
-	Justifies to the left within the specified field
+	Displays the plus or minus sign of a value
blank	Displays a leading blank if the value is positive; displays a minus sign if the value is negative
#	No effect on decimal integers; displays a leading 0X or 0x for hexadecimal integers; displays a leading zero for octal integers; displays the decimal point for reals

Table 7.3. Data type characters used in the format string of `printf`.

Category	Type Character	Outcome
Character	c	Single character
	d	Signed decimal int
	i	Signed decimal int
	o	Unsigned octal int
	u	Unsigned decimal int
	x	Unsigned hexadecimal int; the set of numeric characters used is 01234567890abcdef (note the lowercase letters)
	X	Unsigned hexadecimal int; the set of numeric characters used is 01234567890ABCDEF (note the uppercase letters)
Pointer	p	Displays only the offset for near pointers as 0000; displays far pointers as SSSS:0000
Pointer to int	n	
Real	f	Displays signed value in the format [-]dddd.dddd
	e	Displays signed scientific value in the format [-]d.dddde[+¦-]ddd
	E	Displays signed scientific value in the format [-]d.ddddE[+¦-]ddd

Category	Type Character	Outcome
	g	Displays signed value using either the f or e formats, depending on the value and the specified precision
	G	Displays signed value using either the f or E formats, depending on the value and the specified precision
String pointer	s	Displays characters until the null terminator of the string is reached

Note: Although the function printf plays no role in the output of Windows applications, its sister function, sprintf, does. The latter function creates a string of characters that contains the formatted image of the output. The sprintf function is discussed in a later lesson in which you create a dialog box that contains messages that include numbers.

Consider a simple example. Listing 7.3 shows the source code for the program OUT2.CPP. This program was created by editing the OUT1.CPP in Listing 7.1. The new version displays formatted output using the printf function. The program displays the same floating-point numbers using three different sets of format code.

Listing 7.3. Source code for the program OUT2.CPP.

```
1: // C++ program that uses the printf function for formatted output
2:
3: #include <stdio.h>
4:
5: main()
6: {
7:     short     aShort     = 4;
8:     int       anInt      = 67;
9:     unsigned char aByte = 128;
10:    char      aChar      = '@';
11:    float     aSingle    = 355.0;
12:    double    aDouble     = 1.130e+002;
13:    // display sample expressions
14:    printf("%3d %c %2d = %3d\n",
15:            aByte, '+', anInt, aByte + anInt);
16:
17:    printf("Output uses the %%lf format\n");
18:    printf("%6.4f / %6.4lf = %7.5lf\n", aSingle, aDouble,
19:                                aSingle / aDouble);
20:    printf("Output uses the %%le format\n");
```

Listing 7.3. continued

```
21:    printf("%6.4e / %6.4le = %7.5le\n", aSingle, aDouble,
22:                                        aSingle / aDouble);
23:    printf("Output uses the %%lg format\n");
24:    printf("%6.4g / %6.4lg = %7.5lg\n", aSingle, aDouble,
25:                                        aSingle / aDouble);
26:
27:    printf("The character in variable aChar is %c\n", aChar);
28:    printf("The ASCII code of %c is %d\n", aChar, aChar);
29:      return 0;
30: }
```

Here is a sample session with the program in Listing 7.3.

```
128 + 67 = 195
Output uses the %lf format
355.0000 / 113.0000 = 3.14159
Output uses the %le format
3.5500e+002 / 1.1300e+002 = 3.14159e+000
Output uses the %lg format
355 / 113 = 3.1416
The character in variable aChar is @
The ASCII code of @ is 64
```

The program in Listing 7.3 declares a collection of variables with different data types. The output statement in lines 14 and 15 displays integers and characters using the %d and %c format controls. Table 7.4 shows the effect of the various format controls in the printf statement at line 14. Notice that the printf function converts the first item in output from an unsigned char to an int.

Table 7.4. Effects of the various format controls in the printf statement at line 16.

Format Control	Item	Data Type	Output
%3d	aByte	unsigned char	Integer
%c	'+'	char	Character
%2d	anInt	int	Integer
%3d	aByte + anInt	int	Integer

The output statement in line 18 displays the variable aSingle, the variable aDouble, and the expression aSingle / aDouble using the format controls %6.4f, %6.4lf and %7.5lf. These controls specify precision values of 4, 4, and 5 digits, respectively, and minimum widths of 6, 6, and 7 characters, respectively. The last two format controls indicate that they display a double-typed value.

The output statement in line 21 is similar to that in line 18. The main difference is that the printf in line 21 uses the e format rather than the f format. Consequently, the three items in the printf statement appear in scientific notation.

The output statement in line 24 is similar to that in line 18. The main difference is that the printf in line 24 uses the g format instead of the f format. Consequently, the first two items in the printf statement appear with no decimal places because they are whole numbers.

The output statement in line 27 displays the contents in the variable aChar using the %c format control. The output statement in line 28 displays the contents of variable aChar twice: once as a character and once as an integer (or, to be more exact, the ASCII code of a character). The printf function in line 28 performs this task by using the %c and %d format controls, respectively.

C++ Strings An Overview

C++ (and its parent language C) has no predefined string type. Instead, C++, like C, regards strings as arrays of characters that end with the ASCII 0 null character ('\0').

NEW☞ TERM The '\0' character also is called the *null terminator*. Strings that end with the null terminator sometimes are called *ASCIIZ strings*, with the letter Z standing for zero, the ASCII code of the null terminator. You also will see this character referred to as the NUL character as that's the ASCII name for it.

The null terminator *must* be present in all strings and taken into account when declaring space for a string. When you declare a string variable as an array of characters, be sure to reserve an extra character for the null terminator. The advantage of using the null terminator is that you can create strings that are not restricted by any limit imposed by the C++ implementation. In addition, ASCIIZ strings have very simple structures.

Note: The lesson in Day 4 discusses how pointers can access and manipulate the elements of an array. C and C++ make extensive use of this programming feature in manipulating the characters of a string.

7

DO	**DON'T**

DO include an extra character for the null terminator when specifying the size of a string.

DON'T declare a string variable as a single-character array. Such a variable is useless.

String Input

The programs presented thus far display string literals in output stream statements; C++ supports stream output for strings as a special case for a nonpredefined data type. (You can say the support came by popular demand.) String output using string variables uses the same operator and syntax. With string input, the output operator >> does not work well because strings often contain spaces that are ignored by the output operator. Instead of the output operator, you need to use the getline function. This function reads up to a specified number of characters.

The *getline* Function

The general syntax for the overloaded getline function is

```
istream& getline(signed char* buffer,
int size,
char delimiter = '\n');

istream& getline(unsigned char* buffer,
                int size,
                char delimiter = '\n');

istream& getline(char* buffer,
                int size,
                char delimiter = '\n');
```

The parameter buffer is a pointer to the string receiving the characters from the stream. The parameter size specifies the maximum number of characters to read. The parameter delimiter specifies the delimiting character that causes the string input to stop before reaching the number of characters specified by parameter size. The parameter delimiter has the default argument of '\n', which means that input will end when that character is reached; in the case of a person typing, this character will manifest itself when the person presses the Enter key.

Example

```
#include <iostream.h>
main()
{
    char name[80];
    cout << "Enter your name: ";
    cin.getline(name, sizeof(name)-1);
    cout << "Hello " << name << ", how are you";
    return 0;
}
```

Using the STRING.H Library

The community of C programmers has developed the standard string library STRING.H, which contains the most frequently used string-manipulation functions. The STDIO.H and IOSTREAM.H header file prototype functions also support string I/O. The ANSI/ISO C++

committee has also developed a C++-style string class. This class models strings more in line with the way Pascal and BASIC use them. (You learn more about classes on Day 8 and the C++ string class on Day 10.) The next sections present several (but by no means all) of the functions that are prototyped in the STRING.H header file.

Some of the string functions in STRING.H have more than one version. The extra versions that prepend the characters _f, f, or _ to the function name work with strings that are specifically accessed using far pointers.

Assigning Strings

C++ supports two methods for assigning strings. You can assign a string literal to a string variable when you initialize it. This method is simple and requires using the = operator and the assigning string.

Syntax

Initializing a String

The general syntax for initializing a string is

```
char stringVar[stringSize] = stringLiteral;
```

Example

```
char aString[81] = "Turbo C++ 4.5 in 21 days";
char name[] = "Rene Kinner";
```

The second method for assigning one ASCIIZ string to another actually is just a function that copies the contents of one array to the other, being mindful of the null character on the end of the string—the function strcpy. This function assumes that the copied string ends with null character and stops copying when it's reached.

Syntax

The *strcpy* Function

The prototype for the function strcpy is

```
char* strcpy(char* target, const char* source)
```

The function copies the characters from string source to string target. The function *assumes* that the target string has enough space to contain the source string.

Example

```
char name[41];
strcpy(name,"Turbo C++ 4.5");
```

The variable name contains the string "Turbo C++ 4.5".

The function strdup enables you to copy the characters to another string and allocate required space in the target string.

7

Syntax

The *strdup* Function

The prototype for the function `strdup` is

```
char* strdup(const char* source)
```

The function copies the characters in the source string and returns a pointer to the duplicate string.

Example

```
char* string1 = "The reign in Spain";
char* string2;

string2 = strdup(string1);
```

This example copies the contents of `string1` into `string2` after allocating the memory space for `string2`.

Note: Because `strdup` allocates memory for the new string, you will have to remember to free it later on. This is a nasty "gotcha" that catches a lot of programmers, both novice and expert.

The string library also offers the function `strncpy` to support copying a specified number of characters from one string to another.

Syntax

The *strncpy* Function

The prototype for the function `strncpy` is

```
char* strncpy(char* target, const char* source, size_t num);
```

The function copies *num* characters from the `source` string to the `target` string. Note that the function doesn't perform any character truncation or padding.

Example

```
char str1[] = "Pascal";
char str2[] = "Hello there";

strncpy(str1, str2, 5);
```

The variable `str1` now contains the string `"Hellol"`. Note how the `'l'` from the original string is still in there after the part that we copied.

Using `strncpy` often is preferred over using `strcpy`. The reason, of course, is to make sure that you don't copy more from the source string than there is room in the target string. If, for example, the target was created with room for only 20 characters and then you do a `strcpy` that moves 40 characters, you run the risk of corrupting memory and causing those nifty Windows GPFs.

Note: Using pointers to manipulate strings is a new idea to many novice C++ programmers. In fact, you can use pointers to manipulate the trailing parts of a string by assigning the address of the first character to manipulate. For example, if we declare the string str1 as follows:

```
char str1[41] = "Hello World";
char str2[41];
char* p = str1;

p += 6; // p now points to substring "World" in str
strcpy(str2, p);
cout << str2 << "\n";
```

the output statement displays the string "World". This example shows how using pointers can incorporate an offset number of characters.

The Length of a String

Many string operations require information about the number of characters in a string. The STRING.H library offers the function strlen to return the number of characters, excluding the null terminator, in a string.

Syntax

The *strlen* Function

The prototype for the function strlen is

```
size_t strlen(const char* string)
```

The function strlen returns the number of characters in the parameter string. The result type size_t has a typedef of an unsigned int type.

Example

```
char str[] = "1234567890";
size_t i;
i = strlen(str);
```

These statements assign 10 to the variable i.

7

Concatenating Strings

Often, you build a string by concatenating two or more strings. The function strcat enables you to concatenate one string to another.

NEW☞ TERM When you *concatenate* strings, you join or link them together.

The *strcat* Function

The prototype for the function strcat is

```
char* strcat(char* target, const char* source)
```

The function appends the contents of the source string to the target string and returns the pointer to the target string. The function *assumes* that the target string can accommodate the characters of the source string.

Example

```
char string[81];
strcpy(string, "Turbo");
strcat(string," C++ 4.5")
```

The variable string now contains "Turbo C++ 4.5".

The function strncat concatenates a specified number of characters from the source string to the target strings.

The *strncat* Function

The prototype for the function strncat is

```
char* strncat(char* target, const char* source, size_t num)
```

The function appends *num* characters of the source string to the target string and returns the pointer to the target string.

Example

```
char str1[81] = "Hello I am ";
char str2[41] = "Keith Thompson";

strncat(str1, str2, 5);
```

The variable str1 now contains "Hello I am Keith".

DO	**DON'T**

DO use the function strncat to control the number of concatenated characters, when you are unsure of the capacity of the target string.

DON'T assume that the target string is always adequate to store the characters in the source string.

Look at a program that uses the getline, strlen, and strcat functions. Listing 7.4 contains the source code for the program STRING1.CPP. The program performs the following tasks:

☐ Prompts you to enter a string; your input should not exceed 40 characters

☐ Prompts you to enter a second string; your input should not exceed 40 characters

☐ Displays the number of characters in each of the strings you enter

☐ Concatenates the second string to the first one

☐ Displays the concatenated strings

☐ Displays the number of characters in the concatenated strings

☐ Prompts you to enter a search character

☐ Prompts you to enter a replacement character

☐ Displays the concatenated string after translating all the occurrences of the search character with the replacement character

Listing 7.4. Source code for the program STRING1.CPP.

```
1:  /*
2:    C++ program that demonstrates C-style strings
3:  */
4:
5:  #include <iostream.h>
6:  #include <string.h>
7:
8:  const unsigned MAX1 = 40;
9:  const unsigned MAX2 = 80;
10:
11: int main()
12: {
13:
14:     char smallStr[MAX1+1];
15:     char bigStr[MAX2+1];
16:     char findChar, replChar;
17:
18:     cout << "Enter first string:\n";
19:     cin.getline(bigStr, MAX2);
20:     cout << "Enter second string:\n";
21:     cin.getline(smallStr, MAX1);
22:     cout << "String 1 has " << strlen(bigStr)
23:          << " characters\n";
24:     cout << "String 2 has " << strlen(smallStr)
25:          << " characters\n";
26:     // concatenate bigStr to smallStr
27:     strcat(bigStr, smallStr);
28:     cout << "Concatenated strings are:\n"
29:          << bigStr << "\n";
30:     cout << "New string has " << strlen(bigStr)
31:          << " characters\n";
32:     // get the search and replacement characters
33:     cout << "Enter search character : ";
```

Listing 7.4. continued

```
34:     cin >> findChar;
35:     cout << "Enter replacement character : ";
36:     cin >> replChar;
37:     // replace characters in string bigStr
38:     size_t bigLen = strlen(bigStr);
39:     for (unsigned i = 0; i < bigLen; i++)
40:       if (bigStr[i] == findChar)
41:         bigStr[i] = replChar;
42:     // display the updated string bigStr
43:     cout << "New string is:\n"
44:          << bigStr;
45:     return 0;
46: }
```

Here is a sample session with the program in Listing 7.4.

```
Enter first string:
The rain in Spain stays
Enter second string:
mainly in the plain
String 1 has 23 characters
String 2 has 20 characters
Concatenated strings are:
The rain in Spain stays mainly in the plain
New string has 43 characters
Enter search character : a
Enter replacement character : A
New string is:
The rAin in SpAin stAys mAinly in the plAin
```

The program in Listing 7.4 includes the STRING.H header file for the string manipulation functions. Lines 8 and 9 declare the global constants MAX1 and MAX2, which are used to size a small string and a big string, respectively. The function main declares two strings, smallStr and bigStr. Line 14 declares the variable smallStr to store MAX1+1 characters. (The extra space is for the null character.) Line 15 declares the variable bigStr to store MAX2+1 characters. Line 16 declares the char-typed variable findChar and replChar.

The output statement in line 18 prompts you to enter the first string. The statement in line 19 uses the stream input function getline to obtain your input and to store it in variable bigStr. The function call specifies that you can enter up to MAX2 characters. The output statement in line 20 prompts you to enter the second string. The statement in line 21 uses the stream input function getline to obtain your input and to store it in the variable smallStr. The function call specifies that you can enter up to MAX1 characters.

The output statements in lines 22 through 25 display the number of characters in variables bigStr and smallStr, respectively. Each output statement calls function strlen and passes it a string variable.

The statement in line 27 concatenates the string in the variable smallStr to the variable bigStr. The output statement in lines 28 and 29 displays the updated string bigStr. The output statement in lines 30 and 31 displays the number of characters in the updated string variable bigStr. This statement also uses the function strlen to obtain the number of characters.

The statement in line 33 prompts you to enter the search character. The statement in line 34 obtains your input and stores it in variable findChar. The statement in line 35 prompts you to enter the replacement character. The statement in line 36 obtains your input and stores it in variable replChar.

The for loop in lines 38 to 41 translates the characters in string bigStr. The loop uses the control variable i and iterates, in increments of 1, from 0 to bigLen-1 (which is set on line 38 to be strlen(bigStr)). The if statement in line 40 determines whether character number i in bigStr matches the character in variable findChar. If this condition is true, the program executes the statement in line 41. This statement assigns the character in variable replChar to character number i in variable bigStr. This loop shows how you can manipulate the contents of a string variable by accessing each character in that string.

The output statement in lines 43 and 44 displays the updated string bigStr.

String Comparison

Because strings are arrays of characters, you can't just simply use the == or != operators (or > and <, for that matter) to test for equality. The STRING.H library provides a set of functions to compare strings. These functions compare the characters of two strings using the ASCII value of each character. The functions are strcmp, stricmp, strncmp, and strnicmp.

In general, all the comparison functions return 0 if the two strings compare equally, a negative value if the second string in the comparison is greater, or a positive value if the first string is greater.

The function strcmp performs a case-sensitive comparison of two strings, using every character possible.

The *strcmp* Function

The prototype for the function strcmp is

```
int strcmp(const char* str1, const char* str2);
```

The function compares strings *str1* and *str2*. The integer result indicates the outcome of the comparison.

```
< 0   when str1 is less than str2
= 0   when str1 is equal to str2
> 0   when str1 is greater than str2
```

Example

```
char string1[] = "Turbo C++ 4.5";
char string2[] = "TURBO C++ 4.5";
int i;

i = strcmp(string1, string2);
```

The last statement assigns a positive number to the variable i, because the string in variable string1 is greater than the string in variable string2 (lowercase actually is greater than uppercase in ASCII).

The function stricmp performs a case-insensitive comparison between two strings, using every character possible.

The *stricmp* Function

Syntax

The prototype for the function stricmp is

```
int stricmp(const char* str1, const char* str2);
```

The function compares strings *str1* and *str2* without making a distinction between upper- and lowercase characters. The integer result indicates the outcome of the comparison.

```
< 0   when str1 is less than str2
= 0   when str1 is equal to str2
> 0   when str1 is greater than str2
```

Example

```
char string1[] = "Turbo C++ 4.5";
char string2[] = "TURBO C++ 4.5";
int i;

i = stricmp(string1, string2);
```

The last statement assigns 0 to the variable i because the strings in variables string1 and string2 differ only in their cases.

The function strncmp performs a case-sensitive comparison on specified leading characters in two strings.

The *strncmp* Function

Syntax

The prototype for the function strncmp is

```
int strncmp(const char* str1, const char* str2, size_t num);
```

The function compares the *num* leading characters in two strings, *str1* and *str2*. The integer result indicates the outcome of the comparison, as follows:

```
< 0   when str1 is less than str2
```

```
= 0   when str1 is equal to str2
> 0   when str1 is greater than str2
```

Example

```
char string1[] = "Turbo C++ 4.5";
char string2[] = "Turbo Pascal";
int i;

i = strncmp(string1, string2, 7);
```

This assigns a negative number to the variable i because `"Turbo C"` is less than `"Turbo P"`.

The function `strnicmp` performs a case-insensitive comparison on specified leading characters in two strings.

The *strnicmp* Function

Syntax

The prototype for the function `strnicmp` is

```
int strnicmp(const char* str1, const char* str2, size_t num);
```

The function compares the *num* leading characters in two strings, *str1* and *str2*, regardless of the character case. The integer result indicates the outcome of the comparison, as follows:

```
< 0   when str1 is less than str2
= 0   when str1 is equal to str2
> 0   when str1 is greater than str2
```

Example

```
char string1[] = "Turbo C++ 4.5";
char string2[] = "TURBO Pascal";
int i;

i = strnicmp(string1, string2, 5);
```

This assigns `0` to the variable i because the strings `"Turbo"` and `"TURBO"` differ only in the case of their characters.

Look at an example that compares strings. Listing 7.5 creates an array of strings and initializes it with data. Then the program displays the unordered array of strings, sorts the array, and displays the sorted array.

Listing 7.5. Source code for the program STRING2.CPP.

```
1:  /*
2:     C++ program that demonstrates comparing strings
3:  */
4:
5:  #include <iostream.h>
6:  #include <string.h>
7:
```

continues

225

Listing 7.5. continued

```
8:  const unsigned STR_SIZE = 40;
9:  const unsigned ARRAY_SIZE = 11;
10: const int TRUE = 1;
11: const int FALSE = 0;
12:
13: main()
14: {
15:
16:     char strArr[STR_SIZE][ARRAY_SIZE] =
17:         { "California", "Virginia", "Alaska", "New York",
18:             "Michigan", "Nevada", "Ohio", "Florida",
19:             "Washington", "Oregon", "Arizona" };
20:     char temp[STR_SIZE];
21:     unsigned[]= ARRAY_SIZE;
22:     unsigned offset;
23:     int inOrder;
24:
25:     cout << "Unordered array of strings is:\n";
26:     for (unsigned i = 0; i < ARRAY_SIZE; i++)
27:       cout << strArr[i] << "\n";
28:
29:     cout << "\nEnter a non-space character and press Enter";
30:     cin >> temp[0];
31:     cout << "\n";
32:
33:     offset = n;
34:     do {
35:       offset = (8 * offset) / 11;
36:       offset = (offset == 0) ? 1 : offset;
37:       inOrder = TRUE;
38:       for (unsigned i = 0, j = offset;
39:             i <[]- offset; i++, j++)
40:         if (strcmp(strArr[i], strArr[j]) > 0) {
41:           strcpy(temp, strArr[i]);
42:           strcpy(strArr[i], strArr[j]);
43:           strcpy(strArr[j], temp);
44:           inOrder = FALSE;
45:         }
46:     } while (!(offset == 1 && inOrder));
47:
48:     cout << "Sorted array of strings is:\n";
49:     for (i = 0; i < ARRAY_SIZE; i++)
50:       cout << strArr[i] << "\n";
51:     return 0;
52: }
```

Here is a sample session with the program in Listing 7.5.

```
Unordered array of strings is:
California
Virginia
Alaska
New York
```

```
Michigan
Nevada
Ohio
Florida
Washington
Oregon
Arizona
Enter a non-space character and press Enterc
Sorted array of strings is:
Alaska
Arizona
California
Florida
Michigan
Nevada
New York
Ohio
Oregon
Virginia
Washington
```

 The program in Listing 7.5 declares the global constants STR_SIZE, ARRAY_SIZE, TRUE, and FALSE in lines 8 through 11. The constant STR_SIZE specifies the size of each string. The constant ARRAY_SIZE indicates the number of strings in the array used by the program. The constants TRUE and FALSE represent the Boolean values employed in sorting the array of strings. The function main declares the array strArr (actually, the variable strArr is a matrix of characters) to have ARRAY_SIZE elements and STR_SIZE characters per elements. Notice that the declaration states the size of each string in the first dimension and the size of the array in the second dimension. The function also initializes the array strArr. The function also declares the variable temp as a swap buffer. Lines 21 through 23 declare miscellaneous variables.

The output statement in line 25 shows the title before showing the elements of the unordered array strArr. The for loop in lines 26 and 27 displays the elements. The loop uses the control variable i and iterates, in increments of 1, from 0 to ARRAY_SIZE-1. The output statement in line 27 displays the string at element i, using the expression strArr[i].

The output and input statements in lines 29 and 30 prompt you to enter a nonspace character. This input enables you to examine the unordered array before the program sorts the array and displays its ordered elements.

The statements in lines 33 through 46 implement the Comb sort method. Notice that the if statement in line 40 uses the function strcmp to compare elements number i and j, accessed using the expressions strArr[i] and strArr[j], respectively. The statements in lines 41 through 43 swap the elements i and j, using the function strcpy and the swap buffer temp.

The output statement in line 48 displays the title before showing the elements of the sorted array. The for loop in lines 49 and 50 displays these elements. The loop utilizes the control variable i and iterates, in increments of 1, from 0 to ARRAY_SIZE-1. The output statement in line 50 displays the string at element i, using the expression strArr[i].

Converting Strings

The STRING.H library offers the functions _strlwr and _strupr to convert the characters of a string to lowercase and uppercase, respectively. Note that these functions are more commonly called strlwr and strupr (without the leading underscore character) in C textbooks. I'm showing it with the leading underscore because it's not an ANSI/ISO standard function (probably because it's so trivial to write it on your own). But it's useful enough to mention here.

The _strlwr Function

The prototype for the function _strlwr is

```
char* _strlwr(char* source)
```

The function converts the uppercase characters in the string *source* to lowercase. Other characters are not affected. The function also returns the pointer to the string *source*.

Example

```
char str[] = "HELLO THERE";

_strlwr(str);
```

The variable str now contains the string "hello there".

The _strupr Function

The prototype for the function _strupr is

```
char* _strupr(char* source)
```

The function converts the lowercase characters in the string *source* to uppercase. Other characters are not affected. The function also returns the pointer to the string *source*.

Example

```
char str[] = "Turbo C++ 4.5";
_strupr(str);
```

The variable str now contains the string "TURBO C++ 4.5".

DO	DON'T

DO make copies for the arguments of functions _strlwr and _strupr if you need the original arguments later in a program.

DON'T always assume that applying the function _strlwr and then the function _strupr (or vice versa) to the same variable will succeed in restoring the original characters in that variable.

Reversing Strings

The STRING.H library offers the function strrev to reverse the characters in a string.

Syntax

The *strrev* Function

The prototype for the function strrev is

```
char* strrev(char* str)
```

The function reverses the order of the characters in string str and returns the pointer to the string str.

Example

```
char string[] = "Hello";

strrev(string);
cout << string;
```

This displays "olleH".

Look at a program that manipulates the characters in a string. Listing 7.6 shows the source code for the program STRING3.CPP. The program performs the following tasks:

☐ Prompts you to enter a string

☐ Displays your input

☐ Displays the lowercase version of your input

☐ Displays the uppercase version of your input

☐ Displays the character you typed, in reverse order

☐ Displays a message that your input has no uppercase character, if this is true

☐ Displays a message that your input has no lowercase character, if this is true

☐ Displays a message that your input has symmetrical characters, if this is true

Listing 7.6. Source code for the program STRING3.CPP.

```
1: /*
2:   C++ program that demonstrates manipulating the
3:   characters in a string
4: */
5:
6: #include <iostream.h>
7: #include <string.h>
8:
9:  const unsigned STR_SIZE = 40;
10: const int TRUE = 1;
11: const int FALSE = 0;
12:
13: main()
14: {
```

Listing 7.6. continued

```
15:     char str1[STR_SIZE+1];
16:     char str2[STR_SIZE+1];
17:     int isLowerCase;
18:     int isUpperCase;
19:     int isSymmetrical;
20:
21:
22:     cout << "Enter a string : ";
23:     cin.getline(str1, STR_SIZE);
24:     cout << "Input: " << str1 << "\n";
25:     // copy str1 to str2
26:     strcpy(str2, str1);
27:     // convert to lowercase
28:     strlwr(str2);
29:     isLowerCase = (strcmp(str1, str2) == 0) ? TRUE : FALSE;
30:     cout << "Lowercase: " << str2 << "\n";
31:     // convert to uppercase
32:     strupr(str2);
33:     isUpperCase = (strcmp(str1, str2) == 0) ? TRUE : FALSE;
34:     cout << "Uppercase: " << str2 << "\n";
35:     // copy str1 to str2
36:     strcpy(str2, str1);
37:     // reverse characters
38:     strrev(str2);
39:     isSymmetrical = (strcmp(str1, str2) == 0) ? TRUE : FALSE;
40:     cout << "Reversed: " << str2 << "\n";
41:     if (isLowerCase)
42:       cout << "Your input has no uppercase letters\n";
43:     if (isUpperCase)
44:       cout << "Your input has no lowercase letters\n";
45:     if (isSymmetrical)
46:       cout << "Your input has symmetrical characters\n";
47:     return 0;
48: }
```

Here is a sample session with the program in Listing 7.6.

```
Enter a string : level
Input: level
Lowercase: level
Uppercase: LEVEL
Reversed: level
Your input has no uppercase letters
Your input has symmetrical characters
```

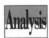

The program in Listing 7.6 declares the string variables str1 and str2 in the function main. Each string stores STR_SIZE + 1 characters (including the null terminator). The function also declares the flags isLowerCase, isUpperCase, and isSymmetrical.

The output statement in line 22 prompts you to enter a string. The statement in line 23 uses the string input function getline to store your input in variable str1. The output statement in line 24 echoes your input.

The statement in line 26 copies the characters in variable str1 to variable str2. The statement in line 26 calls the function strlwr to convert the characters in variable str2. The program manipulates the characters of variable str2, while maintaining the original input in variable str1. The statement in line 29 calls the function strcmp to compare the characters in str1 and str2. The two strings can be equal only if your input has no uppercase characters. The statement uses the conditional operator to assign the constant TRUE to the flag isLowerCase if the above condition is true. Otherwise, the statement assigns FALSE to the flag isLowerCase. The output statement in line 30 displays the characters in variable str2.

The statement in line 32 calls the function strupr and supplies it the argument str2. This function call converts any lowercase character in variable str2 into uppercase. The statement in line 33 calls the function strcmp to compare the characters in str1 and str2. The two strings can be equal only if your input has no lowercase characters. The statement uses the conditional operator to assign the constant TRUE to the flag isUpperCase if that is true. Otherwise, the statement assigns FALSE to the flag isUpperCase. The output statement in line 34 displays the characters in variable str2.

To display the original input in reverse order, the program calls the function strcpy to copy the characters of variable str1 to variable str2 once more. The statement in line 38 calls the function strrev and passes it the argument str2. The statement in line 39 calls the function strcmp to compare the characters in str1 and str2. The two strings can be equal only if your input has symmetrical characters. The statement uses the conditional operator to assign the constant TRUE to the flag isSymmetrical if the characters in str1 and str2 match. Otherwise, the statement assigns FALSE to the flag isSymmetrical. The output statement in line 40 displays the characters in variable str2.

The program uses the if statements in lines 41, 43, and 45 to indicate that your input has special characteristics. The if statement in line 41 comments on the fact that your input has no uppercase letter when the value in variable isLowerCase is TRUE. The if statement in line 43 comments on the fact that your input has no lowercase letter when the value in variable isUpperCase is TRUE. The if statement in line 45 comments on the fact that your input has symmetrical characters when the value in variable isSymmetrical is TRUE.

Locating Characters

The STRING.H library offers a number of functions for locating characters in strings. These functions include strchr, strrchr, strspn, strcspn, and strpbrk. These functions enable you to search for characters and simple character patterns in strings.

The function strchr locates the first occurrence of a character in a string.

The *strchr* Function

The prototype for the function strchr is

```
char* strchr(const char* target, int c)
```

The function locates the first occurrence of pattern c in the string target. The function returns   231 the pointer to the character in string *target* that matches the specified pattern *c*. If character *c* does not occur in the string *target*, the function yields a NULL.

Example

```
char str[81] = "Turbo C++ 4.5";
char* strPtr;

strPtr = strchr(str, '+');
```

The pointer strPtr points to the substring "++ 4.5" in string str.

The function strrchr locates the last occurrence of a character in a string.

The *strrchr* Function

Syntax

The prototype for the function strrchr is

```
char* strrchr(const char* target, int c)
```

The function locates the last occurrence of pattern *c* in the string *target*. The function returns the pointer to the character in string *target* that matches the specified pattern *c*. If character *c* does not occur in the string *target*, the function yields a NULL.

Example

```
char str[81] = "Turbo C++ 4.5 is here";
char* strPtr;

strPtr = strrchr(str, '+');
```

The pointer strPtr points to the substring "+ 4.5 is here" in string str.

The function strspn yields the number of characters in the leading part of a string that matches any character in a pattern of characters.

The *strspn* Function

Syntax

The prototype for the function strspn is

```
size_t strspn(const char* target, const char* pattern)
```

The function returns the number of characters in the leading part of the string *target* that matches any character in the string *pattern*.

Example

```
char str[] = "Turbo C++ 4.5";
char substr[] = "bruTo ";
int index;
```

```
index = strspn(str, substr);
```

This statement assigns 6 to the variable `index` because the characters in `substr` found a match in each of the first six characters of `str`.

The function `strcspn` scans a string and yields the number of leading characters in a string that is totally void of the characters in a substring.

The *strcspn* Function

Syntax

The prototype for the function `strcspn` is

```
size_t strcspn(const char* str1, const char* str2)
```

The function scans *str1* and returns the length of the leftmost substring that is totally void of the characters of the substring *str2*.

Example

```
char strng[] = "The rain in Spain";
int i;

i = strcspn(strng, " in");
```

This example assigns 3 (the location of the first space) to the variable `i`.

The function `strpbrk` searches a string for the first occurrence of any character in a pattern of characters.

The *strpbrk* Function

Syntax

The prototype for the function `strpbrk` is

```
char* strpbrk(const char* target, const char* pattern)
```

The function searches the *target* string for the first occurrence of *any character* among the characters of the string *pattern*. If the characters in the pattern do not occur in the string *target*, the function yields a 0.

Example

```
char* str = "Hello there how are you";
char* substr = "hr";
char* ptr;

ptr = strpbrk(str, substr);
cout << ptr << endl;
```

This displays `"here how are you"`, because the `'h'` is encountered in the string before the `'r'`.

7

Locating Strings

The STRING.H library offers the function strstr to locate a substring in a string.

The *strstr* Function

The prototype for the function strstr is

```
char* strstr(const char* str, const char* substr);
```

The function scans the string *str* for the first occurrence of a string *substr*. The function yields the pointer to the first character in string *str* that matches the parameter *substr*. If the string *substr* does not occur in the string *str*, the function yields a NULL.

Example

```
char str[] = "Hello there! how are you";
char substr[] = "how";
char* ptr;

ptr = strstr(str, substr);
cout << ptr << "\n";
```

This displays "how are you" because the string search matched "how". The pointer ptr points to the rest of the original string, starting with "how".

DO	DON'T
DO use the function strrev before calling the function strstr if you want to search for the last occurrence of a string.	
DON'T forget to reverse both the main and the search strings when using the strrev function to locate the last occurrence of the search string.	

The string library also provides the function strtok, which enables you to break down a string into substrings based on a specified set of delimiting characters.

NEW ☞ Substrings are sometimes called *tokens*.
TERM

The *strtok* Function

The prototype for the function strtok is

```
char* strtok(char* target, const char* delimiters);
```

The function searches the target string for tokens. A string supplies the set of delimiter characters. The following example shows how this function works in returning the tokens in a string. The function strtok modifies the string target by inserting '\0' characters after each token. (Make sure that you store a copy of the original target string in another string variable.)

Example

```c
#include <stdio.h>
#include <string.h>

main()
{
   char* str = "(Base_Cost+Profit) * Margin";
   char* tkn = "+* ()";
   char* ptr = str;

   printf("%s\n", str);
   // the first call looks normal
   ptr = strtok(str, tkn);
   printf("\n\nThis is broken into: %s",ptr);
   while (ptr)
      {
      printf(" ,%s",ptr);
      // must make first argument a 0 character
      ptr = strtok(0, tkn);
      }
   printf("\n\n");
}
```

This example displays the following when the program is run:

```
(Base_Cost+Profit) * Margin
```

This is broken into Base_Cost, Profit, Margin.

DO	**DON'T**
DO remember to supply 0 as the first argument to the function strtok in order to locate the next token.	
DON'T forget to store a copy of the target string in the function strtok.	

Look at an example that searches for characters and strings. Listing 7.7 shows the source code for the program STRING4.CPP. The program performs the following tasks:

☐ Prompts you to enter the main string

☐ Prompts you to enter the search string

☐ Prompts you to enter the search character

☐ Displays a character ruler and the main string

☐ Displays the indices where the search string occurs in the main string

☐ Displays the indices where the search character occurs in the main string

7

Listing 7.7. Source code for the program STRING4.CPP.

```
1:  /*
2:    C++ program that demonstrates searching for the
3:    characters and strings
4:  */
5:
6:  #include <iostream.h>
7:  #include <string.h>
8:
9:  const unsigned STR_SIZE = 40;
10:
11: main()
12: {
13:     char mainStr[STR_SIZE+1];
14:     char subStr[STR_SIZE+1];
15:     char findChar;
16:     char *p;
17:     int index;
18:     int count;
19:
20:     cout << "Enter a string : ";
21:     cin.getline(mainStr, STR_SIZE);
22:     cout << "Enter a search string : ";
23:     cin.getline(subStr, STR_SIZE);
24:     cout << "Enter a search character : ";
25:     cin >> findChar;
26:
27:     cout << "          1         2         3         4\n";
28:     cout << "0123456789012345678901234567890123456789 0\n";
29:     cout << mainStr << "\n";
30:     cout << "Searching for string " << subStr << "\n";
31:     p = strstr(mainStr, subStr);
32:     count = 0;
33:     while (p) {
34:       count++;
35:       index = p - mainStr;
36:       cout << "Match at index " << index << "\n";
37:       p = strstr(++p, subStr);
38:     }
39:     if (count == 0)
40:       cout << "No match for substring in main string\n";
41:
42:     cout << "Searching for character " << findChar << "\n";
43:     p = strchr(mainStr, findChar);
44:     count = 0;
45:     while (p) {
46:       count++;
47:       index = p - mainStr;
48:       cout << "Match at index " << index << "\n";
49:       p = strchr(++p, findChar);
50:     }
51:     if (count == 0)
52:       cout << "No match for search character in main string\n";
53:     return 0;
54: }
```

Here is a sample session with the program in Listing 7.7.

```
Enter a string : here, there, and everywhere
Enter a search string : here
Enter a search character : e
          1         2         3         4
0123456789012345678901234567890123456789 0
here, there, and everywhere
Searching for string here
Match at index 0
Match at index 7
Match at index 23
Searching for character e
Match at index 1
Match at index 3
Match at index 8
Match at index 10
Match at index 17
Match at index 19
Match at index 24
Match at index 26
```

The program in Listing 7.7 declares the strings mainStr and subStr to represent the main and search strings, respectively. The program also declares the variable findChar to store the search character. In addition, the program declares the character pointer p and the int-typed variables index and count.

The output statement in line 20 prompts you to enter a string. The statement in line 21 calls the stream input function getline and stores your input in variable mainStr. The output statement in line 22 prompts you to enter the search string. The statement in line 23 calls the stream input function getline and saves your input in variable subStr. The output statement in line 24 prompts you to enter the search character. The statement in line 25 obtains your input and stores it in the variable findChar.

The output statements in lines 27 through 29 display a ruler, along with your input aligned under the ruler. The output statement in line 30 informs you that the program is searching for the substring you entered. The search begins at the statement in line 31. This statement calls the function strstr to locate the first occurrence of string subStr in the string mainStr. The statement in line 32 assigns 0 to the variable count, which keeps track of the number of times the string mainStr contains the string subStr.

The program uses the while loop in lines 33 through 38 to locate all the occurrences of subStr in mainStr. The condition of the while loop examines the address of pointer p. If that pointer is not NULL, the loop iterates. The first statement inside the loop increments the variable count. The statement in line 35 calculates the index of the string mainStr where the last match occurs. The statement obtains the sought index by subtracting the address of pointer p from the address of the first character in the variable mainStr. (Remember that the expression &mainStr[0] is equivalent to the simpler expression mainStr.) The statement assigns the result to the variable index. The output statement in line 36 displays the value in variable index.

The statement in line 37 searches for the next occurrence of the string subStr in mainStr. Notice that this statement calls strstr and supplies it the pointer p as the first argument. The statement also applies the pre-increment operator to pointer p to store the address of the next character. This action ensures that the call to function strstr finds the next occurrence, if any, and is not stuck at the last occurrence. The if statement outside the while loop examines the value in variable count. If it contains zero, the program executes the output statement in line 40 to inform you that no match was found for the search string.

The output statement in line 42 informs you that the program is now searching for the character you specified in the main string. The process of searching for the character in findChar is very similar to searching for the string subStr. The main difference is that searching for a character involves the function strchr.

Summary

Today's lesson examined the basic input and output operations and functions that are supported by the IOSTREAM.H and STDIO.H header files as well as the C++ strings and their manipulation by functions that are declared in the STRING.H header file. You learned the following:

☐ Formatted stream output uses the precision and width functions to provide some basic formatting output.

☐ Standard stream input supports the insert operator >> to obtain input for the pre-defined data types in C++.

☐ The format codes involved in the format string of the printf function allow the printf function to control the appearance of the output and even perform type conversion.

☐ Strings in C++ are arrays of characters that end with the null character (the ASCII 0 character).

☐ String input requires the use of the getline stream input function. This function requires that you specify the input variable, the maximum number of input characters, and the optional line delimiter.

☐ The STRING.H header file contains the standard string library for the C language. This library contains many versatile functions that support copying, concatenating, converting, reversing, and searching for strings.

☐ C++ supports two methods for assigning strings. The first method assigns a string to another when you declare the latter string. The second method uses the function strcpy to assign one string to another at any stage in the program. The string library also offers the function strdup to copy a string and allocate the needed space.

☐ The function strlen returns the length of a string.

- The `strcat` and `strncat` functions enable you to concatenate two strings. The function `strncat` enables you to specify the number of characters to concatenate.

- The functions `strcmp`, `stricmp`, `strncmp`, and `strnicmp` enable you to perform various types of string comparisons. The function `strcmp` performs a case-insensitive comparison of two strings, using every character possible. The function `stricmp` is a version of the function `strcmp` that performs a case-insensitive comparison. The function `strncmp` is a variant of function `strcmp` that uses a specified number of characters in comparing the strings. The function `strnicmp` is a version of function `strncmp` that also performs a case-insensitive comparison.

- The functions `strlwr` and `strupr` convert the characters of a string into lowercase and uppercase, respectively.

- The function `strrev` reverses the order of characters in a string.

- The functions `strchr`, `strrchr`, `strspn`, `strcspn`, and `strpbrk` enable you to search for characters and simple character patterns in strings.

- The function `strstr` searches for a string in another string. The function `strtok` enables you to break down a string into smaller strings that are delimited by a set of characters that you specify.

Q&A

Q How can I chain >> or << operators?

A Each of these operators returns a special stream data type that can be the input for another similar stream operator.

Q Why can't I use the console stream I/O operators in Windows applications?

A Windows applications have a fundamentally different way of interacting with you. When an EasyWin program (which emulates a non-GUI MS-DOS application) executes an input statement, it goes into a special mode where it monitors the keyboard input. By contrast, Windows programs (which are GUI applications) are always monitoring the mouse (its movements and its button clicks) and the keyboard and reporting the current status to the part of Windows that monitors such events. The vast differences between GUI and non-GUI applications render non-GUI input functions useless in GUI applications.

Q Can a statement initialize a pointer using a string literal?

A Yes. The compiler stores the characters of the string literal in memory and assigns its address to that pointer. Here is an example.

```
const char* p = "I am a small string";
```

Be aware, however, that some compilers may put these strings into a part of memory that is read-only, so you will not be able to modify them. That's why the example assigns a `const char*` instead of a regular `char*`.

7

Q Can a statement declare a constant pointer to a literal string?

A Yes. This kind of declaration resembles the one mentioned previously. Because the statement declares a constant pointer, however, you cannot overwrite the characters of the initializing string literal (you will get a compile-time error). Here is an example.

```
const char* p = "Version 1.0";
```

Use the const char* pointer to store fixed messages and titles.

Q Can a statement declare an array of pointers to a set of string literals?

A Yes. This is the easiest method of using an array of pointers to access a collection of messages, titles, or other types of fixed strings. Here is an example.

```
char* mainMenu[] = { "File", "Edit", "Search", "View",
                     "Debug", "Options", "Windows", "Help"};
```

Thus, the element mainMenu[0] accesses the first string, mainMenu[1] accesses the second string, and so on.

Q How can I use strcmp to compare strings, starting at a specific number of characters?

A Add the offset value to the arguments of the function strcmp. Here is an example.

```
char s1[41] = "Turbo C++ 4.5";
char s2[41] = "TURBO Pascal";
int offset = 5;
int i;
i = strcmp(str1 + offset, str2 + offset);
```

Q How can I use strncmp to compare a specific number of characters in two strings, starting at a specific character?

A Add the offset value to the arguments of the function strcmp. Here is an example.

```
char s1[41] = "Turbo C++ 4.5";
char s2[41] = "TURBO Pascal";
int offset = 5;
int num = 3;
int i;
i = strncmp(str1 + offset, str2 + offset, num);
```

Workshop

The Workshop provides quiz questions to help you solidify your understanding of the material covered and exercises to provide you with experience in using what you've learned. Try to understand the quiz and exercise answers before continuing on to the next day's lesson. Answers are provided in Appendix A.

Quiz

1. What is wrong with the following statement?

   ```
   cout << "Enter a number " >> x;
   ```

2. What happens in the following statement?

   ```
   cout << "Enter three numbers : ";
   cin >> x >> y >> x;
   ```

3. Where is the error in the following program?

   ```
   #include <iostream.h>
   #include <string.h>
   const int MAX = 10;
   main()
   {
     char s1[MAX+1];
     char s2[] = "12345678901234567890123456789012345678890";
     strcpy(s1, s2);
     cout << "String 1 is " << s1
          << "\nString 2 is " << s2;
     return 0;
   }
   ```

4. How can you fix the program in the last question using the function strncpy instead of strcpy?

5. What is the value assigned to variable i in the following statements?

   ```
   char s1[] = "Turbo C++";
   char s2[] = "Turbo Pascal";
   int i;
   i = strcmp(s1, s2);
   ```

6. What is the value assigned to variable i in the following statements?

   ```
   char s1[] = "Turbo C++";
   char s2[] = "Turbo Pascal";
   int offset = strlen("Turbo ");
   int i;
   i = strcmp(s1 + offset, s2 + offset);
   ```

7. True or false? The following function correctly returns 1 if a string does not contain lowercase characters, and yields 0 if otherwise.

```
int hasNoLowerCase(const char* s)
{
  char* s2 = new char[strlen(s)+1];
  strcpy(s2, s);
  strupr(s2);
  return (strcmp(s, s2) == 0)? 1 : 0);
}
```

Exercises

1. Write the program OUT3.CPP, which displays a table of square roots for whole numbers in the range of 2 to 10. Use the MATH.H header file to import the sqrt function, which calculates the square root of a double-typed argument. Because C++ loops have not yet been discussed, use repetitive statements to display the various values. Employ the format controls %3.01f and %3.41f, respectively, to display the number and its square root.

2. Write the program OUT4.CPP, which prompts you for an integer and displays the hexadecimal and octal equivalent forms. Use the printf format controls to perform the conversion between decimal, hexadecimal, and octal numbers.

3. Write your own version of the function strlen. Use a while loop and a character-counting variable to obtain the function result.

4. Write another version of the function strlen. This time use a while loop and a local pointer to obtain the function result.

5. Write the program STRING5.CPP, which uses the function strtok to break down the string "2*(X+Y)/(X+Z) - (X+10)/(Y-5)" into three sets of tokens, using the token delimiter strings "+-*/ ()", "( )", and "+-*/ ".

Each week in this book is accompanied with a game example to help you get a better idea of how to make use of the lessons learned. Thus far, however, you haven't learned enough to look at the game examples supplied with Turbo C++. For this week, you take a look at a simple example that you can type in. The next two weeks address more interesting fare.

This week's example is a simple number-guessing game (shown in Listing R1.1). The program selects a number at random between 1 and 1,000 and prompts you to enter a number in that range. If your input is greater than the secret number, then the program tells you that your guess was higher. By contrast, if your input is less than the secret number, then the program tells you that your guess was lower. If you guess the secret number, then the game ends with your victory. The program allows you up to 10 guesses.

Type — Listing R1.1. Source code for program GUESS.CPP.

```cpp
 1: #include <ctype.h>
 2: #include <iostream.h>
 3: #include <stdlib.h>
 4:
 5: int main()
 6: {
 7:     int guess = 0, number, count;
 8:     char tryagain;
 9:
10:     randomize();
11:     cout << "The object of the game is to guess a number between" << endl
12:         << "1 and 1000.  You will be allowed 10 guesses, after" << endl
13:         << "which you will have lost." << endl;
14:     do
15:         {
16:         number = random(1000) + 1;
17:         for (count = 1; (guess != number) && (count <= 10); ++count)
18:             {
19:             cout << "Please enter try #" << count << ": ";
20:             cin >> guess;
21:             if (guess < number)
22:                 cout << "   You're too low." << endl;
23:             else if (guess > number)
24:                 cout << "   You're too high." << endl;
25:             else
26:                 cout << "   Congratulations!  Pip pip!  Good show, and all
    that!" << endl;
27:             }
28:         if (count > 10)
29:             cout << "   Too bad.  The number was " << number << "." << endl;
30:         cout << "Would you like to try again? ";
31:         cin >> tryagain;
32:         cout << endl;
33:         } while (tolower(tryagain) == 'y');
34:     return 0;
35: }
```

Output — Here is a sample session with the program in Listing R1.1.

```
The object of the game is to guess a number between
1 and 1000.  You will be allowed 10 guesses, after
which you will have lost.
Please enter try #1: 500
   You're too low.
Please enter try #2: 750
   You're too high.
Please enter try #3: 625
   You're too high.
Please enter try #4: 570
   You're too high.
Please enter try #5: 530
   You're too low.
Please enter try #6: 550
   You're too low.
```

```
Please enter try #7: 560
    You're too high.
Please enter try #8: 555
    You're too low.
Please enter try #9: 557
    You're too low.
Please enter try #10: 559
    Too bad.  The number was 558.
Would you like to try again? n
```

The first thing done by the program in Listing R1.1 is to initialize the random number generator with a call to the `randomize` function. This initializes the random number seed, allowing the program to come up with a different random number each time it's run. (If `randomize` was not called, the program would always use the same secret numbers, and the game would become rather boring.) The program then tells the user the object of the game.

Line 14 is the start of the main `do-while` loop. Lines 30 and 31 ask the user whether he or she wants to play the game again, and the conclusion of the loop on line 33 repeats if the user types Y. Note the use of the `tolower` function that enables the user to type the response in either upper- or lowercase. You then do a conversion to the case against which you want to check.

Line 16 sets the secret number via the `random` function. Because the `random` function returns a number from 0 to one less than its argument, you use 1000 for the parameter and then add one immediately afterward to make the range 1 to 1000. The `for` loop that starts on line 17 initializes the count variable to 1, and then has a clause that checks two things: that the current guess isn't correct and that the user hasn't run out of guesses. The final clause in the `for` statement increments the count.

Lines 19 and 20 perform the simple task of retrieving a guess from the user. After that, on lines 21 through 26, the program checks the user's guess against the secret number and lets the user know of his or her proximity in rough terms (can't make it too easy!). Note that if the user guesses correctly, the `for` loop will automatically terminate. If the user makes it out of the loop without guessing the number, then the program lets the user know what that secret number was on line 29.

There is a bug in this program, however. It's rather subtle, and you might not find it immediately. Try mentally running through the code in the case where the user is guessing for the last time (count is 10) and he or she actually gets the right answer. The `if` statement will print out the congratulatory message, and then the `for` loop will exit. Line 28 is designed to tell if the user has exited the loop because he or she ran out of guesses. This works in most cases as it's written; in this case, however, the program is going to assume that the user failed because the count has run out. In order to fix things, you should change line 28 to read `if (guess != number)`.

2

This second week continues teaching you about the C++ language. The topics start with the object-oriented programming (OOP) parts of C++. You learn about classes, components, and the rules for using these components. In addition, you learn about basic file I/O using the C++ stream library. Day 10 introduces you to the string class, which supports strings using C++ classes; you also learn about templates and how they're used in the Borland class library. Day 11 begins your introduction to the ObjectWindows Library (OWL), which allows you to create full-fledged Windows applications. From there you will be taken through some of the basics of Windows programs, including basic windows, controls, and dialog boxes.

Object-Oriented Programming and C++ Classes

Classes provide C++ with object-oriented programming (OOP) constructs. Today's lesson, which marks an important milestone for learning C++, introduces you to building individual classes as well as class hierarchy. You learn about the following topics:

☐ The basics of object-oriented programming

☐ Declaring base classes

☐ Constructors

☐ Destructors

☐ Declaring a class hierarchy

☐ Virtual functions

☐ Friend functions

☐ Operators and friend operators

Basics of Object-Oriented Programming

We live in a world of objects. Each object has its attributes and operations. Some objects are more animated than others. You can categorize objects into classes. For example, a CASIO Data Bank watch is an object that belongs to the class of the CASIO Data Bank watches.

NEW *Object-oriented programming* (*OOP*) uses the notions of real-world objects to develop
TERM applications.

You also can relate individual classes in a class hierarchy. The class of CASIO Data Bank watches is part of the watch class hierarchy. The basics of OOP include classes, objects, methods, inheritance, and polymorphism.

NEW A *class* defines a category of objects. Each *object* is an instance of a class.
TERM

Classes and Objects

An object shares the same attributes and functionality of other objects in the same class. Typically, an object has a unique state, defined by the current values of its attributes. The functionality of a class determines the operations that are possible for the class instances. C++ calls the attributes of the class *data members* and calls the operations of the class *member functions*. Classes encapsulate data members and member functions.

Going back to the CASIO watch example, you can note that the buttons in the watch represent the member functions of the class of CASIO watches, whereas the display represents a data member. You can click certain buttons to edit the date and/or time. In OOP terms, the member functions alter the state of the object by changing its data members.

Messages and Methods

Object-oriented programming models the interaction with objects as events where requests are sent to an object or between objects. The object receiving a request responds by invoking the appropriate method (that's the member function in C++). C++ does not explicitly foster the notion of requests and methods as do other OOP languages, such as SmallTalk. However, some find it easier to discuss invoking member functions using the term "request." The terms *methods* and *member functions* are equivalent.

NEW TERM The *request* is what is done to an object. The *method* is how the object responds to the incoming request.

Inheritance

In object-oriented languages, you can derive a class from another one.

NEW TERM With *inheritance*, the derived class (also called the *descendant class*) inherits the data members and member functions of its *parent* and *ancestor classes*.

Deriving a class refines the parent class by appending new attributes and new operations. The derived class typically declares new data members and new member functions. In addition, the derived class also can override inherited member functions when the operations of these functions are not suitable for the derived class.

To apply the concept of inheritance to the CASIO Data Bank watch, consider the following possible scenario. Suppose that the watch manufacturer decides to create a CASIO Data Comm watch that offers the same features as the CASIO Data Bank plus a beeper! Rather than redesigning the new model (that is the new class, in OOP terms) from scratch, the CASIO engineers start with the existing design of the CASIO Data Bank and build on it. This process may well add new attributes and operations to the existing design and alter some existing operations to fit the new design. Thus, the CASIO Data Comm model inherits the attributes and the operations of the CASIO Data Bank model. In OOP terms, the class of CASIO Data Comm watches is a descendant of the class of CASIO Data Bank watches.

Polymorphism

The OOP feature of polymorphism allows the instances of different classes to react in a particular way to a message (or function invocation, in C++ terms). For example, in a hierarchy of graphical shapes (point, line, square, rectangle, circle, ellipse, and so on), each shape has a Draw function that is responsible for properly responding to a request to draw that shape.

NEW☞ *Polymorphism* enables the instances of different classes to respond to the same function in
TERM ways that are appropriate to each class.

Declaring Base Classes

C++ enables you to declare a class that encapsulates data members and member functions. These
functions alter and/or retrieve the values of the data members as well as perform related tasks.

Syntax

A Base Class

The general syntax for declaring a base class is

```
class className
{
private:
    <private data members>
    <private constructors>
    <private member functions>
protected:
    <protected data members>
    <protected constructors>
    <protected member functions>
public:
    <public data members>
    <public constructors>
    <public destructor>
    <public member functions>
};
```

Example

```
class point
{
protected:
    double x;
    double y;
public:
    point(double xVal, double yVal);
    double getX();
    double getY();
    void assign(double xVal, double yVal);
    point& assign(point& pt);
};
```

The Sections of a Class

The previous syntax shows that the declaration involves the keyword class. C++ classes offer
three levels of visibility for the various members (that is, both data members and member
functions).

☐ The private section

☐ The protected section

☐ The public section

NEW☞
TERM In the *private section*, only the member functions of the class can access the private members. Descendant classes are denied access to private members of its base classes. In the *protected section*, only the member functions of the class and its descendant classes can access members. The *public section* specifies members that are visible to the member functions of the class, class instances, member functions of descendant classes, and their instances.

The following rules apply to the various class sections:

1. The class sections can appear in any order.

2. The class sections may appear more than once.

3. If no class section is specified, the C++ compiler treats the members as private.

4. You should avoid placing data members in the public section unless such a declaration significantly simplifies your design. Data members typically are placed in the protected section to allow their access by member functions of descendant classes.

5. Use member functions to set and/or query the values of data members. The members that set the data members assist in performing validation and updating other data members, if need be.

6. The class may have multiple constructors.

7. The class can have only one destructor, which must be declared in the public section.

8. The member functions (as well as the constructors and destructors) that have multiple statements are defined outside the class declaration. The definition may reside in the same file that declares the class.

NEW☞
TERM *Constructors* are special members that must have the same name as the host class, and they're called when class instances are created. *Destructors* are called when class instances are removed.

> **Note:** It should be mentioned at this point that classes and structures really are the same with one single difference. In a `class`, without specifying a protection level, it starts out with `private`. A `structure` starts out with `public`. All the rules you are used to for putting data in and manipulating structures applies to classes.

In software libraries, the definition of the member functions referred to in rule 8 typically resides in a separate source file (.H and .CPP files). When you define a member function, you must qualify the function name with the class name. The syntax of such a qualification involves using the class name followed by two colons (::) and then the name of a function. For example, consider the following class:

```
class point
{
protected:
   double x;
   double y;
public:
   point(double xVal, double yVal);
   double getX();
   // other member functions
};
```

The definitions of the constructor and member functions are

```
point::point(double xVal, double yVal)
{
   // statements
}

double point::getX()
{
   // statements
}
```

After you declare a class, you can use the class name as a type identifier to declare class instances. The syntax resembles declaring variables.

Look at an example. Listing 8.1 shows the source code for the program CLASS1.CPP. The program prompts you to enter the length and width of a rectangle (which is an object). The program then displays the length, width, and area of the rectangle you specified.

Listing 8.1. Source code for the program CLASS1.CPP.

```
1:  // C++ program that illustrates a class
2:
3:  #include <iostream.h>
4:
5:  class rectangle
6:  {
7:    protected:
8:      double length;
9:      double width;
10:   public:
11:      rectangle() { assign(0, 0); }
12:      rectangle(double len, double wide) { assign(len, wide); }
13:      double getLength() { return length; }
14:      double getWidth() { return width; }
15:      double getArea() { return length * width; }
```

```
16:     void assign(double len, double wide);
17: };
18:
19: void rectangle::assign(double len, double wide)
20: {
21:   length = len;
22:   width = wide;
23: }
24:
25: main()
26: {
27:   rectangle rect;
28:   double len, wide;
29:
30:   cout << "Enter length of rectangle : ";
31:   cin >> len;
32:   cout << "Enter width of rectangle : ";
33:   cin >> wide;
34:   rect.assign(len, wide);
35:   cout << "Rectangle length = " << rect.getLength() << "\n"
36:        << "          width = " << rect.getWidth() << "\n"
37:        << "          area  = " << rect.getArea() << "\n";
38:   return 0;
39: }
```

Here is a sample session with the program in Listing 8.1.

```
Enter length of rectangle : 10
Enter width of rectangle : 12
Rectangle length = 10
width  = 12
area   = 120
```

The program in Listing 8.1 declares the class rectangle, which models a rectangle. The class has two double-typed data members, length and width, which store the dimensions of a rectangle. In addition, the class has two constructors: the default constructor and the nondefault constructor. The class also defines the member functions getLength, getWidth, getArea, and assign.

NEW☛ The *default constructor* creates an instance with 0 dimensions, and the *nondefault*
TERM *constructor* creates an instance with nonzero dimensions.

The function getLength, defined in the class declaration, simply returns the value in member length. The function getWidth, also defined in the class declaration, merely returns the value in member width. The function getArea, defined in the class declaration, simply returns the value of the result of multiplying the members length and width.

The member function assign, defined outside the class declaration, assigns the arguments for its parameters len and wide to the data members length and width, respectively. The implementation of this function is simplified by not checking for negative values.

The function main declares rect as the instance of class rectangle and declares the double-typed variables len and wide. The output statement in line 30 prompts you to enter the length of the rectangle. The statement in line 31 obtains your input and stores it in variable len. The output statement in line 32 prompts you to enter the width of the rectangle. The statement in line 33 obtains your input and stores it in variable wide.

The function main assigns the input values to the instance rect using the assign member function. In OOP terms, we can say that the function main sends the assign message to the object rect. The arguments of the message are variables len and wide. The object rect responds by invoking the method (the member function) rectangle::assign(double, double).

The output statement in lines 35 through 37 displays the length, width, and area of the object rect. This statement sends the messages getLength, getWidth, and getArea to the object rect. In turn, the object rect invokes the appropriate methods (or member functions, if you prefer) to respond to each one of these messages.

Constructors

C++ constructors and destructors work automatically to guarantee the appropriate creation and removal of class instances.

Constructors

The general syntax for constructors is

```
class className
{
public:
    className(); // default constructor
    className(const className& c); // copy constructor
    className(<parameter list>); // another constructor
};
```

Example

```
class point
{
protected:
    double x;
    double y;
public:
    point();
    point(double xVal, double yVal);
    point(const point& pt);
    double getX();
    double getY();
    void assign(double xVal, double yVal);
    point& assign(point& pt);
};
```

```
main()
{
   point p1;
   point p2(10, 20);
   point p3(2);
   p1.assign(p2));
   cout << p1.getX() << " " << p1.getY() << "\n";
   cout << p2.getX() << " " << p2.getY() << "\n";
   cout << p3.getX() << " " << p3.getY() << "\n";
   return 0;
}
```

NEW☛ A *copy constructor* enables you to create class instances by copying the data from existing
TERM instances.

C++ has the following features and rules regarding constructors:

1. The name of the constructor must be identical to the name of its class.

2. You must not include any return type, not even `void`.

3. A class can have any number of constructors, including none. In the latter case, the
   compiler automatically creates one for that class.

4. The default constructor is the one that either has no parameters or possesses a parameter list where all the parameters use default arguments. Here are two examples.

```
// class use parameterless constructor
class point1
{
    protected:
        double x;
        double y;
    public:
        point1();
        // other member functions
};

// class use constructor with default arguments
class point2
{
    protected:
        double x;
        double y;
    public:
        point(double xVal = 0, double yVal = 0);
        // other member functions
};
```

5. The *copy constructor* enables you to create a class instance using an existing instance. Here is an example.

```
class point
{
    protected:
        double x;
        double y;
    public:
        point();
        point(double xVal, double yVal);
        point(const point& pt);
        // other member functions
};
```

6. The declaration of a class instance (which includes function parameters and local instances) involves a constructor. Which constructor is called? The answer depends on how many constructors you have declared for the class and how you declared the class instance. For example, consider the following instances of the last version of the class `point`:

```
point p1; // involves the default constructor
point p2(1.1, 1.3); // uses the second constructor
point p3(p2); // uses the copy constructor
```

Because instance p1 specifies no arguments, the compiler uses the default constructor. The instance p2 specifies two floating-point arguments. Consequently, the compiler uses the second constructor. The instance p3 has the instance p2 as an argument. Therefore, the compiler uses the copy constructor to create instance p3 from instance p2.

DO	DON'T

DO declare copy constructors, especially for classes that model dynamic data structures. These constructors perform what is called a *deep copy*, which includes the dynamic data. By default, the compiler creates what are called *shallow copy* constructors, which copy the data members only.

DON'T rely on the shallow copy constructor to copy instances for classes that have members that are pointers.

Destructors

C++ classes may contain destructors that automatically remove class instances.

Syntax

Destructors

The general syntax for destructors is

```
class className
{
public:
    className(); // default constructor
    // other constructors
    ~className();
    // other member function
};
```

Example

```
class String
{
protected:
    char *str;
    int len;

public:
    String();
    String(const String& s);
    ~String();
    // other member functions
};
```

C++ has the following features and rules regarding destructors:

1. The name of the destructor must begin with a tilde (~). The rest of the destructor name must be identical to the name of its class.

2. You must not include any return type, not even void.

3. A class can have no more than one destructor. In addition, if you omit the destructor, the compiler automatically creates one for you.

4. The destructor cannot have any parameters.

5. The runtime system automatically invokes a class destructor when the instance of that class is out of scope, or when the instance is explicitly deleted.

Examples of Constructors and Destructors

Look at a program that typifies the use of constructors and destructors. Listing 8.2 contains the source code for the CLASS2.CPP program. The program performs the following tasks:

☐ Creates a dynamic array (the object)

☐ Assigns values to the elements of the dynamic array

☐ Displays the values in the dynamic array

☐ Removes the dynamic array

Type **Listing 8.2. Source code for the CLASS2.CPP program.**

```
1:   // Program demonstrates constructors and destructors
2:
3:   #include <iostream.h>
4:
5:   const unsigned MIN_SIZE = 4;
6:
7:   class Array
8:   {
9:      protected:
10:       double *dataPtr;
11:       unsigned size;
12:
13:     public:
14:       Array(unsigned Size = MIN_SIZE);
15:       Array(const Array& a);
16:       ~Array()
17:         { delete [] dataPtr; }
18:       unsigned getSize() const
19:         { return size; }
20:       void store(double x, unsigned index)
21:         { if (index > 0 && index < size) dataPtr[index] = x; }
22:       double recall(unsigned index)
23:         { if (index > 0 and index < size) return dataPtr[index]; }
24:   };
25:
26:   Array::Array(unsigned Size)
27:   {
28:     size = (Size < MIN_SIZE) ? MIN_SIZE : Size;
29:     dataPtr = new double[size];
30:   }
31:
32:   Array::Array(const Array& a)
33:   {
34:     size = a.size;
35:     dataPtr = new double[size];
36:     for (int i = 0; i < size; i++)
37:       dataPtr[i] = a.dataPtr[i];
38:   }
39:
40:   main()
41:   {
42:     Array Arr(10);
43:     double x;
44:     // assign data to array elements
45:     for (unsigned i = 0; i < Arr.getSize(); i++) {
46:       x = double(i);
47:       x = x * x - 5 * x + 10;
48:       Arr.store(x, i);
49:     }
50:     // display data in the array element
51:     cout << "Array Arr has the following values:\n\n";
52:     for (i = 0; i < Arr.getSize(); i++)
53:       cout << "Arr[" << i << "] = " << Arr.recall(i) << "\n";
54:     return 0;
55:   }
```

Here is a sample session with the program in Listing 8.2.

```
Array Arr has the following values:

Arr[0] = 10
Arr[1] = 6
Arr[2] = 4
Arr[3] = 4
Arr[4] = 6
Arr[5] = 10
Arr[6] = 16
Arr[7] = 24
Arr[8] = 34
Arr[9] = 46
```

The program in Listing 8.2 declares the global constant MIN_SIZE in line 5, which specifies the minimum size of dynamic arrays. The program also declares the class Array in line 7. The class has two data members, dataPtr and size. The member dataPtr is the pointer to the array's dynamically allocated elements. The member size stores the number of elements in an instance of class Array.

The class declares a default constructor. (The constructor actually has a parameter with the default value MIN_SIZE.) The program defines the default constructor in lines 26 through 30. The arguments for the parameter Size specify the number of array elements. The statement in line 28 assigns the greater value of parameter Size and the constant MIN_SIZE to the data member size. The statement in line 29 allocates the dynamic space for the array by using the operator new. The statement assigns the base address of the dynamic array to the member dataPtr.

The class also declares a copy constructor. Because there is allocated data involved, it's wise to have this constructor in order to make sure the contents of that data are copied properly. Line 35 allocates the same amount of space as the old Array, and then proceeds to copy the old contents into the new space on lines 36 and 37.

The destructor ~Array removes the dynamic space of the array by applying the operator delete to the member dataPtr.

The member function getSize, defined in the class declaration, returns the value in data member size.

The function store, defined in the class declaration, stores the value passed by parameter x at the element number specified by the parameter index. The implementation of this function is simplified by eliminating the out-of-range index check.

The function recall, defined in the class declaration, returns the value in the element specified by the parameter index. The implementation of this function is simplified by eliminating the out-of-range index check.

The function main declares the object Arr as an instance of class Array. The declaration, located in line 42, specifies that the instance has 10 elements. The function also declares the double-typed variable x. The `for` loop in lines 45 through 49 stores values in the instance `Arr`. The loop uses control variable `i` and iterates from 0 to `Arr.getSize()`-1, in increments of 1. The loop continuation condition sends the `getSize` message to instance `Arr` to obtain the number of elements in the array. The statements in lines 46 and 47 calculate the value to store in an element of instance `Arr`. The statement in line 48 sends the message `store` to instance `Arr` and passes the arguments x and i. The object `Arr` saves the value in variable x at the element number i.

The output statement in line 51 comments on the output of the `for` loop in lines 52 and 53. The loop uses the control variable i and iterates from 0 to `Arr.getSize()` -1, in increments of 1. The output statement in line 53 displays the element in instance `Arr` by sending the message `recall` to that instance. The message has the argument i.

Declaring a Class Hierarchy

The power of the OOP features of C++ comes from the fact that you can derive classes from existing ones. A descendant class inherits the members of its ancestor classes (that is, parent class, grandparent class, and so on) and also can override some of the inherited functions. Inheritance enables you to reuse code in descendant classes.

A Derived Class

The general syntax for declaring a derived class is

```
class className : [public] parentClass
{
    <friend classes>

private:
    <private data members>
    <private constructors>
    <private member functions>

protected:
    <protected data members>
    <protected constructors>
    <protected member functions>

public:
    <public data members>
    <public constructors>
    <public destructor>
    <public member functions>

    <friend functions and friend operators>
};
```

Example

The following example shows the class `cRectangle` and its descendant, the class `cBox`:

```
class cRectangle
{
protected:
   double length;
   double width;
public:
   cRectangle(double len, double wide);
   double getLength() const;
   double getWidth(); const;
   double assign(double len, double wide);
   double calcArea();
};

class cBox : public cRectangle
{
protected:
   double height;

public:
   cBox(double len, double wide, double height);
   double getHeight() const;
   assign(double len, double wide, double height);
   double calcVolume();
};
```

The class lineage is indicated by a colon followed by the optional keyword `public` and then the name of the parent class. When you include the keyword `public`, you allow the instances of the descendant class to access the public members of the parent and other ancestor classes. By contrast, when you omit the keyword `public` or use the private keyword, you deprive the instance of the descendant class from accessing the members of the ancestor classes.

A descendant class inherits the data members of its ancestor classes. C++ has no mechanism for removing unwanted inherited data members—you basically are stuck with them. By contrast, C++ enables you to override inherited member functions. You see more about this topic later in today's lesson. The descendant class declares new data members, new member functions, and overriding member functions. Again, you can place these members in the private, protected, or public sections, as you see fit in your class design.

DO	DON'T

DO reduce the number of constructors by using default argument parameters.

DO use member functions to access the values in the data members. These member functions enable you to control and validate the values in the data members.

DON'T declare all the constructors of a class protected unless you want to force the client programmers (that is, those programs that use the class) to use the class by declaring its descendants with public constructors.

DON'T declare the data members in the public section.

Look at an example that declares a small class hierarchy. Listing 8.3 shows the source code for the CLASS3.CPP program. This program declares classes that contain a hierarchy of two simple geometric shapes: a circle and a cylinder. The program requires no input. Instead, it uses internal data to create the geometric shapes and to display their dimensions, areas, and volume.

Listing 8.3. Source code for the CLASS3.CPP program.

```
 1:  // Program that demonstrates a small hierarchy of classes
 2:
 3:  #include <iostream.h>
 4:  #include <math.h>
 5:
 6:  const double pi = 4 * atan(1);
 7:
 8:  inline double sqr(double x)
 9:  { return x * x; }
10:
11:  class cCircle
12:  {
13:    protected:
14:      double radius;
15:
16:    public:
17:      cCircle(double radiusVal = 0) : radius(radiusVal) {}
18:      void setRadius(double radiusVal)
19:        { radius = radiusVal; }
20:      double getRadius() const
21:        { return radius; }
22:      double area() const
23:        { return pi * sqr(radius); }
24:      void showData();
25:  };
26:
27:  class cCylinder : public cCircle
28:  {
29:    protected:
30:      double height;
31:
32:    public:
33:      cCylinder(double heightVal = 0, double radiusVal = 0)
34:        : height(heightVal), cCircle(radiusVal) {}
35:      void setHeight(double heightVal)
36:        { height = heightVal; }
37:      double getHeight() const
```

```
38:          { return height; }
39:        double area() const
40:          { return 2 * cCircle::area() +
41:                  2 * pi * radius * height; }
42:        void showData();
43: };
44:
45: void cCircle::showData()
46: {
47:    cout << "Circle radius        = " << getRadius() << "\n"
48:         << "Circle area          = " << area() << "\n\n";
49: }
50:
51: void cCylinder::showData()
52: {
53:    cout << "Cylinder radius      = " << getRadius() << "\n"
54:         << "Cylinder height      = " << getHeight() << "\n"
55:         << "Cylinder area        = " << area() << "\n\n";
56: }
57:
58: main()
59: {
60:    cCircle Circle(1);
61:    cCylinder Cylinder(10, 1);
62:
63:    Circle.showData();
64:    Cylinder.showData();
65:    return 0;
66: }
```

Here is a sample session with the program in Listing 8.3.

```
Circle radius        = 1
Circle area          = 3.14159

Cylinder radius      = 1
Cylinder height      = 10
Cylinder area        = 69.115
```

The program in Listing 8.3 declares the classes cCircle and cCylinder. The class cCircle models a circle, whereas the class cCylinder models a cylinder.

The cCircle class declares a single data member, radius, to store the radius of the circle. The class also declares a constructor and a number of member functions. The constructor assigns a value to the data member radius when you declare a class instance. Notice that the constructor uses a new syntax to initialize the member radius. The functions setRadius and getRadius serve to set and query the value in member radius, respectively. The function area returns the area of the circle. The function showData displays the radius and area of a class instance.

The class cCylinder, a descendant of cCircle, declares a single data member, height, to store the height of the cylinder. The class inherits the member radius needed to store the radius of the cylinder. The cCylinder class declares a constructor and a number of member functions. The constructor assigns values to the `radius` and `height` members when creating a class instance. Notice the use of a new syntax to initialize the members—member `height` is initialized, and member `radius` is initialized by invoking the constructor of class `cCircle` with the argument `radiusVal`. The functions `getHeight` and `setHeight` serve to set and query the value in member `height`, respectively. The class uses the inherited functions `setRadius` and `getRadius` to manipulate the inherited member `radius`. The function `area`, which overrides the inherited function `cCircle::area()`, returns the surface area of the cylinder. Notice that this function explicitly invokes the inherited function `cCircle::area()`. The function `showData` displays the radius, height, and area of a class instance.

We also would like to point out that the declarations of the functions `area`, `getHeight`, and `area` in lines 22, 37, and 39 end with the keyword `const`. Using the keyword `const` in this way tells the compiler that the member function cannot change any data member. This feature mainly is aimed at teams of programmers where the team manager sets the specifications for the class and determines which member functions can alter the values of data members.

The function `main` declares the instance `Circle`, of class `cCircle`, and assigns 1 to the circle's radius. In addition, the function also declares the instance `Cylinder`, of class `cCylinder`, and assigns 10 and 1 to the circle's `height` and `radius`, respectively. The function then sends the `showData` message to the instances `Circle` and `Cylinder`. Each object responds to this message by invoking the appropriate member function.

Virtual Functions

As mentioned previously, polymorphism is an important object-oriented programming feature. Consider the following simple classes and the function `main`:

```
#include <iostream.h>
class cA
{
public:
    double A(double x) { return x * x; }
    double B(double x) { return A(x) / 2; }
};

class cB : public cA
{
public:
    double A(double x) { return x * x * x; }
};

main()
{
    cB aB;
    cout << aB.B(3) << "\n";
    return 0;
}
```

Class cA contains functions A and B, where function B calls function A. Class cB, a descendant of class cA, inherits function B, but overrides function A. The intent here is to have the inherited function cA::B call function cB::A in order to support polymorphic behavior. What is the program output? The answer is 4.5 and not 13.5! Why? The answer lies in the fact that the compiler resolves the expression aB.B(3) by using the inherited function cA::B, which in turn calls function cA::A. Therefore, function cB:A is left out and the program fails to support polymorphic behavior.

C++ supports polymorphic behavior by offering virtual functions.

NEW☞ *Virtual functions*, which are bound at runtime, are declared by placing the keyword `virtual`
TERM before the function's return type.

After you declare a function `virtual`, you can override it only with functions in descendant classes. These overriding functions must have the same parameter list. Virtual functions can override nonvirtual functions in ancestor classes. Note that once a function is declared as virtual in a specific class, all descendants of that class will regard the function as virtual, whether or not the `virtual` keyword is used.

Virtual Functions

The general syntax for declaring virtual functions is

```
class className1
{
    // member functions
    virtual returnType functionName(<parameter list>);
};

class className2 : public className1
{
    // member functions
    virtual returnType functionName(<parameter list>);
};
```

Example

This example shows how virtual functions can successfully implement polymorphic behavior in classes cA and cB:

```
#include <iostream.h>
class cA
{
public:
    virtual double A(double x) { return x * x; }
    double B(double x) { return A(x) / 2; }
};

class cB : public cA
{
public:
```

```
   virtual double A(double x) { return x * x * x; }
};

main()
{
   cB aB;
   cout << aB.B(3) << "\n";
   return 0;
}
```

This example displays 13.5, the correct result, because the call to the inherited function cA::B is resolved at runtime by calling cB::A.

DO	DON'T

DO use virtual functions when you have a callable function that implements a class-specific behavior. Declaring such a function as virtual ensures that it provides the correct response that is relevant to the associated class.

DON'T declare a member function as virtual by default. Virtual functions have some additional overhead.

Look at an example. Listing 8.4 shows the source code for the program CLASS4.CPP. The program creates a square and a rectangle and displays their dimensions and areas. No input is required.

Type

Listing 8.4. Source code for the program CLASS4.CPP.

```
1:  // Program that demonstrates virtual functions
2:
3:  #include <iostream.h>
4:
5:  class cSquare
6:  {
7:    protected:
8:      double length;
9:
10:   public:
11:      cSquare(double len) { length = len; }
12:      double getLength() { return length; }
13:      virtual double getWidth() { return length; }
14:      double getArea() { return getLength() * getWidth(); }
15: };
16:
17: class cRectangle : public cSquare
18: {
19:   protected:
20:      double width;
21:
```

```
22:   public:
23:     cRectangle(double len, double wide) :
24:         cSquare(len), width(wide) {}
25:     virtual double getWidth() { return width; }
26: };
27:
28: main()
29: {
30:     cSquare square(10);
31:     cRectangle rectangle(10, 12);
32:
33:     cout << "Square has length = " << square.getLength() << "\n"
34:          << "          and area    = " << square.getArea() << "\n";
35:     cout << "Rectangle has length = "
36:          << rectangle.getLength() << "\n"
37:          << "            and width   = "
38:          << rectangle.getWidth() << "\n"
39:          << "            and area    = "
40:          << rectangle.getArea() << "\n";
41:     return 0;
42: }
```

Here is a sample session with the program in Listing 8.4.

```
Square has length = 10
and area    = 100
Rectangle has length = 10
and width   = 12
and area    = 120
```

The program in Listing 8.4 declares the classes cSquare and cRectangle to model squares and rectangles, respectively. The class cSquare declares a single data member, length, to store the length (and width) of the square. The class declares a constructor with the parameter len, which passes arguments to the member length. The class also declares the functions getLength, getWidth, and getArea. Both functions getLength and getWidth return the value in member length. Notice that the class declares function getWidth as virtual. The function getArea returns the area of the rectangle, calculated by calling the functions getLength and getWidth. We choose to invoke these functions rather than use the data member length in order to demonstrate how the virtual function getWidth works.

The program declares class cRectangle as a descendant of class cSquare. The class cRectangle declares the data member width and inherits the member length. These members enable the class to store the basic dimensions of a rectangle. The class constructor has the parameters len and wide. Notice that the constructor invokes the constructor cSquare and supplies it with the argument len. The constructor initializes the data member width with the value of parameter wide.

The class cRectangle declares the virtual function getWidth. This version returns the value in data member width. The class inherits the member functions getLength and getArea because their implementation is adequate for the cRectangle.

The function `main` declares the object `square` as an instance of class `cSquare`. The instance `square` has a length of 10. The function `main` also declares the object `rectangle` as an instance of class `cRectangle`. The instance `rectangle` has the length of 10 and the width of 12.

The output statement in lines 33 and 34 displays the length and area of the instance `square`. The statement sends the messages `getLength` and `getArea` to the preceding instance in order to obtain the sought values. The instance `square` invokes the function `getArea`, which in turn calls the functions `cSquare::getLength` and `cSquare::getWidth`.

The output statement in lines 35 through 40 displays the length, width, and area of the instance `rectangle`. The statement sends the messages `getLength`, `getWidth`, and `getArea` to this instance. The instance responds by calling the inherited function `cSquare::getLength`, the virtual function `cRectangle::getWidth`, and the inherited function `cSquare::getArea`. The latter function calls the inherited function `cSquare::getLength` and the virtual function `cRectangle::getWidth` to correctly calculate the area of the rectangle.

DO	DON'T

DO declare your destructor as virtual. This ensures polymorphic behavior in destroying class instances. In addition, I highly recommend that you declare a copy constructor and an assignment operator for each class.

DON'T forget that you inherit virtual functions and destructors in the descendant class. You need not declare shell functions and destructors that simply call the corresponding member of the parent class.

Rule for Virtual Functions

The rule for declaring a virtual function is "once virtual, always virtual." In other words, after you declare a function to be virtual in a class, any descendant class that overrides the virtual function must do so using another function that has the same parameter list. If the descendant class fails to use the same parameter list, the base class's version of the virtual function will be inaccessible to the descendant class (and any of its descendants). At first, this rule seems to lock you in. This limitation certainly is true for object-oriented programming languages that support virtual functions but not overloaded functions. In the case of C++, the work-around is interesting. You can declare nonvirtual and overloaded functions that have the same name as the virtual function, but bear a different parameter list. Moreover, you cannot inherit nonvirtual member functions that share the same name with a virtual function. Here is a simple example that illustrates the point.

```
#include <iostream.h>
class cA
{
public:
   cA() {}
   virtual void foo(char c)
      { cout << "virtual cA::foo() returns " << c << '\n'; }
};

class cB : public cA
{
public:
   cB() {}
   void foo(const char* s)
      { cout << "cB::foo() returns " << s << '\n'; }
   void foo(int i)
      { cout << "cB::foo() returns " << i << '\n'; }
   virtual void foo(char c)
      { cout << "virtual cB::foo() returns " << c << '\n'; }
};

class cC : public cB
{
public:
   cC() {}
   void foo(const char* s)
      { cout << "cC::foo() returns " << s << '\n'; }
   void foo(double x)
      { cout << "cC::foo() returns " << x << '\n'; }
   virtual void foo(char c)
      { cout << "virtual cC::foo() returns " << c << '\n'; }
};

main()
{
   int[]= 100;
   cA Aobj;
   cB Bobj;
   cC Cobj;

   Aobj.foo('A');
   Bobj.foo('B');
   Bobj.foo(10);
   Bobj.foo("Bobj");
   Cobj.foo('C');
   // if you uncomment the next statement, program does not compile
   // Cobj.foo(n);
   Cobj.foo(144.123);
   Cobj.foo("Cobj");
   return 0;
}
```

This code declares three classes—cA, cB, and cC—to form a linear hierarchy of classes. Class cA declares function foo(char) as virtual. Class cB also declares its own version of the virtual function foo(char). In addition, class cB declares the nonvirtual overloaded functions foo(const char* s) and foo(int). Class cC, the descendant of class cB, declares the virtual function foo(char) and the nonvirtual and overloaded functions foo(const char*) and foo(double). Notice that class cC must declare the foo(const char*) function if it needs the function because it cannot inherit the member function cB::foo(const char*). C++ supports a different function inheritance scheme when an overloaded function and virtual function are involved. The function main creates an instance for each of the three classes and involves the various versions of the member function foo.

Friend Functions

C++ allows member functions to access all the data members of a class. In addition, C++ grants the same privileged access to friend functions. The declaration of friend functions appears in the class and begins with the keyword friend. Other than using the special keyword, friend functions look very much like member functions, except they cannot access the befriended class automatically because that requires the hidden this pointer. Given a pointer to an instance of the befriended class, however, the function can access all parts of the class. When you define friend functions outside the declaration of their befriended class, you need not qualify the function names with the name of the class.

NEW ☞ *Friend functions* are ordinary functions that have access to all data members of one or **TERM** more classes.

Friend Functions

The general form of friend functions is

```
class className
{
public:
    className();
    // other constructors

    friend returnType friendFunction(<parameter list>);
};
```

Example

```
class String
{
protected:
    char *str;
    int len;

public:
    String();
    ~String();
    // other member functions
```

```
        friend String& append(String& str1, String& str2);
        friend String& append(const char* str1, String& str2);
        friend String& append(String& str1, const char* str2);
};
```

Friend classes can accomplish tasks that are awkward, difficult, and even impossible with member functions.

Look at a simple example for using friend functions. Listing 8.5 contains the source code for the CLASS5.CPP program. This program internally creates two complex numbers, adds them, stores the result in another complex number, and then displays the operands and resulting complex numbers.

 Listing 8.5. Source code for the CLASS5.CPP program.

```
1:  // Program that demonstrates friend functions
2:
3:  #include <iostream.h>
4:
5:  class Complex
6:  {
7:    protected:
8:      double x;
9:      double y;
10:
11:   public:
12:     Complex(double real = 0, double imag = 0);
13:     Complex(Complex& c) { assign(c); }
14:     void assign(Complex& c);
15:     double getReal() const { return x; }
16:     double getImag() const { return y; }
17:     friend Complex add(Complex& c1, Complex& c2);
18: };
19:
20: Complex::Complex(double real, double imag)
21: {
22:   x = real;
23:   y = imag;
24: }
25:
26: void Complex::assign(Complex& c)
27: {
28:   x = c.x;
29:   y = c.y;
30: }
31:
32: Complex add(Complex& c1, Complex& c2)
33: {
34:   Complex result(c1);
35:
36:   result.x += c2.x;
37:   result.y += c2.y;
38:   return result;
39: }
```

continues

Listing 8.5. continued

```
40:
41: main()
42: {
43:   Complex c1(2, 3);
44:   Complex c2(5, 7);
45:   Complex c3;
46:
47:   c3.assign(add(c1, c2));
48:   cout << "(" << c1.getReal() << " + i" << c1.getImag() << ")"
49:        << " + "
50:        << "(" << c2.getReal() << " + i" << c2.getImag() << ")"
51:        << " = "
52:        << "(" << c3.getReal() << " + i" << c3.getImag() << ")"
53:        << "\n\n";
54:   return 0;
55: }
```

Here is a sample session with the program in Listing 8.5.

```
(2 + i3) + (5 + i7) = (7 + i10)
```

The program in Listing 8.5 declares the class Complex, which models complex numbers. This class declares two data members, two constructors, a friend function (the highlight of this example), and a set of member functions. The data members x and y store the real and imaginary components of a complex number, respectively.

The class has two constructors. The first constructor has two parameters (with default arguments) that enable you to build a class instance using the real and imaginary components of a complex number. Because the two parameters have default arguments, the constructor doubles up as the default constructor. The second constructor, complex(complex&), is the copy constructor.

The Complex class declares three member functions. The function assign copies a class instance into another one. The functions getReal and getImag return the value stored in the members real and imag, respectively.

The Complex class declares the friend function add to add two complex numbers. To make the program short, we do not implement complementary friend functions that subtract, multiply, and divide class instances. What is so special about the friend function add? Why not use an ordinary member function to add a class instance? The following declaration of the alternate add member function answers these questions:

```
complex& add(complex& c)
```

This declaration states that the function treats the parameter c as a second operand. Here is how the member function add works.

```
complex c1(3, 4), c2(1.2, 4.5);
c1.add(c2); // adds c2 to c1
```

First, the member function `add` works as an increment and not as an addition function. Second, the targeted class instance is always the first operand. This is not a problem for operations such as addition and multiplication, but it is a problem for subtraction and division. That is why the friend function `add` works better by giving you the freedom of choosing how to add the class instances.

The friend function `add` returns a class instance. The function creates a local instance of class `Complex` and returns that instance.

The function `main` uses the member function `assign` and the friend function `add` to perform basic complex operations. In addition, the function `main` invokes the functions `getReal` and `getImag` with the various instances of class `Complex` to display the components of each instance.

Operators and Friend Operators

The last program used a member function and a friend function to implement complex math operations. The approach is typical in C and Pascal because these languages do not support user-defined operators. By contrast, C++ enables you to declare operators and friend operators. These operators include +, -, *, /, %, ==, !=, <=, <, >=, >, +=, -=, *=, /=, %=, [], (), <<, and >>. Consult a C++ language reference book for more details on the rules of using these operators. C++ treats operators and friend operators as special member functions and friend functions.

Operators and Friend Operators

The general syntax for declaring operators and friend operators is

```
class className
{
public:
    // constructors and destructor
    // member functions

    // unary operator
    returnType operator operatorSymbol();
    // binary operator
    returnType operator operatorSymbol(operand);
    // unary friend operator
    friend returnType operator operatorSymbol(operand);
    // binary operator
    friend returnType operator operatorSymbol(firstOperand,
        secondOperand);
};
```

Example

```
class String
{
protected:
    char *str;
```

```
       int len;

public:
    String();
    ~String();
    // other member functions
    // assignment operator
    String& operator =(String& s);
    String& operator +=(String& s);
    // concatenation operators
    friend String& operator +(String& s1, String& s2);
    friend String& operator +(const char* s1, String& s2);
    friend String& operator +(String& s1, const char* s2);
    // relational operators
    friend int operator >(String& s1, String& s2);
    friend int operator =>(String& s1, String& s2);
    friend int operator <(String& s1, String& s2);
    friend int operator <=(String& s1, String& s2);
    friend int operator ==(String& s1, String& s2);
    friend int operator !=(String& s1, String& s2);
};
```

The functions you write use the operators and friend operators just like predefined operators. Therefore, you can create operators to support the operations of classes that model, for example, complex numbers, strings, arrays, and matrices. These operators enable you to write expressions that are far more readable than expressions that use named functions.

Look at an example. Listing 8.6 contains the source code for the CLASS6.CPP program. We created this program by modifying and expanding Listing 8.5. The new program performs more additions and displays two sets of operands and results.

Listing 8.6. Source code for the CLASS6.CPP program.

```
1:  // Program that demonstrates operators and friend operators
2:
3:  #include <iostream.h>
4:
5:  class Complex
6:  {
7:      protected:
8:         double x;
9:         double y;
10:
11:     public:
12:        Complex(double real = 0, double imag = 0)
13:          { assign(real, imag); }
14:        Complex(Complex& c);
15:        void assign(double real = 0, double imag = 0);
16:        double getReal() const { return x; }
17:        double getImag() const { return y; }
18:        Complex& operator =(Complex& c);
19:        Complex& operator +=(Complex& c);
20:        friend Complex operator +(Complex& c1, Complex& c2);
21:        friend ostream& operator <<(ostream& os, Complex& c);
22:  };
```

```
23:
24: Complex::Complex(Complex& c)
25: {
26:   x = c.x;
27:   y = c.y;
28: }
29:
30: void Complex::assign(double real, double imag)
31: {
32:   x = real;
33:   y = imag;
34: }
35:
36: Complex& Complex::operator =(Complex& c)
37: {
38:   x = c.x;
39:   y = c.y;
40:   return *this;
41: }
42:
43: Complex& Complex::operator +=(Complex& c)
44: {
45:   x += c.x;
46:   y += c.y;
47:   return *this;
48: }
49:
50: Complex operator +(Complex& c1, Complex& c2)
51: {
52:   Complex result(c1);
53:
54:   result.x += c2.x;
55:   result.y += c2.y;
56:   return result;
57: }
58:
59: ostream& operator <<(ostream& os, Complex& c)
60: {
61:   os << "(" << c.x << " + i" << c.y << ")";
62:   return os;
63: }
64:
65: main()
66: {
67:   Complex c1(3, 5);
68:   Complex c2(7, 5);
69:   Complex c3;
70:   Complex c4(2, 3);
71:
72:   c3 = c1 + c2;
73:   cout << c1 << " + " << c2 << " = " << c3 << "\n";
74:   cout << c3 << " + " << c4 << " = ";
75:   c3 += c4;
76:   cout << c3 << "\n";
77:   return 0;
78: }
```

Here is a sample session with the program in Listing 8.6.

```
(3 + i5) + (7 + i5) = (10 + i10)
(10 + i10) + (2 + i3) = (12 + i13)
```

The new class `Complex` replaces the `assign(Complex&)` member function with the operator =. The class also replaces the friend function add with the friend operator +.

```
Complex& operator =(Complex& c);
friend Complex operator +(Complex& c1, Complex& c2);
```

The operator = has one parameter, a reference to an instance of class `Complex`, and also returns a reference to the same class. The friend operator + has two parameters (both are references to instances of class `Complex`) and yields a complex class type.

I also took the opportunity to add two new operators.

```
complex& operator +=(complex& c);
friend ostream& operator <<(ostream& os, complex& c);
```

The operator += is a member of class `Complex`. It takes one parameter, a reference to an instance of class `Complex`, and yields a reference to the same class. The other new operator is the friend operator <<, which illustrates how to write a stream extractor operator for a class. The friend operator has two parameters: a reference to class `ostream` (the output stream class) and a reference to class `Complex`. The operator << returns a reference to class `ostream`. This type of value enables you to chain stream output with other predefined types or other classes (assuming these classes have a friend operator <<). The definition of friend operator << has two statements. The first one outputs strings and the data members of class `Complex` to the output stream parameter `os`. The friendship status of operator << allows it to access the `real` and `imag` data members of its `Complex`-typed parameter c. The second statement in the operator definition returns the first parameter `os`.

The function `main` declares four instances of class `Complex`, c1, c2, c3, and c4. The instances c1, c2, and c4 are created with nondefault values assigned to the data members `real` and `imag`. The function tests use the operators =, +, <<, +=. The program illustrates that you can use operators and friend operators to write code that is more readable and supports a higher level of abstraction.

Summary

Today's lesson introduced you to C++ classes and discussed the following topics:

- [ ] The basics of object-oriented programming include classes, objects, messages, methods, inheritance, and polymorphism.

- [ ] You declare base classes to specify the various private, protected, and public members. C++ classes contain data members and member functions. The data members store the state of a class instance, and the member functions query and manipulate that state.

☐ Constructors and destructors support the automatic creation and removal of class instances. Constructors are special members that must have the same name as the host class. You may declare any number of constructors, or none at all. In the latter case, the compiler creates one for you. Each constructor enables you to create a class instance in a different way. There are two special types of constructors: the default constructor and the copy constructor. In contrast with constructors, C++ enables you to declare only one parameterless destructor. Destructors automatically remove class instances. The runtime system automatically invokes the constructor and destructor when a class instance comes into and goes out of its scope.

☐ Declaring a class hierarchy enables you to derive classes from existing ones. The descendant classes inherit the members of their ancestor classes. C++ classes are able to override inherited member functions by defining their own versions. If you override a nonvirtual function, you may declare the new version using a different parameter list. By contrast, you cannot alter the parameter list of an inherited virtual function.

☐ Virtual member functions enable your classes to support polymorphic behavior. Such behavior offers a response that is suitable for each class in a hierarchy. After you declare a function virtual, you can override it only with a virtual function in a descendant class. All versions of a virtual function in a class hierarchy must have the same signature.

☐ Friend functions are special nonmember functions that may access protected and private data members. These functions enable you to implement operations that are more flexible than those offered by member functions.

☐ Operators and friend operators enable you to support various operations, such as addition, assignment, and indexing. These operators enable you to offer a level of abstraction for your classes. In addition, they assist in making the expressions that manipulate class instances more readable and more intuitive.

Q&A

Q What happens if I declare the default, copy, and other constructors as protected?

A Client programs are unable to create instances of that class. However, client programs can use that class by declaring descendant classes with public constructors.

Q Can I chain messages to an instance?

A Yes, you can as long as the chained messages invoke member functions that return a reference to the same class that receives the message. For example, if you have a class String with the following member functions

```
String& upperCase();
string& reverse();
String& mapChars(char find, char replace);
```

you can write the following statement for the instance of class String s:

```
s.upperCase().reverse().mapChar(' ', '+');
```

Q What happens if a class relies on the copy constructor, which is created by the compiler, to copy instances of a class that has pointers?

A These constructors perform a bit-by-bit copy. Consequently, the corresponding pointer members in both instances end up with the address to the same dynamic data. This kind of duplication is a recipe for trouble!

Q Can I create an array of instances?

A Yes, you can; however, the accompanying class must have a default constructor. The instantiation of the array uses the constructor mentioned previously.

Q Can I use a pointer to create an instance of class?

A Yes, you need to use the operators new and delete to allocate and deallocate the dynamic space for the instance. Here is an example using the class Complex.

```
Complex* pC;
pC = new Complex;
// manipulate the instance accessed by pointer pC
delete pC;

or

Complex* pC = new Complex;
// manipulate the instance accessed by pointer pC
delete pC;
```

Workshop

The Workshop provides quiz questions to help you solidify your understanding of the material covered and exercises to provide you with experience in using what you've learned. Try to understand the quiz and exercise answers before continuing on to the next day's lesson. Answers are provided in Appendix A.

Quiz

1. Where is the error in the following class declaration?

```
class String {
        char *str;
        unsigned len;
        String();
        String(const String& s);
```

```
        String(unsigned size, char = ' ');
        String(unsigned size);
        String& assign(String& s);
        ~String();
        unsigned getLen() const;
        char* getString();
        // other member functions
};
```

2. Where is the error in the following class declaration?

```
class String {
    protected:
      char *str;
      unsigned len;
    public:
      String();
      String(const char* s);
      String(const String& s);
      String(unsigned size, char = ' ');
      String(unsigned size);
      ~String();
      // other member functions
};
```

3. True or false? The following statement, which creates the instance s based on the preceding declaration of class String, is correct:

```
s = String("Hello Turbo C++");
```

4. Looking at the program CLASS6.CPP, if you change the declarations of the instances in function main to the following, will the program still compile?

```
Complex c1 = Complex(3, 5);
Complex c2 = Complex(7, 5);
Complex c3 = c1;
Complex c4 = Complex(2, 3);
```

Exercise

Create the program CLASS7.CPP from CLASS6.CPP by replacing the individual instances c1 to c4 with c, an array of instances.

9

Basic Stream
File I/O

Today's lesson introduces you to file I/O (input/output) operations using the C++ stream library. You have a choice of using file I/O functions in the STDIO.H file or in the C++ stream library. Each of these two I/O libraries offers a lot of power and flexibility. Today's lesson presents basic and practical operations that enable you to read and write data to files. You learn about the following topics:

☐ Common stream I/O functions

☐ Sequential stream I/O for text

☐ Sequential stream I/O for binary data

☐ Random access stream I/O for binary data

To learn more about the C++ stream library, consult a C++ language reference book, such as Tom Swan's *C++ Primer* (Sams Publishing, 1992).

The C++ Stream Library

The C++ stream I/O library (also known as the iostream library) is made up of a hierarchy of classes that are declared in several header files. The IOSTREAM.H header file used thus far is only one of these. Others include ISTREAM.H, OSTREAM.H, IFSTREAM.H, OFSTREAM.H, and FSTREAM.H. The ISTREAM.H and OSTREAM.H files support the basic input and output stream classes. The IOSTREAM.H combines the operations of the classes in the previous two header files. Similarly, the IFSTREAM.H and OFSTREAM.H files support the basic file input and output stream classes. The FSTREAM.H file combines the operations of the classes in the previous two header files. There are additional stream library files that offer even more specialized stream I/O. The ANSI/ISO C++ committee will define the standard stream I/O library, and the committee's work will end any confusion regarding which classes and header files are part of the standard stream library and which ones are not.

Common Stream I/O Functions

This section presents stream I/O member functions that are common to both sequential and random access I/O. These member functions include open, close, good, and fail, in addition to the operator !.

The open member function enables you to open a file stream for input, output, append, and both input and output. The function also permits you to specify whether the related I/O is binary or text.

SAMS
PUBLISHING

Sams
Learning
Center

The *open* Member Function

Syntax

The prototype for the open function is

```
void open(const char* filename,
          int mode,
          int m = filebuf::openprot);
```

The parameter `filename` specifies the name of the file to open. The parameter `mode` indicates the I/O mode. Following is a list of arguments for parameter `mode` that are exported by the FSTREAM.H header file:

in	Open stream for input
out	Open stream for output
ate	Set stream pointer to the end of the file
app	Open stream for append mode
trunc	Truncate file size to 0 if it already exists
nocreate	Raise an error if the file does not already exist
noreplace	Raise an error if the file already exists
binary	Open in binary mode

Example

```
// open stream for input
fstream f;
f.open("\\AUTOEXEC.BAT", ios::in);

// open stream for output
fstream f;
f.open("\\AUTOEXEC.OLD", ios:out);

// open stream for binary input and output
fstream f;
f.open("INCOME.DAT", ios::in | ios::out | ios::binary);
```

Note: The file stream classes offer constructors that include the action (and have the same parameters) of the member function open.

The `close` member function closes the stream and recuperates the resources involved. These resources include the memory buffer used in the stream I/O operations.

Syntax

The *close* Member Function

The prototype for the close function is

```
void close();
```

Example

```
fstream f;
// open stream
f.open("\\AUTOEXEC.BAT", ios::in);
// process file
// now close stream
f.close();
```

The C++ stream library includes a set of basic functions that check the error status of a stream operation. These functions include the following:

1. The good() function returns a nonzero value if there is no error in a stream operation. The declaration of function good is

```
int good();
```

2. The fail() function returns a nonzero value if there is an error in a stream operation. The declaration of function fail is

```
int fail();
```

3. The overloaded operator ! is applied to a stream instance to determine the error status.

The C++ stream libraries offer additional functions to set and query other aspects and types of stream errors.

Sequential Text Stream I/O

The functions and operators involved in sequential text I/O are simple. You already have been exposed to most of them in earlier lessons. The functions and operators include the following:

☐ The stream extractor operator << writes strings and characters to a stream.

☐ The stream inserter operator >> reads characters from a stream.

☐ The getline function reads strings from a stream.

Syntax

The *getline* Member Function

The prototypes for the member function getline are

```
istream& getline(char* buffer,
                 int size,
                 char delimiter = '\n');

istream& getline(signed char* buffer,
                 int size,
                 char delimiter = '\n');
```

```
istream& getline(unsigned char* buffer,
                 int size,
                 char delimiter = '\n');
```

The parameter buffer is a pointer to the string receiving the characters from the stream. The parameter size specifies the maximum number of characters to read. The parameter delimiter specifies the delimiting character, which causes the string input to stop before reaching the number of characters specified by parameter size. The parameter delimiter has the default argument of '\n'.

Example

```
fstream f;
char textLine[MAX];
f.open("\\CONFIG.SYS", ios::in);
while (!f.eof()) {
f.getline(textLine, MAX);
cout << textLine << "\n";
}
f.close();
```

Look at an example. Listing 9.1 shows the source code for the program IO1.CPP. The program performs the following tasks:

☐ Prompts you to enter the name of an input text file.

☐ Prompts you to enter the name of an output text file. (The program detects if the names of the input and output files are the same, and if so, reprompts you for a different output filename.)

☐ Reads the lines from the input files and removes any trailing spaces in these lines.

☐ Writes the lines to the output file and also to the standard output window.

Type

Listing 9.1. Source code for the IO1.CPP program.

```
1:  // C++ program that demonstrates sequential file I/O
2:
3:  #include <iostream.h>
4:  #include <fstream.h>
5:  #include <string.h>
6:
7:  enum boolean { false, true };
8:
9:  const unsigned LINE_SIZE = 128;
10: const unsigned NAME_SIZE = 64;
11:
12: void trimStr(char* s)
13: {
14:   int i = strlen(s) - 1;
15:   // locate the character where the trailing spaces begin
```

continued

287

Listing 9.1. continued

```
16:    while (i >= 0 && s[i] == ' ')
17:      i--;
18:    // truncate string
19:    s[i+1] = '\0';
20: }
21:
22: void getInputFilename(char* inFile, fstream& f)
23: {
24:    boolean ok;
25:
26:    do {
27:      ok = true;
28:      cout << "Enter input file : ";
29:      cin.getline(inFile, NAME_SIZE);
30:      f.open(inFile, ios::in);
31:      if (!f) {
32:        cout << "Cannot open file " << inFile << "\n\n";
33:        ok = false;
34:      }
35:    } while (!ok);
36:
37: }
38:
39: void getOutputFilename(char* outFile, const char* inFile,
40:                        fstream& f)
41: {
42:    boolean ok;
43:
44:    do {
45:      ok = true;
46:      cout << "Enter output file : ";
47:      cin.getline(outFile, NAME_SIZE);
48:      if (stricmp(inFile, outFile) != 0) {
49:        f.open(outFile, ios::out);
50:        if (!f) {
51:          cout << "File " << outFile << " is invalid\n\n";
52:          ok = false;
53:        }
54:      }
55:      else {
56:        cout << "Input and output files must be different!\n";
57:        ok = false;
58:      }
59:    } while (!ok);
60: }
61:
62: void processLines(fstream& fin, fstream& fout)
63: {
64:    char line[LINE_SIZE + 1];
65:
66:    // loop to trim trailing spaces
67:    while (fin.getline(line, LINE_SIZE)) {
68:      trimStr(line);
69:      // write line to the output file
70:      fout << line << "\n";
71:      // echo updated line to the output window
```

```
72:     cout << line << "\n";
73:     }
74:
75: }
76: main()
77: {
78:
79:     fstream fin, fout;
80:     char inFile[NAME_SIZE + 1], outFile[NAME_SIZE + 1];
81:
82:     getInputFilename(inFile, fin);
83:     getOutputFilename(outFile, inFile, fout);
84:     processLines(fin, fout);
85:     // close streams
86:     fin.close();
87:     fout.close();
88:     return 0;
89: }
```

Here is a sample session with the program in Listing 9.1.

```
Enter input file : sample.txt
Enter output file : sample.out
This is line 1
This is line 2
This is line 3
This is line 4
```

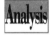

The program in Listing 9.1 declares no classes and, instead, focuses on using file streams to input and output text. The program declares the functions trimStr, getInputFilename, getOutputFilename, processLines, and main.

The function trimStr shaves the trailing spaces in the strings passed by parameter s. The function declares the local variable i and assigns it the index of the character just before the null terminator. The function uses the while loop in line 13 to perform a backward scan of the characters in string s for the first nonspace character. The statement at line 16 assigns the null terminator character to the character located right after the last nonspace character in the string s.

The function getInputFilename obtains the input filename and opens its corresponding input file stream. The parameter inFile passes the name of the input file to the function caller. The reference parameter f passes the opened input stream to the function caller. The function getInputFilename declares the local flag ok. The function uses the do-while loop in lines 26 through 35 to obtain a valid filename and to open that file for input. Line 27 contains the first statement inside the loop, which assigns the enumerated value true to the local variable ok. The output statement in line 28 prompts you for the input filename. The statement in line 29 calls the stream input function getline to obtain your input and to store it in the parameter inFile. The statement in line 30 opens the input file using the stream parameter f. The open statement uses the ios::in value to indicate that the stream is opened for text input. The if statement in line 31 determines whether the stream f is successfully opened. If not, the function executes the statements in lines 32 and 33. These statements display an error message and assign the enumerated value `false` to the local variable `ok`. The loop's `while` clause in line 35 examines the condition `!ok`. The loop iterates until you supply it a valid filename, which must successfully be opened for input.

The function `getOutputFilename` complements the function `getInputFilename` and has three parameters. The parameter `outFile` passes the output filename of the function caller. The parameter `inFile` supplies the function with the input filename. The function uses this parameter to ensure that the input and output filenames are not the same. The parameter `f` passes the output stream to the function caller. The implementation of function `getOutputFilename` is very similar to that of function `getInputFilename`. The main difference is that the function `getOutputFilename` calls the function `stricmp` to compare the values in parameter `inFile` and `outFile`. The function uses the result of `stricmp` to determine whether the names of the input and output files are identical. If so, the function executes the statements in the `else` clause at lines 57 and 58. These statements display an error message and assign `false` to the local variable `ok`.

The function `processLines` reads the lines from the input file stream, trims them, and writes them to the output file stream. The parameters `fin` and `fout` pass the input and output file streams, respectively. The function declares the local string variable `line` and uses the `while` loop in lines 67 through 73 to process the text lines. The `while` clause contains the call to function `getline`, which reads the next line in the input stream `fin` and assigns the input line to variable `line`. The result of function `getline` causes the `while` loop to stop iterating when there are no more input lines. The first statement inside the loop, located at line 68, calls the function `trimStr` and passes it the argument `line`. This function call prunes any existing trailing spaces in the local variable `line`. The statement in line 70 writes the string in variable `line` to the output file stream. The statement in line 72 echoes the string in `line` to the standard output window. (We placed this statement in the program so that you can monitor the progress of the program.)

The function `main` declares the file streams `fin` and `fout`, and the string variables `inFile` and `outFile`. The statement in line 82 calls function `getInputFilename` and passes it the arguments `inFile` and `fin`. This call obtains the name of the input file and the input stream through the arguments `inFile` and `fin`, respectively. The statement in line 83 calls the function `getOutputFilename` and passes it the arguments `outFile`, `inFile`, and `fout`. This call obtains the name of the output file and the output stream through the arguments `outFile` and `fout`, respectively. The statement in line 84 calls function `processLines` and passes it the arguments `fin` and `fout`. This call processes the lines in the input file stream `fin` and writes the results to the output file stream `fout`. The statements in lines 86 and 87 close the input and output file streams, respectively.

Sequential Binary File Stream I/O

The C++ stream library offers the overloaded stream member functions `write` and `read` for sequential binary file stream I/O. The member function `write` sends multiple bytes to an output stream. This function can write any variable or instance to a stream.

The *write* Member Function

The prototypes for the overloaded member function write are

```
ostream& write(const char* buff, int num);
ostream& write(const signed char* buff, int num);
ostream& write(const unsigned char* buff, int num);
```

The parameter buff is the pointer to the buffer that contains the data to be sent to the output stream. The parameter num indicates the number of bytes in the buffer that are sent to the stream.

Example

```
const MAX = 80;
char buff[MAX+1] = "Hello World!";
int len = strlen(buffer) + 1;
fstream f;
f.open("CALC.DAT", ios::out | ios::binary);
f.write((const unsigned char*)&len, sizeof(len));
f.write((const unsigned char*)buff, len);
f.close();
```

The member function read receives multiple bytes from an input stream. This function can read any variable or can read from a stream.

The *read* Member Function

The prototypes for the overloaded member function read are

```
istream& read(char* buff, int num);
istream& read(signed char* buff, int num);
istream& read(unsigned char* buff, int num);
```

The parameter buff is the pointer to the buffer that receives the data from the input stream. The parameter num indicates the number of bytes to read from the stream.

Example

```
const MAX = 80;
char buff[MAX+1];
int len;
fstream f;
f.open("CALC.DAT", ios::in | ios::binary);
f.read((const unsigned char*)&len, sizeof(len));
f.read((const unsigned char*)buff, len);
f.close();
```

Look at an example that performs sequential binary stream I/O. Listing 9.2 shows the source code for the program IO2.CPP. The program declares a class that models dynamic numerical arrays. The stream I/O operations enable the program to read and write both the individual array elements and an entire array in binary files. The program creates the arrays arr1, arr2, and arr3 and then performs the following tasks:

☐ Assigns values to the elements of array arr1. (This array has 10 elements.)

☐ Assigns values to the elements of array arr3. (This array has 20 elements.)

☐ Displays the values in array arr1.

☐ Writes the elements of array arr1 to the file ARR1.DAT, one element at a time.

☐ Reads the elements of arr1 from the file into the array arr2. (The array arr2 has 10 elements—the same size as array arr1.)

☐ Displays the values in array arr2.

☐ Displays the values in array arr3.

☐ Writes the elements of array arr3 to file ARR3.DAT in one swoop.

☐ Reads, in one swoop, the data in file ARR3.DAT and stores them in array arr1.

☐ Displays the values in array arr1. (The output shows that array arr1 has the same size and data as array arr3.)

Type **Listing 9.2. Source code for the IO2.CPP program.**

```
 1:  /*
 2:      C++ program that demonstrates sequential binary file I/O
 3:  */
 4:
 5:  #include <iostream.h>
 6:  #include <fstream.h>
 7:
 8:  const unsigned MIN_SIZE = 10;
 9:  const double BAD_VALUE = -1.0e+30;
10:  enum boolean { false, true };
11:
12:  class Array
13:  {
14:       Array(const Array&);   //prevent copy const. getting called
15:    protected:
16:       double *dataPtr;
17:       unsigned size;
18:       double badIndex;
19:    public:
20:       Array(unsigned Size = MIN_SIZE);
21:       ~Array()
22:         { delete [] dataPtr; }
23:       unsigned getSize() const { return size; }
24:       double& operator [](unsigned index)
25:       { return (index < size) ? *(dataPtr + index) : badIndex; }
26:       boolean writeElem(fstream& os, unsigned index);
27:       boolean readElem(fstream& is, unsigned index);
28:       boolean writeArray(const char* filename);
29:       boolean readArray(const char* filename);
30:  };
31:
32:  Array::Array(unsigned Size)
```

```
33: {
34:    size = (Size < MIN_SIZE) ? MIN_SIZE : Size;
35:    badIndex = BAD_VALUE;
36:    dataPtr = new double[size];
37: }
38:
39: boolean Array::writeElem(fstream& os, unsigned index)
40: {
41:    if (index < size) {
42:      os.write((unsigned char*)(dataPtr + index), sizeof(double));
43:      return (os.good()) ? true : false;
44:    }
45:    else
46:      return false;
47: }
48:
49: boolean Array::readElem(fstream& is, unsigned index)
50: {
51:    if (index < size) {
52:      is.read((unsigned char*)(dataPtr + index), sizeof(double));
53:      return (is.good()) ? true : false;
54:    }
55:    else
56:      return false;
57: }
58:
59: boolean Array::writeArray(const char* filename)
60: {
61:    fstream f(filename, ios::out | ios::binary);
62:
63:    if (f.fail())
64:      return false;
65:    f.write((unsigned char*) &size, sizeof(size));
66:    f.write((unsigned char*)dataPtr, size * sizeof(double));
67:    f.close();
68:    return (f.good()) ? true : false;
69: }
70:
71: boolean Array::readArray(const char* filename)
72: {
73:    fstream f(filename, ios::in | ios::binary);
74:    unsigned sz;
75:
76:    if (f.fail())
77:      return false;
78:    f.read((unsigned char*) &sz, sizeof(sz));
79:    // need to expand the array
80:    if (sz != size) {
81:      delete [] dataPtr;
82:      dataPtr = new double[sz];
83:      size = sz;
84:    }
85:    f.read((unsigned char*)dataPtr, size * sizeof(double));
86:    f.close();
87:    return (f.good()) ? true : false;
88: }
```

continued

Listing 9.2. continued

```
89:
90:  main()
91:  {
92:    const unsigned SIZE1 = 10;
93:    const unsigned SIZE2 = 20;
94:    char* filename1 = "array1.dat";
95:    char* filename2 = "array3.dat";
96:    Array arr1(SIZE1), arr2(SIZE1), arr3(SIZE2);
97:    fstream f(filename1, ios::out | ios::binary);
98:
99:    // assign values to array arr1
100:    for (unsigned i = 0; i < arr1.getSize(); i++)
101:      arr1[i] = 10 * i;
102:
103:    // assign values to array arr3
104:    for (i = 0; i < SIZE2; i++)
105:      arr3[i] = i;
106:
107:    cout << "Array arr1 has the following values:\n";
108:    for (i = 0; i < arr1.getSize(); i++)
109:      cout << arr1[i] << "  ";
110:    cout << "\n\n";
111:
112:    // write elements of array arr1 to the stream
113:    for (i = 0; i < arr1.getSize(); i++)
114:      arr1.writeElem(f, i);
115:    f.close();
116:
117:    // reopen the stream for input
118:    f.open(filename1, ios::in | ios::binary);
119:
120:    for (i = 0; i < arr1.getSize(); i++)
121:      arr2.readElem(f, i);
122:    f.close();
123:
124:    // display the elements of array arr2
125:    cout << "Array arr2 has the following values:\n";
126:    for (i = 0; i < arr2.getSize(); i++)
127:      cout << arr2[i] << "  ";
128:    cout << "\n\n";
129:
130:    // display the elements of array arr3
131:    cout << "Array arr3 has the following values:\n";
132:    for (i = 0; i < arr3.getSize(); i++)
133:      cout << arr3[i] << "  ";
134:    cout << "\n\n";
135:
136:    // write the array arr3 to file ARRAY3.DAT
137:    arr3.writeArray(filename2);
138:    // read the array arr1 from file ARRAY3.DAT
139:    arr1.readArray(filename2);
140:
```

```
141:    // display the elements of array arr1
142:    cout << "Array arr1 now has the following values:\n";
143:    for (i = 0; i < arr1.getSize(); i++)
144:      cout << arr1[i] << "   ";
145:    cout << "\n\n";
146:    return 0;
147: }
```

Here is a sample session with the program in Listing 9.2.

```
Array arr1 has the following values:
0   10  20  30  40  50  60  70  80  90

Array arr2 has the following values:
0   10  20  30  40  50  60  70  80  90

Array arr3 has the following values:
0   1   2   3   4   5   6   7   8   9   10  11  12  13  14  15  16  17  18  19

Array arr1 now has the following values:
0   1   2   3   4   5   6   7   8   9   10  11  12  13  14  15  16  17  18  19
```

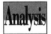

The program in Listing 9.2 declares a version of class Array that resembles the one in Day 8, Listing 8.2. The main difference is that here we use the operator [ ] to replace both the member functions store and recall. This operator checks for valid indices and returns the value in member badIndex if the argument is out of range. In addition to operator [ ], we added the member functions writeElem, readElem, writeArray, and readArray to perform sequential binary file stream I/O.

Also note the copy constructor on line 14, and especially that it isn't actually defined anywhere. This is a trick that can be used to prevent other functions or classes from automatically copying it when you know that it would be a Bad Thing (in this case because of the dynamic data, the contents of which would need to be copied).

The function writeElem, defined in lines 39 through 47, writes a single array element to an output stream. The parameter os represents the output stream. The parameter index specifies the array element to write. The function writeElem yields true if the argument for the index is valid and if the stream output proceeds without any error. After writeElem writes an array element, the internal stream pointer advances to the next location.

The function readElem, defined in lines 49 through 57, reads a single array element from an input stream. The parameter is represents the input stream. The parameter index specifies the array element to read. The function readElem returns true if the argument for the index is valid and if the stream input proceeds without any error. After the readElem reads an array element, the internal stream pointer advances to the next location.

The functions writeElem and readElem permit the same class instance to write and read data elements, respectively, from multiple streams.

The function writeArray, defined in lines 59 through 69, writes the entire elements of the array to a binary file. The parameter filename specifies the name of the output file. The function opens an output stream and writes the value of the data member size and then writes the elements of the dynamic array. The writeArray function returns true if it successfully writes the array to the stream. Otherwise, it yields false. The function opens a local output stream by using the stream function open and supplying it with the filename and I/O mode argument. The I/O mode argument is the expression ios::out ¦ ios::binary, which specifies that the stream is opened for binary output only. The function makes two calls to the stream function write—the first to write the data member size, and the second to write the elements of the dynamic array.

The function readArray, defined in lines 71 through 88, reads the entire elements of the array from a binary file. The parameter filename specifies the name of the input file. The function opens an input stream and reads the value of the data member size and then reads the elements of the dynamic array. The readArray function returns true if it successfully reads the array to the stream. Otherwise, the function yields false. The function opens a local input stream by using the stream function open and supplying it the filename and I/O mode arguments. The I/O mode argument is the expression ios::in ¦ ios::binary, which specifies that the stream is opened for binary input only. The function makes two calls to the stream function read—the first to read the data member size, and the second to read the elements of the dynamic array. Another feature of function readArray is that it resizes the instance of class Array to accommodate the data from the binary file. This means that a dynamic array accessed by the class instance may either shrink or expand, depending on the size of the array stored on file.

The member functions in Listing 9.2 indicate that the program performs two types of sequential binary stream I/O. The first type of I/O, implemented in functions readElem and writeElem, involves items that have the same data type. The second type of I/O, implemented in the functions readArray and writeArray, involves items that have different data types.

In Listing 9.2, the function main performs the following relevant tasks:

☐ Declares, in line 96, three instances of class Array, namely, arr1, arr2, and arr3. (The first two instances have the same dynamic array size, specified by the constant SIZE1, whereas instance arr3 has a larger size, specified by the constant SIZE2.)

☐ Declares, in line 97, the file stream f and opens it (using a stream constructor) to access file ARR1.DAT in binary output mode.

☐ Uses the for loops in lines 100 and 104 to arbitrarily assign values to the instance arr1 and arr3, respectively.

☐ Displays the elements of instance arr1 using the for loop in line 108.

☐ Writes the elements of array arr1 to the output file stream f, using the for loop in line 113 to send the writeElem message to instance arr1 and to supply the message with the output file stream f and the loop control variable i.

☐ Closes the output file stream by sending the close message to the output file stream f.

☐ Opens, in line 118, the file stream f to access the data file ARR1.DAT. (This time, the message open specifies a binary input mode.)

☐ Reads the elements of instance arr2 (which has not yet been assigned any values) from the input file stream f, using the for loop in line 120 to send the message readElem to instance arr2 and to supply the message with the arguments f, the file stream, and i, the loop control variable.

☐ Closes the input file stream, in line 122, by sending the message close to the input file stream f.

☐ Displays the elements of instance arr2 using the for loop in line 126. (These elements match those of instance arr1.)

☐ Displays the elements of instance arr3 by using the for loop in line 132.

☐ Writes the entire instance arr3 by sending the message writeArray to instance arr3. (The message writeArray has the filename argument of ARR3.DAT.)

☐ Reads the array in file ARR3.DAT into instance arr1, sending the message readArray to instance arr1 and supplying the message with the filename argument of ARR3.DAT.

☐ Displays the new elements of instance arr1 using the for loop in line 143.

Random Access File Stream I/O

Random access file stream operations also use the stream member functions read and write that were presented in the preceding section. The stream library offers a number of stream-seeking functions to enable you to move the stream pointer to any valid location. The member function seekg is one of such functions.

The *seekg* Member Function

The prototypes for the overloaded member function seekg are

```
istream& seekg(long pos);
istream& seekg(long pos, seek_dir dir);
```

The parameter pos in the first version specifies the absolute byte position in the stream. In the second version, the parameter pos specifies a relative offset, based on the argument for parameter dir. Following are the arguments for the latter parameter:

ios::begFrom the beginning of the file
ios::curFrom the current position of the file
ios::endFrom the end of the file

Example

```
const BLOCK_SIZE = 80;
char buff[BLOCK_SIZE] = "Hello World!";
fstream f("CALC.DAT", ios::in | ios::out | ios::binary);
f.seekg(3 * BLOCK_SIZE); // seek block # 4
f.read((const unsigned char*)buff, BLOCK_SIZE);
cout << buff <<< "\n";
f.close();
```

NEW TERM A *virtual array* is a disk-based array that stores fixed-size strings on disk.

Look at an example that uses random access file stream I/O. Listing 9.3 shows the source code for the program IO3.CPP and implements a virtual array. The program performs the following tasks:

- [ ] Uses an internal list of names to create a virtual array object
- [ ] Displays the elements in the unordered virtual array object
- [ ] Prompts you to enter a character and press the Return key
- [ ] Sorts the elements of the virtual array object; this process requires random access I/O
- [ ] Displays the elements in the sorted virtual array object

Type

Listing 9.3. Source code for the IO3.CPP program.

```
1:  /*
2:      C++ program that demonstrates random-access binary file I/O
3:  */
4:
5:  #include <iostream.h>
6:  #include <fstream.h>
7:  #include <stdlib.h>
8:  #include <string.h>
9:
10: const unsigned MIN_SIZE = 5;
11: const unsigned STR_SIZE = 31;
12: const double BAD_VALUE = -1.0e+30;
13: enum boolean { false, true };
14:
15: class VmArray
16: {
17:     protected:
18:       fstream f;
19:       unsigned size;
20:       double badIndex;
21:
22:     public:
23:       VmArray(unsigned Size, const char* filename);
24:       ~VmArray()
25:         { f.close(); }
26:       unsigned getSize() const
27:         { return size; }
```

```
28:        boolean writeElem(const char* str, unsigned index);
29:        boolean readElem(char* str, unsigned index);
30:        void Combsort();
31: };
32:
33: VmArray::VmArray(unsigned Size, const char* filename)
34: {
35:    char s[STR_SIZE+1];
36:    size = (Size < MIN_SIZE) ? MIN_SIZE : Size;
37:    badIndex = BAD_VALUE;
38:    f.open(filename, ios::in | ios::out | ios::binary);
39:    if (f.good()) {
40:      // fill the file stream with empty strings
41:      strcpy(s, "");;
42:      f.seekg(0);
43:      for (unsigned i = 0; i < size; i++)
44:        f.write((unsigned char*)s, sizeof(s));
45:    }
46: }
47:
48: boolean VmArray::writeElem(const char* str, unsigned index)
49: {
50:    if (index < size) {
51:      f.seekg(index * (STR_SIZE+1));
52:      f.write((unsigned char*)str, (STR_SIZE+1));
53:      return (f.good()) ? true : false;
54:    }
55:    else
56:      return false;
57: }
58:
59: boolean VmArray::readElem(char* str, unsigned index)
60: {
61:    if (index < size) {
62:      f.seekg(index * (STR_SIZE+1));
63:      f.read((unsigned char*)str, (STR_SIZE+1));
64:      return (f.good()) ? true : false;
65:    }
66:    else
67:      return false;
68: }
69:
70: void VmArray::Combsort()
71: {
72:    unsigned i, j, gap = size;
73:    boolean inOrder;
74:    char strI[STR_SIZE+1], strJ[STR_SIZE+1];
75:
76:    do {
77:      gap = (gap * 8) / 11;
78:      if (gap < 1)
79:        gap = 1;
80:      inOrder = true;
81:      for (i = 0, j = gap; i < (size - gap); i++, j++) {
82:        readElem(strI, i);
83:        readElem(strJ, j);
84:        if (strcmp(strI, strJ) > 0) {
```

continued

Listing 9.3. continued

```
85:            inOrder = false;
86:            writeElem(strI, j);
87:            writeElem(strJ, i);
88:         }
89:       }
90:    } while (!(inOrder && gap == 1));
91: }
92:
93: main()
94: {
95:   char* data[] = { "Michigan", "California", "Virginia", "Maine",
96:                    "New York", "Florida", "Nevada", "Alaska",
97:                    "Ohio", "Maryland" };
98:   VmArray arr(10, "arr.dat");
99:   char str[STR_SIZE+1];
100:  char c;
101:
102:  // assign values to array arr
103:  for (unsigned i = 0; i < arr.getSize(); i++) {
104:    strcpy(str, data[i]);
105:    arr.writeElem(str, i);
106:  }
107:  // display unordered array
108:  cout << "Unsorted arrays is:\n";
109:  for (i = 0; i < arr.getSize(); i++) {
110:    arr.readElem(str, i);
111:    cout << str << "\n";
112:  }
113:  // pause
114:  cout << "\nPress any key and then Return to sort the array...";
115:  cin >> c;
116:  // sort the array
117:  arr.Combsort();
118:  // display sorted array
119:  cout << "Sorted arrays is:\n";
120:  for (i = 0; i < arr.getSize(); i++) {
121:    arr.readElem(str, i);
122:    cout << str << "\n";
123:  }
124:  return 0;
125: }
```

Here is a sample session with the program in Listing 9.3.

```
Unsorted arrays is:
Michigan
California
Virginia
Maine
New York
Florida
Nevada
Alaska
Ohio
Maryland
```

```
Press any key and then Return to sort the array...d
Sorted arrays is:
Alaska
California
Florida
Maine
Maryland
Michigan
Nevada
New York
Ohio
Virginia
```

 The program in Listing 9.3 declares the class VmArray. This class models a disk-based dynamic array that stores all its elements in a random access binary file. Notice that the class declares an instance of class fstream and that there is no pointer to a dynamic array. The class declares a constructor, a destructor, and a number of member functions.

The class constructor has two parameters, namely, Size and filename. The parameter Size specifies the size of the virtual array. The parameter filename names the binary file that stores the elements of a class instance. The constructor opens the stream f using the stream function open and supplies it the argument of parameter filename and the I/O mode expression ios::in ¦ ios::out ¦ ios::binary. This expression specifies that the stream is opened for binary input and output mode (that is, random access mode). If the constructor successfully opens the file stream, it proceeds to fill the file with zeros. The class destructor performs the simple task of closing the file stream f.

The functions writeElem and readElem support the random access of array elements. These functions use the stream function seekg to position the stream pointer at the appropriate array element. The writeElem then calls the stream function write to store an array element (supplied by the parameter str). By contrast, the function readElem calls the stream function read to retrieve an array element (returned by the parameter str). Both functions return Boolean results that indicate the success of the I/O operation.

The VmArray class also declares the Combsort function to sort the elements of the virtual array. This function uses the readElem and writeElem member functions to access and swap the array elements.

The function main performs the following relevant tasks:

☐ Declares the instance arr, of class VmArray. (This instance stores 10 strings in the binary file ARR.DAT.)

☐ Assigns random values to the elements of instance arr, using the for loop in lines 103 through 106, to assign strings accessed by data[i] to the variable str and then to write the value in str to the instance arr by sending it the message writeElem. (The arguments for the message writeElem are the string variable str and the loop control variable i.)

☐ Displays the unsorted elements of instance arr using the for loop in line 109. (The statement in line 110 sends the message readElem to the instance arr to obtain an element in the virtual array.)

☐ Sorts the array by sending the message Combsort to the instance arr.

☐ Displays the sorted elements of instance arr using the for loop in line 120. (The statement in line 121 sends the message readElem to the instance arr to obtain an element in the virtual array.)

Summary

Today's lesson provided a brief introduction to the C++ stream I/O library and discussed the following topics:

☐ Common stream functions include open, close, good, fail, and the operator !. The function open opens a file for stream I/O and supports alternate and multiple I/O modes. The function close shuts down a file stream. The functions good and fail indicate the success or failure, respectively, of a stream I/O operation.

☐ C++ enables you to perform sequential stream I/O for text, using the operators << and >> as well as the stream function getline. The operator << is able to write characters and strings (as well as the other predefined data types). The operator >> is suitable for obtaining characters. The function getline enables your applications to read strings from the keyboard or from a text file.

☐ Sequential stream I/O for binary data uses the stream functions write and read to write and read data from any types of variables.

☐ Random access stream I/O for binary data uses the seekg function in conjunction with the functions read and write. The seekg function enables you to move the stream pointer to either absolute or relative byte locations in the stream.

Q&A

Q How can I emulate the random access of lines in a text file?

A First, read the lines in the file as text, obtain the length of the lines (plus the two characters for the end of each line), and store the cumulative length in a special array. (Call it lineIndex.) This array stores the byte location where each line starts. The last array element should store the size of the file. To access line number i, use the seek or seekg function to locate the offset value in lineIndex[i]. The size of line number i is equal to lineIndex[i+1]-lineIndex[i].

Q How do I write a general-purpose routine to copy between an input and an output file stream?

A You need to use the stream function gcount() to obtain the number of bytes actually read in the last unformatted stream input. The following is the function copyStream:

```
void copyStream(fstream& fin, fstream& fout,
                unsigned char* buffer, int buffSize)
{
  int n;
  while (fin.read(buffer, buffSize) {
    n = fin.gcount();
    fout.write(buffer, n);
  }
}
```

Q **Why declare data members in classes that support exceptions?**

A These data members help the catch blocks to pass information related to the cause and state that lead to the exception. The simplest example is that the exception class has a string-typed data member that passes the error message text.

Workshop

The Workshop provides quiz questions to help you solidify your understanding of the material covered and exercises to provide you with experience in using what you've learned. Try to understand the quiz and exercise answers before continuing on to the next day's lesson. Answers are provided in Appendix A.

Quiz

1. True or false? The stream I/O functions read and write are able to correctly read and write any data type.

2. True or false? The stream I/O functions read and write are able to correctly read and write any data type, as long as the type has no pointer members.

3. True or false? The seek and seekg functions expand the file when you supply them an index that is one byte beyond the current end of file.

4. True or false? The arguments of the functions seek and seekg require no range checking.

Exercise

Create the program IO4.CPP by modifying the program IO3.CPP. The class VmArray in IO4.CPP should have the function binSearch, which conducts a binary search on the members of the sorted array. Add a loop at the end of the function main to search in the array arr, using the unordered data of the initializing list. (The members of this list are accessed using the pointer data.)

10

The C++ *string*
Class, Templates,
and the Class
Library

On Day 7, you learned about strings and the functions in STRING.H that work with them. Turbo C++ 4.5 provides a more powerful method of dealing with strings—the string class. This class conforms to the string class from the ANSI/ISO C++ standards committee and is prototyped in the header file CSTRING.H.

> **Note:** ANSI is American National Standards Institute and ISO is the International Standards Organization. ANSI and ISO are jointly developing a standard for the C++ language.

C-style strings are powerful but require control of many low-level items such as allocation sizes and pointer offsets. The C++ string class is designed to increase the power available above that of C strings, but without need for low-level concerns.

Today you also will learn about templates, the C++ version of a type-checking macro. Hand in hand with templates, you also learn about the class library that comes with Turbo C++ 4.5, which is a useful set of classes for manipulating collections of data.

At the end of today's lesson, you will be familiar with the following:

- [ ] Benefits of the C++ string class
- [ ] I/O with the C++ string class
- [ ] Comparing strings
- [ ] Searching for "tokens"
- [ ] Controlling how string class comparisons are done
- [ ] Searching for substrings inside of larger strings
- [ ] Mixed operations with C/C++ style strings and the string class
- [ ] Templates
- [ ] The Turbo C++ class libraries

Benefits of the C++ *string* Class

The programmer can design a class that inherits from the string class. The newly designed class can use all the power of the string class, as well as whatever else needs to be added.

The result is an object-oriented program design, which is easier to write and maintain. The following shows how the C++ string class provides solutions to C-string difficulties.

Table 10.1. C String difficulties and C ++ class solutions.

C String Difficulty	C++ string Class Solution
C string functions have obscure names, which makes it difficult to find the function you want.	Operators such as != or = are used when possible. When function names are used, they sound like what they do, such as the following: strcmp versus == strcpy versus = strstr versus find strlwr versus to_lower
No variable or function reports the allocated size of a C string. When copying to a string, the programmer must remember the allocated size or allocate a new string large enough to hold the string or strings that he or she wants to store.	The C++ string class handles allocations and knows the allowed size. Operations are checked against the current size, and the allocated size is increased when necessary.
When allocating memory for a string, an additional byte must be allocated for the terminating \0 character. Forgetting to do this is a common error.	String terminating characters are automatically provided.
Comparisons using C-style strings must be done with a call to a function such as strcmp. A frequent error is when the programmer uses logical operators, such as = or <, for C strings, receiving a result that tells of the relationship between the address of the strings in memory rather than of the strings themselves.	Source code to compare C++ strings can be written as if comparing integers, because familiar comparison operators (such as ==, !=, and so on) are provided. An explicit function call is not needed to do a comparison.
Parsing strings into words or finding substrings in C-style strings involves many lines of code with calls to functions such as strtok, the use of which are complicated and detail-intensive.	This work and the consequent debugging are now unnecessary. Powerful functions are in the string class to do such common tasks. For example, read-next word (token) from the keyboard, a file, or from another string is done with a call to read_token. It can be set to skip leading spaces or leave them in the string.

continues

Table 10.1. continued

C String Difficulty	C++ string Class Solution
When an allocation error is made, other memory outside the string array is altered. When that memory is a critical area, it often will cause the program to crash or the computer to lock up.	Exception handling is done by the class. It traps allocation failures and errors, terminating the program safely.

The *string* Class Header File CSTRING.H

The string class uses three other classes. Those classes are as follows:

TStringRef The string class uses this class in reserving and managing memory. Normally the programmer needs not access or use anything from this class. The string class is declared a friend within TStringRef. The string class declares TStringRef as a friend as well.

TSubString This is a class that handles the operations on substrings. Both the string and TSubString classes declare each other as friends. Many of the operations done with a string class actually are performed by TSubString.

TReference A base class used in copy and access operations, TReference is shown in the header file REF.H.

Note: All programs that use the string class must include the header file CSTRING.H.

NEW TERM *NPOS* is used as a value to indicate that no position is specified. It is declared as follows:

```
const size_t NPOS = size_t(-1);
```

Constructors and Copy Constructors

What follows is a list of the public constructors for the string class that can be used to create a new string object instance:

```
string();
string( const string& s);
string( const string& s,  size_t startIndex,
        size_t numChars = NPOS);

string( const char    *cp);
string( const char    *cp, size_t startIndex,
        size_t numChars = NPOS);

string( char          c);
string( char          c,  size_t numChars);
string( signed char   c);
string( signed char   c,  size_t numChars);
string( unsigned char c);
string( unsigned char c,  size_t numChars);

string( const TSubString& ss);

string copy() const; // Note: There are other copy() functions below

string&      operator = (const string& s);
TSubString& operator = (const string& s);
```

The following constructor is only valid for Windows applications. It creates a string object that
is loaded directly from the application's string resources.

```
string( HINSTANCE instance, UINT id, int numChars = 255);
```

Comparing

As stated earlier, the string class provides easier methods of comparison than the strcmp style
functions. The following are the comparison operators defined by the string class:

```
friend int operator == ( const string& s1, const string& s2 );
friend int operator == ( const string& s,  const char    *cp );
friend int operator == ( const char    *cp, const string& s );
int operator == ( const char    *cp );
int operator == ( const string& s );

friend int operator != ( const string& s1, const string& s2 );
friend int operator != ( const string& s,  const char    *cp );
friend int operator != ( const char    *cp, const string& s );
int operator != ( const char    *cp );
int operator != ( const string& s );

friend int operator > ( const string& s1, const string& s2 );
friend int operator > ( const string& s,  const char    *cp );
friend int operator > ( const char    *cp, const string& s );

friend int operator < ( const string& s1, const string& s2 );
friend int operator < ( const string& s,  const char    *cp );
friend int operator < ( const char    *cp, const string& s );


friend int operator <= ( const string& s1, const string& s2 );
friend int operator <= ( const string& s,  const char    *cp );
```

```
friend int operator <= ( const char   *cp, const string& s );


friend int operator >= ( const string& s1, const string& s2 );
friend int operator >= ( const string& s,  const char   *cp );
friend int operator >= ( const char   *cp, const string& s );

int compare ( const string& s) const;
int compare ( const string& s, size_t startIndex,
              size_t numChars = NPOS ) const;
```

Concatenating Strings

The string class provides simpler methods of concatenating strings than using the strcat style of functions. Several of these are implemented as operators, whereas others are implemented with the append member function for adding on to the end of a string and the prepend member function for adding on to the beginning of a string.

```
friend string operator + (  const string& s, const char *cp );

string& operator += ( const string& s );
string& operator += ( const char   *cp );

string& append( const string& s );
string& append( const string&& s, size_t startIndex,
                size_t numChars = NPOS );

string& prepend( const string& s );
string& prepend( const string& s, size_t startIndex,
                 size_t numChars = NPOS )

string& prepend( const char *cp );
string& prepend( const char *cp, size_t startIndex,
                 size_t numChars = NPOS );
```

Inserting Characters into a String

The insert member function enables you to insert other strings into the middle of a string object.

```
string& insert( size_t startInsertAt, const string& s );
string& insert( size_t startInsertAt, const string& s,
                size_t startFrom, size_t numChars = NPOS );
```

Removing Characters from Within a String

There are two member functions for removing characters from within a string. The replace member function replaces characters in a string with the contents of another string. The strip member function removes characters from either the beginning, the ending, or both sides of a string.

```
string& replace( size_t removeFrom, size_t removeCount,
                 const string& s );
string& replace( size_t removeFrom, size_t removeCount,
                 const string& s,    size_t startReplacePosition,
                 size_t replaceCount = NPOS );

TSubString strip( StripType s = Trailing, char c = ' ' );

// Note: strip uses this enum which is defined within the class
//        enum StripType { Leading, Trailing, Both };
//
//        The programmer accesses it as one of
//           string::Leading  string::Trailing  string::Both
```

Addressing Individual Characters in a String

When dealing with regular C-string arrays, it's possible to manipulate single characters within the string by using the array operators [ ]. The C++ string object defines the bracket operators to perform the same function, as well as supplying parentheses operators.

Note in the following syntax that these operators return a reference to the specified character rather than just the character itself. This means that you can assign new characters to that position in the string in the same way you would with a C-string array.

In addition to the bracket and parentheses operators, get_at and put_at are provided for a more primitive method of getting and changing characters in a string object.

```
char& operator [] ( size_t index ); // Note: [] and () both
char& operator () ( size_t index ); //       do the same thing

char operator  [] ( size_t index ) const;
char operator  () ( size_t index ) const;

char get_at( size_t index ) const;
void put_at( size_t index, char c ) const;
```

Getting a Substring from Within a String

The string class provides methods for obtaining substrings from a string. There are two sets of these functions: functions that return results that can be modified and functions that can only be examined. For a result that can be examined, but won't be modified, see the following:

```
const TSubString operator()( size_t startIndex, size_t numChars );

const TSubString substring( const char *cp ) const;
const TSubString substring( const char *cp, size_t start ) const;
```

For a copy that can be examined and modified, see the following:

```
string substr( size_t startIndex ) const;
string substr( size_t startIndex, size_t numChars ) const;

TSubString substring( const char *cp );
TSubString substring( const char *cp, size_t startIndex );
```

311

Searching within a String

Some of the more useful features of the string class are its member functions that enable you to search the contents of a string. The basic member functions are find_first_of, find_first_not_of, find_last_of, and find_last_not_of. One of the most powerful searching functions, however, is in the overloaded parentheses operators, which allows you to supply a regular expression as the search parameter.

```
const TSubString operator()( const TRegexp& pattern ) const;
const TSubString operator()( const TRegexp& pattern,
                             size_t startIndex );

size_t find_first_of     ( const string& s ) const;
size_t find_first_of     ( const string& s, size_t startIndex ) const;
size_t find_first_not_of ( const string& s ) const;
size_t find_first_not_of ( const string& s, size_t startIndex ) const;
size_t find_last_of      ( const string& s ) const;
size_t find_last_of      ( const string& s, size_t startIndex ) const;
size_t find_last_not_of  ( const string& s ) const;
size_t find_last_not_of  ( const string& s, size_t startIndex );
```

Reading the Length

In order to get the length of a C-style string, you use the strlen function. The string class supplies the length member function to obtain the length of the string.

```
size_t length() const;
```

Copying to a C-Style String

Although using the string class is very useful, occasionally it still may be necessary to use a C-style string array. The copy member function copies the contents of a string object into a standard character array.

```
size_t copy( char *cb, size_t numChars );
size_t copy( char *cb, size_t numChars, size_t startIndex );
```

Reading and Setting Parameters for a Single String

A number of internal parameters affect how the string class acts. The reserve member function alternately sets or returns the number of characters reserved for the string; hash returns a hash value that can be used during sorting. The is_null member function can be used to inquire as to whether the string is empty, and resize can either contract or expand a string, appending spaces as necessary.

```
size_t   reserve();
void     reserve( size_t numChars );
unsigned hash() const;
int      is_null() const;
void     resize( size_t numChars );
```

I/O Operations

There are a number of functions for getting strings to interact with input and output streams. Some of these are member functions of the string class (read_token, read_file, read_string, read_line, and read_to_delim), whereas others are just globally declared (operator >>, operator <<, and getline).

```
istream& read_token( istream& is );
istream& read_file( istream& is );
istream& read_string( istream& is );
istream& read_line( istream& is );
istream& read_to_delim( istream& is, char delim = '\n' );

ostream& operator << ( ostream& os, const string& s );
istream& operator >> ( istream& is, string& s );

istream& getline( istream& is, string& s );
istream& getline( istream& is, string& s, char c ); **check**
```

Character Set Conversion

Several functions are available for manipulating such things as the case or the character set of a string. The case manipulators are to_lower and to_upper. There are two versions of these functions: member functions and globally declared functions. The globally declared functions return a copy of the converted string, whereas the member functions modify the string itself.

```
string to_lower( const string &s );
string to_upper( const string &s );

void to_lower();
void to_upper();
```

In the Windows environment, the string can be represented in either the ANSI character set or an OEM character set. The ansi_to_oem and oem_to_ansi member functions convert the string between the two sets.

```
void _RTLENTRY ansi_to_oem();
void _RTLENTRY oem_to_ansi();
```

Reading and Setting Parameters for the Whole Class

The following member functions set internal parameters that affect all string objects as opposed to just a particular instance. Most the parameters affect such things as how searches are undertaken and the initial space reserved for characters when strings are created.

```
static int    set_case_sensitive ( int onOff = 1 );
static int    set_paranoid_check ( int onOff = 1 );
static int    skip_whitespace    ( int onOff = 1 );
static size_t initial_capacity   ( size_t numChars = 63 );
```

```
static size_t resize_increment   ( size_t numChars = 64 );
static size_t max_waste          ( size_t numChars = 63 );

static int    get_case_sensitive_flag();
static int    get_paranoid_check_flag();
static int    get_skip_whitespace_flag();
static size_t get_initial_capacity();
static size_t get_resize_increment();
static size_t get_max_waste();
```

Protected Items (Accessible Only in an Inherited Class)

The following member functions are declared as protected, which means that they can only be accessed from friends or from derived classes.

```
int  valid_element ( size_t pos ) const;
int  valid_index   ( size_t pos ) const;

void assert_element ( size_t pos ) const;
void assert_index   ( size_t pos ) const;

string( const string& s, const char *cb );

void cow();      // Note: "cow" = "copy on write"
```

Declaring a String

Syntax

You can declare variables of string class type (called *instances of the class* or *class instances*). You also can declare pointers or references to a class instance. Any of these can be initialized in the same statement that declares the variable. A string can be declared with an optional initial value.

```
string Str1;
string Str2 = "String 2";
string Str3("String 3");
```

A string pointer or reference also can be allocated with an optional initial value.

```
string *pStr4 = new string;
string *pStr5 = new string("String 5");
string *pStr6;
string &rStr7 = * new string("String Reference");

pStr6 = new string("A New String Is Constructed");
```

Str1, Str2, and Str3 are strings. Str1 has not been given an initial value so it begins as an empty string (as ""). Str2 is set to a value, but the initialization is done with an assignment statement on the same line; it also begins life as an empty string, but that is changed immediately. Str3 takes advantage of the class constructor argument to set the initial value without the additional step of assigning it.

The pStr4, pStr5, and pStr6 are not strings. They are pointers to strings; they each can hold the address of a string.

The pStr4 and pStr5 are assigned the address of a string by a call to the function new. The string to which pStr4 points is empty, and the one to which pStr5 points contains String 5.

The pStr6 begins as pointing to nothing in particular. The assignment statement creates a string with new, initializes it to the given value, and places the address into pStr6.

Bug Busters

Be careful not to use items such as pStr6 until they have been assigned a valid address. Forgetting this is a common programming mistake that can be difficult to track down. Always check that all pointers have been initialized before being used.

The rStr7 is a reference to a string. You can think of it as a pointer to a string, which can be handled in source code as if it were a string.

When new is called to initialize pStr7, a * is placed before it. As new returns a pointer and a reference is treated as an actual string, the * indicates to use the item at the address contained in the pointer.

Reading and Comparing Strings

In C, to copy the contents of one string to another, you place the addresses of the source and destination C strings as calling arguments to the strcpy() function. The string class defines an = operator, so you need only do an assignment, just as with an integer.

Syntax

Assigning Strings

You can assign one string to another using the equals sign (=).

```
string str = initialString;
```

Example

```
string string_1 = "First String";
string string_2 = "Second String";

string_2 = string_1;
```

This places the characters "First String" into string_2. The old contents of string_2 are lost.

As was the case with an assignment statement, the class provides familiar operators for use in performing comparisons. Operators such as == and < free you from calling and interpreting the results of the strcmp function used for C-style strings. In cases where you want to save the comparison results, a strcmp-like function that returns the same kind of positive integer, zero, or negative integer is available. The name is a bit easier to remember than strcmp. It's called compare.

Comparing Strings

Strings can be compared directly as if comparing an integer. Old-style strings can also be compared to C++ strings in this fashion.

The following comparison operators are supplied for strings:

```
==  <=  >=  <   >   !=
```

Example

```cpp
char oldstyle[] = "OLD STYLE STRING";
string newstyle = "new style string";

if (oldstyle < newstyle)
    cout << "oldstyle is lower in value than newstyle" << endl;
```

The message will be displayed because capital letters have smaller values than lowercase letters. The line

```cpp
int compare(const string &compareTo);
```

returns a positive value if the string is greater than compareTo, and a negative value if it is less. If the two strings are equal, then zero is returned. Although using < > and == to compare strings is easy, compare provides a value that can be saved for use later.

Another version of the same function enables you to indicate at what position from the start of the string the comparison should begin, and to specify a maximum number of characters to compare. Although these extra features are more specialized, it is not uncommon to need them.

```cpp
int compare(const string& s,
size_t startIndex, size_t numChars = NPOS);
```

The familiar cin >>, getline, and cout << syntax works well with C++ strings. Because the streams classes also handle file I/O, this works with disk files as well.

Reading and Writing Strings

Normal iostreams functions are provided for the C++ string class. The cin, cout, and file I/O are supported.

Example

```cpp
string textLine;

cin >> textLine;    // Get input from stdin.
```

```
// If "the word" is entered, textLine will become "the"


getline(cin, textLine);
// If "the word" is entered, textLine will become "the word"


ifstream inputFile;
ofstream outputFile;

inputFile.open("FileName.Txt");
outputFile.open("FileName.Out");

getline(inputFile, textLine);
// textLine now contains the first line from the file

outputFile << textLine << endl;
// the string is now stored in the output disk file
```

10

Just as with C style strings, a C++ string can be addressed as if it were an array with an index within square brackets. Readers who have migrated from BASIC or FORTRAN might be pleased to learn that parentheses also can be used.

Examining Individual Characters

C++ strings can be accessed as arrays just as is done with C strings. Remember that the first element is `stringName[0]`. If the value contained in `stringVar` is "0123456789", then `cout << stringVar[7];` will print a 7 to the screen.

For those of you whose first love was FORTRAN or another language that uses parentheses for array subscripts, you can use them as well: `cout << stringVar(7);` would also print a 7.

This example is a small program using some of the previously mentioned syntax. References are used so that the code is more readable.

Three references to string are created. The program reads strings from the keyboard and reports on how they compare. Entering a string of `end` ends the program. Because comparison defaults to being case-sensitive, a value of `END` will not end the program.

Listing 10.1 contains a program that reads and compares C++ `string` class strings.

Listing 10.1. Source code for the program CSTRING1.CPP.

```
1:  #include <iostream.h>
2:  #include <cstring.h>
3:
4:  int main()
5:    {
6:    int result;
7:
8:    string &s1 = * new string; // create 2 references to string
9:    string &s2 = * new string;
```

Listing 10.1. continued

```
10:    string message;              // create an instance of a string
11:
12:    while (1)      // run this loop forever
13:      {
14:      cout << "Enter two lines of text, \"end\" to end program\n";
15:      getline(cin, s1);   // read a line into s1 from the keyboard
16:
17:      if (s1 == "end")     // If ending the program is requested
18:        break;             // break out of the loop
19:
20:      getline(cin, s2);   // read a line into s2
21:
22:      if (s2 == "end")     // If ending the program is requested
23:        break;             // break out of the loop
24:
25:      result = s1.compare(s2); // get and save comparison result
26:
27:      if (result == 0)         // save what we've found in "message"
28:        message = "The strings are equal";
29:      else if (result > 0)
30:        message = "The first string is greater";
31:      else
32:        message = "The second string is greater";
33:
34:      cout << message << endl << endl; // report the result
35:      }
36:
37:   delete &s1;  // References are handled in source code as if they
38:   delete &s2;  // were actual items. This is why the '&' operator
39:   return 0;          // is used to get their address for use by
40:   }                  // delete.
```

Here is a sample session with the example program.

```
Enter two lines of text, "end" to end program
this
that
The first string is greater

Enter two lines of text, "end" to end program
that
this
The second string is greater

Enter two lines of text, "end" to end program
those
those
The strings are equal

Enter two lines of text, "end" to end program
end
```

In lines 8, 9, and 10, the string reference variables s1, s2, and the string variable message are declared, and instances of two of them are allocated by the call to new. The * in front of the new is said to "dereference the pointer." This means that it refers to the value at the address returned by new rather than the address itself. By using reference variables instead of pointers, the variables can be used in the following source lines without the special handling needed when using pointers.

On lines 15 and 20, a full line of text is read into a string. Remember that the getline function removes the end of line character from the input.

On line 22, a string is compared to another with only the == operator. With C-style strings, a call to strcmp would have been necessary. Line 25 uses the string class compare member function to return a value that will be tested on lines 27 and 29. Because it is done this way, the computer only examines the variable result rather than performing a second full-string comparison.

Assigning a new value to a string class item need not call strcpy or strdup. Lines 28, 30, and 32 show message being assigned a value with a simple assignment statement.

Lines 37 through 39 discard the strings you have allocated. Although this program will end and the memory will be recovered by the operating system, in a true application program memory management is of great concern, and objects that have been allocated should be discarded when they are no longer of use. The string variable message is not deleted because it was not created with new. When main ends, message automatically will be destroyed by the compiler's code.

String Search, Substitution, and File I/O

The string class provides powerful tools for searching within strings and substituting parts of strings (substrings). CSTRING2.CPP manipulates the text in a file, substituting alternative text for words and placing this new text in an output file. Listing 10.2 contains the source code for the program CSTRING2.CPP.

 Listing 10.2. Source code for the program CSTRING2.CPP.

```
1:  #include <fstream.h>
2:  #include <cstring.h>
3:
4:  const short True = 1;
5:  const short False = 0;
6:
7:  string    toFind;
8:  string    replaceWith;
9:  char      lineBuf[81];
```

continues

319

Listing 10.2. continued

```
10: ifstream  inFile;
11: ofstream  outFile;
12:
13: short GetFindReplace()
14:    {
15:    char caseFlag;
16:
17:    cout << "Enter the word to find: ";
18:    cin >> toFind;
19:
20:    cout << endl << "Enter replacement word: ";
21:    cin >> replaceWith;
22:
23:    while (1)
24:       {
25:       cout  << "Case sensitive [Y/N]? ";
26:       cin >> caseFlag;
27:       caseFlag = toupper(caseFlag);
28:
29:       if ((caseFlag == 'Y') ¦¦ (caseFlag == 'N'))
30:          {
31:          string::set_case_sensitive(caseFlag == 'Y');
32:          break;
33:          }
34:       }
35:
36:    return (toFind != replaceWith) ? True : False;
37:    } // end GetFindReplace()
38:
39: short ProcessFile()
40:    {
41:    short  findLen;       // Number of characters to find
42:    size_t foundPos;      // Position in string where found
43:    string buffer;        // Holds a line of input data from the file
44:    short  startPos;      // Position in string to start search
45:    short  replaced;      // Set to True if replacement has been done
46:    short  numFound = 0;  // Number of replacements that were made
47:
48:    inFile.open("\\TCWINC45\\README.TXT");
49:    outFile.open("README.NEW");
50:    findLen = toFind.length();        // get # char's in string to find
51:    buffer.skip_whitespace(False);    // don't skip leading spaces
52:
53:    while (inFile)                    // while data left in input file
54:       {
55:       getline(inFile, buffer);       // read one line
56:       replaced = False;              // init flag and position
57:       startPos = 0;
58:
59:       do
60:          {
```

```
61:        foundPos = buffer.find(toFind, startPos);
62:
63:        if (foundPos != NPOS)       // if a match is found
64:          {
65:          buffer.replace(foundPos, findLen, replaceWith);
66:          ++numFound;
67:          replaced = True;
68:          startPos = foundPos + replaceWith.length();
69:          }
70:        } while (foundPos != NPOS);
71:
72:     outFile << buffer << endl;   // copy line to the output file
73:
74:     if (replaced)
75:        cout << buffer << endl;    // show modified lines on screen
76:     }
77:
78:   inFile.close();
79:   outFile.close();
80:   cout << endl;
81:   return numFound;
82:   } // end ProcessFile()
83:
84: int main()
85:    {
86:    if (GetFindReplace())
87:       cout << ProcessFile() << " words were replaced\n";
88:    else
89:       cout << "Error: Find and Replace words are the same\n";
90:
91:    return 0;
92:    }
```

Here is an example session with the CSTRING2 application.

```
Enter the word to find: important

Enter replacement word: unimportant
Case sensitive [Y/N]? y
This README file contains unimportant information about
   Turbo C++.

1 words were replaced
```

This program uses the C++ string class to take the README.TXT file, which came with Turbo C++ 4.5, and to create a new file, README.NEW, in which it has substituted some words. When run, it asks for the word to find, the word to replace it, and whether the search is to be case-sensitive.

Constants are declared for True and False on lines 4 and 5 to make the program more readable.

> **Note:** Windows declares #define macros for TRUE and FALSE in its header file WINDOWS.H. If you declare constants with these names, they will be replaced with 1 and 0, respectively, and could generate an error. To avoid this, True and False are used here instead of TRUE and FALSE.

The main program is small. It calls GetFindReplace on line 86, and if the user's input is valid, it calls ProcessFile on line 87, printing out the number of changes that were made. If the find and replace words are the same, no substitutions would be made, so GetFindReplace returns False, the program prints an error message, and ends.

GetFindReplace, starting on line 13, uses two instances of the C++ string class: toFind and replaceWith. The string class provides overloaded input >> and output >> operators, thus, values to and from the console are handled on lines 18 and 21 just as is done with C-style strings. On line 31, the case-sensitive flag for the string class is adjusted to control the type of comparisons made. In line 36, the function returns True if the two words compare differently.

Case Sensitivity

The following is a member function of the string class. It sets how comparisons will be done.

```
static string::set_case_sensitive(int tf = 1);
```

The calling argument defaults to true. If called with a 0 or false value, it causes all comparisons to ignore uppercase versus lowercase.

Example

```
string s1("THIS IS A STRING")
string s2("this is a string")

string::set_case_sensitive(0);

if (s1 == s2)
cout << "the strings are equal\n"; /* this is printed */

string::set_case_sensitive();

if (s1 != s2)
cout << "the strings are not equal\n"; /* this is printed */
```

> **Note:** There is only one case-sensitive flag for the entire string class. When you change it, *all* instances of the class will have their style of comparisons changed.

If `GetFindReplace` returns `True`, then on line 87 `main` calls `ProcessFile` and prints the returned count of replaced words. That function opens the README.TXT file in the \BC4 directory and creates a README.NEW file in the current directory to receive the program output. On line 50, the `ProcessFile` function uses the `length` member function to have `toFind` report how many characters long the string is.

Number of Characters in a String

Each `string` class variable has a member function called `length` that reports the length of the string in characters. The return value is an `unsigned`. The name `size_t` is defined by the language standards groups, so that it can be set to whatever is appropriate for the current machine. With Turbo C++ 4.5, `size_t` is defined as an `unsigned`. The `stringVar.length();` returns the same value as `strlen(stringVar.c_str());`.

The loop that starts on line 53 and ends on line 76 is where the real work of `ProcessFile` is done. With each pass through the loop, a line of text is read from the input file into the string variable `buffer` (line 55).

Because the string class `skip-whitespace` flag was cleared on line 51, leading spaces are preserved. The variable `replaced` acts as a detector to remember if any words have been replaced on a line and is set to `False`. The `startPos` is the starting position for searching the line and is set to the beginning of the line (to zero).

Searching within a String

The following `string` member functions search for a match with the `toFind` string. The return value is the index of where the match occurred, or `NPOS` if no match is found.

```
size_t find(const string &toFind);
size_t find(const string &toFind, size_t startAt);
```

The second version of the function specifies that, instead of beginning at the start of the string, the search will begin at position `startAt` in the string. Remember that the first character of an array in C or C++ is array index zero. Because of that, if `startAt` were 2, then the third character is where the search would begin.

The `do-while` loop from lines 59 through 70 processes a single line of text from the input file. Starting in character position `startPos`, it searches the string for a match with the `toFind` string. If successful, the `find` function returns the starting character position in `buffer` of the matching characters. In line 63, the position found is compared against the predefined symbol `NPOS`, whose value is used to indicate that no position in the string matches the search string.

Lines 64 through 69 only execute if a match is found. The call to `replace` causes `findLen` characters beginning at position `foundPos` to be deleted and the contents of the string `replaceWith` to be inserted in their place.

String Class I/O

Syntax

The getline member functions using the C++ string class are declared for input and output file streams. The >> and << input and output operators also are provided for file operations with this class.

```
istream &getline(istream &is, string &s);
ostream &getline(istream &is, string &s);
operators >> and <<
```

Controlling Whether Spaces Are Skipped

Syntax

The following two functions enable you to modify the skip_whitespace flag internal to the string class:

```
static int skip_whitespace(int skip = 1);
static int get_skip_whitespace_flag();
```

The skip_whitespace determines if whitespace will be skipped during read operations. The default value is to skip spaces and tabs on input operations such as getline, >>, and read_token. By calling get_skip_whitespace, you can read the current setting of the flag.

Example

```
string  myString;
ifstream myFile("\\TCWIN45\\DOC\\UTILS.TXT");

myString.skip_whitespace(0);
getline(myFile, myString);
```

The string myString will contain "UTILS.TXT".

The string myString would have been "UTILS.TXT" had skip_whitespace not been called. There is only one whitespace setting for the entire string class. Any call to skip_whitespace changes the setting for all.

Changing Part of a C++ String

Syntax

The replace function, a member function of the C++ string class, is overloaded to have two forms.

```
string &replace(size_t      startPos,
                size_t      deleteLen,
                const string &replaceWith);

string &replace(size_t      startPos,
                size_t      deleteLength,
                const string &replaceWith,
                size_t      replaceFrom,
                size_t      replaceLength);
```

The first form will search the string, starting at the index given in startPos, until it finds a match to the string replaceWith. It then will delete deleteLen characters from the string and insert the characters from replaceWith in that position.

If the string to be modified is too short to remove the requested number of characters, then the characters from startPos to the end of the string are removed.

The second form adds two additional arguments: replaceFrom and replaceLength. The replaceLength indicates how many characters from the replacement string will be inserted into the modified one.

"Steven Smith", for example, could be searched for and "Steven" replaced with "George" from the string "George Jones".

10

The replaceFrom argument specifies the starting position in the replacement string to begin in substituting characters. If there are no replaceLength characters in the replacement string, then the number found in the string is used.

The replaceLength can be given the value NPOS and will use all remaining characters in the string if that value is given.

The following two lines, for example, perform the same function:

```
replace(startPos, deleteLen, replaceWith, 0, NPOS);
replace(startPos, deleteLen, replaceWith);
```

Line 72 executes independently of having done any replacements and writes the possibly altered string to the new file. Lines 74 and 75 detect whether any replacements have been done and, if so, writes the changed string to the console.

Lines 78 through 81 perform the clean-up actions of closing files and returning the number of replacements that have been made.

There also are more useful functions in the string class.

Other C++ *string* Class Functions

The following append member function adds characters to the end of a string:

```
string& append(const string &fromStr);
```

This places the characters from fromStr to the end of the string.

Example

```
string firstString("ABC");
string secondString("DEF");

firstString.append(secondString); // firstString is now "ABCDEF"
```

Note that another way to append characters to the end of a string is to use the += operator. The same appending operations could have been done with the following:

```
firstString += secondString;
```

Often it will be necessary to just pass a string object as if it were a C-style string array. The string class provides the c_str member function, which simply returns a const char* to a C-style version of the string.

The contains member function is used to determine whether a particular substring can be found in a string object.

```
int contains(const char *cStyleStr);
```

The member function returns either 1 or 0, depending on whether cStyleStr is found in the string.

After you determine that a substring exists within a string object, it can be useful to determine where in that string the substring can be found. This is done with the find_first_of function.

```
size_t find_first_of(const string &s);
size_t find_first_of(const string &s, size_t startAt);
```

These return the position of the first character found in the string, which is one of the characters in the string s passed to the function. The second overloaded form starts the search at startAt. If nothing is found, then these return NPOS.

In addition to finding the first position in a string at which another string begins, it also is possible to find the first position that isn't a part of another string. This is done with the find_first_not_of member function.

```
xsize_t find_first_not_of(const string &s);
size_t find_first_not_of(const string &s, size_t startAt);
```

These return the first character *not* in the calling argument, or NPOS if nothing is found.

The find_last_of and find_last_not_of member functions are very similar to their find_first equivalents, except that they search starting at the end of the string and work backward.

```
size_t find_last_of(const string &s);
size_t find_last_of(const string &s, size_t startAt);
size_t find_last_not_of(const string &s);
size_t find_last_not_of(const string &s, size_t startAt);
```

These are called in exactly the same manner as the corresponding find_first type functions, and they return the same type of information, except that they work backwards.

When you want to delete characters from a string, you use the remove member function.

```
string &remove(size_t startAt);
string &remove(size_t startAt, size_t howMany);
```

These delete howMany characters from a string, starting at position startAt. The version with only one argument removes all the remaining characters in the string. The stringVar.remove(4); statement is the same as stringVar[4] = '\0';.

Templates

It is common for a language to have many functions, each of which does the same thing but for different data types. Wouldn't it be nice if you could tell the compiler "Here's what I want to do; you figure out how to do it."? C++ has a feature that can do this. It's called a *template*.

> **Note:** AT&T, the original developers of C++, originally added templates to version 2.0 of the C++ specification. That specification currently is at version 3.0 and this is the version used by Turbo C++ 4.5. Templates also have been accepted by the ANSI/ISO committee.

10

NEW TERM A *template* is a method for telling the compiler the algorithm to use to perform a function. The compiler handles the details of the function for the data type being used. Both global functions and classes can be programmed as templates.

When programming a template, you provide a name to use as the symbol for the unknown data type and write the code using that symbol.

Here is a function defined as a template.

```
// return the lowest of 3 values
template <class T> const T& Low(const T& a, const T& b, const T& c)
{
   if (a < b)
      {
      if (a < c)
         return a;
      }
   else if (b < c)
      return b;
   return c;
}
```

The first line of the function is what identifies it as a template (see Figure 10.1).

The word template in the function definition is followed by the characters <class, a symbol to use for the type, and then by a >. Although a single character is most often used for the symbol, it can be any legal C++ name.

Figure 10.1.

A template function's declaration.

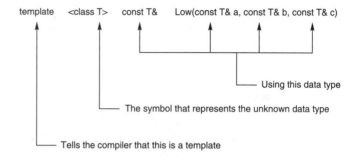

This template function is used as any other function would be. For example, this returns the lowest of three C++ string items.

```
string s1("6543");
string s2("5432");
string s3("4321");
cout << Low(s1, s2, s3) << endl;
```

Although use of the word `class` is required when defining a template, templates are not limited to having classes as arguments. They can be used as fundamental data types also. `Low(1, 2, 3);`, for example, uses integers and is a valid call of the `Low` function.

A class can be defined in terms of templates. The syntax for doing this is the same as with the preceding function, but some changes are required when declaring instances of the class.

```
template <class TypeSymbol> class ArrayType
{
protected:
    TypeSymbol *items;
    int        numItems;
public:
    ArrayType(const TypeSymbol& firstItem);
    ~ArrayType();
    int AddItem(TypeSymbol& toAdd);
    TypeSymbol& operator [] (int index);
};
```

When you declare an instance of this class, the compiler must know what data type is to be used with this class. The declaration for `iArray` shows this, as the angle brackets enclose the type to use.

```
ArrayType<int> iArray(1);
```

Look at Listing 10.3, which is an example of using templates. It implements a template class that can hold up to five items, gives them values, and prints them to the screen. Versions of the class are used for float and integer types. It also uses a template function that is not in a class. That function reports the size of the data type.

Type Listing 10.3. An example that uses templates.

```cpp
1:  #include <iostream.h>
2:
3:
4:  const int True = 1;
5:  const int False = 0;
6:
7:
8:  template <class X> class ArrayType
9:     {
10: protected:
11:    int maxItems; // maximum number of items this will hold
12:    int numItems; // number of items it is holding now
13:    X  *items;    // array of items
14:
15: public:
16:    ArrayType(int capacity);
17:    ~ArrayType()       { delete [] items; }
18:
19:    int InRange(int n) { return((n >= 0) && (n < numItems)); }
20:    int Capacity()     { return maxItems; }
21:    int AddItem(X& toAdd);
22:    X& operator [] (int index) { return items[index]; }
23:    }
24:
25:
26: template <class X> ArrayType<X>::ArrayType(int capacity)
27:    {
28:    maxItems = capacity;
29:    items = new X[capacity];
30:    numItems = 0;
31:    } // end ArrayType::ArrayType()
32:
33:
34: template <class a> int ArrayType<a>::AddItem(a& toAdd)
35:    {
36:    if (numItems < maxItems)
37:       {
38:       items[numItems++] = toAdd;
39:       return True;
40:       }
41:
42:    return False;
43:    } // end ArrayType::AddItem()
44:
45:
46: template <class SomeType> size_t Size(const SomeType&)
47:    {
48:    return sizeof(SomeType);
49:    } // end Size()
50:
51:
52: template <class D, class X> void Report(const char *s, D& d, X& x)
```

continues

329

Listing 10.3. continued

```
53:    {
54:    cout << endl << s << "has space for " << d.Capacity()
55:        << " items.  Each item uses " << Size(x) << " bytes.\n";
56:
57:    for (int i = 0; d.InRange(i); i++)
58:      cout << "\t" << s << "[" << i << "] " << d[i] << endl;
59:    } // end Report()
60:
61:
62: int main()
63:    {
64:    int              iVal;
65:    float            fVal;
66:    ArrayType <int>   iArray(3);
67:    ArrayType <float> fArray(5);
68:
69:    for (iVal = 0, fVal = 0.0; iVal < 10; ++iVal, fVal += 1.11)
70:      {
71:      iArray.AddItem(iVal);
72:      fArray.AddItem(fVal);
73:      }
74:
75:    Report("iArray: ", iArray, iArray[0]);
76:    Report("fArray: ", fArray, fArray[0]);
77:
78:    return 0;
79:    }
```

When you run this example, the results are as follows:

```
iArray: has space for 3 items. Each item uses 2 bytes.
iArray: [0] 0
iArray: [1] 1
iArray: [2] 2

fArray: has space for 5 items. Each item uses 4 bytes.
fArray: [0] 0
fArray: [1] 1.11
fArray: [2] 2.22
fArray: [3] 3.33
fArray: [4] 4.44
```

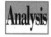

Beginning with line 8, the template class is defined. The symbol X is declared to be used for the type and is used within the body of the definition wherever the type name is needed.

The X is only valid within the block to which the template word refers. It is not related to what is used in other blocks. In line 34, a is used as the symbol for the type, and although the AddItem() function with which it is used is a member of the ArrayType class that uses an X in its template, there is no confusion. The compiler is content to use a for the function block.

The inline functions InRange(), Capacity(), operator [ ], and ~ArrayType() don't need a separate template word applied to them, because they are contained in the same one that is used for the class.

Both ArrayType() (line 26) and AddItem() (line 34) need template in their definition, because the lines of code for them are not located within the class and are not covered by the class use of the word template.

Line 46 has a template function that is neither a class nor a class member. The syntax of C++ still requires the word class in the function header. SomeType is used as the type symbol, but X or any other valid C++ name would work as well. The calling argument to Size() is described as a type without a variable name applied to it. Unlike C, C++ does not require that a variable name be placed there; the Size() function only needs to know the type, not an actual variable.

The function Report() (line 52) has an interesting variation on the template system. Two dummy type names are provided, and both types are used by the function. When called from lines 75 and 76, the function makes calls to Capacity() and InRange(). If the data type for the d calling argument in Report() did not have functions with those names, an error would be generated.

The main() function is in line 62. In lines 66 and 67 it declares two instances of ArrayType: one that will hold up to three items of type int and one that will hold up to three items of type float.

Between lines 69 and 73, the items in the two classes are initialized. Ten initializations are done for each, relying on the AddItem() function to detect and ignore initializations following those that have already filled the class to capacity.

Lines 75 and 76 call the Report() function to tell some things about the classes. Report() uses the Capacity() member function of the class to print the maximum number of items it can hold. It also calls Size() (line 55) to show the number of bytes used for each member.

Lines 57 through 59 then perform a for loop to display the data members of each class, stopping when the InRange() function returns False.

This example is a bit contrived in order to illustrate using templates. For container classes that you can use for general arrays and so on, the Turbo C++ 4.5 class library provides a multitude of better choices.

The Class Libraries

There are a number of data structures for holding on to data that have been developed over the years. These various structures are referred to as *containers*, and Borland supplies a set of these called the Class Libraries. Table 10.2 shows the types of containers provided with the Turbo C++ compiler.

Table 10.2. Turbo C++ Class Library Containers.

Container	Header File	Usage
Array	arrays.h	Mimics the standard C++ arrays in which objects are contained in a contiguous block of memory, but with the addition of being expandable in size after they already have been declared.
Association	assoc.h	Stores a key value with each object, allowing you to use the key to locate and retrieve the object.
Bag	bags.h	This is the least structured of all the containers in that it just stores objects in any order.
Binary search tree	binimp.h	Binary trees are a method of storing sorted data in an easy to search way. Objects are stored in such a way that each object can have up to two children. The child on the "left" of the parent must be less than the parent, and the "right" child greater than the parent.
Dequeue	deques.h	Contains a "train" of objects; you store objects at either end of the container and then access them in the order in which they were stored. As you access either end of the container, the objects are removed.
Dictionary	dict.h	Simple storage of objects as they're added to the container.
Double-linked list	dlistimp.h	A double-linked list contains objects in non-contiguous memory. Traversing the list involves following pointers in each entry that point to the previous and next entries in the list.
Hash table	hashimp.h	This is similar to an association container, except that the associated keys (the hash values) are calculated based on the object being stored rather than specified directly.
Queue	queues.h	Queus allow objects to be stored in one end and retrieved from the other end. This sometimes is referred to as a FIFO (First In, First Out) container.
Set	sets.h	Sets are similar to bags in that they store objects in an unordered format, but sets can contain only one of any object.

Container	Header File	Usage
Single-linked list	listimp.h	Single-linked lists, like double-linked lists, contain objects that aren't stored in contiguous memory. Single-linked list entries, however, only contain a pointer to the next entry and no pointer to the previous.
Stack	stacks.h	A stack is a way of storing objects one on top of each other, so that the most recently added object will be the one that can be retrieved. This sometimes is referred to as a LIFO (Last In, First Out) container.
Vector	vectimp.h	Vectors contain objects in contiguous memory. It usually is used simply as a storage method for the other classes.

Each of these types of classes has several different versions. These different versions are created to reflect the differing conditions in which they are used. In order to help the programmer distinguish between the different versions of each class, there is a standard set of characters that are used at the beginning of class names (see Table 10.3). By looking at the classes provided and decoding the abbreviation characters, you can deduce the differences of the container.

Table 10.3. Container class name abbreviations.

Abbreviation	Meaning	Description
T	Class Library Prefix	All Borland-supplied classes (including OWL, which is described on Day 11) start with this letter.
M	User-supplied mem-mgt.	The programmer must supply to the container a class that will handle the memory management for the contained objects.
I	Indirect	The container holds a pointer to the object rather than to the object itself.
C	Counted	The container keeps a running count of the number of objects stored within it.
S	Sorted	The container sorts its objects. In order to achieve this, the objects must have valid comparison operators.

Each container has specific iterators associated with it. These iterators act much in the same way as the simple integers you have used before in for loops, except that they are written specifically for manipulating and accessing the data of a container. While each iterator can have any number of functions, there are a few that are common amongst all the iterators (see Table 10.4).

Table 10.4. Common container iterator member-functions.

Function	Description
constructor	The constructor typically takes one argument: a reference to the specific container for which it is to manipulate. The constructor initializes the iterator to point at the "beginning" of the container. (Note that the term "beginning" doesn't apply very well to some containers.)
Current	This returns the object currently being pointed to by the iterator.
Restart	This restarts the iterator to point at the "beginning" of the list.
operator int	When you need to know whether a container has been completely traversed, you can just compare it to 0, which will invoke a conversion operator. If the iterator is equal to 0, then the "end" of the container has been reached.
operator ++	Obviously, traversing a container involves incrementing its iterator, and this is the function that does it. Just use the regular ++ increment operator.

Space constraints prevent me from providing a full list of all the various classes in the class libraries; there are a great deal of them. Instead, I will present one example that goes through using a double-linked list for storing strings in Listing 10.4.

Listing 10.4. A demonstration of double-linked lists.

```
1:      #include <cstring.h>
2:      #include <classlib\dlistimp.h>
3:      #include <iostream.h>
4:
5:      // Create some typedefs to make things easier
6:      // later on when we create the list and its
7:      // iterator.
8:      //
9:      typedef TDoubleListImp<string> strList;
10:     typedef TDoubleListIteratorImp<string> strIter;
11:
12:     int main()
13:     {
14:         strList list;
15:
```

```
16:          // Add some strings
17:          //
18:          list.Add("first");
19:          list.Add("second");
20:          list.Add("third");
21:          list.Add("fourth");
22:          list.Add("fifth");
23:          list.AddAtHead("Head");    // Add at Head
24:          list.AddAtTail("Tail");    // Add at Tail
25:
26:          // Print out the list
27:          //
28:          strIter i(list);
29:          while (i != 0)
30:             {
31:             cout << i.Current() << endl;
32:             ++i;
33:             }
34:          cout << endl;              // Add a blank line
35:
36:          // Get rid of one of the entries
37:          //
38:          list.Detach("third");
39:
40:          // Now show what's left in reverse
41:          //
42:          for (i.RestartAtTail(); i != 0; --i)
43:             cout << i.Current() << endl;
44:
45:          return 0;
46:       }
```

Here is the output produced by Listing 10.4.

```
Head
fifth
fourth
third
second
first
Tail

Tail
first
second
fourth
fifth
Head
```

Analysis Taking a look at the program, you can see that on lines 9 and 10 that two typedefs are used to create easy access to the new template list and iterator. The names for these template classes can become rather long, so it's a common practice to create shorter typedefs of the more complicated names for easier typing and identification during programming.

On line 14 is a declaration for the list itself. As you can see, it's a fairly simple line with no special parameters needed for the constructor. Immediately following this are some calls to the class member functions Add, AddAtHead, and AddAtTail. These are passing literal strings which are, in turn, being passed to the string constructor, which then is passed to the various add routines. The template nature of the class libraries means that each container class is specially made to match the type of its contained objects, so the add functions take string parameters and passing a literal string just creates a string object to be added to the container.

Note the AddAtHead and AddAtTail functions on lines 23 and 24. The normal Add function actually adds items to the head of the list by default, as you can see in the output where the "Head" string is displayed next to the "fifth" string. Using AddAtHead and AddAtTail allows for finer control of where objects are placed in the list.

NEW☞
TERM
The *head* and *tail* of a linked list are the beginning and ending, respectively. Since there's no real sense of a 0 index or a maximum size, it's necessary to keep track of the beginning and ending of the list differently.

Next, on line 28, you can see how an iterator is instantiated with the list to which it should be associated. Following this, you can see how the iterator is used to traverse the list, displaying each item in turn, and then displaying an additional blank line in preparation for the next list.

On line 38, the string "third" is removed from the list. Note that it isn't necessary to search for the item before detaching it; the container automatically searches for the requested item and then removes it.

Starting on line 42, another method of traversing the list is shown: a for loop. Here you use the initializing portion of the for loop expression to restart the iterator at the list's tail, and you then decrement the iterator as you traverse the list backwards. Note how the output shows the contents of the list in reverse order from which its contents were initially added.

Altogether, the class libraries provide for a very easy method of using powerful data structures. Many versions of these will automatically sort items as they are added to the containers, and some provide very fast searching mechanisms. Take some time to read the documentation for a full list of the various containers provided by the class libraries.

Summary

This chapter presented the C++ string class, templates, and a glimpse at the class library. You should now be familiar with the following:

☐ The string class handles allocation and manipulation of strings without need for the low-level issues necessary when working with C-style strings.

- When declaring a string variable, the initial value can be placed in parentheses immediately after (as in `string myStr("Init Value");`). When you assign a new value to it, any necessary size adjustment is handled for you.

- Simple comparison operators can be used with the `string` class. There is no need to call functions such as `strcmp` or `strncmp`.

- C++ templates can be used with functions and classes to work with any kind of data type. You define a template with "generic" arguments and use a template giving specific arguments. The compiler generates code appropriate to the actual argument types.

- Creating an instance of a template class requires that you specify the type(s) as part of the class name.

- The class libraries provide a rich set of easy-to-use classes for creating containers. These containers can store objects in a variety of useful formats.

Q&A

Q Can I get the value of a character in a string as I can in C?

A Yes, and in the same way. If `strC` is a C-style array and `strCpp` is a C++ string class and both are set to `"ABC"`, then both `strC[1]` and `strCpp[1]` are equal to the character `'B'`.

Q What happens if I assign a `char` to a string index that is beyond the end of an array?

A In C, when you write to a character that is past the end of an array, the character is stored in the position where it would have been, had the array been large enough. If that memory contains critical information, then the computer could lock up, but only after it has run further, destroying the symptoms of where the problem occurred.

With a C++ string when you write past the end of the array, the over-write is detected and the exception handling system is called. If running a DOS program, the program ends with an `Abnormal program termination` error. If you were stepping through the program with Turbo Debugger, the error would be displayed at the line where it occurred, not elsewhere.

Q What happens if I copy to a string and the size is larger than has been allocated?

A The C++ string class detects that and expands the array to fit. If you were using C-style strings, a DOS Abnormal Termination would be presented or an equivalent complaint would be shown by Windows. If debugging, Turbo Debugger would stop at the line where the problem occurred, telling you of the problem.

Q I found a function that operates on C-style strings and does what I want. How can I use it with C++ string class items?

A Use the c_str function. For example, if strCpp is a C++ string, then strlen(strCpp.c_str()); will find the length of the string.

Q Can I use templates with my own structures and classes, or am I limited to using C++'s built-in types?

A Templates can use any type, as in the following example:

```
template <class T> const T& Dump(const T& objectToDump);

int a = 100;

struct {
  int p;
  long q;
  double r;
} b;

Dump(a);
Dump(b);
```

Q Can I create a template with more than one type?

A Yes. Just separate the types with commas, as in the following example:

```
template <class Form, class Printer> class SpecialFormPrinter
{
  ...
};

InsuranceFormLaserPrinter = new SpecialFormPrinter<InsuranceForm,
LaserPrinter>;
```

Q Can I create a double-linked list that automatically sorts the items added to it?

A Yes. Use the TSDoubleListImp and TSDoubleListIteratorImp classes to create and traverse such a list.

Workshop

The Workshop provides quiz questions to help you solidify your understanding of the material covered and exercises to provide you with experience in using what you've learned. Try to understand the quiz and exercise answers before continuing on to the next day's lesson. Answers are provided in Appendix A.

Quiz

1. What header file must be included to use the C++ string class?
2. How is a C++ string class variable declared?
3. How do you compare a string to a C-style string?
4. What string class function will find and replace text in one call?
5. To read the second character in a string, what array index is used?
6. Declare a string named myString with an initial value of 12.
7. Assuming that you have two string class variables, s1 and s2, and that s1 contains "11" and s2 contains "2112", what is the result of the following code lines?

   a. s1 + s2;

   b. s2.contains(s1);

   c. s1 > s2

   d. s2.find(s1, 0);

8. True or false? Templates let you use any type, including your own classes, without ever having to provide any extra code.

Exercises

1. Write a line of code that declares a C-style string of value 12, and another that declares a C++ string class variable with the same value.
2. Write a function that accepts a reference to a string as its calling argument and writes that string to the computer screen.
3. Modify the function written for the previous exercise to perform a loop, writing all the characters from the string, one per pass through the loop, and to return the size of the string.
4. Write a line of code that uses the function strrev, which reverses the characters in a C-style string, to reverse the characters contained in a C++ string class variable.

Tip: If myCstr is a C-style string, a would do this.

Programming Windows with OWL 2.5

ObjectWindows version 2.5 (or OWL 2.5) is included with Turbo C++ 4.5. It is a C++ library that shortens the time and effort needed to develop a Windows program. OWL uses a feature of the C++ language called *templates*. Today, you will learn about the following:

☐ OWL and basic Windows issues
☐ Hungarian notation
☐ The basic structure of OWL
☐ Windows messages and OWL
☐ Developing a real OWL program, complete with resources, menus, screen writing

OWL and Windows Issues

Although using OWL means that you need not worry about many of the details of Windows, you still need some knowledge of how Windows does things and especially of some of the symbols used in Windows programs.

Under DOS, there can only be one program running at a time (with the exception of TSR programs, such as Print). That program owns the screen, keyboard, and mouse. Under Windows, several programs can be running at a time, and normally each one has screen, keyboard, and mouse I/O capability. To force these programs to cooperate, Windows enforces strict conditions on program structure, handling each task almost as if it were a function in a larger application of which Windows itself is the main program.

Windows administers a communication channel called the *message loop*, which acts as a type of "party line" by which it communicates with all the executing tasks. When a task writes to the screen or the user provides some keyboard or mouse input, Windows gathers up the information and calls a function in whichever task it has decided should receive the appropriate message.

The complexity of having independently executing functions for each of your program's screen windows, along with a main program that never calls any of them directly, is what OWL addresses. The problem is that no interface library can totally hide what is underneath. Windows uses an extensive set of macros that substitute for data types and other items. Table 11.1 is a list of some of the more important ones. You might want to put a bookmark at this page so that you can refer back to it.

Table 11.1. Some common Windows MACRO names.

Macro	Meaning	Equivalent
TRUE	Used for function return values	1
FALSE	Used for function return values	0
NULL	A null pointer, as in the C language	0

Macro	Meaning	Equivalent
UINT	An unsigned 16-bit integer value	unsigned int
BYTE	An unsigned 8-bit value	unsigned char
WORD	An unsigned 16-bit value	unsigned short
DWORD	An unsigned 32-bit value	unsigned long
LONG	A signed 32-bit value	long
VOID	As a function return, it means that it returns nothing; as a pointer, it means that the data type it points to is not specified	void
LPSTR	Long pointer to a string	char far *
LPCSTR	Long pointer to a constant string	const char far *

Type	Meaning
HANDLE	A generic handle to some form of Windows item
HWND	A handle to a window
PASCAL	Specifies that the function to which it applies uses the Pascal calling method. Most Windows API functions use this calling convention because it allows Pascal programs to use the API and because it is a slightly more efficient method of passing parameters to a function (the reasons for which are beyond the scope of this book).
WPARAM	A word parameter, used to define a data type as a calling argument to a function; defined as a UINT
LPARAM	A long parameter, used to define a data type as a calling argument to a function; defined as a LONG LRESULT used to define the data type a function returns
HINSTANCE	Handle to the instance or copy of the program that is currently running

Hungarian Notation

Microsoft has been developing Windows since the early 1980s. At its inception, the ANSI standard for C compilers did not exist and type-checking was minimal. Microsoft programmers adopted a naming convention for variables that had the data type indicated as the first few characters of the variable name. It was called *Hungarian notation* because its inventor was from Hungary.

With the introduction of the ANSI C standard with its stronger type-checking, and especially with C++, a strongly typed language, Hungarian notation is no longer needed; still, it is not uncommon.

In a variable name such as lpszFilename, the lpsz means long pointer to zero-terminated string. Many programmers feel confident that they would know a variable called Filename is a string without having to add lpsz to the name. Because Windows documentation uses Hungarian notation, however, it is important to have some feel for what the leading characters in the names are, so Table 11.2 shows the prefixes used in Hungarian notation. Nonetheless, your program will run as well without them as with them.

Table 11.2. Hungarian notation prefixes.

Prefix	Data Type
c	char
by	BYTE (unsigned char)
n	short or int
i	int
x, y	short (used as x-coordinate or y-coordinate)
cx, cy	short (used as x or y length; the c stands for "count")
b	BOOL (int)
w	UINT (unsigned int) or WORD (unsigned short)
l	LONG (long)
dw	DWORD (unsigned long)
fn	function
s	C string
sz	C string terminated by 0 byte

The Basic Structure of OWL

OWL has groups of classes, each of which addresses a certain phase of Windows programming. The structure uses multiple inheritance to allow classes to encapsulate those combinations of functionality they need.

Event Handling, *TEventHandler*

The programmer does little with this directly. The functions it provides are available in many of the other program groups because of C++ inheritance. It manages the messages that constantly flow in a Windows program.

Streamable or Persistent Objects, *TStreamableBase*

This actually is part of the regular class library and not an OWL class. It allows a class to be viewed as a stream and saved to memory or disk for later use in the current run of the program or at another time that the program is run. This is exotic for small programs but is of great value in more advanced programs, such as those using the document-view architecture.

Module Management, *TModule* and *TApplication*

TModule and TApplication are in the module management group. TModule is responsible for loading and unloading DLLs while TApplication is responsible for initializing the program, managing it while it runs, and handling the tasks that are needed when the program ends.

Window Management, *TWindow*

TWindow is the base window class and inherits from TEventHandler and TStreamableBase. There are various types of windows that you might want to use in your program, and they all build on TWindow.

- [ ] TFrameWindow is a simple framed window with menu capability.
- [ ] TDecoratedFrame adds capabilities to use other items, such as status bars and tool bars.
- [ ] TMDIFrame, TMDIChild, and TDecoratedMDIFrame are Multiple Document Interface (MDI) classes used to present multiple windows in a single application.

Other functional groups are provided for the graphics, menu handling, dialog boxes, printing, and exception handling.

A Sample OWL Program

Our first OWL program only displays a window with a title. You have to press Alt+F4 or open the system menu and select Close to end it.

This program has two elements: a class to manage the window and a class to manage the application.

A class called MainApp is derived from TApplication, the class that manages the startup, the continuing message handling, and the ending tasks. TApplication has a virtual function called InitMainWindow(). In MainApp, you overload that function and provide your own. Within the function, you make a call setting the main window to a frame window with your window title.

Windows applications normally do not start with a function called main(). Instead they use a function that is declared as follows:

```
int PASCAL WinMain(HINSTANCE hInstance, HINSTANCE hPrevInstance,
                   LPSTR lpszCmdLine, int cmdShow);
```

OWL allows a main() function similar to what you're used to with other C and C++ programs, as follows:

```
int OwlMain(int argc, char *argv[]);
```

> **Note:** On the first day, when EasyWin was described, it was mentioned that when a so-called real Windows program was created, the EasyWin flag needed to be turned off in the IDE's option screens. Because OWL applications are considered real Windows applications, you will need to access the IDE's TargetExpert by clicking the right mouse button and selecting the option from the pop-up menu. A dialog box will appear with a list box titled Target Type. You need to select the Application [.exe] item in this list box and then click the OK button.

 Listing 11.1. FIRST.CPP, a first OWL program.

```
1:  #include <owl\framewin.h>
2:  #include <owl\applicat.h>
3:
4:  class MainApp : public TApplication
5:  {
6:  public:
7:      MainApp() : TApplication() {}
8:      void InitMainWindow();        // overload TApplication function
9:  };
10:
11: void MainApp::InitMainWindow()
12: {
13:     SetMainWindow(new TFrameWindow(0, "First OWL Program"));
14: }
15:
16: int OwlMain(int, char **)
17: {
18:     return MainApp().Run();
19: }
```

Figure 11.1 shows what the first OWL program does.

Figure 11.1.
The minimalist OWL program.

OwlMain begins in line 16. It calls the Run() function, and OWL's default processing does the rest. (Run() is a function within TApplication.)

The "magic" of how this operates is hidden in how the classes are set up. MainApp calls the constructor for TApplication on line 7, inside of its own constructor. That triggers default processing for all maintenance functions except the InitMainWindow() function, which has been overloaded by declaring a member function of the same name in line 8.

In line 13, the InitMainWindow() function calls SetMainWindow() to allocate a TFrameWindow and link the application with this window object. The same line allocates the TFrameWindow by calling new for it and passes the window caption to it in the constructor call.

The two header files that are included are for TFrameWindow (framewin.H) and TApplication (applicat.H). A Windows program should have a .DEF file to tell the linker what to do with the segments and stack. Turbo C++ supplies one for you, \TCWIN45\LIB\DEFAULT.DEF, and it was used for this program. It should be added to the list in your project file by following the instructions for project management on Day 1.

Windows Messages and OWL

The Windows system calls the function in your program that it has logged as the handling function for an open window. Several calling arguments are passed to the function, one of which is called the message. The other calling parameters are WPARAM and LPARAM. What they mean varies depending upon what the message was.

Messages are all named with #define macros. Two of the more common ones are

WM_CHAR, which reports a normal key is pressed. WPARAM argument contains the value of the key. LPARAM argument contains the number of times it has been pressed in the lower 16 bits, and has an array of bit flags in the upper 16 bits to indicate other data about the keyboard.

WM_SIZE, which says window size has changed. WPARAM argument contains a value defining the type of size change, such as if it has been minimized. LPARAM argument has the new width in the lower 16 bits and the new height in the upper 16 bits.

OWL provides two macros and an array of functions that know about Windows messages. When an event occurs for which Windows calls the OWL window procedure, OWL parses the information from the calling arguments and calls any function you may have provided to handle that event. You know the name to use for the function because it is derived from the name of the message, such as the following:

Windows Message	Event-handler Function Name
WM_CHAR	void EvChar(UINT key, UINT repeat, UINT flags);
WM_SIZE	void EvSize(UINT sizeType, TSize& newSize); TSize is a structure with an x and a y member called cx and cy, respectively. It holds the new dimensions of the window.

In the OWL handlers, the other calling parameters are said to be "cracked"—broken down into more easily understood parameters and not buried into the middle of a parameter value. The cracking of messages avoids many common code bugs. OWL's handling of the repetitive overhead needed by each message avoids many more bugs.

The way you tell OWL that you have supplied an event handler is done with two macros and a declaration. Within your class derived from TWindow, you declare the function itself. Also within the class definition, you place a macro to tell it that the overloading of functions is being done. In a typical class definition, those lines would look like the following:

```
class BaseWindow : public TWindow
{
protected:
    void EvChar(UINT key, UINT repeatCount, UINT flags);
    :
public:
    :
DECLARE_RESPONSE_TABLE(BaseWindow);
};
```

Later in the code, you define the response table with one entry for each function that you need.

```
DEFINE_RESPONSE_TABLE1(BaseWindow, TWindow)
    EV_WM_CHAR,
    EV_WM_SIZE,
END_RESPONSE_TABLE;
```

The macro used here is DEFINE_RESPONSE_TABLE1 because there is only one immediate class from which BaseWindow inherits. Were there to be two classes, then DEFINE_RESPONSE_TABLE2 would be used and the second class also would be listed as an argument to the macro. Macros are available for up to three inherited classes.

The Windows message name has EV_ placed in front of it to help in the macro parsing, but otherwise it is the same name as the message.

As described on Day 1, a helpful feature of the Turbo C++ IDE is that if the cursor is placed on a name such as EvChar and Ctrl+F1 is pressed, the online Help will display the function, its calling arguments, and an explanation of what each argument means.

A Real OWL Program Resources, Menus, Screen Writing

A demo that only puts a window on the screen is not very useful. Menus and screen writing have been added to the next example. It demonstrates techniques for handling normal Windows messages and messages from menus.

Menus are a feature that you can add to a window. The Windows system runs them for you, returning a number corresponding to the user selection. The message that Windows sends in response to a menu selection is WM_COMMAND, with the WPARAM parameter set to the value of the selected item. Because the selections in a menu that you create would not be part of the operating system, OWL has no built-in detection for them. What it does have is an EV_COMMAND macro that enables you to specify response functions for nonstandard events.

There are three source files involved in adding a menu to an application. The source file for the program is involved, but you also need a resource file.

Resources are predefined items that will be added to the executable as a last step. As the program is already compiled and linked when they are added, this arrangement enables resources to be more easily changed—a great advantage when changing a menu from English to German, for example. Because a resource file normally has the file extension .RC, they often are called .RC files.

The third file involved is a header file listing the macros used for menu selections, along with their number equivalents. By including the same header file in the source code and the .RC file, any changes in the selection numbers will track through to the C++ compilation as well as to the resource compiler's handling of the .RC file. As you did with DEFAULT.DEF, add the name REAL.RC to the IDE project file list. Listing 11.2 shows a resource file.

Listing 11.2. REAL.RC, a resource file.

```
 1:  #include "real.rh"
 2:
 3:  MENU_1 MENU
 4:    {
 5:    POPUP "&File"
 6:      {
 7:      MENUITEM "&Clear",  CM_CLEAR
 8:      MENUITEM "E&xit",   CM_FILEEXIT
 9:      }
10:
11:    MENUITEM "&About",   CM_ABOUT
12:    }
```

   Figure 11.2 shows what it looks like.

Figure 11.2.
From REAL.RC,
a resource file.

   Later you will use Resource Workshop to create .RC files containing menus and other items. For now, there is little value in using that tool unless you have some feel for what is being created with it, so this text file is what you will use instead.

On line 3, the MENU_1 item is not referenced in the header file or the source file. With the available information, the resource compiler will make it a text string. You can take advantage of this name string in the program when you load a menu identified as MENU_1.

Line 5 starts defining a pop-up menu. A *pop-up* is a menu that, when selected, opens to display more menu selections. It does not return a value, although the newly shown selections often do.

The first pop-up item in the menu is given the name &File. The & character flags the F as special. In the menu it will be shown underlined, and pressing Alt+F will cause it to be selected.

The pop-up contains two menu items on lines 7 and 8. A menu item does return a value to the program. In this, case the displayed names for the menu items are **C**lear and E**x**it with the **C** and **x** underlined. You can use Alt+C and Alt+X to select these items when the pop-up is opened. If **C**lear is selected, CM_CLEAR is returned. The following header file assigns the number 1125 to CM_CLEAR, but the program doesn't care what that number is. All it cares about is if it receives a message with the WPARAM set equal to whatever the macro CM_CLEAR stands for.

On line 9, the curly brace after E&xit ends the pop-up. Following that on line 10 is another menu item selection for About. If selected, the value CM_ABOUT will be sent to the program, which will display an About box that tells the name of the program.

When the program is running, OWL doesn't have any knowledge of what the CM_CLEAR, CM_FILEEXIT or CM_ABOUT values accompanying a WM_COMMAND message are, so it ignores them. You can change this with additions to the response table, which tells OWL what to do with those messages.

Along with predefined messages such as WM_SIZE and WM_CHAR, you can use the EV_COMMAND macro to say that you have a command message that you want OWL to handle. It is used as follows:

```
DEFINE_RESPONSE_TABLE1(BaseWindow, TWindow)
    EV_WM_CHAR,
    EV_WM_SIZE,
    EV_COMMAND( CM_ABOUT, CmAbout),
END_RESPONSE_TABLE;
```

The function is expected to take no parameters and return no value—in other words, void CmAbout(). OWL programmers commonly use a certain way of naming such functions, and if you follow that convention, your code will be more understandable to others and you will be getting used to the same type of naming that is used in the documentation that came with Turbo C++. To name the function, delete any underscores and capitalize the first letter of each word. For example, CM_ABOUT becomes CmAbout(). Windows event handlers drop the WM_ entirely and put Ev at the beginning of the name; thus WM_CHAR becomes EvChar. Remember that event handlers usually take some parameters. When you use one, look it up in the online Help to check that you have the arguments correct.

REAL.CPP writes to the screen what you have typed. OWL provides an entire class, called TEdit, which can edit and capture your input far better than REAL.CPP does. This and other controls will be covered in later chapters. This example's writing to the screen is meant to illustrate how one paints a window under Windows—which is very different than under DOS.

 NEW TERM Windows uses an item called a *device context*, also called a *DC*. A DC is a structure containing information about a device such as a screen, a printer, or a block of memory.

You can write to anything for which you have asked Windows to provide a DC. Windows only has a limited number of DC blocks, so they are handled by requesting one, using it, and then calling Windows to free it for other uses. Forgetting to release DCs can result in Windows apparently stopping. With OWL, you needn't worry unless requesting a DC yourself. OWL automatically checks out a DC when it's time to paint the screen and returns it afterward. OWL expands upon this by placing the device context into a class called TDC along with functions that use DCs. Those functions already know what device you are writing to when you call them. Listing 11.3 shows a header file.

Listing 11.3. REAL.RH, a header file.

```
1: #define CM_CLEAR    1125
2: #define CM_FILEEXIT 1126
3: #define CM_ABOUT    1127
```

REAL.RH does not get listed in the compiler's project file. The compiler will discover what header files are used by itself.

Listing 11.4 shows a program that uses a menu, accepts keyboard input, and writes the input to the screen.

Listing 11.4. REAL.CPP, a real OWL program.

```
1:  #include <owl\framewin.h>
2:  #include <owl\applicat.h>
3:  #include <owl\dc.h>
4:  #include <mem.h>
5:
6:  #pragma hdrstop
7:
8:  #include "real.rh"
9:
10: const int maxLines = 25;
11: const int maxWidth = 80;
12: const int maxData = maxLines * (maxWidth + 1);
13:
14: class BaseWindow : public TWindow
15: {
16: protected:
17:    int   currentLine;        // line being typed in now
18:    int   lineLen[maxLines];  // length of each line
19:    char *linePtrs[maxLines]; // string for each line
20:    BOOL  isMinimized;        // TRUE if window is an icon
21:    TSize windowSize;         // structure with size in pixels
22:
23:    void EvChar(UINT key, UINT repeatCount, UINT flags);
24:    void Paint(TDC& dc, BOOL, TRect&);
25:    void EvSize(UINT sizeType, TSize& size);
26:
27:    void CmAbout();
28:    void CmClear();
```

```
29:
30:    // Menu choice, end the program
31:    void CmFileExit() { PostQuitMessage(0); }
32:
33: public:
34:    BaseWindow(TWindow *parent = 0);
35:    ~BaseWindow() {}
36:    DECLARE_RESPONSE_TABLE(BaseWindow); // says we'll have a
37: };                                    // response table
38:
39: DEFINE_RESPONSE_TABLE1(BaseWindow, TWindow)
40:    EV_WM_CHAR,
41:    EV_WM_SIZE,
42:    EV_COMMAND( CM_ABOUT,    CmAbout),
43:    EV_COMMAND( CM_FILEEXIT, CmFileExit),
44:    EV_COMMAND( CM_CLEAR,    CmClear),
45: END_RESPONSE_TABLE;
46:
47: class MyApp : public TApplication
48: {
49: public:
50:    MyApp() : TApplication() {}
51:
52:    void InitMainWindow();
53: };
54:
55: BaseWindow::BaseWindow(TWindow *parent)
56: {
57:    int lineNum;
58:
59:    Init(parent, 0, 0);
60:    linePtrs[0] = new char[maxData]; // allocate edit buffer
61:    lineLen[0] = currentLine = 0;
62:
63:    // apportion the buffer out to the line pointer array
64:    for (lineNum = 1; lineNum < maxLines; ++lineNum)
65:        {
66:        linePtrs[lineNum] = linePtrs[lineNum - 1] + maxWidth;
67:        lineLen[lineNum] = 0;
68:        }
69: }
70:
71: // Menu choice, display an About box, use a message box to do it
72: void BaseWindow::CmAbout()
73: {
74:    MessageBox("Teach Yourself Turbo C++ 4.5 in 21 Days", "About");
75: }
76:
77:    // Menu choice, clear the display
78:    void BaseWindow::CmClear()
79:    {
80:    for (int lineNum = 0; lineNum < maxLines; ++lineNum)
81:        lineLen[lineNum] = 0;    // empty all lines
82:
83:    currentLine = 0;             // move back to top line
84:    Invalidate();                // window is invalid, repaint
```

continues

11

Listing 11.4. continued

```
85:    }
86:
87:    // this is called whenever the window changes size
88:    void BaseWindow::EvSize(UINT sizeType, TSize& size)
89:    {
90:      if (sizeType == SIZE_MINIMIZED) // if shrunk to icon
91:          isMinimized = TRUE;
92:      else
93:          {
94:          windowSize = size;              // save window size
95:          isMinimized = FALSE;
96:          }
97:    }
98:
99:    // called when time to update (paint) the screen
100:   void BaseWindow::Paint(TDC& dc, BOOL, TRect&)
101:   {
102:     int   lineNum;           // line number to write
103:     int   yPos;              // vertical position on screen
104:     int   displayedLines;    // number of linePtrs in this window
105:     TSize textSize;          // used to get char height in pixels
106:
107:     if (isMinimized)         // don't write to an icon
108:         return;
109:
110:     // get char sizes so that height is saved
111:     textSize = dc.GetTextExtent("W", 1);
112:     displayedLines = windowSize.cy / textSize.cy;
113:
114:     if (displayedLines > maxLines)
115:         displayedLines = maxLines;
116:
117:     for (lineNum = yPos = 0; lineNum < displayedLines; ++lineNum)
118:         {
119:         if (lineLen[lineNum] > 0)  // if any text on the line
120:             dc.TextOut(0, yPos, linePtrs[lineNum], lineLen[lineNum]);
121:
122:         yPos += textSize.cy;   // adjust screen line position
123:         }
124:   }
125:
126:   // called when a normal key is pressed
127:   void BaseWindow::EvChar(UINT key, UINT repeatCount, UINT)
128:   {
129:     BOOL invalidDisplay = FALSE;
130:     BOOL eraseBackground = FALSE;
131:
132:     while (repeatCount—)
133:         {
134:         if ((key >= ' ') && (key <= '~')) // if a printable key
135:             {
136:             if (currentLine >= maxLines)    // if buffer full
137:                 {
138:                 MessageBeep(-1);                // complain
139:                 break;
140:                 }
```

```
141:        else                              // else
142:            {                             //    add char
143:            linePtrs[currentLine][lineLen[currentLine]] = (char)key;
144:
145:            if (++lineLen[currentLine] >= maxWidth)
146:                ++currentLine;
147:
148:            invalidDisplay = TRUE;
149:            }
150:        }
151:    else if (key == '\b')  // rubout, delete char
152:        {
153:        if (currentLine >= maxLines)
154:            break;
155:        else if (lineLen[currentLine] == 0)
156:            {
157:            if (currentLine > 0)
158:                -currentLine;
159:            }
160:        else
161:            -lineLen[currentLine];
162:
163:        invalidDisplay = eraseBackground = TRUE;
164:        }
165:    else if (key == '\r') // if carriage return (Enter key)
166:        ++currentLine;
167:    }
168:
169:    if (currentLine >= maxLines)
170:        currentLine = maxLines - 1;
171:
172:    if (invalidDisplay)                 // if buffer has changed
173:        Invalidate(eraseBackground); //   force window repaint
174: }
175:
176: void MyApp::InitMainWindow()
177: {
178:    SetMainWindow(new TFrameWindow(0, "A Real Windows Program",
179:                                    new BaseWindow()));
180:    GetMainWindow()->AssignMenu("MENU_1");
181: }
182:
183:
184: int OwlMain(int, char **)
185: {
186:    return MyApp().Run();
187: }
```

Before running this application, you may want to get a feel for how it looks by examining Figure 11.1. Three instances of this program are shown on-screen, one each for an About box displayed, data typed in, and the pop-up menu opened.

As with the first program, this begins in OwlMain(). Line 186 calls the constructor for MyApp, and then calls Run().

The constructor is declared on line 52. It in turn calls the constructor for TApplication. Line 54 has a function called InitMainWindow() that overloads the virtual function of the same name in the inherited class.

TApplication's constructor calls InitMainWindow() (lines 176 through 181). That function makes two calls to new, creating a base window and then a frame window to handle the items on the base window's borders. The GetMainWindow() call on the next line assigns the menu to the main window. From then on, the application runs on its own, with Windows driving it by way of messages about menu selections and keyboard events.

The response table on lines 39 through 45 declared response functions for a character being entered, a window size change, and any of the three menu selections. Also, BaseWindow's inheritance chain includes a virtual function called Paint(), which has been overloaded.

The data in the BaseWindow class is for keyboard input. Such input causes EvChar() on line 127 to be called. The calling arguments are the value of the key, the number of times it has been entered since you were last called, and a flag's variable that you don't use. The repeat count is important because a long process such as saving a disk file could allow the keyboard to insert several keys into the keyboard buffer.

This function passes through a loop as many times as the repeat count directs, adding keys to the keyboard buffer. When a line is full, it skips to the next line and begins entering there. If the buffer is full, the computer beeps at you (line 138).

If the user chooses the Backspace button, it deletes the last character entered (if one exists). The end of the function calls Invalidate(), a function that tells Windows that the whole window must be updated. The eraseBackground variable is only set to TRUE if a character is deleted. This minimizes screen blinking.

In response to the Invalidate() call, Windows sends the window procedure a message to paint the window. In the process, it sets things up and calls Paint().

Paint() gets the text size. Fonts in Windows often are of variable width, but the measurement you are interested in is the vertical, which doesn't vary. You also calculate the number of displayable lines. It's a waste of time to paint more than that, because additional lines won't be placed on the screen.

A loop starting on line 118 passes through each line, writing any data in it to the screen. Note that linePtrs[lineNum] is an array of characters, not a string. No '\0' has been placed at the end. It relies on the lineLen array to handle how long the string is.

Note the TDC argument to Paint(). That is the device context you are to use in writing the screen. OWL has assigned it and will delete it after your function ends.

If you grab the corner of the window with the mouse cursor and resize it, EvSize() from line 88 will be called. If the application is minimized (shrunk to an icon), it merely sets a flag and returns.

If it is not minimized, it captures the window dimensions into the TSize structure called windowSize for later use by the Paint() function.

Menu operation is straightforward. Select any menu item and OWL calls the corresponding function. The CMClear() function (starting on line 78) sets the line length for all strings to zero and moves the current line number to point at the first line (linePtrs[0]). It then invalidates the window so that Paint() will be called. When called with no arguments, Invalidate() defaults to TRUE so the background will also be erased.

CmAbout calls a message box—a built-in Windows function—to show the name of the book.

CmFileExit() on line 31 calls a true Windows function, PostQuitMessage(). This function ends the program, and the return value (which Windows ignores in version 3.1) is the function argument.

Summary

Today's lesson introduced you to Borland's ObjectWindows application framework/class library and discussed the following topics:

- ☐ Windows requires special programming techniques because it allows multiple programs to run at the same time (unlike DOS).
- ☐ Windows communicates with programs via messages, and programs receive and process these messages in their message loop.
- ☐ Windows defines several shorthand names for common types of variables.
- ☐ Hungarian notation is a style of naming variables to indicate the type of data they hold and it helps in preventing bugs caused by mixing incompatible types. It's somewhat old-fashioned, as Turbo C++ implements very strong C++ type checking, but Windows still uses some of its notations.
- ☐ OWL consists of groups of classes used to represent Windows structures, including event handling, module management, and window management.
- ☐ OWL processes Windows messages by executing the appropriate functions found in a window object's response table. OWL also "cracks" the parameters that Windows sends into more meaningful values.
- ☐ Adding a menu to a window requires that you create a menu resource, tell OWL to load it, and process the menu items using the EV_COMMAND macro.

Q&A

Q I have a DOS program I'd like to port to Windows. Do I have to rewrite it to use Windows techniques like message loops?

A Yes. It won't be a Windows program if it doesn't follow Windows rules. However, you can use Turbo C++'s EasyWin library, which enables you to use DOS-style input and output functions. The result is a Windows program that looks like a DOS program.

Q The shorthand type names like DWORD and LPCSTR are confusing; can't I just use the normal C++ types?

A Yes, you can, but you have to make sure you do everything exactly the same. For example, everywhere you would normally use LPCSTR, make sure you use const char far *. Although learning the types takes some time, it usually is worth the extra effort, if only in saving the time it takes to type!

Q What function in my program is called first?

A DOS programs start at the main() function, which has arguments for the command-line parameters. Windows instead looks for a WinMain() function, with several arguments for instance handles, command-line parameters, and main window sizes. OWL simplifies it by providing an OwlMain() function that takes the same parameters as main() does.

Q Do I have to use a resource editor like Resource Workshop to create my resources?

A No. Resource files (with a .RC extension) are text files, so you can create and edit them with any text editor. However, Resource Workshop greatly simplifies editing resources, especially graphical ones.

Workshop

The Workshop provides quiz questions to help you solidify your understanding of the material covered and exercises to provide you with experience in using what you've learned. Try to understand the answers before continuing on to the next day's lesson. Answers are provided in Appendix A.

Quiz

1. True or false? The underlying types of Windows types like WORD and UINT will never change.

2. True or false? Even though an OWL program is quite different from a program written in C, it still is a normal Windows program.

Exercise

Create the program REAL2.CPP by using the TWindow::MessageBox function to display a message when the user types an invalid key.

12

Basic Windows

The most relevant aspect of the Windows environment, as the name suggests, is the use of windows. Windows are the holders of information. The application is responsible for maintaining information when you resize, move, or use existing scroll bars. In today's lesson, you learn about the following:

☐ Creating read-only text windows

☐ Scrolling through text using scroll bars

☐ Changing the scroll bar metrics (units, line size, page size, and ranges)

☐ Optimizing the `Paint` member function

Creating a Read-Only Text Window

Day 11 presented a number of menu-driven OWL applications. However, there was very little explanation concerning how information was displayed in windows. This section presents an OWL application that displays read-only text in its windows. The basic notion of the application is similar to that of the read-only online Help windows.

The purpose of the program is to demonstrate how to display text and maintain that text after one or more of the following has occurred:

☐ Resizing the window

☐ Minimizing, restoring, or maximizing the window

☐ Moving a window or dialog box over the text area

The main tools to implement the application's features are the member functions `TDC::TextOut` and `TWindow::Paint`. The function `TDC::TextOut` draws a character string on the specified display. The text appears in the currently selected font and at the specified window coordinates.

The *TextOut* Function

The declarations for the overloaded `TDC` member function `TextOut` are

```
bool TextOut(int x, int y, const char far* str, int count = -1);
bool TextOut(const TPoint& p, const char far* str, int count = -1);
```

The x and y parameters identify the window location where the first character appears. The `str` parameter points to the string to be displayed in the window. The `count` parameter indicates the leading number of characters of `str` to display. The argument for the last parameter is usually the size of the displayed string argument. Note that this has a default of -1, which means to display all the characters of `str`. In the second version of the function `TextOut`, the x and y parameters are replaced by a reference to a `TPoint` structure. The function returns a nonzero value when successful and `0` when it fails.

Example

```
char s[81] = "Hello";
string str("Guten Tag!");
TPoint pt(10, 20);
dc.TextOut(20, 10, s);
dc.TextOut(pt, str.c_str());
```

As expected, the function `TDC::TextOut` displays text once. This means that altering the viewing area of the window or moving another window over the displayed text erases that text. What is needed is a mechanism that updates the display of text in the window. Enter the member function `TWindow::Paint`. This function enables you to display and maintain the contents of a window (both text and graphics). The versatility of the function `TWindow::Paint` comes from the fact that it responds to a `WM_PAINT` message whenever Windows determines that the window needs repainting. This repainting feature includes the initial creation of the window. Consequently, the versatility of `TWindow::Paint` includes setting the initial display as well as maintaining it.

Note: You need to declare your own version of the `Paint` member function in your derived window class. The code you place inside your version of the `Paint` function determines what information appears, remains, and disappears.

In the case of this OWL application, the same information is displayed from start to finish. The general form of the `Paint` member function is

```
void MyWindow::Paint(TDC& dc, bool erase, TRect& rect)
{
    // declarations

    // statements using the TextOut member function
    // e.g.
    //      dc.TextOut(x, y, s, strlen(s));
}
```

The parameter `dc` that is passed to the `Paint` member function is referred to as the device context, and it's the link to the display of the window. The `dc.TextOut` function can be used as needed to place text on the window. Interestingly, if you come across a C-coded Windows application that uses the `TextOut` API function, you note that a similar text output requires initializing the device-context object and then promptly releasing it once it has finished its task. These steps are performed automatically by the `TWindow::EvPaint` function, which in turn calls the `Paint` function.

NEW☛ A *device context* (or DC for short) is the place in which all output goes. Anything that needs
TERM to be painted, such as text or graphics, must go onto DCs. These DCs can directly represent physical pixels on the screen, or they can be *memory DCs*. These memory DCs typically are used

361

as temporary space in which to create such things as bitmaps before actually putting them on the screen by copying to another DC.

Now look at the code for the OWL application. Listing 12.1 contains the script for the resource file WINDOW1.RC. This resource file defines a menu with a single menu item, Exit, to exit the application. Listing 12.2 shows the source code for the WINDOW1.CPP program.

Create the directory WINDOW1 as a subdirectory of \TCWIN45\TC21DAY and store all the project's files in the new directory. The project's IDE file should contain the files WINDOW1.CPP and WINDOW1.RC.

Compile and run the application. Notice that the lines of text appear when the window is created. Alter the window by resizing it, minimizing it, and then restoring it to normal. The lines of text are always visible (or at least a portion of them) as long as the upper-left portion of the screen is not obscured by another window. You also can click the left mouse button to display a message box. Drag that message box over the text lines and release the mouse. Then, drag the message box away from the text location. What do you see? The text lines reappear; Paint is constantly at work.

 Listing 12.1. Script code for WINDOW1.RC.

```
1: #include <windows.h>
2: #include <owl\window.rh>
3:
4: EXITMENU MENU LOADONCALL MOVEABLE PURE DISCARDABLE
5: BEGIN
6:     MENUITEM "E&xit", CM_EXIT
7: END
```

Listing 12.2. Source code for WINDOW1.CPP.

```
1:  #include <owl\applicat.h>
2:  #include <owl\dc.h>
3:  #include <owl\framewin.h>
4:  #include <owl\window.h>
5:  #include <owl\window.rh>
6:  #include <stdio.h>
7:
8:  const MAX_LINES = 30;
9:
10: class TMyWindow : public TWindow
11: {
12: public:
13:     TMyWindow(TWindow* parent = 0);
14:
15: protected:
16:     bool CanClose();
17:
18:     void CmExit();
```

```
19:     void EvLButtonDown(UINT, TPoint &);
20:
21:     void Paint(TDC &, bool, TRect &);
22:
23:     DECLARE_RESPONSE_TABLE(TMyWindow);
24: };
25: DEFINE_RESPONSE_TABLE1(TMyWindow, TWindow)
26:     EV_WM_LBUTTONDOWN,
27:     EV_COMMAND(CM_EXIT, CmExit),
28: END_RESPONSE_TABLE;
29:
30: class TMyApp : public TApplication
31: {
32: public:
33:     TMyApp() : TApplication() {}
34:
35:     void InitMainWindow()
36:         {
37:         SetMainWindow(new TFrameWindow(  0,
38:                             "A Simple Read-Only Text Window",
39:                             new TMyWindow ));
40:         GetMainWindow()->AssignMenu("EXITMENU");
41:         }
42: };
43:
44: TMyWindow::TMyWindow(TWindow* parent)
45: {
46:     Init(parent, 0, 0);
47: }
48:
49: bool TMyWindow::CanClose()
50: {
51:     return IDYES == MessageBox("Want to close this application?",
52:                                 "Query",
53:                                 MB_YESNO | MB_ICONQUESTION );
54: }
55:
56: void TMyWindow::CmExit()
57: {
58:     SendMessage(WM_CLOSE);
59: }
60:
61: void TMyWindow::EvLButtonDown(UINT, TPoint &)
62: {
63:     MessageBox( "You clicked the left button!",
64:                 "Mouse Click Event",
65:                 MB_OK );
66: }
67:
68: void TMyWindow::Paint(TDC& dc, bool /*erase*/, TRect& /*rect*/)
69: {
70:     char s[81];
71:     bool ok = true;
72:     int y = 0;
73:
74:     for (int i = 0; i < MAX_LINES && ok; ++i)
```

continues

363

Listing 12.2. continued

```
75:        {
76:        sprintf(s, "This is line number %d", i);
77:        ok = dc.TextOut(0, y, s);
78:        y += dc.GetTextExtent(s, lstrlen(s)).cy;
79:        }
80: }
81:
82: int OwlMain(int, char *[])
83: {
84:    return TMyApp().Run();
85: }
```

 Figure 12.1 shows a sample session with the program WINDOW1.EXE.

Figure 12.1.

A sample session with the program WINDOW1.EXE.

 Listing 12.2 shows the source code for the WINDOW1.CPP program file. The part of the program that is relevant to this application is the TMyWindow class and its member functions, declared on lines 10 through 28. The window class declares a constructor and three member functions, namely EvLButtonDown, CmClose, and Paint. The constructor creates a window on line 37 with the title "A Simple Read-Only Text Window" that has default size and location, and that uses the EXITMENU menu resource.

The main point of interest is the Paint function that starts on line 68. The function declares the constant MAX_LINES, the string variable s, and the bool-typed variable ok. The Paint function displays the lines using the for loop on lines 74 through 79. Each loop iteration executes two statements. The first statement calls the sprintf function (prototyped in the STDIO.H header file) to create the image of a formatted output and store it in the variable s. The next statement calls the dc's TextOut member function, which places the formatted output on the window. Notice the first two arguments of the TextOut function. They are 0 (for parameter X) and y. These values result in displaying the text, starting with the left margin of the window. The next function called is the dc's GetTextExtent member function. This is used to determine the height of the text and any line spacing and to use that information by adding it to the y variable so that the next time through the loop, the next line is placed appropriately below the previous line.

Scrolling Through Text

One of the versatile features of windows is the capability to scroll information, if that information cannot be contained in the current viewing portion of the window. The scroll bars are the visual components of a window that assist in scrolling through the window's contents. Recall that a window can have a vertical scroll bar, horizontal scroll bar, or both. A scroll bar has an arrow box at each end and a scroll thumb. The arrow boxes enable you to scroll the window's contents to either end or to either side. In today's lesson, you learn about scrolling windows that contain text drawn using device-context objects.

NEW☞
TERM The *scroll thumb* serves two purposes. First, it shows where you are relative to the entire width or length of the viewed information. Second, when you drag the thumb with the mouse, you can move to a specific portion of the viewed information.

The scrolling effect mentioned at the beginning of today's lesson is supported by a visual interface and an internal "engine." You can easily include the visual scroll bars in a window by incorporating the WS_VSCROLL and WS_HSCROLL styles in the Attr.Style member data from the window's constructor. To create a window with both vertical and horizontal scroll bars, for example, use the following statement:

```
// both vertical and horizontal scroll bars
Attr.Style |= WS_VSCROLL | WS_HSCROLL;
```

The WS_VSCROLL and WS_HSCROLL constants add the visual aspect of the scroll bars. The functionality is supported by overriding the EvVScroll, EvHScroll, and EvSize functions, and then adjusting your Paint function to take advantage of any scrolling changes. OWL provides an integrated class that does just this, called TScroller. An object of this class, when assigned the TWindow's Scroller member function, provides scrolling by working with the TWindow class to automatically sense the setting of the scroll bars and adjusts the window's viewport accordingly.

NEW☞
TERM The *viewport* is that portion of the window that is visible at any one time. It is possible to paint on a window outside of the visible portion, but that will be *clipped* from view. By adjusting the viewport's origin, the clipped region will change, and offsets within the window

will be adjusted accordingly. For example, given a standard window, when a string of text is drawn at (10,10), the text will appear offset down and to the right of the upper-left corner of the window. By adjusting the viewport origin to begin at (10,10), drawing that same text at the same location now will make it appear in the upper-left corner.

The constructor for the TScroller class looks like this.

```
TScroller(TWindow* window, int xUnit, int yUnit,
long xRange, long yRange);
```

The window parameter is a pointer to the window for which the TScroller object is being created. The xUnit and yUnit parameters specify how many device units to scroll in each direction. In the case of textual information, this usually is going to be the size of a single character, so that scrolling goes by lines. Note, however, that because most fonts in Windows are variable (each of the characters are of differing widths), the horizontal unit tends to be the average width of all the characters. Finally, the xRange and yRange parameters specify how many scrolling positions exist. For example, a yRange of 20 would mean that the down arrow on the scroll bar could be clicked 20 times.

It is easy to add an additional include file at the top,

```
#include <owl\scroller.h>
```

and the following two lines to the constructor of the TMyWindow class from the last example:

```
Attr.Style |= WS_VSCROLL | WS_HSCROLL;
Scroller = new TScroller(7, 16, 20, MAX_LINES - 1);
```

If you add those two lines and recompile, you will find that your window now has scroll bars on the bottom and right side, and you can scroll to the right 20 columns and down as many lines as are drawn (minus one, so at least one of the lines stays on-screen). The two more interesting functions of the TScroller class are the VScroll and HScroll member functions.

Manually Scrolling with *TScroller*

Syntax

The declarations of TScroller's VScroll and HScroll member functions are

```
void VScroll(UINT scrollEvent, int thumbPos);
void HScroll(UINT scrollEvent, int thumbPos);
```

The scrollEvent specifies the scrolling request. Table 12.1 shows the predefined constants for the various scrolling requests. The thumbPos parameter specifies the position of the thumb box when the argument for scrollEvent is either SB_THUMBPOSITION or SB_THUMBTRACK.

Example

```
Scroller->VScroll(SB_LINEDOWN, 0);
Scroller->HScroll(SB_THUMBPOSITION, 23);
```

Table 12.1. Predefined constants for vertical scrolling requests.

Value	Meaning
SB_BOTTOM	Scroll to the bottom
SB_ENDSCROLL	End scroll
SB_LINEDOWN	Scroll one line down
SB_LINEUP	Scroll one line up
SB_PAGEDOWN	Scroll one page down
SB_PAGEUP	Scroll one page up
SB_THUMBPOSITION	Scroll to the nPos position
SB_THUMBTRACK	Drag the scroll thumb box to the nPos position
SB_TOP	Scroll to the top

In the preceding short example, the 7 and 16 are approximations of a character's width and height. They will work when using the default font on most standard VGA screens, but you will run into problems when you try to use different fonts or when you run on screens that use a smaller font (such as an 800×600 or 1024×768 screen). The solution is to figure out the size of the font beforehand and set the scroll units accordingly.

A Scrolling Window

This section presents a program that defines general scrollable windows. WINDOW2.EXE has two main menu items: Exit and Char Sets. The second menu item is a pop-up menu that has three selections: Set 1, Set 2, and Set 3. These options produce text lines that have a different line spacing and different maximum number of lines. The text fonts are the same for all three sets. Initially, the client area of the application window is clear. Therefore, you must select one of the three character sets. The application also supports the cursor movement keys to scroll the text. The <Home> and <End> keys scroll vertically to the top and bottom, respectively. Similarly, the <PgUp> and <PgDn> keys scroll up and down one page. The up- and down-arrow keys scroll one line at a time. The left- and right-arrow keys scroll horizontally by pages.

This program illustrates two main aspects of scrolling windows:

☐ Declaring a scrolling window class with additional member functions that manage the assignment, access, and use of scrolling-related data

☐ Using assigned values to control vertical scrolling, and relying on the current window metrics to control the horizontal scrolling

Look at the code for the general text scroller window application. Listings 12.3 and 12.4 show the header file WINDOW2.H and the resource file WINDOW2.RC, respectively. Listing 12.5 contains the source code for the WINDOW2.CPP program.

Create the directory WINDOW2 as a subdirectory of \TCWIN45\TC21DAY and store all the project's files in the new directory. The project should contain the files WINDOW2.CPP and WINDOW2.RC.

Listing 12.3. Source code for WINDOW2.H.

```
1:  #define  CM_HEIGHT8    (WM_USER + 100)
2:  #define  CM_HEIGHT10   (WM_USER + 101)
3:  #define  CM_HEIGHT14   (WM_USER + 102)
4:  #define  CM_HEIGHT20   (WM_USER + 103)
5:  #define  CM_HEIGHT26   (WM_USER + 104)
```

Listing 12.4. Script code for WINDOW2.RC.

```
1:  #include <windows.h>
2:  #include <owl\window.rh>
3:  #include "window2.h"
4:
5:  EXITMENU MENU LOADONCALL MOVEABLE PURE DISCARDABLE
6:  BEGIN
7:      MENUITEM "E&xit", CM_EXIT
8:      POPUP "&Char Heights"
9:      BEGIN
10:         MENUITEM "&8", CM_HEIGHT8
11:         MENUITEM "1&0", CM_HEIGHT10
12:         MENUITEM "1&4", CM_HEIGHT14
13:         MENUITEM "&20", CM_HEIGHT20
14:         MENUITEM "2&6", CM_HEIGHT26
15:     END
16: END
```

Listing 12.5. Source code for WINDOW2.CPP.

```
1:  #include <owl\applicat.h>
2:  #include <owl\dc.h>
3:  #include <owl\framewin.h>
4:  #include <owl\scroller.h>
5:  #include <owl\window.h>
6:  #include <owl\window.rh>
7:  #include <stdio.h>
8:
9:  #include "window2.h"
10:
11: const MAX_LINES = 30;
12:
13: class TMyWindow : public TWindow
14: {
15: public:
16:     TMyWindow(TWindow* parent = 0);
17:     ~TMyWindow();
18:
19: protected:
```

```
20:    virtual void SetupWindow();
21:
22:    bool CanClose();
23:
24:    void CmExit();
25:    void CmHeight8();
26:    void CmHeight10();
27:    void CmHeight14();
28:    void CmHeight20();
29:    void CmHeight26();
30:    void EvKeyDown(UINT, UINT, UINT);
31:    void EvLButtonDown(UINT, TPoint &);
32:
33:    void Paint(TDC &, bool, TRect &);
34:
35: private:
36:    TFont* pFont;
37:
38:    void NewFont(int);
39:
40:    DECLARE_RESPONSE_TABLE(TMyWindow);
41: };
42: DEFINE_RESPONSE_TABLE1(TMyWindow, TWindow)
43:    EV_WM_KEYDOWN,
44:    EV_WM_LBUTTONDOWN,
45:    EV_COMMAND(CM_EXIT, CmExit),
46:    EV_COMMAND(CM_HEIGHT8, CmHeight8),
47:    EV_COMMAND(CM_HEIGHT10, CmHeight10),
48:    EV_COMMAND(CM_HEIGHT14, CmHeight14),
49:    EV_COMMAND(CM_HEIGHT20, CmHeight20),
50:    EV_COMMAND(CM_HEIGHT26, CmHeight26),
51: END_RESPONSE_TABLE;
52:
53: class TMyApp : public TApplication
54: {
55: public:
56:    TMyApp() : TApplication() {}
57:
58:    void InitMainWindow()
59:        {
60:        SetMainWindow(new TFrameWindow(  0,
61:                            "A Simple Read-Only Text Window",
62:                            new TMyWindow ));
63:        GetMainWindow()->AssignMenu("EXITMENU");
64:        }
65: };
66:
67: TMyWindow::TMyWindow(TWindow* parent)
68: {
69:    Init(parent, 0, 0);
70:    Attr.Style |= WS_VSCROLL | WS_HSCROLL;    // Add scroll bars
71:    pFont = NULL;
72: }
73:
74: TMyWindow::~TMyWindow()
75: {
76:    if (pFont)
```

continues

Listing 12.5. continued

```
77:         delete pFont;
78: }
79:
80: void TMyWindow::SetupWindow()
81: {
82:     TWindow::SetupWindow();
83:
84:     // Set up the scroller and font.  Note that
85:     // dummy values of 7 and 16 are used for the
86:     // scroll bar's units, but they'll be reset
87:     // as soon as the font is set.
88:     //
89:     Scroller = new TScroller(this, 7, 16, 20, MAX_LINES - 1);
90:     NewFont(8);                              // Initialize our font
91: }
92:
93: bool TMyWindow::CanClose()
94: {
95:     return IDYES == MessageBox("Want to close this application?",
96:                               "Query",
97:                               MB_YESNO | MB_ICONQUESTION );
98: }
99:
100: void TMyWindow::CmExit()
101: {
102:     SendMessage(WM_CLOSE);
103: }
104:
105: void TMyWindow::CmHeight8()
106: {
107:     NewFont(8);
108: }
109:
110: void TMyWindow::CmHeight10()
111: {
112:     NewFont(10);
113: }
114:
115: void TMyWindow::CmHeight14()
116: {
117:     NewFont(14);
118: }
119:
120: void TMyWindow::CmHeight20()
121: {
122:     NewFont(20);
123: }
124:
125: void TMyWindow::CmHeight26()
126: {
127:     NewFont(26);
128: }
129:
130: void TMyWindow::EvKeyDown( UINT key,
131:                           UINT /*repeatCount*/,
```

```
132:                         UINT /*flags*/ )
133: {
134:     if (Scroller)          // Can't scroll if it ain't there!
135:         switch (key)
136:             {
137:             case VK_HOME:
138:                 Scroller->VScroll(SB_TOP, 0);
139:                 break;
140:             case VK_END:
141:                 Scroller->VScroll(SB_BOTTOM, 0);
142:                 break;
143:             case VK_PRIOR:
144:                 Scroller->VScroll(SB_PAGEUP, 0);
145:                 break;
146:             case VK_NEXT:
147:                 Scroller->VScroll(SB_PAGEDOWN, 0);
148:                 break;
149:             case VK_UP:
150:                 Scroller->VScroll(SB_LINEUP, 0);
151:                 break;
152:             case VK_DOWN:
153:                 Scroller->VScroll(SB_LINEDOWN, 0);
154:                 break;
155:             }
156: }
157:
158: void TMyWindow::EvLButtonDown(UINT, TPoint &)
159: {
160:     MessageBox( "You clicked the left button!",
161:                 "Mouse Click Event",
162:                 MB_OK );
163: }
164:
165: void TMyWindow::Paint(TDC& dc, bool /*erase*/, TRect& /*rect*/)
166: {
167:     char s[81];
168:     bool ok = true;
169:     int y = 0;
170:
171:     for (int i = 0; i < MAX_LINES && ok; ++i)
172:         {
173:         if (pFont)
174:             dc.SelectObject(*pFont);
175:         sprintf(s, "This is line number %d", i);
176:         ok = dc.TextOut(0, y, s);
177:         y += dc.GetTextExtent(s, lstrlen(s)).cy;
178:         if (pFont)
179:             dc.RestoreFont();
180:         }
181: }
182:
183: void TMyWindow::NewFont(int nHeight)
184: {
185:     if (pFont)
186:         delete pFont;
187:     pFont = new TFont("Arial", nHeight);
188:
```

continues

12

Listing 12.5. continued

```
189:     // Now reset the scroller's units
190:     if (pFont && Scroller)
191:         {
192:         TClientDC dc(*this);
193:         TEXTMETRIC tm;
194:
195:         dc.SelectObject(*pFont);
196:         dc.GetTextMetrics(tm);
197:         dc.RestoreFont();
198:
199:         Scroller->SetUnits(  tm.tmAveCharWidth,
200:                              tm.tmHeight + tm.tmExternalLeading );
201:
202:         Invalidate();
203:         }
204: }
205:
206: int OwlMain(int, char *[])
207: {
208:     return TMyApp().Run();
209: }
```

 Figure 12.2 shows a sample session with the program WINDOW2.EXE.

Figure 12.2.

A sample session with the program WINDOW2.EXE.

 This program is very similar to the first one presented in this chapter. The major differences are the addition of the scroll bars on the right and bottom of the window and the new menu item enabling the user to change the font as it is displayed on-screen.

NEW A *font* is a description of the type of characters used to display text. This description
TERM includes what the characters look like, called the *typeface*, as well as their size, referred to
as their *point size*. Some common typefaces are *Arial* and *Times New Roman*, both of which come
with Windows. Also, such things as italics and bold characters are described by fonts.

The `TMyWindow` class on lines 13 through 51 declares a new data member and a new function
member, both private, for use in displaying using different point-sized fonts:

☐ The `pFont` member on line 36 stores a pointer to the font used to display the text.
This variable is preset to `NULL` in the class's constructor on line 71 and initialized in the
`SetupWindow` function on line 90. It then is reset by the user via the menus.

☐ The `NewFont` function starting on line 183 is used to change the font. It takes an
integer value that is used as the point size, and it then creates a `TFont` object, assigning
it to the `pFont` data member.

☐ The `Paint` function starting on line 165 first selects the `pFont` object into the device
context before writing to the window. After it's done, it reselects the original font back
into the window.

> **Note:** When dealing with windows and selecting objects into device contexts such
> as fonts or text colors, it's always a good idea to make sure you leave the DC in the
> same condition as you found it. If you change the font, make sure you change it
> back to whatever it might have been before you modified it.

12

Note that the `pFont` is only preset to `NULL` in the constructor, but the real initialization occurs
in the `SetupWindow` member function. This is a very important distinction, as creating the font
requires the existence of a window.

The *SetupWindow* Member Function

Although the `TWindow` class has the usual constructor where things can be initialized as in any
other class, it also has the member function `SetupWindow` for all initializations that rely on an
actual window to be there. The `SetupWindow` function looks like this.

```
void SetupWindow(void);
```

When the `TWindow` class is first created, all that exists is the interface object or C++ object. For
many initializations, an actual interface element or Windows object (a window) may need to
exist. During the course of the window's initialization, the `SetupWindow` will be called. This
function does the actual initialization of the Windows object to which the C++ object is to be
connected; this includes the creation of any child windows contained within the window. This

is why it is vitally important for any derived versions of SetupWindow to call the parent's version. Until the actual TWindow::SetupWindow function is called, there will be no Windows object.

This program enables the user to use the keyboard to scroll the window. It does this through a single member function EvKeyDown starting on line 130. In this function is a switch statement that checks for the keys on the keypad. For each of these, it sends the Scroller object the appropriate command (refer to Table 12.1) to scroll the window. The Scroller object is closely tied to the TWindow object, of which TMyWindow is directly descended, so it handles all the dirty work of changing the scroll bars and telling the window to update itself, which then calls Paint to paint the right portions of the screen.

In order to enable the user to change the font, the Char Heights pop-up menu item has been added with various selections, enabling the user to select specific point sizes for the fonts. The program responds to these menu selections through the various CmHeightXX member functions on lines 105 through 128. These functions serve only to call the NewFont member function with the appropriate point size, as specified by the user.

Finally, the NewFont member function, starting on line 183, handles the creation of the fonts used in painting the window:

☐ First, it checks to see if the pFont data member has been set yet. If so, it deletes the old one in preparation for replacing the old one with a new version, which it does immediately. It allocates a new TFont object with the typeface *Arial* and a point size of nHeight.

Note: Although it is safe to delete a NULL pointer in Turbo C++, it still is a good idea to check first, because not all compilers are as safe.

☐ Assuming that the Scroller object exists and the creation of pFont succeeded, the function proceeds to set the Scroller with new values to let it know how big the characters are now. To do this, it first gets a device context from the window and selects the new pFont into it. The font's attributes are placed into the TEXTMETRIC object and that information is used in the TScroller's SetUnits function.

☐ Finally, because the font you use to paint the window has changed, you need to tell the window to update itself with the new font. This is done with the Invalidate function, which tells the window that its contents are no longer valid and need repainting. Windows automatically tells the window to repaint itself, at which time the Paint function will be entered.

Summary

Today's lesson discussed the mechanics of creating windows that show fixed and scrollable text. The lesson included the following topics:

☐ Read-only text windows that display information are the basis of help screens

☐ You can write text in a window using the versatile TDC::TextOut member function.

☐ You can create scrollable windows with vertical and horizontal scroll bars. These windows scroll using either the mouse or the cursor-control keys. The classes of scrollable windows use the TScroller class assigned to the TWindow's Scroller data member, as well as other functions to manage the text metrics.

Q&A

Q Is the member function Paint needed to maintain windows with visual controls such as command buttons?

A No. You need only to write the function Paint to maintain windows that draw text and graphics. In the case of windows with controls, you do not need to declare your own version of function Paint.

Workshop

The Workshop provides quiz questions to help you solidify your understanding of the material covered and exercises to provide you with experience in using what you've learned. Try to understand the quiz and exercise answers before continuing on to the next day's lesson. Answers are provided in Appendix A.

Quiz

1. True or false? The member function Paint redraws the window only when needed.

2. True or false? The TWindow::Scroller data member offers default scrolling features.

3. True or false? Omitting the EvKeyDown member function in program WINDOW2.CPP disables the vertical scrolling feature altogether.

Exercise

Experiment with modifying the WINDOW2.CPP program by adding cases to the EvKeyDown function that will enable the window to scroll horizontally in response to the right- and left-arrow keys being pressed. In addition, you can experiment with adding more CmHeightXX member functions and the corresponding menu selections.

13

WEEK
2

OWL Controls

Interacting with Windows applications often involves dialog boxes that contain various types of controls, such as the list box, the edit control (also called edit box), and the pushbutton. These controls can be included in windows or, more frequently, in dialog boxes. Today's lesson and the next three look at the controls as they appear in windows and focus on the basic properties of these controls. Day 14 presents dialog boxes and views how the controls work with these boxes. Today, you learn about the following topics:

☐ The TControl object

☐ Static text control

☐ Edit control

☐ Pushbutton control

Understanding the various controls and mastering how they behave and interact enables you to implement highly interactive Windows applications. Today's lesson and the two that follow discuss the constructors and relevant member functions for the control classes.

The *TControl* Object

To learn about OWL controls, it's best to start with the TControl object. This object is the base from which all other control objects are derived. Note that you will never have any need to create a TControl object directly, but a discussion of it here helps you to understand the control objects derived from it.

The TControl object is derived from the TWindow class, which means that it has much of the same functionality as the TWindow class. This actually is a direct mapping of the Windows environment where controls are, indeed, just specialized child windows. Because the TControl class merely is meant as a common base class for the rest of the control classes, the only public function is the constructor.

Syntax

The *TControl* Constructor

The constructor of the TControl class is

```
TControl(TWindow*      parent,
         int           id,
         const char far* title,
         int           x,
         int           y,
         int           w,
         int           h,
         TModule*      module = 0);
```

The parent parameter is a pointer to the parent window in which the control will be placed. The id represents the control's ID, which is used in communication between the parent window and the control itself (more on this later, when specific controls are discussed). Next comes the title of the control. This parameter isn't always displayed by the particular control created, but it's always set. The four parameters x, y, w, and h describe the position and size of the control to be created. Finally, the module parameter specifies the DLL with which the control is associated. This has a default value of 0, and you will rarely find a need to override that.

You will see the parameters to this class duplicated repeatedly in the various control classes derived from TControl. Added on to these standard parameters will be other parameters specific to the particular class being created.

The Static Text Control

The static text control provides a window or a dialog box with static text. The TStatic class implements the static text control. Look at the class constructor and members.

NEW☞ *Static text* is text that the application user cannot easily and readily change. Static text does
TERM not necessarily mean text etched in stone! In fact, static text controls allow your OWL applications to alter the text at any time, or you still can specify that the text be permanent and unchangeable. The choice ultimately is yours.

The TStatic class, a descendant of TControl (which, in turn, is descended from TWindow), offers static text that is defined by a display area, text to display, and text attributes. Of these three components, you can alter only the displayed text during runtime.

The *TStatic* Constructor

The constructor of the TStatic control is

```
TStatic(TWindow*       parent,
        int            id,
        const char far *title,
        int            x,
        int            y,
        int            w,
        int            h,
        uint           textLen = 0,
        TModule*       module = 0 );
TStatic(TWindow*       parent,
        int            resourceId,
        uint           textLen = 0,
        TModule*       module = 0 );
```

Example

```
pText = new TStatic(this, -1, "Sample Text", 10, 10, 75, 25);
pText->Attr.Style &=~SS_LEFT;
pText->Attr.Style !=SS_SIMPLE;
```

The parent parameter specifies the parent window into which the static control will be placed. The id is used to give the static control a unique identifier. A control's ID typically is used when the static text needs to be changed by the application. In the case of a static control, this is a very rare occasion, so the id parameter is usually set to -1. The title sets an initial text string that will appear within the control. The next four parameters—x, y, w, and h—describe the location and size of the control as it will appear within its parent window. The textLen parameter is used for advanced transfer and streaming capabilities, and the module pointer is used for specifying the DLL with which the static control is associated. Note that these last two both have default values of 0, and you rarely will find a need to override that.

The second constructor is used when connecting a TStatic object with a static control that has been loaded from a resource (in a dialog box). In this case, the resourceId must be the same as the one specified in the resource. Dialog boxes and how this constructor is used are discussed on Day 14.

In addition to the usual WS_CHILD and WS_VISIBLE styles that go along with all controls, static controls have their own special set of SS_XXX styles, as shown in Table 13.1. Note that the TStatic class automatically includes the SS_LEFT style.

Table 13.1. Values for static text styles.

Value	Meaning
SS_BLACKFRAME	Designates a box with a frame drawn with the color matching that of the window frame (black, in the default Windows color scheme).
SS_BLACKRECT	Specifies a rectangle filled with the color matching that of the window frame (black, in the default Windows color scheme).
SS_CENTER	Centers the static text characters; text is wrappable.
SS_GRAYFRAME	Specifies a box with a frame that has the same color as the screen background (gray, in the default Windows color scheme).
SS_GRAYRECT	Selects a rectangle filled with the same color as the screen background (gray, in the default Windows color scheme).
SS_ICON	Specifies an icon that is to be displayed in the control. The text is interpreted as the resource name of the icon. (Note that the width and height of the control are ignored as the icon automatically is sized.)
SS_LEFT	Indicates left-justified text; text is wrappable.
SS_LEFTNOWORDWRAP	Indicates left-justified text that cannot be wrapped.
SS_NOPREFIX	Specifies that the ampersand character (&) in the static text string should not be a hot key designator character, but rather part of the static text character.

Value	Meaning
SS_RIGHT	Selects right-justified text that is wrappable.
SS_SIMPLE	Indicates that the static text characters cannot be altered at runtime and that the static text is displayed on a single line with line breaks ignored.
SS_WHITEFRAME	Specifies a box with a frame that has the same color as the window background (white, in the default Windows color scheme).
SS_WHITERECT	Selects a rectangle filled with the same color as the window background (white, in the default Windows color scheme).

The string accessed by the `title` pointer in the constructor may include the ampersand (`&`) character to visually specify a hot key. The hot-key character appears as an underlined character. The ampersand should be placed before the hot key character. If the string contains more than one ampersand character, only the last occurrence is effective. The other occurrences of the ampersand are not displayed and are ignored. To display the `&` character, you need to specify the `SS_NOPREFIX` style. The price you pay for using this style is the inability to display a hot key character.

Now focus on the component of the static text control that you can change during runtime, namely, the text itself. If you specify the `SS_SIMPLE` style in the control's `Attr.Style` data member, you cannot alter its text. In this sense, the instance of `TStatic` is, indeed, etched in stone. The `TStatic` class enables you to set, query, and clear the characters of the static text using the `GetTextLen`, `GetText`, `SetText`, and `Clear` functions.

13

The *GetTextLen* Function

The parameterless `GetTextLen` member function returns the length of the control's text.

```
int GetTextLen()
```

Example

```
int nLen = pText->GetTextLen();
```

The *GetText* Function

The `GetText` member function enables you to access the static text characters. The declaration of the function is

```
int GetText(char far* text, int maxChars);
```

Syntax

Syntax

The text parameter is a pointer to the string that receives a copy of the static text characters. The maxChars parameter specifies the maximum number of static text characters to copy. The function result returns the actual number of characters copied to the string accessed by the pointer text.

Example

```
char s[128];
pText->GetText(s, sizeof(s) - 1);
```

Syntax

The *SetText* Function

The SetText member function overwrites the current static text characters with those of a new string. The declaration of the function is

```
void SetText(const char far* str);
```

The str parameter is the pointer to the new text for the control. If the new text is an empty string, the SetText function call simply clears the text in the static text control instance.

Example

```
pText->SetText("New Text");
```

Syntax

The *Clear* Function

The Clear member function is simply a wrapper that passes an empty string to the SetText member function. The declaration of the function is

```
void Clear();
```

Its existence is there to make code look a little cleaner by enabling you to call the Clear function rather than SetText("");.

The Edit Control

The ObjectWindows Library offers the TEdit class that implements an edit control. The edit control enables the user to type in and edit the text in the input dialog box. This section discusses the functionality of class TEdit in more detail, because implementing customized text editors in your OWL application requires you to become quite familiar with the TEdit member functions.

The *TEdit* Class

The TEdit class is derived from the TStatic class and implements a versatile edit control that supports single-line and multiline text, as well as the capability to cut, paste, copy, delete, and clear text. The edit control also can undo the last text changes and exchange text with the Clipboard.

The *TEdit* Constructor

The declaration of the TEdit constructor is

```
TEdit(TWindow*      parent,
      int           id,
      const char far* text,
      int           x,
      int           y,
      int           w,
      int           h,
      uint          textLen = 0,
      bool          multiline = false,
      TModule*      module = 0 );
TEdit(TWindow*      parent,
      int           resourceId,
      uint          textLen = 0,
      TModule*      module = 0 );
```

The parameters to the first constructor are almost identical to the ones for the TStatic constructor. The only difference is the addition of a multiline parameter. This tells whether the edit control should have more than one input line, like a text editor. Unlike the TStatic control, however, it never makes sense to use an invalid number in the id parameter of the TEdit control, as the TEdit control will need to send notification messages back to its parent window.

The second constructor is identical in usage to the second constructor for the TStatic control. It is used to associate a C++ class object with a control loaded with a dialog resource. Again, this will be discussed on Day 14.

Example

```
const IDE_INPUT = 101;
pInput = new TEdit(this, IDE_INPUT, "", 10, 10, 100, 25);
```

The TEdit control also has its own set of special styles, ES_XXX, that can be used to modify its behavior (see Table 13.2). When you create a TEdit object, the ES_LEFT and ES_AUTOHSCROLL automatically are added in. If the multiline parameter is set, then the ES_MULTILINE and ES_AUTOVSCROLL also are automatically set.

13

Table 13.2. Values for edit control styles.

Value	Meaning
ES_AUTOHSCROLL	Allows the text to automatically scroll to the right by 10 characters when the user enters a character at the end of the line; when the user presses the Enter key, text scrolls back to the left.
ES_AUTOVSCROLL	Permits the text to scroll up by one page when the user presses the Enter key on the last visible line.
ES_CENTER	Centers the text in a multiline edit control.

continues

Table 13.2. continued

Value	Meaning
ES_LEFT	Justifies the text to the left.
ES_LOWERCASE	Converts into lowercase all the letters that the user types.
ES_MULTILINE	Specifies a multiline edit control that recognizes line breaks (designated by the sequence of carriage return and line feed characters).
ES_NOHIDESEL	By default, hides the selected text when it loses focus and shows the selection when it gains focus again; prevents edit control from restoring the selected text.
ES_OEMCONVERT	Converts the entered text from the Windows character set to the OEM character set and back again. This is useful for controls that receive filenames.
ES_PASSWORD	Displays all characters as asterisks (*) as they are typed. Note that this only affects the display; what the user types is stored accurately in the control.
ES_READONLY	Prevents the user from modifying the contents of the control, although it is still possible to select text in the control.
ES_RIGHT	Justifies the text to the right in multiline edit controls.
ES_UPPERCASE	Converts into uppercase all the letters that the user types.
ES_WANTRETURN	Normally, the Enter key will click the default button. When this style is set in an edit control, however, pressing Enter while editing text will insert a new line. This applies only to multiline edit controls.

Clipboard-Related Editing Functions

The TEdit class includes a set of member functions that handle Clipboard-related text editing commands. These commands are available in typical menu options: Cut, Copy, Paste, Clear, Undo, and Delete. Table 13.3 shows the TEdit member functions and their purpose. These functions work with the Clipboard in the CF_TEXT format.

Table 13.3. `TEdit` member functions that support Clipboard-related editing menu commands.

Member Function	Purpose
CanUndo	Returns whether an undo operation is possible at the moment. It is used to enable and disable the Undo menu item accordingly.
Cut	Deletes the current selection in the edit control and copies the text to the Clipboard.
Copy	Copies the current selection to the Clipboard.
Paste	Inserts the text from the Clipboard to the current cursor position in the edit control.
Clear	Deletes all the text in the control; this does not affect the Clipboard.
Undo	Undoes the last change made to the text of the edit control.

Query of Edit Controls

The `TEdit` class has a family of text query member functions. These functions enable you to retrieve either the entire control text or parts of it, or they permit you to obtain information on the text statistics (number of lines, length of lines, and so on). Two of these functions are inherited directly from the `TStatic` class. They are `GetTextLen` and `GetText`. They are used to retrieve the contents of edit controls and are declared and used in the same way as they are in the `TStatic` class.

Because edit controls allow for both multiple lines and user manipulation, additional functions are used to get text from different lines and for manipulating the selection.

The *GetNumLines* Function

Syntax

The `GetNumLines` member function returns the number of lines in the edit control. The declaration is

```
int GetNumLines() const;
```

Example

```
nLineCount = pEdit->GetNumLines();
```

13

> **Note:** In the case of `multiline` edit controls, you should take into account the characters involved in either the soft or hard line breaks.
>
> Hard line breaks use pairs of carriage return and line feed characters (`"\r\n"`) at the end of each line. Soft line breaks use two carriage returns and a line feed at line breaks (`"\r\r\n"`).
>
> This information is relevant when you are counting the number of characters to process.

The *GetLineFromPos* Function

The `GetLineFromPos` member function returns the line number of a specified character index. Its declaration is

```
int GetLineFromPos(uint charPos) const;
```

If the `charPos` argument is `-1`, then the function will return either of the following two values:

- [ ] If there is selected text, the function yields the line number where the first selected character is located.
- [ ] If there is no selected text, the function returns the line number where the caret is, where character insertion occurs.

Example

```
nLineNum = pEdit->GetLineFromPos(-1);
```

The *GetLineIndex* Function

The `GetLineIndex` member function returns the character index of a specific line. The character index also is the size of the text in the edit control up to the specified line number. Its declaration is

```
uint GetLineIndex(int lineNumber) const;
```

The `lineNumber` parameter specifies the line index. If it is `-1`, then it represents the current line as represented by the caret, which marks the user's current position. The function returns the number of characters from the first line through to the specified line. If the argument of `lineNumber` is greater than the actual number of lines, then the function will return `-1`.

Example

```
nCharIndex = pEdit->GetLineIndex(-1);
```

The *GetLineLength* Function

Syntax

The `GetLineLength` member function returns the length of a line for a specific line number. Its declaration is

```
int GetLineLength(int lineNumber) const;
```

The `lineNumber` parameter specifies the line number from which to get the length. If `lineNumber` is `-1`, then the function will return one of the following:

☐ If no text is selected, the length of the current line is returned.

☐ If text is selected, the length of the line, minus the length of the currently selected text, is returned.

Example

```
nLen = pEdit->GetLineLength(1);
```

The *GetSelection* Function

Syntax

The `GetSelection` member function returns the starting and ending character positions of the selected text. The starting character position is the index of the first selected character. The ending position is the index of the first character *after* the selected text. The declaration of the function is

```
void GetSelection(uint& startPos, uint& endPos) const;
```

The function fills in the passed `startPos` and `endPos` with the corresponding selection locations. If these two values are equal, there is no selected text, because both `uint`s are the character indices to the current position.

Example

```
pEdit->GetSelection(start, end);
```

The *GetLine* Function

Syntax

The `GetLine` member function returns a line from a multiline edit control. Its declaration is

```
bool GetLine(char far* str, int strSize, int lineNumber) const;
```

The `str` parameter points to a buffer that is to receive the text of the line; `strSize` is the number of characters to receive; and `lineNumber` is the line to retrieve. If there is a problem copying the line or if the line is longer than `strSize`, the function will return `false`; otherwise it will return `true`.

Example

```
char s[128];
pEdit->GetLine(s, sizeof(s) - 1, 22);
```

Altering the Edit Controls

Now focus on the member functions of TEdit that alter the edit control text. The operations of these member functions include writing new text to the control, selecting text, and replacing the selected text.

☐ The SetText member function that is inherited from the parent TStatic class acts in the same manner; it overwrites the current edit control characters with those of a new string.

☐ The SetSelection member function defines a block of characters as the new selected text.

☐ The Insert member function replaces the selected text with new characters.

The *SetSelection* Function

The declaration of the SetSelection function is

```
bool SetSelection(uint startPos, uint endPos);
```

The startPos and endPos parameters define the range of characters that make up the new selected text. If the starting and ending positions are 0 and -1, respectively, then the entire text in the edit control is selected. If startPos is -1, then any selection is removed. The current position is placed at the greater of the two parameters.

Example

```
pEdit->SetSelection(0, -1);
```

The *Insert* Function

The declaration of the Insert function is

```
void Insert(const char far* str);
```

The str parameter is the pointer to the new selected text that replaces the current selection. If there is no selected text, the function simply inserts the text accessed by str at the current insertion point.

Example

```
pEdit->Insert("New Text");
```

Note: You can use the Insert function to delete parts of the edit control text by first selecting that part and then replacing it with an empty string.

The Pushbutton Control

The *pushbutton control* is, perhaps, psychologically the most powerful control (you never hear about the nuclear list box or the nuclear check box). In a sense, the pushbutton control represents the fundamental notion of a control—you click on the control and something happens. The rest of today's lesson focuses on the aspects of the class TButton that deal with the pushbutton controls.

NEW **TERM**   There basically are two types of pushbutton controls: *default buttons* and *nondefault buttons*. Default buttons have slightly thicker edges than nondefault buttons. Pressing the Enter key is equivalent to clicking the default button in a dialog box. There can be only one default button in a dialog box. You can select a new default button by pressing the Tab key. This feature works only when the buttons are in a dialog box. If a nondialog box window owns a pushbutton control, it can only visually display a default button—the functionality is not supported.

The *TButton* Class

The TButton class, a descendant of TControl, does not declare any public member functions other than its constructors.

The *Tbutton* Constructor

Syntax

The declaration for the TButton constructor is

```
TButton(TWindow*      parent,
        int           id,
        const char far* text,
        int           X,
        int           Y,
        int           W,
        int           H,
        bool          isDefault = false,
        TModule*      module = 0 );
TButton(TWindow* parent, int resourceId, TModule* module = 0);
```

The first seven parameters to this function now should be relatively familiar to you, as they're identical to the ones in both the TStatic and TEdit controls. In fact, you'll find that most of these controls are descendants of the TControl class; the parameters virtually will be the same across the control classes. In this case, the difference is the addition of an isDefault parameter. This parameter specifies whether or not the button is default.

Example

```
pOk = new TButton(this, IDOK, "&OK", 10, 10, 50, 25, true);
pCancel = new TButton(this, IDCANCEL, "&Cancel", 70, 10, 50, 25);
```

13

Handling Button Messages

When you click a button, the control sends the BN_CLICKED notification message to its parent window. The parent window responds to this message by invoking a message response member function based on the ID of the button. If you have a button that was created with an ID of IDB_EXIT, for example, the message handler function is

```
// Other declarations
void HandleExitBtn();
// Other declarations

DEFINE_RESPONSE_TABLE1(TMyWindow, TWindow)
    // Other possible message mapping macros
    EV_BN_CLICKED(IDB_EXIT, HandleExitBtn),
    // Other possible message mapping macros
END_RESPONSE_TABLE;
```

This example shows that the message map macro EV_BN_CLICKED is used to map the IDB_EXIT notification message with the HandleExitBtn member function.

Manipulating Buttons

You can disable and enable a button by using the EnableWindow function, which is inherited from the TWindow ancestor. A disabled button has a faded gray caption and does not respond to mouse clicks or keyboard input. The TWindow::EnableWindow function enables you to enable or disable a button. The function accepts a single argument, a Boolean argument that specifies whether the button is enabled (when the argument is true) or disabled (when the argument is false). Sample calls to the EnableWindow member function are

```
pOk->EnableWindow(false);
pCalculate->EnableWindow(true);
```

You can query the enabled state of a button by using the Boolean IsWindowEnabled function, which takes no arguments. A sample call to IsWindowEnabled is

```
// Toggle the enabled state of a button
pButton->EnableWindow(!pButton->IsWindowEnabled());
```

You also can hide and show a button using the ShowWindow function. The function takes one argument, either the SW_HIDE constant to hide the button or the SW_SHOW constant to show the button. Other constant values are defined for this function, but the SW_HIDE and SW_SHOW are the only two that apply to pushbuttons. The Boolean IsWindowVisible function queries the visibility of a button. This function takes no arguments. A sample call to the ShowWindow and IsWindowVisible functions is

```
// Toggle the visibility of a button
pButton->ShowWindow(pButton->IsWindowVisible() ? SW_HIDE : SW_SHOW);
```

Mr. Calculator

Look at an application that uses static text, single-line edit controls, multiline edit controls, and pushbuttons—*Mr. Calculator.* This nontrivial application implements a floating-point calculator that uses edit controls rather than buttons. This type of interface is somewhat visually inferior to the typical button-populated calculator Windows applications. This interface, however, can support more mathematical functions without requiring the addition of the buttons for those extra functions. In Mr. Calculator, the calculator is made up of the following controls:

- ☐ Two edit controls for the first and second operands to accept integers, floating-point numbers, and the names of single-letter variables, A to Z

- ☐ One edit control for the operator supports the calculator's four basic math operations and the exponentiation (using a caret, ^)

- ☐ One edit control displays the result of the math operation

- ☐ One edit control displays any error messages

- ☐ One multiline edit control that enables you to store a number in the Result edit control in one of 26 single-letter variables, A to Z. The multiline edit displays the current values stored in these variables and enables you to view and edit these numbers. You can use the vertical scroll bar to inspect the values in the different variables.

- ☐ Multiple static text controls serve to label the various edit controls. Of particular interest is the static control for the Error Message box. If you click the accompanying static text, the Error Message is cleared of any text.

- ☐ A menu has the single Exit option.

- ☐ A pushbutton with the caption "Calc" performs the operation specified in the Operator edit control, using the operands in the operand edit controls.

- ☐ A pushbutton with the caption "Store" stores the contents of the result edit control in the currently selected line of the multiline edit control.

- ☐ A pushbutton with the caption "Exit" exits the application.

The program supports the following special features for the Store button control:

- ☐ The Store pushbutton is disabled if the application attempts to execute an invalid operator. This feature illustrates an example of disabling a pushbutton when a certain condition arises (in this case, a specific calculation error).

- ☐ The Store pushbutton is enabled if you click the Error Message static text. The same button is enabled when you successfully execute a math operation.

13

The calculator application demonstrates the following tasks:

- [ ] Using single-line edit controls for simple input
- [ ] Using a multiline edit control to view and edit information
- [ ] Accessing and editing line-oriented text
- [ ] Simulating static text that responds to mouse clicks
- [ ] Using pushbuttons
- [ ] Disabling and enabling pushbuttons

Create the directory MRCALC as a subdirectory of \TCWIN45\TC21DAY and store all the project's files in the new directory. The project's .IDE file should contain the files MRCALC.CPP and MRCALC.RC.

First, compile and run the application to get a good sense for how the calculator application works. Experiment with typing different numeric operands and the supported operators and click the Calc button. Each time, the result appears in the Result box, overwriting the previous result. Try dividing a number by zero to experiment with the error handling features.

Using the single-letter variables is easy. All these variables are initialized with 0. Therefore, the first step to using them is to store a nonzero value. Perform an operation and then click inside the Variables edit box. Select the first line that contains the variable A. Now click the Store button and watch the number in the Result box appear in the first line of the Variables edit box. The name of the variable and the colon and space characters that follow reappear with the new text line. Now replace the contents of the Operand1 edit box with the variable A, and then click the Calc button. The Result edit box displays the result of the latest operation.

Listing 13.1 shows the source code for the MRCALC.H header file. The header file declares the command constants for the menu item and the various controls. Listing 13.2 contains the script for the MRCALC.RC resource file. Listing 13.3 contains the source code for the MRCALC.CPP program file.

 Listing 13.1. Source code for the MRCALC.H header file.

```
1:  #define IDB_CALC      101
2:  #define IDB_STORE     102
3:  #define IDB_EXIT      103
4:  #define IDE_OPERAND1  104
5:  #define IDE_OPERATOR  105
6:  #define IDE_OPERAND2  106
7:  #define IDE_RESULT    107
8:  #define IDE_ERRMSG    108
9:  #define IDE_VARIABLE  109
```

Listing 13.2. Script for the MRCALC.RC resource file.

```
1:  #include <windows.h>
2:  #include <owl\window.rh>
3:
4:  EXITMENU MENU LOADONCALL MOVEABLE PURE DISCARDABLE
5:  BEGIN
6:      MENUITEM "E&xit", CM_EXIT
7:  END
```

Listing 13.3. Source code for the MRCALC.CPP program file.

```
1:  #include <ctype.h>
2:  #include <math.h>
3:  #include <stdio.h>
4:  #include <owl\applicat.h>
5:  #include <owl\button.h>
6:  #include <owl\edit.h>
7:  #include <owl\framewin.h>
8:  #include <owl\static.h>
9:  #include <owl\window.h>
10: #include <owl\window.rh>
11:
12: #include "mrcalc.h"
13:
14: class TCalcWindow : public TWindow
15: {
16: public:
17:     TCalcWindow(TWindow* parent = 0);
18:     ~TCalcWindow();
19:
20: protected:
21:     virtual void SetupWindow();
22:     virtual void EvLButtonDown(uint modKeys, TPoint &point);
23:
24:     void CmCalc();
25:     void CmStore();
26:     void CmExit();
27:
28: private:
29:     TStatic  *ErrMsgLabel;
30:     TEdit    *Operand1, *Operator, *Operand2, *Result,
31:              *ErrMsg, *Variable;
32:     TButton  *Store;
33:
34:     double get_number(TEdit* edit);
35:     double get_var(int line);
36:     void put_var(double val);
37:
38:     DECLARE_RESPONSE_TABLE(TCalcWindow);
39: };
40: DEFINE_RESPONSE_TABLE1(TCalcWindow, TWindow)
41:     EV_WM_LBUTTONDOWN,
42:     EV_COMMAND(CM_EXIT, CmExit),
```

Listing 13.3. continued

```
43:     EV_BN_CLICKED(IDB_CALC, CmCalc),
44:     EV_BN_CLICKED(IDB_STORE, CmStore),
45:     EV_BN_CLICKED(IDB_EXIT, CmExit),
46: END_RESPONSE_TABLE;
47:
48: TCalcWindow::TCalcWindow(TWindow* parent)
49: {
50:     Init(parent, 0, 0);
51:
52:     int   wlblspacing = 40,
53:           hlblspacing = 5,
54:           wlbl = 100,
55:           hlbl = 20,
56:           wbox = 100,
57:           hbox = 30,
58:           wboxspacing = 40,
59:           hboxspacing = 40,
60:           wbtn = 80,
61:           hbtn = 30,
62:           wbtnspacing = 30;
63:     int   wlongbox = 4 * (wbox + wboxspacing);
64:     int   wvarbox = 2 * wbox,
65:           hvarbox = 3 * hbox;
66:     int   x0 = 20, y0 = 30;
67:     int   x, y;
68:
69:     // First, create the labels for the edit text boxes.
70:     //
71:     x = x0;
72:     y = y0;
73:     new TStatic(this, -1, "Operand1", x, y, wlbl, hlbl);
74:     x += wlbl + wlblspacing;
75:     new TStatic(this, -1, "Operator", x, y, wlbl, hlbl);
76:     x += wlbl + wlblspacing;
77:     new TStatic(this, -1, "Operand2", x, y, wlbl, hlbl);
78:     x += wlbl + wlblspacing;
79:     new TStatic(this, -1, "Result", x, y, wlbl, hlbl);
80:     x += wlbl + wlblspacing;
81:
82:     // Now create the edit text boxes
83:     //
84:     x = x0;
85:     y += hlbl + hlblspacing;
86:     if (NULL != (Operand1 = new TEdit(this, IDE_OPERAND1, "",
87:                                             x, y, wbox, hbox)))
88:         Operand1->Attr.Style |= ES_UPPERCASE;
89:     x += wbox + wboxspacing;
90:     if (NULL != (Operator = new TEdit(this, IDE_OPERATOR, "",
91:                                             x, y, wbox, hbox)))
92:         Operator->Attr.Style |= ES_UPPERCASE;
93:     x += wbox + wboxspacing;
94:     if (NULL != (Operand2 = new TEdit(this, IDE_OPERAND2, "",
95:                                             x, y, wbox, hbox)))
96:         Operand2->Attr.Style |= ES_UPPERCASE;
97:     x += wbox + wboxspacing;
98:     Result = new TEdit(this, IDE_RESULT, "", x, y, wbox, hbox);
99:     x += wbox + wboxspacing;
```

```
100:
101:     // Now create the label and box for the error message
102:     //
103:     x = x0;
104:     y += hbox + hboxspacing;
105:     ErrMsgLabel = new TStatic( this, -1, "Error Message", x, y,
106:                                 wlbl, hlbl );
107:     y += hlbl + hlblspacing;
108:     ErrMsg = new TEdit(this, IDE_ERRMSG, "", x, y, wlongbox, hbox);
109:
110:     // Create the label and box for the single-letter
111:     // variable selection
112:     //
113:     y += hbox + hboxspacing;
114:     new TStatic(this, -1, "Variables", x, y, wlbl, hlbl);
115:     y += hlbl + hlblspacing;
116:     char str[6 * ('Z' - 'A' + 1) + 1];
117:     char *p = str;
118:     for (char ch = 'A'; ch <= 'Z'; ++ch)
119:         p += sprintf(p, "%c: 0\r\n", ch);
120:     Variable = new TEdit(this, IDE_VARIABLE, str, x, y,
121:                           wvarbox, hvarbox, 0, true );
122:
123:     // Finally create some buttons
124:     //
125:     x += wvarbox + wbtnspacing;
126:     new TButton(this, IDB_CALC, "Calc", x, y, wbtn, hbtn);
127:     x += wbtn + wbtnspacing;
128:     Store = new TButton(this, IDB_STORE, "Store", x, y, wbtn, hbtn);
129:     x += wbtn + wbtnspacing;
130:     new TButton(this, IDB_EXIT, "Exit", x, y, wbtn, hbtn);
131: }
132:
133: TCalcWindow::~TCalcWindow()
134: {
135: }
136:
137: void TCalcWindow::SetupWindow()
138: {
139:     TWindow::SetupWindow();     // Initialize the visual element
140:
141:     // Keep the users out of the destination areas.
142:     //
143:     if (Result)
144:         Result->SetReadOnly(true);
145:     if (ErrMsg)
146:         ErrMsg->SetReadOnly(true);
147:     if (Variable)
148:         Variable->SetReadOnly(true);
149: }
150:
151: void TCalcWindow::EvLButtonDown(uint /*modKeys*/, TPoint& point)
152: {
153:     if (       ErrMsgLabel
154:          && (ErrMsgLabel->HWindow == ChildWindowFromPoint(point)) )
155:         {
156:         if (ErrMsg)
```

Listing 13.3. continued

```
157:            ErrMsg->Clear();
158:         if (Store)
159:            Store->EnableWindow(true);
160:         }
161: }
162:
163: double TCalcWindow::get_number(TEdit *edit)
164: {
165:     double rslt;
166:     char *str;
167:     int size;
168:
169:     if (edit)
170:         {
171:         str = new char[size = edit->GetWindowTextLength() + 1];
172:         if (str)
173:             {
174:             edit->GetWindowText(str, size);
175:             if (isalpha(str[0]))
176:                 rslt = get_var(tolower(str[0]) - 'a');
177:             else
178:                 rslt = atof(str);
179:             delete str;
180:             }
181:         }
182:     return rslt;
183: }
184:
185: double TCalcWindow::get_var(int line)
186: {
187:     double rslt = 0;
188:
189:     if (Variable)
190:         {
191:         int size = Variable->GetLineLength(line) + 1;
192:         char *str = new char[size];
193:         if (str)
194:             {
195:             Variable->GetLine(str, size, line);
196:             rslt = atof(str + 3);        // Don't want first 3 chars
197:             delete str;
198:             }
199:         }
200:     return rslt;
201: }
202:
203: void TCalcWindow::put_var(double var)
204: {
205:     if (Variable)
206:         {
207:         uint start, end;
208:         Variable->GetSelection(start, end);
209:         if (start != end)
210:             Variable->SetSelection(start, start);
211:         int line = Variable->GetLineFromPos(-1);
212:         int size = Variable->GetLineLength(line) + 1;
213:         char *str = new char[size];
```

```
214:        if (str)
215:            {
216:            Variable->GetLine(str, size, line);
217:            sprintf(str, "%c: %g", str[0], var);
218:            start = Variable->GetLineIndex(-1);
219:            end = start + Variable->GetLineLength(-1);
220:            Variable->SetSelection(start, end);
221:            Variable->Insert(str);
222:            delete str;
223:            }
224:        }
225:
226: }
227:
228: void TCalcWindow::CmCalc()
229: {
230:    double x, y, z = 0;
231:    char  *str, *err = NULL;
232:    int   size;
233:
234:    x = get_number(Operand1);
235:    y = get_number(Operand2);
236:
237:    if (Operator)
238:        {
239:        str = new char[size = Operator->GetWindowTextLength() + 1];
240:        if (str)
241:            {
242:            Operator->GetWindowText(str, size);
243:            if (str[1] != '\0')
244:                err = "Invalid operator";
245:            else
246:                switch (str[0])
247:                    {
248:                    case '+':
249:                        z = x + y;
250:                        break;
251:                    case '-':
252:                        z = x - y;
253:                        break;
254:                    case '*':
255:                        z = x * y;
256:                        break;
257:                    case '/':
258:                        if (y)
259:                            z = x / y;
260:                        else
261:                            err = "Division by zero error";
262:                        break;
263:                    case '^':
264:                        if (x > 0)
265:                            z = exp(y * log(x));
266:                        else
267:                            err = "Can't raise power of negative numbers";
268:                        break;
269:                    default:
270:                        err = "Invalid operator";
```

continues

Listing 13.3. continued

```
271:                break;
272:            }
273:            if (ErrMsg)
274:                if (!err)
275:                    ErrMsg->Clear();
276:                else
277:                    ErrMsg->SetWindowText(err);
278:            if (Store)
279:                Store->EnableWindow(!err);
280:            if (!err && Result)
281:                {
282:                char dest[81];
283:                sprintf(dest, "%g", z);
284:                Result->SetWindowText(dest);
285:                }
286:        delete str;
287:        }
288:    }
289: }
290:
291: void TCalcWindow::CmStore()
292: {
293:    if (Result)
294:        {
295:        int size = Result->GetWindowTextLength() + 1;
296:        char *str = new char[size];
297:        if (str)
298:            {
299:            Result->GetWindowText(str, size);
300:            put_var(atof(str));
301:            delete str;
302:            }
303:        }
304: }
305:
306: void TCalcWindow::CmExit()
307: {
308:    SendMessage(WM_CLOSE);
309: }
310:
311: class TCalcApp : public TApplication
312: {
313: public:
314:    TCalcApp() : TApplication()
315:        { nCmdShow = SW_SHOWMAXIMIZED; }
316:
317:    void InitMainWindow()
318:        {
319:        SetMainWindow(new TFrameWindow(  0,
320:                            "Mr. Calculator",
321:                            new TCalcWindow ));
322:        GetMainWindow()->AssignMenu("EXITMENU");
323:        }
324: };
325:
326: int OwlMain(int, char *[])
```

```
327: {
328:     return TCalcApp().Run();
329: }
330:
```

 Figure 13.1 shows a sample session with the Mr. Calculator program.

Figure 13.1.
A sample session with
MRCALC.EXE.

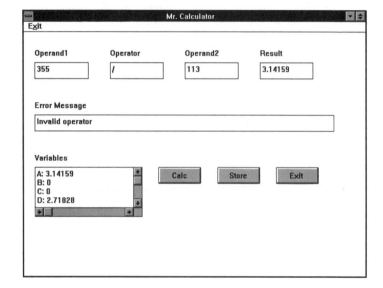

The program in Listing 13.3 contains a number of data members in the TCalcWindow class, each of which is a pointer to a control class. These are the TStatic, TEdit, and TButton controls, declared on lines 29 through 32. In general, there is no real need to keep track of these controls because OWL will automatically take care of deleting these controls when their corresponding Windows elements are destroyed. If you have some need to access them during the duration of their existence, however, you will need a pointer in order to affect them.

Note that as the operand and operator edit boxes are created on lines 82 through 96, they are given the style of ES_UPPERCASE. This style results in automatically converting into uppercase the single-letter variable names that you type in these edit controls.

Usually, controls such as TButton and especially TStatic can be created without bothering to keep a pointer to them; a button will automatically send notifications to its parent and, because static text controls are usually used as labels, there rarely is a need to keep track of them. In this case, however, you need to keep track of the Store button so that you can enable and disable it according to error conditions. You also need to keep track of the Error Message label so that you can tell when the user has clicked it, at which point you need to clear the error message and re-enable the Store button.

In the constructor of `TCalcWindow` are a number of declarations between lines 52 and 57. These are used when placing the controls as they are created. The declarations define the various widths and heights of the controls as well as the space in between them. As the controls are created, the local variables `x` and `y` are updated to the location of the next control.

In the `SetupWindow` member function of `TCalcWindow` starting on line 37, the `Result`, `ErrMsg`, and `Variable` edit controls are set to read-only by calling the `TEdit::SetReadOnly` member function. This is done to prevent the user from modifying the parts of the screen that should be updated only by the program itself. The user can still place the caret in these edit controls, even select text and scroll around in them, but Windows will prevent the user from changing any of the contents.

On lines 110 through 121, the `Variable` edit box is created somewhat differently from the other edit boxes. First, an elaborate initializing string is made up for it. This string consists of 26 letters (`'A'` through `'Z'`), each followed by a colon, a space, the number `0`, and finally the characters `"\r\n"`. This makes up the format of the list box and later will be changed dynamically by the user clicking the Store button.

Secondly, the `Variable` edit box constructor receives two extra parameters on lines 120 through 121. The first of the two extra parameters, `0`, is the same as the default parameter that is used whenever the constructor is called without passing anything for that argument. The next parameter, however, is the one stating that you want a multiline edit control. This automatically sets the control to allowing for multiple lines, as well as adding the horizontal and vertical scroll bars.

The `EvLButtonDown` member function starting on line 151 performs a simple task. It checks whether the mouse click occurs in the rectangle occupied by the error message static text control. If this condition is true, then the function performs the following tasks:

☐ Uses the `ChildWindowFromPoint` function starting on line 154 to determine in which window the mouse was clicked, and then checks that against the window of `ErrMsgLabel`

☐ Clears the error message box by invoking the function `Clear` on line 157

☐ Enables the Store button by invoking the function `EnableWindow` on line 159

Because you will have two edit boxes from which you will want to get either a number or a value associated with a variable, it makes sense to have only one function that performs this action and is called for in each edit box. This is the purpose of the `get_number` private member function starting on line 163. Its single parameter is a pointer to a `TEdit` object. From this, the function obtains the text that is stored in that edit box on line 174. If the first character in that edit box is an alphabetic character (checked through the ANSI C function `isalpha` on line 175), then the private `get_var` function is called on line 176; otherwise, the contents are converted to a floating point number with the `atof` function on line 178.

The get_var function starting on line 185 is used to obtain the value associated with a specific variable in the Variable edit control. Given a line number, it gets the text from that line in the edit control, and then passes that line, skipping the first three characters (the variable letter, the colon, and the space), to the atof function for conversion to a floating point number.

The put_var function starting on line 203 changes a variable in the Variable edit box. It does so with the following steps:

1. Check for a selection in the Variable edit box on lines 208 and 209. If there is one, then you remove that selection and set the current insertion point to the beginning of the selection.

2. Using the GetLineFromPos function, you get the line of the insertion point on line 211.

3. After creating a string large enough to hold the line, you get the line and then change it to include the new value on lines 212 through 217.

4. By passing -1 to the GetLineIndex function on line 218, you obtain the character location of the start of the current line. Adding the length of the line, you get the start of the next line.

5. Using the SetSelection function on line 220, you select the current line. You then Insert the new string on line 221, replacing the current selection.

The CmCalc member function starting on line 228 responds to the notification message emitted by the Calc button. You told the window to have the function called by using the EV_BN_CLICKED macro during the TCalcWindow's response table declaration on line 43. The function performs the following tasks:

1. Obtains the two operands from the Operand1 and Operand2 edit boxes with the get_number private member function on lines 234 and 235

2. Copies the text in the Operator edit box into the local variable str on line 242

3. Determines and performs the requested operation by using a switch statement on lines 246 through 272, checking the first character of the string for the supported operators +, −, *, / and ^ (power)

4. If at any time an error is detected, the err local variable is set to a string describing the error, and at the end on line 273, if this variable is non-NULL, its value is placed in the Error Message edit box, and the Store button is disabled.

The CmStore member function, starting on line 291, stores the contents of the Result box in a single-letter variable. The function first obtains the string from the Result edit box by calling the GetWindowText function on line 299. Then, the function invokes the private member function put_var on line 300 to actually store the result string at the current insertion point in the Variables edit box.

13

The CmExit member function, starting on line 306, responds to the notification message of both the Exit button and the Exit menu item. It sends a WM_CLOSE message to the window, which effectively terminates the program.

Summary

Today's lesson looked at the static text, edit box, and pushbutton controls. Using these and other controls animates the Windows applications and provides a more consistent user interface. You learned about the following topics:

☐ You can create static text controls and manipulate their text at runtime.

☐ Single-line and multiline edit box controls enable you to type in and edit the text in the input dialog box.

Day 15 presents the grouped controls, the classes for group, check box, and radio controls. These controls are used to fine-tune the execution of a specified task, such as searching and replacing text in a text editor.

Q&A

Q How do I create a string for a multiline static text control?

A You build a multiline string, such as "This is\r\na multiline" (notice the embedded \r\n characters, which break the line) and pass it as the third argument to the TStatic class's constructor.

Q Why does program MRCALC.CPP use local variables such as x and y to specify the location of a control? Why not replace these variables with numeric constants?

A Using variables, such as x and y, enables you to specify the location of the controls relative to one another. This method enables you to shift controls very easily. By contrast, using numeric constants specifies the absolute values for the control locations. Shifting controls, in this case, means plugging in a new set of numbers.

Q What do .RC resource files compile into?

A The .RC resource files are compiled into .RES files. Also, note that the Resource Workshop is quite capable of saving your various dialog boxes and other resources in an .RES file as well as an .RC file. This precompiled file then could be included in your .IDE file instead of the .RC.

Workshop

The Workshop provides quiz questions to help you solidify your understanding of the material covered and exercises to provide you with experience in using what you've learned. Try to understand the quiz and exercise answers before continuing on to the next day's lesson. Answers are provided in Appendix A.

Quiz

1. True or false? The text for all static text controls is unchangeable.

2. True or false? The SS_CENTER style centers each line of a multiline static text control.

3. True or false? A static text control needs an accompanying pointer for access only when the program needs to set or query the text in the control.

4. True or false? Every edit control needs an accompanying pointer for access.

5. True or false? The API Windows function EnableWindow can disable any control.

6. True or false? The Windows messages emitted by a pushbutton can be mapped using the EV_COMMAND map.

Exercises

1. Experiment with the program MRCALC.CPP to add trigonometric functions, inverse trigonometric functions, hyperbolic functions, and inverse hyperbolic functions.

2. Experiment with a copy of the program MRCALC.CPP by changing values assigned to the constants that specify the size and spacing of the various controls.

13

14

Dialog Boxes

Dialog boxes are special pop-up windows that contain controls serving to display information or to input data. Windows applications use dialog boxes to exchange information with the user. The nicest feature of dialog boxes is that they can be created with all their controls by using a screen painter (the resource workshop), and then accessed simply by loading them in from resources.

Today's lesson looks at the modal and modeless dialog boxes supported by Windows.

NEW☞ TERM *Modal dialog boxes* require you to close them before you can proceed any further with the application because they are meant to perform a critical exchange of data. In fact, modal dialog boxes disable their parent windows while they have the focus. Modeless dialog boxes do not need to be closed to continue using the application. You need merely to click on another of the application's windows to continue.

Today you learn about the following topics:

☐ Constructing instances of the class TDialog

☐ Executing a modal dialog box

☐ Transferring control data

☐ Transferring data for modal dialog boxes

☐ Transferring data for modeless dialog boxes

Constructing Dialog Boxes

OWL declares the TDialog class to support both modeless and modal dialog boxes. The TDialog class, a descendant of TWindow, has a class constructor and a number of member functions, including the Create and Execute functions. The TDialog constructor is declared as follows:

```
TDialog(TWindow* parent, TResId resId, TModule* module = 0);
```

The parent parameter is a pointer to the parent window. The resId parameter describes the dialog box's resource name or ID. The module parameter, which normally is left out of calls to the constructor, can be used to specify different locations from which to load the resource (for example, loading from a separate DLL).

The TResId class is a method used by OWL to encapsulate the different ways that a resource can be named in an application's resources. For example, one could specify a dialog template as having either a number or a name. The useful TResId class has three overloaded constructors. The first one, the default constructor, takes no arguments and initializes the class to a 0 value. The other two constructors look like the following:

```
TResId(LPCSTR resString);
TResId(int resNum);
```

This means that you can easily create a `TResId` by simply passing the appropriate value for the constructor. Also, if you use it as a temporary object, you can have `TDialog` constructors that look something like this.

```
TDialog* errdlg = new TDialog(this, "ErrorDlg");
TDialog* newdlg = new TDialog(this, 101);
```

> **Note:** Using resources to define dialog boxes and their controls enables you to define the location, dimensions, style, and caption of a control outside the Windows application source code. Thus, you can change the resource file, recompile it, and then incorporate it in the .EXE application file without recompiling the source file itself. This approach enables you to develop different resource versions with varying colors, styles, and even languages while maintaining a single copy of the application code. Furthermore, this approach does away with the need to write all that complicated code for creating and placing controls in the constructor of a `TWindow` class.
>
> The Turbo C++ package includes the *Resource Workshop*, which enables you to create dialog boxes by drawing the controls in the dialog boxes. The Resource Workshop creates .RC resource files that then are bound in your Windows applications. If you are a novice Windows programmer, first learn about the .RC file and its script. Using the Resource Workshop is easy and intuitive. Knowing about the .RC resource script makes working with the output of the Resource Workshop even easier.

Creating Dialog Boxes

Typically, modal dialog boxes are created and removed more frequently than modeless dialog boxes and much more frequently than windows. Executing modal dialog boxes involves the following steps:

1. Create a dialog box object by using `TDialog` constructor.

2. Call the `Execute` member function, declared in the class `TDialog`, to display the dialog box. Typically, dialog boxes contain the OK and Cancel pushbuttons, with the OK button as the default button. The OK and Cancel buttons have the predefined IDs of `IDOK` and `IDCANCEL`, respectively. You can use pushbutton controls with different captions other than OK and Cancel; however, you still should use the `IDOK` and `IDCANCEL` with these renamed buttons. Using these IDs enable you to take advantage of the automatic response to `IDOK` and `IDCANCEL` provided by the `CmOk` and `CmCancel` member functions defined in the `TDialog` class. Clicking OK or pressing the Enter

key usually signals your acceptance of the current (that is, the default or edited) data in the dialog box. By contrast, clicking the Cancel button signals your dissatisfaction with the current data. Following is the declaration of the Execute function:

```
int Execute();
```

The function returns an integer that represents the outcome. This typically is the value of a pushbutton ID, such as IDOK and IDCANCEL.

3. Compare the result of the Execute function with IDOK (or, less frequently, IDCANCEL). The outcome of this comparison determines the steps to take. Such steps usually involve accessing data that you entered in the dialog box controls.

Creating modeless dialog boxes takes only a little more effort. First, they must be created on the heap with a call to new. Then its Create and ShowWindow member functions must be called, as in the following:

```
TDialog* pdlg = new TDialog(this, "My Dialog");
pdlg -> Create();
pdlg -> ShowWindow(SW_SHOW);
```

Unlike with modal dialog boxes, the modeless dialog object will not be deleted automatically when the dialog box is closed. Be sure to delete the object when you know the dialog box is gone. This *can* be done automatically, however, if you set the wfDeleteOnClose flag in the window with the following member-function call:

```
pdlg->SetFlag(wfDeleteOnClose);
```

Like the TWindow class, from which much of TDialog's functionality is inherited, the SetupWindow, CanClose, and Destroy member functions support the execution of both modal and modeless dialog boxes. The SetupWindow member function serves to initialize the dialog box and its controls. The declaration of the SetupWindow function is as follows:

```
virtual void SetupWindow();
```

Typically, the SetupWindow function initializes the controls of the dialog box. This initialization usually involves copying data from buffers or data members.

The CanClose function is called whenever the user presses the OK button. Following is the declaration of the CanClose function:

```
virtual bool CanClose();
```

The CanClose acts to copy data from the dialog box controls to data members or buffers after deciding whether it's all right to close the dialog. This function returns either true or false, depending on whether the user is allowed to close the dialog box, given the data entered.

The Destroy member function handles the closing of the dialog box. Following is the declaration of the Destroy:

```
virtual void Destroy(int retValue = IDCANCEL);
```

The Destroy function serves to clean up before the dialog box is closed, which may involve closing data files, for example. Usually, the last statement in the Destroy member function definition is a call to the Destroy function of its parent class.

The next example is a simple OWL program that uses a dialog box defined in resource files. It also uses resource files to create alternate forms of the same dialog box; the first uses modern English and the second uses old English. The application is simple and is made up of an empty window with a single menu item, Exit. When you click the Exit menu item (or press the Alt+X keys), a dialog box appears and asks you whether you want to exit the application. The dialog box has a title, a message, and the two buttons (in fact, we purposely made it so that it resembles the dialog boxes spawned by the MessageBox function). The program alternates between the two versions of the dialog box. When you first click the Exit menu, you get the modern English version (with OK and Cancel buttons), shown in Figure 14.1. If you click the Cancel button and then click the Exit menu again, you get the old English version of the dialog box (with Yea and Nay buttons), shown in Figure 14.2. Every time you select the Cancel or Nay button and then click the Exit menu, you toggle between the two versions of the dialog box. To exit the application, click the OK or Yea button, depending on the current dialog box version.

Listing 14.1 shows the DIALOG1.RC resource file. Listing 14.2 shows the source code for the DIALOG1.CPP program.

Listing 14.1. Script for the DIALOG1.RC resource file.

```
1:   #include <windows.h>
2:   #include <owl\window.rh>
3:
4:   EXITMENU MENU LOADONCALL MOVEABLE PURE DISCARDABLE
5:   BEGIN
6:     MENUITEM "E&xit", CM_EXIT
7:   END
8:
9:   ModernEnglish DIALOG DISCARDABLE LOADONCALL PURE MOVEABLE 20, 50, 200, 100
10:  STYLE WS_POP-UP ¦ DS_MODALFRAME
11:  CAPTION "Message"
12:  BEGIN
13:    CTEXT "Exit the application?", -1, 10, 10, 170, 15
14:    DEFPUSHBUTTON "OK", IDOK, 20, 50, 70, 15, WS_VISIBLE ¦ WS_TABSTOP
15:    PUSHBUTTON "Cancel", IDCANCEL, 110, 50, 70, 15, WS_VISIBLE ¦ WS_TABSTOP
16:  END
17:
18:  OldeEnglish DIALOG DISCARDABLE LOADONCALL PURE MOVEABLE 20, 50, 200, 100
19:  STYLE WS_POP-UP ¦ DS_MODALFRAME
20:  CAPTION "Message"
21:  BEGIN
22:    CTEXT "Leavest thou now?", -1, 10, 10, 170, 15
23:    DEFPUSHBUTTON "Yea", IDOK, 20, 50, 70, 15, WS_VISIBLE ¦  WS_TABSTOP
24:    PUSHBUTTON "Nay", IDCANCEL, 110, 50, 70, 15, WS_VISIBLE ¦  WS_TABSTOP
25:  END
```

14

Listing 14.2. Source code for the DIALOG1.CPP program file.

```
1: #include <windows.h>
2: #include <owl\applicat.h>
3: #include <owl\dialog.h>
4: #include <owl\framewin.h>
5: #include <owl\window.h>
6: #include <owl\window.rh>
7:
8: class TMyWindow : public TWindow
9: {
10: public:
11:     TMyWindow(TWindow* parent = 0);
12:
13:     virtual bool CanClose();
14:
15: protected:
16:     void CmExit();
17:
18:     DECLARE_RESPONSE_TABLE(TMyWindow);
19: };
20: DEFINE_RESPONSE_TABLE1(TMyWindow, TWindow)
21:     EV_COMMAND(CM_EXIT, CmExit),
22: END_RESPONSE_TABLE;
23:
24: TMyWindow::TMyWindow(TWindow* parent)
25:     : TWindow(parent)
26: {
27: }
28:
29: bool TMyWindow::CanClose()
30: {
31:     static bool bFlag = false;
32:
33:     bFlag = !bFlag;
34:     if (bFlag)
35:        return TDialog(this, "ModernEnglish").Execute() == IDOK;
36:     else
37:        return TDialog(this, "OldeEnglish").Execute() == IDOK;
38: }
39:
40: void TMyWindow::CmExit()
41: {
42:     SendMessage(WM_CLOSE);
43: }
44:
45: class TDialogApp : public TApplication
46: {
47: public:
48:     TDialogApp() : TApplication()
49:        { nCmdShow = SW_SHOWMAXIMIZED; }
50:
```

```
51:     void InitMainWindow()
52:         {
53:         SetMainWindow(new TFrameWindow(  0,
54:                             "Simple Dialog Box Tester Application",
55:                             new TMyWindow ));
56:         GetMainWindow()->AssignMenu("EXITMENU");
57:         }
58: };
59:
60: int OwlMain(int, char *[])
61: {
62:     return TDialogApp().Run();
63: }
```

Figure 14.1 shows a sample session.

Figure 14.1.
*A sample session with the
DIALOG1.EXE application
showing the dialog box with
modern English wording.*

Listing 14.1 shows the script for the DIALOG1.RC resource file, which defines the
following resources:

☐ The menu resource, EXITMENU, which displays a single menu with the single item Exit

☐ The dialog box resource starting on line 9, ModernEnglish, which has a defined style,
caption, and list of child controls. The specified style indicates that the dialog box is a
modal pop-up child window. The caption specified on line 11 is the string Message.
The dialog box contains three controls: a centered static text (for the dialog box
message), a default OK pushbutton, and an ordinary Cancel button. The OK button
has the resource ID of the predefined IDOK constant, and the Cancel button has the
resource ID of the predefined IDCANCEL constant.

Figure 14.2 shows a sample session.

14

Figure 14.2.

A sample session with the DIALOG1.EXE application showing the dialog box with the old English wording.

☐ The dialog box resource starting on line 18, `OldeEnglish`, which is similar to the `ModernEnglish` dialog box resource, except that it uses old English wording. The Yea button has the resource ID of the predefined `IDOK` constant. The Nay button has the resource ID of the predefined `IDCANCEL` constant. These buttons are examples of exit buttons with atypical captions.

The `CTEXT` keyword specifies centered text. The `DEFPUSHBUTTON` keyword enables you to define any control and requires the caption, ID, location, dimensions, and control style of the control. The `PUSHBUTTON` definition is identical to the `DEFPUSHBUTTON` keyword's definition, but it describes an ordinary button instead of a default pushbutton.

Until now, you have been creating resources by manually creating the .RC file. When making dialog boxes, it is far easier to use the Resource Workshop. This provides an easy interface by which dialog boxes can be painted on-screen exactly the way you want them to appear when your application is run.

Listing 14.2 shows the source code for the DIALOG1.CPP program file. The source code declares two classes: an application class starting on line 45 and a window class starting on line 8. The application uses the standard `TDialog` class; it does not derive a specialized descendant, because no additional dialog box functionality is required.

The most relevant member function is `CanClose` starting on line 29, which responds to the user's request to close the window (triggered by the `CmExit` function on line 40, which in turn is triggered by the Exit menu choice). The function uses the Boolean static local variable, `bFlag`, to toggle between the two dialog box resources `ModernEnglish` and `OldeEnglish`. The modern English dialog box is invoked in the following statement:

```
return TDialog(this, "ModernEnglish").Execute() == IDOK;
```

The dialog box object is executed using the `Execute` function, disabling the parent window until you click either pushbutton control. The value returned by the `Execute` member function is compared with the `IDOK` constant, and the result is returned to the caller to let it know what the user selected, and whether to close the application window.

The instance of the old English version of the dialog box is similarly created, as shown in the following statement:

```
return TDialog(this, "OldeEnglish").Execute() == IDOK;
```

Connecting OWL Objects with Windows Controls

Until now, the constructors for the various controls you have learned have had the same general look of the constructor of the TControl class from which they are descendants.

```
TControl( TWindow* parent,
          int id,
          const char far* title,
          int x,
          int y,
          int w,
          int h,
          TModule* module = 0 );
```

Occasionally, there have been additional parameters after the h and before the module parameters, as the various controls needed. These all assume that the controls needed to be created from scratch, including their positions in their parent window.

When creating a dialog box from a resource file, however, these controls will be created automatically from the resource script at the same time as the dialog box. In order to have access to the controls from an OWL object, there is a second constructor for each control class that enables you to create an object that has a direct correspondence with the actual Windows control. They're all based on the following constructor for the TControl class.

```
TControl(TWindow* parent, int resourceId, TModule* module = 0);
```

The following are the constructors for creating the various controls that have already been introduced:

```
TStatic( TWindow* parent, int resourceId, uint textLen = 0,
        TModule* module = 0);
TEdit( TWindow* parent, int resourceId, uint textLen = 0,
      TModule* module = 0 );
TButton(TWindow* parent, int resourceId, TModule* module = 0);
```

In addition, there are a number of other controls that will be introduced formally in the next few days. Since I am assuming you are at least marginally familiar with the controls themselves, I will introduce their constructors here so that you can easily create them in your dialog boxes.

```
TCheckBox( TWindow* parent, int resourceId, TGroupBox* group = 0,
          TModule* module = 0 );
TRadioButton( TWindow* parent, int resourceId, TGroupBox* group = 0,
             TModule* module = 0 );
TGroupBox(TWindow* parent, int resourceId, TModule* module = 0);
TListBox(TWindow* parent, int resourceId, TModule* module = 0);
TComboBox( TWindow* parent, int resourceId, uint textLen = 0,
          TModule* module = 0 );
TScrollBar(TWindow* parent, int resourceId, TModule* module = 0);
```

14

The control objects, as with the full versions, should be created in a dialog's constructor. The following is an example of creating an OWL object to interface with a window's Cancel button:

```
cancel = new TButton(this, IDCANCEL);
```

413

Transferring Control Data

Dialog boxes serve mainly as pop-up windows to request input from the application user. This input often includes a variety of settings that use radio buttons, check boxes, and edit boxes. Because dialog boxes are frequently created, it makes sense to preserve the latest values in the dialog's controls for the next time it appears. The Search and Replace dialog boxes that are found in many Windows editors are typical examples. These dialog boxes remember the settings of all or some of their controls from the last time the dialog box was executed. You also can use the transfer mechanism as an easy way to set and retrieve data in the dialog box for simple initialization and retrieval purposes.

To implement this feature in dialog boxes, you need a data transfer mechanism between the dialog box and a buffer. This buffer usually is a data member of the parent window. Therefore, the first step in supporting data transfer is to define a transfer buffer type. The buffer declares the data fields to buffer the controls that transfer their data. These controls typically include the edit box, list box, combo box, scroll bar, check box, and radio button. The static text, group box, and pushbutton controls usually have no data to transfer and, therefore, do not enter in the declaration of the data transfer buffer type because OWL has them disabled by default. Following is a sample data buffer type that includes a single instance of each allowable control:

```
struct TAppTransferBuffer
{
    char EditBox[MaxEditLen];
    TListBoxData ListBoxData;
    TComboBoxData ComboBoxData;
    TScrollBarData ScrollBarData;
    uint CheckBox;
    uint RadioButton;
};
```

The buffer structure needs only to include the controls that actually transfer data. You do not need to declare the fields of the buffer structure in any particular order, so long as the controls they match are created in the same order. This sample buffer type includes three special classes that transfer data between dialog boxes and list boxes, combo boxes, and scroll bars. You will see more about these classes later in this section.

Look at the various members of the data transfer buffer type.

- [ ] The `EditBox` member assists in moving data between the edit control and the data buffer. The data member defines a character array that should be equal to or greater than the number of characters in the edit control.

- [ ] The `ListBoxData` member helps to transfer data between a list box control and the data buffer. The `ListBoxData` is an instance of the `TListBoxData` class that OWL provides for keeping track of the contents of a list box, including any selections.

- [ ] The `ComboBoxData` member helps to move data between a combo box control and the data buffer. The `ComboBoxData` is an instance of the `TComboBoxData` class. This, too, is provided by OWL to keep track of the contents and state of a combo box.

- [ ] The `ScrollBarData` member is an instance of the `TScrollBarData` class that assists in transferring data between a scroll bar control and the data buffer.

- [ ] The `CheckBox` member stores the current check state of a check box in a `uint` type.

- [ ] The `RadioButton` member stores the current check state of a radio button in a `uint` type.

Data Transfer for Modal Dialog Boxes

The next application is a simple example of transferring data between the controls of a modal dialog box and a buffer. It creates a typical dialog box that is used in replacing characters in a text editor. The dialog box contains the following controls:

- [ ] Find edit box
- [ ] Replace edit box
- [ ] Scope group box that contains the Global and Selected Text radio button controls
- [ ] Case-Sensitive check box
- [ ] The Whole Word check box
- [ ] The OK pushbutton control
- [ ] The Cancel pushbutton control

The application has a main menu with the Exit and Dialog menu items. To invoke the dialog box, click the Dialog menu item or press Alt+D. When you invoke the dialog box for the first time, the controls have the following initial values and states:

- [ ] The Find edit box contains the string DOS.
- [ ] The Replace edit box has the string Windows.
- [ ] The Global radio button is checked.
- [ ] The Case-Sensitive check box is checked.
- [ ] The Whole Word check box is checked.

Type new strings in the edit box and alter the check states of the radio buttons and check boxes. Now, click the OK button (or press Alt+O) to close the dialog box. Invoke the Dialog menu item again to pop up the dialog box. Notice that the controls of the dialog box have the same values and states as when you last closed the dialog box.

Listing 14.3 shows the source code for the DIALOG2.H header file. Listing 14.4 contains the script for the DIALOG2.RC resource file. Listing 14.5 shows the source code for the DIALOG2.CPP program file.

14

Listing 14.3. Source code for the DIALOG2.H header file.

```
1: #define CM_DIALOG (WM_USER + 100)
2:
3: #define IDE_FIND        101
4: #define IDE_REPLACE     102
5: #define IDR_GLOBAL      103
6: #define IDR_SELTEXT     104
7: #define IDC_CASE        105
8: #define IDC_WHOLEWORD   106
```

 Listing 14.4. Script for the DIALOG2.RC resource file.

```
1:  #include <windows.h>
2:  #include <owl\window.rh>
3:  #include "dialog2.h"
4:
5:  Search DIALOG DISCARDABLE LOADONCALL PURE MOVEABLE 10, 10, 200, 150
6:  STYLE DS_MODALFRAME ¦ WS_POP-UP ¦ WS_VISIBLE ¦ WS_CAPTION ¦
        WS_SYSMENU
7:  CAPTION "Controls Demo"
8:  BEGIN
9:    LTEXT "Find", -1, 20, 10, 100, 15, NOT WS_GROUP
10:    EDITTEXT IDE_FIND, 20, 25, 100, 15
11:    LTEXT "Replace", -1, 20, 45, 100, 15, NOT WS_GROUP
12:    EDITTEXT IDE_REPLACE, 20, 60, 100, 15
13:    GROUPBOX " Scope ", -1, 20, 80, 90, 50, BS_GROUPBOX
14:    RADIOBUTTON "Global", IDR_GLOBAL, 30, 90, 50, 15,
           BS_AUTORADIOBUTTON
15:    RADIOBUTTON "Selected Text", IDR_SELTEXT, 30, 105, 60, 15,
16:       BS_AUTORADIOBUTTON
17:    CHECKBOX "Case Sensitive", IDC_CASE, 20, 130, 80, 15,
           BS_AUTOCHECKBOX ¦
18:       WS_TABSTOP
19:    CHECKBOX "Whole Word", IDC_WHOLEWORD, 100, 130, 80, 15,
           BS_AUTOCHECKBOX
20:       ¦ WS_TABSTOP
21:    DEFPUSHBUTTON "&OK", IDOK, 120, 90, 30, 20
22:    PUSHBUTTON "&Cancel", IDCANCEL, 160, 90, 30, 20
23: END
24:
25: MainMenu MENU LOADONCALL MOVEABLE PURE DISCARDABLE
26: BEGIN
27:    MENUITEM "E&xit", CM_EXIT
28:    MENUITEM "&Dialog", CM_DIALOG
29: END
```

 **Listing 14.5. Source code for the DIALOG2.CPP
program file.**

```
1: #include <cstring.h>
2: #include <windows.h>
3: #include <owl\applicat.h>
```

```
 4:  #include <owl\checkbox.h>
 5:  #include <owl\dialog.h>
 6:  #include <owl\edit.h>
 7:  #include <owl\framewin.h>
 8:  #include <owl\radiobut.h>
 9:  #include <owl\window.h>
10:  #include <owl\window.rh>
11:
12:  #include "dialog2.h"
13:
14:  const MaxEditLen = 30;
15:
16:  struct TTransferBuffer
17:  {
18:      char find[MaxEditLen];
19:      char replace[MaxEditLen];
20:      uint global, seltext, csensitive, wholeword;
21:  };
22:
23:  class TSearchDialog : public TDialog
24:  {
25:  public:
26:      TSearchDialog( TWindow* parent,
27:                     TTransferBuffer* xfer,
28:                     TModule* module = 0);
29:
30:  };
31:
32:  TSearchDialog::TSearchDialog( TWindow* parent,
33:                               TTransferBuffer* xfer,
34:                               TModule* module)
35:      : TDialog(parent, "Search", module)
36:  {
37:      new TEdit(this, IDE_FIND, MaxEditLen);
38:      new TEdit(this, IDE_REPLACE, MaxEditLen);
39:      new TRadioButton(this, IDR_GLOBAL);
40:      new TRadioButton(this, IDR_SELTEXT);
41:      new TCheckBox(this, IDC_CASE);
42:      new TCheckBox(this, IDC_WHOLEWORD);
43:      SetTransferBuffer(xfer);
44:  }
45:
46:  class TMyWindow : public TWindow
47:  {
48:  public:
49:      TMyWindow(TWindow* parent = 0);
50:
51:  protected:
52:      void CmExit();
53:      void CmDialog();
54:
55:  private:
56:      TTransferBuffer xfer;
57:
58:      DECLARE_RESPONSE_TABLE(TMyWindow);
59:  };
60:  DEFINE_RESPONSE_TABLE1(TMyWindow, TWindow)
```

14

Listing 14.5. continued

```
61:    EV_COMMAND(CM_EXIT, CmExit),
62:    EV_COMMAND(CM_DIALOG, CmDialog),
63: END_RESPONSE_TABLE;
64:
65: TMyWindow::TMyWindow(TWindow* parent)
66:    : TWindow(parent)
67: {
68:    memset(&xfer, 0, sizeof(xfer));
69:    lstrcpy(xfer.find, "DOS");
70:    lstrcpy(xfer.replace, "Replace");
71:    xfer.global = BF_CHECKED;
72:    xfer.csensitive = BF_CHECKED;
73:    xfer.wholeword = BF_CHECKED;
74: }
75:
76: void TMyWindow::CmExit()
77: {
78:    SendMessage(WM_CLOSE);
79: }
80:
81: void TMyWindow::CmDialog()
82: {
83:    if (TSearchDialog(this, &xfer).Execute() == IDOK)
84:       {
85:       string msg("Find String: ");
86:       msg += xfer.find;
87:       msg += "\n\nReplace String: ";
88:       msg += xfer.replace;
89:       MessageBox(msg.c_str(), "Dialog Box Data");
90:       }
91: }
92:
93:    class TDialogApp : public TApplication
94:    {
95:    public:
96:       TDialogApp() : TApplication()
97:          { nCmdShow = SW_SHOWMAXIMIZED; }
98:
99:       void InitMainWindow()
100:          {
101:          SetMainWindow(new TFrameWindow(  0,
102:                              "Modal Dialog Box Data Transfer Tester",
103:                              new TMyWindow ));
104:          GetMainWindow()->AssignMenu("MainMenu");
105:          }
106: };
107:
108: int OwlMain(int, char *[])
109: {
110:    return TDialogApp().Run();
111: }
```

Figure 14.3 shows a sample session with the DIALOG2.EXE application.

Figure 14.3.
A sample session with
the DIALOG2.EXE
application.

 Listing 14.4 contains the script for the DIALOG2.RC resource file. This file defines the resources for the menu and the dialog box, including its controls. In the dialog box resource definition on lines 21 and 22, the OK and Cancel pushbuttons have the predefined IDOK and IDCANCEL IDs, respectively.

Listing 14.5 shows the source code for the DIALOG2.CPP program file. The program declares the data transfer type TTransferBuffer starting on line 16 and includes members for the edit boxes, radio buttons, and check boxes.

Starting on line 23, the application declares the TSearchDialog class as a descendant of the TDialog class. Notice that it doesn't have any member data, and the only function declared is its constructor. This constructor starts on line 32 and, in turn, does nothing more than create some OWL interface objects to be associated with the various controls created from the dialog resource. The constructor then makes a call to the SetTransferBuffer function on line 43, passing the xfer parameter along. OWL takes over from here and performs automatically all the transfers between xfer and the actual controls.

Starting on line 43, the TMyWindow class declares its constructor, two functions to respond to the menu, and a data member of type TTransferBuffer. This data member is initialized in the constructor, first with a call to the memset function on line 68. This call fills the xfer data member with zeros. We recommend that you systematically call the memset function to perform a basic initialization of buffers and structures before assigning specific values to them. Then the xfer's data members are set to some initial values. Another way to ensure an empty structure is to provide it with a default constructor that clears all the data members.

Starting on line 81, the CmDialog function, which responds to the Dialog menu item, creates a modal dialog of type TSearchDialog on line 83, passing the xfer data member as a parameter. If the user clicks the OK button to exit this dialog box, it will return IDOK, and the CmDialog function then will build and display a message string that reflects the current Find and Replace text on lines 85 through 89.

Transferring Data for Modeless Dialog Boxes

The method of transferring data from modeless dialog boxes almost is the same as that used for modal dialog boxes. The main difference is that the mechanism that automatically transfers the data between the controls, and the transfer buffer is only called when the dialog window is modal. The programmer needs to make the call, explicitly in the case of a modeless dialog box. This can be done by overriding the CloseWindow member function in the dialog box's descendant class.

```
void TMyDialog::CloseWindow(int retValue)
{
    TransferData(tdGetData);
    TDialog::CloseWindow(retValue);
}
```

At this point, all the control data will be transferred to the buffer that was sent to the SetTransferBuffer in the dialog box's constructor.

Another possible action might be to have a Send button in the dialog box, with a response function that looks similar to the following:

```
void TMyDialog::CmSend()
{
    TransferData(tdGetData);
    Parent->HandleMessage(WM_COMMAND, IDB_SEND);
}
```

Then, in the dialog box's parent's window class, add a member function to handle the Send button in the same way you did for the dialog class. This function will be called automatically when the dialog box simulates the press of the Send button via the call to its parent's HandleMessage function.

Summary

Today's lesson presented you with powerful dialog boxes that serve as input tools. You learned about the following topics:

☐ You can construct instances of class TDialog to create modeless or modal dialog boxes.

☐ You can construct instances of the various control classes that give access to the controls created automatically from the dialog resource.

☐ Modal dialog boxes are executed with the Execute member function.

☐ The basics of transferring control data include declaring the data transfer buffer type, declaring the buffer, creating the controls in a sequence that matches their buffers, and establishing the buffer link with the SetTransferBuffer member function.

☐ The first step in supporting data transfer is to define a transfer buffer type. You can transfer data for modal dialog boxes and modeless dialog boxes.

Q&A

Q **Does OWL support specialized dialog boxes?**

A Yes. OWL has a set of classes that implement dialog boxes for selecting files, selecting colors, selecting fonts, printing, and searching/replacing text. The classes that model these dialog boxes are all descendants of the class `TDialog` and display the common dialog boxes.

Q **Is the data transfer buffer necessary for modeless dialog boxes?**

A Not always. You can have an application that pops up multiple modeless dialog boxes and have them communicate with each other directly, without the need of a data transfer buffer.

Workshop

The Workshop provides quiz questions to help you solidify your understanding of the material covered and exercises to provide you with experience in using what you've learned. Try to understand the quiz and exercise answers before continuing on to the next day's lesson. Answers are provided in Appendix A.

Quiz

1. True or false? You must compile all the .RC files into .RES files before or during the creation of the application.
2. True or false? The OK and Cancel buttons in a dialog box are optional.
3. True or false? You can create a dialog box with buttons labeled Yes and No.
4. True or false? Nested dialog boxes are not allowed by Windows.
5. True or false? Dialog boxes must always have a nondialog window parent.

Exercises

1. Create a version of the MrCalc application (from Day 13) that uses a dialog box as a stand-alone window.
2. Use the Resource Workshop to create the dialog box resource for the DIALOG2 program.

As you end the second week of learning to program with Turbo C++ 4.5, look at the Turbo Blocks example provided with the package. This is a Tetris clone, and it can be found in the TCWIN45\EXAMPLES\OWL\GAMES\BLOCKS directory. The file of most importance, the one with all the C++ source code, is BLOCKS.CPP. Accompanying this example also is a BLOCKS.RC file, which contains the program's menu, an About dialog box, and the program's icon. To run this program, open the BLOCKS.IDE file with Turbo C++. You'll be able to see the files that make up the project, and you'll be able to build and run the application.

One of the first items in the file is the declaration and definition of the TBlock structure. Notice that, although this is declared as a struct, it includes a member function. You'll remember from Day 8 that structures are really just classes, except a structure's member starts out with the public default, while classes start out as private. The TBlock structure declares two items of member data, size and elements. The first of these two is an indicator of just how large the block is, and the second holds an array of characters that are used to define the actual shape of the block. The rotate member function is used to rotate the shape 90 degrees to the left. Note that four rotations will bring the block back to its initial state, so there's no real need for a function that will rotate to the right: just rotate it to the left three times.

Immediately following the rotate member function is the declaration of the global variable blocks. This holds the definition of all the blocks that will be used in the game. There also are the global variables pen and brush, which will be used to draw the blocks in the window. We'll get to those in a bit. Notice, however, that there is one more entry in each of pen and brush than there is in blocks. Next is the enumeration GameState, which provides values for the different states in which the game can be at any one time: an idle state (no game running), a block dropping (game in progress), paused (the user needs a break), and when lines are flashing or being removed.

Now we start to get into the meat of the program with the TBlocksWindow class. This class is a descendant of TWindow, and so inherits all the functionality thereof. The first members of the new class are data items, each of which is labeled quite well, so I'll skip their descriptions here, and instead mention them as they're used.

An interesting member function is EvEraseBkgnd. All it does is return true, but that has a lot of significance in the Windows world. Normally, when Windows goes to redraw a window (just before sending the WM_PAINT message, which triggers the OWL Paint member function), it sends the WM_ERASEBKGND message. The default response to this message is to completely erase the background of the window. This is normally a "good thing," but when you're trying to do animation, you don't want the flicker this action creates; the window would briefly clear before being redrawn. So, in order to prevent Windows from performing its default action, you return true, thus keeping the window's painting all to yourself.

You'll notice that the SetupWindow is rather simple, in that it merely calls the base class's version (a requirement) then proceeds to set up a timer. Timers are discussed more completely on Day 17, but suffice it to say that this call sets up a Windows timer that will call us back every hundredth of a second with a message that triggers the EvTimer member function. The timer is destroyed by the CleanupWindow member function, which is called when the window is closed.

The PauseEnabler member function is called whenever the user tries to use the program's menu. This function allows the program to enable or change the text of the menu item for which it's associated. This association occurs in the response table definition on the line that reads EV_COMMAND_ENABLE(CM_GAMEPAUSE, PauseEnabler). The PauseEnabler function disables the menu item if there's no game in progress, and it sets the text of the menu item to reflect whether the user can pause or resume the game in progress.

The constructor simply resets the size of the window to the size of the board before clearing the board and initializing various member data. The RemoveLines member function is sort of interesting to look at. It initializes one counter to the bottom line of the board, then checks each line to see if it's full of blocks. If so, the function removes that line by copying the contents of all the lines above down by one line, and then clears the top. There's no need to actually remove the full line because the copy operation will cover it up. Note that the while loop doesn't iterate to the previous line if there was a copy operation; if it did, it might skip a full line that had just been copied from its old location down to the current line. Instead, the next iteration of the loop looks at the very same line.

The NewGame member function is a little less interesting. It simply clears the board before creating a new falling block at random. It then sets the game state to that of one in progress and invalidates the window. This last action tells Windows that the window needs to be repainted, and the Paint function will get called in short order. Similarly uninteresting is the ClearBoard member function. It just goes through all the blocks and sets them to 0 while setting the invisible borders to -1 (the latter action is done so it will be easy to tell when a falling block hits it).

The EvTimer function, which is called intermittently by Windows, performs different actions depending on the current game state. If no game is going on, or the if current game is paused, or if the game is in the process of removing lines, the function does nothing. If, however, the game is in progress and a block is dropping, then the timer function must act to animate the block. First it increments the dropCount data member, which is used to further subdivide the timer intervals. If either dropCount has reached its maximum value or if the user has asked to drop the current block (signified by the dropping data member), then the function needs to move the block down a line. First, dropCount is reset for the next run-through with the timer. Then, the block's location is moved down a line by incrementing its y component. If the HitTest function returns true, then it signifies that the block has hit something and must be placed onto the board. This is done with the PlaceBlock function. After that, you make sure to remove lines and start a new block falling. Finally, the window is invalidated to make sure everything gets redrawn properly.

The EvKeyUp and EvKeyDown functions handle keypresses. Rather than wait for the standard keypress that results in an EvChar message, you want to watch as the keys are actually pressed and held down, and then watch them be released. This allows the player to press a key and have it affect the game for the duration of time it is pressed. The various keys do some rather obvious things, such as move the block over to the left or right, if possible, or rotate the block. With the matching sections of both EvKeyDown and EvKeyUp, the dropping data member is set to true as long as the down arrow key is pressed, and then is reset to false the moment it's released.

The HitTest function actually is quite simple. It first sets up a pair of nested loops that runs through the contents of the current block, and then performs a series of three if statements. The first statement checks to make sure that the part block it's about to check actually is in range on the board; because pieces don't always take up the whole space of the block, there could be parts that extend off the board. The second test is to see if something already is on the board in the selected location. If so, then you check the block itself to see if there's a piece of it there as well. If all of these conditions are true, then the function returns that condition.

The NewBlock function sets the currentBlock according to the blockType parameter and the current color accordingly. Because the player could be about to lose, it also checks to see if the new block is hitting something at the top of the screen. If so, it then places the block and ends the game. PlaceBlock simply copies the contents of the current block to the board and then removes any full lines that might exist.

DrawBlock actually paints a block on-screen. First it selects a brush and pen of the appropriate color into the supplied device context. For objects such as rectangles (which is what this function draws), you use the pen to draw the outline, and use the brush to fill that in. This makes it quite easy to create those nice-looking segmented squares of which each block is made. After selecting the drawing objects, a pair of nested loops goes through all the elements of the block and puts a rectangle on the DC for each occupied element.

Finally you get to the Paint function—the workhorse function that is responsible for all the drawing on the window. First it creates a memory DC and then selects a new bitmap in it. The reasoning behind this is to minimize any flicker on-screen and make the drawing as smooth as possible. If you were to draw to the screen DC directly, the user might be able to see the drawing process as it happened. By drawing to the memory DC instead, and then copying that memory DC directly to the screen, you make the whole screen-drawing process happen in one quick step.

Next, Paint takes care of the case in which the game is paused. If you allowed users to pause the game and study the screen, the game would become a little easier, and consequently less fair. So, in this case, the DC is cleared with a call to FillRect and then the string " * * P A U S E D * * " is written in the middle. The resulting DC is copied to the screen with the BitBlt function and Paint returns.

If the game isn't paused, Paint goes through the process of drawing the board. It draws a square for each position on the board, doing so in the color that had been assigned to it either during initialization or in the PlaceBlock function. Finally, if the game is in progress, it calls DrawBlock to show the currently falling block. When all this is done, Paint copies the memory DC to the screen.

The rest of the program should look quite familiar to you by now. A TApplication descendant is defined that creates a frame window with our specially defined window as its client. This TBlocksApp object then is instantiated in the OwlMain function and run.

This last week presents topics that cover more aspects of creating Windows applications using various classes in the OWL library. You will learn about more complicated Windows controls, including check boxes, radio buttons, list boxes, combo boxes, and scroll bars. You also will learn how to include Visual Basic Controls (VBXs) in your application. These controls make up most of the visual controls that are common to Windows applications. You then will be introduced to MDI windows and OLE 2 applications.

Along with this basic information on Windows programming, you also will be introduced to the Application and Class Experts, features of the Turbo C++ IDE that enable you to quickly and easily generate and maintain complex Windows programs. After that will be a chapter with a walkthrough of a debugging session, giving you some useful tips on fixing a broken program.

15

Grouped Controls

Windows supports check box and radio button controls that act as software switches. These controls appear in typical Search and Replace dialog boxes and influence certain aspects of the text search or replacement. These aspects include the scope, direction, and case-sensitivity of searching or replacing text. In today's lesson, you learn about the following topics:

☐ The check box control

☐ The radio button control

☐ The group control

Today's lesson also shows you how to respond to the messages emitted by these controls as well as how to use the ForEach iterators to manipulate the check box and radio button controls.

NEW☞ The *group box control* is a special control that visually and logically groups the check box
TERM and radio button controls.

The Check Box Control

The check box control is a special button that toggles a check mark. The control instances appear with a small rectangular button and a title that appears, by default, to the right side of the square. When you click the square, you toggle the control's check mark. Think of the check box as a binary digit that can be either set or cleared. The instances of a check box can appear inside or outside a group box and are not mutually exclusive—toggling any check box does not affect the check state of other check boxes.

> **Note:** Placing check boxes inside groups (inside a dialog box) serves two purposes. First, the group box provides a visual grouping that clarifies the purpose of the check boxes to the application user. Second, you can streamline the notification messages emitted by the check boxes in a group to detect any change in the checked state of the check boxes.

NEW☞ Windows enables you to specify a check box that can have one of three states: checked,
TERM unchecked, and *grayed.* The grayed state fills the control's rectangular button with a gray color. This third state can serve to indicate that the check box control is in an indeterminate (or "don't care") state.

The *TCheckBox* Class

The ObjectWindows Library offers the TCheckBox class, a descendant of TButton, as the class that provides the instances of check box controls. Day 13 introduced you to the TButton class and discussed the aspects of that class that are related to the pushbutton controls. Because check boxes really are just specialized buttons, much of what applies to buttons also applies to check boxes. By deriving the TCheckBox class from the TButton class, you ensure that TCheckBox inherits much of the parent's functionality. The check box styles shown in Table 15.1 indicate that there are two basic modes for managing the check state of a check box control: automatic and nonautomatic (manual, if you prefer). In automatic mode (specified by BS_AUTOCHECKBOX and BS_AUTO3STATE), Windows toggles the check state when you click the control. In manual mode, your application code is responsible for managing the check state of the check box.

Table 15.1. Check box control styles.

Style	Meaning
BS_CHECKBOX	Specifies a check box with the title to the right of the rectangular button
BS_AUTOCHECKBOX	Same as BS_CHECKBOX, except the button is automatically toggled when you click it. This is the default setting for the TCheckBox class.
BS_3STATE	Same as BS_CHECKBOX, except that the control has three states: checked, unchecked, and grayed
BS_AUTO3STATE	Same as BS_3STATE, except the button is automatically toggled when you click it
BS_LEFTTEXT	Sets the control's title to the left of the button. Note that this is the only style that can be ORed into the style.

The TCheckBox class provides member functions to set and query the state of the check box. The GetCheck member function returns a state of the check box control and is declared as follows:

```
uint GetCheck() const;
```

The function returns a uint-typed value that represents the check state. A value of BF_UNCHECKED indicates that the control is not checked. A value of BF_CHECKED signals that the control is checked. A value of BF_GRAYED indicates that the control is in an indeterminate state. The latter value is valid for the BS_3STATE and BS_AUTO3STATE styles.

The SetCheck member function enables you to set the check state of a check box control. The declaration of the SetCheck function is

```
void SetCheck(uint check);
```

The check parameter specifies the new state of the check box control and should be one of the BF_XXX values.

Responding to Check Box Messages

Because check boxes are descendants of TButton with a BS_CHECKBOX or BS_AUTOCHECKBOX style, your OWL application responds to the messages emitted by check boxes in a manner similar to the pushbuttons. The EV_BN_CLICKED macro maps the message sent by the check box control with the member function that responds to that message.

The Radio Button Control

Radio buttons typically enable you to select an option from two or more options. This type of control comes with a circular button and a title that appears, by default, to the right of the button. When you check a radio button, a tiny, filled circle appears inside the circular button. Radio buttons need to be placed in group boxes that visually and logically group them. In each group of radio buttons, only one button can be selected. Therefore, radio buttons are mutually exclusive.

The *TRadioButton* Class

OWL applications use the TRadioButton class, a descendant of TCheckBox, to create radio button controls by specifying BS_RADIOBUTTON or BS_AUTORADIOBUTTON. Table 15.2 contains the radio button styles. The constructor creates a radio button with the BS_AUTORADIOBUTTON style. Like the check box controls, the radio buttons use the GetCheck and SetCheck member functions to query and set the state. Unlike the check box, the radio button has only two states: checked and unchecked.

Table 15.2. Radio button control styles.

Style	Meaning
BS_RADIOBUTTON	Specifies a radio button with the title to the right of the circular button
BS_AUTORADIOBUTTON	Same as BS_RADIOBUTTON, except the button is automatically toggled when you click it. This is the default style for the TRadioButton class.
BS_LEFTTEXT	Sets the control's title to the left of the button. This is the only style that can be ORed into the style.

The radio button controls send the same type of notification messages to their parent windows as do the check box controls. Handling these messages for radio buttons is identical to that of check box and pushbutton controls.

The Group Control

The group box control encloses radio buttons and check boxes. The group box performs the following tasks:

☐ Visually groups radio buttons or check boxes, which makes relating these controls to each other clearer for the application user, by placing a box around them. Note that you don't necessarily need controls in a box to get the visual effect.

☐ Logically groups multiple radio buttons so that when you select one radio button, the other buttons in the same group are automatically deselected.

NEW☞
TERM
The group box control is a special type of control known as a *container control.*

You can code your OWL application so that the controls inside a group box notify the parent of the group box that you have changed the state of its controls.

The *TGroupBox* Class

Your OWL applications can create group boxes with the TGroupBox class, descended from TControl. This automatically creates the visual element and provides access via its SelectionChanged member function. The declaration of the SelectionChanged function is

```
void SelectionChanged(int controlId);
```

When an item in the group is changed, this function is called. By default, the SelectionChanged function checks the TGroupBox's NotifyParent data member. If it's TRUE, then the function notifies the parent window of the group box that one of its selections has changed by sending it a child-ID-based message. By deriving your own version of TGroupBox and redefining SelectionChanged, you can handle selection changes from the group box itself.

The Widget Selection Application

Here's a short application that demonstrates a possible use for the controls introduced in this chapter. The program shows a sample order form for the World-Wide Widget Weilders company. On it, the user can select one each of Type A, Type B, and Type C widgets. For each of those widget types, there are several different models from which the user can choose. In each case, the different models are disabled so long as the widget type is not checked.

This program illustrates the following:

☐ The basic use of check box controls
☐ The basic use of radio buttons

- [ ] Responding to check box notification messages
- [ ] Overriding a group box to keep track of changes in radio button selections
- [ ] Making initial radio button selections

Listing 15.1 contains the source code for the WIDGETS.H header file, listing 15.2 shows the source code for the WIDGETS.RC resource file, and listing 15.3 shows the WIDGETS.CPP program file. Create the directory WIDGETS as a subdirectory of \TCWIN45\TC21DAY and store all the project's files in the new directory. The project's .IDE file should contain the file WIDGETS.CPP and WIDGETS.RC.

Listing 15.1. Source code for the WIDGETS.H header file.

```
 1:  #define IDC_TYPEA       101
 2:  #define IDC_TYPEB       102
 3:  #define IDC_TYPEC       103
 4:  #define IDR_ETCHED      104
 5:  #define IDR_POLISHED    105
 6:  #define IDR_WOODGRAIN   106
 7:  #define IDR_VARNISHED   107
 8:  #define IDR_ENGRAVED    108
 9:  #define IDR_MEDIOCRE    109
10:  #define IDR_DELUXE      110
11:  #define IDG_TYPEA       111
12:  #define IDG_TYPEB       112
13:  #define IDG_TYPEC       113
```

Listing 15.2. Source code for the WIDGETS.RC resource file.

```
 1: /*****************************************************************************
 2:
 3:
 4: WIDGETS.RC
 5:
 6: produced by Borland Resource Workshop
 7:
 8:
 9: *****************************************************************************/
10:
11:        #include "widgets.h"
12:
13:        WWWW DIALOG 8, 15, 241, 165
14:        STYLE DS_MODALFRAME ¦ WS_POPUP ¦ WS_VISIBLE ¦ WS_CAPTION ¦ WS_SYSMENU
15:        CAPTION "World-Wide Widget Weilders"
16:        FONT 8, "MS Sans Serif"
17:        {
18:         CHECKBOX "Type A", IDC_TYPEA, 10, 12, 40, 12, BS_AUTOCHECKBOX ¦
            WS_TABSTOP
19:         CONTROL "", IDG_TYPEA, "static", SS_BLACKFRAME ¦ WS_GROUP, 67, 6, 160,
25
```

```
20:          CONTROL "Etched", IDR_ETCHED, "BUTTON", BS_AUTORADIOBUTTON, 77, 12, 60,
             12
21:          CONTROL "Polished", IDR_POLISHED, "BUTTON", BS_AUTORADIOBUTTON, 147,
             12, 60, 12
22:          CHECKBOX "Type B", IDC_TYPEB, 10, 59, 40, 12, BS_AUTOCHECKBOX ¦
             WS_TABSTOP
23:          CONTROL "", IDG_TYPEB, "static", SS_BLACKFRAME ¦ WS_GROUP, 67, 48, 160,
34
24:          CONTROL "Wood-Grain", IDR_WOODGRAIN, "BUTTON", BS_AUTORADIOBUTTON, 77,
             49, 60, 12
25:          CONTROL "Varnished", IDR_VARNISHED, "BUTTON", BS_AUTORADIOBUTTON, 150,
             49, 60, 12
26:          CONTROL "Engraved", IDR_ENGRAVED, "BUTTON", BS_AUTORADIOBUTTON, 77, 68,
             60, 12
27:          CHECKBOX "Type C", IDC_TYPEC, 10, 105, 40, 12, BS_AUTOCHECKBOX ¦
             WS_TABSTOP
28:          CONTROL "", IDG_TYPEC, "static", SS_BLACKFRAME ¦ WS_GROUP, 67, 97, 160,
28
29:          CONTROL "Mediocre", IDR_MEDIOCRE, "BUTTON", BS_AUTORADIOBUTTON, 77,
             105, 60, 12
30:          CONTROL "Deluxe", IDR_DELUXE, "BUTTON", BS_AUTORADIOBUTTON, 153, 105,
             60, 12
31:          DEFPUSHBUTTON "Done", IDOK, 47, 134, 50, 14
32:          PUSHBUTTON "Cancel", IDCANCEL, 144, 134, 50, 14
33:          }
```

Listing 15.3. Source code for the WIDGETS.CPP program file.

```
1:       #include <stdio.h>
2:       #include <owl\applicat.h>
3:       #include <owl\button.h>
4:       #include <owl\checkbox.h>
5:       #include <owl\dialog.h>
6:       #include <owl\framewin.h>
7:       #include <owl\groupbox.h>
8:       #include <owl\radiobut.h>
9:       #include <owl\window.h>
10:      #include <owl\window.rh>
11:
12:      #include "widgets.h"
13:
14:      class TMyGroup : public TGroupBox
15:      {
16:      public:
17:        TMyGroup(TWindow*      parent,
18:                 int          id,
19:                 TModule*     module = 0 )
20:          : TGroupBox(parent, id, module), cur(-1)
21:          { }
22:
23:        LPCSTR GetCurCheck();
```

continues

435

Listing 15.3. continued

```
24:
25:             virtual void SelectionChanged(int controlId)
26:                 { TGroupBox::SelectionChanged(cur = controlId); }
27:
28:         private:
29:             int cur;
30:         };
31:
32:         LPCSTR TMyGroup::GetCurCheck()
33:         {
34:             TWindow* w = Parent->ChildWithId(cur);
35:             return w ? w->Title : NULL;
36:         }
37:
38:         class TWidgetDialog : public TDialog
39:         {
40:         public:
41:             TWidgetDialog(TWindow* parent = 0, TModule* module = 0);
42:
43:         protected:
44:             virtual void SetupWindow();
45:
46:             void EnableGroupA(bool enable);
47:             void EnableGroupB(bool enable);
48:             void EnableGroupC(bool enable);
49:
50:             bool BuildStr( LPSTR str,
51:                            LPCSTR name,
52:                            TCheckBox* check,
53:                            TMyGroup* group );
54:
55:             void CmDone();
56:             void CmCancel();
57:             void CmTypeA();
58:             void CmTypeB();
59:             void CmTypeC();
60:
61:         private:
62:             TCheckBox      *TypeA, *TypeB, *TypeC;
63:             TMyGroup       *GroupA, *GroupB, *GroupC;
64:             TRadioButton   *Etched, *Polished,
65:                            *WoodGrain, *Varnished, *Engraved,
66:                            *Mediocre, *Deluxe;
67:
68:             DECLARE_RESPONSE_TABLE(TWidgetDialog);
69:         };
70:         DEFINE_RESPONSE_TABLE1(TWidgetDialog, TDialog)
71:             EV_BN_CLICKED(IDOK, CmDone),
72:             EV_BN_CLICKED(IDCANCEL, CmCancel),
73:             EV_BN_CLICKED(IDC_TYPEA, CmTypeA),
74:             EV_BN_CLICKED(IDC_TYPEB, CmTypeB),
75:             EV_BN_CLICKED(IDC_TYPEC, CmTypeC),
76:         END_RESPONSE_TABLE;
77:
```

```
78:     TWidgetDialog::TWidgetDialog(TWindow* parent, TModule* module)
79:        : TDialog(parent, "WWWW", module)
80:     {
81:        TypeA = new TCheckBox(this, IDC_TYPEA);
82:        GroupA = new TMyGroup(this, IDG_TYPEA);
83:        Etched = new TRadioButton(this, IDR_ETCHED);
84:        Polished = new TRadioButton(this, IDR_POLISHED);
85:
86:        TypeB = new TCheckBox(this, IDC_TYPEB);
87:        GroupB = new TMyGroup(this, IDG_TYPEB);
88:        WoodGrain = new TRadioButton(this, IDR_WOODGRAIN);
89:        Varnished = new TRadioButton(this, IDR_VARNISHED);
90:        Engraved = new TRadioButton(this, IDR_ENGRAVED);
91:
92:        TypeC = new TCheckBox(this, IDC_TYPEC);
93:        GroupC = new TMyGroup(this, IDG_TYPEC);
94:        Mediocre = new TRadioButton(this, IDR_MEDIOCRE);
95:        Deluxe = new TRadioButton(this, IDR_DELUXE);
96:     }
97:
98:     void TWidgetDialog::SetupWindow()
99:     {
100:        TDialog::SetupWindow();      // Initialize the visual element
101:
102:        EnableGroupA(false);
103:        EnableGroupB(false);
104:        EnableGroupC(false);
105:     }
106:
107:     void TWidgetDialog::EnableGroupA(bool enable)
108:     {
109:        if (Etched)
110:            Etched->EnableWindow(enable);
111:        if (Polished)
112:            Polished->EnableWindow(enable);
113:     }
114:
115:     void TWidgetDialog::EnableGroupB(bool enable)
116:     {
117:        if (WoodGrain)
118:            WoodGrain->EnableWindow(enable);
119:        if (Varnished)
120:            Varnished->EnableWindow(enable);
121:        if (Engraved)
122:            Engraved->EnableWindow(enable);
123:     }
124:
125:     void TWidgetDialog::EnableGroupC(bool enable)
126:     {
127:        if (Mediocre)
128:            Mediocre->EnableWindow(enable);
129:        if (Deluxe)
130:            Deluxe->EnableWindow(enable);
131:     }
132:
```

continues

Listing 15.3. continued

```
133:    bool TWidgetDialog::BuildStr( LPSTR str,
134:                                  LPCSTR name,
135:                                  TCheckBox* check,
136:                                  TMyGroup* group )
137:    {
138:        bool rslt = false;
139:        if (str && check && check->GetCheck())
140:            {
141:            rslt = true;
142:            LPCSTR groupname;
143:
144:            str += lstrlen(str);    // point to end of str
145:            sprintf(str, "\n   %s: ", name);
146:            if (group && (NULL != (groupname = group->GetCurCheck())))
147:                strcat(str, groupname);
148:            }
149:        return rslt;
150:    }
151:
152:    void TWidgetDialog::CmDone()
153:    {
154:        char          str[256] = "";
155:        int           sels = 0;
156:
157:        strcpy(str, "You have selected the following:");
158:        sels += BuildStr(str, "Widget A", TypeA, GroupA);
159:        sels += BuildStr(str, "Widget B", TypeB, GroupB);
160:        sels += BuildStr(str, "Widget C", TypeC, GroupC);
161:        if (!sels)
162:            strcat(str, "\n   << No selections >>");
163:        MessageBox(str, "Widget Selection", MB_OK);
164:        SendMessage(WM_CLOSE);
165:    }
166:
167:    void TWidgetDialog::CmCancel()
168:    {
169:        SendMessage(WM_CLOSE);
170:    }
171:
172:    void TWidgetDialog::CmTypeA()
173:    {
174:        if (TypeA)
175:            EnableGroupA(TypeA->GetCheck());
176:        if (GroupA && !GroupA->GetCurCheck() && Etched)
177:            Etched->Check();
178:    }
179:
180:    void TWidgetDialog::CmTypeB()
181:    {
182:        if (TypeB)
183:            EnableGroupB(TypeB->GetCheck());
184:        if (GroupB && !GroupB->GetCurCheck() && WoodGrain)
185:            WoodGrain->Check();
186:    }
```

```
187:
188:        void TWidgetDialog::CmTypeC()
189:        {
190:          if (TypeC)
191:            EnableGroupC(TypeC->GetCheck());
192:          if (GroupC && !GroupC->GetCurCheck() && Mediocre)
193:            Mediocre->Check();
194:        }
195:
196:        class TWidgetApp : public TApplication
197:        {
198:        public:
199:          TWidgetApp() : TApplication()
200:            { nCmdShow = SW_SHOWMAXIMIZED; }
201:
202:          void InitMainWindow()
203:          {
204:            SetMainWindow(new TFrameWindow(  0,
205:                    "World-Wide Widget Weilders",
206:                    new TWidgetDialog ));
207:          }
208:        };
209:
210:        int OwlMain(int, char *[])
211:        {
212:          return TWidgetApp().Run();
213:        }
```

 Figure 15.1 shows a sample session with the WIDGETS.EXE program.

Figure 15.1.
A sample session with program WIDGETS.EXE.

The program starts off on line 14 of Listing 15.3 by declaring a descendant of TGroupBox called TMyGroup. The purpose of this is to keep track of the selections made by the controls contained within it. The class initializes its cur data member to −1 in the constructor on line 20. This signifies that no control has yet been selected inside the group. This value is changed in the overridden SelectionChanged member function on line 26. This function, as described earlier, is called whenever a control inside the group is selected. Our version of the function simply passes the single parameter along to the parent's version of the function while assigning the value of that parameter to our cur data member. Finally, the TMyGroup class defines the GetCurCheck member function starting on line 32. This function uses the parent window's ChildWithId function to obtain a TWindow pointer to the control with the ID recorded in cur. If a control was found, then its Title data member is returned.

The main dialog TWidgetDialog then is declared, starting on line 38. As usual, there is a constructor and a SetupWindow member function. The constructor creates all the various controls that are to appear on the screen, starting on line 78: three check boxes, each with a group next to it, and then between two and three radio buttons inside that group. The SetupWindow member function that starts on line 98, after calling its parent's version of the function, makes calls to three functions to initially disable the various groups of radio buttons.

Next are the helper functions EnableGroupA, EnableGroupB, and EnableGroupC on lines 107 through 131. These are used to enable and disable whole groups of controls via TDialog's EnableWindow member function. They each take a single bool-typed enable parameter that determines whether the controls are to be enabled or disabled. This parameter is passed directly on to the individual control's EnableWindow function.

The two functions CmDone and CmCancel on lines 152 through 170 come next. They respond to the two buttons Done and Cancel, respectively. In both cases, they send the WM_CLOSE message to the main window in order to shut the application down, but the CmDone function first creates and displays a message box informing the user of the selections made. It builds this string by doing the following:

☐ First, it fills in the str variable on line 157 with an initial string, letting the user know what information follows.

☐ Next, the BuildStr member function (discussed next) is called for each of the three check boxes and group boxes on lines 158 through 160. The return values of these calls are added to the sels variable and BuildStr modifies str.

☐ After filling up the string with results of the user's selections, the sels variable is checked. If it's still 0, then nothing was selected, and the str variable is filled to reflect that on lines 161 and 162. This bit of code works because true is defined to be 1 and false to be 0. So, when the bool return values from multiple calls to BuildStr are added together in sels, we're checking to see if any of the return values were true without actually caring about which one.

- [ ] The `str` variable is then sent to the `MessageBox` function on line 163 for display to the user.
- [ ] Finally, the `WM_CLOSE` message is sent to the window via the `SendMessage` function on line 164 to effectively terminate the window and, thus, the program.

The `BuildStr` member function, starting on line 133, works by taking a destination string in its `str` parameter, the name of the check box to be reported to the user in the `name` parameter, and the pointers to the check box and group box controls in the `check` and `group` parameters, respectively. The function does the following things:

- [ ] First, it checks on line 139 to make sure it received valid `str` and `check` parameters. It's always a good idea to check parameters before trying to use them to help prevent unwanted bugs in the program. In the same statement, it also calls `check`'s `GetCheck` function. If that returns `true`, then the check box has been checked, and you need to start filling in the `str` parameter.
- [ ] In order to keep from overwriting the previous contents of the `str` parameter, `str` is made to point at its end by adding the value obtained from the `lstrlen` function on line 144.
- [ ] The name of the check box is printed into the `str`, along with some formatting characters on line 145.
- [ ] If you have a valid `group` parameter and you are able to get the title of its selected radio button, then that title is concatenated to the `str` parameter on line 147.
- [ ] Finally, the result of whether anything was actually added to `str` is returned on line 149.

The last functions of interest are the `CmTypeA`, `CmTypeB`, and `CmTypeC` member functions on lines 172 through 194. These each respond, in turn, to the Type A, Type B, and Type C check boxes respectively. In each one, first the appropriate `EnableGroupX` is called with the check box's check state to either enable or disable the appropriate group's radio buttons. The function then attempts to find out the title of the currently selected radio button. If this value isn't set, then you know that this is the first time the check box has been set, so you initialize the radio buttons by setting the first one with its `Check` member function.

Summary

Today's lesson discussed the special switch controls: group box, check box, and radio button. You learned about the following:

- [ ] Check box and radio button controls act as software switches.
- [ ] You can set and query the check state for the check box and radio button controls.

☐ Notification messages can be sent by these controls to their parent window.

☐ Group box controls enclose radio buttons and check boxes.

☐ Switch controls can be selectively manipulated.

Day 16 presents the list box, and Day 17 presents the scroll bar and combo box controls. These controls are value selectors because they enable you to select from a list or range of values.

Q&A

Q The check box has the states `BF_UNCHECKED`, `BF_CHECKED`, and `BF_GRAYED`. What can I use the third state for?

A You can use the `BF_GRAYED` state as a "don't care" or as an undetermined state.

Q Does it make any difference if I place check box controls in a group control?

A Placing check box controls in a group control affects the logical grouping of such controls as the user sees it. Consequently, this can enhance the interface for the user.

Workshop

The Workshop provides quiz questions to help you solidify your understanding of the material covered and exercises to provide you with experience in using what you've learned. Try to understand the quiz and exercise answers before continuing on to the next day's lesson. Answers are provided in Appendix A.

Quiz

1. True or false? A check box can replace any two radio buttons in a group control.
2. True or false? You should use radio buttons in a group control when you have three or more options.
3. True or false? A set of check boxes parallels the bits in a byte or word.
4. True or false? Radio buttons, in a group control, are mutually nonexclusive.

Exercise

Expand on program WIDGETS.CPP by adding more widget types and more design types for each widget.

16

List Box Controls

List box controls are input tools that conveniently provide you with items from which to choose. This feature makes list box controls popular because they absolve you from remembering the list members—especially when computer programs expect exact spelling. Experience with DOS programs has shown that the various DOS utilities that display lists of files and directories are far easier and friendlier to use than their counterparts that assume the user knows all the names of the files and directories. Using list box controls gradually has become a routine method for retrieving information. Today's lesson discusses the single-selection and multiple-selection list boxes. You will learn about the following topics:

☐ The list box control

☐ Handling single-selection list boxes

☐ Handling multiple-selection list boxes

The List Box Control

List boxes typically are framed and include a vertical scroll bar. When you select an item by clicking it, the selection is highlighted. Microsoft suggests the following guidelines for making a selection:

☐ Use a single mouse click to select a new or an additional item. A separate button control retrieves the selected item.

☐ Use a double-click as a shortcut for selecting an item and retrieving it.

NEW☞ The *list box* is an input control that permits the application user to select from a list of
TERM items.

A list box control supports multiple selections only if you specify the multiple-selection style when you create the control. Making multiple selections is convenient when you want to process the selected items in a similar manner. For example, selecting multiple files for deletion speeds up the process and reduces the effort you have to make.

The *TListBox* Class

The Borland ObjectWindows Library offers the TListBox class, a descendant of TControl, to implement list box controls. The TListBox class has a set of member functions that enable you to easily manipulate and query both the contents of the list box and the selected item. As with many other classes in OWL, the class TListBox uses a default constructor to create list box instances.

The *TListBox* Constructor

Syntax

The declarations of the TListBox constructors are

```
TListBox(TWindow* parent,
         int      id,
         int      x,
         int      y,
         int      w,
         int      h,
         TModule* module = 0 );
TListBox(TWindow* parent, int resourceId, TModule* module = 0);
```

Notice that the TListBox class constructor looks very much like the other controls descended from TControl (such as TEdit, TButton, and so on). You specify the control's parent window, its control ID, and its dimensions within that window, or you specify its id in the dialog box as loaded from a resource file.

Example

```
TListBox* pFiles = new TListBox(this, IDL_FILES, 10, 10, 75, 250);
TListBox* pFolders = new TListBox(this, IDL_FOLDERS);
```

Along with the regular WS_XXX styles, the list box makes use of the special LBS_XXX styles (see Table 16.1). The TListBox class, by default, sets the LBS_STANDARD style. This is equivalent to the WS_BORDER, WS_VSCROLL, LBS_SORT, and LBS_NOTIFY styles. You can remove the LBS_SORT style from the list box controls to maintain a list of items that is not automatically sorted. Such a list enables you to maintain items in a chronological fashion. You also can use this type of list to maintain the items sorted in descending order (you are responsible for maintaining the list items in that order). Removing the WS_VSCROLL style gives you a list box without the vertical scroll bar. The next section presents a demonstration program that uses this type of list box to implement the synchronized scrolling of multiple list boxes.

Table 16.1. List box control styles.

Style	Meaning
LBS_DISABLENOSCROLL	Specifies that the list box is to always have a scroll bar that is gray when there is nothing to scroll. Normally, the scroll bar disappears when not needed.
LBS_EXTENDEDSEL	Allows the extension of multiple-selections in the list box by using the Shift key.
LBS_HASSTRINGS	Used in owner-drawn list boxes to have the control maintain a copy of the strings added.
LBS_MULTICOLUMN	Designates a multicolumn list box that scrolls horizontally.
LBS_MULTIPLESEL	Supports multiple selections in a list box.

continues

Table 16.1. continued

Style	Meaning
LBS_NOINTEGRALHEIGHT	Allows showing parts of an item if it doesn't fit within the displayed portion of the list box.
LBS_NOREDRAW	Prevents the list box from being updated when the selection is changed. (You can use the SetRedraw member function to change this at will.)
LBS_NOTIFY	Notifies the parent window when you click or double-click in the list box.
LBS_OWNERDRAWFIXED	Used to specify an owner-drawn list box (a list box for which the application is responsible for drawing, instead of the automatic Windows functions). Specifies that the list box items all will be the same height.
LBS_OWNERDRAWVARIABLE	Specifies an owner-drawn list box that contains items of differing heights.
LBS_SORT	Specifies that the items inserted in the list box be automatically sorted in ascending alphanumeric order.
LBS_STANDARD	Sets the WS_BORDER, WS_VSCROLL, LBS_SORT, and LBS_NOTIFY styles.
LBS_USETABSTOPS	Allows the tab character to be expanded within the list box control.
LBS_WANTKEYBOARDINPUT	Permits the list box owner to receive WM_VKEYTOITEM or WM_CHARTOITEM messages when a key is pressed while the list box has the focus (allows the application to manipulate the items in the list box).

The TListBox class enables you to refer to the items in a list box by index. The index of the first item is 0. The TListBox class offers the following member functions to set and query ordinary and selected list members:

☐ The AddString member function adds a string to the list box.

☐ The DeleteString member function removes a list member from a specified position.

☐ The parameterless ClearList member function clears the list of strings in the list box control in one swoop. This function serves to reset the contents of a list box before building up a new list.

☐ The FindExactString and FindString member functions perform case-insensitive searches for items in the list box. The first searches the list box for an exact match to a string, whereas the second searches for a list box entry that begins with a string.

- [ ] The parameterless GetCount member function returns the number of items in the list box. The function returns a negative number if there is an error.

- [ ] The parameterless GetSelIndex member function returns the position of the selected item in a single-selection list box. If there is no selected item, the function yields a negative value. This function is aimed at single-selection list boxes only.

- [ ] The GetSel member function returns the selection state of a list box item, specified by an index.

- [ ] The parameterless GetSelCount member function returns the number of selected items in the list box. For single-selection list boxes, the number will be either 0 or 1.

- [ ] The GetSelIndexes member function returns the number and positions of the selected items in a multiple-selection list box.

- [ ] The GetString member function obtains an item in a list box by specifying its index.

- [ ] The GetStringLen member function returns the length of a list item specified by its position in the list.

- [ ] The GetTopIndex member function returns the index of the first visible list box item.

- [ ] The InsertString member function inserts a string in a list box.

- [ ] The SetSelString member function selects a list box item that matches a search string.

- [ ] The SetSelItemRange member function enables you to select a range of items in one call.

- [ ] The SetSelIndex member function chooses a list item as the new selection in a single-selection list box.

- [ ] The SetSel member function makes or clears a selection in a multiple-selection list box.

- [ ] The SetTopIndex member function selects the list box entry that becomes the first visible item in the list box control.

- [ ] The DirectoryList member function is a special member function that enables you to automatically insert filenames in a list box.

Note: Many of the TListBox functions return either LB_ERR or LB_ERRSPACE. Note that both of these values are negative, so just checking a return value to see if it's less than 0 is often enough.

The *AddString* Function

The declaration of the AddString member function is

```
int AddString(const char far* str);
```

The str parameter is the pointer to the added string. The function returns the position of the added string in the control. If there is any error in adding the string, the function yields an LB_ERR or LB_ERRSPACE value (out-of-memory error). If the LBS_SORT style is set, then the string is inserted so that the list order is maintained. If the LBS_SORT style is not set, then the added string is inserted at the end of the list.

Example

```
pList->AddString("MS-DOS");
```

The *DeleteString* Function

The declaration of the DeleteString member function is

```
int DeleteString(int index);
```

The index parameter specifies the position of the item to delete. The function returns the number of remaining list members. If errors occur, then DeleteString yields the value LB_ERR.

Example

```
pList->DeleteString(0); //Deletes item 0
```

The *FindExactString* and *FindString* Functions

The declarations of the FindExactString and FindString functions are

```
int FindExactString(const char far* str, int searchIndex) const;
int FindString(const char far* str, int searchIndex) const;
```

In both cases, the searchIndex parameter specifies the index of the first list box member to be searched, and the str parameter is the pointer to the searched string. The functions search the entire list, beginning with position searchIndex and resuming at the beginning of the list, if needed. The search stops when either a list member matches the search string or the entire list is searched. Passing an argument of 1 to searchIndex forces the functions to start searching from the beginning. The functions return the position of the matching list item, or they yield the LB_ERR value if no match is found or when an error occurs.

The difference between the two functions is that, although FindExactString looks for an exact match of the parameter str to an entry in the list box, FindString will stop as soon as it finds an entry that begins with str.

Example

```
int msdos = pList->FindString("MS-DOS", -1);
int anti = pList->FindString("anti", -1);
```

> **Note:** The interesting search method used by `FindExactString` and `FindString` enables you to speed up the search by specifying a position that comes closely before the most likely location for a match. For example, if you happen to know where the first item starting with an s is located, and you're searching for something that begins with the same character, you can specify that initial index in an attempt to speed up the search.
>
> The beauty of this method is that if you specify a position that actually is beyond that of the string you seek, you cannot miss finding that string because the function resumes searching at the beginning of the list. Another benefit of `FindExactString` and `FindString` is their capability to find duplicate strings.

16

The *GetSel* Function

The declaration of the function `GetSel` is

```
bool GetSel(int index) const;
```

The `index` parameter specifies the index of the queried list box item. The function returns a `TRUE` if the item is selected, `FALSE` if the item is not selected.

Example

```
pList->SetSel(0, !pList->GetSel(0)); //toggles sel state of item 0
```

The *GetSelIndexes* Function

The declaration of the `GetSelIndexes` function is

```
int GetSelIndexes(int* indexes, int maxCount) const;
```

The `maxCount` parameter specifies the size of the array accessed by the `indexes` pointer. The `indexes` parameter is the pointer to an array of integers that stores the positions of the selected items. The function returns the current number of selections. The function yields `LB_ERR` with single-selection list boxes.

Example

```
int num_items = pList->GetSelCount();
int* items = new int[num_items];
pList->GetSelIndexes(items, num_items);
```

Syntax

The *GetString* Function

The declaration for the GetString function is

```
int GetString(char far* str, int index) const;
```

The index parameter specifies the index of the retrieved item. The first list box item has the index of 0. The str parameter points to a buffer that receives the retrieved item.

You are responsible for ensuring that the buffer has enough space for the retrieved item (for example, using GetStringLen when allocating a receiving buffer). The function returns the number of characters retrieved from the list box.

Example

```
char* s = NULL;
int size = pList->GetStringLen(ix);
if ((size > 0) && (NULL != (s = new char[size + 1])))
    pList->GetString(s, ix);
```

Syntax

The *GetStringLen* Function

The declaration of the GetStringLen function is

```
int GetStringLen(int index) const;
```

The parameter index specifies the index of the target list item. The function returns the length of the target item, or the LB_ERR result if an error occurs.

Example

See the example for GetString.

Syntax

The *InsertString* Function

The declaration of the InsertString function is

```
int InsertString(const char far* str, int index);
```

The index parameter specifies the requested insertion position. The str parameter is the pointer to the inserted string. The function returns the actual insertion position, or it yields the LB_ERR value if an error occurs. If the argument for index is 1, then the string is simply appended to the end of the list.

Example

```
pList->InsertString("Windows", 0);
```

Warning: In general, do not use the `InsertString` member function with list boxes that have the `LBS_SORT` style set. Using this function with ordered list boxes will most likely corrupt the sort order of the list.

The *SetSelString* Function

The declaration of the `SetSelString` function is

```
int SetSelString(const char far* str, int searchIndex);
```

The parameters and search mechanism of `SetSelString` are identical to those of `FindString`. The difference is that `SetSelString` selects the list box item that matches the string accessed by parameter `str`.

Example

```
int ix = pList->SetSelString("MS-DOS", -1);
```

The *SetSelItemRange* Function

The declaration of the `SetSelItemRange` function is

```
int SetSelItemRange(bool select, int first, int last);
```

The `select` parameter acts as a switch used to select or deselect the range of list box items defined by parameters of `first` and `last`. The number returned is the number of items actually selected between and including `first` and `last`.

Example

```
pList->SetSelItemRange(TRUE, 0, 10);
```

The *SetSelIndex* Function

The declaration of the `SetSelIndex` function is

```
int SetSelIndex(int index);
```

The parameter `index` specifies the position of the new selection. To clear a list box from any selection, pass a 1 argument as the `select` parameter. The function returns `LB_ERR` if an error occurs. This is used for single-selection list boxes.

Example

```
pList-SetSelIndex(-1);        // clear current selection
```

451

Syntax

The *SetSel* Function

The declaration of the `SetSel` function is

```
int SetSel(int index, bool select);
```

The `index` parameter specifies the list box item to either select, if `select` is `TRUE`, or deselect, if `select` is `FALSE`. The function returns `LB_ERR` if an error occurs. The function result serves only to flag a selection/deselection error. You can use the `SetSel` function to toggle the selection of multiple items in a multiple-selection list box, one at a time.

Example

```
pList->SetSel(0, TRUE);        // select first item in list
```

Syntax

The *SetTopIndex* Function

The declaration of the function `SetTopIndex` is

```
int SetTopIndex(int index);
```

The `index` parameter specifies the index of the list box item that becomes the first visible item. This selection scrolls the list box, unless the item `index` is already the first visible item. The function returns `LB_ERR` if an error occurs. Otherwise, the result is meaningless.

Example

```
pList->SetTopIndex(10);
```

Syntax

The *DirectoryList* Function

The declaration of the `DirectoryList` function is

```
int DirectoryList(uint attrs, const char far* fileSpec);
```

The `attrs` parameter specifies the combination of attributes, as shown in Table 16.2. The table also shows the equivalent file attribute constants that are declared in the DOS.H header file. The `fileSpec` parameter is the pointer to the filename specification, such as `*.*`, `L*.EXE`, or `A???.CPP`. The return value is the number of files added to the list box.

Example

```
int numFiles = pList->DirectoryList(DDL_ARCHIVE, "CTL*.CPP");
```

Table 16.2. Attributes for the `attrs` parameter in the `TListbox::DirectoryList` member function.

Attribute Value	Equivalent Constant in DOS.H Header File	Meaning
DDL_READWRITE	FA_NORMAL or _A_NORMAL	File can be used for input and output.
DDL_READONLY	FA_RDONLY or _A_RDONLY	File is read only.
DDL_HIDDEN	FA_HIDDEN or _A_HIDDEN	File is hidden.
DDL_SYSTEM	FA_SYSTEM or _A_SYSTEM	File is system file.
DDL_DIRECTORY	FA_DIREC or _A_SUBDIR	Name indicated by parameter `fileSpec` also supplies the directory.
DDL_ARCHIVE	FA_ARCH or _A_ARCH	File has the archive bit set.
DDL_POSTMSGS		Posts messages to the application instead of sending them directly to the list box.
DDL_DRIVES		Includes all the drives that match the filename supplied by `fileSpec`.
DDL_EXCLUSIVE		Exclusive flag (prevents normal files from being included with specified files).

Note that in the preceding table, there are two constants defined in the DOS.H header file for each item. The first is the value defined by Borland. The second is the one defined for the Microsoft compiler. Borland defines these to help with compatibility to make programs more easily portable between the two compilers.

Responding to List Box Notification Messages

The list box control emits various types of messages, as shown in Table 16.3. The table also shows the message-mapping macros that are associated with the various command and notification messages. Each type of command or notification message requires a separate member function declared in the control's parent window class.

Table 16.3. List box notification messages.

Message	Macro	Meaning
WM_COMMAND	EV_COMMAND	The Windows command message through which all the LBN_*xxx* sub-commands are passed; they're specified in the wParam parameter.
LBN_DBLCLK	EV_LBN_DBLCLK	A list item is selected with a mouse double-click.
LBN_ERRSPACE	EV_LBN_ERRSPACE	The list box cannot allocate more dynamic memory to accommodate new list items.
LBN_KILLFOCUS	EV_LBN_KILLFOCUS	The list box has lost focus.
LBN_SELCHANGE	EV_LBN_SELCHANGE	A list item is selected with a mouse click.
LBN_SETFOCUS	EV_LBN_SETFOCUS	The list box has gained focus.

The List Manipulation Tester

The next program demonstrates how to set and query normal and selected strings, and how to set and query the current selection in a single-selection list box—a simple list manipulation tester. This program focuses on illustrating how to use most of the TListBox member functions presented earlier in this section. The program contains the following controls that offer the indicated test features:

- [ ] A list box control
- [ ] A String Box edit control that enables you to type in and retrieve a list member
- [ ] An Index Box edit control that enables you to key in and retrieve the position of the current selection
- [ ] An Add String pushbutton to add the contents of the String Box to the list box (the program does not enable you to add duplicate names, and, if you attempt to do so, the program displays a warning message)
- [ ] A Delete String pushbutton to delete the current selection in the list box (the program automatically selects another list member)
- [ ] The Get Selected String pushbutton that copies the current list selection to the String Box
- [ ] The Set Selected String pushbutton that overwrites the current selection with the string in the String Box
- [ ] The Get Selected Index pushbutton that writes the position of the current selection in the Index Box
- [ ] The Set Selected Index pushbutton that uses the integer value in the Index Box as the position of the new list box selection

☐ The Get String button that copies the string whose position appears in the Index Box into the String Box

☐ The Exit pushbutton

These controls exercise various aspects of manipulating a sorted list box and its members. The program is coded to retain a current selection and to prevent the insertion of duplicate names.

Listings 16.1, 16.2, and 16.3 show the header file CTLLST.H, the script for the CTLLST.RC resource file, and the source code for the CTLLST.CPP program file, respectively. The resource file contains a single-item menu resource.

Create the directory CTLLST as a subdirectory of TCWIN45\TC21DAY and store all the project's files in the new directory. The project's IDE file should contain the files CTLLST.CPP and the CTLLST.RC.

Compile and run the program. When the program starts running, it places a set of names in the list box. Experiment with the various pushbutton controls to add, delete, and obtain strings. The program is straightforward and easy to run.

Listing 16.1. Source code for the CTLLST.H header file.

```
 1: #define IDL_STRINGS      101
 2: #define IDE_STRING       102
 3: #define IDE_INDEX        103
 4: #define IDB_ADD          104
 5: #define IDB_DEL          105
 6: #define IDB_GETSELSTR    106
 7: #define IDB_SETSELSTR    107
 8: #define IDB_GETSELIDX    108
 9: #define IDB_SETSELIDX    109
10: #define IDB_GETSTR       110
11: #define IDB_EXIT         111
```

Listing 16.2. Script for the CTLLST.RC resource file.

```
 1:    #include <windows.h>
 2:    #include <owl\window.rh>
 3:    #include "ctllst.h"
 4:
 5:    EXITMENU MENU LOADONCALL MOVEABLE PURE DISCARDABLE
 6:    BEGIN
 7:       MENUITEM "E&xit", CM_EXIT
 8:    END
 9:
10:       CTLLST DIALOG 7, 18, 288, 209
11:    STYLE DS_MODALFRAME ¦ WS_POPUP ¦ WS_VISIBLE ¦ WS_CAPTION ¦ WS_SYSMENU
12:    CAPTION "Simple List Box Tester Application"
13:    FONT 8, "MS Sans Serif"
14:    {
15:    LTEXT "List Box", -1, 10, 20, 60, 8
```

Listing 16.2. continued

```
16:    LISTBOX IDL_STRINGS, 10, 31, 74, 137, LBS_STANDARD
17:    LTEXT "String Box", -1, 100, 20, 60, 8
18:    EDITTEXT IDE_STRING, 100, 31, 180, 12
19:    LTEXT "Index Box", -1, 100, 63, 62, 8
20:    EDITTEXT IDE_INDEX, 100, 74, 180, 12
21:    PUSHBUTTON "Add String", IDB_ADD, 100, 111, 80, 14
22:    PUSHBUTTON "Delete String", IDB_DEL, 100, 136, 80, 14
23:    PUSHBUTTON "Get Selected String", IDB_GETSELSTR, 100, 161, 80, 14
24:    PUSHBUTTON "Set Selected String", IDB_SETSELSTR, 100, 186, 80, 14
25:    PUSHBUTTON "Get Selected Index", IDB_GETSELIDX, 200, 111, 80, 14
26:    PUSHBUTTON "Set Selected Index", IDB_SETSELIDX, 200, 136, 80, 14
27:    PUSHBUTTON "Get String by Index", IDB_GETSTR, 200, 161, 80, 14
28:    PUSHBUTTON "Exit", IDB_EXIT, 200, 186, 80, 14
29: }
```

Type

Listing 16.3. Source code for the CTLLST.CPP program file.

```
1:     #include <stdio.h>
2:     #include <owl\applicat.h>
3:     #include <owl\button.h>
4:     #include <owl\dialog.h>
5:     #include <owl\edit.h>
6:     #include <owl\framewin.h>
7:     #include <owl\listbox.h>
8:     #include <owl\static.h>
9:     #include <owl\window.h>
10:    #include <owl\window.rh>
11:
12:    #include "ctllst.h"
13:
14:    class TMyDialog : public TDialog
15:    {
16:    public:
17:        TMyDialog(TWindow* parent = 0, TModule* module = 0);
18:        virtual ~TMyDialog();
19:
20:    protected:
21:        virtual void SetupWindow();
22:
23:        void CbAdd();
24:        void CbDel();
25:        void CbGetSelStr();
26:        void CbSetSelStr();
27:        void CbGetSelIdx();
28:        void CbSetSelIdx();
29:        void CbGetStr();
30:        void CmExit();
31:
32:    private:
33:        TListBox *list;
34:        TEdit *strbox, *idxbox;
35:
36:        DECLARE_RESPONSE_TABLE(TMyDialog);
37:    };
```

```
38:    DEFINE_RESPONSE_TABLE1(TMyDialog, TDialog)
39:      EV_COMMAND(CM_EXIT, CmExit),
40:      EV_BN_CLICKED(IDB_ADD, CbAdd),
41:      EV_BN_CLICKED(IDB_DEL, CbDel),
42:      EV_BN_CLICKED(IDB_GETSELSTR, CbGetSelStr),
43:      EV_BN_CLICKED(IDB_SETSELSTR, CbSetSelStr),
44:      EV_BN_CLICKED(IDB_GETSELIDX, CbGetSelIdx),
45:      EV_BN_CLICKED(IDB_SETSELIDX, CbSetSelIdx),
46:      EV_BN_CLICKED(IDB_GETSTR, CbGetStr),
47:      EV_BN_CLICKED(IDB_EXIT, CmExit),
48:    END_RESPONSE_TABLE;
49:
50:    TMyDialog::TMyDialog(TWindow* parent, TModule* module)
51:      : TDialog(parent, "CTLLST", module)
52:    {
53:      list = new TListBox(this, IDL_STRINGS);
54:      strbox = new TEdit(this, IDE_STRING);
55:      idxbox = new TEdit(this, IDE_INDEX);
56:    }
57:
58:    TMyDialog::~TMyDialog()
59:    {
60:    }
61:
62:    void TMyDialog::SetupWindow()
63:    {
64:      TDialog::SetupWindow();     // Initialize the visual element
65:
66:      // Initialize the list box with some data and
67:      // select the second item
68:      //
69:      if (list)
70:          {
71:          list->AddString("Keith");
72:          list->AddString("Kevin");
73:          list->AddString("Ingrid");
74:          list->AddString("Roger");
75:          list->AddString("Rick");
76:          list->AddString("Beth");
77:          list->AddString("Kate");
78:          list->AddString("James");
79:          list->SetSelIndex(1);
80:          }
81:    }
82:
83:    void TMyDialog::CbAdd()
84:    {
85:      if (strbox && list)
86:          {
87:          char* str;
88:          int size = strbox->GetWindowTextLength() + 1;
89:          if ((size > 1) && (NULL != (str = new char[size])))
90:              {
91:              strbox->GetWindowText(str, size);
92:              if (list->FindExactString(str, -1) >= 0)
93:                  MessageBox("Cannot add duplicate names", "Bad Data");
94:              else
```

Listing 16.3. continued

```
 95:                    {
 96:                    int ix = list->AddString(str);
 97:                    list->SetSelIndex(ix);
 98:                    }
 99:                delete str;
100:                }
101:            }
102:    }
103:
104:    void TMyDialog::CbDel()
105:    {
106:        if (list)
107:            {
108:            int ix = list->GetSelIndex();
109:            list->DeleteString(ix);
110:            list->SetSelIndex((ix > 0) ? (ix - 1) : 0);
111:            }
112:    }
113:
114:    void TMyDialog::CbGetSelStr()
115:    {
116:        if (list && strbox)
117:            {
118:            char* str;
119:            int ix = list->GetSelIndex();
120:            if (ix >= 0)
121:                {
122:                if (NULL != (str = new char[list->GetStringLen(ix) + 1]))
123:                    {
124:                    list->GetString(str, ix);
125:                    strbox->SetWindowText(str);
126:                    delete str;
127:                    }
128:                }
129:            }
130:    }
131:
132:    void TMyDialog::CbSetSelStr()
133:    {
134:        if (list && strbox)
135:            {
136:            int ix = list->GetSelIndex();
137:
138:            char* str;
139:            int size = strbox->GetWindowTextLength() + 1;
140:            if ((size > 1) && (NULL != (str = new char[size])))
141:                {
142:                strbox->GetWindowText(str, size);
143:                if (list->FindExactString(str, -1) >= 0)
144:                    MessageBox("Cannot add duplicate names", "Bad Data");
145:                else
146:                    {
147:                    list->DeleteString(ix);
148:                    ix = list->AddString(str);
149:                    list->SetSelIndex(ix);
```

```
150:                    }
151:                delete str;
152:                }
153:            }
154:    }
155:
156:    void TMyDialog::CbGetSelIdx()
157:    {
158:        if (list && idxbox)
159:            {
160:            char str[15];
161:            sprintf(str, "%d", list->GetSelIndex());
162:            idxbox->SetWindowText(str);
163:            }
164:    }
165:
166:    void TMyDialog::CbSetSelIdx()
167:    {
168:        if (list && idxbox)
169:            {
170:            char* str;
171:            int size = idxbox->GetWindowTextLength() + 1;
172:            if ((size > 1) && (NULL != (str = new char[size])))
173:                {
174:                idxbox->GetWindowText(str, size);
175:                list->SetSelIndex(atoi(str));
176:                delete str;
177:                }
178:            }
179:    }
180:
181:    void TMyDialog::CbGetStr()
182:    {
183:        if (list && idxbox && strbox)
184:            {
185:            char* str;
186:            int ix = -1;
187:            int size = idxbox->GetWindowTextLength() + 1;
188:            if ((size > 1) && (NULL != (str = new char[size])))
189:                {
190:                idxbox->GetWindowText(str, size);
191:                ix = atoi(str);
192:                delete str;
193:                }
194:            if ((ix >= 0) && (NULL != (str = new char[list->GetStringLen(ix) +
              ➡ 1])))
195:                {
196:                list->GetString(str, ix);
197:                strbox->SetWindowText(str);
198:                delete str;
199:                }
200:            }
201:    }
202:
203:    void TMyDialog::CmExit()
204:    {
```

continues

Listing 16.3. continued

```
205:        SendMessage(WM_CLOSE);
206:    }
207:
208:    class TListApp : public TApplication
209:    {
210:    public:
211:        TListApp() : TApplication()
212:            { nCmdShow = SW_SHOWMAXIMIZED; }
213:
214:        void InitMainWindow()
215:            {
216:            SetMainWindow(new TFrameWindow(  0,
217:                    "Simple List Box Tester Application",
218:                    new TMyDialog ));
219:            GetMainWindow()->AssignMenu("EXITMENU");
220:            }
221:    };
222:
223:    int OwlMain(int, char *[])
224:    {
225:        return TListApp().Run();
226:    }
```

Output Figure 16.1 shows a sample session with the CTLLST.EXE application.

Figure 16.1.
A sample session with the CTLLST.EXE application.

The program in Listing 16.3 declares the dialog class TMyDialog, starting on line 14, which contains a number of data members that are pointers to the controls owned by the main dialog. The class also declares a SetupWindow member function and several member functions that respond to the notification messages emitted by the various pushbutton controls.

The TMyDialog constructor, starting on line 50, performs the creation of interface elements that can connect with the resources loaded in the dialog box. Then the SetupWindow member function initializes the list box, starting on line 62.

The member function CbAdd, starting on line 83, adds the string of the String Box in the list box control. The function performs the following tasks:

- [ ] Ensures that the list box and edit box were created properly on line 85.
- [ ] If the String Box edit control isn't empty, then the function creates room for copying the contents of the edit control and then places those contents in the str variable on lines 87 through 91.
- [ ] Verifies that the added string does not already exist in the list box, using the FindExactString function on line 92 to detect an attempt to add duplicate strings, and complains with a message box on line 93 if a duplicate is found.
- [ ] Adds the string in str to the list box and assigns the position of the string to the local variable ix using the AddString function on line 96.
- [ ] Makes the added string the current selection by invoking the SetSelIndex function with the argument ix on line 97.

The member function CbDel, starting on line 104, deletes the current selection by carrying out the following tasks:

- [ ] After ensuring the list pointer was created properly on line 106, obtains the position of the current selection by invoking the GetSelIndex function on line 108, and stores the selection position in the local variable ix
- [ ] Deletes the selection by calling the DeleteString function and supplying it the argument ix on line 109
- [ ] Selects another list item on line 110 as the new selection at position ix - 1 (if the variable ix already contains 0, the new first list item becomes the new selection)

The member function CbGetSelStr starting on line 114 copies the current selection to the String Box edit control. The function performs the following tasks:

- [ ] Creates room for and copies the contents of the list box's current selection using the GetSelIndex, GetStringLen, and GetString functions on lines 118 through 124
- [ ] Overwrites the contents of the String Box with the characters retrieved from the list box on line 125

The member function CbSetSelStr, starting on line 132, overwrites the current selection with the string in the String Box edit control. Because the list maintains sorted items, the replacement string likely has a different position from the original selection. The function performs the following tasks:

- [ ] Obtains the position of the current selection, using the GetSelIndex function, and assigns that value to the local variable ix on line 136.

☐ Copies the text in the String Box to the newly allocated str variable on line 142.

☐ Verifies that the string in str does not already exist in the list box, using the FindExactString function on line 143, displaying a message box if the string already exists on line 144.

☐ If the string is new to the list, then the function uses the DeleteString function to delete the current selection on line 147, uses the AddString function to add the string on line 198, and then uses SetSelIndex to select the added string on line 149.

If the string has a matching list item, the function displays a message informing you that you cannot add duplicate strings in the list box. This warning also appears if you attempt to overwrite the current selection with the same string.

The member function CbGetSelIdx, starting on line 156, writes the position of the current selection to the Index Box edit box on line 162. The function uses the GetSelIndex function to obtain the sought position on line 161.

The member function CbSetSelIdx, starting on line 166, reads the value in the Index Box edit control and uses that value to set the new current selection. The function uses the SetSelIndex function to make the new selection on line 175.

The member function CbGetStr, starting on line 181, enables you to retrieve the list item whose position appears in the Index Box edit control. The function performs the following tasks:

☐ Copies the characters of the Index Box to an allocated string in the str data member on line 190

☐ Converts the string in str to the int-typed local variable ix on line 191

☐ Copies the characters of the list item at position ix to a reallocated str on line 196

☐ Writes the characters of str to the String Box edit control on line 197

Handling Multiple-Selection Lists

This section demonstrates the use of multiple-selection lists and focuses on getting and setting the selection strings and their indices. There are two modes for making multiple selections in a list box. These modes depend on whether you set the LBS_EXTENDEDSEL style when you create a TListBox instance. Setting this style enables you to quickly extend the range of selected items by holding down the Shift key and clicking the mouse. The disadvantage of this style is that you are committed to selecting blocks of contiguous items in the list box manually (that is, using the mouse or cursor keys). Using the SetSel or SetSelItemRange member functions, you can make your program select noncontiguous items. However, this approach requires extra effort on behalf of the application user and a few extra controls. By contrast, if you do not set the LBS_EXTENDEDSEL style, then you can make dispersed selections easily by clicking the mouse button on the individual items that you want to select. The disadvantage of this selection mode is that you must click every item to select it, including neighboring items. Choose the selection mode that you feel best meets the user-interface requirements for your OWL applications.

The Multiple-Selection List Tester

Figure 16.2 shows a sample session with the XFERLIST.EXE application—a program that demonstrates how to query multiple selections in a list box—and also shows the controls used by that application. Following are the controls used by the test program and the operations they support:

□ Two multiple-selection list boxes that have the LBS_MULTIPLESEL style selected, but not the LBS_EXTENDEDSEL style

□ Two pushbuttons, one with the caption "<" and the other with the caption ">", that transfer the selected items of one list box to the other

□ Static text controls that label the list boxes

Figure 16.2.
A sample session with the XFERLIST.EXE application.

The multiple-selection list tester application basically enables the user to transfer the contents of one list box to the other and then back again. Listings 16.4, 16.5, and 16.6 contain the source code for the XFERLIST.H, XFERLIST.RC, and XFERLIST.CPP files, respectively.

Create the directory XFERLIST as a subdirectory of \TCWIN45\TC21DAY and store all the project's files in the new directory. As before, the project's IDE file should contain the files XFERLIST.CPP and XFERLIST.RC.

Compile and run the program. The application initializes the list box with many names. Select a few list items in the Source list box and click the > pushbutton. The selected strings appear in the Destination list box and disappear from the Source list box. Now select a few names in the Destination list box and click the < pushbutton. The names move over to the Source list box. When you have finished experimenting with the program, click the Exit menu item or press Alt+X.

Listing 16.4. Source code for the XFERLIST.H header file.

```
1:  #define IDL_SRC    101
2:  #define IDL_DST    102
3:  #define IDB_TOSRC 103
4:  #define IDB_TODST 104
```

Listing 16.5. Script for the XFERLIST.RC resource file.

```
1:  #include <windows.h>
2:  #include <owl\window.rh>
3:  #include "xferlist.h"
4:
5:  EXITMENU MENU LOADONCALL MOVEABLE PURE DISCARDABLE
6:  BEGIN
7:      MENUITEM "E&xit", CM_EXIT
8:  END
9:
10: XFERLIST DIALOG 6, 15, 219, 170
11: STYLE DS_MODALFRAME ¦ WS_POPUP ¦ WS_VISIBLE ¦ WS_CAPTION ¦ WS_SYSMENU
12: CAPTION "Multiple Selection List Tester"
13: FONT 8, "MS Sans Serif"
14: {
15:   LTEXT "Source", -1, 9, 15, 60, 8
16:   LISTBOX IDL_SRC, 9, 27, 78, 130, LBS_STANDARD ¦ LBS_MULTIPLESEL
17:   PUSHBUTTON "—>", IDB_TODST, 95, 62, 30, 14
18:   PUSHBUTTON "<—", IDB_TOSRC, 95, 92, 30, 14
19:   LTEXT "Destination", -1, 135, 15, 60, 8
20:   LISTBOX IDL_DST, 135, 27, 78, 130, LBS_STANDARD ¦ LBS_MULTIPLESEL
21: }
```

Listing 16.6. Source code for the XFERLIST.CPP program file.

```
0:  #include <owl\applicat.h>
1:  #include <owl\button.h>
2:  #include <owl\dialog.h>
3:  #include <owl\framewin.h>
4:  #include <owl\listbox.h>
5:  #include <owl\static.h>
6:  #include <owl\window.h>
7:  #include <owl\window.rh>
8:
9:  #include "xferlist.h"
10:
11: class TMyDialog : public TDialog
12: {
13: public:
14:     TMyDialog(TWindow* parent = 0, TModule* module = 0);
15:     virtual ~TMyDialog();
16:
17: protected:
18:     virtual void SetupWindow();
```

```
19:
20:     void CbToDst();
21:     void CbToSrc();
22:     void CmExit();
23:
24: private:
25:     TListBox *src, *dst;
26:
27:     void MoveSels(TListBox* src, TListBox* dst);
28:
29:     DECLARE_RESPONSE_TABLE(TMyDialog);
30: };
31: DEFINE_RESPONSE_TABLE1(TMyDialog, TDialog)
32:     EV_COMMAND(CM_EXIT, CmExit),
33:     EV_BN_CLICKED(IDB_TODST, CbToDst),
34:     EV_BN_CLICKED(IDB_TOSRC, CbToSrc),
35: END_RESPONSE_TABLE;
36:
37: TMyDialog::TMyDialog(TWindow* parent, TModule* module)
38:     : TDialog(parent, "XFERLIST", module)
39: {
40:     src = new TListBox(this, IDL_SRC);
41:     dst = new TListBox(this, IDL_DST);
42: }
43:
44: TMyDialog::~TMyDialog()
45: {
46: }
47:
48: void TMyDialog::SetupWindow()
49: {
50:     static char *names[] =
51:         { "Keith", "Bruce", "Kevin", "Bridget", "Kate",
52:           "Kay", "Roger", "Marie", "Kathleen", "Liz",
53:           "Ingrid", "Craig", "George", "Janet", "Gary",
54:           "Helen", "Candace",
55:           NULL };
56:
57:     TWindow::SetupWindow();
58:
59:     if (src)
60:         for (int ix = 0; names[ix]; ++ix)
61:             src->AddString(names[ix]);
62: }
63:
64: void TMyDialog::MoveSels(TListBox* src, TListBox* dst)
65: {
66:     if (src && dst)
67:         {
68:         int *sels, numsels = src->GetSelCount();
69:         if ((numsels > 0) && (NULL != (sels = new int[numsels])))
70:             {
71:             int ix;
72:
73:             src->GetSelIndexes(sels, numsels);
74:             for (ix = 0; ix < numsels; ++ix)
75:                 {
```

Listing 16.6. continued

```
76:                char* str;
77:                int size = src->GetStringLen(sels[ix]) + 1;
78:                if ((size > 1) && (NULL != (str = new char[size])))
79:                    {
80:                    src->GetString(str, sels[ix]);
81:                    dst->AddString(str);
82:                    delete str;
83:                    }
84:                }
85:            for (ix = numsels - 1; ix >= 0; -ix)
86:                src->DeleteString(sels[ix]);
87:
88:            delete sels;
89:            }
90:        }
91: }
92:
93: void TMyDialog::CbToDst()
94: {
95:     MoveSels(src, dst);
96: }
97:
98: void TMyDialog::CbToSrc()
99: {
100:    MoveSels(dst, src);
101: }
102:
103: void TMyDialog::CmExit()
104: {
105:     SendMessage(WM_CLOSE);
106: }
107:
108: class TXferApp : public TApplication
109: {
110: public:
111:     TXferApp() : TApplication()
112:         { nCmdShow = SW_SHOWMAXIMIZED; }
113:
114:     void InitMainWindow()
115:         {
116:         SetMainWindow(new TFrameWindow( 0,
117:                "Multiple Selection List Tester",
118:                new TMyDialog ));
119:         GetMainWindow()->AssignMenu("EXITMENU");
120:         }
121: };
122:
123: int OwlMain(int, char *[])
124: {
125:     return TXferApp().Run();
126: }
```

The program in Listing 16.6 works similarly to the other programs presented so far. It declares an application class TXferApp on line 108 and a dialog class TMyDialog on line 11.

The dialog class creates a couple of interface controls in its constructor and then does its initialization in the SetupWindow member function.

The TMyDialog dialog class declares two data members, src and dst on line 25, which are pointers to class objects of type TListBox. These are used to access the source and destination list boxes after they are created.

The function MoveSels, starting on line 64, is the main workhorse of the program. It does the following:

16

- [ ] It takes two parameters: the source list box src and the destination list box dst.
- [ ] After making sure it was given valid TListBox pointers, it obtains the number of selections from the source list box on line 68 and creates an array to hold those indices on line 69. It then retrieves those indices and stores them in the newly created sels array on line 73.
- [ ] The function iterates through the list of selections on lines 74 through 84 and gets a string for each entry with the GetString function on line 80. It then adds this string to the destination list box with the AddString function on line 81.
- [ ] Finally, the function iterates through the list of selections again, this time backwards, and deletes them from the source list box with the DeleteString function on lines 85 and 86.

Note that when the MoveSels function deletes the selections from the source list box, it does so in reverse order. The reason for this is that, as the function deletes an entry, every item after the now-deleted one in the list box has its index decreased by one. If the function were to delete the strings forwards, then all but the first selection would be incorrect, because the retrieved list became out of sync with the list box itself.

The two functions that respond to the buttons, CbToDst on line 93 and CbToSrc on line 98, both call the MoveSels function, and they both pass the same arguments; however, they each pass them in a different order. By doing this, you can use the MoveSels function for both buttons, but have it move the selections between opposite list boxes as the parameters are switched.

Summary

Today's lesson presented the list box control, which enables an application user to choose from a collection of values. You learned about the following topics:

- [ ] The single-selection list box control provides you with a list of items from which to select. This type of list box enables you to select only one item at a time.
- [ ] The multiple-selection list box enables you to select multiple items in a list box for collective processing. Setting the LBS_EXTENDEDSEL style when you create the list box enables you to quickly extend the range of selected items by holding down the Shift key and clicking the mouse.

Q&A

Q Can the argument for the `fileSpec` parameter in function
`TListBox::DirectoryList` contain multiple wildcards, such as `"*.CPP *.H"`?

A No, the argument list for `fileSpec` is limited to one filename wildcard.

Q Does OWL support intercepting the messages related to the movement of the
thumb box in a list box control?

A Yes, but the standard `ListBox` control doesn't have any default notifications for these
events. You can intercept the `WM_HSCROLL` and `WM_VSCROLL` messages to track the thumb.
You'll learn a bit more about scroll bars on Day 17.

Q What is the general approach to implementing a program with two list boxes
that scroll simultaneously?

A The general approach is to intercept the `WM_HSCROLL` and `WM_VSCROLL` messages in each
list box and then adjust the other accordingly. Again, you learn more about handling
scroll bars on Day 17.

Q Should I use `InsertString` in a list box created with the `LBS_SORT` style?

A No, you shouldn't because the `LBS_SORT` style maintains the list box items in order.
Using `InsertString` corrupts the order in the list box. Instead, use the `AddString`
member function.

Workshop

The Workshop provides quiz questions to help you solidify your understanding of the material
covered and exercises to provide you with experience in using what you've learned. Try to
understand the quiz and exercise answers before continuing on to the next day's lesson. Answers
are provided in Appendix A.

Quiz

1. True or false? The list box notification message `LBN_SETFOCUS` is suitable for optional
   initializing related to selecting a list box control.

2. True or false? The list box notification message `LBN_KILLFOCUS` is suitable for optional
   validation after you deselect a list box control.

3. True or false? The list box enables you to detect only the final selection, using the
   `LBN_KILLFOCUS` notification.

4. True or false? You should use LBN_SELCHANGE with a special flag to detect mouse double-clicks on a list box item.

5. True or false? LBS_STANDARD creates a list box control with unordered items.

Exercise

Modify the XFERLIST program to initialize the source list box with a directory listing, and then have it enable and disable the appropriate pushbuttons depending on whether there is anything selected in the corresponding list boxes.

Scroll Bars, Combo Boxes, and VBX Controls

Day 16 presented list box controls. Today's lesson presents two somewhat similar controls: the scroll bar and the combo box. The scroll bar control enables you to select a numeric value quickly, usually in a wide range of values. The combo box control combines the edit control and the list box, enabling the user to select a value from the list box component or to enter a new value in the edit control part.

Today, you also will learn about the Visual Basic Controls (VBXs). The VBX interface was designed to allow for a standard method of creating custom controls for Visual Basic, allowing third-party vendors to supply interesting, original controls in addition to those supplied by standard Windows. VBXs are wide and varied, and Borland supplies a set of classes to allow the programmer to implement them easily.

You will learn about the following topics:

- The scroll bar control
- The combo box control in its various styles
- VBX controls

The Scroll Bar Control

Windows allows the scroll bar to exist as a separate control as well as to be incorporated in windows, lists, and combo boxes. The scroll bar control appears and behaves much like the scroll bar of a window. The control has a thumb box that keeps track of the current value; when the user clicks and drags the thumb box, the display can be changed with a fine control. This thumb box mechanism is supported by the EvVScroll or EvHScroll member functions. In addition, the scroll bar responds to cursor control keys, such as Home, End, PageUp, and PageDown. This feature is supported by the EvKeyDown member function. The main purpose of the scroll bar control is to enable you to quickly and efficiently select an integer value in a predefined range of values. Windows, for example, uses scroll bars to fine-tune the color palette, the keyboard rate, and the mouse sensitivity.

The *TScrollBar* Class

The ObjectWindows Library offers the TScrollBar class, a descendant of TControl, as the class that models the scroll bar controls. The TScrollBar class declares a class constructor and a number of member functions to set and query the control's current position and range of values.

The class constructors appear similar to all the other classes derived from TControl.

The *TScrollBar* Constructor

The declaration of the TScrollBar constructor is

```
TScrollBar( TWindow* parent,
            int id,
            int x,
            int y,
            int w,
            int h,
            bool isHScrollBar,
            TModule* module = 0 );
TScrollBar(TWindow* parent, int resourceId, TModule* module = 0);
```

As with the other control class constructors, the parent refers to the parent window that contains the control, and id is the identifier used in differentiating the control from others. The x, y, w, and h parameters describe the location and size of the scroll bar control. The isHScrollBar parameter is used to specify in which direction the scroll bar will be. If the parameter is true, then the scroll bar will extend horizontally; false will mean a vertical scroll bar. The resourceId parameter is used to associate the OWL object with a dialog box's interface element.

Note that the type of scroll bar that appears will be the same regardless of the values specified in the w and h parameters. If you specify a width and height for a vertical scroll bar, but specify true for the isHScrollBar parameter, you'll end up with a very oddly shaped horizontal scroll bar. For this reason, the constructor will automatically set either the width or height of the control if the appropriate parameter is set to 0. When creating a horizontal scroll bar, for example, specifying 0 for the h parameter will give the control a standard height.

There are several styles, described in Table 17.1, that can be used to control the display of the scroll bar with respect to the rectangle you define in the constructor. Only two of them, the SBS_HORZ and SBS_VERT styles, are automatically set, depending on the state of the isHScrollBar parameter.

Example

```
TScrollBar* pThermometer = TScrollBar( this,
                                       IDSB_THERMOMETER,
                                       10, 10, 180, 0,
                                       true );
```

Table 17.1. SBS_XXX styles for the scroll bar control.

Value	Meaning
SBS_BOTTOMALIGN	Specifies a style used with SBS_HORZ to align the bottom of the scroll bar with the bottom edge of the rectangle specified in the TScrollBar constructor.
SBS_HORZ	Specifies a horizontal scroll bar whose location, width, and height are specified by the parameters in the constructor, if neither SBS_BOTTOMALIGN nor SBS_TOPALIGN.

continues

Table 17.1. continued

Value	Meaning
SBS_LEFTALIGN	Specifies a style used with the SBS_VERT to align the left edge of the scroll bar with the left edge of the rectangle specified in the constructor.
SBS_RIGHTALIGN	Specifies a style used with SBS_VERT to align the right edge of the scroll bar with the right edge of the rectangle specified in the constructor.
SBS_SIZEBOX	Specifies a size box whose location, width, and height are specified by the parameters in the constructor, if neither one of the next two SBS_XXX styles is specified.
SBS_SIZEBOXBOTTOMRIGHTALIGN	Specifies a style used with SBS_SIZEBOX to align the lower right corner of the size box with the lower right corner of the rectangle specified in the constructor.
SBS_SIZEBOXTOPLEFTALIGN	Specifies a style used with the SBS_SIZEBOX style to align the upper left corner of the size box with the upper left corner of the rectangle specified in the constructor.
SBS_TOPALIGN	Specifies a style used with SBS_HORZ to align the top of the scroll bar with the top edge of the rectangle specified in the constructor.
SBS_VERT	Specifies a vertical scroll bar whose location, width, and height are specified by the parameters in the constructor, if neither SBS_RIGHTALIGN nor SBS_LEFTALIGN is specified.

The TScrollBar class declares a number of member functions. The following are some of the more useful functions:

☐ The first member function that you will most likely use after creating a TScrollBar instance is SetRange. This function enables you to set the range of values for the scroll bar.

☐ The GetRange member function enables you to query the current range of values for the scroll bar.

☐ The parameterless GetPosition member function returns the current position of the thumb box.

☐ The SetPosition member function moves the thumb box to the specified position. You are responsible for ensuring that the new thumb position is within the current scroll bar range.

Syntax

The *SetRange* Function

The declaration of the SetRange function is

```
void SetRange(int min, int max);
```

The arguments for the min and max parameters designate the new range of values for the scroll bar control.

Example

```
pThermometer->SetRange(32,212);      // Freezing to boiling
```

Syntax

The *GetRange* Function

The declaration of the GetRange function is

```
void GetRange(int& min, int& max) const;
```

The parameters min and max are filled in by the GetRange member function with the minimum and maximum of the current range values for the scroll bar control.

Example

```
int freezing, boiling;
pThermometer->GetRange(freezing, boiling);
```

Syntax

The *SetPosition* Function

The declaration of the member function SetPosition is

```
void SetPosition(int thumbPos);
```

The parameter thumbPos specifies the new thumb box position.

Example

```
pThermometer->SetPosition(72);     // a comfortable temp
```

Responding to Scroll Bar Notification Messages

There are several methods by which a program can handle scroll bar notifications. The first is by creating a descendant class of the TScrollBar class, and then overriding the various member functions that are called in response to the SB_XXX notification messages as listed in Day 15's lesson. The following table associates the notification messages with their corresponding TScrollBar member functions:

Table 17.2. SBS_XXX and TScrollBar member functions.

Notification Message	TScrollBar member function
SB_LINEUP	SBLineUp
SB_LINEDOWN	SBLineDown
SB_PAGEUP	SBPageUp
SB_PAGEDOWN	SBPageDown
SB_THUMBPOSITION	SBThumbPosition
SB_THUMBTRACK	SBThumbTrack
SB_TOP	SBTop
SB_BOTTOM	SBBottom

You must remember, however, that when overriding a descendant class's version of a response function, the parent's version must be called first. It is that version that keeps the scroll bar updated. Consider the following example:

```
void TMyScrollBar::SBTop()
{
   TScrollBar::SBTop();     // Make sure our parent gets a chance
   sndPlaySound("TOP.WAV", SND_ASYNC);   // Play a sound
}
```

Another method of responding to scroll bar notification messages is by intercepting the EvHScroll or EvVScroll member functions in the scroll bar's parent class. There, you can interrogate the scroll bar as to its current position and then act accordingly.

```
void TMyWindow::EvVScroll(uint code, uint pos, HWND hwnd)
{
   TWindow::EvVScroll(code, pos, hwnd);  // Give our parent a chance
   int newpos = scrollbar->GetPosition(); // get the updated position
   switch (code)
      {
      case SB_TOP:
         sndPlaySound("TOP.WAV", SND_ASYNC);
         break;
      }
}
```

Finally, if one uses the EV_CHILD_NOTIFY_ALL_CODES macro when defining the response table to assign a function response to the scroll bar's ID, the assigned function will be called for all notification messages coming from the scroll bar. The response function looks and acts similarly to the EvXScroll functions, but in this case it isn't necessary to call the parent's version of the function.

```
DEFINE_RESPONSE_TABLE1(TMyWindow, TWindow)
   EV_CHILD_NOTIFY_ALL_CODES(IDSC_THERMOMETER, EvScrollBar),
END_RESPONSE_TABLE;
```

```
void TMyWindow::EvScrollBar(uint code)
{
   switch (code)
      {
      case SB_TOP:
         sndPlaySound("TOP.WAV", SND_ASYNC);
         break;
      }
}
```

The Count Down Timer

The *count down timer* application contains the following controls:

- ☐ A timer scroll bar control that has a default range of 0 to 60 seconds
- ☐ Two static text controls that label the range of values for the timer scroll bar
- ☐ A static text control to show the current setting of the scroll bar
- ☐ Start and Exit buttons

You can set the number of seconds by using the scroll bar. When you move the scroll bar thumb box, the current thumb position appears in a static box. To trigger the countdown process, click the Start button. During the countdown, the application decrements the number of seconds in the edit box and moves the scroll bar's thumb box upward. When the countdown ends, the program sounds a beep and restores the scroll bar to its starting value.

The countdown timer application illustrates the following scroll bar manipulations:

- ☐ Setting and altering the scroll bar range of values
- ☐ Moving and changing the scroll bar thumb box position (the program illustrates how these tasks are performed internally or with the mouse)
- ☐ Using the scroll bar to supply a value

Listing 17.1 shows the source code for the COUNTDN.H header file, Listing 17.2 shows the source code for the COUNTDN.RC resource file, and Listing 17.3 shows the source code for the COUNTDN.CPP program file.

Listing 17.1. Source code for the COUNTDN.H header file.

```
1:    #define IDB_START    101
2:    #define IDB_EXIT     102
3:    #define IDS_STATUS   103
4:    #define IDSC_TIMER   104
```

Listing 17.2. Source code for the COUNTDN.RC resource file.

```
1: /**************************************************************************
2:
3:
4: COUNTDN.RC
5:
6: produced by Borland Resource Workshop
7:
8:
9: **************************************************************************/
10:
11:        #include "countdn.h"
12:
13:        COUNTDN DIALOG 6, 15, 272, 182
14:        STYLE DS_MODALFRAME | WS_POPUP | WS_VISIBLE | WS_CAPTION | WS_SYSMENU
15:        CAPTION "Count Down Timer"
16:        FONT 8, "MS Sans Serif"
17:        {
18:         RTEXT "Countdown: ", -1, 42, 20, 52, 8
19:         LTEXT "50", IDS_STATUS, 94, 20, 29, 8
20:         PUSHBUTTON "Start", IDB_START, 19, 65, 30, 20
21:         PUSHBUTTON "Exit", IDB_EXIT, 62, 65, 30, 20
22:         SCROLLBAR IDSC_TIMER, 131, 32, 9, 100, SBS_VERT
23:         LTEXT "0", -1, 145, 33, 13, 8
24:         LTEXT "60", -1, 145, 124, 13, 8
25:        }
```

Listing 17.3. Source code for the COUNTDN.CPP program file.

```
0: #include <stdio.h>
1: #include <owl\applicat.h>
2: #include <owl\button.h>
3: #include <owl\dialog.h>
4: #include <owl\framewin.h>
5: #include <owl\scrollba.h>
6: #include <owl\static.h>
7: #include <owl\window.h>
8: #include <owl\window.rh>
9:
10:        #include "countdn.h"
11:
12:        class TMyDialog : public TDialog
13:        {
14:        public:
15:            TMyDialog(TWindow *parent = 0, TModule* module = 0);
16:
17:        protected:
18:            virtual void SetupWindow();
19:
20:            void EvTimerBar(uint code);
21:            void CbStart();
```

```
22:              void CbExit();
23:
24:          private:
25:              TScrollBar  *timerbar;
26:              TStatic     *status;
27:
28:              DECLARE_RESPONSE_TABLE(TMyDialog);
29:          };
30:          DEFINE_RESPONSE_TABLE1(TMyDialog, TDialog)
31:              EV_CHILD_NOTIFY_ALL_CODES(IDSC_TIMER, EvTimerBar),
32:              EV_BN_CLICKED(IDB_START, CbStart),
33:              EV_BN_CLICKED(IDB_EXIT, CbExit),
34:          END_RESPONSE_TABLE;
35:
36:          TMyDialog::TMyDialog(TWindow *parent, TModule* module)
37:              : TDialog(parent, "COUNTDN", module)
38:          {
39:              status = new TStatic(this, IDS_STATUS);
40:              timerbar = new TScrollBar(this, IDSC_TIMER);
41:          }
42:
43:          void TMyDialog::SetupWindow()
44:          {
45:              TWindow::SetupWindow();     // Initialize the visual element
46:
47:              if (timerbar)
48:                  {
49:                  timerbar->SetRange(0, 60);
50:                  timerbar->SetPosition(15);
51:                  EvTimerBar(SB_THUMBPOSITION);
52:                  }
53:          }
54:
55:          void TMyDialog::EvTimerBar(uint /*code*/)
56:          {
57:              if (status)
58:                  {
59:                  char text[25];
60:                  sprintf(text, "%d", timerbar ? timerbar->GetPosition() : 0);
61:                  status->SetText(text);
62:                  }
63:          }
64:
65:          void DelaySecs(DWORD dwSecs)
66:          {
67:              DWORD dwTime = GetTickCount() + (dwSecs * 1000L);
68:              while (GetTickCount() < dwTime)
69:                  /* Just wait a while. */;
70:          }
71:
72:          void TMyDialog::CbStart()
73:          {
74:              if (timerbar)
75:                  {
76:                  // First, let the user know that we're stopping the
77:                  // system for a time.
78:                  //
```

continues

479

Listing 17.3. continued

```
79:                    ::SetCursor(::LoadCursor(NULL, IDC_WAIT));
80:
81:                    int start = timerbar->GetPosition();
82:                    for (int ix = start - 1; ix >= 0; —ix)
83:                        {
84:                        timerbar->SetPosition(ix);
85:                        EvTimerBar(SB_THUMBPOSITION);
86:                        DelaySecs(1);
87:                        }
88:                    timerbar->SetPosition(start);
89:                    EvTimerBar(SB_THUMBPOSITION);
90:                    }
91:            }
92:
93:        void TMyDialog::CbExit()
94:        {
95:            SendMessage(WM_CLOSE);
96:        }
97:
98:        class TCountDownApp : public TApplication
99:        {
100:        public:
101:            TCountDownApp() : TApplication()
102:                { nCmdShow = SW_SHOWMAXIMIZED; }
103:
104:            void InitMainWindow()
105:                {
106:                SetMainWindow(new TFrameWindow(  0,
107:                        "Count Down Timer",
108:                        new TMyDialog ));
109:                }
110:        };
111:
112:        int OwlMain(int, char *[])
113:        {
114:            return TCountDownApp().Run();
115:        }
```

Analysis The interesting parts of the program in Listing 17.3 on line 92 start with the SetupWindow member function starting on line 43. First make sure to call the parent's version to create the actual visual elements. After making sure you can create the timerbar object, its range and position are initialized on lines 49 and 50, and the EvTimerBar member function is called with the parameter SB_THUMBPOSITION on line 51. Although EvTimerBar doesn't actually make use of the parameter it's passed, you should be sure that you send an accurate value, just in case some future version of this program *does* make use of the parameter.

The EvTimerBar member function that starts on line 55 responds to any notification message that might be sent by the scroll bar, as well as the various times it's called explicitly by the program itself. Its sole purpose at this point is to keep the status static text box updated with the current position of the scroll bar.

Figure 17.1 shows a sample session with the COUNTDN.EXE application.

Figure 17.1.

A sample session with the COUNTDN.EXE application.

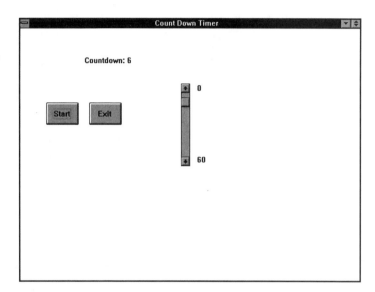

The next function is the nonmember function DelaySecs starting on line 65. This simply sits on its laurels for the number of seconds specified in the dwSecs parameter. It does this by calling the Windows GetTickCount function. This function returns the number of milliseconds elapsed since Windows was started. By multiplying dwSecs by 1000L and then adding that to the result of the GetTickCount call on line 67, you get the end time. From there, all that's needed is a small loop that keeps calling the GetTickCount function as long as its result is less than the end time.

It's the CbStart function that provides the real meat of the program starting on line 72. After ensuring on line 74 that you have a valid pointer to the timerbar object, you set the cursor to the hourglass on line 79. Because you'll be delaying the entire Windows system for the duration of the countdown, it's polite to let the user know that you are taking over for a while by changing the cursor to the hourglass. As soon as you exit the loop and go back to Windows, the cursor will automatically be changed back to the regular arrow. Note the use of the scope modifier on the calls to SetCursor and LoadCursor. This is used to make sure we get the original Windows functions instead of the TWindow member functions, which behave slightly differently.

On line 81 you initialize the start variable with the current position of the scroll bar and start a countdown to 0 from there. As you count down, you set the scroll bar's position, update the static text box, and then call the DelaySecs function on lines 94 through 86. Once the loop is finished, you reset the scroll bar to its original position on line 88 and update the static text control on line 89.

The Combo Box Control

Windows supports the combo box control, which combines an edit box with a list box. Thus, a combo box enables you either to select an item in the list box component (or part, if you prefer) or to enter your own input. In a sense, the list box part of the combo box contains convenient or frequently used selections. A combo box, unlike a list box, does not confine you to choosing items in the list box. There are three types of combo boxes: simple, drop-down, and drop-down list.

NEW☞ TERM The *simple combo box* includes the edit box and the list box that are always displayed. The *drop-down combo box* differs from the simple type by the fact that the list box appears only when you click the down scroll arrow. The *drop-down list combo box* provides a drop-down list that appears when you click the down scroll arrow. There is no edit box in this type of combo box.

Syntax

The *TComboBox* Class

OWL offers the TComboBox class, a descendant of TListBox, to support the combo box controls. The TComboBox class declares a constructor and a rich set of member functions to support both the edit control components, in addition to all the inherited list box member functions.

The declaration of the constructor is

```
TComboBox( TWindow* parent,
           int     id,
           int     x, int y, int w, in h,
           uint32  style,
           uint    textLen,
           TModule* module = 0 );
TComboBox(TWindow* parent, int resourceId, uint testLen, TModule* module = 0);
```

The new parameters to this control class are the style and textLen parameter. The TComboBox control is the only control class whose constructor takes a parameter for specifying the style. This is because it is the one class in which you will most often want to modify the style. These styles are described in Table 17.3, and only the CBS_SORT and CBS_AUTOHSCROLL styles are set automatically; anything else you might want must be passed via the style parameter. The textLen parameter works similarly to the one sent to the TEdit class from Day 13. When the combo box has an edit box at the top, this parameter specifies the text length for that box to be textLen - 1. Specifying 0 for textLen will allow up to 64K of text in the edit box.

Example

```
pcb = new TComboBox(this, 101, 10, 10, 100, 150, CBS_DROPDOWN, 0);
```

The style parameter may include either CBS_SIMPLE for a simple combo box, CBS_DROPDOWN for a drop-down combo box, or CBS_DROPDOWNLIST for a drop-down list combo box.

Table 17.3. Combo box control styles.

Style	Meaning
CBS_AUTOHSCROLL	Automatically scrolls the text in the edit control to the right when you enter a character at the end of the line (removing this style limits the text to the characters that fit inside the rectangular boundary of the edit control).
CBS_DISABLENOSCROLL	Causes the scroll bar of the dropped-down list box portion of the combo box simply to become disabled and gray when scrolling is not allowed. By default, the scroll bar disappears.
CBS_DROPDOWN	Specifies a drop-down combo box.
CBS_DROPDOWNLIST	Specifies a drop-down list combo box.
CBS_HASSTRINGS	When used with an owner-drawn combo box, it causes the strings added to the combo box to be copied internally by the standard Windows routines. This always is the case when Windows does the drawing of the combo box.
CBS_NOINTEGRALHEIGHT	Tells the combo box that its drop-down list box portion need not be truncated to fit the height of its items; partial displays of items may be displayed.
CBS_OEMCONVERT	Allows Windows to convert the character sets as appropriate (useful for filenames).
CBS_OWNERDRAWFIXED	Creates an owner-drawn combo box; the programmer must create routines to display the items in the combo box. All items in the drop-down list box portion will be the same height.
CBS_OWNERDRAWVARIABLE	Exactly the same as CBS_OWNERDRAWFIXED, except the display items may be of differing heights.
CBS_SIMPLE	Specifies a simple combo box.
CBS_SORT	Automatically sorts the items in the list box.

The TComboBox class declares member functions to manage the edit box component and overrides member functions to manage the list box components. Most of these functions are similar to the corresponding members of the TEdit and TListBox classes.

In addition to the inherited TListBox member functions, the TComboBox class declares some extra member functions to handle the drop-down specifics of the combo box control. Among these are the following:

☐ The parameterless `ShowList` and `HideList` functions to drop down and roll up the combo box, respectively. Note that these are just wrapper functions that call the version of the `ShowList` function that takes a `bool` parameter, `ShowList` passing `TRUE` and `HideList` passing `FALSE`.

☐ The `GetDroppedControlRect` member function to obtain the size of the dropped-down control

☐ The parameterless `GetDroppedState` member function that returns a `bool` to tell whether the combo box is currently dropped down

☐ The pair of member functions `GetExtendedUI` and `SetExtendedUI` that get and set the extended user interface for the combo box

The *GetDroppedControlRect* Function

Syntax

The declaration of the `GetDroppedControlRect` function is

```
void GetDroppedControlRect(TRect& Rect) const;
```

When this function is called, the `Rect` parameter is filled with the screen coordinates of the dropped-down list box.

Example

```
TRect rct;
pcb->GetDroppedControlRect(rct);
```

Although the `TComboBox` class isn't directly derived from the `TEdit` class, it has member functions to manipulate the edit control that comes as part of the combo box:

☐ The parameterless `GetTextLen` member function that returns an integer specifying the length of the text in the edit box

☐ The `GetText` and `SetText` member functions for modifying the edit text

☐ The `GetEditSel` and `SetEditSel` member functions that allow the manipulation of the starting and ending character position (that is, the index of the first selected character and the index of the first selected character that is not in the selected text)

☐ The parameterless `Clear` member function that clears the selected text

The *GetText* Function

Syntax

The declaration of the `GetText` function is

```
int GetText(char far* str, int maxChars) const;
```

The parameter `str` is a pointer to a buffer into which `GetText` will copy the contents of the edit box, and `maxChars` is the maximum number of characters to copy (the size of the input buffer).

Example

```
int len = pcb->GetTextLen() + 1;
char* str = new char[len];
if (str)
    pcb->GetText(str, len);
```

Responding to Combo Box Notification Messages

The combo box control emits various types of messages (see Table 17.4). The table also shows the message-mapping macros that are associated with the various command and notification messages. Each type of command or notification message requires a separate member function declared in the control's parent window class.

17

Table 17.4. Combo box notification messages.

Message	Macro	Meaning
CBN_CLOSEUP	EV_CBN_CLOSEUP	The combo box has been closed up.
CBN_DBLCLK	EV_CBN_DBLCLK	A combo item is selected with a mouse double-click.
CBN_DROPDOWN	EV_CBN_DROPDOWN	The combo box has been dropped down.
CBN_EDITCHANGE	EV_CBN_EDITCHANGE	The contents of the edit box are changed.
CBN_EDITUPDATE	EV_CBN_EDITUPDATE	The contents of the edit box are updated.
CBN_ERRSPACE	EV_CBN_ERRSPACE	The combo box cannot allocate more dynamic memory to accommodate new list items.
CBN_KILLFOCUS	EV_CBN_KILLFOCUS	The combo box has lost focus.
CBN_SELCHANGE	EV_CBN_SELCHANGE	A combo item is selected or deselected with a mouse click.
CBN_SELENDCANCEL	EV_CBN_SELENDCANCEL	The user has just selected an item and then selected another control or closed the window.
CBN_SELENDOK	EV_CBN_SELENDOK	The user has just clicked a list item or selected an item and closed the list. This is sent before every CBN_SELCHANGE message.
CBN_SETFOCUS	EV_CBN_SETFOCUS	The combo box has gained focus.

Combo Boxes as History List Boxes

A combo box also can be a history list box. History list boxes typically follow these rules of operation.

☐ The combo list box removes the CBS_SORT style to insert the list items in a chronological fashion. New items are inserted at position 0, pushing the older items farther down the list. The oldest item is the one at the bottom of the list.

☐ History boxes usually have a limit on the number of items you can insert, to prevent bleeding memory. This conservation scheme requires that oldest list items be removed after the number of list items reaches a maximum limit.

☐ If the edit control contains a string that does not have an exact match in the accompanying list box, the edit control string is inserted as a new member at position 0.

☐ If the edit control contains a string that has an exact match in the accompanying list box, the matching list member is moved to position 0, the top of the list. This process involves first deleting the matching list member from its current position and then reinserting it at position 0.

A history list box is really a combo box that manipulates its edit control and list box items in a certain way. There is no need to derive a descendant of TComboBox to add new member functions, although if you use a history list box enough, it might make sense to create a descendant class that automates the functionality. Furthermore, for additional functionality, the descendant class could save the history list to disk for future invocations of the program.

The Son of Mr. Calculator Application

This section presents an updated version of the calculator application—*Son of Mr. Calculator*. This new version adds functionality to Day 13's version by using history combo boxes for the operands and result, instead of the standard edit boxes, and uses a simple combo box that contains the list of supported operators and functions. Figure 17.2 shows a sample session with the CALCJR.EXE application and indicates the controls that are used.

Compile and run the program. Experiment with entering and executing numbers and operators or functions. Notice that combo boxes for the operands and the result fill in their accompanying list boxes in a chronological order. The Operand and Result combo boxes remember the last 30 different operands you entered. In a way, the Result combo box acts as temporary memory.

Listing 17.4 shows the source code for the CALCJR.H header file, Listing 17.5 contains the source code for the CALCJR.RC resource file, and Listing 17.6 contains the source code for the CALCJR.CPP program file. The resource file defines the accelerator keys and menu resources.

Figure 17.2.
A sample session with the CALCJR.EXE application.

17

Type **Listing 17.4. Source code for the CALCJR.H header file.**

```
1:    #define IDB_CALC     101
2:    #define IDB_EXIT     102
3:    #define IDC_OPERAND1 103
4:    #define IDC_OPERATOR 104
5:    #define IDC_OPERAND2 105
6:    #define IDC_RESULT   106
7:    #define IDE_ERRMSG   107
```

Type **Listing 17.5. Source code for the CALCJR.RC resource file.**

```
1: /*****************************************************************************
2:
3:
4: CALCJR.RC
5:
6: produced by Borland Resource Workshop
7:
8:
9: *****************************************************************************/
10:
11:        #include "calcjr.h"
12:
13:        CALCJR DIALOG 6, 19, 326, 205
14:        STYLE DS_MODALFRAME ¦ WS_POPUP ¦ WS_VISIBLE ¦ WS_CAPTION ¦ WS_SYSMENU
15:        CAPTION "Son of Mr. Calculator"
16:        FONT 8, "MS Sans Serif"
17:        {
```

continues

487

Listing 17.5. continued

```
18:          LTEXT "Operand1", -1, 10, 15, 60, 8
19:          LTEXT "Operator", -1, 85, 15, 60, 8
20:          LTEXT "Operand2", -1, 160, 14, 60, 8
21:          LTEXT "Result", -1, 235, 15, 60, 8
22:          COMBOBOX IDC_OPERAND1, 10, 27, 60, 95, CBS_DROPDOWN | WS_TABSTOP
23:          COMBOBOX IDC_OPERATOR, 85, 27, 60, 95, CBS_DROPDOWNLIST | WS_TABSTOP
24:          COMBOBOX IDC_OPERAND2, 160, 26, 60, 95, CBS_DROPDOWN | WS_TABSTOP
25:          COMBOBOX IDC_RESULT, 235, 27, 60, 95, CBS_DROPDOWN | WS_TABSTOP
26:          LTEXT "Error Message", -1, 10, 133, 60, 8
27:          EDITTEXT IDE_ERRMSG, 10, 145, 301, 12
28:          PUSHBUTTON "Calc", IDB_CALC, 10, 169, 50, 15
29:          PUSHBUTTON "Exit", IDB_EXIT, 76, 169, 50, 15
30:        }
```

 Listing 17.6. Source code for the CALCJR.CPP program file.

```
 1: #include <ctype.h>
 2: #include <math.h>
 3: #include <stdio.h>
 4: #include <owl\applicat.h>
 5: #include <owl\button.h>
 6: #include <owl\dialog.h>
 7: #include <owl\combobox.h>
 8: #include <owl\edit.h>
 9: #include <owl\framewin.h>
10:     #include <owl\static.h>
11:     #include <owl\window.h>
12:     #include <owl\window.rh>
13:
14:     #include "calcjr.h"
15:
16:     class THistoryBox : public TComboBox
17:     {
18:     public:
19:        THistoryBox(TWindow* parent,
20:                    int       id,
21:                    int x, int y, int w, int h,
22:                    int       historyLen,
23:                    uint      textLen = 0,
24:                    TModule* module = 0);
25:        THistoryBox(TWindow* parent,
26:                    int       resourceId,
27:                    int       historyLen,
28:                    uint      textLen = 0,
29:                    TModule* module = 0);
30:
31:        void EvKillFocus(HWND);
32:
33:     private:
34:        int history;
35:
36:        DECLARE_RESPONSE_TABLE(THistoryBox);
37:     };
```

```
38:        DEFINE_RESPONSE_TABLE1(THistoryBox, TComboBox)
39:          EV_WM_KILLFOCUS,
40:        END_RESPONSE_TABLE;
41:
42:        THistoryBox::THistoryBox(  TWindow* parent,
43:                                   int      id,
44:                                   int x, int y, int w, int h,
45:                                   int      historyLen,
46:                                   uint     textLen,
47:                                   TModule* module )
48:          : TComboBox(parent, id, x, y, w, h, CBS_DROPDOWN, textLen, module)
49:        {
50:          Attr.Style &= ~CBS_SORT;        // We don't want to sort
51:          history = historyLen;
52:        }
53:
54:        THistoryBox::THistoryBox(TWindow* parent,
55:                                 int      resourceId,
56:                                 int      historyLen,
57:                                 uint     textLen,
58:                                 TModule* module )
59:          : TComboBox(parent, resourceId, textLen, module)
60:        {
61:          Attr.Style |= CBS_DROPDOWN;   // Make sure it's a drop-down
62:          Attr.Style &= ~CBS_SORT;                // We don't want to sort
63:          history = historyLen;
64:        }
65:
66:        void THistoryBox::EvKillFocus(HWND)
67:        {
68:          int len = GetTextLen() + 1;
69:          char* str = new char[len];
70:          if (str)
71:              {
72:              GetText(str, len);
73:              int ix = FindExactString(str, -1);
74:              if (ix < 0)
75:                  {
76:                  InsertString(str, 0);
77:                  while (GetCount() >= history)
78:                      DeleteString(GetCount() - 1);
79:                  }
80:              else if (ix > 0)
81:                  {
82:                  DeleteString(ix);
83:                  InsertString(str, 0);
84:                  SetSelIndex(0);
85:                  }
86:              delete str;
87:              }
88:        }
89:
90:        class TCalcJrDialog : public TDialog
91:        {
92:        public:
93:          TCalcJrDialog(TWindow* parent = 0, TModule* module = 0);
94:
```

continues

489

Listing 17.6. continued

```
95:         protected:
96:             virtual void SetupWindow();
97:
98:             void CmCalc();
99:             void CmExit();
100:
101:        private:
102:            TComboBox    *Operator;
103:            THistoryBox *Operand1, *Operand2, *Result;
104:            TEdit        *ErrMsg;
105:
106:            DECLARE_RESPONSE_TABLE(TCalcJrDialog);
107:        };
108:        DEFINE_RESPONSE_TABLE1(TCalcJrDialog, TDialog)
109:            EV_BN_CLICKED(IDB_CALC, CmCalc),
110:            EV_BN_CLICKED(IDB_EXIT, CmExit),
111:        END_RESPONSE_TABLE;
112:
113:        TCalcJrDialog::TCalcJrDialog(TWindow* parent, TModule* module)
114:            : TDialog(parent, "CALCJR", module)
115:        {
116:            Operand1 = new THistoryBox(this, IDC_OPERAND1, 30);
117:            Operator = new TComboBox(this, IDC_OPERATOR);
118:            Operand2 = new THistoryBox(this, IDC_OPERAND2, 30);
119:            Result = new THistoryBox(this, IDC_RESULT, 30);
120:            ErrMsg = new TEdit(this, IDE_ERRMSG);
121:        }
122:
123:        void TCalcJrDialog::SetupWindow()
124:        {
125:            TWindow::SetupWindow();     // Initialize the visual element
126:
127:            // Fill up out Operator combo box with a variety
128:            // of operators for our users compuational pleasure.
129:            //
130:            if (Operator)
131:                {
132:                static char* p[] =
133:                    { "+", "-", "*", "/", "^", "log", "exp", "sqrt", NULL };
134:                for (int ix = 0; p[ix]; ++ix)
135:                    Operator->AddString(p[ix]);
136:                }
137:
138:            // Keep the users out of the error box.
139:            //
140:            if (ErrMsg)
141:                ErrMsg->SetReadOnly(TRUE);
142:        }
143:
144:        double get_number(TComboBox *numbox)
145:        {
146:            double rslt = 0;          // default to 0
147:            char* str;
148:            int size;
149:
```

```
150:        if (numbox)
151:            {
152:            str = new char[size = numbox->GetTextLen() + 1];
153:            if (str)
154:                {
155:                numbox->GetText(str, size);
156:                rslt = atof(str);
157:                delete str;
158:                }
159:            }
160:        return rslt;
161:    }
162:
163:    void TCalcJrDialog::CmCalc()
164:    {
165:        double x, y, z = 0;
166:
167:        x = get_number(Operand1);
168:        y = get_number(Operand2);
169:
170:        if (Operator)
171:            {
172:            int   ix = Operator->GetSelIndex();
173:            if (ix >= 0)
174:                {
175:                char* err = 0;
176:
177:                switch (ix)
178:                    {
179:                    case 0:     // + operator
180:                        z = x + y;
181:                        break;
182:                    case 1:     // - operator
183:                        z = x - y;
184:                        break;
185:                    case 2:     // * operator
186:                        z = x * y;
187:                        break;
188:                    case 3:     // / operator
189:                        if (y)
190:                            z = x / y;
191:                        else
192:                            err = "Can't divide by zero.";
193:                        break;
194:                    case 4:     // ^ operator
195:                        if (x > 0)
196:                            z = exp(y * log(x));
197:                        else
198:                            err = "Need positive number to raise power.";
199:                        break;
200:                    case 5:     // log function
201:                        if (x > 0)
202:                            z = log(x);
203:                        else
204:                            err = "Need positive number for log.";
205:                        break;
206:                    case 6:     // exp function
```

continues

Listing 17.6. continued

```
207:                        if (x < 230)
208:                            z = exp(x);
209:                        else
210:                            err = "Need a smaller number for exp.";
211:                        break;
212:                    case 7:     // sqrt function
213:                        if (x >= 0)
214:                            z = sqrt(x);
215:                        else
216:                            err = "Can't do sqrt of negative number.";
217:                        break;
218:                    default:
219:                        err = "Unknown operator";
220:                        break;
221:                    }
222:
223:                if (ErrMsg)
224:                    if (!err)
225:                        ErrMsg->Clear();
226:                    else
227:                        ErrMsg->SetWindowText(err);
228:                if (!err && Result)
229:                    {
230:                    char dest[81];
231:                    sprintf(dest, "%g", z);
232:                    Result->SetWindowText(dest);
233:                    Result->EvKillFocus(NULL);    // Force history addition
234:                    }
235:                }
236:            }
237:        }
238:
239:    void TCalcJrDialog::CmExit()
240:    {
241:        SendMessage(WM_CLOSE);
242:    }
243:
244:    class TCalcJrApp : public TApplication
245:    {
246:    public:
247:        TCalcJrApp() : TApplication()
248:            { nCmdShow = SW_SHOWMAXIMIZED; }
249:
250:        void InitMainWindow()
251:            {
252:            SetMainWindow(new TFrameWindow(  0,
253:                    "Son of Mr. Calulator",
254:                    new TCalcJrDialog ));
255:            }
256:    };
257:
258:    int OwlMain(int, char *[])
259:    {
260:        return TCalcJrApp().Run();
261:    }
```

Analysis The program in Listing 17.6 begins by declaring, starting on line 16, a descendant of TComboBox called THistoryBox. This descendant declares its constructors, a single member function, and a single data member. The constructor that creates a brand new control specifies the CBS_DROPDOWN style when calling the parent TComboBox constructor on line 48, and then turns off the CBS_SORT style and initializes the history member data with the historyLen parameter on lines 50 and 51.

The constructor that simply associates the OWL object with the pre-existing dialog control works similarly to the other constructor, except this needs to move the CBS_DROPDOWN setting into the constructor's body, rather than the call to the base class' constructor.

The EvKillFocus member function of THistoryBox that starts on line 66 is called in response to the WM_KILLFOCUS Windows message. At this time, the function inserts the string of the edit control part in the list box part. This insertion occurs only if the string is not already in the list box part. In this case, the string is inserted at index 0 and becomes the new top-of-the-list item. If the targeted string already is in the list box part, then the function deletes the existing item in the list box and reinserts it at index 0. Thus, the targeted string appears to have moved up to the top of the list box part.

The TCalcJrDialog's constructor that starts on line 113 does the usual creation of controls. The SetupWindow member function then initializes the Operator combo box by filling its list box component with the supported operators and functions on lines 130 through 136.

The get_number function, starting on line 144, is used, as in Day 13, to obtain a double value from a control. This time, it receives a TComboBox pointer, gets the contents of its edit box, then uses the atof function to obtain the double value that is returned.

The Calc button causes the CmCalc member function, starting on line 163, to be called. This is the function that does all the following work of the application:

- [ ] Retrieves the values from the Operand1 and Operand2 combo boxes and places their values in the x and y variables, respectively, on lines 167 and 168.
- [ ] Obtains the index of the selected operator in the Operator combo box on line 172.
- [ ] If something is actually selected, a switch statement is used to determine the requested operation or math function, then the case statement performs the requested task and assigns the result to variable z, or sets the err pointer to an appropriate error string.
- [ ] Sets the Error Message edit box if an error occurred or clears that same edit box if no error was detected on lines 223 through 227.
- [ ] If no error occurred, displays the result of the operation or function evaluation in the edit control box of the Result combo box, then calls its EvKillFocus function directly to have that value inserted into its list box component on lines 228 through 234.

VBX Controls

VBX is an acronym for *Visual Basic eXchange* and describes the host of controls written to the Visual Basic control format. The VBX interface is rather complex, but OWL makes it easy to use with support classes that can be mixed in to the standard ones you've been using so far. There really are just a few simple steps to using VBX controls:

☐ Declare an instance of the class `TBIVbxLibrary`. This initializes the VBX subsystem that is required to interface with the VBX controls, and is usually done in the `OwlMain` function.

☐ Use the mixin class `TVbxEventHandler`, multiply inheriting from it and the regular interface class (such as `TWindow` or `TDialog`) and specifying it when defining the response table.

☐ Use the `EV_VBXEVENTNAME` macro when defining a response table for your interface.

☐ Create OWL objects to connect with the VBX interface elements that appear on the screen.

Initializing the VBX Subsystem

The initialization and termination of the VBX subsystem occurs with calls to two simple functions: `VBXInit` and `VBXTerm`. Here is a sample `OwlMain` function in which these functions are called.

```
int OwlMain(int argc, char* argv[])
{
    TBIVbxLibrary vbxLib;
    return TApplication().Run();
}
```

As you can see, there really isn't all that much to it. The `TBIVbxLibrary`'s constructor does the initialization, and its destructor shuts down the system when the program closes.

Using the VBX Mixin Class

Mixin classes are ones that can add functionality to a base class simply by being co-declared as multiply-inherited base class. For example, the following code snippet adds VBX control functionality to a descendent dialog class by simply adding `TVbxEventHandler` to the list of base classes:

```
class MyVbxDialog : public TDialog, public TVbxEventHandler
{
    // ... member functions and data go here ...
DECLARE_RESPONSE_TABLE(MyVbxDialog);
}
```

Defining a VBX Response Table

The response table for a dialog box that uses VBX controls looks very much like the ones you've already created, except for a few additions.

```
DEFINE_RESPONSE_TABLE2(MyVbxDialog, TDialog, TVbxEventHandler)
    // ... other response functions go here ...
    EV_VBX_EVENTNAME(ID_CONTROL1, "DragDrop", EvControl1),
    EV_VBX_EVENTINDEX(ID_CONTROL1, 1, EvControl1),
END_RESPONSE_TABLE;
```

Take careful note of the DEFINE_RESPONSE_TABLE2 line. So far, your response tables have been defined with a 1, but because this is multiply-inherited from two separate classes, you need to specify this when defining the response table by using a 2. (Note that if this were for a TWindow descendant, then TWindow would have been used in place of TDialog.) Then the response table entries themselves use the EV_VBX_EVENTNAME or EV_VBX_EVENTINDEX macros, which have the following basic definitions:

```
EV_VBX_EVENTNAME(controlID, eventName, EvHandler)
EV_VBX_EVENTINDEX(controlID, eventIndex, EvHandler)
```

The controlId parameter is the typical control ID parameter used in defining other response-table entries; it refers to the ID assigned to the control when it's created by Windows, typically the ID used in the resource file describing the dialog in which the control resides. eventName is a string holding the name of the event itself. VBX controls identify their separate events with both indexes and with string labels; these are what belong here. Finally, the EvHandler is the name of the member function to be called whenever the event occurs, much like you've already defined in earlier response tables.

The response function for a VBX event is rather simple and looks like the following:

```
void EvHandler(VBXEVENT far* event);
```

Because the VBX events have so much information associated with them, they're passed in a structure rather than as individual arguments to the function. Here is the definition of the VBXEVENT structure.

```
struct VBXEVENT
{
    HCTL    Control;
    HWND    Window;
    int     ID;
    int     EventIndex;
    LPCSTR  EventName;
    int     NumParams;
    LPVOID  ParamList;
};
```

Following is the breakdown of the various items in the structure:

☐ Control is the handle of the sending VBX control. Be careful not to confuse this with a window control; this is a special handle used to refer to the VBX control alone.

17

☐ Window is a handle to the control window itself.

☐ ID is the ID of the VBX control, the same one defined in the resource file, and so on.

☐ EventIndex is the event index. All VBX controls have their individual events numbered, and this is the number associated with this particular VBX control's event.

☐ EventName is the name of the event. The name is provided, mainly, for the programmer's convenience so the VBX control authors can more easily communicate the purpose of the event.

☐ NumParams is the number of parameters for this event. Each event can have a number of different parameters (VBXEVENT is just a wrapper that describes the event itself) that are encoded in the next structure item.

☐ ParamList is a pointer to an array containing the pointers to the parameter values for this event. The number of parameters is defined by the previous parameter, and they are indexed from 0 to NumParams - 1. You need to know the details of the VBX control itself to be able to identify the types of the parameters. These are supplied by the VBX control vendor.

There are two macros that can be used to access the parameters passed in ParamList. Both of them require the parameters up to the one accessed be the same as the one accessed. Here are the two macros.

```
VBX_EVENTARGNUM(event, type, index)
VBX_EVENTARGSTR(event, index)
```

The event parameter is the same as the one passed to an event handler of the type VBXEVENT far*. The type parameter in the first macro should be the type of the argument to retrieve. index is the 0-based number of the argument. Since strings are such a common item to retrieve, VBX_EVENTARGSTR is provided which already knows the type of argument to access. The types are all based upon Visual Basic types, and have C++ equivalents as shown in Table 17.5.

Table 17.5. VBX argument types.

Basic	C++
Boolean	bool
Control	HCTL
Double	double
Enum	short
Integer	short
Long	long
Single	float
String	HLSTR

Note that the string is referred to as an HLSTR. This is not a standard C++ character array or even a reference to the C++ string class. These are handles to Visual Basic strings, and they need to be accessed with the following special functions:

```
HLSTR   VBXCreateBasicString(LPVOID buffer, USHORT len);
VOID    VBXDestroyBasicString(HLSTR string);
int     VBXGetBasicStringBuf(HLSTR string, LPSTR buffer, int len);
USHORT  VBXGetBasicStringLength(HLSTR string);
ERR     VBXSetBasicString(HLSTR far *string, LPVOID buffer, USHORT len);
```

Based on your previous experiences in this book, I would imagine the functions and how they're used are fairly obvious after reading just the function names. In order, they create strings, destroy them, copy them to a character array, obtain a string's length, and copy a character array into a string. If you need more information, you can check out the online help provided with Turbo C++.

The *TVbxControl* OWL Interface Class

When it finally comes time to instantiate an interface object to communicate with the VBX control, you need to use the TVbxControl class. The following are the two constructors for this object:

```
TVbxControl(TWindow*        parent,
            int             id,
            const char far* vbxName,
            const char far* vbxClass,
            const char far* title,
            int             x,
            int             y,
            int             w,
            int             h,
            long            initLen = 0,
            void far*       initData = 0,
            TModule*        module = 0);
TVbxControl(TWindow* parent, int resourceId, TModule* module = 0);
```

Notice that the second constructor looks just like all the other constructors used to associate an OWL class with a resource control, and that's just exactly what it is. Looking back at the first constructor, you'll see that many of the parameters are the same as those used to create other controls (parent, id, title, x, y, w, h, and module). The vbxName parameter specifies the filename of the VBX control library and the vbxClass parameter specifies the class name of the control (libraries can contain multiple controls, and the class name enables you to select the particular one in which you're interested).

There are two additional parameters towards the end of the list called initLen and initData, both of which have default values of 0. These are used to supply specific information to the VBX control as it is being initialized. This information is control-specific, and its exact makeup needs to be defined by the author of the VBX control.

Unlike the other controls, however, VBX controls have a number of properties which describe their appearance and actions. These properties, like the response functions, are defined by the VBX control author and you will need to consult the documentation for the specific control you want to use.

Once you know which properties you want to manipulate, you can do so with a variety of `GetProp` and `SetProp` functions. There are a substantial number of these overloaded functions, enabling you to access properties of varying types, either by index or name.

> **Note:** As you might have noticed before with the response functions, all VBX controls use both indexes and names together to provide easier access to the programmer.

Here are the general formats of the property manipulation functions.

```
bool GetProp(int propIndex, type& value, int arrayIndex = -1);
bool GetProp(const char far* name, type& value, int arrayIndex = -1);
bool SetProp(int propIndex, type value, int arrayIndex = -1);
bool SetProp(const char far* name, type value, int arrayIndex = -1);
```

Note that I didn't specify a particular type for each of these functions. As stated earlier, these functions are overloaded to accept a number of different types: `int`, `long`, `bool`, `ENUM`, `HPIC`, `float`, `string`, and `COLORREF`. The `arrayIndex` parameter can be used to access different elements of an array property. By default, you access the first property, whether or not there are any more to access.

In addition to the functions for changing the different properties, you can ask the VBX to tell you which properties it contains, and even what the property types are.

```
int GetNumProps();
int GetPropIndex(const char far* name);
void GetPropName(int propIndex, string& str);
int GetPropType(int propIndex);
int GetPropType(char far* name);
bool IsArrayProp(int propIndex);
bool IsArrayProp(char far* name);
```

The `GetNumProps` function returns the number of properties associated with the control, while `GetPropName` will supply the name of the indexed control. `GetPropIndex` will search the control's properties for the supplied name and return the associated index. You can determine a property's type by using the `GetPropType` function. This returns a value that can be checked against one of the macros described in Table 17.6. Checking the `IsArrayProp` function tells you whether or not the specified property is stored as an array.

Table 17.6. VBX Property Types

Property Type	Equivalent C++ Type
PTYPE_CSTRING	HSZ
PTYPE_SHORT	short
PTYPE_LONG	LONG
PTYPE_BOOL	bool
PTYPE_COLOR	DWORD or COLORREF
PTYPE_ENUM	BYTE or ENUM
PTYPE_REAL	float
PTYPE_XPOS	LONG (Twips)
PTYPE_XSIZE	LONG (Twips)
PTYPE_YPOS	LONG (Twips)
PTYPE_YSIZE	LONG (Twips)
PTYPE_PICTURE	HPIC
PTYPE_BSTRING	HLSTR

While this listing of and inquiry of the various properties of a VBX control can be useful, you probably won't have much call for it. Usually you will need to determine the properties beforehand by reading the VBX's documentation and then make use of the properties as described.

Summary

Today's lesson presented the scroll bar and combo box controls. These controls share the common factor of being input objects. You learned about the following topics:

- [ ] The scroll bar control enables you to select quickly from a wide range of integers.
- [ ] There are various types of combo box controls: simple, drop-down, and drop-down list.
- [ ] You can make a history list box out of a drop-down combo box.
- [ ] VBX controls can be easily controlled with OWL classes and, with a few minor differences, can be treated like ordinary Windows controls.

Q&A

Q Do the scroll bars strictly select integers?

A Yes. However, these integers can be indices to arrays, items in list box controls, and other integer codes to various attributes such as colors. Therefore, in a sense, the scroll bar can be used to select nonintegers.

Q Can I create a scroll bar control with an excluded subrange of values?

A No. You may want to use a list box control instead and have that control list the value numbers.

Workshop

The Workshop provides quiz questions to help you solidify your understanding of the material covered and exercises to provide you with experience in using what you've learned. Try to understand the quiz and exercise answers before continuing on to the next day's lesson. Answers are provided in Appendix A.

Quiz

1. True or false? If you do not include the CBS_AUTOHSCROLL style in creating a combo list box, you limit the text to the characters that fit inside the rectangular boundary of the edit control.

2. True or false? You can handle the CBN_SELCHANGE notification message to monitor every keystroke in the edit control of a combo box.

3. True or false? Setting CBS_SORT creates a combo box whose list box items are sorted and unique.

4. True or false? To emulate a history list box, a combo box must be created without the CBS_SORT style.

5. True or false? A history list may have duplicate items.

6. True or false? COUNTDN.CPP demonstrates how to implement a two-way connection between the current value of a scroll bar control and the numeric value in a text box.

7. True or false? The range of values for a scroll bar control are fixed when you create the control.

Exercise

Modify the CALCJR.CPP program by adding a Variables multiline box and a Store pushbutton.

Write a wrapper class to simulate the VBX HLSTR object, allowing programmers to act on it like it was a C++ string.

MDI Windows

The *Multiple Document Interface* (*MDI*) is a standard Windows interface used by many popular Windows applications and utilities, such as the Windows Program Manager, the Windows File Manager, and even the Turbo C++ IDE. The MDI interface also is part of the Common User Access (CUA) standard set by IBM. Each MDI-compliant application enables you to open child windows for file-specific tasks such as editing text, managing a database, or working with a spreadsheet. Today, you will learn the following topics on managing MDI windows and objects:

- [ ] The basic features and components of an MDI-compliant application
- [ ] Basics of building an MDI-compliant application
- [ ] The class `TMDIFrame`
- [ ] The class `TMDIClient`
- [ ] Building MDI client windows
- [ ] The class `TMDIChild`
- [ ] Building MDI child windows
- [ ] Managing messages in an MDI-compliant application

The MDI Application Features and Components

An MDI-compliant application is made up of the following objects:

- [ ] The visible *MDI frame window* that contains all other MDI objects. The MDI frame window is an instance of the class `TMDIFrame` or its descendants. Each MDI application has one MDI frame window.

- [ ] The invisible *MDI client window* that performs underlying management of the MDI child windows that are dynamically created and removed. The MDI client window is an instance of the class `TMDIClient`. Each MDI application has one MDI client window.

- [ ] The dynamic and visible *MDI child window*. An MDI application dynamically creates and removes multiple instances of MDI child windows. An MDI child window is an instance of `TMDIChild` or its descendant. These windows are located, moved, resized, maximized, and minimized inside the area defined by the MDI frame window. At any given time (and while there is at least one MDI child window), there is only one active MDI child window.

When you maximize an MDI child window, it occupies the area defined by the client area of the MDI frame window. When you minimize an MDI child window, the icon of that window appears at the bottom area of the MDI frame window.

> **Note:** The MDI frame window has a menu that manipulates the MDI child windows and their contents. The MDI child windows cannot have a menu, but they may contain controls. In any other respect, you can think of an MDI child window as an instance of TFrameWindow or its descendants.

Basics of Building an MDI Application

Before discussing in more detail the creation of the various components that make up an MDI application, focus on the basic strategy involved. In the last section, you learned that the basic ingredients for an MDI application are the TMDIFrame, TMDIClient, and TMDIChild (or a TMDIChild descendant) classes. The TMDIFrame class supports the creation and handling of the MDI client window as well as menu management.

The MDIClient class focuses on the creation and underlying management of MDI child windows. The TMDIChild class offers the functionality for the MDI child windows.

At this stage you might ask, "Do I typically derive descendants for all three classes to create an MDI application?" The answer is no. You normally need to derive descendants only for the TMDIFrame and TWindow classes. The functionality of the TMDIClient class is adequate for most MDI-compliant applications.

The *TMDIFrame* Class

ObjectWindows offers the TMDIFrame class, a descendant of TFrameWindow, to implement the MDI frame window of an MDI application. The declaration of the TMDIFrame class is as follows:

```
class _OWLCLASS TMDIFrame : virtual public TFrameWindow {
public:
   TMDIFrame(const char far* title,
             TResId         menuResId,
             TMDIClient&    clientWnd = *new TMDIClient,
             TModule*       module = 0);


   TMDIFrame(HWND hWindow, HWND clientHWnd, TModule* module = 0);

   //
   // override virtual functions defined by TFrameWindow
   //
   bool        SetMenu(HMENU);
   TMDIClient* GetClientWindow();
   virtual HWND GetCommandTarget();
   void        PerformCreate(int menuOrId);
```

```
    //
    // find & return the child menu of an MDI frame's (or anyone's) menu
    // bar.
    //
    static HMENU FindChildMenu(HMENU);

protected:
    //
    // call ::DefFrameProc() instead of ::DefWindowProc()
    //
    LRESULT DefWindowProc(uint message, WPARAM wParam, LPARAM lParam);

private:
    //
    // hidden to prevent accidental copying or assignment
    //
    TMDIFrame(const TMDIFrame&);
    TMDIFrame& operator=(const TMDIFrame&);

    DECLARE_RESPONSE_TABLE(TMDIFrame);
    DECLARE_STREAMABLE(_OWLCLASS, TMDIFrame, 1);
};
```

The TMDIFrame class has public, protected, and private members. The MDI frame window class has three constructors, one of which is private. The first constructor creates a class instance by specifying the title, associated menu resource ID, and reference to the associated MDI client window. The second constructor creates a class instance from an existing non-OWL window. The third constructor, which is declared private and thus is used only internally in the class, creates an instance of class TMDIFrame using another existing instance.

The class TMDIFrame declares the public member functions SetMenu, GetClientWindow, and FindChildMenu. The function SetMenu looks for the MDI submenu in the new menu bar and updates member ChildMenuPos if the menu is found. The function searches for the MDI submenu in the menu bar and updates the position in the MDI window's top-level menu of the child window submenu. The function GetClientWindow returns a pointer to the associated MDI client window. The function FindChildMenu searches for the child menu of an MDI frame's menu bar.

The class TMDIFrame declares the single protected member function DefWindowProc. This function overrides the inherited function TWindow::DefWindowProc and invokes the Windows API function DefFrameProc. The API function provides the default processing for any incoming Windows message that is not handled by the MDI frame window.

Building MDI Frame Windows

The usual approach for creating the objects that make up an ObjectWindows application starts with creating the application instance and then its main window instance. In the case of an MDI-compliant application, the application's main window is typically a descendant of class TMDIFrame. The InitMainWindow member function of the application class creates this window.

Looking at the first two TMDIFrame constructors, you can tell that creating the main MDI window involves a title and menu resource—there is no pointer to a parent window because MDI frame windows have no parent windows. The MDI frame window, unlike most descendants of class TWindow, must have a menu associated with it. This menu typically includes the items shown in Table 18.1, needed to manipulate the MDI children. In addition, the menu of the MDI frame window is dynamically and automatically updated to include the current MDI children.

The constructor of the descendant of TMDIFrame (call it the application frame class) can, in many cases, simply invoke the parent class constructor. This invocation occurs if the steps taken by the parent class are adequate for creating the MDI frame window instance. In the case in which you want to modify the behavior of the application frame class, you need to include the required statements. Such statements might assign initial values to data members declared in the application frame class.

The SetupWindow member function invokes the InitClientWindow to create the TMDIClient instance. You can modify the SetupWindow function to automatically create the first child MDI window, for example.

The *TMDIClient* Class

ObjectWindows offers the TMDIClient class, a descendant of TWindow, to implement the MDI client window. The declaration of the TMDIClient class is as follows:

```
class _OWLCLASS TMDIClient : public virtual TWindow {
public:
    LPCLIENTCREATESTRUCT  ClientAttr;

    TMDIClient(TModule* module = 0);
    ~TMDIClient();

    virtual bool CloseChildren();

    TMDIChild* GetActiveMDIChild();

    //
    // member functions to arrange the MDI children
    //
    virtual void ArrangeIcons();
    virtual void CascadeChildren();
    virtual void TileChildren(int tile = MDITILE_VERTICAL);

    //
    // override member functions defined by TWindow
    //
    bool PreProcessMsg(MSG& msg);
    bool Create();

    virtual TWindow* CreateChild();
```

18

```
    //
    // constructs a new MDI child window object. By default, constructs
    // an instance of TWindow as an MDI child window object
    //
    // will almost always be overridden by derived classes to construct
    // an instance of a user-defined TWindow derived class as an MDI
    // child window object
    //
    virtual TMDIChild* InitChild();

protected:
    char far* GetClassName();

    //
    // menu command handlers & enabler
    //
    void CmCreateChild()
        { CreateChild(); }  // CM_CREATECHILD
    void CmTileChildren()
        { TileChildren(); }  // CM_TILECHILDREN
    void CmTileChildrenHoriz()
        { TileChildren(MDITILE_HORIZONTAL); }  // CM_TILECHILDREN
    void CmCascadeChildren()
        { CascadeChildren(); }  // CM_CASCADECHILDREN
    void CmArrangeIcons()
        { ArrangeIcons(); }  // CM_ARRANGEICONS
    void CmCloseChildren()
        { CloseChildren(); }  // CM_CLOSECHILDREN
    void CmChildActionEnable(TCommandEnabler& commandEnabler);

    LRESULT EvMDICreate(MDICREATESTRUCT far& createStruct);
    void    EvMDIDestroy(hwnd hWnd);

private:
    friend class TMDIFrame;
    TMDIClient(HWND hWnd, TModule* module = 0);

    //
    // hidden to prevent accidental copying or assignment
    //
    TMDIClient(const TMDIClient&);
    TMDIClient& operator =(const TMDIClient&);

    DECLARE_RESPONSE_TABLE(TMDIClient);
    DECLARE_STREAMABLE(_OWLCLASS, TMDIClient, 1);
};
```

The class TMDIClient declares a public constructor and destructor. The MDI client class declares a number of member functions that handle Windows and menu command messages for activating an MDI child window; arranging the MDI child icons; cascading and tiling MDI children; closing MDI children; and creating an MDI child window. These message response functions use sibling member functions. Table 18.1 shows the predefined menu ID constants and the TMDIClient member functions that respond to them.

Table 18.1. The predefined menu command messages for manipulating MDI children.

Action	Menu ID Constant	Responding `TMDIClient` Member Function
Tile	`CM_TILECHILDREN`	`CmTileChildren`
Tile Horizon	`CM_TILECHILDRENHORIZ`	`CmTileChildrenHoriz`
Cascade	`CM_CASCASDECHILDREN`	`CmCascadeChildren`
Arrange Icons	`CM_ARRANGEICONS`	`CmArrangeIcons`
Close All	`CM_CLOSECHILDREN`	`CmCloseChildren`

There are a number of member functions in the class `TMDIClient` that you may want to modify when you create class descendants. The list of such member functions includes `CreateChild`, `SetupWindow`, `CanClose`, and `CloseChildren`. These functions enable you to modify how to create, set up, and close MDI children.

The MDI Child Window Class

The class `TMDIChild` models the basic operations of all MDI child windows. The declaration for the class `TMDIChild` is as follows:

```
class _OWLCLASS TMDIChild : virtual public TFrameWindow {
public:
   TMDIChild(TMDIClient&    parent,
             const char far* title = 0,
             TWindow*        clientWnd = 0,
             bool            shrinkToClient = false,
             TModule*        module = 0);

             TMDIChild(HWND hWnd, TModule* module = 0);

             ~TMDIChild() {}

   //
   // override method defined by TWindow
   //
   bool PreProcessMsg(MSG& msg);
   bool ShowWindow(int cmdShow);
   bool EnableWindow(bool enable);
   void Destroy(int retVal = 0);

protected:
   void PerformCreate(int menuOrId);
   LRESULT DefWindowProc(uint msg, WPARAM wParam, LPARAM lParam);
   void EvMDIActivate(HWND hWndActivated,
                      HWND hWndDeactivated);
   bool EvNCActivate(bool active);
```

18

```
private:
   //
   // hidden to prevent accidental copying or assignment
   //
   TMDIChild(const TMDIChild&);
   TMDIChild& operator =(const TMDIChild&);

   DECLARE_RESPONSE_TABLE(TMDIChild);
   DECLARE_STREAMABLE(_OWLCLASS, TMDIChild, 1);
};
```

The class TMDIChild declares three constructors (one of which is private) and a destructor. The first constructor enables you to create a class instance by specifying the parent MDI client window, MDI child window title, the client window, and whether the MDI child window shrinks to fit the client window. The second constructor creates a class instance using an existing non-OWL MDI child window. The third constructor, which is declared private and used only internally within the class, creates a TMDIChild class instance using an existing instance.

The MDI child window class declares the single public member function PreProcessMsg. This function preprocesses the Windows messages sent to the MDI child windows. The class TMDIChild offers a set of protected functions that create, destroy, and activate MDI child windows. In addition, the class provides its own version of function DefWindowProc to handle default Windows message processing.

Building MDI Child Windows

Building MDI child windows is very similar to building application windows in the programs presented earlier. Following are the differences:

☐ An MDI child window cannot have its own menu. The menu of the MDI frame window is the one that manipulates the currently active MDI child window or all of the MDI children.

Note: The keyboard handler must not be enabled. It actually causes the reverse effect in the MDI children and antagonizes the proper operations of the MDI application.

☐ An MDI child window can have controls—this is unusual but certainly allowed.

Managing MDI Messages

The message loop directs the command messages first to the current focus window, and then after that to the active MDI child window to allow it to respond. If that window does not respond, then the message is sent to the parent MDI frame window. The active MDI child window responds to the notification messages sent by its controls, just as any window or dialog box would.

Simple Text Viewer

Look at a simple MDI-compliant application. Because MDI applications frequently are used as text viewer and text editors, we present the next application that emulates a simple text viewer. We say "emulates" because the application actually displays random text rather than text that you can retrieve from a file. This approach keeps the program simple and helps you to focus on implementing the various MDI objects. Figure 18.1, which appears after Listing 18.4, shows a sample session with the MDI1.EXE program. The MDI application has a simple menu containing the Exit and MDI Children items.

Compile and run the application. Experiment with creating MDI children. Notice that the text in odd-numbered MDI child windows is static, whereas the text in even-numbered windows can be edited. This feature is implemented to illustrate how to create a simple form of text viewer and text editor (with no Save option, to keep the example short). Try to tile, cascade, maximize, and minimize these windows. Also test closing individual MDI child windows as well as closing all of the MDI children.

Examine the code that implements this simple MDI application. Listing 18.1 shows the contents of the MDI1.DEF definition file. Listing 18.2 shows the source code for the MDI1.H header file. This file declares the command message constants and a control ID constant. Listing 18.3 contains the script for the MDI1.RC resource file. The file defines the menu resource required by the MDI frame window. The menu has two menu items, Exit and MDI Children. The latter menu item is a pop-up menu with several options. The commands, except the option Count Children, use predefined command message constants. Listing 18.4 shows the source code for the MDI1.CPP program file.

 Listing 18.1. The contents of the MDI1.DEF definition file.

```
1:  NAME          MDI1
2:  DESCRIPTION   'An OWL Windows Application'
3:  EXETYPE       WINDOWS
4:  CODE          PRELOAD MOVEABLE DISCARDABLE
5:  DATA          PRELOAD MOVEABLE MULTIPLE
6:  HEAPSIZE      1024
7:  STACKSIZE     8192
```

Listing 18.2. The source code for the MDI1.H header file.

```
1:  #define CM_COUNTCHILDREN 101
2:  #define ID_TEXT_EDIT     102
3:  #define IDM_COMMANDS     400
```

Listing 18.3. The script for the MDI1.RC resource file.

```
1:  #include <windows.h>
2:  #include <owl\window.rh>
3:  #include <owl\mdi.rh>
4:  #include "mdi1.h"
5:  IDM_COMMANDS MENU LOADONCALL MOVEABLE PURE DISCARDABLE
6:  BEGIN
7:    MENUITEM "E&xit", CM_EXIT
8:    POPUP "&MDI Children"
9:    BEGIN
10:     MENUITEM  "C&reate", CM_CREATECHILD
11:     MENUITEM  "&Cascade", CM_CASCADECHILDREN
12:     MENUITEM  "&Tile", CM_TILECHILDREN
13:     MENUITEM  "Arrange &Icons", CM_ARRANGEICONS
14:     MENUITEM  "C&lose All", CM_CLOSECHILDREN
15:     MENUITEM  "C&ount Children", CM_COUNTCHILDREN
16:    END
17:  END
```

Listing 18.4. The source code for the MDI1.CPP program file.

```
1:  /*
2:    Program to illustrate simple MDI windows
3:  */
4:  #include <owl\mdi.rh>
5:  #include <owl\applicat.h>
6:  #include <owl\framewin.h>
7:  #include <owl\mdi.h>
8:  #include <owl\static.h>
9:  #include <owl\edit.h>
10: #include <owl\scroller.h>
11: #include "mdi1.h"
12: #include <stdio.h>
13: #include <string.h>
14:
15: const MaxWords = 100;
16: const WordsPerLine = 12;
17: const NumWords = 10;
18: char* Words[NumWords] = { "The ", "friend ", "saw ", "the ",
19:                 "girl ", "drink ", "milk ", "boy ",
20:                 "cake ", "bread " };
21:
22: bool ExpressClose = false;
23: int NumMDIChild = 0;
```

```
24:    int HighMDIindex = 0;
25:
26:    class TWinApp : public TApplication
27:    {
28:    public:
29:      TWinApp() : TApplication() {}
30:
31:    protected:
32:      virtual void InitMainWindow();
33:    };
34:
35:    class TAppMDIChild : public TMDIChild
36:    {
37:    public:
38:      // pointer to the edit box control
39:      TEdit* TextBox;
40:      TStatic* TextTxt;
41:
42:      TAppMDIChild(TMDIClient& parent, int ChildNum);
43:
44:    protected:
45:
46:      // handle closing the MDI child window
47:      virtual bool CanClose();
48:    };
49:
50:    class TAppMDIClient : public TMDIClient
51:    {
52:    public:
53:
54:      TAppMDIClient() : TMDIClient() {}
55:
56:     protected:
57:
58:      // create a new child
59:      virtual TMDIChild* InitChild();
60:
61:      // close all MDI children
62:      virtual bool CloseChildren();
63:
64:      // handle the command for counting the MDI children
65:      void CMCountChildren();
66:
67:      // handle closing the MDI frame window
68:      virtual bool CanClose();
69:
70:      // declare response table
71:      DECLARE_RESPONSE_TABLE(TAppMDIClient);
72:    };
73:
74:    DEFINE_RESPONSE_TABLE1(TAppMDIClient, TMDIClient)
75:      EV_COMMAND(CM_COUNTCHILDREN, CMCountChildren),
76:      END_RESPONSE_TABLE;
77:
78:    TAppMDIChild::TAppMDIChild(TMDIClient& parent, int ChildNum)
79:      : TMDIChild(parent),
```

continues

511

18

Listing 18.4. continued

```
80:          TFrameWindow(&parent),
81:          TWindow(&parent)
82:    {
83:      char s[1024];
84:
85:      // set the scrollers in the window
86:      Attr.Style |= WS_VSCROLL | WS_HSCROLL;
87:      // create the TScroller instance
88:      Scroller = new TScroller(this, 200, 15, 10, 50);
89:
90:      // set MDI child window title
91:      sprintf(s, "%s%i", "MDI Child #", ChildNum);
92:      Title = _fstrdup(s);
93:
94:      // randomize the seed for the random-number generator
95:      randomize();
96:
97:      // assign a null string to the variable s
98:      strcpy(s, "");
99:      // build the list of random words
100:     for (int i = 0; i < MaxWords; i++) {
101:         if (i > 0 && i % WordsPerLine == 0)
102:             strcat(s, "\r\n");
103:         strcat(s, Words[random(NumWords)]);
104:     }
105:     // create a static text object in the child window if the
106:     // ChildNum variable stores an odd number. Otherwise,
107:     // create an edit box control
108:     if (ChildNum % 2 == 0) {
109:         // create the edit box
110:         TextBox = new TEdit(this, ID_TEXT_EDIT, s,
111:                   10, 10, 300, 400, 0, true);
112:         // remove borders and scroll bars
113:         TextBox->Attr.Style &= ~WS_BORDER;
114:         TextBox->Attr.Style &= ~WS_VSCROLL;
115:         TextBox->Attr.Style &= ~WS_HSCROLL;
116:     }
117:     else
118:         // create static text
119:         TextTxt = new TStatic(this, -1, s, 10, 10, 300, 400,
120:                             strlen(s));
121:   }
122:
123:   bool TAppMDIChild::CanClose()
124:   {
125:     // return true if the ExpressClose member of the
126:     // parent MDI frame window is true
127:     if (ExpressClose == true) {
128:       NumMDIChild—;
129:       return true;
130:     }
131:     else
132:       // prompt the user and return the prompt result
133:       if (MessageBox("Close this MDI window?",
134:           "Query", MB_YESNO | MB_ICONQUESTION) == IDYES) {
```

```
135:        NumMDIChild—;
136:        return true;
137:      }
138:    else
139:      return false;
140: }
141:
142: TMDIChild* TAppMDIClient::InitChild()
143: {
144:   ++NumMDIChild;
145:   return new TAppMDIChild(*this, ++HighMDIindex);
146: }
147:
148: bool TAppMDIClient::CloseChildren()
149: {
150:   bool result;
151:   // set the ExpressClose flag
152:   ExpressClose = true;
153:   // invoke the parent class CloseChildren() member function
154:   result = TMDIClient::CloseChildren();
155:   // clear the ExpressClose flag
156:   ExpressClose = false;
157:   NumMDIChild = 0;
158:   HighMDIindex = 0;
159:   return result;
160: }
161:
162: //  display a message box that shows the number of children
163: void TAppMDIClient::CMCountChildren()
164: {
165:   char msgStr[81];
166:
167:   sprintf(msgStr, "There are %i MDI child windows", NumMDIChild);
168:   MessageBox(msgStr, "Information", MB_OK | MB_ICONINFORMATION);
169: }
170:
171: bool TAppMDIClient::CanClose()
172: {
173:   return MessageBox("Close this application?", "Query",
174:                  MB_YESNO | MB_ICONQUESTION) == IDYES;
175: }
176:
177: void TWinApp::InitMainWindow()
178: {
179:   MainWindow = new TMDIFrame("Simple MDI Text Viewer",
180:                     TResID(IDM_COMMANDS),
181:                     *new TAppMDIClient);
182: }
183:
184: int OwlMain(int /* argc */, char** /*argv[] */)
185: {
186:   TWinApp app;
187:   return app.Run();
188: }
189:
```

18

Figure 18.1.
A sample session with the MDI1.EXE program.

The program in Listing 18.4 declares a set of global constants used in generating the random text in each MDI child window. The global array of pointer Words contains the program's somewhat restricted vocabulary. The listing also declares the global variables ExpressClose, NumMDIChild, and HighMDIindex. These variables provide a simple solution for sharing information between the descendants of branched-out OWL classes. The variable ExpressClose assists in closing all of the child MDI windows in one swoop. The variable NumMDIChild maintains the actual number of MDI child windows. The variable HighMDIindex stores the index of the last MDI child window created.

The program listing declares three classes: the application class, TWinApp, in line 26; the MDI client class, TAppMDIClient, in line 50; and the MDI child window class, TAppMDIChild, in line 35. We will discuss these classes in order.

The code for the application class looks very much like the ones in previous programs, with one exception. The InitMainWindow member function, defined in lines 177 to 182, creates an instance of the stock MDI frame class, TMDIFrame. The TMDIFrame constructor call has the following arguments: title of the application; the name of the menu resource, COMMANDS; and the pointer to the dynamically allocated instances of TAppMDIClient.

The TAppMDIClient class declares a constructor and a group of protected member functions. The member functions are as follows:

☐ The member function InitChild (defined in lines 142 to 146) initializes an MDI child window. The function increments the global variable NumMDIChild and then returns a dynamically allocated instance of TAppMDIChild. The arguments of creating this instance are *this (a reference to the object itself) and ++HighMDIindex. The second argument pre-increments the global variable HighMDIindex, which keeps track of the highest index for an MDI child window.

☐ The member function CloseChildren (defined in lines 148 to 160) alters the behavior of the inherited CloseChildren function. The new version performs the following tasks:

    ☐ Assigns true to the global variable ExpressClose (see line 152)

- [ ] Invokes the parent class version of `CloseChildren` and stores the result of that function call in the local variable result

- [ ] Assigns `false` to the variable `ExpressClose` in line 156

- [ ] Assigns `0` to the global variable `NumMDIChild` in line 157

- [ ] Assigns `0` to the global variable `HighMDIindex` in line 157. This task resets the value in variable `HighMDIindex` when you close all of the MDI child windows.

- [ ] Returns the value stored in the variable result

- [ ] The member function `CMCountChildren` (defined in lines 163 to 168) responds to the Windows command message `CM_COUNTCHILDREN` generated by the menu option Count Children. The function displays the number of MDI child windows in a message dialog box. The function first builds the string `msgStr` to contain the formatted image of the global variable `NumMDIChild`. Then, the function invokes the member function `MessageBox` to display the sought information.

- [ ] The virtual member function `CanClose` (defined in lines 171 to 175) prompts you to confirm closing the MDI-compliant application.

The MDI child window class, `TAppMDIChild`, declares the `TextBox` and `TextTxt` data members, a constructor, and the `CanClose` member function. The member `TextBox` is the pointer to the `TEdit` instance created to store the random text in one kind of the MDI child windows. The member `TextTxt` is the pointer to the `TStatic` instance created to store random text in the other type of MDI child windows.

The `TAppMDIChild` constructor (defined in lines 78 to 121) performs a variety of tasks, as follows:

- [ ] Sets the window style to include the vertical and horizontal scroll bars (see line 86).

- [ ] Creates an instance of `TScroller` to animate the window's scroll bars (see line 88).

- [ ] Sets the window title to include the MDI child window number, using the statements in lines 91 and 92.

- [ ] Randomizes the seed for the random-number generator function, `random`.

- [ ] Creates the random text and stores it in the local string variable s. This task uses the `for` loop in lines 100 to 104.

- [ ] If the MDI child window number is even, creates a multiline instance of `TEdit` in lines 110 and 111. This instance contains a copy of the text stored in variable s. In addition, the constructor disables the border, vertical scroll bar, and horizontal scroll bar styles (see the statements in lines 113 to 115). These scroll bars are not needed because the MDI child window itself has scroll bars. In the case of an odd-numbered MDI child window number, the constructor creates static text using the characters in variable s (see the statement in lines 119 and 120).

The `CanClose` member function regulates closing an MDI child window. When you close such a window using the Close option in its own system menu, the function requires your confirmation. If the request to close comes from the Close All menu command in the parent   515 window, the MDI child window closes without confirmation. The function decrements the global variable NumMDIChild in two cases: first, when the global variable ExpressClose is true; and second, when the function MessageBox, which prompts you to confirm closing the window, returns IDYES.

Revised Text Viewer

Let's expand on the MDI1.EXE program to illustrate other aspects of managing MDI windows. The next application also creates MDI children that contain edit box controls with random text. However, each MDI child window has the following additional controls:

☐ An UpperCase pushbutton control that converts the text in the MDI child window into uppercase.

☐ A LowerCase pushbutton control that converts the text in the MDI child window into lowercase.

☐ A Can Close check box. Using this box replaces using the confirmation dialog box that appears when you want to close the MDI child window. The check box enables you to predetermine whether the MDI child window can be closed.

The application menu adds a new pop-up menu item, Current MDI Child. This menu item has options that work on the current MDI child window. The commands enable you to clear, convert to uppercase, convert to lowercase, or rewrite the characters in the MDI child window. The new pop-up menu shows how you can manipulate MDI children with custom menus.

Compile and run the application. Create a few MDI children and use their pushbutton controls to toggle the case of characters in these windows. Also use the Current MDI Child commands to further manipulate the text in the currently active MDI child window. Try to close the MDI children with the Can Close check box marked and unmarked. Only the MDI children with the Can Close control checked close individually. Use the Close All option in the MDI Children pop-up menu and watch all of the MDI children close, regardless of the check state of the Can Close control. Figure 18.2, which appears after Listing 18.8, shows a sample session with the MDI2.EXE program.

Listing 18.5 shows the contents of the MDI2.DEF definition file. Listing 18.6 shows the source code for the MDI2.H header file. The file contains the constants for the menu commands and the control IDs. Listing 18.7 contains the script for the MDI2.RC resource file and shows the resource for the expanded menu. Listing 18.8 contains the source code for the MDI2.CPP program file.

 Listing 18.5. The contents of the MDI2.DEF definition file.

```
1:  NAME         MDI2
2:  DESCRIPTION  'An OWL Windows Application'
3:  EXETYPE      WINDOWS
4:  CODE         PRELOAD MOVEABLE DISCARDABLE
```

```
5:   DATA          PRELOAD MOVEABLE MULTIPLE
6:   HEAPSIZE      1024
7:   STACKSIZE     8192
```

 Listing 18.6. The source code for the MDI2.H header file.

```
1:   #define CM_COUNTCHILDREN 101
2:   #define CM_CLEAR          102
3:   #define CM_UPPERCASE      103
4:   #define CM_LOWERCASE      104
5:   #define CM_RESET          105
6:   #define ID_TEXT_EDIT      106
7:   #define ID_CANCLOSE_CHK   107
8:   #define ID_UPPERCASE_BTN  108
9:   #define ID_LOWERCASE_BTN  109
10:  #define IDM_COMMANDS      400
```

Type **Listing 18.7. The script for the MDI2.RC resource file.**

```
1:   #include <windows.h>
2:   #include <owl\window.rh>
3:   #include <owl\mdi.rh>
4:   #include "mdi2.h"
5:   IDM_COMMANDS MENU LOADONCALL MOVEABLE PURE DISCARDABLE
6:   BEGIN
7:     MENUITEM "E&xit", CM_EXIT
8:     POPUP "&MDI Children"
9:     BEGIN
10:      MENUITEM  "C&reate", CM_CREATECHILD
11:      MENUITEM  "&Cascade", CM_CASCADECHILDREN
12:      MENUITEM  "&Tile", CM_TILECHILDREN
13:      MENUITEM  "Arrange &Icons", CM_ARRANGEICONS
14:      MENUITEM  "C&lose All", CM_CLOSECHILDREN
15:      MENUITEM  "C&ount Children", CM_COUNTCHILDREN
16:    END
17:    POPUP "&Current MDI Child"
18:    BEGIN
19:      MENUITEM  "&Clear", CM_CLEAR
20:      MENUITEM  "&Uppercase", CM_UPPERCASE
21:      MENUITEM  "&Lowercase", CM_LOWERCASE
22:      MENUITEM  "&Reset", CM_RESET
23:    END
24:  END
```

Type **Listing 18.8. The source code for the MDI2.CPP program file.**

```
1:   /*
2:      Program to demonstrate MDI windows with controls
3:   */
```

Listing 18.8. continued

```
4:    #include <owl\mdi.rh>
5:    #include <owl\applicat.h>
6:    #include <owl\framewin.h>
7:    #include <owl\button.h>
8:    #include <owl\edit.h>
9:    #include <owl\checkbox.h>
10:   #include <owl\scroller.h>
11:   #include <owl\mdi.h>
12:   #include "mdi2.h"
13:   #include <stdio.h>
14:   #include <string.h>
15:
16:   // declare constants for sizing and spacing the controls
17:   // in the MDI child window
18:   const Wbtn = 50 * 3;
19:   const Hbtn = 30;
20:   const BtnHorzSpacing = 20;
21:   const BtnVertSpacing = 10;
22:   const Wchk = 200 * 3;
23:   const Hchk = 20;
24:   const ChkVertSpacing = 10;
25:   const Wbox = 400 * 3;
26:   const Hbox = 200 * 3;
27:
28:   // declare the constants for the random text that appears
29:   // in the MDI child window
30:   const MaxWords = 200;
31:   const WordsPerLine = 10;
32:   const NumWords = 10;
33:   const BufferSize = 1024;
34:   char AppBuffer[BufferSize];
35:   char* Words[NumWords] = { "The ", "friend ", "saw ", "the ",
36:                    "girl ", "drink ", "milk ", "boy ",
37:                    "cake ", "bread " };
38:
39:
40:   bool ExpressClose = false;
41:   int NumMDIChild = 0;
42:   int HighMDIindex = 0;
43:
44:   class TWinApp : public TApplication
45:   {
46:   public:
47:     TWinApp() : TApplication() {}
48:
49:   protected:
50:     virtual void InitMainWindow();
51:   };
52:
53:   class TAppMDIChild : public TMDIChild
54:   {
55:   public:
56:
57:
58:     TAppMDIChild(TMDIClient& parent, int ChildNum);
```

```
59:
60:    protected:
61:
62:      TEdit* TextBox;
63:      TCheckBox* CanCloseChk;
64:
65:      // handle the UpperCase button
66:      void HandleUpperCaseBtn()
67:        { CMUpperCase(); }
68:
69:      // handle the LowerCase button
70:      void HandleLowerCaseBtn()
71:        { CMLowerCase(); }
72:
73:      // handle clear the active MDI child
74:      void CMClear()
75:        { TextBox->Clear(); }
76:
77:      // handle converting the text of the active
78:      // MDI child to uppercase
79:      void CMUpperCase();
80:
81:      // handle converting the text of the active
82:      // MDI child to lowercase
83:      void CMLowerCase();
84:
85:      // handle resetting the text of the active MDI child
86:      void CMReset();
87:
88:      // reset the text in an MDI child window
89:      void InitText();
90:
91:       // handle closing the MDI child window
92:       virtual bool CanClose();
93:
94:       // declare response table
95:       DECLARE_RESPONSE_TABLE(TAppMDIChild);
96:    };
97:
98:    DEFINE_RESPONSE_TABLE1(TAppMDIChild, TMDIChild)
99:      EV_COMMAND(ID_UPPERCASE_BTN, HandleUpperCaseBtn),
100:     EV_COMMAND(ID_LOWERCASE_BTN, HandleLowerCaseBtn),
101:     EV_COMMAND(CM_CLEAR, CMClear),
102:     EV_COMMAND(CM_UPPERCASE, CMUpperCase),
103:     EV_COMMAND(CM_LOWERCASE, CMLowerCase),
104:     EV_COMMAND(CM_RESET, CMReset),
105:   END_RESPONSE_TABLE;
106:
107:   class TAppMDIClient : public TMDIClient
108:   {
109:   public:
110:
111:     TAppMDIClient() : TMDIClient() {}
112:
113:     protected:
114:
```

18

continues

Listing 18.8. continued

```
115:     // create a new child
116:     virtual TMDIChild* InitChild();
117:
118:     // close all MDI children
119:     virtual bool CloseChildren();
120:
121:     // handle the command for counting the MDI children
122:     void CMCountChildren();
123:
124:     // handle closing the MDI frame window
125:     virtual bool CanClose();
126:
127:     // declare response table
128:     DECLARE_RESPONSE_TABLE(TAppMDIClient);
129: };
130:
131: DEFINE_RESPONSE_TABLE1(TAppMDIClient, TMDIClient)
132:   EV_COMMAND(CM_COUNTCHILDREN, CMCountChildren),
133: END_RESPONSE_TABLE;
134:
135: TAppMDIChild::TAppMDIChild(TMDIClient& parent, int ChildNum)
136:     : TMDIChild(parent),
137:       TFrameWindow(&parent),
138:       TWindow(&parent)
139: {
140:     char s[41];
141:     int x0 = 10;
142:     int y0 = 10;
143:     int x = x0;
144:     int y = y0;
145:
146:     // set the scrollers in the window
147:     Attr.Style |= WS_VSCROLL | WS_HSCROLL;
148:     // create the TScroller instance
149:     Scroller = new TScroller(this, 200, 15, 10, 50);
150:
151:     // set MDI child window title
152:     sprintf(s, "%s%i", "Child #", ChildNum);
153:     Title = _fstrdup(s);
154:
155:     // create the push button controls
156:     new TButton(this, ID_UPPERCASE_BTN, "->UpperCase",
157:                 x, y, Wbtn, Hbtn, true);
158:     x += Wbtn + BtnHorzSpacing;
159:     new TButton(this, ID_LOWERCASE_BTN, "->LowerCase",
160:                 x, y, Wbtn, Hbtn, false);
161:
162:     x = x0;
163:     y += Hbtn + BtnVertSpacing;
164:     CanCloseChk = new TCheckBox(this, ID_CANCLOSE_CHK, "Can Close",
165:                                 x, y, Wchk, Hchk, NULL);
166:     y += Hchk + ChkVertSpacing;
167:     InitText();
168:     // create the edit box
169:     TextBox = new TEdit(this, ID_TEXT_EDIT, AppBuffer,
170:                         x, y, Wbox, Hbox, 0, true);
```

```
171:     // remove borders and scroll bars
172:     TextBox->Attr.Style &= ~WS_BORDER;
173:     TextBox->Attr.Style &= ~WS_VSCROLL;
174:     TextBox->Attr.Style &= ~WS_HSCROLL;
175:   }
176:
177:   void TAppMDIChild::CMUpperCase()
178:   {
179:     TextBox->GetText(AppBuffer, BufferSize);
180:     strupr(AppBuffer);
181:     TextBox->SetText(AppBuffer);
182:   }
183:
184:   void TAppMDIChild::CMLowerCase()
185:   {
186:     TextBox->GetText(AppBuffer, BufferSize);
187:     strlwr(AppBuffer);
188:     TextBox->SetText(AppBuffer);
189:   }
190:
191:   void TAppMDIChild::CMReset()
192:   {
193:     InitText();
194:     TextBox->SetText(AppBuffer);
195:   }
196:
197:   bool TAppMDIChild::CanClose()
198:   {
199:     // return true if the ExpressClose member of the
200:     // parent MDI frame window is true
201:     if (ExpressClose == true) {
202:       NumMDIChild—;
203:       return true;
204:     }
205:     else
206:     // do not close the MDi child window if the Can Close is
207:     // not checked
208:     if (CanCloseChk->GetCheck() == BF_UNCHECKED)
209:       return false;
210:     else {
211:       NumMDIChild—;
212:       return true;
213:     }
214:   }
215:
216:   void TAppMDIChild::InitText()
217:   {
218:     // randomize the seed for the random-number generator
219:     randomize();
220:
221:     // assign a null string to the buffer
222:     AppBuffer[0] = '\0';
223:     // build the list of random words
224:     for (int i = 0;
225:          i < MaxWords && strlen(AppBuffer) <= (BufferSize - 10);
226:          i++) {
```

continues

Listing 18.8. continued

```
227:        if (i > 0 && i % WordsPerLine == 0)
228:          strcat(AppBuffer, "\r\n");
229:          strcat(AppBuffer, Words[random(NumWords)]);
230:      }
231:  }
232:
233:  TMDIChild* TAppMDIClient::InitChild()
234:  {
235:    ++NumMDIChild;
236:    return new TAppMDIChild(*this, ++HighMDIindex);
237:  }
238:
239:  bool TAppMDIClient::CloseChildren()
240:  {
241:    bool result;
242:    // set the ExpressClose flag
243:    ExpressClose = true;
244:    // invoke the parent class CloseChildren() member function
245:    result = TMDIClient::CloseChildren();
246:    // clear the ExpressClose flag
247:    ExpressClose = false;
248:    NumMDIChild = 0;
249:    HighMDIindex = 0;
250:    return result;
251:  }
252:
253:  //  display a message box that shows the number of children
254:  void TAppMDIClient::CMCountChildren()
255:  {
256:    char msgStr[81];
257:
258:    sprintf(msgStr, "There are %i MDI children", NumMDIChild);
259:    MessageBox(msgStr, "Information", MB_OK | MB_ICONINFORMATION);
260:  }
261:
262:  bool TAppMDIClient::CanClose()
263:  {
264:    return MessageBox("Close this application?",
265:             "Query", MB_YESNO | MB_ICONQUESTION) == IDYES;
266:  }
267:
268:  void TWinApp::InitMainWindow()
269:  {
270:    MainWindow = new TMDIFrame("Simple MDI Text Viewer (version 2)",
271:                    TResID(IDM_COMMANDS),
272:                    *new TAppMDIClient);
273:  }
274:
275:  int OwlMain(int /* argc */, char** /*argv[] */)
276:  {
277:    TWinApp app;
278:    return app.Run();
279:  }
```

Figure 18.2.
A sample session with the MDI2.EXE program.

The program in Listing 18.8 declares two sets of constants. The first set is used for sizing and spacing the controls of each MDI child window. The second set of constants is used to manage the random text. The program also declares variable AppBuffer as a single 1KB text buffer. We chose to make the buffer global instead of a class data member mainly to reduce the buffer space—the application classes need only one shared buffer at any time. The program listing also declares the global variables ExpressClose, NumMDIChild, and HighMDIindex—another set of components carried over from the program in file MDI1.CPP.

The new application maintains the same three classes described in the last program. However, the MDI child class has different members in this program. The new members manage the response to the control notification messages as well as the Current MDI Child menu command messages.

The TAppMDIChild constructor (defined in lines 135 to 175) performs the following tasks:

☐ Sets the window style to include the vertical and horizontal scroll bars, using the statement in line 147

☐ Creates an instance of TScroller to animate the window's scroll bars, using the statement in line 149

☐ Sets the window title to include the MDI child window number using the statements in lines 152 and 153

☐ Creates the LowerCase and UpperCase pushbutton controls using the statements in lines 156 to 160

☐ Creates the Can Close check box control using the statements in lines 162 to 165

☐ Calls the InitText member function to generate random text in the application buffer AppBuffer

☐ Creates a multiline instance of TEdit in statement located in lines 169 and 170. This instance contains a copy of the text stored in the application buffer.

☐ Disables the border, vertical scroll bar, and horizontal scroll bar styles of the edit control. This task uses the statements in lines 172 to 174.

The member function CMUpperCase (defined in lines 177 to 182) responds to the command message emitted by the UpperCase command. The function copies the text in the MDI child window to the application's buffer, converts the characters in the buffer to uppercase, and then writes the buffer back to the MDI child window.

The member function CMLowerCase (defined in lines 184 to 189) responds to the command message emitted by the LowerCase command. The function performs similar steps to those in CMUpperCase—except the text is converted into lowercase.

The member function CanClose (defined in lines 197 to 214) responds to the WM_CLOSE message emitted by the Close option in the system menu available in each MDI child window. If the MDI frame window's ExpressClose variable is true, then the function decrements the global variable NumMDIChild and returns true. Otherwise, the function returns false if the Can Close check box is unchecked, or it decrements the global variable NumMDIChild and then returns false if the control is not checked.

The member function InitText (defined in lines 233 to 237) is an auxiliary routine that fills the application buffer with random text. The function creates up to MaxWords words or enough that the buffer limit is closely reached (within 10 bytes). Checking the number of characters in the buffer ensures that the program does not corrupt the memory while attempting to add MaxWords words to the buffer.

The member functions HandleUpperCaseBtn and HandleLowerCase respond to the notification messages sent by the pushbuttons of an MDI child window. These functions perform the same tasks of CMUpperCase and CMLowerCase, respectively. Therefore, the notification response functions call their respective command-message response member functions.

The member function CMClear (defined in lines 74 and 75) responds to the command message emitted by the Clear command in the Current MDI Child menu item. The function simply invokes the TextBox->Clear() function call.

The member function CMReset (defined in lines 191 to 195) responds to the command message emitted by the Reset command in the Current MDI Child menu item. The function calls the InitText member function to create a new batch of random text and then copies the buffer's text to the edit control of the MDI child window.

Note: The Current MDI Child pop-up menu has four options that manipulate the currently active MDI child window. The command messages emitted by these options are handled by the MDI child window instances and not the MDI frame instance—which is what a window instance normally does regarding its own menu commands. This order of handling the command messages is preferred and makes use of the fact that the menu-based messages do reach the currently active MDI child window first. You can rewrite the program such that the functions CMClear, CMUpperCase, CMLowerCase, and CMReset appear as member functions of class TAppMDIFrame.

Summary

This chapter presented the Multiple Document Interface (MDI), which is an interface standard in Windows. The chapter discussed the following subjects:

- [ ] The basic features and components of an MDI-compliant application. These components include the MDI frame window, the invisible MDI client window, and the dynamically created MDI child windows.
- [ ] Basics of building an MDI application
- [ ] The TMDIFrame class, which manages the MDI client window, the MDI child windows, and the execution of the menu commands
- [ ] Building MDI frame windows as objects that are owned by the application and that own the MDI client window
- [ ] The TMDIClient class, which owns the MDI child windows
- [ ] Building MDI child windows as an instance of a TMDIChild descendant and using customized client windows as instances of TWindow descendants
- [ ] Managing messages in an MDI-compliant application. The currently active MDI child window has a higher priority for handling menu-based command messages than its parent, the MDI client window

18

Q&A

Q Should each MDI child window have an ID?

A Yes. Associating each MDI child window with an ID gives you more control over managing these windows, especially if they vary in relevance. Thus, you can use the ID to exclude special MDI child windows from collective operations.

Q Can I hide MDI child windows?

A Yes. You can use the inherited member function TWindow::ShowWindow to show and hide one MDI child window or more.

Workshop

The Workshop provides quiz questions to help you solidify your understanding of the material covered and exercises to provide you with experience in using what you've learned. Try to understand the quiz and exercise answers before continuing on to the bonus chapters. Answers are provided in Appendix A.

Quiz

1. True or false? MDI child windows can have their own menus.
2. True or false? MDI child windows can be moved outside the area of the frame window.
3. True or false? The MFC library supports nested MDI child windows.

Exercises

1. Experiment with the expanding vocabulary of programs MDI1.EXE and MDI2.EXE.
2. Add a control that inserts the date and time in MDI child windows of program MDI1.EXE.

The Application and Class Experts

The AppExpert utility is a versatile tool that helps you create project source code files quickly and systematically. The utility generates functioning skeleton-code that you then can customize to meet the needs of your Windows applications. Thus, rather than starting from scratch or from adapting similar existing code, you can rely on the AppExpert utility to do much of the systematic work for you, freeing you to concentrate on implementing the code that supports your application's special features. It's like having a consultant inside Turbo C++! This chapter focuses on the following topics:

- Using the AppExpert utility
- Examining the source code output that is generated by selecting some project options in AppExpert
- Using the ClassExpert utility to modify the AppExpert output

Note: The listings generated by AppExpert were edited to better fit the pages in this book.

Using the AppExpert Utility

To use the *AppExpert utility*, invoke the AppExpert option in the Project menu. The IDE brings up the project file-selection dialog box. This dialog box is very similar to the Open A File dialog box. Select an .IDE filename or type in the name of a new .IDE file and then click the OK button. If you type in the name of a new .IDE file, the AppExpert utility creates a new project file. On the other hand, if you choose an existing .IDE file, the AppExpert utility merely adds the new target to that project file. Next, the AppExpert utility displays the AppExpert Application Generation Options dialog box (called the AppExpert dialog box for short), as shown in Figure 19.1. This dialog box has three topics in its left hand list box: Application, Main Window, and MDI Child/View.

Note: It is important to know that the AppExpert dialog box hides and shows different controls based on the currently selected topic or subtopic in the same way as the options dialog box. As you select different items in the left hand list box, the options on the right side of the dialog will change.

The Application Topic

Figure 19.1 shows the options of the *Application topic.* You will be working with these options in this chapter and the following chapter to generate projects with the AppExpert utility. The options of the Application topic are as follows:

- ☐ The choice between an application that supports SDI or MDI child windows, or one that supports a dialog client
- ☐ The use of document and view classes in the text editor
- ☐ The inclusion of a toolbar
- ☐ The inclusion of a status line
- ☐ The support for the drag-and-drop feature
- ☐ The support for printing and print-previewing features

Figure 19.1.
The AppExpert Application Generation Options dialog box.

If you click the + sign located to the left of the Application topic (or double-click the Application topic itself), you expand the Application subtopics. Figure 19.2 shows the options offered by the Application subtopics:

- ☐ Basic Options
- ☐ OLE 2 Options
- ☐ Code Gen Control
- ☐ Admin Options

The Basic Options Subtopic

Figure 19.2 shows the options offered by the *Basic Options subtopic.* The option choices include the following:

- ☐ The name of the target
- ☐ The base directory for the target
- ☐ The option to provide online help with its corresponding help file
- ☐ The application's startup state
- ☐ The control styles

Figure 19.2.

The AppExpert dialog box showing the Basic Options subtopic in the Application topic.

The dialog box offers three edit box controls for you to enter the preceding information. In addition, the dialog box shows a Browse pushbutton, which enables you to invoke a dialog box for selecting a new base directory. As for the help file, the AppExpert dialog box contains a check box that enables you to either support or prevent the creation of the help file.

The radio buttons for setting the startup options allow you to have the application automatically minimized or maximized when it starts up, or to start up in the normal manner. The radio buttons for the control styles default to the standard Windows setting, which shows a white background on dialog boxes. The BWCC style refers to Borland's set of "chiseled steel" dialog boxes with the mottled background and controls with a more three-dimensional appearance. The MS Control 3D appearance is used in standard Microsoft applications.

The OLE 2 Options Subtopic

The *OLE 2 Options* offered by the Application Generator are shown in figure 19.3. They include the following:

☐ Whether an application is an OLE 2 container

☐ Whether an application is an OLE 2 server, and whether it's an EXE or a DLL server

☐ Whether the application should be automated

☐ The server ID to be used in registering the application

The first option is obvious; an application either is or isn't an OLE 2 container. With the server, however, an application may have the OLE 2 server routines reside in either an EXE or a DLL, and the application generator will handle both cases. The automation routines allow one application to be controlled from another. Finally, the server ID is a unique number, guaranteed to be different from all other IDs that might exist. OLE 2 is described in more detail on Day 20.

Figure 19.3.

The AppExpert dialog box showing the OLE 2 Options subtopic in the Application topic.

The Code Gen Control Subtopic

The *Code Gen Control subtopic* offers the options shown in Figure 19.4. When you select this subtopic, the AppExpert dialog box displays the target name and the base directory. In addition, the dialog box offers edit-box controls to select the following:

☐ The source directory

☐ The header directory

☐ The main source file

☐ The main header file

☐ The application class

☐ The About dialog class

The dialog box offers browse buttons for the preceding source and header directory options. In addition, the dialog box presents a frame with two radio buttons that enable you to select between verbose or terse comments. The default setting enables verbose comments.

Figure 19.4.

The AppExpert dialog box showing the Code Generation Control subtopic.

The Admin Options Subtopic

The *Admin Options subtopic*, shown in Figure 19.5, handles the administrative side of the project. The AppExpert dialog box provides you with edit box controls to enter the following information:

☐ The version number (the default is 1.0)

☐ The copyright notice (the dialog box offers a default wording for the copyright notice)

☐ The description (the default description is the target name)

☐ The name of the target author

☐ The name of the company

Figure 19.5.
The AppExpert dialog box showing the Administrative Options subtopic.

The Main Window Topic

The *Main Window topic* alters the AppExpert dialog box to offer you options that set the window title and background (see Figure 19.6). The dialog box also presents a Set background color pushbutton for altering the background color.

Figure 19.6.
The AppExpert dialog box showing the Main Window topic.

The Main Window topic has the following subtopics:

- [ ] Basic Options
- [ ] SDI Client
- [ ] MDI Client
- [ ] Dialog Client

The Basic Options Subtopic

The *Basic Options subtopic* in the Main Window topic permits you to select the window style. Figure 19.7 shows the options offered by this subtopic, as follows:

- [ ] **Caption:** Creates a single thin border and a title bar that can display a caption.
- [ ] **Border:** Creates a single thin border that has no title bar.
- [ ] **Max box:** Adds a maximize button to the right side of the title bar that belongs to the application's main window.
- [ ] **Min box:** Adds a minimize button to the right side of the title bar that belongs to the application's main window.
- [ ] **Vertical scroll:** Includes a vertical scroll on the right side of the main window.
- [ ] **Horizontal scroll:** Includes a horizontal scroll on the bottom of the main window.
- [ ] **System menu:** Includes the system-menu button located to the left side of the title bar in the main window. The Caption option must be selected to make this option available.
- [ ] **Visible:** Makes the main window visible.
- [ ] **Disabled:** Disables the main window.
- [ ] **Thick frame:** Displays the main window as a dialog box, with a double border. Consequently, you cannot resize the main window.
- [ ] **Clip siblings:** Protects the sibling windows of the main window.
- [ ] **Clip children:** Ensures that the main window is not painted over by the child windows.

Figure 19.7.
The AppExpert dialog box showing the Basic Options subtopic in the Main Window topic.

The SDI Client Subtopic

The *SDI Client subtopic* offers options that define the class, which in turn models the client area of an SDI-compliant main window. These options are effective only if you select the Single Document Interface option in the opening AppExpert dialog box. Figure 19.8 shows the AppExpert dialog box displaying the SDI Client subtopic with the following options:

- [ ] The drop-down combo box that enables you to select the Client/View class
- [ ] The drop-down combo box that permits you to select the Document class
- [ ] The three edit boxes to enter the file-type filters. These controls accept the file description, filters, and default extensions.
- [ ] An edit box allowing you to set the name of the SDI view class
- [ ] Two edit boxes to set the names of the header file and the source file for the SDI class

Figure 19.8.
The AppExpert dialog box showing the SDI Client subtopic.

The MDI Client Subtopic

The *MDI Client subtopic* offers options to define the class that models the client area of an MDI-compliant frame window. These options are effective only if you select the Multiple Document Interface option in the opening AppExpert dialog box. Figure 19.9 shows the AppExpert dialog box displaying the MDI Client subtopic with the following options:

☐ The name of the MDI client window class

☐ The source (which we are calling *implementation* in this book, because we mean *source* in a broad sense) filename

☐ The header filename

Figure 19.9.

The AppExpert dialog box showing the MDI Client subtopic.

The Dialog Client Subtopic

The *Dialog Client subtopic* offers options to define the class that models the client area of a dialog frame window. You can select the resource ID of the dialog box to load, and you can select whether to include a menu bar. These options are effective only if you select the Dialog Client option in the opening AppExpert dialog box. Figure 19.10 shows the AppExpert dialog box displaying the MDI Client subtopic with the following options:

☐ The name of the MDI client window class

☐ The source (which we are calling *implementation* in this book, because we mean source in a broad sense) filename

☐ The header filename

☐ The resource ID of the dialog box to load into the client

☐ Whether to include a menu bar in the frame

19

Figure 19.10.
The AppExpert dialog box showing the MDI Client subtopic.

The MDI Child/View Topic

The MDI Child/View topic, shown in Figure 19.11, has options that enable you to specify the following:

☐ The name of the MDI child-window class

☐ The source file that contains the implementation of the MDI child-window class

☐ The header file that contains the declaration of the MDI child-window class

Figure 19.11.
The AppExpert dialog box showing the MDI Child/View topic.

The AppExpert dialog box offers the Customize child and view pushbutton control, which simply invokes the Basic Options subtopic that is discussed next.

The Basic Options Subtopic

The *Basic Options subtopic* offers options to define the class that models the client area of an MDI child window. These options are effective only if you select the Multiple Document Interface option in the opening AppExpert dialog box. Figure 19.12 shows the AppExpert dialog box displaying the Basic Options subtopic with the following options:

- ☐ The drop-down combo box that enables you to select the MDI Client/view class.
- ☐ The drop-down combo box that enables you to select the Document class.
- ☐ The three edit boxes to enter the file-type filters. These controls accept the file description, filters, and default extensions.
- ☐ The class name, header file, and source file.

Figure 19.12.
The AppExpert dialog box showing the Basic Options subtopic in the MDI Child/ View topic.

Studying the AppExpert Output

You've just seen that the AppExpert utility offers many options to determine the kind of source code files that can be generated. Now I present an SDI-compliant project generated by altering the AppExpert options. Because the total number of possible source-code listings is rather large, we will focus on a selection of source-code files generated by AppExpert.

> **Note:** Although the AppExpert creates a sizable amount of source code very quickly, you should nonetheless study the output. Acquainting yourself with the output enables you to quickly and efficiently customize the AppExpert output. This approach shortens the overall process of developing your applications. By contrast, not becoming familiar with the emitted source code will cost you extra time in debugging your programs.

The ideal study of the source-code files generated by AppExpert would include varying each of the AppExpert options, one at a time, and covering all of the possible combinations. Because the total number of these combinations is relatively large, we will examine just one set of the possible output source-code that is generated. The AppExpert generates a minimally functioning text editor. Please do not interpret the words *minimally functioning* to mean that it's a real dud. In fact, the generated text editors offer an acceptable level of operations, because the various OWL classes used in these editors support these operations. I would like to point out that working with all the different combinations is a good independent exercise. I suggest that you experiment with these various combinations to see what kind of program each combination generates.

The *Expert* Project

The sample project is *Expert.* This project generates an SDI-compliant text editor with no toolbar, no status line, no drag-and-drop feature support, and no printing-related features. In other words, the Expert project is the simplest text editor generated by AppExpert.

When you invoke the AppExpert utility from the IDE Project menu, set the name of the project to "Expert." When the AppExpert dialog appears, select the SDI option and turn off the other options in the first section "Application." The utility generates the following set of files.

Filename	Size	Description
applsdi.ico	1,086	Application icon
expert.apx	18,572	AppExpert reference file
expert.ide	27,138	IDE project file
exprtapp.rc	13,331	Resource source
exprtapp.rh	4,404	Resource header
exprtapp.def	503	Application definition file
exprtapp.cpp	4,325	Main application source
exprtapp.h	1,533	Main application header
xprtabtd.cpp	4,974	About box source
xprtabtd.h	1,480	About box header
xprtedtf.cpp	1,137	TEditFile descendant class source
xprtedtf.h	1,010	TEditFile descendant class header

The preceding files contains icon, header, definition, resource header, resource, implementation, and IDE files. Look at the .DEF, .H, .RH, .RC, and .CPP files. Build the EXPERT project and experiment with its text-editing features.

Type **Listing 19.1. The contents of the EXPRTAPP.DEF definition file.**

```
;------------------------------------------------
;   Project expert
;
;   Copyright © 1994. All Rights Reserved.
;
;   SUBSYSTEM:    expert.exe Module Defintion File
;   FILE:         exprtapp.def
;   AUTHOR:
;
;------------------------------------------------

NAME expert

DESCRIPTION 'expert Application - Copyright © 1994. All Rights Reserved.'
EXETYPE     WINDOWS
CODE        PRELOAD MOVEABLE DISCARDABLE
DATA        PRELOAD MOVEABLE
HEAPSIZE    4096
STACKSIZE   8192
```

Type **Listing 19.2. The source code for the EXPRTAPP.RH resource header file.**

19

```
//#if !defined(__exprtapp_rh)              // Sentry use file only if it's not
➥already included.
//#define __exprtapp_rh

/*  Project expert

Copyright © 1994. All Rights Reserved.

SUBSYSTEM:    expert.exe Application
FILE:         exprtapp.h
AUTHOR:


OVERVIEW
========
Constant definitions for all resources defined in exprtapp.rc.
*/


//
// IDHELP BorButton for BWCC dialogs.
//
#define IDHELP                    998              // Id of help button
```

Listing 19.2. continued

```
//
// Application specific definitions:
//
#define IDI_SDIAPPLICATION      1001              // Application icon

#define SDI_MENU                100               // Menu resource ID and Accelerator
➥IDs

//
// CM_FILEnnnn commands (include\owl\editfile.rh except for CM_FILEPRINTPREVIEW)
//
#define CM_FILENEW              24331             // SDI New
#define CM_FILEOPEN             24332             // SDI Open
#define CM_FILECLOSE            24339
#define CM_FILESAVE             24333
#define CM_FILESAVEAS           24334


//
// Window commands (include\owl\window.rh)
//
#define CM_EXIT                 24310


//
// CM_EDITnnnn commands (include\owl\window.rh)
//
#define CM_EDITUNDO             24321
#define CM_EDITCUT              24322
#define CM_EDITCOPY             24323
#define CM_EDITPASTE            24324
#define CM_EDITDELETE           24325
#define CM_EDITCLEAR            24326
#define CM_EDITADD              24327
#define CM_EDITEDIT             24328


//
// Search menu commands (include\owl\editsear.rh)
//
#define CM_EDITFIND             24351
#define CM_EDITREPLACE          24352
#define CM_EDITFINDNEXT         24353


//
// Help menu commands.
//
#define CM_HELPABOUT            2009


//
// About Dialogs
//
```

```
#define IDD_ABOUT              22000
#define IDC_VERSION            22001
#define IDC_COPYRIGHT          22002
#define IDC_DEBUG              22003


//
// OWL defined strings
//

// Statusbar
#define IDS_MODES              32530
#define IDS_MODESOFF           32531


// EditFile
#define IDS_UNTITLED           32550
#define IDS_UNABLEREAD         32551
#define IDS_UNABLEWRITE        32552
#define IDS_FILECHANGED        32553
#define IDS_FILEFILTER         32554

// EditSearch
#define IDS_CANNOTFIND         32540


//
// General & application exception messages (include\owl\except.rh)
//
#define IDS_UNKNOWNEXCEPTION   32767
#define IDS_OWLEXCEPTION       32766
#define IDS_OKTORESUME         32765
#define IDS_UNHANDLEDXMSG      32764
#define IDS_UNKNOWNERROR       32763
#define IDS_NOAPP              32762
#define IDS_OUTOFMEMORY        32761
#define IDS_INVALIDMODULE      32760
#define IDS_INVALIDMAINWINDOW  32759
#define IDS_VBXLIBRARYFAIL     32758

//
// Owl 1 compatibility messages
//
#define IDS_INVALIDWINDOW       32756
#define IDS_INVALIDCHILDWINDOW  32755
#define IDS_INVALIDCLIENTWINDOW 32754

//
// TXWindow messages
//
#define IDS_CLASSREGISTERFAIL   32749
#define IDS_CHILDREGISTERFAIL   32748
#define IDS_WINDOWCREATEFAIL    32747
#define IDS_WINDOWEXECUTEFAIL   32746
#define IDS_CHILDCREATEFAIL     32745
```

continues

19

Listing 19.2. continued

```
#define IDS_MENUFAILURE          32744
#define IDS_VALIDATORSYNTAX      32743
#define IDS_PRINTERERROR         32742

#define IDS_LAYOUTINCOMPLETE     32741
#define IDS_LAYOUTBADRELWIN      32740

//
// TXGdi messages
//
#define IDS_GDIFAILURE           32739
#define IDS_GDIALLOCFAIL         32738
#define IDS_GDICREATEFAIL        32737
#define IDS_GDIRESLOADFAIL       32736
#define IDS_GDIFILEREADFAIL      32735
#define IDS_GDIDELETEFAIL        32734
#define IDS_GDIDESTROYFAIL       32733
#define IDS_INVALIDDIBHANDLE     32732


// TInputDialog DIALOG resource (include\owl\inputdia.rh)
#define IDD_INPUTDIALOG          32514
#define ID_PROMPT                4091
#define ID_INPUT                 4090


// TSlider bitmaps (horizontal and vertical) (include\owl\slider.rh)
#define IDB_HSLIDERTHUMB         32000
#define IDB_VSLIDERTHUMB         32001


// Validation messages (include\owl\validate.rh)
#define IDS_VALPXPCONFORM        32520
#define IDS_VALINVALIDCHAR       32521
#define IDS_VALNOTINRANGE        32522
#define IDS_VALNOTINLIST         32523


//#endif          // __exprtapp_rh sentry.
```

Analysis

Listing 19.2 shows the source code for the EXPRTAPP.RH resource header file. The file contains the definitions of constants used to manage the following menu commands and resources:

- [ ] The File menu options
- [ ] The Edit menu options
- [ ] The Help menu options
- [ ] The About dialog box
- [ ] The edit file messages
- [ ] The general and application exception messages

- [ ] The GDI exception messages
- [ ] The input dialog box resources
- [ ] The slider bitmaps
- [ ] The validation messages

Listing 19.3. The source code for the EXPRTAPP.H header file.

```
#if !defined(__exprtapp_h)              // Sentry, use file only if it's not
➥already included.
#define __exprtapp_h

/*  Project expert

Copyright © 1994. All Rights Reserved.

SUBSYSTEM:    expert.exe Application
FILE:         exprtapp.h
AUTHOR:


OVERVIEW
========
Class definition for expertApp (TApplication).
*/


#include <owl\owlpch.h>
#pragma hdrstop


#include "exprtapp.rh"            // Definition of all resources.


//
// FrameWindow must be derived to override Paint for Preview and Print.
//
//{{TDecoratedFrame = SDIDecFrame}}
class SDIDecFrame : public TDecoratedFrame {
public:
SDIDecFrame (TWindow *parent, const char far *title, TWindow *clientWnd, bool
➥trackMenuSelection = false, TModule *module = 0);
~SDIDecFrame ();
};    //{{SDIDecFrame}}


//{{TApplication = expertApp}}
class expertApp : public TApplication {
private:

public:
expertApp ();
virtual ~expertApp ();
```

continues

545

Listing 19.3. continued

```
TOpenSaveDialog::TData FileData;                  // Data to control open/saveas
➥standard dialog.
void OpenFile (const char *fileName = 0);
//{{expertAppVIRTUAL_BEGIN}}
public:
virtual void InitMainWindow();
//{{expertAppVIRTUAL_END}}

//{{expertAppRSP_TBL_BEGIN}}
protected:
void CmFileNew ();
void CmFileOpen ();
void CmHelpAbout ();
//{{expertAppRSP_TBL_END}}
DECLARE_RESPONSE_TABLE(expertApp);
};      //{{expertApp}}


#endif                                            // __exprtapp_h sentry.
```

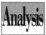

Listing 19.3 shows the source code for the EXPRTAPP.H header file. This file declares the text-editor application class expertApp as a descendant of TApplication. The class has public, protected, and private members. The public members include the constructor, destructor, and member function InitMainWindow. The protected members include the CmXXXX functions that respond to various menu commands. Note the data member FileData, an instance of class TOpenSaveDialog::TData, which stores the data for the File Open and File Save dialog boxes.

Listing 19.4. The source code for the XPRTABTD.H header file.

```
#if !defined(__xprtabtd_h)          // Sentry, use file only if it's not
➥already included.
#define __xprtabtd_h

/*  Project expert

Copyright © 1994. All Rights Reserved.

SUBSYSTEM:    expert.exe Application
FILE:         xprtabtd.h
AUTHOR:


OVERVIEW
========
Class definition for expertAboutDlg (TDialog).
*/
```

```
#include <owl\owlpch.h>
#pragma hdrstop

#include "exprtapp.rh"                      // Definition of all resources.


//{{TDialog = expertAboutDlg}}
class expertAboutDlg : public TDialog {
public:
expertAboutDlg (TWindow *parent, TResId resId = IDD_ABOUT, TModule *module = 0);
virtual ~expertAboutDlg ();

//{{expertAboutDlgVIRTUAL_BEGIN}}
public:
void SetupWindow ();
//{{expertAboutDlgVIRTUAL_END}}
};      //{{expertAboutDlg}}


// Reading the VERSIONINFO resource.
class ProjectRCVersion {
public:
ProjectRCVersion (TModule *module);
virtual ~ProjectRCVersion ();

bool GetProductName (LPSTR &prodName);
bool GetProductVersion (LPSTR &prodVersion);
bool GetCopyright (LPSTR &copyright);
bool GetDebug (LPSTR &debug);

protected:
LPBYTE      TransBlock;
void FAR    *FVData;

private:
// Don't allow this object to be copied.
ProjectRCVersion (const ProjectRCVersion &);
ProjectRCVersion & operator =(const ProjectRCVersion &);
};


#endif                                      // __xprtabtd_h sentry.
```

Analysis Listing 19.4. shows the source code for the XPRTABTD.H header file. This header file contains the declaration of the About dialog box class, expertAboutDlg. This class is a descendant of the class TDialog and declares a constructor, destructor, and the member function SetupWindow. Whereas many of the generated files will change from project to project, the About dialog source code will remain fairly constant. The only real difference will be in the name of the dialog box class, which is derived from the project name.

Type

Listing 19.5. The script for the EXPRTAPP.RC resource file.

```
/*   Project expert

Copyright © 1994. All Rights Reserved.

SUBSYSTEM:    expert.exe Application
FILE:         exprtapp.rc
AUTHOR:


OVERVIEW
========
All resources defined here.
*/

#if !defined(WORKSHOP_INVOKED)
#include <windows.h>
#endif
#include "exprtapp.rh"

SDI_MENU MENU
BEGIN
POPUP "&File"
BEGIN
MENUITEM "&New", CM_FILENEW
MENUITEM "&Open...", CM_FILEOPEN
MENUITEM SEPARATOR
MENUITEM "&Save", CM_FILESAVE, GRAYED
MENUITEM "Save &As...", CM_FILESAVEAS, GRAYED
MENUITEM SEPARATOR
MENUITEM "E&xit\tAlt+F4", CM_EXIT
END

MENUITEM SEPARATOR

POPUP "&Edit"
BEGIN
MENUITEM "&Undo\tAlt+BkSp", CM_EDITUNDO, GRAYED
MENUITEM SEPARATOR
MENUITEM "Cu&t\tShift+Del", CM_EDITCUT, GRAYED
MENUITEM "&Copy\tCtrl+Ins", CM_EDITCOPY, GRAYED
MENUITEM "&Paste\tShift+Ins", CM_EDITPASTE, GRAYED
MENUITEM SEPARATOR
MENUITEM "Clear &All\tCtrl+Del", CM_EDITCLEAR, GRAYED
MENUITEM "&Delete\tDel", CM_EDITDELETE, GRAYED
END

POPUP "&Search"
BEGIN
MENUITEM "&Find...", CM_EDITFIND, GRAYED
MENUITEM "&Replace...", CM_EDITREPLACE, GRAYED
MENUITEM "&Next\aF3", CM_EDITFINDNEXT, GRAYED
END

MENUITEM SEPARATOR
```

```
MENUITEM SEPARATOR

MENUITEM SEPARATOR

MENUITEM SEPARATOR

POPUP "&Help"
BEGIN
MENUITEM "&About...", CM_HELPABOUT
END

END


// Accelerator table for short-cut to menu commands. (include\owl\editfile.rc)
SDI_MENU ACCELERATORS
BEGIN
VK_DELETE, CM_EDITDELETE, VIRTKEY
VK_DELETE, CM_EDITCUT, VIRTKEY, SHIFT
VK_INSERT, CM_EDITCOPY, VIRTKEY, CONTROL
VK_INSERT, CM_EDITPASTE, VIRTKEY, SHIFT
VK_DELETE, CM_EDITCLEAR, VIRTKEY, CONTROL
VK_BACK,   CM_EDITUNDO, VIRTKEY, ALT
VK_F3,     CM_EDITFINDNEXT, VIRTKEY
END


//
// Table of help hints displayed in the status bar.
//
STRINGTABLE
BEGIN
                         "File/document operations"
CM_FILENEW,                "Creates a new window"
CM_FILEOPEN,               "Opens a window"
CM_FILECLOSE,              "Close this document"
CM_FILESAVE,               "Saves this document"
CM_FILESAVEAS,             "Saves this document with a new name"
CM_EXIT,                   "Quits expertApp and prompts to save the documents"
CM_EDITUNDO-1,             "Edit operations"
CM_EDITUNDO,               "Reverses the last operation"
CM_EDITCUT,                "Cuts the selection and puts it on the Clipboard"
CM_EDITCOPY,               "Copies the selection and puts it on the Clipboard"
CM_EDITPASTE,              "Inserts the clipboard contents at the insertion point"
CM_EDITDELETE,             "Deletes the selection"
CM_EDITCLEAR,              "Clear the document"
CM_EDITADD,                "Insert a new line"
CM_EDITEDIT,               "Edit the current line"
CM_EDITFIND-1,             "Search/replace operations"
CM_EDITFIND,               "Finds the specified text"
CM_EDITREPLACE,            "Finds the specified text and changes it"
CM_EDITFINDNEXT,           "Finds the next match"
CM_HELPABOUT-1,            "Access About"
CM_HELPABOUT,              "About the expert application"
END
```

continues

Listing 19.5. continued

```
//
// OWL string table
//

// EditFile (include\owl\editfile.rc and include\owl\editsear.rc)
STRINGTABLE LOADONCALL MOVEABLE DISCARDABLE
BEGIN
IDS_CANNOTFIND,              "Cannot find ""%s""."
IDS_UNTITLED,               "Document"
IDS_UNABLEREAD,             "Unable to read file %s from disk."
IDS_UNABLEWRITE,            "Unable to write file %s to disk."
IDS_FILECHANGED,            "The text in the %s file has changed.\n\nDo you want to
➥save the changes?"
IDS_FILEFILTER,             "Text files (*.TXT)¦*.TXT¦AllFiles (*.*)¦*.*¦"
END


// Exception string resources (include\owl\except.rc)
STRINGTABLE LOADONCALL MOVEABLE DISCARDABLE
BEGIN
IDS_OWLEXCEPTION,           "ObjectWindows Exception"
IDS_UNHANDLEDXMSG,          "Unhandled Exception"
IDS_OKTORESUME,             "OK to resume?"
IDS_UNKNOWNEXCEPTION,       "Unknown exception"

IDS_UNKNOWNERROR,           "Unknown error"
IDS_NOAPP,                  "No application object"
IDS_OUTOFMEMORY,            "Out of memory"
IDS_INVALIDMODULE,          "Invalid module specified for window"
IDS_INVALIDMAINWINDOW,      "Invalid MainWindow"
IDS_VBXLIBRARYFAIL,         "VBX Library init failure"

IDS_INVALIDWINDOW,          "Invalid window %s"
IDS_INVALIDCHILDWINDOW,     "Invalid child window %s"
IDS_INVALIDCLIENTWINDOW,    "Invalid client window %s"

IDS_CLASSREGISTERFAIL,      "Class registration fail for window %s"
IDS_CHILDREGISTERFAIL,      "Child class registration fail for window %s"
IDS_WINDOWCREATEFAIL,       "Create fail for window %s"
IDS_WINDOWEXECUTEFAIL,      "Execute fail for window %s"
IDS_CHILDCREATEFAIL,        "Child create fail for window %s"

IDS_MENUFAILURE,            "Menu creation failure"
IDS_VALIDATORSYNTAX,        "Validator syntax error"
IDS_PRINTERERROR,           "Printer error"

IDS_LAYOUTINCOMPLETE,       "Incomplete layout constraints specified in window %s"
IDS_LAYOUTBADRELWIN,        "Invalid relative window specified in layout constraint
➥in window %s"

IDS_GDIFAILURE,             "GDI failure"
IDS_GDIALLOCFAIL,           "GDI allocate failure"
IDS_GDICREATEFAIL,          "GDI creation failure"
IDS_GDIRESLOADFAIL,         "GDI resource load failure"
```

```
IDS_GDIFILEREADFAIL,        "GDI file read failure"
IDS_GDIDELETEFAIL,          "GDI object %X delete failure"
IDS_GDIDESTROYFAIL,         "GDI object %X destroy failure"
IDS_INVALIDDIBHANDLE,       "Invalid DIB handle %X"
END


// General Window's status bar messages. (include\owl\statusba.rc)
STRINGTABLE
BEGIN
IDS_MODES                   "EXT¦CAPS¦NUM¦SCRL¦OVR¦REC"
IDS_MODESOFF                "    ¦    ¦   ¦    ¦   ¦   "
SC_SIZE,                    "Changes the size of the window"
SC_MOVE,                    "Moves the window to another position"
SC_MINIMIZE,                "Reduces the window to an icon"
SC_MAXIMIZE,                "Enlarges the window to its maximum size"
SC_RESTORE,                 "Restores the window to its previous size"
SC_CLOSE,                   "Closes the window"
SC_TASKLIST,                "Opens task list"
SC_NEXTWINDOW,              "Switches to next window"
END


// Validator messages (include\owl\validate.rc)
STRINGTABLE LOADONCALL MOVEABLE DISCARDABLE
BEGIN
IDS_VALPXPCONFORM           "Input does not conform to picture:\n""%s"""
IDS_VALINVALIDCHAR          "Invalid character in input"
IDS_VALNOTINRANGE           "Value is not in the range %ld to %ld."
IDS_VALNOTINLIST            "Input is not in valid-list"
END


//
// Misc application definitions
//

// Application ICON
IDI_SDIAPPLICATION ICON "applsdi.ico"


// About box.
IDD_ABOUT DIALOG 12, 17, 204, 65
STYLE DS_MODALFRAME ¦ WS_POPUP ¦ WS_CAPTION ¦ WS_SYSMENU
CAPTION "About expert"
FONT 8, "MS Sans Serif"
BEGIN
CTEXT "Version", IDC_VERSION, 2, 14, 200, 8, SS_NOPREFIX
CTEXT "My Application", -1, 2, 4, 200, 8, SS_NOPREFIX
CTEXT "", IDC_COPYRIGHT, 2, 27, 200, 17, SS_NOPREFIX
RTEXT "", IDC_DEBUG, 136, 55, 66, 8, SS_NOPREFIX
ICON IDI_SDIAPPLICATION, -1, 2, 2, 34, 34
DEFPUSHBUTTON "OK", IDOK, 82, 48, 40, 14
END
```

19

continues

Listing 19.5. continued

```
// TInputDialog class dialog box.
IDD_INPUTDIALOG DIALOG 20, 24, 180, 64
STYLE WS_POPUP | WS_CAPTION | DS_SETFONT
FONT 8, "Helv"
BEGIN
LTEXT "", ID_PROMPT, 10, 8, 160, 10, SS_NOPREFIX
CONTROL "", ID_INPUT, "EDIT", WS_CHILD | WS_VISIBLE | WS_BORDER | WS_TABSTOP |
➥ES_AUTOHSCROLL, 10, 20, 160, 12
DEFPUSHBUTTON "&OK", IDOK, 47, 42, 40, 14
PUSHBUTTON "&Cancel", IDCANCEL, 93, 42, 40, 14
END


// Horizontal slider thumb bitmap for TSlider and VSlider (include\owl\slider.rc)
IDB_HSLIDERTHUMB BITMAP PRELOAD MOVEABLE DISCARDABLE
BEGIN
'42 4D 66 01 00 00 00 00 00 00 76 00 00 00 28 00'
'00 00 12 00 00 00 14 00 00 00 01 00 04 00 00 00'
'00 00 F0 00 00 00 00 00 00 00 00 00 00 00 00 00'
'00 00 10 00 00 00 00 00 00 00 00 00 C0 00 00 C0'
'00 00 00 C0 C0 00 C0 00 00 00 C0 00 00 C0 C0'
'00 00 C0 C0 C0 00 80 80 80 00 00 00 FF 00 00 FF'
'00 00 00 FF FF 00 FF 00 00 00 FF 00 FF 00 FF FF'
'00 00 FF FF FF 00 BB BB 0B BB BB BB B0 BB BB 00'
'00 00 BB B0 80 BB BB BB 08 0B BB 00 00 00 BB 08'
'F8 0B BB B0 87 70 BB 00 00 00 B0 8F F8 80 BB 08'
'77 77 0B 00 00 00 08 F8 88 88 00 88 88 87 70 00'
'00 00 0F F7 77 88 00 88 77 77 70 00 00 00 0F F8'
'88 88 00 88 88 87 70 00 00 00 0F F7 77 88 00 88'
'77 77 70 00 00 00 0F F8 88 88 00 88 88 87 70 00'
'00 00 0F F7 77 88 00 88 77 77 70 00 00 00 0F F8'
'88 88 00 88 88 87 70 00 00 00 0F F7 77 88 00 88'
'77 77 70 00 00 00 0F F8 88 88 00 88 88 87 70 00'
'00 00 0F F7 77 88 00 88 77 77 70 00 00 00 0F F8'
'88 88 00 88 88 87 70 00 00 00 0F F7 77 88 00 88'
'77 77 70 00 00 00 0F F8 88 88 00 88 88 87 70 00'
'00 00 0F F7 77 78 00 88 77 77 70 00 00 00 0F FF'
'FF FF 00 88 88 88 80 00 00 00 B0 00 00 00 BB 00'
'00 00 0B 00 00 00'
END


// Vertical slider thumb bitmap for TSlider and HSlider (include\owl\slider.rc)
IDB_VSLIDERTHUMB BITMAP PRELOAD MOVEABLE DISCARDABLE
BEGIN
'42 4D 2A 01 00 00 00 00 00 00 76 00 00 00 28 00'
'00 00 28 00 00 00 09 00 00 00 01 00 04 00 00 00'
'00 00 B4 00 00 00 00 00 00 00 00 00 00 00 00 00'
'00 00 10 00 00 00 00 00 00 00 00 00 C0 00 00 C0'
'00 00 00 C0 C0 00 C0 00 00 00 C0 00 00 C0 C0'
'00 00 C0 C0 C0 00 80 80 80 00 00 00 FF 00 00 FF'
'00 00 00 FF FF 00 FF 00 00 00 FF 00 FF 00 FF FF'
'00 00 FF FF FF 00 B0 00 00 00 00 00 00 00 00 0B'
'B0 00 00 00 00 00 00 00 00 0B 0F 88 88 88 88 88'
'88 88 88 80 08 88 88 88 88 88 88 88 80 0F 77'
'77 77 77 77 77 77 80 08 77 77 77 77 77 77 77'
END
```

```
'77 80 0F 77 FF FF FF FF FF FF F7 80 08 77 FF FF'
'FF FF FF FF F7 80 0F 70 00 00 00 00 00 00 77 80'
'08 70 00 00 00 00 00 00 77 80 0F 77 77 77 77 77'
'77 77 77 80 08 77 77 77 77 77 77 77 77 80 0F 77'
'77 77 77 77 77 77 80 08 77 77 77 77 77 77 77 77'
'77 80 0F FF FF FF FF FF FF FF F0 08 88 88 88'
'88 88 88 88 88 80 B0 00 00 00 00 00 00 00 00 0B'
'B0 00 00 00 00 00 00 00 00 0B'
END


// Version info.
//
#if !defined(__DEBUG_)
// Non-Debug VERSIONINFO
VERSIONINFO LOADONCALL MOVEABLE
FILEVERSION 1, 0, 0, 0
PRODUCTVERSION 1, 0, 0, 0
FILEFLAGSMASK 0
FILEFLAGS VS_FFI_FILEFLAGSMASK
FILEOS VOS__WINDOWS16
FILETYPE VFT_APP
BEGIN
BLOCK "StringFileInfo"
BEGIN
// Language type = U.S. English (0x0409) and Character Set = Windows,
Multilingual(0x04e4)
BLOCK "040904E4"                           // Matches VarFileInfo Translation hex
➥value.
BEGIN
VALUE "CompanyName", "\000"
VALUE "FileDescription", "expert for Windows\000"
VALUE "FileVersion", "1.0\000"
VALUE "InternalName", "expert\000"
VALUE "LegalCopyright", "Copyright © 1994. All Rights Reserved.\000"
VALUE "LegalTrademarks", "Windows (TM) is a trademark of Microsoft Corporation\000"
VALUE "OriginalFilename", "expert.EXE\000"
VALUE "ProductName", "expert\000"
VALUE "ProductVersion", "1.0\000"
END
END

BLOCK "VarFileInfo"
BEGIN
VALUE "Translation", 0x0409, 0x04e4        // U.S. English(0x0409) & Windows
➥Multilingual(0x04e4) 1252
END

END
#else

// Debug VERSIONINFO
VERSIONINFO LOADONCALL MOVEABLE
FILEVERSION 1, 0, 0, 0
PRODUCTVERSION 1, 0, 0, 0
FILEFLAGSMASK VS_FF_DEBUG | VS_FF_PRERELEASE | VS_FF_PATCHED | VS_FF_PRIVATEBUILD |
➥VS_FF_SPECIALBUILD
```

19

Listing 19.5. continued

```
FILEFLAGS VS_FFI_FILEFLAGSMASK
FILEOS VOS__WINDOWS16
FILETYPE VFT_APP
BEGIN
BLOCK "StringFileInfo"
BEGIN
// Language type = U.S. English (0x0409) and Character Set = Windows,
Multilingual(0x04e4)
BLOCK "040904E4"                              // Matches VarFileInfo Translation hex
➥value.
BEGIN
VALUE "CompanyName", "\000"
VALUE "FileDescription", "expert for Windows\000"
VALUE "FileVersion", "1.0\000"
VALUE "InternalName", "expert\000"
VALUE "LegalCopyright", "Copyright © 1994. All Rights Reserved.\000"
VALUE "LegalTrademarks", "Windows (TM) is a trademark of Microsoft Corporation\000"
VALUE "OriginalFilename", "expert.EXE\000"
VALUE "ProductName", "expert\000"
VALUE "ProductVersion", "1.0\000"
VALUE "SpecialBuild", "Debug Version\000"
VALUE "PrivateBuild", "Built by \000"
END
END

BLOCK "VarFileInfo"
BEGIN
VALUE "Translation", 0x0409, 0x04e4      // U.S. English(0x0409) & Windows
Multilingual(0x04e4) 1252
END

END
#endif
```

Listing 19.5 contains the script for the EXPRTAPP.RC resource file. This file contains the definition of the various menu, accelerator, string, icon, and dialog box resources.

Listing 19.6. The source code for the XPRTABTD.CPP implementation file.

```
/*  Project expert

Copyright © 1994. All Rights Reserved.

SUBSYSTEM:    expert.exe Application
FILE:         xprtabtd.cpp
AUTHOR:


OVERVIEW
========
Source file for implementation of expertAboutDlg (TDialog).
*/
```

```
#include <owl\owlpch.h>
#pragma hdrstop

#if !defined(__FLAT__)
#include <ver.h>
#endif

#include "exprtapp.h"
#include "xprtabtd.h"


ProjectRCVersion::ProjectRCVersion (TModule *module)
{
char     appFName[255];
char     subBlockName[255];
DWORD    fvHandle;
UINT     vSize;

FVData = 0;

module->GetModuleFileName(appFName, sizeof(appFName));
OemToAnsi(appFName, appFName);
DWORD dwSize = ::GetFileVersionInfoSize(appFName, &fvHandle);
if (dwSize) {
FVData  = (void FAR *)new char[(UINT)dwSize];
if (::GetFileVersionInfo(appFName, fvHandle, dwSize, FVData)) {
// Copy string to buffer so if the -dc compiler switch (Put constant strings in
➥code segments)
// is on VerQueryValue will work under Win16.  This works around a problem in
➥Microsoft's ver.dll
// which writes to the string pointed to by subBlockName.
strcpy(subBlockName, "\\VarFileInfo\\Translation");
if (!::VerQueryValue(FVData, subBlockName, (void FAR* FAR*)&TransBlock, &vSize)) {
delete FVData;
FVData = 0;
} else
// Swap the words so wsprintf will print the lang-charset in the correct format.
*(DWORD *)TransBlock = MAKELONG(HIWORD(*(DWORD *)TransBlock), LOWORD(*(DWORD
➥*)TransBlock));
}
}
}


ProjectRCVersion::~ProjectRCVersion ()
{
if (FVData)
delete FVData;
}


bool ProjectRCVersion::GetProductName (LPSTR &prodName)
{
UINT     vSize;
char     subBlockName[255];
```

Listing 19.6. continued

```
wsprintf(subBlockName, "\\StringFileInfo\\%08lx\\%s", *(DWORD *)TransBlock,
➥(LPSTR)"ProductName");
return FVData ? ::VerQueryValue(FVData, subBlockName, (void FAR* FAR*)&prodName,
➥&vSize) : false;
}


bool ProjectRCVersion::GetProductVersion (LPSTR &prodVersion)
{
UINT    vSize;
char    subBlockName[255];

wsprintf(subBlockName, "\\StringFileInfo\\%08lx\\%s", *(DWORD *)TransBlock,
➥(LPSTR)"ProductVersion");
return FVData ? ::VerQueryValue(FVData, subBlockName, (void FAR* FAR*)&prodVersion,
➥&vSize) : false;
}


bool ProjectRCVersion::GetCopyright (LPSTR &copyright)
{
UINT    vSize;
char    subBlockName[255];

wsprintf(subBlockName, "\\StringFileInfo\\%08lx\\%s", *(DWORD *)TransBlock,
➥(LPSTR)"LegalCopyright");
return FVData ? ::VerQueryValue(FVData, subBlockName, (void FAR* FAR*)&copyright,
➥&vSize) : false;
}


bool ProjectRCVersion::GetDebug (LPSTR &debug)
{
UINT    vSize;
char    subBlockName[255];

wsprintf(subBlockName, "\\StringFileInfo\\%08lx\\%s", *(DWORD *)TransBlock,
➥(LPSTR)"SpecialBuild");
return FVData ? ::VerQueryValue(FVData, subBlockName, (void FAR* FAR*)&debug,
➥&vSize) : false;
}


//{{expertAboutDlg Implementation}}


/////////////////////////////////////////////////////////
// expertAboutDlg
// ==========
// Construction/Destruction handling.
expertAboutDlg::expertAboutDlg (TWindow *parent, TResId resId, TModule *module)
: TDialog(parent, resId, module)
{
// INSERT>> Your constructor code here.
}
```

```
expertAboutDlg::~expertAboutDlg ()
{
Destroy();

// INSERT>> Your destructor code here.
}


void expertAboutDlg::SetupWindow ()
{
LPSTR prodName = 0, prodVersion = 0, copyright = 0, debug = 0;

// Get the static text for the value based on VERSIONINFO.
TStatic *versionCtrl = new TStatic(this, IDC_VERSION, 255);
TStatic *copyrightCtrl = new TStatic(this, IDC_COPYRIGHT, 255);
TStatic *debugCtrl = new TStatic(this, IDC_DEBUG, 255);

TDialog::SetupWindow();

// Process the VERSIONINFO.
ProjectRCVersion applVersion(GetModule());

// Get the product name and product version strings.
if (applVersion.GetProductName(prodName) &&
➥applVersion.GetProductVersion(prodVersion)) {
// IDC_VERSION is the product name and version number, the initial value of
➥IDC_VERSION is
// the word Version (in whatever language) product name VERSION product version.
char    buffer[255];
char    versionName[128];

buffer[0] = '\0';
versionName[0] = '\0';

versionCtrl->GetText(versionName, sizeof(versionName));
wsprintf(buffer, "%s %s %s", prodName, versionName, prodVersion);

versionCtrl->SetText(buffer);
}

//Get the legal copyright string.
if (applVersion.GetCopyright(copyright))
copyrightCtrl->SetText(copyright);

// Only get the SpecialBuild text if the VERSIONINFO resource is there.
if (applVersion.GetDebug(debug))
debugCtrl->SetText(debug);
}
```

Listing 19.6 shows the source code for the XPRTABTD.CPP implementation file. This file defines the class expertAboutDlg, which implements the About dialog box. In addition, the file declares and defines the project resource version class, ProjectRCVersion. Look

briefly at this class first. The class defines a constructor, destructor, a set of public member functions, and two protected data members. The class `ProjectRCVersion` supports operations that extract the information about the product name, version, and copyright.

The About dialog box class defines the following members:

- ☐ The constructor simply invokes the constructor of the parent class `TDialog`. The constructor has no executable statements and contains a comment that indicates where to place your code to support additional initialization.

- ☐ The destructor simply calls the inherited member function `Destroy`. The definition contains a comment that indicates where to place your code to support additional cleanup.

- ☐ The member function `SetupWindow` is a bit more interesting; it sets up the About dialog box by carrying out the following tasks:

  - ☐ Creates three static text control objects for the version, copyright, and debug information. The function assigns the addresses of these controls to the local pointers `versionCtrl`, `copyrightCtrl`, and `debugCtrl`. These objects are surrogate objects for the statics created in the dialog resource.

  - ☐ Invokes the `SetupWindow` member function of the parent dialog box class.

  - ☐ Creates the instance `applVersion` of the class `ProjectRCVersion`.

  - ☐ Calls `applVersion`'s `GetProductName` and `GetProductVersion` to obtain the product name and version. If successful in getting these, the function then sets the `versionCtrl` static text box with the names.

  - ☐ Calls `applVersion`'s `GetCopyright` to obtain the copyright information from the dialog box resource. If successful, it then sets the corresponding static text box.

  - ☐ Assigns the debug information to the debug static text control if `applVersion`'s `GetDebug` function returns a nonzero value.

 Listing 19.7. The source code for the EXPRTAPP.CPP implementation file.

```
/*  Project expert

Copyright © 1994. All Rights Reserved.

SUBSYSTEM:    expert.exe Application
FILE:         exprtapp.cpp
AUTHOR:


OVERVIEW
========
Source file for implementation of expertApp (TApplication).
*/
```

```
#include <owl\owlpch.h>
#pragma hdrstop


#include "exprtapp.h"
#include "xprtedtf.h"                          // Definition of client class.
#include "xprtabtd.h"                          // Definition of about dialog.


//{{expertApp Implementation}}


//
// Build a response table for all messages/commands handled
// by the application.
//
DEFINE_RESPONSE_TABLE1(expertApp, TApplication)
//{{expertAppRSP_TBL_BEGIN}}
EV_COMMAND(CM_FILENEW, CmFileNew),
EV_COMMAND(CM_FILEOPEN, CmFileOpen),
EV_COMMAND(CM_HELPABOUT, CmHelpAbout),
//{{expertAppRSP_TBL_END}}
END_RESPONSE_TABLE;


//////////////////////////////////////////////////////////
// expertApp
// =====
//
expertApp::expertApp () : TApplication("expert")
{

// Common file file flags and filters for Open/Save As dialogs.  Filename and
➥directory are
// computed in the member functions CmFileOpen, and CmFileSaveAs.
FileData.Flags = OFN_FILEMUSTEXIST ¦ OFN_HIDEREADONLY ¦ OFN_OVERWRITEPROMPT;
FileData.SetFilter("All Files (*.*)¦*.*¦");

// INSERT>> Your constructor code here.
}


expertApp::~expertApp ()
{
// INSERT>> Your destructor code here.
}


//////////////////////////////////////////////////////////
// expertApp
// =====
// Application intialization.
//
void expertApp::InitMainWindow ()
```

continues

Listing 19.7. continued

```
{
if (nCmdShow != SW_HIDE)
nCmdShow = (nCmdShow != SW_SHOWMINNOACTIVE) ? SW_SHOWNORMAL : nCmdShow;

SDIDecFrame *frame = new SDIDecFrame(0, GetName(), 0, false);

//
// Assign ICON w/ this application.
//
frame->SetIcon(this, IDI_SDIAPPLICATION);

//
// Menu associated with window and accelerator table associated with table.
//
frame->AssignMenu(SDI_MENU);

//
// Associate with the accelerator table.
//
frame->Attr.AccelTable = SDI_MENU;


SetMainWindow(frame);

frame->SetMenuDescr(TMenuDescr(SDI_MENU));
}


/////////////////////////////////////////////////////////
// expertApp
// ==========
// Menu File New command
void expertApp::CmFileNew ()
{
expertEditFile *client = TYPESAFE_DOWNCAST(GetMainWindow()->GetClientWindow(),
➥expertEditFile);     // Client window for the frame.
client->NewFile();
}


/////////////////////////////////////////////////////////
// expertApp
// ==========
// Menu File Open command
void expertApp::CmFileOpen ()
{
//
// Display standard Open dialog box to select a file name.
//
*FileData.FileName = 0;

expertEditFile *client = TYPESAFE_DOWNCAST(GetMainWindow()->GetClientWindow(),
➥expertEditFile);     // Client window for the frame.
if (client->CanClose())
if (TFileOpenDialog(GetMainWindow(), FileData).Execute() == IDOK)
```

```
OpenFile();
}


void expertApp::OpenFile (const char *fileName)
{
if (fileName)
strcpy(FileData.FileName, fileName);

expertEditFile *client = TYPESAFE_DOWNCAST(GetMainWindow()->GetClientWindow(),
➡expertEditFile);    // Client window for the frame.
client->ReplaceWith(FileData.FileName);
}


//{{SDIDecFrame Implementation}}


SDIDecFrame::SDIDecFrame (TWindow *parent, const char far *title, TWindow
➡*clientWnd, bool trackMenuSelection, TModule *module)
: TDecoratedFrame(parent, title, clientWnd == 0 ? new expertEditFile(0, 0, 0) :
➡clientWnd, trackMenuSelection, module)
{
// INSERT>> Your constructor code here.

}


SDIDecFrame::~SDIDecFrame ()
{
// INSERT>> Your destructor code here.

}


////////////////////////////////////////////////////////////
// expertApp
// ===========
// Menu Help About expert.exe command
void expertApp::CmHelpAbout ()
{
//
// Show the modal dialog.
//
expertAboutDlg(MainWindow).Execute();
}
int OwlMain (int , char* [])
{
try {
expertApp    app;
return app.Run();
}
catch (xmsg& x) {
::MessageBox(0, x.why().c_str(), "Exception", MB_OK);
}

return -1;
}
```

19

Listing 19.7 shows the source code for the EXPRTAPP.CPP implementation file. The listing includes the XPRTABTD.H header file to access the definition of the application and About dialog box classes. In addition, the listing contains the declaration of a class that models a decorated SDI window frame.

The listing contains the definition of the message-response table for the application class expertApp. The table includes a set of EV_COMMAND macros to map the various CM_*XXXX* commands with their respective Cm*XXXX* member functions.

The listing contains the definitions of the following members:

☐ The constructor, which performs the following minimal initialization:

    ☐ Assigns an expression of bitwise ORed OFN_*XXXX* constants to the Flags member of the data member FileData.

    ☐ Calls the data member FileData's SetFilter member function with a string literal argument that assigns the file-type filters to the member FileData.

        The preceding assignments initialize the data member FileData to prepare it for the dialog boxes that open and save files. The constructor contains a comment that indicates where to place statements for additional initialization.

☐ The destructor merely contains a comment that indicates where to place statements for application clean-up.

☐ The member function InitMainWindow initializes the main window by carrying out the following tasks:

    ☐ Assigns a value to the inherited data member nCmdShow such that the window appears in its normal state.

    ☐ Creates a new decorated SDI frame window by allocating an instance of class SDIDecFrame. The function assigns the address of this instance to the local pointer frame.

    ☐ Assigns the application's icon using the icon resource IDI_SDIAPPLICATION. This involves calling the member function SetIcon of the SDI window accessed by the pointer frame.

    ☐ Assigns the application's menu using the menu resource SDI_MENU using the frame's AssignMenu member function.

    ☐ Assigns the accelerator table SDI_MENU to the frame window.

    ☐ Uses the SetMainWindow member function to set the main window to frame.

    ☐ Sets the menu descriptor to the SDI_MENU resource.

☐ The member function CmFileNew responds to the New menu option by sending the C++ message NewFile to the window client area accessed by pointer client.

- The member function `CmFileOpen` responds to the Open menu option. The function contains nested `if` statements. The outer `if` statement sends the C++ message `CanClose` to the client area. If this message returns a nonzero value, the function `CmFileOpen` executes the nested `if` statement. This statement creates a dynamic instance of the class `TFileOpenDialog` and sends it the C++ message `Execute`. The `if` statement compares the result of the message with the predefined constant `IDOK`. If the two values match, the function invokes the member function `OpenFile`.

- The member function `OpenFile` performs two simple tasks. The first task assigns the string in the parameter `fileName` to the member `FileName` of data member `FileData`. The second task updates the title of the window with the name of the newly opened file. The function performs this task by sending the C++ message `ReplaceWith` to the window client area object. The argument of this message is the member `FileName` of the data member `FileData`.

- The listing offers the definition of class `SDIDecFrame`. This class, a descendant of class `TDecoratedFrame`, models the decorated SDI frame window. The AppExpert comments remind you that this class needs to override the member functions that support the printing and print-previewing features. The class declares a constructor and a dummy destructor.

- The `expertApp`'s member function `CmHelpAbout` responds to the Help | About menu option. The function creates a new instance of class `expertAboutDlg` to invoke the About dialog box. The function invokes this modal dialog box by sending it the C++ message `Execute`.

Finally, the typical `OwlMain` is presented in which an `expertApp` object is created and run. Note that this is enclosed automatically in a `try/catch` block to keep exceptions from getting out of hand.

Altering AppExpert's Options

As mentioned before, the potential output from the AppExpert is varied. I go over some different output on Day 20 when I use the AppExpert to jump-start the creation of an OLE2 application. In the meantime, you really need to experiment with all the various options.

For one thing, letting the AppExpert generate code for you, and then studying that output is a great way of figuring out how to get certain things done with Turbo C++, such as generating an application that uses a toolbar (there's a check box on the first AppExpert option screen). You see many extra files generated, particularly .BMP files with bitmaps, that will be displayed on the buttons in the toolbar. You also will see how the toolbar is set up and used.

Invoking ClassExpert

To use the *ClassExpert*, invoke the ClassExpert menu option in the View menu selection. Figure 19.13 shows a sample session with the ClassExpert utility in a project created by AppExpert. The ClassExpert window contains three panes: the Classes pane, the Events pane, and the editor pane. The Classes pane lists the classes in the current project. If there are too many classes to fit in this pane, the ClassExpert window displays vertical scroll bars. The Events pane shows an outline of the various messages for the selected class in the Classes pane. These messages include command notifications, control notifications, virtual functions, and Windows messages. The thick + symbol indicates that an outline item is hiding sub-items. The thick – symbol indicates that the item is expanded. The editor pane is supported by a BRIEF-like smart editor that enables you to enter, edit, and delete statements.

When you select a different class in the Class pane, the contents of the Events pane automatically change to reflect the events available for the newly selected class.

When you expand the outlines in the Events pane, notice check marks to the left of certain outline items. These check marks indicate that the event has a handler in the project's source code.

Figure 19.13.
A sample session with the ClassExpert utility.

Note: The right mouse button offers versatile, context-sensitive pop-up menus that enable you to perform various tasks. (The pop-up menus are so context-sensitive that they vary not only from one pane to another, but also between one type of selection and another in the same pane.)

The following sections describe how to add new member functions and classes.

Adding New Member Functions

Use the simple SDI-compliant text editor you just finished. First, add an additional menu in the Resource Workshop. This new menu should support the following features:

- ☐ Converting the selected text or the entire contents of the file (if there is no selected text) to lowercase characters
- ☐ Converting the selected text or the entire contents of the file (if there is no selected text) to uppercase characters
- ☐ Reversing the characters of the selected text or the entire contents of the file (if there is no selected text)
- ☐ Inserting the current date
- ☐ Inserting the current time
- ☐ Inserting the current date and time

Each of the preceding features is supported by a menu option. Each menu option has an event-handler member function. To create the new application, follow these general steps:

1. Use the Resource Workshop to add the menu selection Special and its nested menu options Lowercase, UpperCase, Reverse, Insert Date, Insert Time, and Insert Date/Time. (Consult Part II of the *Turbo C++ User's Guide* manual to learn more about using this utility.) Use the identifiers CM_LOWERCASE, CM_UPPERCASE, CM_REVERSE, CM_INSDATE, CM_INSTIME, and CM_INSDATETIME, respectively, for the menu options. Insert a separator menu item between the first three and last three menu options in the menu selection. The targeted menu resource is the one with the ID SDI_MENU. When you finish adding the preceding menu items, save the updated resources.

2. Use the ClassExpert utility to add the member functions needed to handle the six new menu options. Click on expertApp in the Classes pane, and then on the plus sign of the Command Notifications item in the Events pane to expand that outline item.

3. Search for the CM_LOWERCASE identifier, which represents the commands for the new menu option Lowercase.

4. Click in the + symbol located to the left of the identifier CM_LOWERCASE. This action reveals two nested outline items: Command and Command Enable.

5. Select the Command outline and click the right mouse button to access the pop-up menu.

6. Select and invoke the Add Handler menu option. This option prompts you with a simple input dialog box, which requests that you enter the name of the handler

member function. Type **CMLowerCase** and then click the OK button of the dialog box. The ClassExpert responds by creating the following:

☐ The declaration of member function CMLowerCase in the declaration of class expertApp (located in the header file EXPRTAPP.H)

☐ The event response-table macro that links the command CM_LOWERCASE with the member function CMLowerCase (located in the implementation file EXPRTAPP.CPP)

☐ The empty definition of member function CMLowerCase (located in the implementation file EXPRTAPP.CPP)

7. Repeat steps 4 through 7 for the other CM_XXXX constants that handle the remaining new menu options. Specify the member functions CmUppercase, CmInsertDate, CmInsertTime, CmInsertDateTime, and CmReverse to handle the Windows commands CM_UPPERCASE, CM_INSDATE, CM_INSTIME, CM_INSDATETIME, and CM_REVERSE, respectively.

8. Add the header files STDIO.H, STRING.H, and DOS.H, along with the statements for the member function CmXXXX in file EXPRTAPP.CPP. (More about these statements later.)

9. Add the functionality for each of these new member functions by double-clicking on the appropriate Command members for each of the new events. You then can use the editor window on the bottom of the ClassExpert window to modify the empty member-function stubs.

If you take a look at EXPRTAPP.RH, you'll see the new CM_XXXX identifiers, and EXPRTAPP.RC contains an updated menu. EXPRTAPP.H has the new CmXXXX member functions added to the expertApp class, and EXPRTAPP.CPP now has the new code for those member functions. Listing 19.8 shows the new version of EXPRTAPP.CPP with the new member functions that implement the text manipulation.

Type

Listing 19.8. The new source code for the EXPRTAPP.CPP implementation file.

```
 1:     /*  Project expert
 2:
 3:     Copyright © 1994. All Rights Reserved.
 4:
 5:     SUBSYSTEM:    expert.exe Application
 6:     FILE:         exprtapp.cpp
 7:     AUTHOR:
 8:
 9:
10:     OVERVIEW
11:     ========
12:     Source file for implementation of expertApp (TApplication).
13:     */
14:
15:
```

```
16:        #include <owl\owlpch.h>
17:        #pragma hdrstop
18:
19:        #include <dos.h>
20:        #include <stdio.h>
21:        #include <string.h>
22:
23:        #include "exprtapp.h"
24:        #include "xprtedtf.h"                          // Definition of client class.
25:        #include "xprtabtd.h"                          // Definition of about dialog.
26:
27:
28:        //{{expertApp Implementation}}
29:
30:
31:        //
32:        // Build a response table for all messages/commands handled
33:        // by the application.
34:        //
35:        DEFINE_RESPONSE_TABLE1(expertApp, TApplication)
36:        //{{expertAppRSP_TBL_BEGIN}}
37:        EV_COMMAND(CM_FILENEW, CmFileNew),
38:        EV_COMMAND(CM_FILEOPEN, CmFileOpen),
39:        EV_COMMAND(CM_HELPABOUT, CmHelpAbout),
40:        EV_COMMAND(CM_LOWERCASE, CmLowercase),
41:        EV_COMMAND(CM_UPPERCASE, CmUppercase),
42:        EV_COMMAND(CM_REVERSE, CmReverse),
43:        EV_COMMAND(CM_INSDATE, CmInsertDate),
44:        EV_COMMAND(CM_INSTIME, CmInsertTime),
45:        EV_COMMAND(CM_INSDATETIME, CmInsertDateTime),
46:        //{{expertAppRSP_TBL_END}}
47:        END_RESPONSE_TABLE;
48:
49:
50:        ////////////////////////////////////////////////////////////
51:        // expertApp
52:        // =====
53:        //
54:        expertApp::expertApp () : TApplication("expert")
55:        {
56:
57:        // Common file file flags and filters for Open/Save As dialogs.
                ➥Filename and directory are
58:        // computed in the member functions CmFileOpen, and CmFileSaveAs.
59:        FileData.Flags = OFN_FILEMUSTEXIST ¦ OFN_HIDEREADONLY ¦
                ➥OFN_OVERWRITEPROMPT;
60:        FileData.SetFilter("All Files (*.*)¦*.*¦");
61:
62:        // INSERT>> Your constructor code here.
63:        }
64:
65:
66:        expertApp::~expertApp ()
67:        {
68:        // INSERT>> Your destructor code here.
69:        }
70:
```

Listing 19.8. continued

```
71:
72:     //////////////////////////////////////////////////////
73:     // expertApp
74:     // =====
75:     // Application intialization.
76:     //
77:     void expertApp::InitMainWindow ()
78:     {
79:     if (nCmdShow != SW_HIDE)
80:     nCmdShow = (nCmdShow != SW_SHOWMINNOACTIVE) ? SW_SHOWNORMAL : nCmdShow;
81:
82:     SDIDecFrame *frame = new SDIDecFrame(0, GetName(), 0, false);
83:
84:     //
85:     // Assign ICON w/ this application.
86:     //
87:     frame->SetIcon(this, IDI_SDIAPPLICATION);
88:
89:     //
90:     // Menu associated with window and accelerator table associated with
            ➥table.
91:     //
92:     frame->AssignMenu(SDI_MENU);
93:
94:     //
95:     // Associate with the accelerator table.
96:     //
97:     frame->Attr.AccelTable = SDI_MENU;
98:
99:
100:    SetMainWindow(frame);
101:
102:    frame->SetMenuDescr(TMenuDescr(SDI_MENU));
103:    }
104:
105:
106:    //////////////////////////////////////////////////////
107:    // expertApp
108:    // ===========
109:    // Menu File New command
110:    void expertApp::CmFileNew ()
111:    {
112:    expertEditFile *client = TYPESAFE_DOWNCAST(GetMainWindow()->
        ➥GetClientWindow(), expertEditFile);    // Client window for the frame.
113:    client->NewFile();
114:    }
115:
116:
117:    //////////////////////////////////////////////////////
118:    // expertApp
119:    // ===========
120:    // Menu File Open command
121:    void expertApp::CmFileOpen ()
122:    {
123:    //
```

```
124:      // Display standard Open dialog box to select a file name.
125:      //
126:      *FileData.FileName = 0;
127:
128:      expertEditFile *client = TYPESAFE_DOWNCAST(GetMainWindow()->
          ➥GetClientWindow(), expertEditFile);      // Client window for the frame.
129:      if (client->CanClose())
130:      if (TFileOpenDialog(GetMainWindow(), FileData).Execute() == IDOK)
131:      OpenFile();
132:      }
133:
134:
135:      void expertApp::OpenFile (const char *fileName)
136:      {
137:      if (fileName)
138:      strcpy(FileData.FileName, fileName);
139:
140:      expertEditFile *client = TYPESAFE_DOWNCAST(GetMainWindow()->
          ➥GetClientWindow(), expertEditFile);      // Client window for the frame.
141:      client->ReplaceWith(FileData.FileName);
142:      }
143:
144:
145:      //{{SDIDecFrame Implementation}}
146:
147:
148:      SDIDecFrame::SDIDecFrame (TWindow *parent, const char far *title,
          ➥TWindow *clientWnd, bool trackMenuSelection, TModule *module)
149:      : TDecoratedFrame(parent, title, clientWnd == 0 ? new expertEditFile(0,
          ➥ 0, 0) : clientWnd, trackMenuSelection, module)
150:      {
151:      // INSERT>> Your constructor code here.
152:
153:      }
154:
155:
156:      SDIDecFrame::~SDIDecFrame ()
157:      {
158:      // INSERT>> Your destructor code here.
159:
160:      }
161:
162:
163:      //////////////////////////////////////////////////////////
164:      // expertApp
165:      // ==========
166:      // Menu Help About expert.exe command
167:      void expertApp::CmHelpAbout ()
168:      {
169:      //
170:      // Show the modal dialog.
171:      //
172:      expertAboutDlg(MainWindow).Execute();
173:      }
174:      int OwlMain (int , char* [])
```

continues

Listing 19.8. continued

```
175:        {
176:        try {
177:        expertApp     app;
178:        return app.Run();
179:        }
180:        catch (xmsg& x) {
181:        ::MessageBox(0, x.why().c_str(), "Exception", MB_OK);
182:        }
183:
184:        return -1;
185:        }
186:
187:        void expertApp::CmLowercase ()
188:        {
189:        uint startPos, endPos;
190:        int numChars;
191:        char* str;
192:        expertEditFile *client = TYPESAFE_DOWNCAST(GetMainWindow()->
           ↪GetClientWindow(), expertEditFile);     // Client window for the frame.
193:
194:        client->GetSelection(startPos, endPos);
195:        if (startPos < endPos)
196:        {
197:        numChars = endPos - startPos + 1;
198:        str = new char[numChars + 1];
199:        client->GetSubText(str, startPos, endPos);
200:        strlwr(str);
201:        client->Insert(str);
202:        client->SetSelection(startPos, endPos);
203:        delete[] str;
204:        }
205:        else
206:        {
207:        numChars = client->GetWindowTextLength();
208:        str = new char[numChars + 1];
209:        client->GetSubText(str, 0, (uint)numChars);
210:        strlwr(str);
211:        client->DeleteSubText(0, (uint)numChars);
212:        client->SetSelection(0, 0);
213:        client->Insert(str);
214:        delete[] str;
215:        }
216:        }
217:
218:
219:        void expertApp::CmUppercase ()
220:        {
221:        uint startPos, endPos;
222:        int numChars;
223:        char* str;
224:        expertEditFile *client = TYPESAFE_DOWNCAST(GetMainWindow()->
           ↪GetClientWindow(), expertEditFile);     // Client window for the frame.
225:
226:        client->GetSelection(startPos, endPos);
227:        if (startPos < endPos)
```

```
228:        {
229:        numChars = endPos - startPos + 1;
230:        str = new char[numChars + 1];
231:        client->GetSubText(str, startPos, endPos);
232:        strupr(str);
233:        client->Insert(str);
234:        client->SetSelection(startPos, endPos);
235:        delete[] str;
236:        }
237:        else
238:        {
239:        numChars = client->GetWindowTextLength();
240:        str = new char[numChars + 1];
241:        client->GetSubText(str, 0, (uint)numChars);
242:        strupr(str);
243:        client->DeleteSubText(0, (uint)numChars);
244:        client->SetSelection(0, 0);
245:        client->Insert(str);
246:        delete[] str;
247:        }
248:        }
249:
250:
251:        void expertApp::CmReverse ()
252:        {
253:        uint startPos, endPos;
254:        int numChars;
255:        char swap, *str;
256:        expertEditFile *client = TYPESAFE_DOWNCAST(GetMainWindow()->
           ►GetClientWindow(), expertEditFile);      // Client window for the frame.
257:
258:        client->GetSelection(startPos, endPos);
259:        if (startPos < endPos)
260:        {
261:        numChars = endPos - startPos + 1;
262:        str = new char[numChars + 1];
263:        client->GetSubText(str, startPos, endPos);
264:        for (int i = 0, j = strlen(str) - 1; i < j; ++i, --j)
265:        {
266:        swap = str[i];
267:        str[i] = str[j];
268:        str[j] = swap;
269:        }
270:        client->Insert(str);
271:        client->SetSelection(startPos, endPos);
272:        delete[] str;
273:        }
274:        else
275:        {
276:        numChars = client->GetWindowTextLength();
277:        str = new char[numChars + 1];
278:        client->GetSubText(str, 0, (uint)numChars);
279:        for (int i = 0, j = strlen(str) - 1; i < j; ++i, --j)
280:        {
281:        swap = str[i];
282:        str[i] = str[j];
```

19

continues

Listing 19.8. continued

```
283:      str[j] = swap;
284:      }
285:      client->DeleteSubText(0, (uint)numChars);
286:      client->SetSelection(0, 0);
287:      client->Insert(str);
288:      delete[] str;
289:      }
290:      }
291:
292:
293:      void expertApp::CmInsertDate ()
294:      {
295:      struct date dt;
296:      char str[41];
297:      expertEditFile *client = TYPESAFE_DOWNCAST(GetMainWindow()->
          ➥GetClientWindow(), expertEditFile);     // Client window for the frame.
298:
299:      getdate(&dt);
300:      sprintf(str, "%02d/%02d/%02d",
301:      dt.da_mon, dt.da_day, dt.da_year % 100 );
302:      client->Insert(str);
303:      }
304:
305:      void expertApp::CmInsertTime ()
306:      {
307:      struct time tm;
308:      char str[41];
309:      expertEditFile *client = TYPESAFE_DOWNCAST(GetMainWindow()->
          ➥GetClientWindow(), expertEditFile);     // Client window for the frame.
310:
311:      gettime(&tm);
312:      sprintf(str, "%02d:%02d:%02d",
313:      tm.ti_hour, tm.ti_min, tm.ti_sec );
314:      client->Insert(str);
315:      }
316:
317:
318:      void expertApp::CmInsertDateTime ()
319:      {
320:      expertEditFile *client = TYPESAFE_DOWNCAST(GetMainWindow()->
          ➥GetClientWindow(), expertEditFile);     // Client window for the frame.
321:      CmInsertDate();
322:      client->Insert(" ");
323:      CmInsertTime();
324:      }
```

The implementation file in Listing 19.8 shows the definitions of the CmXXXX member functions
that handle the new menu options. The file contains the #include statements that we added to
include the header files STDIO.H, STRING.H, and DOS.H. Also, notice the response table
macros that were inserted by the ClassExpert utility. We added the code for the following
member functions:

1. The member function CMLowerCase (defined on lines 187 to 216) responds to the
   Lowercase menu option by performing the following tasks:

□ Obtains the currently selected text (if any). This task involves sending the C++ message `GetSelection` (on line 194) to the client. The arguments for this message are the local variables `startPos` and `endPos`.

□ Performs the following sequence of subtasks (found on lines 197 to 203) if the value in variable `startPos` is less than that in `endPos` (which indicates that there is selected text):

  □ Calculates the number of characters in the selected text and assigns this number to the local variable `numChars`

  □ Creates a dynamic string with `numChars+1` characters and assigns the address of that string to the local pointer `str`

  □ Copies the selected text into the dynamic string. This task involves sending the C++ message `GetSubText` to the client window. The arguments for this message are `str`, `startPos`, and `endPos`.

  □ Converts the characters of the dynamic string to lowercase by using the string function `strlwr`

  □ Replaces the selected text with the contents of the dynamic string. This task involves sending the C++ message `Insert` to the client window. The argument for this message is the pointer `str`.

  □ Selects the newly inserted text by sending the C++ message `SetSelection` to the client window. The arguments for this message are the local variables `startPos` and `endPos`.

  □ Deletes the dynamic string accessed by pointer `str`

□ If there is no selection, the function converts all of the characters in the file to lowercase by performing the following subtasks (using the statements in lines 207 to 214):

  □ Obtains the size of the edited text by sending the C++ message `GetWindowTextLength` to the client window. This task assigns the result of the message to the local variable `numChars`.

  □ Creates a dynamic string with `numChars+1` characters and assigns the address of that string to the local pointer `str`

  □ Obtains the entire edited text by sending the C++ message `GetSubText` to the client area. The arguments for this message are `str` (the text copy buffer), `0`, and `(uint)numChars`.

  □ Converts the characters of the dynamic string to lowercase by using the string function `strlwr`

  □ Deletes the entire edited text by sending the C++ message `DeleteSubText` to the client window. The arguments for this message are `0` and `(uint)numChars`.

19

☐ Selects the start of the file as the insertion point by sending the C++ message SetSelection to the client window. The arguments for this message are the integers 0 and 0.

☐ Inserts the characters of the dynamic string into the client window. This task involves sending the C++ message Insert to the client area. The argument for this message is the pointer str.

☐ Deletes the dynamic string accessed by pointer str.

> **Note:** The program implements the various text-edit operations using the data member client, which is a pointer to the class expertEditFile. This class includes TEdit as one of its base classes. This lineage enables the pointer client to receive C++ editing messages implemented by the member functions of class TEdit.

2. The member function CmUppercase (defined on lines 219 to 248) responds to the menu option UpperCase. The function is very similar to the function CMLowerCase and differs only by its use of the string function strupr instead of the function strlwr.

3. The member function CmInsertDate (defined on lines 293 to 303) responds to the Insert Date menu option by performing the following options:

☐ Obtains the current system date by calling the function getdate (prototyped in the DOS.H header file). The argument for this function call is the address of the structured variable dt. This variable has the date structure.

☐ Creates a formatted string image of the month number, day number, and year number. This task uses the function sprintf and assigns the formatted string to the local string variable str.

☐ Inserts the string image into the client window by sending that window the C++ message Insert. The argument for this message is the variable str.

4. The member function CmInsertTime (defined in lines 305 to 315) responds to the Insert Time menu option by performing the following options:

☐ Obtains the current system time by calling the function gettime (prototyped in the DOS.H header file). The argument for this function call is the address of the structured variable tm. This variable has the time structure.

☐ Creates a formatted string image of the hour, minute, and second. This task uses the function sprintf and assigns the formatted string to the local string variable str.

☐ Inserts the string image into the client window by sending that window the C++ message Insert. The argument for this message is the variable str.

5. The member function `CmInsertDateTime` responds to the Insert Date/Time menu option. This function simply calls the `CmInsertDate` and `CmInsertTime` functions, inserting a space in between them.

6. The member function `CmReverse` (defined on lines 251 to 290) responds to the Reverse menu option. This function performs the following tasks:

   ☐ Obtains the currently selected text (if any). This task involves sending the C++ message `GetSelection` to the client window. The arguments for this message are the local variables `startPos` and `endPos`.

   ☐ Performs the following sequence of subtasks (in lines 261 to 272) if the value in variable `startPos` is less than that in `endPos` (which indicates that there is selected text):

     ☐ Calculates the number of characters in the selected text and assigns this number to the local variable `numChars`.

     ☐ Creates a dynamic string with `numChars+1` characters and assigns the address of that string to the local pointer `str`.

     ☐ Copies the selected text into the dynamic string. This task involves sending the C++ message `GetSubText` to the client window. The arguments for this message are `str`, `startPos`, and `endPos`.

     ☐ Reverses the characters in the dynamic string. This task involves using a `for` loop with two control variables: `i` and `j`. The loop statements swap characters using the local variable `swap`. The loop initializes the variable `i` and `j` to `0` and `strlen(str)-1`, respectively, and iterates until variable `i` is equal to or is greater than variable `j`.

     ☐ Replaces the selected text with the contents of the dynamic string. This task involves sending the C++ message `Insert` to the client window. The argument for this message is the pointer `str`.

     ☐ Selects the newly inserted text by sending the C++ message `SetSelection` to the client window. The arguments for this message are the local variables `startPos` and `endPos`.

     ☐ Deletes the dynamic string accessed by pointer `str`.

   ☐ If there is no selection, the function converts all the characters in the file to uppercase by performing the following subtasks (using the statements on lines 276 to 288):

     ☐ Obtains the size of the edited text by sending the C++ message `GetWindowTextLength` to the client window. This task assigns the result of the message to the local variable `numChars`.

     ☐ Creates a dynamic string with `numChars+1` characters and assigns the address of that string to the local pointer `str`.

19

☐ Obtains the entire edited text by sending the C++ message GetSubText to the client area. The arguments for this message are str (the text copy buffer), 0, and (uint)numChars.

☐ Reverses the characters in the dynamic string. This task involves using a for loop with two control variables: i and j. The loop statements swap characters using the local variable swap. The loop initializes the variable i and j to 0 and strlen(str)-1, respectively, and iterates until variable i is equal to or is greater than variable j.

☐ Deletes the entire edited text by sending the C++ message DeleteSubText to the client window. The arguments for this message are 0 and (uint)numChars.

☐ Selects the start of the file as the insertion point by sending the C++ message SetSelection to the client window. The arguments for this message are the integers 0 and 1.

☐ Inserts the characters of the dynamic string into the client window. This task involves sending the C++ message Insert to the client area. The argument for this message is the pointer str.

☐ Deletes the dynamic string accessed by pointer str

Compile and run the program EXPERT.EXE. Load a small text file and experiment with converting and reversing the characters of selected text and of the entire file. In addition, experiment with inserting the date, the time, or both. When you are done experimenting, exit the file without saving it. Figure 19.14 shows a sample session with the EXPERT.EXE program.

Figure 19.14.
A sample session with the EXPERT.EXE program.

Summary

This chapter introduced you to using the AppExpert utility and offered sample SDI-compliant, text-editor applications generated by that utility. You learned about the following topics:

- [ ] Working with the AppExpert utility, which you invoke from inside the IDE.
- [ ] The Application topics in AppExpert, which enable you to make main selections about the type of application you want AppExpert to generate.
- [ ] The Main Window topics in AppExpert, which enable you to fine-tune the window styles and the SDI or MDI client windows.
- [ ] The MDI Child/View options in AppExpert, which enable you to control the creation of the MDI child windows.
- [ ] The EXPERT project, which implements an SDI-compliant, minimally functioning text editor generated by the AppExpert utility. The project implements the simplest type of text editor that you can create with the AppExpert utility.

Q&A

Q How does the ClassExpert utility complement the source code generated by AppExpert?

A The ClassExpert enables you to fine-tune the source code of AppExpert by adding new classes and/or member functions that support custom operations of your program.

Q Can I customize the code generated by AppExpert without using ClassExpert?

A Yes. However, depending on how you manually customize the code, it may be difficult to use ClassExpert later for further customization.

Q How can I change the menus and other resources?

A Use the Resource Workshop utility.

Exercises

1. Use the AppExpert utility to create a text editor that supports the drag/drop and printing features. Compare the output code with the listings in this chapter.
2. Use the AppExpert utility to create a text editor that supports the speed bar, status line, drag/drop, and printing features. Compare the output code with the listings in this chapter.
3. Use the AppExpert utility to create a text editor that uses the document/view feature. Compare the output code with the listings in this chapter.

20

OLE 2

Object Linking and Embedding (OLE) is the Windows system for enabling several programs to work together, and OLE 2 represents a further degree of refinement and increase in function over the original OLE system. With Turbo C++ 4.5, new classes have been provided to support OLE 2. Today, you explore the following topics:

☐ The Borland solution to implementing OLE 2

☐ Embedding objects the OWL way

☐ Passing data between programs—OLE Automation

What Is OLE 2?

NEW☞ TERM With *object linking and embedding*, objects can be linked together. Thus, a document or other object can be composed of many objects from different applications, and the data that represents the objects can be embedded into the document.

A *linked* object holds sufficient information in the client to invoke another application with the reference for the data to be operated on.

An *embedded* object has the data of the object held in the client.

Before going into detail, let's examine why a user would want linking and embedding. From the early days of PC programs, users wanted the capability of joining information from different applications. For example, every word-processed sales report needs that sales-up-in-the-third-quarter pie chart. The original solutions of integration, such as Lotus Symphony, tried to do everything in one large application. Similarly, most of the industry-standard word processors, spreadsheets, and presentation graphics programs have a tremendous overlap of function—in Excel, you can draw on your spreadsheet; in Word, you can make a simple spreadsheet in a word processing table. Of course, the user does not want cut-down functionality in these add-on features. The solution in Windows is to provide the capability of inserting the output from other applications into documents.

OLE 2 is not just about providing the user with desktop publishing, however. The question could better be phrased "What *are* OLE 2?" OLE 2 comes in two forms:

☐ A system of data exchange called *Automation* that enables programs to pass data between themselves

☐ A system of joining programs and data together to create a compound document

NEW☞ TERM Throughout the rest of the day, the term *OLE* means OLE 2 unless explicit reference is made to OLE 1.

There is a significant difference between the two activities. With Automation, the two programs must have a defined interface and know about the data that is being passed between them, as with DDEML. The client transaction processes the data provided by the Automation server.

With object linking and embedding, the principle is that the container knows nothing about the object being contained; rather, it interacts with the OLE system only. However, an OLE container must provide certain features to enable an object to cohabit.

NEW☞ The correct terminology for the user of an OLE object is a *container*. The provider of an
TERM OLE object is a *server*.

To the user, OLE means being able to edit a document or graphic and place other objects on the screen. An object is inserted into a container either by an Insert Object command, the Clipboard using the special OLE options, or drag-and-drop. The container is responsible for providing the space for the object; the object's server is responsible for drawing it. Similarly, when saving an embedded object, the server is responsible for writing the object to the file provided by the container.

> **Note:** Once an OLE object has been linked or embedded, the server is no longer required. The OLE container keeps an image of the object (drawn using a Windows metafile) so it can reproduce the object. This includes scaling to fit the page and printing it—true WYSIWYG fashion.

There are two different processes. In linking, the container stores a reference to another application with instructions as to how to access the server. One linked document can be shared among several containers. A change to a linked document can be updated across several containers—and, if the document is moved to another machine, the linked document needs to go with it and the links may need to be reestablished. In embedding, all the data is held in the container document. This means that the object is safely owned by the document, and it can be copied from one place to another without losing the embedded data. Only one document owns the data, however—other documents are not kept up to date. The appropriate method for linking is a user decision, depending on why the object is being inserted.

OLE gets in everywhere. OLE 2 defines a standard for the format for storing objects. The storage is divided into compartments, which can contain other compartments. The main document contains a subcompartment for each embedded object. The advantages of the standardization of the storage are that containers can identify the server data mixed in with its own data and that the container can use the OLE file structure so that it reads only objects that are needed. For example, if the object is a 24-bit screen print that is displayed on the second page of a document, it may not be necessary to read the picture when opening a document to view the first page. More importantly, the storage structure is hierarchical and can be used by an object to contain other objects. Finally, the storage concept is independent of the medium in which the objects are saved; a storage can be on disk or in memory or held in a blob on a Paradox database, for example.

20

NEW☞ The OLE name for a compartment is a *storage*.
TERM

An OLE object is made of two separate components: the data and the view. As you have seen, the data can be stored separately from the application that displays the object. An object also can be viewed in a number of different ways, as with Clipboard formats. So, for an extreme (but actual) example, an embedded wave file may provide a visual "view" for its representation in a document and a sound "view" to play it.

The level of integration in OLE is very high. A true OLE 2 container embedding or linking an OLE object enables its menu, toolbar, and status bar to be taken over by the server for in-place editing, effectively appearing to be the server application. The object, when activated (when it has focus, rather than being edited), can add options to menus, provides for pop-up menus over the object, and can be moved and sized within a document. Originally, OLE 1 enabled embedded objects, but, to edit them, a separate application window had to be opened. Figure 20.1 shows an ancient Word 2 processor doing simple embedding.

Figure 20.1.
The WordArt object opens as a separate application from Word 2.

OLE applications can work as containers, servers, or both. Even more confusing is that an OLE embedded object with in-place editing can itself open an in-place edited object, as in Figure 20.2. OLE 2 provides backwards compatibility with OLE 1 so that you can embed OLE 2 objects in an OLE 1 application (without in-place editing). Similarly, OLE 2 can insert OLE 1 objects; they just cannot provide in-place editing.

There are two ways you can provide an OLE server: as an executable and as a DLL. Even as an executable, you may not want to provide your object as a stand-alone application—to save implementing the stand-alone requirements of printing and file management, for example. Providing a server as a DLL has large performance improvements. This enables OLE to call server functions directly. With an OLE executable, OLE has a problem. Because OLE is designed for true multitasking systems, it has to organize calls between tasks properly; it cannot simply send messages. Therefore, OLE has to convert its commands into task-independent messages to ensure that it can edit the object without having the container aware of the object implementation. Furthermore, the intention is that the OLE implementation can be extended to enable objects to be implemented across networks so that the OLE tasks might run on different computers—all transparent to the user and the programmer.

Figure 20.2.
The OLE 2 way of
embedding.

How Does Borland Implement OLE 2?

OCF stands for *Object Components Framework.* This is Borland's high-level C++ wrapper around OLE, which converts between a simplified C++ OOP interface and the OLE API. It is similar to the ObjectWindows Library that acts as a wrapper around the standard Windows API.

OLE contains many features. However, "there ain't no such thing as a free lunch." To provide all these features, a container application must provide the correct interaction with OLE. This, as you might imagine, is hard work, considering the tremendous number of different situations with which the application has to cope. OCF simplifies the work required by providing a number of classes that support the basic function in the same way that OWL supports the Windows API. Aside from the classes, OCF provides a number of macros to simplify the definition of the OLE registration data and class definitions. It does so in a way similar to the way that OWL uses macros for the response tables, and it also defines its own special messages to enable a simplified OCF event to be handled.

20

> **Note:** OCF is a separate set of classes from OWL. OWL 2.5 provides classes that make use of OCF to build OLE applications, but OCF does not require the use of OWL.

OCF provides class support for OLE servers, OLE containers, and OLE Automation. OCF helps implement the following:

- *Linking and embedding.* OCF provides support for both server and container.
- *The Clipboard.* OCF provides all the cut-and-paste options.
- *Drag-and-drop.* This is the capability of dragging an object and, when placed in a drag-and-drop enabled window, placing the object in that window.
- *OLE interface.* OCF provides standard components to build OLE dialog boxes, and also provides the capability of modifying the container window if it is written to conform to OCF's requirements.
- OLE compound files

OCF places a layer of abstraction over the standard Microsoft OLE interface. If you were to program in straight C++ without OWL, OCF would provide a simplified way of programming OLE. For OLE Automation, OCF provides all the function required to pass data between a client and server object. OCF also provides additional help to the application to enable it to handle the command line correctly, which is used to instruct an OLE application as to the mode in which it should run. However, there still is a lot of work to do in managing a linking and embedding application.

Building on the OCF classes, OWL then provides a number of classes to ease the programming of OLE via OCF. There are OLE-enabled frames, `TOleFrame` and `TOleMDIFrame`, and OLE container windows—for example, `TOleWindow`. `TOleDocument` and `TOleView` represent the container and views of the container. There also have been some modifications to the `TApplication` class to enable it to run in the different ways required by OLE.

OWL provides support for these OCF functions, but wraps them further still to the point that you need very little code in your program to support OLE.

AppExpert (discussed on Day 19) has been revised to support the OLE classes and you can quickly generate the framework of an OLE application for both an OLE container and server.

OLE *Doc/View*

For the rest of the look at OLE linking and embedding, you study the `TOleDocument` and `TOleView` implementation of OLE. The `Doc/View` model has been present in OWL 2 since its original release. The principle of the `Doc/View` model is that the storing of data and the presentation of data are two different tasks.

NEW☞ For simplicity, *Doc/View* refers to TOleDocument and TOleView throughout the rest of
TERM today's lesson.

Defining a *TOleDocument* Class

There are several steps to follow in defining a TOleDocument class.

Step 1: Define the Document Storage

TOleDocument understands how to store OLE documents and provides the container with access
to the storage medium so that the programmer can easily add specific data to the document.

> **OWL Note:** Transparently, you write to the special OLE storage format. This
> means that you do not need to do anything special to store data in either embedded
> or stand-alone file format.

Normally, you derive a class and provide Open and Commit functions to enable the document to
read and write its data. You also provide a Close function to clear the document, and you may
want to provide a Revert function to reset your document to a cleared or as-originally-read state.
In each of these, you need to call the base TOleDocument function. You access the file by using
the Instream function to return a TInStream for reading and the OutStream function for getting
a TOutStream. When writing the file, you should place markers or read a fixed number of objects,
which you note before writing so that you can safely reread the data.

> **Warning:** At the end of writing out data in the Commit function, make sure you call
> TOleDocument::CommitTransactedStorage, which updates the storage to disk. If you
> do not do this, the file you write will be incomplete and cannot be opened.

Step 2: Define Notifications to Tell Views to Update Themselves

You are likely to need some notifications to tell the document views of any changes to the
document that might affect them. At any time, a document may have several views open,
although only one will be active. When a document changes, it uses the NotifyViews function,
which sends the notification to all the views that are open; it does this via the standard message
response table. There are a number of standard notifications. Additionally, you can define your

own document-specific notifications for which you need to define a notification value, a response function signature (via a macro that OWL provides), and a response table entry. This code snippet, for example, defines document notifications for when the document has been added to or been cleared:

```
//
// Custom Doc/View notifications
//
const int vnDrawAppend = vnCustomBase+0;
const int vnDrawClear = vnCustomBase+1;
//
// Custom Doc/View signatures
//
NOTIFY_SIG(vnDrawAppend, uint)
NOTIFY_SIG(vnDrawClear, void)
//
// Response table macros
//
#define EV_VN_DRAWAPPEND  VN_DEFINE(vnDrawAppend,  VnAppend,  int)
#define EV_VN_DRAWCLEAR   VN_DEFINE(vnDrawClear,  VnClear,  void)
```

Step 3 is to provide data access functions for views.

Defining a *TOleView* Class

Next, you need to provide access functions so that the various views can get at the data. Their exact form is up to you, but normally, you require at least something to add data and to get the data from the document. More sophisticated applications provide more functions.

Creating a TOleView class requires a bit more work. How much work depends on whether the view is intended to contain OLE objects (remember that an OLE server can itself contain objects if you want). TOleView contains all the work to contain objects.

OWL Note: When building your TOleView class, you should store a pointer or reference to your document class. There already is such a pointer, but it is of the generic TOleDocument type and needs down-casting to use.

Step 1: Define the Presentation

Defining the presentation is based on accessing data from the document. Generally, this consists of having the Paint function retrieve data from the document. You may have more than one method of presenting the data. If so, you can either create separate TOleView classes or, more likely, derive further classes from a common class of your own devising. The special trick to an

OLE server is that the view may not be presented in device units. OWL looks after the scaling, but it means that any interaction you have with the screen needs to be managed in logical window units—not pixels as you would expect.

Step 2: Add Data Editing Methods

How the view accepts data is up to the view. However, because there may be several views open on the document at once, take care as to how you handle this. The general approach is to handle the editing in the view, and when the object is complete, store it in the document, using the document access functions you provide. The document accepts the data and sends a notification message. In a PaintBrush example, you might type text on the picture only in the active view and when the text is accepted by the user, add the text to the document. Then, in the notification response, invalidate the window to ensure that the screen is redisplayed. By using custom notifications, you can refine the process so that when adding data, all the views can, if possible, modify their screen rather than entirely redrawing it.

Step 3: Add Notification Responses

The view should handle all document notifications to ensure that the display matches the document data. The normal response often is to invalidate the screen (by calling `Invalidate`), but, if the object is a server, the view should also call `InvalidatePart` to ensure that the container is kept in step with the editing.

Note: It's important to remember that if you edit an OLE object (rather than opening for in-place editing), you can observe your embedded object being updated as you edit the object in a separate application.

20

Step 4: Support Embedded Objects, if Required

OWL supports embedded objects for you in `TOleView`; however, you need to avoid interfering with how it works. Essentially, OWL provides a default place to dump new objects, then uses `EvLButtonDown`, `EvMouseMove`, and `EvLButtonUp` to manage moving and sizing the embedded objects. There are a few traps to mouse handling.

☐ You need to enable the mouse messages to be responded to by the base class to enable contained objects to be handled.

☐ The `EvLButtonDown` and `EvMouseMove` messages convert the `TPoint` mouse position parameter into logical units, dependent on the view. The DC view is provided by the `DragDC` member of the view. The mouse down always creates a `DragDC` for you. If you are drawing on the view, you need to use the `DragDC` to get the correct scaling for an embedded edit. If you are storing the position of the object based on the `EvLButtonUp`, you need to convert the mouse coordinates to logical units yourself.

☐ You should use the mouse only if the mouse hasn't selected an embedded object. You can test for this by testing whether a `DragDC` exists (it will unless your mouse has been moved over the window, having first been pressed outside). Then you should check whether the mouse is holding the object. You do this by calling `SelectEmbedded`, which returns `true` if the `TOleView` is currently handling an embedded object.

By default, you have no control over the placement of the objects (which is normal for many embedding applications). You can provide a current position for insertion by providing a `GetInsertPosition` function (for example, this might return the current cursor position in a word processor).

You provide the rest of the OLE container functionality by giving the appropriate menu options—all the OLE function is built in whether you are building a server or a container.

As you can see, the steps using the `Doc`/`View` model are nearly identical for a container or server.

The OLE Registry

The first thing an OLE application does when it starts up is to register itself with Windows, letting the operating system know just what parts of OLE the program can handle. The standard method has been to fill in all sorts of long complicated parameters to all manner of OLE API functions. With OCF, however, the information still can be rather complicated; the information is created in a structure with the aid of special registration macros. The structure then is passed into the OCF object constructors, which make sure that your application's program is registered properly with the operating system.

Note: The actual registry information is stored in the REG.DAT file in Windows 3.1. In Windows NT and Windows 95, the information is stored in the system registry.

Although there are several registry functions, the most common ones—the ones in which you're interested—are listed in Table 20.1. These are used to build the registration structures that describe both the application and the various document formats.

Table 20.1. OCF registry macros.

Macro	Meaning
BEGIN_REGISTRATION	This is used to start defining a structure. This is similar to the DEFINE_RESPONSE_TABLEx macro used in OWL. The single parameter to this macro is the name of the structure to be defined.
END_REGISTRATION	This is used to end the definition of a structure. It is similar to OWL's END_RESPONSE_TABLE macro.
REGDATA	This is the main workhorse macro that adds a keyed entry to the structure. The first parameter to this macro is the key. The second parameter is a value to associate with the key.
REGDOCFLAGS	This adds an entry containing flags for a document template. These flags are used in the Doc/View model of OLE programming. The parameter is an ORed together bunch of dtxxx flags.
REGFORMAT	Each document needs to let the OLE registry know what formats, such as metafiles, bitmaps, and so on, it can handle. This adds information regarding a document's capabilities to the structure.
REGISTRATION_FORMAT_BUFFER	Some of the macros used to create the registration structure require some temporary space in order to properly expand. This macro provides that temporary space, the size of which is based on its single parameter.

In the description of the REGDATA macro, I mentioned that it registers keyed entries. There are quite a number of keys available to be registered, some of which are required for various structures. Table 20.2 describes some of the keys.

Table 20.2. OCF registry keys.

Key Name	Entry Value
clsid	This defines the Globally Unique Identifier (GUID) needed to differentiate each OLE application from one another. The GUIDs are generated automatically by the IDE's AppExpert. If you create an OLE application on your own, you can use the GUIDGEN.EXE program supplied with the compiler to generate a GUID for this field.

continues

Table 20.2. continued

Key Name	Entry Value
progid	This is a string that identifies the structure. This is used for both documents and for applications, and it typically consists of three parts: a program name, an object name, and a version number.
description	When OLE puts up a string for the user to see, it shows the contents of this entry, which can be up to 40 characters long.
cmdline	This describes the arguments that OLE should place on the program's command line when OLE starts the application. It's often just an empty string.
appname	This usually is the title that shows up in the application's main window.
docfilter	This is represented as a file mask, such as *.SPT, and generally uses the same letters as in the document's extension. That file mask is used in the common dialogs, along with a file type (see menuname and description) when OLE asks the user to open or save files.
usage	This is a flag that lets OLE know whether it should start up a new instance of the application server for each client that requests it. If ocrSingleUse is used here, the application will be started once for each OLE client that needs it. ocrMultipleUse means that the server application will be opened only once, no matter how many clients ask for it.
insertable	The key for this entry is always an empty string; its presence is used in a structure to identify a document as one that can be inserted into other container documents. It will appear in the list of available documents when the user selects the Insert Object menu item.
menuname	This is a short name that shows up as a menu item in container programs. In order to keep menu sizes short and readable, the suggested maximum length for this entry is 15 characters.
verbN	This describes the verbs used for documents, ones that will appear in pop-up menus. N represents a number that should begin with 0 and go no further than 7. Typical entries are &Edit and &Open.
extension	This is used to identify filename extensions for OLE documents. When OLE is asked to open a file, it matches the extension of the file with the various servers associated with extensions and then uses the matching one.

It's important to note that this list is by no means complete. There are a number of other keys that can be used, but the ones listed so far are enough to get a program up and running with full OLE functionality.

Creating an OLE Application

The previous discussion has created only the Doc/View components and described the registry in general terms, but this has not explained how documents and views are managed. OWL provides a document manager, called TDocManager. It is this class (which you normally don't need to amend in any way) that looks after documents and views. There are a few simple steps that you take to enable the document manager to understand your class.

Step 1: Declare a *Doc/View* Template and Register its Details

You do not need to worry about the internals of declaring a Doc/View template. There are three components you need to define. (You don't use these yourself, they are used by the TDocManager.) The DEFINE_DOC_TEMPLATE_CLASS macro associates the documents and the views. You declare one of these for each combination:

```
DEFINE_DOC_TEMPLATE_CLASS(SpotDoc, SpotView, SpotTemplate);
```

Then you need to declare some important OLE registration details for each document.

```
BEGIN_REGISTRATION(__SpotRegistration)
    REGDATA(progid, "Spot.Container.1")
    REGDATA(description, "Spot Container Version 1")
    REGDATA(extension, "SPT")
    REGDATA(docfilter, "*.SPT")
    REGDOCFLAGS(dtAutoDelete ¦ dtUpdateDir
                ¦ dtAutoOpen ¦ dtRegisterExt)
    REGDATA(menuname, "Spot container")
    REGDATA(insertable, "")
    REGDATA(verb0, "&Edit")
    REGDATA(verb1, "&Open")
    REGFORMAT(0, ocrEmbedSource,  ocrContent,
                 ocrIStorage, ocrGet)
    REGFORMAT(1, ocrMetafilePict, ocrContent,
                 ocrMfPict ¦ ocrStaticMed, ocrGet)
    REGFORMAT(2, ocrBitmap, ocrContent,
                 ocrGDI ¦ ocrStaticMed, ocrGet)
    REGFORMAT(3, ocrDib, ocrContent,  ocrHGlobal
                 ¦ ocrStaticMed, ocrGet)
    REGFORMAT(4, ocrLinkSource, ocrContent,
                 ocrIStream, ocrGet)
END_REGISTRATION
```

This table is passed to Windows so that your application is entered into the system. This enables other applications to know of your existence. Important entries (well, they are all important!) are the progid and description, which appear when the user accesses the object (for example, via Insert Object). insertable is a placeholder to indicate that this object can be inserted—that is, the document is an OLE server. extension, docfilter, and the REGDOCFLAGS line all tell the document manager (and OLE) what files can be handled by the Doc/View combination. The REGFORMATs tell OLE what formats the server can produce for linking and embedding. OWL Doc/View can provide all these formats for you.

Having created this information, you then declare a global static instance of the Doc/View template. The instance looks after associating itself with the manager, so you can call it what you like. It takes the registration information as a parameter (you pass the registration details even if you decide not to provide OLE support).

```
SpotTemplate __spotTemplate(__SpotRegistration);
```

You now have created your Doc/View classes.

Step 2: Add the Application Registration Details

Next, you need to sort out the application. There are a number of new features for this. First, you need a static TAppDictionary. This manages OWL internal information. This must be called AppDictionary to ensure that certain OWL features work.

Second, you need to register the application (by the way, place this before your Doc/View registration).

```
//
// Ole 2 linking and embedding apps need a TOcRegistrar
//
static TPointer<TOcRegistrar> Registrar;

REGISTRATION_FORMAT_BUFFER(100)

BEGIN_REGISTRATION(ApplicationReg)
//
// The following must be unique per Ole 2 application
//
    REGDATA(clsid, "{FE91A8E0-DBDA-101B-A585-040224007802}")
    REGDATA(appname, "Spot Container & Server")
    REGDATA(description, "Spot Container & Server Application")
    REGDATA(cmdline, "")
    REGDATA(usage, ocrMultipleUse)
END_REGISTRATION
```

Create a TOcRegistrar pointer, which must be called Registrar. OCF uses templates that rely on this. You will set up the Registrar in OwlMain.

> **Note:** The TPointer class is a cunning ruse to ensure that dynamically allocated objects get cleaned up. It accepts a pointer of the type of the object specified and deletes the object if the instance goes out of scope, a new object is assigned to it, or zero is assigned to it. This improves the capability of cleaning up objects if something goes wrong. You can use this class yourself. Typically, you use it where you would declare a variable, but, because of size, you want to declare it using new. One

place it works well is where an exception may be thrown—objects declared on the stack are cleaned up, but dynamically allocated objects are not. By wrapping the pointer in an object, dynamically allocatable objects can now be cleaned up.

Next, create the application registration. `appname` and `description` are self-explanatory. `usage` enables multiple clients to use the same application, and `cmdline` indicates that there are no arguments needed on the command line. The important one is `clsid`.

Warning: The class id must be absolutely unique to ensure that OLE starts the correct program. The Globally Unique Identifier is unique around the world, and you should never copy someone else's—especially if you are going to distribute your application.

This horrible long number can easily be generated. Merely run GUIDGEN (which lives in your Turbo C++ BIN directory). This places a new GUID in your Clipboard and you can then paste it into your code.

Step 3: Implement the Application Class

You now can move and look at the class. A `Doc`/`View` application handles a couple of responses for the document manager:

```
DEFINE_RESPONSE_TABLE1(SpotApp, TApplication)
    EV_OWLVIEW(dnCreate, EvNewView),
    EV_OWLVIEW(dnClose,  EvCloseView),
    EV_COMMAND(CM_HELPABOUT, CmHelpAbout),
END_RESPONSE_TABLE;
```

The application itself is multi-derived from `TApplication` and `TOcModule`. The `TOcModule` is transparent, but you do need to use a special `TApplication` constructor:

```
SpotApp::SpotApp () : TApplication
   (::ApplicationReg["description"], ::Module, &::AppDictionary)
{
    SetDocManager(new TDocManager(dmSDI ¦ dmMenu, this));
}
```

The constructor is identical for any OLE application you write, using the global objects you created earlier. In the constructor, set up the document manager. This needs to be set for whether you are using SDI or MDI (it controls whether multiple documents can be open).

`InitMainWindow` is fairly standard, except that you cannot create a client at this point; OLE is not yet ready. You use a `TOleFrame`, which is a special `TDecoratedFrame` that can handle the OLE

20

toolbar interface. You would create your toolbar for a stand-alone application here, setting the toolbar's Attr.Id to IDW_TOOLBAR. This enables OWL to swap it if another application takes over your application.

In TApplication::InitInstance, the application can now have its client window set up if required. If the application is not embedding, you can open the file based on the command line, or you can open a blank document. To open files, you ask the document manager. In the following snippet, if not embedding, the application finds out whether the document manager recognizes the filename that has been sent via MatchTemplate. If so, it attempts to open the file by creating a document. It uses the document template to construct an empty document, then uses the document manager to initialize it, which, in turn, opens a view. Similarly, if there is no document, the application merely opens a new view.

```
if (!::Registrar->IsOptionSet(amEmbedding))
  {
      TDocTemplate* tpl = GetDocManager()
         ->MatchTemplate(GetCmdLine().c_str());
      if (tpl)
        {
          TDocument* doc = tpl->ConstructDoc();
          if (doc)
            {
              doc->SetTemplate(tpl);
              GetDocManager()->InitDoc(doc,
                   GetCmdLine().c_str(), 0);
              return;
            }
        }
      GetDocManager()->CreateAnyDoc(0, dtNewDoc);
  }
```

The document manager opens the view. Recall that the application response table defined two document notifications. Once a view has been created, it has to be associated with a window. Because the application may operate in an embedded mode, this view may be a window in the container document. So, to handle the notification, the application needs to test whether the document is embedded. If the document is embedded, it creates a view parented to a special window; otherwise, the view is created as a standard client (in this case, an SDI client).

```
TOleView* ov = dynamic_cast<TOleView*>(&view);
if (ov && view.GetDocument().IsEmbedded() &&
    !ov->GetOcRemView()->IsOpenEditing())
  {
    //
    // Embedded view window
    //
    TWindow* vw = view.GetWindow();
    vw->SetParent(dynamic_cast<TOleFrame*>(GetMainWindow())
                  ->GetRemViewBucket());
    vw->Create();
  }
else
  {
    //
```

```
    // Normal window - associate with MainWindow
    //
    GetMainWindow()->SetClientWindow(view.GetWindow());
    if (!view.IsOK())
      GetMainWindow()->SetClientWindow(0);
    else
        if (view.GetViewMenu())
            GetMainWindow()->MergeMenu(*view.GetViewMenu());
}
```

Note: In Doc/View menu merging is used even in an SDI application, because different views can be placed as a client.

Step 4: Implement an OLE *OwlMain*

The OwlMain is changed around. This is to enable the OLE system to call your application correctly. When you run an OLE application, it receives a variety of command-line options. It is responsible for registering and unregistering itself, and also for interpreting the command-line options that OLE might have passed. OWL strips these out for you, leaving a simplified command line with only non-OLE information. This saves you from having to decode the flags yourself. You can interrogate the flags by calling TRegistrar::IsOptionSet. This tests for any flags you send, which are enumerated. The main test you need is to decide whether your application is operating in embedded mode. Normally, the command line can contain the filename to enable File Manager to start your application via its associations. It also normally passes the filename and a flag to request printing a document.

```
int OwlMain (int , char* [])
{
    try
      {
        ::Registrar = new TOcRegistrar(::ApplicationReg,
                          TOleDocViewFactory<SpotApp>(),
                          TApplication::GetCmdLine(),
                          ::DocTemplateStaticHead);
        if (!::Registrar->IsOptionSet(amAnyRegOption))
          ::Registrar->Run();
        ::Registrar = 0;
        return 0;
      }
    catch (xmsg& x)
      {
        ::MessageBox(0, x.why().c_str(), "Exception", MB_OK);
      }
    return -1;
}
```

The main trick here is the use of the ::Registrar object. For an OLE application that does linking and embedding, you need a TOcRegistrar object. The ::ApplicationReg and

`TApplication::GetCommandLine()` are all standard objects that you use. `::DocTemplateStaticHead` represents a special link for the registration to find the document template registration details. The special part is the `TOleDocViewFactory`. This is a template class that generates a hidden callback function. This callback function is what actually is called by the `::Registrar->Run()` call. OWL provides a number of different callbacks depending on the sort of application you are building. The name `Factory` implies that this is the OLE object generator. When building an OLE application, your target needs to include the OCF libraries. (When distributing an OLE application, you also need to distribute the OLE libraries.)

Put all that together, and then run your application. However, before you run an OLE-enabled server, you should run it in register mode. The proper way to do this is to run it with a `-RegServer` command line. The IDE makes this easy for you; there are two special commands on the SpeedMenu for a target node. Choose SpeedMenu | Special | Register or Unregister, and the IDE will run your application in registration mode. In this mode, it does not create windows; it merely performs the registration and then immediately exits.

Creating OLE Applications with AppExpert

The following application initially was generated using AppExpert, although it has been substantially tidied up. With Turbo C++ 4.5, AppExpert is OLE-enabled. You can create `Doc/View` servers or containers with all the usual features that you would expect to be able to generate. ClassExpert understands the OLE `Doc/View` model. You are familiar with AppExpert, so you will find it simple to amend OLE applications. At the time of writing, AppExpert gives a derived `TOleView` object to work with, but does not provide a derived `TOleDocument` class. This always is required for all but trivial examples. This can easily be derived by using ClassExpert. (Remember to use the SpeedMenu from the class pane; this enables you to derive from any class that the ClassExpert knows about.)

Another suggestion is to amend the derived `TOleView` class manually so that it accepts a derived `TOleDocument` as a parameter rather than the `TOleDocument` set as the parameter. This saves downcasting the document each time you access it.

If you want to create an OLE container to play with, press the generate button and compile the result. You will find that you can make an application that provides a nearly complete OLE implementation. AppExpert is useful, because an OLE application normally needs to support toolbars and status bars, and it will generate all the different menus and registration tables.

Note: Do not select Automation support in the OLE 2 options yet. This option is covered in the second part of today's lesson.

Listings 20.1 through 20.12, SPOT.EXE, provide a practical and stimulating example.

 Listing 20.1. Source code for the SPOTAPP.H header file.

```
#if !defined(__spotapp_h)
#define __spotapp_h

//     Class definition for SpotApp (TApplication).

#include <owl\owlpch.h>
#pragma hdrstop


#include "spotapp.rh"
//
// For OLE2 linking & embedding, need TOcModule,
// which coordinates with OCF
//
class SpotApp : public TApplication, public TOcModule
  {
    public:
      SpotApp ();
      virtual void InitMainWindow ();
      virtual void InitInstance ();
    protected:
      void EvNewView (TView& view);
      void EvCloseView (TView& view);
      void CmHelpAbout ();
    DECLARE_RESPONSE_TABLE(SpotApp);
};

#endif
```

 Listing 20.2. Source code for the SPOTAPP.CPP program file.

```
#include <owl\owlpch.h>
#pragma hdrstop
#include "spotdoc.h"
#include "spotapp.h"
#include "spotview.h"
#include "sptabtdl.h"
//
// Ole 2 linking & embedding apps (may need to) use a special
// dictionary.
//
DEFINE_APP_DICTIONARY(AppDictionary);
//
// Ole 2 linking and embedding apps need a TOcRegistrar
//
static TPointer<TOcRegistrar> Registrar;

REGISTRATION_FORMAT_BUFFER(100)
```

Listing 20.2. continued

```
BEGIN_REGISTRATION(ApplicationReg)
//
// The following must be unique per Ole 2 application
// Use GUIDGEN to make one.
//
    REGDATA(clsid, "{FE91A8E0-DBDA-101B-A585-040224007802}")
    REGDATA(appname, "Spot Container & Server")
    REGDATA(description, "Spot Container & Server Application")
    REGDATA(cmdline, "")
    REGDATA(usage, ocrMultipleUse)
END_REGISTRATION


//
// This builds the relationship between the document
// and the view.
//
DEFINE_DOC_TEMPLATE_CLASS(SpotDoc, SpotView, SpotTemplate);

BEGIN_REGISTRATION(__SpotRegistration)
    REGDATA(progid, "Spot.Container.1")
    REGDATA(description, "Spot Container Version 1")
    REGDATA(extension, "SPT")
    REGDATA(docfilter, "*.SPT")
    REGDOCFLAGS(dtAutoDelete | dtUpdateDir | dtAutoOpen |
                dtRegisterExt)
    REGDATA(menuname, "Spot container")
    REGDATA(insertable, "")
    REGDATA(verb0, "&Edit")
    REGDATA(verb1, "&Open")
    REGFORMAT(0, ocrEmbedSource,  ocrContent,  ocrIStorage,
                ocrGet)
    REGFORMAT(1, ocrMetafilePict, ocrContent,  ocrMfPict |
                ocrStaticMed, ocrGet)
    REGFORMAT(2, ocrBitmap, ocrContent,  ocrGDI | ocrStaticMed,
                ocrGet)
    REGFORMAT(3, ocrDib, ocrContent,  ocrHGlobal | ocrStaticMed,
                ocrGet)
    REGFORMAT(4, ocrLinkSource, ocrContent,  ocrIStream, ocrGet)
END_REGISTRATION
SpotTemplate __spotTemplate(__SpotRegistration);


//
// Build a response table for all messages/commands handled
// by the application.
//
DEFINE_RESPONSE_TABLE1(SpotApp, TApplication)
    EV_OWLVIEW(dnCreate, EvNewView),
    EV_OWLVIEW(dnClose,  EvCloseView),
    EV_COMMAND(CM_HELPABOUT, CmHelpAbout),
END_RESPONSE_TABLE;


//
// Note the special constructor
//
SpotApp::SpotApp () : TApplication
```

```
               (::ApplicationReg["description"], ::Module, &::AppDictionary)
{
    //
    // Tell the doc manager what sort of application it is
    // dealing with - SDI in this case
    //
    SetDocManager(new TDocManager(dmSDI | dmMenu, this));
}


//
// Application intialization.
//
void SpotApp::InitMainWindow ()
{
//
// AppExpert likes to set this in a complicated way...
//
    if (nCmdShow != SW_HIDE)
      nCmdShow = (nCmdShow != SW_SHOWMINNOACTIVE) ?
                            SW_SHOWNORMAL : nCmdShow;

    TOleFrame *frame = new TOleFrame(GetName(), 0, false, this);
    //
    // Assign ICON w/ this application.
    //
    frame->SetIcon(this, IDI_SDIAPPLICATION);
    //
    //  Menu and accelerator
    //
    frame->AssignMenu(SDI_MENU);
    frame->Attr.AccelTable = SDI_MENU;

    SetMainWindow(frame);
    //
    // OLE 2 needs to use menu descriptors for
    // easy merging of menus
    //
    frame->SetMenuDescr(TMenuDescr(SDI_MENU));
    EnableCtl3d(true);
    }
void SpotApp::InitInstance ()
{
    TApplication::InitInstance();

    if (!::Registrar->IsOptionSet(amEmbedding))
      {
          TDocTemplate* tpl = GetDocManager()
            ->MatchTemplate(GetCmdLine().c_str());
          if (tpl)
            {
              TDocument* doc = tpl->ConstructDoc();
              if (doc)
                {
                  doc->SetTemplate(tpl);
                  GetDocManager()->InitDoc(doc,
                      GetCmdLine().c_str(), 0);
                  return;
```

20

Listing 20.2. continued

```
                    }
                }
            GetDocManager()->CreateAnyDoc(0, dtNewDoc);
        }

}
// Response Table handlers:
//
void SpotApp::EvNewView (TView& view)
{
    //
    // When a new view is opened - need to associate with
    // correct window. If the object is embedded and is
    // using in-place editing - get the in-place window.
    // (Can be embedded and do full-screen editing)
    //
    // Only OLE servers need this test
    //
    TOleView* ov = dynamic_cast<TOleView*>(&view);
    if (ov && view.GetDocument().IsEmbedded() &&
        !ov->GetOcRemView()->IsOpenEditing())
      {
          //
          // Embedded view window
          //
          TWindow* vw = view.GetWindow();
          vw->SetParent(dynamic_cast<TOleFrame*>(GetMainWindow())
                    ->GetRemViewBucket());
          vw->Create();
      }
    else
      {
          //
          // Normal window - associate with application
          // main window frame.
          //
          GetMainWindow()->SetClientWindow(view.GetWindow());
          if (!view.IsOK())
            GetMainWindow()->SetClientWindow(0);
          else
            if (view.GetViewMenu())
              GetMainWindow()->MergeMenu(*view.GetViewMenu());
      }
}


void SpotApp::EvCloseView (TView&)
{
    GetMainWindow()->SetClientWindow(0);
    //
    // Set caption back to just title
    //
    GetMainWindow()->SetCaption("Spot");
}
//
// Menu Help About spot.exe command
```

```
void SpotApp::CmHelpAbout ()
{
    //
    // Show the modal dialog.
    //
    // Note the special parenting command
    //
    SpotAboutDlg(&TWindow(GetMainWindow()->
        GetCommandTarget())).Execute();
}


int OwlMain (int , char* [])
{
    try
      {
        ::Registrar = new TOcRegistrar(::ApplicationReg,
                            TOleDocViewFactory<SpotApp>(),
                            TApplication::GetCmdLine(),
                            ::DocTemplateStaticHead);
        if (!::Registrar->IsOptionSet(amAnyRegOption))
        // If this is an exe server normal run, run the app now.
          ::Registrar->Run();
        ::Registrar = 0; // Explicitly free registrar
        return 0;
      }
    catch (xmsg& x)
      {
        ::MessageBox(0, x.why().c_str(), "Exception", MB_OK);
      }
    return -1;
}
```

 Listing 20.3. Source code for the SPOTDOC.H header file.

```
#if !defined(__spotdoc_h)
#define __spotdoc_h

//    Class definition for SpotDoc (TOleDocument).

#include <owl\owlpch.h>
#pragma hdrstop
#include "spotapp.rh"
//
// Custom Doc/View notifications
//
const int vnDrawAppend = vnCustomBase+0;
const int vnDrawClear  = vnCustomBase+1;
//
// Custom Doc/View signatures
//
NOTIFY_SIG(vnDrawAppend, uint)
NOTIFY_SIG(vnDrawClear, void)
//
// Response table macros
```

Listing 20.3. continued

```
    //
    #define EV_VN_DRAWAPPEND VN_DEFINE(vnDrawAppend,  VnAppend,  int)
    #define EV_VN_DRAWCLEAR  VN_DEFINE(vnDrawClear,  VnClear,  void)

    typedef TArray<TPoint> Points;
    //
    // Underlying OLE-capable document - uses OLE2 storage
    // format
    //
    class SpotDoc : public TOleDocument
      {
        public:
          SpotDoc (TDocument* parent = 0);
          virtual ~SpotDoc ();
    //
    // SpotView helper functions
    //
          TPoint* GetSpot(uint index);
          void    AddSpot(TPoint& point);
          void    Clear();
    //
    // Document manager functions
    //
          virtual bool Open (int mode, const char far* path = 0);
          virtual bool Commit (bool force);
          virtual bool Close ();
        protected:
          Points* points;
      };
    #endif
```

Type

Listing 20.4. Source code for the SPOTDOC.CPP program file.

```
#include <owl\owlpch.h>
#pragma hdrstop
#include "spotdoc.h"
SpotDoc::SpotDoc (TDocument* parent):
    TOleDocument(parent)
{
    points = new Points(10,0,10);
}


SpotDoc::~SpotDoc ()
{
    delete points;
}
//
// Warning! Open is called and path is never
// populated!
//
bool SpotDoc::Open (int mode, const char far* path)
{
```

```
        points->Flush();
        //
        // If new - GetDocPath() will return 0
        //
        if (GetDocPath())
          {
            //
            // Read base storage for any contained
            // objects
            //
            TOleDocument::Open(mode,path);
            //
            // Get the file stream
            //
            TInStream* is = (TInStream*)InStream(ofRead);
            //
            // If cannot open file, will be zero
            //
            if (!is)
              return false;
            // reference for convenience
            TInStream& in = *is;
            //
            // Check how many points to read
            //
            //
            uint pointCount;
            in >> pointCount;
            //
            // Read specified number of points
            //
            TPoint p;
            for (int i = 0; i < pointCount; i++)
              {
                in >> p;
                points->Add(p); // Add to container
              }
            delete is;
          }
        SetDirty(false);        // Mark as unchanged
        return true;
    }
bool SpotDoc::Commit (bool force)
{
    bool result;
    //
    // Write out contained objects
    //
    result = TOleDocument::Commit(force);
    //
    // Get output stream to write own data
    //
    TOutStream* os = OutStream(ofWrite);
    if (!os)
      return false;
    TOutStream& out = *os; // reference for convenience
    //
    // Write out number of points
```

20

Listing 20.4. continued

```
        //
        out << points->GetItemsInContainer();
        //
        // For each point, write out to stream
        //
        for (int i = 0; i < points->GetItemsInContainer();i++)
          out << (*points)[i];
        delete os;
        //
        // Mark document as matching
        //
        SetDirty(false);
        //
        // Very important line! This forces write to disk;
        // without this, the file IS created but is corrupt.
        //
        TOleDocument::CommitTransactedStorage();
        return true;
}

//
// Close document
//
bool SpotDoc::Close()
  {
    points->Flush();
    return TOleDocument::Close();
  }
//
// View service functions
//
//   GetSpot returns a point at index
//
TPoint* SpotDoc::GetSpot(uint index)
  {
    if (points && index < points->GetItemsInContainer())
      return &(*points)[index];
    else
      return 0;
  }
//
// Add spot to collection
//
void SpotDoc::AddSpot(TPoint& point)
  {
    points->Add(point);
    // Picture has changed - set dirty flag
    SetDirty(true);
    //
    // Notify all views that the view has changed
    // Pass the index of the new point so that the
    // views can draw the new spot without redrawing
    // the entire screen.
    //
    // vnDrawAppend is defined in the header
    //
    NotifyViews(vnDrawAppend, points->GetItemsInContainer() - 1);
```

```
  }
//
// Entirely clear document
//
void SpotDoc::Clear()
  {
    //
    // Clear the document data
    //
    points->Flush();
    SetDirty(true);
    //
    // Tell view to empty container
    //

    NotifyViews(vnDrawClear,0);
  }
```

  Listing 20.5. Source code for the SPOTVIEW.H header file.

```
#if !defined(__spotview_h)
#define __spotview_h
#include <owl\owlpch.h>
#pragma hdrstop


#include "spotapp.rh"              // Definition of all resources.
#include "spotdoc.h"
//
// View class (may be several instances of this per
// document)
//
class SpotView : public TOleView
  {
    public:
      SpotView (SpotDoc& doc, TWindow* parent = 0);
      virtual ~SpotView ();
      virtual void Paint (TDC& dc, bool erase, TRect& rect);
      virtual const char far* GetViewName ();
      static const char far* StaticName ();
    protected:
      SpotDoc& spotDoc;  // Parent document
      TBrush* backBrush;
      TBrush* spotBrush;
      TPoint storePoint;
      TControlBar * toolBar;
      //
      // Draw a spot from a view
      //
      void SpotView::DrawSpot(TDC& dc, const TPoint& point);
      void EvLButtonDown (uint modKeys, TPoint& point);
      void EvMouseMove (uint modKeys, TPoint& point);
      void EvLButtonUp (uint modKeys, TPoint& point);
      void CmClear ();
      void CmEditCopy ();
      void CmEditCut ();
```

20

Listing 20.5. continued

```
        bool EvOcViewPartSize(TOcPartSize far& ps);
        bool EvOcViewShowTools(TOcToolBarInfo far& tbi);

    // Document notifications
        bool VnCommit(bool force); // Document saved
        bool VnRevert(bool clear); // Document restored
        bool VnAppend(uint index); // Document amended
        bool VnClear();            // document blanked
        DECLARE_RESPONSE_TABLE(SpotView);
};


#endif
```

 Listing 20.6. Source code for the SPOTVIEW.CPP program file.

```
#include <owl\owlpch.h>
#pragma hdrstop

#include "sptabtdl.h"
#include "spotapp.h"
#include "spotview.h"
#include "spotapp.rh"
#include <stdio.h>

const int spotRadius = 10; // Spot size
//
// Build a response table for all messages/commands handled
// by the application.
//
DEFINE_RESPONSE_TABLE1(SpotView, TOleView)
  //
  // Standard messages
  //
  EV_WM_LBUTTONDOWN,
  EV_WM_MOUSEMOVE,
  EV_WM_LBUTTONUP,
  EV_COMMAND(CM_EDITCLEAR, CmClear),
  EV_COMMAND(CM_EDITCOPY, CmEditCopy),
  EV_COMMAND(CM_EDITCUT, CmEditCut),
  //
  // View notifications
  //
  EV_VN_COMMIT,
  EV_VN_REVERT,
  EV_VN_DRAWAPPEND,
  EV_VN_DRAWCLEAR,
  //
  // OCF notifications
  //
  EV_OC_VIEWPARTSIZE,
  EV_OC_VIEWSHOWTOOLS,
END_RESPONSE_TABLE;
```

```
// SpotView
// =========
// Construction/Destruction handling.
SpotView::SpotView (SpotDoc& doc, TWindow* parent)
    : TOleView(doc, parent),
      spotDoc(doc)
{
    backBrush = new TBrush(TColor::LtMagenta);
    spotBrush = new TBrush(TColor::LtYellow);
    toolBar = 0;
}


SpotView::~SpotView ()
{
    delete backBrush;
    delete spotBrush;
    delete toolbar;   // Just in case
}
//
// Class and View names
//
const char far* SpotView::GetViewName ()
{
    return "SpotViewClass";
}
const char far* SpotView::StaticName ()
{
    return "Spot View";
}
//
// Paint is not only called for window, but also to update
// OLE2 metafile
//
void SpotView::Paint (TDC& dc, bool erase, TRect& rect)
{
    TPoint* spot;
    //
    TRect clientRect(0,0,GetSystemMetrics(SM_CXSCREEN),
                         GetSystemMetrics(SM_CYSCREEN));
    dc.FillRect(clientRect,*backBrush);

    //
    // This line paints the OLE embedded objects
    // (note: OLE objects are painted from a metafile and
    // do not require the server to be present)
    //
    TOleView::Paint(dc, false, rect);
    //
    // Spots before your eyes...
    //
    dc.SelectObject(*spotBrush);
    int i = 0;
    do
      {
        spot = spotDoc.GetSpot(i++);
        if (spot)
          DrawSpot(dc,*spot);
```

continues   607

Listing 20.6. continued

```
            }
        while (spot);

        dc.RestoreBrush();
    }
    void SpotView::DrawSpot(TDC& dc, const TPoint& point)
      {
        int radius = spotRadius;
        TRect spotRect(point.x - radius,
                       point.y - radius,
                       point.x + radius,
                       point.y + radius);
        dc.Ellipse(spotRect);

      }


    void SpotView::EvLButtonDown (uint modKeys, TPoint& point)
    {
        //
        // Base call sets up DragDC - it also modifies point
        // to be in logical units. This enables in-place editing
        // to work when the window has been stretched
        //
        TOleView::EvLButtonDown(modKeys, point);
        if (DragDC && !SelectEmbedded())
          {
            //
            // If haven't hit an OLE object -
            // capture mouse and draw temporary spot
            //
            SetCapture();
            DragDC->SetROP2(R2_XORPEN);      // Invert drawing
            storePoint = point;             // store point
            DragDC->SelectObject(*spotBrush);
            DrawSpot(*DragDC,storePoint);   // Draw spot inverted
          }
      }


    void SpotView::EvMouseMove (uint modKeys, TPoint& point)
    {
        TOleView::EvMouseMove(modKeys, point); // point modified
        if (DragDC&& !SelectEmbedded())  // If not dragging OLE object
          {
            DrawSpot(*DragDC,storePoint); // Clear up spot
            storePoint = point;
            DrawSpot(*DragDC,storePoint); // Spot breaks out again
          }

    }


    void SpotView::EvLButtonUp (uint modKeys, TPoint& point)
    {
        if (DragDC && !SelectEmbedded()) // Not OLE2 object
```

```
        {
          DrawSpot(*DragDC,storePoint); // Clear up spot
          storePoint = point;          // Store point
          DragDC->DPtoLP(&storePoint); // Convert to LPs
          ReleaseCapture();
          spotDoc.AddSpot(storePoint);
        }
                                    // Inconsistent:
      TOleView::EvLButtonUp(modKeys, point);
                                    // Does not convert point
                                    // except if using itself
}
//
// Let container know about the server view size in pixels
//
bool
SpotView::EvOcViewPartSize(TOcPartSize far& ps)
{
  TClientDC dc(*this);
  // Set minimum size...
  TRect rect(0, 0, 0, 0);
  // a 2" x 2" extent for server
  //
  rect.right  = dc.GetDeviceCaps(LOGPIXELSX) * 2;
  rect.bottom = dc.GetDeviceCaps(LOGPIXELSY) * 2;
  //
  // Note: this would be better calculated on open of
  // view and when data changed - but for simplicity, I have
  // just done it a nasty way.
  //
  // Declare picture size to be a minimum of 2" x 2"
  // but enable user to add more points for scaling
  //
  // Iterate through all the points and calculate the
  // most extreme
  //
  uint i = 0;
  TPoint* point = spotDoc.GetSpot(i++);
  while (point)
    {
      if (point->x > rect.bottom)
        rect.bottom = point->x;
      if (point->y > rect.right)
        rect.right = point->y;
      point = spotDoc.GetSpot(i++);
    }
  ps.PartRect = rect;
  return true;
}
//
// Give toolbar to container application.
// Note: to emphasize the point, when executing, the
// server does not have a toolbar - only when embedding.
// For the application, create a toolbar in the standard
// fashion. (Give it an Attr.Id of IDW_TOOLBAR)
//
bool
SpotView::EvOcViewShowTools(TOcToolBarInfo far& tbi)
```

20

Listing 20.6. continued

```
    {
      //
      // Construct & create a control bar for show;
      // destroy our bar for hide
      //
      if (tbi.Show)
        {
          if (!toolBar)
            {
              toolBar = new TControlBar(this);
              toolBar->Insert(*new TButtonGadget(CM_EDITCLEAR,
                        CM_EDITCLEAR, TButtonGadget::Command));
              toolBar->Insert(*new TSeparatorGadget);
              toolBar->Insert(*new TButtonGadget(CM_HELPABOUT,
                        CM_HELPABOUT, TButtonGadget::Command));
            }
          toolBar->Create();
          tbi.HTopTB = (HWND)*toolBar;
        }
      else
        {
          if (toolBar)
            {
              toolBar->Destroy();
              delete toolBar;
              toolBar = 0;
            }
        }
      return true;
    }


    bool SpotView::VnCommit(bool /*force*/)
    {
      // nothing to do here; no data held in view
      return true;
    }

    bool SpotView::VnRevert(bool /*clear*/)
    {
      Invalidate();  // force full repaint
      return true;
    }
    //
    // View notification that the document has been
    // emptied
    //
    bool SpotView::VnClear()
      {
      Invalidate();  // force full repaint
      //
      // Component parts are held in a collection
      // iterate the collection to remove the data
      //
      for (TOcPartCollectionIter i(GetOcDoc()->GetParts()); i; i++)
        {
```

```
          TOcPart* p = i.Current();
          TOcPartChangeInfo changeInfo(p, invData¦invView);
          EvOcViewPartInvalid(changeInfo);
          GetOcDoc()->GetParts().Detach(p,true);
      }
    InvalidatePart(invData¦invView);
    return true;
}
//
// View notiification that the document has been added to
//
bool SpotView::VnAppend(uint index)
{
  //
  // Append a spot onto current views - could be a metafile
  //
  // Get a dc for the view window
  TClientDC dc(*this);
  //
  // Get the spot notified at index
  //
  const TPoint* spot = spotDoc.GetSpot(index);
  bool metafile = dc.GetDeviceCaps(TECHNOLOGY) == DT_METAFILE;
  //
  // If drawing to metafile, need to scale
  //
  SetupDC(dc, !metafile);
  dc.SelectObject(*spotBrush);
  DrawSpot(dc,*spot);
  //
  // Tell container to redraw
  //
  InvalidatePart(invView);
  return true;
}


void SpotView::CmClear ()
{
    //
    // Tell document to clear down
    //
    spotDoc.Clear();
}


void SpotView::CmEditCopy ()
{
  //
  // Supposed to be able to copy view to Clipboard
  //
  // Not implemented at time of writing
  //
    TOcRemView* orv = GetOcRemView();
//  if (orv)
//    orv->Copy();
}
```

Listing 20.6. continued

```
void SpotView::CmEditCut ()
{
    // Do nothing... nothing sensible to do
}
```

 Listing 20.7. Source code for the SPOTAB.H header file.

```
#if !defined(__sptab_h)
#define __sptab_h

#include <owl\owlpch.h>
#pragma hdrstop

#include "spotapp.rh"
class SpotAboutDlg : public TDialog
 {
  public:
    SpotAboutDlg (TWindow *parent, TResId resId = IDD_ABOUT,
                  TModule *module = 0);
    virtual ~SpotAboutDlg ();
  public:
    void SetupWindow ();
};
// Reading the VERSIONINFO resource.
class ProjectRCVersion
  {
    public:
      ProjectRCVersion (TModule *module);
      virtual ~ProjectRCVersion ();

      bool GetProductName (LPSTR &prodName);
      bool GetProductVersion (LPSTR &prodVersion);
      bool GetCopyright (LPSTR &copyright);
      bool GetDebug (LPSTR &debug);

    protected:
      LPBYTE      TransBlock;
      void FAR    *FVData;

    private:
    // Don't enable this object to be copied.
    ProjectRCVersion (const ProjectRCVersion &);
    ProjectRCVersion & operator =(const ProjectRCVersion &);
  };

#endif
```

Listing 20.8. Source code for the SPOTAB.CPP program file.

```cpp
#include <owl\owlpch.h>
#pragma hdrstop

#if !defined(__FLAT__)
#include <ver.h>
#endif

#include "spotapp.h"
#include "spotab.h"
//
// AppExpert generated About box
//
ProjectRCVersion::ProjectRCVersion (TModule *module)
{
    char     appFName[255];
    char     subBlockName[255];
    DWORD    fvHandle;
    uint     vSize;

    FVData = 0;

    module->GetModuleFileName(appFName, sizeof(appFName));
    DWORD dwSize = ::GetFileVersionInfoSize(appFName,&fvHandle);
    if (dwSize)
      {
        FVData  = (void FAR *)new char[(uint)dwSize];
        if (::GetFileVersionInfo(appFName, fvHandle, dwSize,
                              FVData))
          {
            strcpy(subBlockName, "\\VarFileInfo\\Translation");
            if (!::VerQueryValue(FVData, subBlockName,
                          (void FAR* FAR*)&TransBlock, &vSize))
              {
                delete FVData;
                FVData = 0;
              }
            else
                *(DWORD *)TransBlock =
                            MAKELONG(HIWORD(*(DWORD *)TransBlock),
                            LOWORD(*(DWORD *)TransBlock));
          }
      }
  }


ProjectRCVersion::~ProjectRCVersion ()
  {
    if (FVData)
        delete FVData;
  }


bool ProjectRCVersion::GetProductName (LPSTR &prodName)
```

continues

20

Listing 20.8. continued

```
    {
        uint    vSize;
        char    subBlockName[255];

        wsprintf(subBlockName, "\\StringFileInfo\\%08lx\\%s",
          *(DWORD *)TransBlock, (LPSTR)"ProductName");
        return FVData ? ::VerQueryValue(FVData, subBlockName,
                            (void FAR* FAR*)&prodName, &vSize) : false;
    }


bool ProjectRCVersion::GetProductVersion (LPSTR &prodVersion)
    {
        uint    vSize;
        char    subBlockName[255];

        wsprintf(subBlockName, "\\StringFileInfo\\%08lx\\%s",
                *(DWORD *)TransBlock, (LPSTR)"ProductVersion");
        return FVData ? ::VerQueryValue(FVData, subBlockName,
                (void FAR* FAR*)&prodVersion, &vSize) : false;
    }


bool ProjectRCVersion::GetCopyright (LPSTR &copyright)
    {
        uint    vSize;
        char    subBlockName[255];

        wsprintf(subBlockName, "\\StringFileInfo\\%08lx\\%s",
                *(DWORD *)TransBlock, (LPSTR)"LegalCopyright");
        return FVData ? ::VerQueryValue(FVData, subBlockName,
                (void FAR* FAR*)&copyright, &vSize) : false;
    }


bool ProjectRCVersion::GetDebug (LPSTR &debug)
{
        uint    vSize;
        char    subBlockName[255];

        wsprintf(subBlockName, "\\StringFileInfo\\%08lx\\%s",
                *(DWORD *)TransBlock, (LPSTR)"SpecialBuild");
        return FVData ? ::VerQueryValue(FVData, subBlockName,
                (void FAR* FAR*)&debug, &vSize) : false;
}


SpotAboutDlg::SpotAboutDlg (TWindow *parent, TResId resId,
                                TModule *module)
        : TDialog(parent, resId, module)
    {
    }

SpotAboutDlg::~SpotAboutDlg ()
    {
        Destroy();
```

```
    }

void SpotAboutDlg::SetupWindow ()
{
    LPSTR prodName = 0, prodVersion = 0, copyright = 0, debug = 0;

    // Get the static text for the value based on VERSIONINFO.
    TStatic *versionCtrl = new TStatic(this, IDC_VERSION, 255);
    TStatic *copyrightCtrl = new TStatic(this, IDC_COPYRIGHT,
                                         255);
    TStatic *debugCtrl = new TStatic(this, IDC_DEBUG, 255);
    TDialog::SetupWindow();
    // Process the VERSIONINFO.
    ProjectRCVersion applVersion(GetModule());
    // Get the product name and product version strings.
    if (applVersion.GetProductName(prodName) &&
        applVersion.GetProductVersion(prodVersion)) {
        char    buffer[255];
        char    versionName[128];
        buffer[0] = '\0';
        versionName[0] = '\0';
        versionCtrl->GetText(versionName, sizeof(versionName));
        wsprintf(buffer, "%s %s %s", prodName,
                 versionName, prodVersion);
        versionCtrl->SetText(buffer);
    }
    //Get the legal copyright string.
    if (applVersion.GetCopyright(copyright))
        copyrightCtrl->SetText(copyright);
    if (applVersion.GetDebug(debug))
        debugCtrl->SetText(debug);
}
```

Listing 20.9. Source code for the SPOTAPP.RH resource header file.

```
//#if !defined(__spotapp_rh)
//#define __spotapp_rh
//
// IDHELP BorButton for BWCC dialogs.
//
#define IDHELP        998                // Id of help button


//
// Application-specific definitions:
//
#define IDI_SDIAPPLICATION    1001  // Application icon

#define SDI_MENU              100   // Menu and Accelerator IDs

#define IDM_DOCMANAGERFILE    32401
                              // Menu for DocManager merging.

//
```

Listing 20.9. continued

```
// OleView merged menus (include\owl\oleview.rh)
//
#define IDM_OLEPOPUP            32405
#define IDM_OLEVIEW             32406


//
// CM_FILEnnnn commands
//   (include\owl\editfile.rh except for CM_FILEPRINTPREVIEW)
//
#define CM_FILENEW              24331          // SDI New
#define CM_FILEOPEN             24332          // SDI Open
#define CM_FILECLOSE            24339
#define CM_FILESAVE             24333
#define CM_FILESAVEAS           24334
#define CM_FILEREVERT           24335
#define CM_VIEWCREATE           24341


//
// Window commands (include\owl\window.rh)
//
#define CM_EXIT                 24310


//
// CM_EDITnnnn commands (include\owl\window.rh)
//
#define CM_EDITUNDO             24321
#define CM_EDITCUT              24322
#define CM_EDITCOPY             24323
#define CM_EDITPASTE            24324
#define CM_EDITDELETE           24325
#define CM_EDITCLEAR            24326
#define CM_EDITADD              24327
#define CM_EDITEDIT             24328
#define CM_EDITPASTESPECIAL     24311
#define CM_EDITPASTELINK         24312
#define CM_EDITINSERTOBJECT     24313
#define CM_EDITLINKS            24314

#define CM_EDITOBJECT           24370
#define CM_EDITFIRSTVERB        24371          // 20 verbs at most
#define CM_EDITLASTVERB         24390

#define CM_EDITCONVERT          24391
#define CM_EDITSHOWOBJECTS      24392


//
// Search menu commands (include\owl\editsear.rh)
//
#define CM_EDITFIND             24351
#define CM_EDITREPLACE          24352
#define CM_EDITFINDNEXT         24353
```

```
//
// Help menu commands.
//
#define CM_HELPABOUT              2009


//
// About Dialogs
//
#define IDD_ABOUT                 22000
#define IDC_VERSION               22001
#define IDC_COPYRIGHT             22002
#define IDC_DEBUG                 22003


//
// OWL defined strings
//

// Status bar
#define IDS_MODES                 32530
#define IDS_MODESOFF              32531


// EditFile
#define IDS_UNABLEREAD            32551
#define IDS_UNABLEWRITE           32552
#define IDS_FILECHANGED           32553
#define IDS_FILEFILTER            32554

// EditSearch
#define IDS_CANNOTFIND            32540


//
// General & application exception messages
//    (include\owl\except.rh)
//
#define IDS_UNKNOWNEXCEPTION      32767
#define IDS_OWLEXCEPTION          32766
#define IDS_OKTORESUME            32765
#define IDS_UNHANDLEDXMSG         32764
#define IDS_UNKNOWNERROR          32763
#define IDS_NOAPP                 32762
#define IDS_OUTOFMEMORY           32761
#define IDS_INVALIDMODULE         32760
#define IDS_INVALIDMAINWINDOW     32759
#define IDS_VBXLIBRARYFAIL        32758


//
// Owl 1 compatibility messages
//
#define IDS_INVALIDWINDOW         32756
#define IDS_INVALIDCHILDWINDOW    32755
#define IDS_INVALIDCLIENTWINDOW   32754

//
```

Listing 20.9. continued

```
// TXWindow messages
//
#define IDS_CLASSREGISTERFAIL    32749
#define IDS_CHILDREGISTERFAIL    32748
#define IDS_WINDOWCREATEFAIL     32747
#define IDS_WINDOWEXECUTEFAIL    32746
#define IDS_CHILDCREATEFAIL      32745

#define IDS_MENUFAILURE          32744
#define IDS_VALIDATORSYNTAX      32743
#define IDS_PRINTERERROR         32742

#define IDS_LAYOUTINCOMPLETE     32741
#define IDS_LAYOUTBADRELWIN      32740

//
// TXGdi messages
//
#define IDS_GDIFAILURE           32739
#define IDS_GDIALLOCFAIL         32738
#define IDS_GDICREATEFAIL        32737
#define IDS_GDIRESLOADFAIL       32736
#define IDS_GDIFILEREADFAIL      32735
#define IDS_GDIDELETEFAIL        32734
#define IDS_GDIDESTROYFAIL       32733
#define IDS_INVALIDDIBHANDLE     32732


// ListView (include\owl\listview.rh)
#define IDS_LISTNUM              32584


// DocView (include\owl\docview.rh)
#define IDS_DOCMANAGERFILE       32500
#define IDS_DOCLIST              32501
#define IDS_VIEWLIST             32502
#define IDS_UNTITLED             32503
#define IDS_UNABLEOPEN           32504
#define IDS_UNABLECLOSE          32505
#define IDS_READERROR            32506
#define IDS_WRITEERROR           32507
#define IDS_DOCCHANGED           32508
#define IDS_NOTCHANGED           32509
#define IDS_NODOCMANAGER         32510
#define IDS_NOMEMORYFORVIEW      32511
#define IDS_DUPLICATEDOC         32512
#define IDS_EDITOBJECT           32600
#define IDS_EDITCONVERT          32601
#define IDS_CLOSESERVER          32602
#define IDS_EXITSERVER           32603

// Text for Clipboard format names
#define IDS_CFTEXT               32610
#define IDS_CFBITMAP             32611
#define IDS_CFMETAFILE           32612
#define IDS_CFSYLK               32613
```

```
#define IDS_CFDIF              32614
#define IDS_CFTIFF             32615
#define IDS_CFOEMTEXT          32616
#define IDS_CFDIB              32617
#define IDS_CFPALETTE          32618
#define IDS_CFPENDATA          32619
#define IDS_CFRIFF             32620
#define IDS_CFWAVE             32621
#define IDS_CFUNICODETEXT      32622
#define IDS_CFENHMETAFILE      32623

#define IDS_IN          32700


//#endif
```

Type   Listing 20.10. Script for the SPOTAPP.RC resource file.

```
#if !defined(WORKSHOP_INVOKED)
#include <windows.h>
#endif
#include "spotapp.rh"
//
// Standard application menu
//
SDI_MENU MENU
{
 POPUP "&File"
 {
  MENUITEM "&New", CM_FILENEW
  MENUITEM "&Open...", CM_FILEOPEN
  MENUITEM SEPARATOR
  MENUITEM "&Save", CM_FILESAVE, GRAYED
  MENUITEM "Save &As...", CM_FILESAVEAS, GRAYED
  MENUITEM SEPARATOR
  MENUITEM "E&xit\tAlt+F4", CM_EXIT
 }

 MENUITEM SEPARATOR
 POPUP "&Edit"
 {
  MENUITEM "&Undo\tAlt+BkSp", CM_EDITUNDO, GRAYED
  MENUITEM SEPARATOR
  MENUITEM "Cu&t\tShift+Del", CM_EDITCUT, GRAYED
  MENUITEM "&Copy\tCtrl+Ins", CM_EDITCOPY, GRAYED
  MENUITEM "&Paste\tShift+Ins", CM_EDITPASTE, GRAYED
  MENUITEM "Paste &Special...",    CM_EDITPASTESPECIAL
  MENUITEM "Paste &Link",          CM_EDITPASTELINK
  MENUITEM SEPARATOR
  MENUITEM "Clear &All\tCtrl+Del", CM_EDITCLEAR, GRAYED
  MENUITEM Separator
  MENUITEM "&Insert Object...",    CM_EDITINSERTOBJECT
  MENUITEM "&Links...",            CM_EDITLINKS
  MENUITEM "&Object",              CM_EDITOBJECT
  MENUITEM Separator
```

continues

20

Listing 20.10. continued

```
      MENUITEM "&Show Objects",          CM_EDITSHOWOBJECTS
      }

    MENUITEM SEPARATOR
    MENUITEM SEPARATOR
    MENUITEM SEPARATOR
    MENUITEM SEPARATOR
    POPUP "&Help"
    {
     MENUITEM "&About...", CM_HELPABOUT
    }

    }


    // Accelerator table for short-cut to menu commands. (include\owl\editfile.rc)
    SDI_MENU ACCELERATORS
    BEGIN
      VK_DELETE, CM_EDITDELETE, VIRTKEY
      VK_DELETE, CM_EDITCUT, VIRTKEY, SHIFT
      VK_INSERT, CM_EDITCOPY, VIRTKEY, CONTROL
      VK_INSERT, CM_EDITPASTE, VIRTKEY, SHIFT
      VK_DELETE, CM_EDITCLEAR, VIRTKEY, CONTROL
      VK_BACK,   CM_EDITUNDO, VIRTKEY, ALT
      VK_F3,     CM_EDITFINDNEXT, VIRTKEY
    END


    // DocManager File menu

    IDM_DOCMANAGERFILE MENU LOADONCALL MOVEABLE PURE DISCARDABLE
    BEGIN
        MENUITEM "&New", CM_FILENEW
        MENUITEM "&Open...", CM_FILEOPEN
        MENUITEM "&Close", CM_FILECLOSE
        MENUITEM SEPARATOR
        MENUITEM "&Save", CM_FILESAVE, GRAYED
        MENUITEM "Save &As...", CM_FILESAVEAS, GRAYED
        MENUITEM SEPARATOR
        MENUITEM "E&xit\tAlt+F4", CM_EXIT
    END


    // Menu merged in when TOleView is active;
    // notice the extra MENUITEM SEPARATORs, which are
    // for menu negotation.  These separators are used as group
    // markers by OWL.
    IDM_OLEVIEW MENU
    {
     MENUITEM SEPARATOR
     POPUP "&Edit"
     {
      MENUITEM "&Undo\aCtrl+Z", CM_EDITUNDO
      MENUITEM SEPARATOR
      MENUITEM "&Cut\aCtrl+X", CM_EDITCUT
      MENUITEM "C&opy\aCtrl+C", CM_EDITCOPY
```

```
     MENUITEM "&Paste\aCtrl+V", CM_EDITPASTE
     MENUITEM "Paste &Special...", CM_EDITPASTESPECIAL
     MENUITEM "Paste &Link", CM_EDITPASTELINK
     MENUITEM "Clear &All\aCtrl+Del", CM_EDITCLEAR
     MENUITEM Separator
     MENUITEM "&Insert Object...",    CM_EDITINSERTOBJECT
     MENUITEM "&Links...",            CM_EDITLINKS
     MENUITEM "&Object",              CM_EDITOBJECT
     MENUITEM Separator
     MENUITEM "&Show Objects",        CM_EDITSHOWOBJECTS

  }

  MENUITEM SEPARATOR
  MENUITEM SEPARATOR
  MENUITEM SEPARATOR
  MENUITEM SEPARATOR
  POPUP "&Help"
  {
   MENUITEM "&About...", CM_HELPABOUT
  }

}
//
// OLE pop-up
//

IDM_OLEPOPUP MENU LOADONCALL MOVEABLE PURE DISCARDABLE
BEGIN
    POPUP "OLE"
    BEGIN
        MENUITEM "&Cut\aCtrl+X", CM_EDITCUT
        MENUITEM "C&opy\aCtrl+C", CM_EDITCOPY
        MENUITEM "&Delete\aDel", CM_EDITDELETE
        MENUITEM SEPARATOR
        MENUITEM "&Object", CM_EDITOBJECT
    END
END


//
// Table of help hints displayed in the status bar.
//
STRINGTABLE
BEGIN
    -1,             "File/document operations"
    CM_FILENEW,     "Creates a new document"
    CM_FILEOPEN,    "Opens an existing document"
    CM_VIEWCREATE,  "Create a new view for this document"
    CM_FILEREVERT,  "Reverts changes to last document save"
    CM_FILECLOSE,   "Close this document"
    CM_FILESAVE,    "Saves this document"
    CM_FILESAVEAS,  "Saves this document with a new name"
    CM_EXIT,        "Quits Spot and prompts to save the documents"
    CM_EDITUNDO-1,  "Edit operations"
    CM_EDITUNDO,    "Reverses the last operation"
    CM_EDITCUT,   "Cuts the selection and puts it on the Clipboard"
```

20

continues

621

Listing 20.10. continued

```
        CM_EDITCOPY,   "Copies selection and puts it on the Clipboard"
        CM_EDITPASTE,  "Inserts clipboard contents at insertion point"
        CM_EDITPASTESPECIAL, "Select paste option and format"
        CM_EDITPASTELINK,    "Link with object on the clipboard"
        CM_EDITDELETE,  "Deletes the selection"
        CM_EDITCLEAR,   "Clear the document"
        CM_EDITLINKS,   "Edit links to the document"
        CM_EDITINSERTOBJECT,    "Insert an object into the document"
        CM_EDITOBJECT,  "Ask the selected object to perform an action"
        CM_EDITSHOWOBJECTS,      "Hilight selected object"
        CM_EDITADD,       "Insert a new line"
        CM_EDITEDIT,      "Edit the current line"
        CM_EDITFIND-1,   "Search/replace operations"
        CM_EDITFIND,     "Finds the specified text"
        CM_EDITREPLACE,  "Finds the specified text and changes it"
        CM_EDITFINDNEXT, "Finds the next match"
        CM_HELPABOUT-1,  "Access About"
        CM_HELPABOUT,    "About the Spot application"
    END


    //
    // OWL string table
    //

    // EditFile (include\owl\editfile.rc and include\owl\editsear.rc)
    STRINGTABLE LOADONCALL MOVEABLE DISCARDABLE
    BEGIN
        IDS_CANNOTFIND,  "Cannot find ""%s""."
        IDS_UNABLEREAD,  "Unable to read file %s from disk."
        IDS_UNABLEWRITE, "Unable to write file %s to disk."
        IDS_FILECHANGED, "The text in the %s file has changed."
                         "\n\nDo you want to save the changes?"
        IDS_FILEFILTER,  "Text files (*.TXT)¦*.TXT¦AllFiles
                          "(*.*)¦*.*¦"
    END



    // ListView (include\owl\listview.rc)
    STRINGTABLE LOADONCALL MOVEABLE DISCARDABLE
    BEGIN
      IDS_LISTNUM,  "Line number %d"
    END



    // Doc/View (include\owl\docview.rc)
    STRINGTABLE LOADONCALL MOVEABLE DISCARDABLE
    BEGIN
        IDS_DOCMANAGERFILE,         "&File"
        IDS_DOCLIST,                "--Document Type--"
        IDS_VIEWLIST,               "--View Type--"
        IDS_UNTITLED,               "Document"
        IDS_UNABLEOPEN,             "Unable to open document."
        IDS_UNABLECLOSE,            "Unable to close document."
        IDS_READERROR,              "Document read error."
        IDS_WRITEERROR,             "Document write error."
        IDS_DOCCHANGED,             "The document has been"
                "changed.\n\nDo you want to save the changes?"
```

```
        IDS_NOTCHANGED,          "The document has not been changed."
        IDS_NODOCMANAGER,          "Document Manager not present."
        IDS_NOMEMORYFORVIEW,          "Insufficient memory for view."
        IDS_DUPLICATEDOC,          "Document already loaded."
END


// OLEView (include\owl\oleview.rc)
STRINGTABLE LOADONCALL MOVEABLE DISCARDABLE
BEGIN
        IDS_EDITOBJECT,          "&Object"
        IDS_EDITCONVERT,          "Convert..."
        IDS_CLOSESERVER,          "Close and Return to "
        IDS_EXITSERVER,          "Exit and Return to "
END


STRINGTABLE LOADONCALL MOVEABLE DISCARDABLE
BEGIN
        IDS_CFTEXT,          "Text\nplain text"
        IDS_CFBITMAP,          "Bitmap\na bitmap image"
        IDS_CFMETAFILE,          "Metafile Picture\na static picture"
        IDS_CFSYLK,          "Sylk\na spreadsheet"
        IDS_CFDIF,          "DIF\na document"
        IDS_CFTIFF,          "Tagged Image File Format\na "
                             "TIFF image file"
        IDS_CFOEMTEXT,          "OEM Text\nan OEM text"
        IDS_CFDIB,          "DIB\na device independent bitmap"
                             "image"
        IDS_CFPALETTE,          "Palette\na color palette"
        IDS_CFPENDATA,          "Pen Data\npen data"
        IDS_CFRIFF,          "RIFF\na RIFF media file"
        IDS_CFWAVE,          "Wave\na sound wave file"
        IDS_CFUNICODETEXT,          "UniCode Text\nUnicode text"
        IDS_CFENHMETAFILE,          "Enhanced Metafile\nan "
                             "enhanced metafile picture"
        IDS_IN,          " in "
END


// Exception string resources (include\owl\except.rc)
STRINGTABLE LOADONCALL MOVEABLE DISCARDABLE
BEGIN
        IDS_OWLEXCEPTION,          "ObjectWindows Exception"
        IDS_UNHANDLEDXMSG,          "Unhandled Exception"
        IDS_OKTORESUME,          "OK to resume?"
        IDS_UNKNOWNEXCEPTION,          "Unknown exception"

        IDS_UNKNOWNERROR,          "Unknown error"
        IDS_NOAPP,          "No application object"
        IDS_OUTOFMEMORY,          "Out of memory"
        IDS_INVALIDMODULE,     "Invalid module specified for window"
        IDS_INVALIDMAINWINDOW,          "Invalid MainWindow"
        IDS_VBXLIBRARYFAIL,          "VBX Library init failure"

        IDS_INVALIDWINDOW,          "Invalid window %s"
        IDS_INVALIDCHILDWINDOW,          "Invalid child window %s"
        IDS_INVALIDCLIENTWINDOW,          "Invalid client window %s"
```

Listing 20.10. continued

```
            IDS_CLASSREGISTERFAIL,
                    "Class registration fail for window %s"
            IDS_CHILDREGISTERFAIL,
                    "Child class registration fail for window %s"
            IDS_WINDOWCREATEFAIL,       "Create fail for window %s"
            IDS_WINDOWEXECUTEFAIL,      "Execute fail for window %s"
            IDS_CHILDCREATEFAIL,        "Child create fail for window %s"

            IDS_MENUFAILURE,            "Menu creation failure"
            IDS_VALIDATORSYNTAX,        "Validator syntax error"
            IDS_PRINTERERROR,           "Printer error"

            IDS_LAYOUTINCOMPLETE,
                "Incomplete layout constraints specified in window %s"
            IDS_LAYOUTBADRELWIN,
                "Invalid relative window specified in layout constraint
                in window %s"

            IDS_GDIFAILURE,             "GDI failure"
            IDS_GDIALLOCFAIL,           "GDI allocate failure"
            IDS_GDICREATEFAIL,          "GDI creation failure"
            IDS_GDIRESLOADFAIL,         "GDI resource load failure"
            IDS_GDIFILEREADFAIL,        "GDI file read failure"
            IDS_GDIDELETEFAIL,          "GDI object %X delete failure"
            IDS_GDIDESTROYFAIL,         "GDI object %X destroy failure"
            IDS_INVALIDDIBHANDLE,       "Invalid DIB handle %X"
        END


        // General Window's status bar messages. (include\owl\statusba.rc)
        STRINGTABLE
        BEGIN
            IDS_MODES                   "EXT¦CAPS¦NUM¦SCRL¦OVR¦REC"
            IDS_MODESOFF                "   ¦    ¦   ¦    ¦   ¦   "
            SC_SIZE,            "Changes the size of the window"
            SC_MOVE,            "Moves the window to another position"
            SC_MINIMIZE,        "Reduces the window to an icon"
            SC_MAXIMIZE,        "Enlarges the window to it maximum size"
            SC_RESTORE,         "Restores the window to its previous size"
            SC_CLOSE,                   "Closes the window"
            SC_TASKLIST,                "Opens task list"
            SC_NEXTWINDOW,              "Switches to next window"
        END



        //
        // Misc application definitions
        //

        // Application ICON
        IDI_SDIAPPLICATION ICON "applsdi.ico"


        // About box.
        IDD_ABOUT DIALOG 12, 17, 204, 65
        STYLE DS_MODALFRAME ¦ WS_POPUP ¦ WS_CAPTION ¦ WS_SYSMENU
```

```
CAPTION "About Spot"
FONT 8, "MS Sans Serif"
BEGIN
    CTEXT "Version", IDC_VERSION, 2, 14, 200, 8, SS_NOPREFIX
    CTEXT "Expert OWL Application", -1, 2, 4, 200, 8, SS_NOPREFIX
    CTEXT "", IDC_COPYRIGHT, 2, 27, 200, 17, SS_NOPREFIX
    RTEXT "", IDC_DEBUG, 136, 55, 66, 8, SS_NOPREFIX
    ICON IDI_SDIAPPLICATION, -1, 2, 2, 34, 34
    DEFPUSHBUTTON "OK", IDOK, 82, 48, 40, 14
END

CM_EDITCLEAR BITMAP LOADONCALL MOVEABLE
{
 '42 4D 66 01 00 00 00 00 00 00 76 00 00 00 28 00'
 '00 00 14 00 00 00 14 00 00 00 01 00 04 00 00 00'
 '00 00 F0 00 00 00 00 00 00 00 00 00 00 00 00 00'
 '00 00 00 00 00 00 00 00 00 00 00 00 80 00 00 80'
 '00 00 00 80 80 00 80 00 00 00 80 00 80 00 80 80'
 '00 00 80 80 80 00 C0 C0 C0 00 00 00 FF 00 00 FF'
 '00 00 00 FF FF 00 FF 00 00 00 FF 00 FF 00 FF FF'
 '00 00 FF FF FF 00 88 88 88 88 88 88 88 88 88 88'
 '40 00 88 88 88 88 88 88 88 88 88 88 90 00 88 88'
 '88 88 88 88 88 88 20 00 88 88 88 88 88 88'
 '88 88 88 88 40 18 88 88 88 88 88 88 88 88 88 88'
 '00 00 88 88 88 88 88 88 88 88 88 00 00 88 88'
 '88 88 88 88 88 88 00 00 88 88 88 88 88 88'
 '88 88 88 88 0B 00 88 80 08 88 88 88 88 88 88 88'
 '00 00 88 80 08 88 88 88 88 88 88 00 00 88 80'
 '08 88 88 84 44 44 44 48 00 00 88 80 08 80 88 84'
 'EF EF EF 48 0B 00 88 80 07 80 08 84 FE FE FE 48'
 '00 00 88 87 00 00 00 84 EF EF EF 48 00 00 88 88'
 '70 00 00 84 FE FE FE 48 00 00 88 88 80 08 84'
 'EF EF EF 48 0B 00 88 88 88 80 88 84 FE FE 44 48'
 'FF FF 88 88 88 88 88 84 EF EF 44 88 FF FF 88 88'
 '88 88 88 84 44 44 48 88 00 00 88 88 88 88 88 88'
 '88 88 88 88 0B 00'
}
CM_HELPABOUT BITMAP
{
 42 4D 66 01 00 00 00 00 00 00 76 00 00 00 28 00'
 '00 00 14 00 00 00 14 00 00 00 01 00 04 00 00 00'
 '00 00 F0 00 00 00 00 00 00 00 00 00 00 00 00 00'
 '00 00 00 00 00 00 00 00 00 00 00 00 80 00 00 80'
 '00 00 00 80 80 00 80 00 00 00 80 00 80 00 80 80'
 '00 00 80 80 80 00 C0 C0 C0 00 00 00 FF 00 00 FF'
 '00 00 00 FF FF 00 FF 00 00 00 FF 00 FF 00 FF FF'
 '00 00 FF FF FF 00 88 88 88 88 88 88 88 88 88 88'
 '00 00 88 88 88 84 44 44 48 88 88 88 00 00 88 88'
 '84 44 44 44 44 48 88 88 00 00 88 88 44 46 FF 64'
 '44 44 88 88 00 00 88 84 44 4F FF F6 44 44 48 88'
 '00 00 88 44 44 4F F6 48 44 44 44 88 00 00 88 44'
 '44 46 FF 44 44 44 44 88 01 01 84 44 44 44 FF 64'
 '44 44 44 48 08 33 84 44 44 44 6F F4 44 44 44 48'
 '00 00 84 44 44 44 4F F6 44 44 44 48 00 00 84 44'
 '44 48 46 FF 44 44 44 48 00 00 84 44 44 46 FF FF'
 '44 44 44 48 00 00 84 44 44 44 6F F6 44 44 44 48'
 '00 00 88 44 44 44 44 44 44 44 88 00 00 88 44'
 '44 44 66 44 44 44 88 00 00 88 84 44 44 46 FF'
```

Listing 20.10. continued

```
'64 44 48 88 00 00 88 88 44 44 46 FF 64 44 88 88'
'00 00 88 88 84 44 44 66 44 48 88 88 00 00 88 88'
'88 84 44 44 48 88 88 88 00 00 88 88 88 88 88 88'
'88 88 88 88 00 00'
}
// Version info.
//
#if !defined(__DEBUG_)
// Non-Debug VERSIONINFO
1 VERSIONINFO LOADONCALL MOVEABLE
FILEVERSION 1, 0, 0, 0
PRODUCTVERSION 1, 0, 0, 0
FILEFLAGSMASK 0
FILEFLAGS VS_FFI_FILEFLAGSMASK
FILEOS VOS__WINDOWS16
FILETYPE VFT_APP
BEGIN
    BLOCK "StringFileInfo"
    BEGIN
        // Language type = U.S. English (0x0409) and
        // Character Set = Windows, Multilingual(0x04e4)
        BLOCK "040904E4"
            // Matches VarFileInfo Translation hex value.
        BEGIN
            VALUE "CompanyName", "Honor Oak Systems\000"
            VALUE "FileDescription", "Spot for Windows\000"
            VALUE "FileVersion", "1.0\000"
            VALUE "InternalName", "Spot\000"
            VALUE "LegalCopyright",
                "Copyright   1994 by Honor Oak Systems. \000"
            VALUE "LegalTrademarks", "Windows (TM)\000"
            VALUE "OriginalFilename", "Spot.EXE\000"
            VALUE "ProductName", "Spot\000"
            VALUE "ProductVersion", "1.0\000"
        END
    END

    BLOCK "VarFileInfo"
    BEGIN
        VALUE "Translation", 0x0409, 0x04e4
    // U.S. English(0x0409) & Windows Multilingual(0x04e4) 1252
    END

END
#else

// Debug VERSIONINFO
1 VERSIONINFO LOADONCALL MOVEABLE
FILEVERSION 1, 0, 0, 0
PRODUCTVERSION 1, 0, 0, 0
FILEFLAGSMASK VS_FF_DEBUG ¦ VS_FF_PRERELEASE ¦ VS_FF_PATCHED ¦
VS_FF_PRIVATEBUILD ¦ VS_FF_SPECIALBUILD
FILEFLAGS VS_FFI_FILEFLAGSMASK
FILEOS VOS__WINDOWS16
FILETYPE VFT_APP
BEGIN
```

```
        BLOCK "StringFileInfo"
        BEGIN
            // Language type = U.S. English (0x0409)
            // and Character Set = Windows, Multilingual(0x04e4)
            BLOCK "040904E4"
            // Matches VarFileInfo Translation hex value.
            BEGIN
                VALUE "CompanyName", "Honor Oak Systems\000"
                VALUE "FileDescription", "Spot for Windows\000"
                VALUE "FileVersion", "1.0\000"
                VALUE "InternalName", "Spot\000"
                VALUE "LegalCopyright",
                    "Copyright 1994 by Honor Oak Systems.  \000"
                VALUE "LegalTrademarks", "Windows (TM)\000"
                VALUE "OriginalFilename", "Spot.EXE\000"
                VALUE "ProductName", "Spot\000"
                VALUE "ProductVersion", "1.0\000"
                VALUE "SpecialBuild", "Debug Version\000"
                VALUE "PrivateBuild", "Built by Ian Spencer\000"
            END
        END

        BLOCK "VarFileInfo"
        BEGIN
            VALUE "Translation", 0x0409, 0x04e4
        // U.S. English(0x0409) & Windows Multilingual(0x04e4) 1252
        END

END
#endif

IDM_OLEVIEW ACCELERATORS
{
 VK_DELETE, CM_EDITDELETE, VIRTKEY, CONTROL
}
```

Type

Listing 20.11. Source code for the SPOTAPP.DEF definition file.

20

```
NAME spot

DESCRIPTION 'Spot - Copyright 1994 by Honor Oak Systems.'
EXETYPE     WINDOWS
CODE        PRELOAD MOVEABLE DISCARDABLE
DATA        PRELOAD MOVEABLE
HEAPSIZE    4096
STACKSIZE   20000
```

Type

Listing 20.12. Contents of the SPOT.IDE project file.

```
SPOT[.EXE] OWL + OCF LIBRARIES
  SPOTAPP[.CPP]
  SPOTDOC[.CPP]
  SPOTVIEW[.CPP]
```

continues 627

Listing 20.12. continued

```
SPOTAB[.CPP]
SPOTAPP[.RC]
SPOTAPP[.DEF]
```

Analysis First, ensure that you have registered the server. You may want to build some of the OLE samples in the EXAMPLES directory to give you a test bed, unless you have a modern application. Running it as a stand-alone application might give you a result like the one in Figure 20.3. Running in another OLE application, STEP14.EXE (provided as an example in the OWL tutorial directory), gives the appearance shown in Figure 20.4.

Figure 20.3.
The SPOT application running as a stand-alone application.

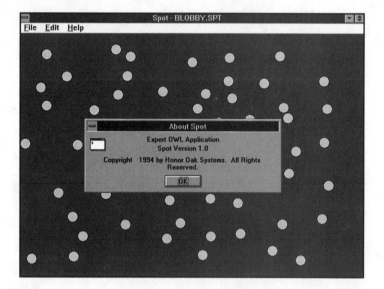

Analysis Looking first to the application class in Listing 20.2 (SPOTAPP.CPP), you see that there was no toolbar created in the InitMainWindow. This emphasizes that, when running as an in-place editor, you provide a toolbar specifically for the application. In fact, if you can guarantee that the instance will be only single-use (set by the registration option usage for the application), you can borrow the control bar for your main application. OWL ToleView does this by default in response to EvOcShowTools. You should always provide a toolbar—if you don't, the screen jumps about while switching in the container application as the client window is repositioned.

Note also that OWL expects to use menu merging even for an SDI application. For OWL to manage the menus for you, you merely need to create menus of the correct identity. OWL creates the TMenuDescr objects for you, except for the main menu, as long as you use the predefined menu identifiers.

Figure 20.4.
The SPOT application running with in-place editing.

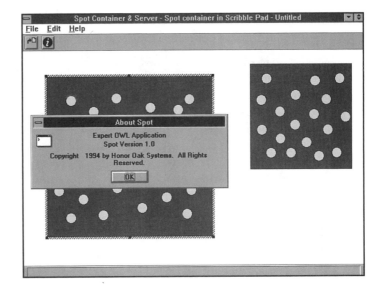

Take a look at the InitInstance. If the application starts as an embedding application, OWL looks after creating the view. In this SDI application, there should always be a client view by first attempting to open a command-line document (this could be optimized to avoid opening for obviously invalid command lines).

The trivialities of the About box bring out an important point about embedded objects. You may want to bring up dialog boxes. GetCommandTarget can be used to provide a suitable parent in place of GetMainWindow, which may, in fact, be hidden during embedding. This should ensure that the dialog stays modal over the container application.

In Listing 20.4 (SPOTDOC.CPP), the first catch is in writing the Open function. Although the path appears to be passed in as a parameter, it is not used. You should use GetDocPath, which is filled in before Open is called in TOleDocument::InitDoc.

You can detect a failure to open a file by using the result of the InStream function. In SpotDoc, the spots are held in a TArray container. They can easily be read in from and out to this container.

Warning: Failure to read a document can occur because the document was improperly written. Check that the Commit function is properly structured and ends with a call to TOleDocument::CommitTransactedStorage.

AddSpot uses a custom notification to get the views updated. This is a good optimization, because, for this application, the views need to add the item to their current display, rather than redrawing the entire screen. Note the interaction of the view and the document. The view captures the data and passes it to the document, which then tells the view to draw it.

Moving on to Paint in Listing 20.6 (SPOTVIEW.CPP), the drawing here requires care. Your Paint functions up to now have almost always been able to rely on having the mapping mode be MM_TEXT when drawing to a window. Because the OLE container may have scaled the image, when you edit in place, your window may not be pixel-based. OWL sorts out the scaling for you. However, this means that you must be careful that you draw in logical units, not pixels. The Paint function also is called by OWL to create the metafile that OLE stores in the embedded document for viewing and printing. This does not provide the usual functions you might expect to determine the drawing area—it is up to you to define the drawing area. The view always obtains its data from the document; it does not store its own data. The other unusual thing to note is the call to TOleView::Paint. This is how the embedded objects that are not active get redisplayed. (Therefore, it is not required for a server-only application.)

The mouse handling needs consideration. TOleView handles matching the mouse with the current display mapping mode. To handle its embedded objects, it provides a DC to enable it to draw and to scale its mouse movements. The tricky part is in the use of the EvLButtonUp response. Unlike the other two mouse events, TOleView does not scale the mouse coordinates. Also, unlike the other two responses, your code needs to happen before the base class processing so that you can test for the presence of the DC. (Again, if the application is not a container, it does not need to worry about the base class processing.)

There are two OCF events you might like to handle, which are specific for an OLE server.

The first is declaring the size of your view to OLE with EvOcViewPartSize. The implementation here is quick and dirty. Normally, good programming practice dictates avoiding recalculating the view size each time the message is called. In this case, the view expands if data is placed outside the declared bounds. To avoid problems, the minimum view is declared to be a two-inch square.

NEW☛ TERM In OCF, the embedded objects are known as *parts*.

Second, there is the placing of the toolbar. This is requested when OLE opens the object for in-place editing. You create a standard toolbar. (By default, TOleView assumes that it can borrow the application MainWindow toolbar on the assumption that the application instance is single-use.) This toolbar is likely to be slightly different from a normal stand-alone application toolbar, leaving out File Save and other items. Hidden away is the OWL processing, which updates the menu and manages the status bar. Much of the processing is enabled merely by placing the correct options on the menu and toolbar.

There is a whole raft of functions that OWL provides. You should spend some time experimenting with the effects of the different embedding options. Try dragging objects around, resizing their borders when selected, resizing when open for editing, pasting links and so on. It is worth remembering that, in OWL, most of the Doc/View control is provided by the document manager (TDocManager). The controlling of the window is mainly provided by TOleView through TOleWindow. With luck, investigating these classes should provide you with the information you need to go beyond this quick look at OLE linking and embedding.

Consider what the changes would be to take away the container functionality—a very few statements, removing a few menu items and a few base class calls. Consider what it would take to take away server function—some registration options and some spare notifications. Finally, compare that with a stand-alone application—using the Doc/View model. OLE Doc/View provides a surprisingly high degree of implementation independence. It is possible to write OWL OLE applications without the Doc/View model; however, your application needs to be quite specialized to make it worthwhile.

There is a wealth of issues not covered here. OLE 2 provides language independence for the interface. Doc/View is a very high-level abstraction—OWL does enable closer control of the OLE process. You can go on to explore enabling your application to control object positioning or laying out objects around the embedded parts. Finally, don't get so involved with providing OLE support that you forget to develop a useful application. There already are a lot of container applications out there—what is needed are useful servers.

OLE Automation

As the final part of your tour of OLE, you look at OLE Automation. OLE Automation provides a method of linking application data across the OLE interface. This acts as a replacement for DDEML. When you study Automation, the most noticeable thing you find in the OCF implementation is the ease of use of these objects—unlike the low level of DDEML. The big difference is that Automation understands classes. Using OCF, your server provides a C++ class that can use all the usual features. The client uses another C++ class that maps onto the server class behind the scenes, using OCF magic. In both applications, the class is handled the same way as a normal C++ class. An Automation object interface is not limited in the same way as VBX. You can call functions and pass data, which includes your own C++ classes.

NEW☞ TERM Under Automation, you provide an *Automation server* to supply services and an *Automation controller* to ask for them.

A server can provide methods (or callable functions), properties (data members accessed by function), direct access to data members, or even automated objects it is accessing from another server.

NEW☞ TERM Declaring a member, function, or class to be visible via Automation is called *exposing*.

Using Automation is surprisingly simple. Just follow a few simple steps.

Step 1: Design the Server Class

The server class may be a new class especially designed for the Automation server, or you can provide some elements of an existing class or a whole new class. You should design it in the first instance without consideration of having it operated remotely.

Step 2: Declare the Class to Be Automatic

Note: It is recommended that the class be derived from TAutoClass, which merely ensures that OLE is notified of the class' destruction if the class instance is deleted when still in use by OLE. This is not essential.

Within the class declaration, a series of macros are used to declare the services to be exposed. For example, this code snippet

```
DECLARE_AUTOCLASS(DataServer)
  AUTOPROPRO(Value, GetValue, int,)
  AUTOPROPRO(Text, GetText, TAutoString,)
  AUTOFUNC0(Throw,Throw,int,)
```

exposes two read-only properties and a function with no parameters that returns an int. There is a set of macros that includes the following:

Declaration Macro	Member
AUTODATA	Data
AUTODATARO	Data, read-only
AUTOFLAG	A bit flag
AUTOFUNC*n*	Function returning a value with *n* parameters
AUTOFUNC*n*V	Function returning void with *n* parameters
AUTOITERATOR	Iterator object
AUTOPROP	Property
AUTOPROPRO	Property, read-only
AUTOPROXY	Property containing an automated object
AUTOSTAT	Static member function or global function
AUTOTHIS	*this

Warning: These macros look similar but are organized differently from response tables. In particular, note that there is no comma at the end of the line and that there is an optional last parameter, where you must specify the comma that precedes it even if you do not give the final parameter.

For example, `AUTOFUNC1(OleFunction,CalledFuction,int,bool,)` calls the class member function int `CalledFunction(bool)`. The first parameter of the macro represents the OLE name for the object and is used by the controlling application. The only rule on types is that if the type is a character array, declare it as a `TAutoString`, and if the object is a pointer or reference to a C++ object, wrap it up in a `TAutoObject<>` wrapper.

> **Note:** OCF uses the `TAuto...` templates to enable it to convert types using RTTI (Run Time Type Information). RTTI gets the type information from the actual object, not from pointers and references, so it is hard to handle. The special auto classes, therefore, create an actual object of a known type that contains a pointer or reference of a type known by template generation.

These macros allow an option to be their last parameter to enable you to hook the command—that is, execute some action when OLE accesses the exposed member. These are quite complicated except for `AUTOVALIDATE`. This enables you to place a boolean expression, which is called whenever the function or data is accessed. *Val* is used to represent the value when a member is accessed, *Arg1*, *Arg2*, and so forth are used to represent function parameters. For example, if the value of one pair of dice is exposed, this snippet

```
AUTODATA(DiceValue,value,int,
                AUTOVALIDATE(Val>0 && Val <= 6))
```

ensures that a value between 1 and 6 is set; otherwise, an OLE error occurs in the controlling application.

Step 3: Define the Automatic Methods and Properties

Having exposed the members, it is necessary to describe the members to OLE.

```
DEFINE_AUTOCLASS(DataServer)
  EXPOSE_METHOD(Throw,TAutoShort,"Throw","Throw the dice",)
  EXPOSE_PROPRO(Value,TAutoShort,"Value","Last throw",)
  EXPOSE_PROPRO(Text,TAutoString,"Text","Last throw as text",)
  EXPOSE_APPLICATION(DataServer,"Dice","Dice application",)
  EXPOSE_QUIT("Quit","Quit",)
END_AUTOCLASS(DataServer,"Dice","Dice throwing class",0)
```

> **Note:** Exposing methods enables multilingual support. This is beyond the scope of this book.

The END_AUTOCLASS(`cls`, `name`, `desc`, `help`) defines that the C++ class `cls` is given to OLE as `name`, described as `desc`, with a help index of `help`.

> **Note:** You can provide a help interface by registering a help file. The identifier on the macro enables the controlling application to request context-sensitive help from WinHelp.

The macros implement methods for a class nested within your automated class, which OCF uses to communicate with the class.

Macro	Member Declaration
EXPOSE_APPLICATION	Automated application name—just for interest
EXPOSE_METHOD	Method
EXPOSE_PROPRO	Read-only property
EXPOSE_PROPRW	Read-write property
EXPOSE_PROPWO	Write-only property
EXPOSE_QUIT	Shutdown method (provided by TAutoBase)

In addition, functions with parameters need to be followed with REQUIRED_ARG and OPTIONAL_ARG macros. Remember that required arguments cannot follow optional arguments. The datatypes in the table must be special TAuto... data types. Refer to your *ObjectWindows Programmers' Guide*, Chapter 4, to understand the conversion table.

Step 4: Build the Application Engine

Having built the table, all that remains is to build the server application. Because this does not require object linking and embedding, the registration is much simpler. The key item is registering the application with the command-line flag of -Automation. The application also can use a simple hidden window so the OWL bit is trivial.

OWL doesn't provide a ComponentFactory macro that works with a plain TApplication object. Take an opportunity to write one. A ComponentFactory is a callback that is called three times in an executing server: to register, run, and shut down the application. However, it also may have to cope with a standard execution. The example that follows shows a simple callback. It uses a static member to store the data server object between callbacks and uses the application to run the message loop. Note that the registrar is a TRegistrar and that the includes required are simple, too. You also must include a TOleAllocator(0) object in your OwlMain procedure. Your target needs to include the OCF libraries.

Step 5: Build a Type Library and C++ Class

It is almost time to move on to building the controller, but first you build and run the controller with a parameter of -TypeLib. This does two things. It registers the automatic objects with OLE, and it builds a type library in the directory of the executable. Then, by running AutoGen (provided with Turbo C++ 4.5) and picking up the type library (selecting the Automation option), you can generate a C++ class, which can be used by the Automation controller. These are given in a C++ source and header that you can include directly in your project.

Step 6: Use the C++ Class

The AutoGen application produces a C++ class with names taken from the exposed functions. You normally can use this class without amendment merely by including the generated code in your application. AutoGen does an excellent job of generating function names, because it can take the name that you declared for each member and use that as a proxy class member. The salient points are that the class is derived from TAutoProxy. The function calls and class members are declared as normal C++ members. OCF then provides some simple AUTO... macros that combine to translate the calling function into a call to OCF. For example, here is the other end of the DataServer class—note that the class declaration is simple.

```cpp
class Dice : public TAutoProxy {
  public:
    Dice() : TAutoProxy(0x409) {}
    // Throw the dice
    short Throw(); // [id(1), method]
    // Last throw of the dice
    short GetValue(); // [id(2), propget]
    // Last throw of dice in text
    TAutoString GetText(); // [id(3), propget]
    // Dice-throwing application
    void GetDice(Dice&); // [id(4), propget]
    // Quit
    void Quit(); // [id(5), method]
};
short Dice::Throw()
{
  AUTONAMES0("Throw")
  AUTOARGS0()
  AUTOCALL_METHOD_RET
}

short Dice::GetValue()
{
  AUTONAMES0("Value")
  AUTOARGS0()
  AUTOCALL_PROP_GET
}

TAutoString Dice::GetText()
{
```

20

```
AUTONAMES0("Text")
AUTOARGS0()
AUTOCALL_PROP_GET
}
```

NEW☞ TERM A class used by an Automation controller that is supplied by an Automation server is called a *proxy class*.

Don't worry about the TAutoString; it converts quite nicely to a char *. The types aren't quite identical at the other end of the OLE conversation, but they are compatible.

To use a proxy class, you merely declare it; call the TAutoProxy::Bind member with the name of the application—which AutoGen even supplies at the top of the include file if you've forgotten it. Having included the CXX file in your application, use the class as a normal class. The only change required to the rest of the application is to declare a TOleAllocator(0) in OwlMain. You also need to include the OCF libraries.

Here are the applications; one will be very familiar. The first one, Listing 20.13, is DICESVR.EXE.

Listing 20.13. Source code for the DICESVR.CPP program file.

```cpp
#include <owl\applicat.h>
#include <ocf/appdesc.h>
#include <ocf/automacr.h>
#include <ocf/ocreg.h>
#include <owl\framewin.h>

TPointer<TRegistrar> Registrar;

REGISTRATION_FORMAT_BUFFER(100)
BEGIN_REGISTRATION(AppReg)
  REGDATA(clsid,"{82F153C0-DCB6-101B-A585-040224007802}")
  REGDATA(progid,"Dice.Server")
  REGDATA(description,"Dice Thrower")
  REGDATA(cmdline, "-Automation")
END_REGISTRATION

class OleServerApp;

class DataServer: public TAutoBase
   {
     public:
     DataServer();
     ~DataServer();
     int GetValue() {return value;}
     const char* GetText();
     int Throw();
     private:
       int value;
     DECLARE_AUTOCLASS(DataServer)
       AUTOPROPRO(Value, GetValue, int,)
       AUTOPROPRO(Text, GetText, TAutoString,)
       AUTOFUNC0(Throw,Throw,int,)
```

```
    };
  DEFINE_AUTOCLASS(DataServer)
    EXPOSE_METHOD(Throw,TAutoShort,"Throw","Throw the dice",)
    EXPOSE_PROPRO(Value,TAutoShort,"Value","Last throw of the dice",)
    EXPOSE_PROPRO(Text,TAutoString,"Text","Last throw of dice in text",)
    EXPOSE_APPLICATION(DataServer,"Dice","Dice throwing application",)
    EXPOSE_QUIT("Quit","Quit",)
  END_AUTOCLASS(DataServer,"Dice","Dice throwing class",0)

  DataServer::DataServer():TAutoBase()
    {
      value = 0;
      randomize();
    }
  DataServer::~DataServer()
    {
      ::GetAppDescriptor()->InvalidateObject(this);
    }
  const char* DataServer::GetText()
    {
      const char * throwText[] = {"","One","Two","Three","Four","Five","Six"};
      return throwText[value];
    }
int DataServer::Throw()
  {
    value = rand() % 6 + 1;
    return value;
  }


class OleServerApp:public TApplication
  {
    public:
      void InitMainWindow()
        {
          SetMainWindow(new TFrameWindow(0,"Dice Throw"));
          if (Registrar->IsOptionSet(amAutomation))
            nCmdShow = SW_HIDE;
        }
  };
IUnknown* ComponentFactory(IUnknown* outer, uint32 options, uint32 /*id*/ = 0)
{
  static DataServer* dataServer = 0;      // used to hold EXE object until OLE
factory call
  IUnknown* ifc = 0;
  if (options & amShutdown)
      return (options & amServedApp) ? 0 : outer;
  //
  // Must be first time through - make server App
  // or we are going through once and running
  //
  if (!dataServer)
    dataServer = new DataServer();

  //
  // If not Automation (so is going to drop through to run)
  // or callback, is request to register use
```

continues

Listing 20.13. continued

```
   //
   if (!(options & amAutomation) ||(options & amServedApp))
   //
   // Do OLE stuff
   //
     ifc = *::Registrar->CreateAutoApp
          (TAutoObjectDelete<DataServer>(dataServer),
          options, outer); // does an AddRef
   //
   // If this is a call to just run the app
   //
   if (options & amRun)
      OleServerApp().Run();
   return ifc;
}
int OwlMain(int,char*[])
   {
     TOleAllocator oleAllocator(0);
     try
       {
         Registrar = new TRegistrar(AppReg, ComponentFactory,
                                    TApplication::GetCmdLine());
         if (!Registrar->IsOptionSet(amAnyRegOption))
           Registrar->Run();
         Registrar = 0;
       }
     catch(...)
       {
       }
     return 0;
   }
```

Finally, here are Listings 20.14 through 20.19, DICECLIE.EXE, which is a client that uses an OLE-served dice throw.

 Listing 20.14. Source code for the DICE.H header file.

```
#ifndef _DICE_H
#define _DICE_H
#include <owl\owlall.h>
// stdio for sprintf
#include <stdio.h>
#include "dice.rh"
#include "dicedlg.h"

#endif
```

 Listing 20.15. Source code for the DICE.CPP program file.

```
#include "dice.h"
//
// The usual TApplication derivative, this time
```

```
//  putting in the dice client
//
class DiceApp:public TApplication
  {
  public:
  void InitMainWindow()
        {
            TDialog* dice = new DiceDialog();
            //
            // The proper way to handle MainWindow...
            //
            SetMainWindow(new TFrameWindow(0,"Dice",dice,TRUE));
            GetMainWindow()->SetIcon(this,IDI_DICE);
            GetMainWindow()->Attr.Style
                &= ~WS_THICKFRAME & ~WS_MAXIMIZEBOX;

        }
  };
int OwlMain(int,char*[])
  {
    TOleAllocator oleAlloc(0); // NEW!
    DiceApp diceApp;
    try
      {
          return diceApp.Run(); // Standard TApplication::Run
       }
    catch (TXBase be)
      {
         MessageBox(0,be.why().c_str(),0,MB_OK);
      }
    return 0;
  }
```

Type

Listing 20.16. Source code for the DICEDLG.H header file.

```
#ifndef _DICEDIAL_H
#define _DICEDIAL_H
// Forward declaration for Dice pointer
class Dice;
class DiceDialog:public TDialog
  {
  public:
  DiceDialog();
  // new destructor
  ~DiceDialog();
  protected:
  Dice* diceThrow; // Pointer to proxy class
  TStatic* dice1;
  TStatic* dice2;
  TStatic* diceText1;
  TStatic* diceText2;
  TEdit* sum;
  TButton* pushButton;
   void SetupWindow();
  void PushButton();
  void EvTimer(uint timerId);
```

Listing 20.16. continued

```
    void EvPaint();
    void Paint(TDC&,bool,TRect&);

    private:
    bool roll;
    int sumValue;
    int diceValue1;
    int diceValue2;
    TRect rectDice1;
    TRect rectDice2;
    TDib* dice;
    DECLARE_RESPONSE_TABLE(DiceDialog);
    };


#endif
```

Listing 20.17. Source code for the DICEDLG.CPP program file.

```
#include "dice.h"
// Include dicesvr source code
#include "dicesvr.cxx"
DEFINE_RESPONSE_TABLE1(DiceDialog,TDialog)
  EV_WM_TIMER,
  EV_WM_PAINT,
  EV_BN_CLICKED(IDC_PUSHBUTTON1,PushButton),
END_RESPONSE_TABLE;
DiceDialog::DiceDialog()
  :TDialog(0,DICE)
  {
    diceThrow = new Dice();          // Create proxy class
//
// Declare the controls - add some text this time
//
    dice1 = new TStatic(this,IDC_DICE1);
    diceText1 = new TStatic(this,IDC_DICETEXT1);
    dice2 = new TStatic(this,IDC_DICE2);
    diceText2 = new TStatic(this,IDC_DICETEXT2);
    sum = new TEdit(this,IDC_EDIT3);

    pushButton = new TButton(this,IDC_PUSHBUTTON1);
//
// Initialize the dice
//
    roll = FALSE;
    sumValue = 0;
    dice = new TDib(TBitmap(GetModule()->GetInstance(),
         IDB_DICE));
    diceValue1 = 0;
    diceValue2 = 0;
  };
//
```

```
// Destructor - called when instance deleted
//
DiceDialog::~DiceDialog()
  {
//
// Delete some brushes
//
   delete dice;
   diceThrow->Quit(); // Force the closure of the proxy
                      // object
   delete diceThrow;
  }
void DiceDialog::SetupWindow()
  {
  TDialog::SetupWindow();
  rectDice1 = dice1->GetWindowRect();
  rectDice2 = dice2->GetWindowRect();
  dice1->Destroy();
  dice2->Destroy();
  ScreenToClient(rectDice1.TopLeft());
  ScreenToClient(rectDice2.TopLeft());
  ScreenToClient(rectDice1.BottomRight());
  ScreenToClient(rectDice2.BottomRight());
  diceThrow->Bind("Dice.Server"); // bind to server
                                  // throws an exception
                                  // if fails
}

void DiceDialog::PushButton()
  {
   if (roll)
    {
      char diceString[5];
      KillTimer(1);
      roll = FALSE;
      pushButton->SetCaption("&Spin");
      sprintf(diceString,"%i",sumValue);
      sum->SetText(diceString);
    }
   else
    {
      roll = TRUE;
      pushButton->SetCaption("&Stop");
      sum->SetText("");
      SetTimer(1,100);
      EvTimer(1);
    }

  }
void DiceDialog::EvTimer(uint /*timerId*/)
  {
  TClientDC dc(*this);
  //
  // Four calls to the proxy class - that's
  // all that is new, replacing the call to
  // the local random number generator.
  //
```

continues

Listing 20.17. continued

```
    diceValue1 = diceThrow->Throw();
    diceText1->SetText(diceThrow->GetText());
    diceValue2 = diceThrow->Throw();
    diceText2->SetText(diceThrow->GetText());
    sumValue = diceValue1 + diceValue2;
    Paint(dc,TRUE,TRect(0,0,0,0));
  };
void DiceDialog::EvPaint()
  {
  TPaintDC dc(*this);
  TRect&   rect = *(TRect*)&dc.Ps.rcPaint;
  Paint(dc, dc.Ps.fErase, rect);
  }
void DiceDialog::Paint(TDC& dc,bool,TRect&)
  {
    TRect source1(0,0,dice->Height(),dice->Height());
    source1.Offset(dice->Height()*diceValue1,0);
    dc.StretchDIBits(rectDice1,source1,*dice);
    TRect source2(0,0,dice->Height(),dice->Height());
    source2.Offset(dice->Height()*diceValue2,0);
    dc.StretchDIBits(rectDice2,source2,*dice);
  }
```

 Listing 20.18. Source code for the DICE.RH resource header file.

```
#define IDI_DICE   1
#define IDB_DICE   1
#define DICE   1
#define IDC_EDIT3   103
#define IDC_PUSHBUTTON1   104
#define IDC_DICE1   120
#define IDC_DICE2   121
#define IDC_DICETEXT1   131
#define IDC_DICETEXT2   132
```

 Listing 20.19. Script for the DICE.RC resource file.

```
#include "dice.rh"
DICE DIALOG 7, 15, 85, 58
STYLE WS_CHILD | WS_VISIBLE | WS_BORDER
FONT 8, "MS Sans Serif"
{
 EDITTEXT IDC_EDIT3, 60, 6, 16, 12, ES_READONLY |
          NOT WS_TABSTOP | WS_BORDER
 LTEXT "+", -1, 25, 8, 6, 8
 LTEXT "=", -1, 52, 9, 7, 8
 DEFPUSHBUTTON "&Spin", IDC_PUSHBUTTON1, 17, 39, 50, 14
 CONTROL "", IDC_DICE1, "static", SS_BLACKFRAME | WS_CHILD
         | WS_VISIBLE, 6, 6, 16, 17
 CONTROL "", IDC_DICE2, "static", SS_BLACKFRAME | WS_CHILD
         | WS_VISIBLE, 35, 6, 16, 17
```

```
 CTEXT "", IDC_DICETEXT1, 2, 25, 25, 8
 CTEXT "", IDC_DICETEXT2, 30, 26, 25, 8
}

IDB_DICE BITMAP
{
 '42 4D F6 03 00 00 00 00 00 00 76 00 00 00 28 00'
 '00 00 70 00 00 00 10 00 00 00 01 00 04 00 00 00'
 '00 00 80 03 00 00 00 00 00 00 00 00 00 00 00 00'
 '00 00 10 00 00 00 00 00 00 00 00 00 BF 00 00 BF'
 '00 00 00 BF BF 00 BF 00 00 00 BF 00 BF 00 BF BF'
 '00 00 C0 C0 C0 00 80 80 80 00 00 00 FF 00 00 FF'
 '00 00 00 FF FF 00 FF 00 00 00 FF 00 FF 00 FF FF'
 '00 00 FF FF FF 00 91 11 11 11 11 11 11 11 91 11'
 '11 11 11 11 11 11 91 11 11 11 11 11 11 11 91 11'
 '11 11 11 11 11 11 91 11 11 11 11 11 11 11 91 11'
 '11 11 11 11 11 11 91 11 11 11 11 11 11 11 79 99'
 '99 99 99 99 99 91 79 99 99 99 99 99 99 91 79 99'
 '99 99 99 99 99 91 79 99 99 99 99 99 99 91 79 99'
 '99 99 99 99 99 91 79 99 99 99 99 99 99 91 79 99'
 '99 99 99 99 99 91 79 99 99 99 99 99 99 91 79 99'
 '99 99 99 99 99 91 79 99 99 99 99 9B BB 91 79 99'
 '99 99 99 9B BB 91 79 BB B9 99 99 9B BB 91 79 BB'
 'B9 99 99 9B BB 91 79 BB B9 99 99 9B BB 91 79 99'
 '99 99 99 99 99 91 79 99 99 99 99 99 99 91 79 99'
 '99 99 99 9B BB 91 79 99 99 99 99 9B BB 91 79 BB'
 'B9 99 99 9B BB 91 79 BB B9 99 99 9B BB 91 79 BB'
 'B9 99 99 9B BB 91 79 99 99 99 99 99 99 91 79 99'
 '99 99 99 99 99 91 79 99 99 99 99 9B BB 91 79 99'
 '99 99 99 9B BB 91 79 BB B9 99 99 9B BB 91 79 BB'
 'B9 99 99 9B BB 91 79 BB B9 99 99 9B BB 91 79 99'
 '99 99 99 99 99 91 79 99 99 99 99 99 99 91 79 99'
 '99 99 99 99 99 91 79 99 99 99 99 99 99 91 79 99'
 '99 99 99 99 99 91 79 99 99 99 99 99 99 91 79 99'
 '99 99 99 99 99 91 79 99 99 99 99 99 99 91 79 99'
 '99 99 99 99 99 91 79 99 99 99 99 99 99 91 79 99'
 '99 99 99 99 99 91 79 99 99 99 99 99 99 91 79 99'
 '99 99 99 99 99 91 79 99 99 99 9B BB 99 99 91 79 99'
 '99 99 99 99 99 91 79 99 99 9B BB 99 99 91 79 99'
 '99 99 99 99 99 91 79 99 99 9B BB 99 99 91 79 BB'
 'B9 99 99 9B BB 91 79 99 99 99 99 99 99 91 79 99'
 '99 9B BB 99 99 91 79 99 99 99 99 99 99 91 79 99'
 '99 9B BB 99 99 91 79 99 99 99 99 99 99 91 79 99'
 '99 9B BB 99 99 91 79 BB B9 99 99 9B BB 91 79 99'
 '99 99 99 99 99 91 79 99 99 9B BB 99 99 91 79 99'
 '99 99 99 99 99 91 79 99 99 9B BB 99 99 91 79 99'
 '99 99 99 99 99 91 79 99 99 9B BB 99 99 91 79 BB'
 'B9 99 99 9B BB 91 79 99 99 99 99 99 99 91 79 99'
 '99 99 99 99 99 91 79 99 99 99 99 99 99 91 79 99'
 '99 99 99 99 99 91 79 99 99 99 99 99 99 91 79 99'
 '99 99 99 99 99 91 79 99 99 99 99 99 99 91 79 99'
 '99 99 99 99 99 91 79 99 99 99 99 99 99 91 79 99'
 '99 99 99 99 99 91 79 99 99 99 99 99 99 91 79 99'
 '99 99 99 99 99 91 79 99 99 99 99 99 99 91 79 99'
 '99 99 99 99 99 91 79 BB B9 99 99 99 99 91 79 BB'
 'B9 99 99 99 99 91 79 BB B9 99 99 9B BB 91 79 BB'
```

20

continues

Listing 20.19. continued

```
        'B9 99 99 9B BB 91 79 BB B9 99 99 9B BB 91 79 99'
        '99 99 99 99 99 91 79 99 99 99 99 99 99 91 79 BB'
        'B9 99 99 99 99 91 79 BB B9 99 99 99 99 91 79 BB'
        'B9 99 99 9B BB 91 79 BB B9 99 99 9B BB 91 79 BB'
        'B9 99 99 9B BB 91 79 99 99 99 99 99 99 91 79 99'
        '99 99 99 99 99 91 79 BB B9 99 99 99 99 91 79 BB'
        'B9 99 99 99 99 91 79 BB B9 99 99 9B BB 91 79 BB'
        'B9 99 99 9B BB 91 79 BB B9 99 99 9B BB 91 77 77'
        '77 77 77 77 77 79 77 77 77 77 77 77 77 79 77 77'
        '77 77 77 77 77 79 77 77 77 77 77 77 77 79 77 77'
        '77 77 77 77 77 79 77 77 77 77 77 77 77 79 77 77'
        '77 77 77 77 77 79'
}


IDI_DICE ICON
{
        '00 00 01 00 01 00 20 20 10 00 00 00 00 00 E8 02'
        '00 00 16 00 00 00 28 00 00 00 20 00 00 00 40 00'
        '00 00 01 00 04 00 00 00 00 00 80 02 00 00 00 00'
        '00 00 00 00 00 00 00 00 00 00 00 00 00 00 00 00'
        '00 00 00 00 BF 00 00 BF 00 00 00 BF BF 00 BF 00'
        '00 00 BF 00 BF 00 BF BF 00 00 C0 C0 C0 00 80 80'
        '80 00 00 00 FF 00 00 FF 00 00 00 FF FF 00 FF 00'
        '00 00 FF 00 FF 00 FF FF 00 00 FF FF FF 00 00 00'
        '00 00 00 00 00 00 00 00 00 00 00 00 00 00 00 00'
        '00 00 00 00 00 00 00 00 00 00 00 00 00 00 00 00'
        '00 00 00 00 00 00 00 00 00 00 00 00 00 00 00 00'
        '00 00 00 00 00 00 00 00 00 00 00 00 00 00 00 00'
        '00 00 01 11 11 11 11 11 11 11 33 31 00 00 00 00'
        '00 01 11 11 11 11 33 31 11 11 11 11 10 00 00 00'
        '00 11 33 31 11 11 11 11 11 11 11 11 10 00 00 00'
        '00 19 99 99 99 99 99 99 99 99 91 11 10 00 00 00'
        '0D 99 99 99 99 99 99 99 99 99 99 11 10 00 00 00'
        '0D 99 99 99 99 99 99 99 9B B9 99 11 10 00 00 00'
        '0D 99 99 99 99 99 99 99 BB BB 99 11 10 00 00 00'
        '0D 99 99 99 99 99 99 99 BB BB 99 11 10 00 00 00'
        '0D 99 99 99 99 99 99 99 9B B9 99 11 10 00 00 00'
        '0D 99 99 99 99 99 99 99 99 99 99 11 10 00 00 00'
        '0D 99 99 99 99 99 99 99 99 99 99 13 10 00 00 00'
        '0D 99 99 99 99 99 99 99 99 99 99 13 10 00 00 00'
        '0D 99 99 99 99 99 99 99 99 99 99 13 10 00 00 00'
        '0D 99 99 99 99 99 99 99 99 99 99 11 10 00 00 00'
        '0D 99 99 99 99 99 99 99 99 99 99 11 10 00 00 00'
        '0D 99 99 99 99 99 99 99 99 99 99 11 10 00 00 00'
        '0D 99 99 99 99 99 99 99 99 99 99 11 10 00 00 00'
        '0D 99 99 99 99 99 99 99 99 99 99 11 10 00 00 00'
        '0D 99 BB 99 99 99 99 99 99 99 99 11 10 00 00 00'
        '0D 9B BB B9 99 99 99 99 99 99 99 11 10 00 00 00'
        '0D 9B BB B9 99 99 99 99 99 99 99 11 00 00 00 00'
        '0D 99 BB 99 99 99 99 99 99 99 99 11 00 00 00 00'
        '0D D9 99 99 99 99 99 99 99 99 99 10 00 00 00 00'
        '00 DD DD DD DD DD DD DD DD DD D0 00 00 00 00 00'
        '00 00 00 00 00 00 00 00 00 00 00 00 00 00 00 00'
        '00 00 00 00 00 00 00 00 00 00 00 00 00 00 00 00'
```

```
'00 00 00 00 00 00 00 00 00 00 00 00 00 00 00 00'
'00 00 00 00 00 00 00 00 00 00 00 00 00 00 FF FF'
'FF FF FF FF FF FF FF FF FF FF FF FF FF FF FF 80'
'00 0F FE 00 00 07 FC 00 00 07 FC 00 00 07 F8 00'
'00 07 F8 00 00 07 F8 00 00 07 F8 00 00 07 F8 00'
'00 07 F8 00 00 07 F8 00 00 07 F8 00 00 07 F8 00'
'00 07 F8 00 00 07 F8 00 00 07 F8 00 00 07 F8 00'
'00 07 F8 00 00 07 F8 00 00 07 F8 00 00 07 F8 00'
'00 0F F8 00 00 0F F8 00 00 1F FC 00 00 7F FF FF'
'FF FF FF FF FF FF FF FF FF FF FF FF FF FF'
}
```

The application appears in Figure 20.5.

Figure 20.5.
The automatic dice.

I am sure you are surprised at how easy it is to use a proxy class with the help of OCF. Assuming that OLE can find the server, you should have no difficulty using the class. The Bind statement makes the connection through OLE. The destructor of the object should disconnect, but it is safest to call the Quit method to ensure that OLE disconnects the server. The function calls themselves are almost transparent.

For the server, the hard work is not in defining the class, but in matching up the OCF macros to the server class. This is a tedious rather than difficult task.

Whither Automation?

This was a simple example. Obviously, data exchange using Automation through OCF is simplicity itself compared to DDEML. However, at the time of writing, there isn't a proper way to send notifications back to the proxy object. Automation objects are the core of OCX, the replacement for VBX controls for 32-bit Windows. OLE defines quite a number of other features for Automation, including help file support and international translation via resources. OLE embedding servers can also provide automation.

Summary

Today, you got a taste of OLE 2. Specifically, you explored the following topics:

☐ OLE 2 as a method for communicating between programs and for linking and embedding views and data

☐ How ObjectWindows and Object Components Framework work together to provide a high-level programming solution to OLE 2

☐ How OWL provides tremendous support for OLE embedding via its OLE Doc/View model—you can concentrate on your application rather than OLE

☐ Using OLE Automation via OCF as a simple way to pass data between programs (for the programmer!)

Q&A

Q Can an OLE Automation server pass across more than one class?

A Yes, by using aggregation. Effectively, this means defining a controlling class that inherits or contains other classes. The aggregate class can then delegate the task of responding to requests to its component classes.

Q How do I set up an advise loop as I would in DDEML?

A The interface for notifying events is not supported yet. Eventually, this will be part of the emerging capabilities of the specification of OCX. In the meantime, one can use a more limited version of advise loops with the server informing the client when data has changed and the latter then retrieving that information via the IDataObject and IAdviseSink interfaces.

Q How do I find out more about OLE?

A If possible, work through the examples in the Borland manuals on OCF that do not use the OWL classes. These highlight some of the mechanics of OLE. I recommend that you avoid books on pure OLE as these will not explain the OCF interface. There is a full tutorial included with the Borland package; it is well worth working through it. The OWL manuals and online help are full of information about OLE and OCF.

Workshop

The Workshop provides quiz questions to help you consolidate your understanding of the material covered, and exercises to provide you with experience in using what you've learned. Try to understand the quiz and exercise answers before continuing on to the next day's lesson. Answers are provided in the Appendix A.

Quiz

1. What method of joining documents should a user use to place a document in several other documents?
2. What OWL class is responsible for managing the display of embedded objects?
3. What must you do before you can access an OLE 2 server from a container?

Exercise

Generate a copy of the SPOT application with AppExpert with all the decorations.

20

21

Debugging

No matter how well you may try to write a program, and no matter how good at writing programs you ever become, you will always make mistakes and cause bugs to appear in your program. The easiest bugs to locate and fix are those caught by the compiler as it shows you your syntax and other related errors. However, it is quite possible to have a program compile flawlessly, even without any warnings, and still fail in some miserable ways. When a program fails, a debugger can be the best tool for figuring out what went wrong. In today's lesson, you learn about the following:

- ☐ The integrated debugger commands
- ☐ How to debug a simple program
- ☐ Other debugging tools

The Integrated Debugger

Built into the Integrated Development Environment (IDE) are several debugging functions. You can use these to stop a running program in the middle of its execution, to view the values of variables and member data, and to watch how programming constructs are executed on a line-by-line basis.

In the IDE's top-level menu are two submenus that can be used in debugging. The first is the Debug menu. This menu provides a number of commands that control the execution of programs and enable you to view individual variables and structures. The second menu is the View menu. Inside this menu are, among other items, commands to open various debugging windows.

The Debug Menu

The principal commands for debugging are located in the Debug menu. These are the commands that enable you to execute your program on a line-by-line basis, to set breakpoints, and evaluate individual expressions.

NEW ☞ A *breakpoint* is a point in a program at which execution will stop or break. Once a
TERM   breakpoint is set, you can go ahead and let the program run. When the line of code where the breakpoint is set is reached, the program will pause, and the debugger will come up with the specified line highlighted. At this point, you can evaluate expressions and execute the code one line at a time.

- ☐ The Run command starts a program's execution. If the source code has changed and the program isn't already in a suspended state of execution, the IDE goes through the rebuild process, compiling and linking as necessary.

- ☐ The Step over command is used to *single-step* through the program code on a line-by-line basis. Each time you select Step over, the highlighted line is executed. If that line contains a function call, the function is called, and when it returns, the debugger will stop again on the next line.

☐ If you want to actually go into the function instead of skipping over it, you can use the `Trace into` command. This is the same as stepping over lines of code, except that this will follow into function calls, enabling you to step through them. If there is no function call, the trace acts exactly like a step. Note, however, that some function calls aren't as visible as others. For example, when an object is created, its constructor function will be called, even if there doesn't appear to be any direct call to that function.

☐ The `Toggle breakpoint` command sets or clears a breakpoint on the line of code with the cursor. If the program is executing freely when it reaches this line of code (you aren't stepping or tracing through the code), then the program will pause and the debugger will come up with the cursor on this line of code.

☐ If your program is paused and you move the cursor around, or perhaps you look at some other files, you might lose track of the line of code at which the program was paused. In this case, you can use the `Find execution point` command to place the cursor on the current line of executing code.

☐ Sometimes, you might have started a program running, and then later decided that you need to pause the program, but you didn't set any breakpoints. You can use the `Pause program` command to pause the program at its current execution point. At this point, you will be able to evaluate expressions and look at various global variables. Unfortunately, you will not always be able to locate the current execution point in the code. Also, you may not always be able to use the `Pause program` command to stop the program if, say, it's in an infinite loop. In these cases, you can sometimes use the Ctrl+Alt+SysRq key sequence to pause the program and return to the debugger.

☐ The `Terminate program` command stops the program's execution and then resets it to the beginning. This means that the next time you might try to run or step into the program, it will be at the beginning.

☐ There is a window in the debugger called the Watch window. When you use the `Add watch...` command, you are given a dialog box, shown in Figure 21.1, that enables you to add an expression. This expression will be placed in the Watch window and will be updated as the program continues execution. The watch expressions are excellent ways to see how certain variables change over the course of the program.

☐ Figure 21.2 shows the dialog box that is brought up when you select the `Add breakpoint...` command. This sets a breakpoint on the current line in the same way as `Toggle breakpoint`, except that you are allowed to add some parameters to the breakpoint. For example, you can have the debugger break out only when a certain condition is true (for example, a variable being equal to a certain value).

21

Figure 21.1.
The dialog box from which a watch expression may be added.

Figure 21.2.
The dialog box on which breakpoint properties may be modified.

☐ The `Evaluate/Modify...` command opens a dialog box that enables you to enter expressions and see what they evaluate to. It also enables you to change the value of certain variables by first evaluating them and then changing their contents.

☐ The `Inspect...` command yields a window for each item you inspect. This window is customized to the type of variable being inspected. If you're looking at a variable, for example, you get simple information showing the name of the variable, its location in memory, and its value. Classes, on the other hand, display all the same data in addition to their member data, their values, and the locations and names of their member functions. Figure 21.3 shows a sample inspection window.

Figure 21.3.
A sample session in the IDE's debugger with an inspection window.

☐ Finally, the `Load symbol table...` command enables you to load a symbol table when you try to debug something like a DLL. In this case, the symbol table for the application you debug will be loaded automatically, but you will have to load the DLL's symbols by hand.

The View Menu

The View menu contains commands that display different windows. One section of that menu enables you to display windows associated with debugging. These are the Watch, Breakpoint, Call Stack, Register, and Event Log windows.

☐ The Watch window shows a list of expressions you've entered and their evaluation. As the program runs and the variables mentioned in the expressions change, so will the evaluations.

☐ The Breakpoint window shows a list of all the breakpoints set in the program. Also, when you double-click a breakpoint entry in this window, you are allowed to bring up the breakpoint properties window, enabling you to modify the breakpoint's settings.

☐ When you've stopped in the middle of a program, it's often helpful to see where you've come from. For example, if you find yourself in a function that could be called by any of a number of other locations, it would be useful to know which particular function called the current function and, in turn, who called that. This progression of calls is in the Call Stack window, along with the parameters of the functions for which debugging information is available.

☐ Although you are using C++ here, the machine itself actually deals on a much lower level, with machine code and assembly language. Basic to this lower level are registers that act like a limited set of variables for assembly language. Occasionally, it is useful to be able to view the contents of those registers during the execution of a program, and these are displayed in the Registers window. Note, however, that this usually is not very useful unless you know how your program works on the lower-level translated assembly language.

☐ The Event Log window displays a list of such things as when breakpoints were reached, or debugging information is displayed by the program (with the Windows `OutputDebugString` function).

In addition to all these menu commands, there is also the `Locate function...` command found under the Search menu. This brings up a dialog box that prompts you to enter a function name. The IDE's debugger will then attempt to find the requested function and place the cursor at that point. In order for the debugger to find the function, it must be listed in the loaded debugging information.

21

Debugging a Program

When debugging a program, you first must make sure that debugging information is included when the program is compiled and built. With that done, you'll be able to step through the program a line at a time, view the contents of variables as you go, set breakpoints, and so on.

Unfortunately, the standard libraries (the runtime library, the class library, and the Object Windows Library) don't come with debugging information included in them by default. Because of this, you won't be able to step or trace into its code, just as you won't be able to step or trace into the internal Windows code. You can, however, rebuild the Borland libraries to include debugging information if you have the source code. The class library and OWL source code is included with the Turbo C++ for Windows package, but the runtime library source code is available only on the CD version or at an extra cost.

The best way to learn how to debug a program is to sit down and do it. To start, type in and compile the program in Listings 21.1 and 21.2. You'll notice that it compiles with no warnings or errors, but if you try to run it and select the Dialog menu item, you'll get either a GP fault or, barring that, an hourglass that doesn't go away. In any case, the program certainly isn't doing what you would want it to do.

Listing 21.1. Script for the BUG.RC resource file.

```
 1:  #include <windows.h>
 2:  #include <owl\window.rh>
 3:
 4:  TheDialog DIALOG 6, 15, 207, 111
 5:  STYLE DS_MODALFRAME | WS_POPUP | WS_VISIBLE | WS_CAPTION |
             WS_SYSMENU
 6:  CAPTION "Dialog of the Century"
 7:  FONT 8, "MS Sans Serif"
 8:  BEGIN
 9:     LISTBOX 101, 27, 8, 49, 88, LBS_STANDARD | WS_TABSTOP
10:     DEFPUSHBUTTON "OK", IDOK, 148, 6, 50, 14
11:     PUSHBUTTON "Cancel", IDCANCEL, 148, 24, 50, 14
12: END
13:
14: MainMenu MENU LOADONCALL MOVEABLE PURE DISCARDABLE
15: BEGIN
16:    MENUITEM "E&xit", CM_EXIT
17:    MENUITEM "&Dialog", 100
18: END
```

Listing 21.2. Source code for the BUG.CPP program file.

```
 1:  #include <stdio.h>
 2:  #include <windows.h>
 3:  #include <owl\applicat.h>
 4:  #include <owl\dialog.h>
 5:  #include <owl\framewin.h>
```

```
 6:   #include <owl\listbox.h>
 7:   #include <owl\window.h>
 8:   #include <owl\window.rh>
 9:
10:   class TMyDialog : public TDialog
11:   {
12:   public:
13:       TMyDialog(TWindow* parent, TModule* module = 0);
14:
15:       void SetupWindow();
16:
17:   private:
18:       TListBox* numbers;
19:   };
20:
21:   TMyDialog::TMyDialog(TWindow* parent, TModule* module)
22:       : TDialog(parent, "TheDialog", module)
23:   {
24:   }
25:
26:   void fill_lb(TListBox* plb, int count)
27:   {
28:      for (int ix = 0; ix < count; ++count)
29:          {
30:          char str[25];
31:          sprintf(str, "%d", ix + 1);
32:          plb->AddString(str);
33:          }
34:   }
35:
36:   void TMyDialog::SetupWindow()
37:   {
38:       fill_lb(numbers, 20);
39:   }
40:
41:   class TMyWindow : public TWindow
42:   {
43:   public:
44:       TMyWindow(TWindow* parent = 0);
45:
46:   protected:
47:       void CmExit();
48:       void CmDialog();
49:
50:   private:
51:       DECLARE_RESPONSE_TABLE(TMyWindow);
52:   };
53:   DEFINE_RESPONSE_TABLE1(TMyWindow, TWindow)
54:       EV_COMMAND(CM_EXIT, CmExit),
55:       EV_COMMAND(100, CmDialog),
56:   END_RESPONSE_TABLE;
57:
58:   TMyWindow::TMyWindow(TWindow* parent)
59:       : TWindow(parent)
60:   {
61:   }
62:
```

continues

Listing 21.2. continued

```
63:  void TMyWindow::CmExit()
64:  {
65:      SendMessage(WM_CLOSE);
66:  }
67:
68:  void TMyWindow::CmDialog()
69:  {
70:      TMyDialog(this).Execute();
71:  }
72:
73:  class TDialogApp : public TApplication
74:  {
75:  public:
76:      TDialogApp() : TApplication()
77:          { nCmdShow = SW_SHOWMAXIMIZED; }
78:
79:      void InitMainWindow()
80:          {
81:          SetMainWindow(new TFrameWindow(  0,
82:                                  "Dialog Testers, Inc.",
83:                                  new TMyWindow ));
84:          GetMainWindow()->AssignMenu("MainMenu");
85:          }
86:  };
87:
88:  int OwlMain(int, char *[])
89:  {
90:      return TDialogApp().Run();
91:  }
```

If you run the program from the IDE, and then select the Dialog menu item, you are likely to get a dialog box that comes up entitled Unhandled Exception, with the message that a General Protection Exception occurred in BUG.CPP on line 32. By clicking OK, the IDE will come back up and place you on line 32 of the BUG.CPP file.

NEW☞ TERM A *general protection violation* or *general protection fault* occurs when some code attempts to read or write to a part of memory that it isn't allowed. In C++, this usually means that a pointer is used that hasn't been initialized or is still pointing at memory that has been deleted and no longer exists. When running under the IDE, a general protection fault, which is Windows terminology, is reported as a general protection *exception* in keeping with C++ terminology.

Line 32 of BUG.CPP contains the following code:

```
plb->AddString(str);
```

So, remembering that a general protection exception usually has something to do with accessing memory that is off limits, you might think that the str variable probably is at fault, because it's a pointer. The only problem with that theory is that str is really a pointer to a local area of memory that's just been set up. You know that it still exists because it's still in scope.

The only other pointer here is the plb parameter. Considering, however, that you're just calling one of its member functions, how could it possibly be the problem? Take a look at the function it is calling, AddString. This function is declared in the TListBox class in the following manner:

```
virtual int AddString(const char far* str);
```

Note that the function is declared as virtual. This means that when the code to call it is compiled, a direct call to the member function isn't generated; rather, code to look up the location of the function is generated. The reason is that because a derived class could have written its own version of the function, the base class will need to be able to access that new function, without necessarily knowing where this function resides. So, when the pointer is used to call AddString, it really does use plb as a pointer, by looking up the function's address in the virtual table.

NEW🖝 TERM The *virtual table* is a list of pointers to virtual functions. Each class has a virtual table associated with it, in which all the virtual functions have their addresses listed. Along with each object is a *virtual table pointer*, which points to the virtual table for the appropriate class. When some code attempts to call a virtual function, the generated assembly code first looks up the virtual table, then the virtual function's address, and then actually calls the function.

The only possibility at this point is the plb parameter. This pointer appears to be invalid for some reason. The next step is to see who gave us this pointer. Go into the View menu and select Call Stack. A window appears that shows the current function fill_lb at the top. The next function down is TMyDialog::SetupWindow. Double-click that next line to position the cursor at the place where the fill_lb function was called.

You now are placed directly into the middle of the SetupWindow function on the following line:

```
fill_lb(numbers, 20);
```

It appears that the numbers member data is invalid, because that is the parameter that becomes plb in the fill_lb function. If you take a look around, you'll notice that you forgot to set numbers to anything. It's declared in the class, but nobody ever assigns it any value. Oops! This must be fixed before you can continue trying to run the program. Obviously, you needed to initialize numbers in the constructor to connect with the list box interface element in the dialog box you load from the resource. Go up to the constructor and add the following line:

```
numbers = new TListBox(this, 101, module);
```

Now if you take a look at the Debug menu, you'll notice that the Run item is grayed out. This is because you've changed the file and trying to continue running would make little sense. So use the Terminate program option to stop the program and then rebuild and run the application.

This time when you select the Dialog menu item, an hourglass that seems to hang around forever appears. After a while you may be getting the idea that something is wrong. The only way to stop the program now is to do the "three-fingered salute" and press the Ctrl+Alt+Del keys. Windows will give you a choice of going back and waiting a little longer, ending the program, or rebooting

21

Windows. Because waiting a little longer for the program to do something looks a little hopeless and restarting Windows seems a bit drastic, just end the program. In this case, when you get back to the IDE, the program already will have been terminated, and there will be no reason to use the Terminate program menu item.

In finding this problem, you're going to have to look at a bit of code to help narrow down where the problem might be. You know the bug occurs after you select the Dialog menu option but before the dialog box actually appears on-screen. At times like this, it's a good idea to set breakpoints on some likely areas and run through the code, one line at a time, to see what happens.

Position the cursor on the TMyWindow::CmDialog function and select Toggle breakpoint from the Debug menu (or press Ctrl+F8). Notice how the line changes color to reflect the state of the breakpoint. Now set breakpoints on the TMyDialog constructor and its SetupWindow function, and then run the program.

When you select the Dialog menu item now, you are returned to the IDE with the cursor on the line where you set the breakpoint, the line where TMyWindow::CmDialog is declared. Select the Step over command in the Debug menu. The screen flashes to the application and then flashes back to the source code, with the cursor on the next line, where the dialog is actually created and executed. This line looks okay, so you can step over it as well.

Now look at the TMyDialog constructor. Looking at the code, there doesn't seem to be anything out of the ordinary. Here you run into the nonlinearity of Windows. If you simply keep stepping, you'll end up running through the constructor and then back to the TMyWindow::CmDialog function. You know you have a breakpoint on the next bit of code you want to look at, so it's a good idea to just continue running from here.

When next you break into the source code, you're on the TMyDialog::SetupWindow function. There's only one function call in here, and it's something we wrote, so there probably is good reason to suspect that that might have inadvertently caused a problem in there. Use the Trace function in the Debug menu now. Your first trace takes you onto the call to fill_lb, and your next trace takes you right inside it.

Inside here you will see a for loop. It might be a good idea to walk through that one step at a time, watching the relevant variables plb, count, d, and str. Place the cursor on each of these variables and select the Add Watch item from the Debug menu. You are not particularly interested in any fancy displays at this point in time, so just click OK on the resultant Watch Properties dialog box. You may notice that some of the values are weird or possibly even undefined, but that's okay for right now. You are not really in the function yet, so the debugger hasn't had a chance to figure out what those values are. Also, because the str variable has not been declared yet, it will be listed as undefined until you get to where it is declared, at which point the Watch window will become synchronized properly.

Step over the beginning of the function. The cursor is placed on the first line of the for loop, and the count variable shows up as the number 20 in the Watch window. This is good. We specified 20 when we called this function. Step again and see that the ix variable is now set to 0 and the str variable is now recognized.

Notice how str is uninitialized at this point, showing random data. Stepping once more will fill str with what should be more reasonable data. Note, however, that the data isn't in a very readable format. It would be better if you could see it as a string. If you double-click the data item, you will bring back the Watch Properties dialog box. If you take a look in the Display As section, you will see a radio button marked String. Select this item and then click OK. When you get back to the Watch window, you'll see a string containing something a little more akin to what you expected.

Stepping again calls the AddString member function and brings you back to the line with the sprintf. Take another look at the Watch window and see how things are doing.

Wait a minute!

Why is count now 21, and why is ix still 0? Take a look at that for loop again.

```
for (int ix = 0; ix < count; ++count)
```

Oops, again! Incrementing the limit rather than the counter is a common mistake. No wonder the program seemed to have stopped. It was never leaving the loop and was trying to keep filling the list box with ever-increasing numbers. To fix that, change the line to the following:

```
for (int ix = 0; ix < count; ++ix)
```

Now terminate the application, remove the breakpoints, rebuild, and start over again. When you select the Dialog menu item now, the dialog box at least appears on-screen. Unfortunately, the list box appears to be completely empty.

The question here comes down to figuring out from where the failure is coming. You know that the pointer to the list box is valid; otherwise, you would have had another general protection exception. So the problem must be somewhere with the portion that is adding the string. Set a breakpoint on the line that reads

```
plb->AddString(str);
```

Start the program and select the Dialog menu item. When you reach the breakpoint, take a closer look at the plb parameter. Place the cursor over the plb variable and select the Inspect item from the Debug menu.

Looking at the inspection window, you can clearly see that, although you were obviously capable of creating the class object, it doesn't appear to be hooked up to the actual Windows interface item. The TWindow::HWindow data member is NULL, and the TWindow::Attr data member is mostly empty, except for the 101 that you passed to it earlier.

21

If you remember, the SetupWindow function is the location in which class objects become associated with their Windows counterparts. Taking a look at the TMyDialog's version of the function, you can see that you forgot to call the parent's version of the SetupWindow function. Without that call, the actual work that connects the class with the interface element never gets done. To fix this, simply change the function to look like the following:

```
void TMyDialog::SetupWindow()
{
    TDialog::SetupWindow();
    fill_lb(numbers, 20);
}
```

Now, when you next compile and run the program, you will see a fully functional, if boring, application that enables you to display a dialog box that contains a list box of numbers 1 to 20.

Other Debugging Tools

Along with the integrated debugger included in the IDE, other tools are useful in finding and fixing problems with your applications. The first is *WinSight*. This program can display a listing of all the windows currently registered with Windows, whether those windows are visible or not. You can even see the hierarchy of the windows—which windows are children of which others. From there, you can select one or more windows and watch the messages received by them.

Of course, WinSight requires some knowledge of the lower-level Windows API that hasn't been covered in this book. OWL really does do an admirable job of hiding some of the truly messy details of the Windows API, allowing you to use an easy interface. The drawback is that, when there are problems with your code that involves the lower-level Windows API, it sometimes is difficult to track down the problem due to OWL's interface hiding.

One of the most useful programs is WinSpector. Normally, whenever you run your application from outside the IDE, general-protection (GP) faults simply will display a nasty error window and terminate your program. If you have WinSpector running when that GP fault occurs, WinSpector will record the location in your application that caused the GP fault. WinSpector also will attempt to figure out what other sections of your application had been executed immediately prior to the fault occurring, by performing a stack trace. The results of this then can be run through the DFA program to match up the memory locations with the debugging information of your program. The final results often can tell you exactly what line in your application's source code died and what functions had been called before.

Summary

Today's lesson presented a short tutorial on some of the debugging techniques provided by the IDE. You learned about the following subjects:

☐ The debugging commands available in the Integrated Development Environment

☐ Examples of some of the more common programming mistakes

☐ Some of the techniques used to track down and exterminate bugs

Q&A

Q Do my watches need to be limited to variables?

A No. You may supply whole expressions, such as `(count + 1) * 2`.

Q If I set a breakpoint on a line of code, do I have to stop there every single time the program comes to that line?

A No. You can set up conditions on the breakpoint so that, for example, if you are in the middle of a loop, the debugger will break in only when the iterator is equal to a certain value.

21

3

For this review, you look at the Turbo Cribbage game supplied with the Turbo C++ 4.5 package in the TCWIN45\EXAMPLES\OWL\GAMES\CRIBBAGE directory. This implements, as the name suggests, the card game of cribbage. It includes routines for displaying cards and a pegboard, and routines for totaling scores.

How to Play

Before beginning a discussion of the program that implements the game, it probably would be useful (if not downright required) to first have a discussion about how to play the game.

The roots of cribbage extend back to the 1600s and Briton John Suckling. Cribbage is a two-person card game (actually, up to six people could play, but this version is for two players, known as the *Dealer* and the *Pone*). The rules are rather simple, but the variety and strategy still continue to make the game exciting. The numbers and point-counting make it an ideal game for children as well as adults.

Here are the stages of the game.

- ☐ The deal
- ☐ The discard
- ☐ The turn
- ☐ The play
- ☐ Counting player hands
- ☐ Counting the crib

The stages of the game are repeated until one player has acquired 121 points. As soon as 121 points are achieved, the game is over—there is no need to wait until the end of a hand.

Scoring

Different stages of the game involve different scoring possibilities, but most are used throughout the game.

15	Any combination of two or more cards whose sum is 15 (face cards count as 10). Two points are awarded.
Two, three, or four of a kind	If two, three, or four cards have the same face value, 2 points are awarded for each pair combination—the points awarded for 2, 3, and 4 of a kind are 2, 6, and 12 points, respectively.
Run	A sequential series of three or more cards. One point is awarded for each card in the run.
His Nobs	If a player holds a Jack in his or her hand (or in the crib while they're the dealer) that has the same suit as the turned extra card, one point is awarded.
His Heels	If the Starter (extra card) revealed by the Pone is a Jack, the Dealer receives two points.

31	Any combination of cards whose sum is 31 (again, face cards count as 10) scores 2 points.
Flush	Four or more cards of the same suit. One point is awarded for each card in the flush. The crib only allows a five-card flush.
Go	During the play, a player who cannot play declares "Go" and his or her opponent can receive one point if they cannot play.
Last Card	The last player to lay down a card during the play receives one point for the last card.

The Deal

The deal alternates between players every hand. In the two-player version, each player receives six cards face down.

The Discard

Each player selects two cards to discard (face down) into the *crib*. The crib is a bonus hand that awards the points to the Dealer. Because the deal alternates between players, so do the points in the crib. Throwing to the crib involves a bit of strategy because neither player can control the other's crib contribution, and the Starter, which is used as a fifth card for scoring, will not be revealed until after the throw has been made. The Pone will not want to throw obvious points to the crib, but the Dealer has the capability to throw away points to be received when they count the crib. The scoring combinations are explained in a later section ("Counting Player Hands"), but a couple of obvious bad throws would be a 5, cards which add up to 15, or a pair (all of which give points or guarantee points for the Dealer).

The Turn

After both players have thrown to the crib, the Pone cuts the remaining (undealt) cards and the top card is turned over and then is known as the *Starter*. This card is used as a fifth card for counting points in each player's hand and the crib. If a Jack (of any suit) is revealed, then the Dealer receives two points for *His Heels*.

The Play

The Play is an opportunity for both players to play the four cards they kept in their hands in a head-to-head duel. Play begins with the Pone, who plays a card face up from his or her hand and continues with each player alternating cards. Scoring occurs during *The Play* by looking at the cards played by each player as a single sequence of cards—one big hand. Scoring opportunities are available for each player in the form of sums of fifteen; two, three, or four of a kind; runs; Go, Last Card, and 31. Play continues until neither player has any cards left in his or her hand.

Each cycle of play ends when neither player can legally make a play because to do so would cause the total value of upturned cards to exceed the limit of 31 (face cards are counted as 10) or a total of 31 occurs. At the end of each playing cycle the upturned cards are turned over and a new cycle begins with the remaining cards.

As the total approaches 31, a player who cannot play declares, "Go!" and the opponent can continue playing cards (and collecting points, if possible) or collect 1 point for the Go. If a player plays a card that causes the total to become 31, then that player receives 2 points and all overturned cards are turned over for the next playing cycle.

Counting Player Hands

After the play, each player counts the points in their hand, using the Starter as a fifth, extra card. Players can earn points for 15s (commonly counted aloud as "Fifteen-two, fifteen-four", and so on); 2, 3, or 4 of a kind; a flush; runs (of 3 or more cards); or Nobs. Because the Dealer has the advantage of counting the crib's points, the Pone counts his or her hand first.

Counting the Crib

After both players have counted their hands, the Dealer picks up the crib and counts the points (again, including the Starter). The scoring opportunities available when counting the crib are the same as a regular player hand except for the Flush, which is awarded only if all five cards are the same suit.

The Cribbage Example

The base of the program starts in the CARDS.H and CARDS.CPP files where the TCard, TCardGroup, and TDeck classes are declared and defined. The first class models a single card and has data members to describe the card's face value (ace through king), its suit (hearts, spades, diamonds, and clubs), its back style (the card can have one of 13 styles on its back), and whether the card is faceup. All these data members are public, and the two constructors are there simply to make the object's creation simpler.

The TCardGroup class is used to model several cards together as a unit (such as a player's hand or a specific pile of cards). The maximum number of cards allowable in the group must be specified when instances of the class are created, and then you can insert and remove cards from the group via the Insert and Remove member functions, respectively. The Insert member function is overloaded to allow you to add either a single card or another group. This class also defines the array operator (operator[]) in order to provide easy access to the cards contained in the group.

Finally, TDeck is a descendant of TCardGroup that is used to model an entire deck of cards. Because it's derived from TCardGroup, it can make use of all the insertion and removal methods of its base, and TDeck also adds a little extra functionality. The new class has methods for shuffling the deck, cutting it, and for initializing it. This last method, Initialize, is called by the class constructor and simply inserts a card for each member of a standard 52-card deck. The DealCard member function acts to simply remove the top card from the deck.

TDeck also has the two methods EncodeDeck and DecodeDeck. The first function creates a 52-byte string with the contents of the current deck encoded into it. This encoding is done by placing the suit of each card into the upper four bits of a byte while filling the lower four bits with the card's face value. The encoding is done so that the contents of the deck can be saved into an INI file for future retrieval.

These classes so far only model cards and card groups in general terms. In a Windows program, we're going to want to display it. Here's where our friendly neighborhood VBX comes in. Turbo C++ 4.5 automatically installs the MHCD200.VBX file that provides routines for displaying playing cards. For each of these cards you can specify which face value and suit it's to have, and you can select from a variety of back styles. In order to use the VBX, Turbo C++ 4.5 also supplies the VBXGEN program. This reads in a VBX file and automatically creates a header file with the appropriate classes and definitions for using the VBX file. This has been done to create the MHCD200.H header file, which declares the class TVbxMhCardDeck as a descendant of TVbxControl.

The files that make use of this to actually display cards are the CARDDISP.H and CARDDISP.CPP files. These declare and define the TCardDisplay class as a descendant of both TWindow and TCardGroup. This particular window has its style set to that of a child in the constructor, thus making it easy to include within other windows in much the same way as child controls (pushbuttons, list boxes, and so on) can be included within windows; just create a TCardDisplay object in the desired location, and then use it the same way you use other controls, calling member functions to change aspects of its appearance.

The data members of the TCardDisplay class include a list of pointers to VBX card display objects (cardvbx); whether to draw a rectangle around the outside of the control (rectangle); the size of the border between the edge of the control and any rectangle that gets drawn (borderSize); a label for the control and a position for that label (label and labelPos); an array of positions for the cards in the group (cardPos); and an ID that can be used to distinguish this control from others (id).

Table R3.1 lists the member functions of the TCardDisplay class.

Table R3.1. TCardDisplay member functions.

Member Function	Usage
TCardDisplay	Initializes the members of the class and sets the size of the window to that specified by the parameters to the function. Also creates arrays to hold the VBX card objects and their positions.
~TCardDisplay	Cleans up the arrays allocated in the constructor.
Paint	Displays the main parts of the card display, including its border (if specified) and the label.
SetupWindow	Sets the background color for the window, and then hides all the VBX cards whilst setting their backs' colors to the background.
FaceUp	Resets the specified card to its face-up value.
SetCardPosition	Sets the position of the specified card.
Show	This is the function that actually shows a card by setting the VBX properties for the rank, suit, and back-style. The function then calls the VBX's ShowWindow member function.
SetLabel	Resets the label of the card display window.
Insert	Calls the base class TCardGroup's Insert member function, and then calls the Show member function to display the newly inserted card.
Remove	Like Insert, this calls the base class' version of this function, and then proceeds to update the display with the new status of the cards.
operator[]	Accesses a card without removing it.
VBXEventHandler	This is the main entry from the VBX controls. In this case, the function checks to see if it was triggered by a mouse click. If so, it then passes that message along to its parent in the form of a WM_CARD_SELECTED message.

The overall effect of all these member functions, especially with the inclusion of the base classes' functionality and member functions, is that of presenting an encapsulated object that provides for all the needs of an apparent card display control. As you will see shortly, you only create this near-control in a window, and the cards will show themselves with very little prompting.

The cribbage game also includes a pegboard you use to keep track of the scoring. Like the card display, this is achieved in the program via a special child window encapsulated in a single object TCribbageBoard as defined in the BOARD.H and BOARD.CPP files. The data members of the TCribbageBoard class consist of an array to hold the players' names (playerName), an array to hold the players' current points (points), an array to hold the players' previous points (oldpoints), and an array that holds the locations of all the holes in the pegboard (holes). There also is an enum (PegType) that defines the various peg types that can be used (ptPlayer0, ptPlayer1, and ptEmpty). Table R3.2 describes the member functions in this TWindow descendant.

Table R3.2. Member functions of TCribbageBoard.

Member Function	Usage
TCribbageBoard	This constructor initializes several members and sets its window to a specific size. Most of all, though, it fills in the holes array with the locations of all the holes in the pegboard.
SetupWindow	Simply calls the base class' SetupWindow and then initializes the background color for the window.
Reset	Resets the point values to their initial values of 0 for the current points and -1 for the previous points.
PegHole	This actually is what draws an individual peg hole. It does this by referring to the holes array and then either drawing red boxes for Player 0, drawing blue boxes for Player 1, or copying the EMPTY_HOLE bitmap into the specified location. Note the addition of an extra PegHole function that takes an int type for the pegType parameter, and then simply calls the real version of the function, casting pegType to the appropriate PegType enumeration.
AddToScore	Calling this member function adds a specific amount to a specific player's score. At the same time, the pegboard's peg display is updated along with the textual representation of the score. Note how the window's DC is obtained simply by declaring an instance of TClientDC, which then is passed to the PegHole and TextOut functions for drawing.
SetPlayerName	A simple function that sets a specific player's name and then makes sure it's reflected properly in the window.
GetPlayerName	An even simpler function that returns a specific player's name.
Paint	This begins by copying the PEGBOARD bitmap into the window, followed immediately by writing the two players' names and their scores. Finally, the member function calls PegHole to display the two players' scores on the pegboard.

669

Throughout the course of the game, a number of dialog boxes need to be displayed, the source code for which can be found in the DIALOGS.H and DIALOGS.CPP files. The dialog boxes include one that prompts the user to cut the cards (TCutDeckDialog); it displays the backs of 52 cards and responds to a user's click by returning to the position in the deck where the user clicked. After the user has selected a card from the deck, the TCutResultDialog is displayed, which shows both the card the user selected and the one selected by the computer.

The TGoDialog class opens a simple dialog with a single button that reads either OK or Take 1 Point depending upon whether the player can play more cards. This is used when the computer has signified that it cannot play any more cards.

The TQuickPointsDialog displays a number of buttons that allow the player to select the number of points he or she is entitled to. It's rather a simple dialog box, but the interesting part is where the constructor creates an array of 15 TButton objects to represent buttons 15 through 29. These objects will be used to hide those buttons in certain versions of the dialog, when it wouldn't be possible to select more than 14 points.

When it's time to display the total points for either the computer's hand or a hand in which the player miscounted, the TShowPointsDialog appears. This consists of a simple text box filled with the number of points counted and a button that enables the player to request details. If that button is pressed, the height of the dialog box is increased and the extra space at the bottom is filled with a new list box. That list box is filled with the details of the points as passed to the class constructor in the aDetail parameter.

Up to now I've only discussed the lower-level tools that help get the game running. The real meat is contained in the TGameWindow class as defined and declared in the CRIBBAGE.H and CRIBBAGE.CPP files. Just as a simple deck of cards doesn't define the game of cribbage, neither does the TDeck class define the cribbage game in this program; the TGameWindow class has all the actual functionality that defines the cribbage game itself. You should take careful note here of how the lower-level classes have been designed to model real-world objects that are then used in the main game itself. This is the kind of thing for which C++ and other object-oriented programming languages were designed.

Table R3.4 contains a brief list of the member functions contained in the TGameWindow class and their usage. They all act on the member data described in Table R3.3.

Table R3.3. TGameWindow member data.

Member Data	Meaning
handCardPos	An array holding the positions of all the cards that can be displayed in a player's hand
cribCardPos	An array holding the positions of all the cards that can be displayed in the crib

Member Data	Meaning
pegCardPos	An array holding the positions of all the cards that can be displayed in the playing field
topCardPos	An array (of one element) that holds the position of the extra card
player	An array holding the two TCardDisplay objects used as the two player hands
crib	The crib display
pegCards	The playing field cards
topCards	The extra card
board	The pegboard display
deal	One of the buttons used during game play
go	One of the buttons used during game play
done	One of the buttons used during game play
take1	One of the buttons used during game play
take2	One of the buttons used during game play
instructions	A static control that is updated throughout the game with instructions concerning the next move for the player
state	The current state of the game, as defined by the TGameState enumeration
dealer	A number that indicates the current dealer
deck	The main deck of cards being played
currentCribPos	Indicates the current owner of the crib
cardBackStyle	Holds the current style of the card backs
pegCardOwner	Keeps track of the owner of each card played. This is used after the game play is over to move the played cards back to their original players for point scoring.
greenBrush	Because green is such a heavily used color in this game (ever played at a real gambling table without green felt?), it's saved here to keep it from being recreated all the time.
detail	As points are tallied by the computer, their details are recorded here for the player to examine upon request.
detailCount	Holds the current number of lines in the detail list

Table R3.4. `TGameWindow` **member functions.**

Member Function	Usage
TGameWindow	The constructor initializes the window to its set size and inserts all the player controls, buttons, static text areas, and so on.
~TGameWindow	Deallocates the objects created in the constructor
SetupWindow	Sets the background color of the window to green and initializes the game state to that of waiting for a new game
FaceValue	Returns the face value of a card (1 through 10 for Ace through 10 and 10 for all the face cards)
RunSize	Checks to see if a sequence of cards form a run (a sequential list of cards)
ComputeHandPoints	Adds up the points in a given hand and lists the breakdown of those points in a details buffer. This looks for all combinations that total 15, series that form runs, pairs of cards, flushes, and Nobs (a Jack that matches the extra card's suit).
ComputePegPoints	Computes any points that might have been generated by the last card played on the playing field
ResetPegCardDisplay	Clears out the arrays used to keep track of the playing field and the cards' original owners
ReclaimPegCards	Redistributes the cards from the playing field back into their original decks
PegCard	Adds a card from a player to the playing field
ScoreComputerPegPoints	Adds points to the computer's peg score, displaying a message box to let the user know the amount of points
ComputerPlayPegCard	Plays a card onto the playing field for the computer
TurnOverPegCards	Turns over the cards on the playing field to hide their faces
PlayableCards	Searches a group of cards for all that can be played on the playing field without going over the maximum total of 31. It returns an index to the first one playable, and optionally fills in an array with the indices of all those that are playable.
SetState	Changes the game state, showing the appropriate buttons and filling the instruction box with appropriate text

Member Function	Usage
Deal	Shuffles the deck and deals the top card out as the extra card. Then, if it's the computer's turn to deal, Deal actually deals the cards to the two players. If it's the player's turn to deal, then this just sets the game state to gsDeal and waits for the player to click the Deal button.
ShowPoints	Moves the playing field cards back into their respective decks and then counts the total points for each hand. If the player miscounts, then the computer takes the missing points.
NewGame	Responds to the New | Game menu item by reinitializing the playing field and deck, asking the player for his or her name, asking the player to cut the deck, and then dealing the first hand
DealButton	Responds to the Deal button (which is visible during the gsDeal game state) by dealing the hands, discarding the computer's two cards, and then waiting for the user to discard
FixDeck	Moves all the cards from the playing field, as well as the players' hands, the crib, and the extra card back into the deck
SaveGame	Saves the current game state
Exit	Exits the program
SaveGameEnabler	Enables/disables the Save | Game menu item depending upon whether or not a game is currently in progress
AboutBox	Displays the about box dialog box
LoadGame	Loads a saved game
Paint	Draws the DECK bitmap. Note that all the other painting is done automatically by the other classes created.
EvCtlColor	Ensures that the background looks green, especially with regards to a slight idiosyncrasy with button controls (described in the source code)
CardSelected	This is a handler for the WM_CARD_SELECTED message generated by the TCardDisplay class in response to a VBX message. If the player currently is discarding cards to the crib, then this moves the selected cards. If the player is playing a card to the playing field, then this moves the selected card appropriately.

Table R3.4. `TGameWindow` member functions.

Member Function	Usage
PegCardsSum	Computes the total value of all the cards in the playing field
CanClose	This function, which is called whenever the program is asked to quit, checks to make sure the user doesn't want to abandon any game that might currently be in progress.
GoButton	Responds to the Go button and checks to see if the player is capable of playing a card. If this verifies that the player is capable at this point, then it issues a warning. Otherwise it just sends the game play over to the computer.
DoneButton	Responds to the Done button, which is available while the player is moving cards into the crib. This checks to make sure the player moved exactly two cards into the crib and then turns the crib cards face down, the extra card face up, and then has the computer play a card.
Take1Button	When the computer can't play any more cards and the player can, the player is allowed to take either one or two points (if they're below or at 31 points, respectively). The Take 1 and Take 2 buttons are visible at these points and simply add the corresponding number of points to the player's score.
Take2Button	*See `Take1Button`*
ComputerDiscard	Discards two cards from the computers hand to the crib
ComputerPlayCard	Has the computer play a card. This includes logic to account for the times when the player has specified that he or she can't play any more cards to the playing field.
CountPoints	Counts the points in the playing field after the player has just played a card. This then displays a dialog box that enables the player to select the number of points gained in the last turn, and it checks to make sure the player counted properly.

There are many interrelationships within the `TGameWindow` class. Many of the functions are there simply for the use of other functions, which is evidenced by the fact that there are so few listed in the response table. The most important lesson to learn here is how all the other classes are brought together in the main window and used to represent the various parts of the game to the user. It also is an interesting game to learn to play.

Variations and Expanding the Game

A number of variations in the game exist, including the number of players and how many points to play for in a game (achieving 121 points before your opponent scores 61 or scoring 61 before they get 31 is known as a *lurch*). Tournaments are available and special awards exist for those who receive a perfect hand (containing 29 points), those who have 0-point hands, receiving a hand whose digits are those of their ZIP code, and so on. Other variations include awarding points overlooked by one player and discovered by the other in an act known as *Muggins*.

A good project for you now would be to figure out how to implement some of the above variations or, better yet, to give the computer a little more strategy when it plays its game against you. I mean, you don't want to be able to win *all* the time, do you?

Answers

> **Note:** Because of space limitations, not every Exercise has an answer presented here.

Answers to Day 1, "Getting Started"

Quiz

1. The program generates the string C++ in 21 Days?.

2. The program generates no output because the cout statement appears inside a comment! The function main simply returns 0.

3. The cout statement is missing the semicolon.

Exercise

```
// Exercise program

#include <iostream.h>

main()
{
   cout << "I am a C++ Programmer";
   return 0;
}
```

Answers to Day 2, "C++ The Preprocessor, Variables, and Operators"

Quiz

1. The following table indicates which identifiers are valid and which are not (and why).

Identifiers	Valid?	Reason (If Invalid)
numFiles	Yes	
n0Distance_02_Line	Yes	
0Weight	No	Starts with a digit
Bin Number	No	Contains a space
static	No	Reserved keyword
Static	Yes	

2. The output is

12

8

2

3.64851

150.5

3. The output is

12

8

2

4. The output is

12

27

5. The output is

TRUE

TRUE

TRUE

FALSE

Exercise

1. Here is my version of the function max.

```
int max(int i, int j)
{

    return (i > j) ? i : j;
}
```

2. Here is my version of the function min.

```
int min(int i, int j)
{
    return (i < j) ? i : j;
}
```

3. Here is my version of the function abs.

```
int abs(int i)
{
    return (i > 0) ? i : -i;
}
```

4. Here is my version of the function isOdd.

```
int isOdd(int i)
{
    return (i % 2 != 0) ? 1 : 0;
}
```

Answers to Day 3, "The Decision-Making Constructs and Loops"

Quiz

1. The simpler version is

```
if (i > 0 && i < 10)
   cout << "i = " << i << endl;
```

2. The simpler version is

```
if (i > 0) {
   j = i * i;
   cout << "j = " << j << endl;
}
else if (i < 0) {
   j = 4 * i;
   cout << "j = " << j << endl;
}
else {
   j = 10 + i;
   cout << "j = " << j << endl;
}
```

3. False. When the variable i stores values between -10 and -1, the statements in the clauses of the two if statements execute. In this case, all the assignment statements are executed. By contrast, it is impossible to execute the statements in both the if and else clauses of the supposedly equivalent if-else statement.

4. The simplified version is

```
if (i > 0 && i < 100)
     j = i * i;
else if (i >= 100)
     j = i;
else
     j = 1;
```

Notice that I eliminate the original first else if clause because the tested condition is a subset of the first tested condition. Consequently, the condition in the first else if never gets examined and the associated assign statement never gets executed. This is an example of what is called *dead code*.

5. The tested condition is always false. Consequently, the statements in the clause never are executed. This is another example of dead code.

6. The statements inside the loop fail to alter the value of i. Consequently, the tested condition is always true and the loop iterates endlessly.

7. The output of the program consists of the numbers 3, 5, and 7.

8. The output of the program is an endless sequence of lines that display the value of 3. The reason for the indefinite looping is that the loop control variable is not incremented.

9. The nested `for` loops use the same loop control variable. This program will not run.

10. Both `for` loops declare the variable `i` as their loop control variable. The compiler generates an error for this duplication.

11. The condition of the `while` loop is always true. Therefore, the loop iterates endlessly.

12. The program lacks a statement which explicitly initializes the variable `factorial` to 1. Without this statement, the program automatically initializes the variable `factorial` to 0—the wrong value. Consequently, the `for` loop ends up assigning 0 to the variable `factorial` in every iteration. Here is the correct version of the code.

```
int n;
double factorial = 1;
cout << "Enter positive integer: ";
cin >> n;
for (int i = 1; i <= n; i++)
   factorial *= i;
cout << n << "! = " << factorial;
```

Exercises

1. Here is my version of program IF5.CPP.

```
// C++ program to solve quadratic equation

#include <iostream.h>
#include <math.h>

main()
{
  double A, B, C, discrim, root1, root2, twoA;

  cout << "Enter coefficients for equation A*X^2 + B*X + C\n";
  cout << "Enter A: ";
  cin >> A;
  cout << "Enter B: ";
  cin >> B;
  cout << "Enter C: ";
  cin >> C;

  if (A != 0) {
    twoA = 2 * A;
    discrim = B * B - 4 * A * C;
    if (discrim > 0) {
      root1 = (-B + sqrt(discrim)) / twoA;
      root2 = (-B - sqrt(discrim)) / twoA;
      cout << "root1 = " << root1 << endl;
      cout << "root2 = " << root2 << endl
    }
    else if (discrim < 0) {

      discrim = -discrim;
      cout << "root1 = (" << -B/twoA
           << ") + i (" << sqrt(discrim) / twoA <<")\n";
```

```
      cout << "root2 = (" << -B/twoA
           << ") - i (" << sqrt(discrim) / twoA << ")\n";
    }
    else {
      root1 = -B / 2 / A;
      root2 = root1;
      cout << "root1 = " << root1 << endl;
      cout << "root2 = " << root2 << endl;
    }
  }
  else
    cout << "root = " << (-C / B) << endl;


  return 0;
}
```

2. Here is my version of program SWITCH2.CPP.

```
// C++ program which uses the switch statement to implement
// a simple four-function calculator program

#include <iostream.h>

const int TRUE = 1;
const int FALSE = 0;

main()
{
  double x, y, z;
  char op;
  int error = FALSE;

  cout << "Enter the first operand: ";
  cin >> x;
  cout << "Enter the operator: ";
  cin >> op;
  cout << "Enter the second operand: ";
  cin >> y;

  switch (op) {
    case '+':
      z = x + y;
      break;
    case '-':
      z = x - y;
      break;
    case '*':
      z = x * y;
      break;
    case '/':
      if (y != 0)
        z = x / y;
      else
        error = TRUE;
      break;
```

```
      default:
        error = TRUE;
    }

    if (!error)
      cout << x << " " << op << " " << y << " = " << z << endl;
    else
      cout << "Bad operator or division-by-zero error\n";

    return 0;
  }
```

3. Here is my version of program FOR5.CPP.

```
// Program calculates a sum of odd integers in
// the range of 11 to 121

#include <iostream.h>

const int FIRST = 11;
const int LAST = 121;

main()
{
    double sum = 0;
    for (int i = FIRST; i <= LAST; i += 2)
      sum += (double)i;

    cout << "Sum of odd integers from "
         << FIRST << " to " << LAST << " = "
         << sum << endl;
    return 0;
}
```

4. Here is my version of program WHILE2.CPP.

```
// Program calculates a sum of squared odd integers in
// the range of 11 to 121

#include <iostream.h>

const int FIRST = 11;
const int LAST = 121;

main()
{
    double sum = 0;
    int i = FIRST;
    while (i <= LAST) {
      sum += double(i * i++);
    }
    cout << "Sum of squared odd integers from "
         << FIRST << " to " << LAST << " = "
         << sum << endl;
    return 0;
}
```

5. Here is my version of program DOWHILE2.CPP.

```
// Program calculates a sum of squared odd integers in
// the range of 11 to 121

#include <iostream.h>

const int FIRST = 11;
const int LAST = 121;

main()
{
    double sum = 0;
    int i = FIRST;
    do {
      sum += double(i * i++);
    } while (i <= LAST);
    cout << "Sum of squared odd integers from "
         << FIRST << " to " << LAST << " = "
         << sum << endl;
    return 0;
}
```

Answers to Day 4, "User-Defined Types and Pointers"

Quiz

1. The enumerated values on and off appear in two different enumerated types. Here is a correct version of these statements.

```
enum Boolean { false, true };
enum State { state_on, state_off };
enum YesNo { yes, no };
enum DiskDriveStatus { drive_on , drive_off };
```

2. False. The enumerated type YesNo is correctly declared.

3. The program lacks a delete statement before the return statement. Here is the correct version.

```
#include <iostream.h>
main()
{
  int *p = new int;
  cout << "Enter a number : ";
  cin >> *p;
  cout << "The square of " << *p << " = " << (*p * *p);
  delete p;
  return 0;
}
```

Exercises

1. Here is my version of PTR6.CPP.

```cpp
/* C++ program that demonstrates pointers to structured types */

#include <iostream.h>
#include <stdio.h>
#include <math.h>

const MAX_RECT = 4;
const TRUE = 1;
const FALSE = -1;

struct point {
  double x;
  double y;
};

struct rect {
  point ulc; // upper left corner
  point lrc; // lower right corner
  double area;
  int id;
};

typedef rect rectArr[MAX_RECT];

main()
{
  rectArr r;
  rect temp;
  rect* pr = r;
  rect* pr2;
  double length, width;
  int offset;
  int inOrder;

  for (int i = 0; i < MAX_RECT; i++, pr++) {
    cout << "Enter (X,Y) coord. for ULC of rect. # "
         << i << " : ";
    cin >> pr->ulc.x >> pr->ulc.y;
    cout << "Enter (X,Y) coord. for LRC of rect. # "
         << i << " : ";
    cin >> pr->lrc.x >> pr->lrc.y;
    pr->id = i;
    length = fabs(pr->ulc.x - pr->lrc.x);
    width = fabs(pr->ulc.y - pr->lrc.y);
    pr->area = length * width;
  }

  // sort the rectangles by areas
  offset = MAX_RECT;
  do {
    offset = (8 * offset) / 11;
    offset = (offset == 0) ? 1 : offset;
    inOrder = TRUE;
```

Answers

```
            pr = r;
            pr2 = r + offset;
            for (int i = 0;
                 i < MAX_RECT - offset;
                 i++, pr++, pr2++)
              if (pr->area > pr2->area) {
                inOrder = FALSE;
                temp = *pr;
                *pr = *pr2;
                *pr2 = temp;
              }
        } while (!(offset == 1 && inOrder));

        pr = r; // reset pointer
        // display rectangles sorted by area
        for (i = 0; i < MAX_RECT; i++, pr++)
          printf("Rect # %d has area %5.4lf\n", pr->id, pr->area);
        return 0;
    }
```

2. Here is my version of structure intArrStruct.

```
struct intArrStruct {
  int* dataPtr;
  unsigned size;
};
```

3. Here is my version of structure matStruct.

```
struct matStruct {
  double* dataPtr;
  unsigned rows;
  unsigned columns;
};
```

Answers to Day 5, "Functions"

Quiz

1. The output of the program is

   ```
   a = 10 and b = 3
   ```

   The function swap fails to swap the arguments a and b because it only swaps a copy of their values.

2. The output of the program is

   ```
   a = 3 and b = 10
   ```

   The function swap succeeds in swapping the arguments a and b because it uses reference parameters. Consequently, the changes in the values of parameters i and j go beyond the scope of the function itself.

3. The second version of function inc has a default argument, which, when used, hinders the compiler from determining which version of inc to call. The compiler flags a compile-time error for such functions.

4. Because the second parameter has a default argument, the third one must also have a default argument. Here is one version of the correct definition of function `volume`.

```
double volume(double length, double width = 1, double height = 1)
{
    return length * width * height;
}
```

5. The parameter `i` is a lowercase letter. However, the function uses the uppercase `I` in the assignment statement. The compiler complains that the identifier `I` is not defined.

6. The function main requires a prototype of function `sqr`. The correct version of the program is

```
#include <iostream.h>

// declare prototype of function sqr
double sqr(double);

main()
{
    double x = 5.2;

    cout << x << "^2 = " << sqr(x);
    return 0;
}

double sqr(double x)
{ return x * x; }
```

7. The function is

```
double factorial(int i)
{ return (i > 1) ? double(i) * factorial(i-1) : 1; }
```

Exercises

Here is my version of program OVERLOD2.CPP.

```
// C++ program illustrates function overloading
// and default arguments

#include <iostream.h>

// inc version for int types
void inc(int& i, int diff = 1)
{
    i = i + diff;
}

// inc version for double types
void inc(double& x, double diff = 1)
{
    x = x + diff;
}
```

```
// inc version for char types
void inc(char& c, int diff = 1)
   c = c + diff;
}

main()
{
   char c = 'A';
   int i = 10;
   double x = 10.2;

   // discplay initial valus
   cout << "c = " << c << endl
        << "i = " << i << endl
        << "x = " << x << endl;

   // invoke the inc functions using default arguments
   inc(c);
   inc(i);
   inc(x);

   // display updatecd values
   cout << "After using the overloaded inc function" << endl
        << "c = " << c << endl
        << "i = " << i << endl
        << "x = " << x << endl;
   return 0;
}
```

Answers to Day 6, "Arrays"

Quiz

1. The program displays the factorials for the numbers 0 to 4.

   ```
   x[0] = 1
   x[1] = 1
   x[2] = 2
   x[3] = 6
   x[4] = 24
   ```

2. The program displays the square roots for the numbers 0 to 4.

   ```
   x[0] = 0
   x[1] = 1
   x[2] = 1.41421
   x[3] = 1.73205
   x[4] = 2
   ```

3. The first for loop should iterate between 1 and MAX-1 and not between 0 and MAX-1. The first loop iteration uses an out-of-range index.

Exercise

Here is my version of program ARRAY7.CPP.

```cpp
// C++ program that sorts arrays using the Comb sort method
#include <iostream.h>

const int MAX = 10;
const int TRUE = 1;
const int FALSE = 0;

int obtainNumData()
{
   int m;
   do { // obtain number of data points
      cout << "Enter number of data points [2 to "
           << MAX << "] : ";
      cin >> m;
      cout << endl;
   } while (m < 2 || m > MAX);
   return m;
}

void inputArray(int intArr[], int n)
{
   // prompt user for data
   for (int i = 0; i < n; i++) {
      cout << "arr[" << i << "] : ";
      cin >> intArr[i];
   }
}

void showArray(int intArr[], int n)
{
   for (int i = 0; i < n; i++) {
      cout.width(5);
      cout << intArr[i] << " ";
   }
   cout << endl;
}

void sortArray(int intArr[], int n)
{
   int offset, temp, inOrder;

   offset = n;
   while (offset > 1) {
      offset /= 2;
      do {
         inOrder = TRUE;
         for (int i = 0, j = offset; i < (n - offset); i++, j++) {
            if (intArr[i] > intArr[j]) {
               inOrder = FALSE;
               temp = intArr[i];
               intArr[i] = intArr[j];
               intArr[j] = temp;
            }
         }
```

```
        } while (!inOrder);
    }
}

main()
{
    int arr[MAX];
    int n;

    n = obtainNumData();
    inputArray(arr, n);
    cout << "Unordered array is:\n";
    showArray(arr, n);
    sortArray(arr, n);
    cout << "\nSorted array is:\n";
    showArray(arr, n);
    return 0;
}
```

Answers to Day 7, "Strings and Managing I/O"

Quiz

1. The output statement cannot contain the inserter operator >>. The statement can be corrected as follows:

    ```
    cout << "Enter a number ";
    cin >> x;
    ```

2. Because the variable x appears in the first and last items, the last number overwrites the first number.

3. The string s1 is smaller than string s2. Consequently, the call to function strcpy causes a program bug.

4. Using the function strncpy to include the constant MAX as the third argument ensures that string s1 receives MAX characters (excluding the null terminator) from string s1:

    ```
    #include <iostream.h>
    #include <string.h>
    const in MAX = 10;
    main()
    {
      char s1[MAX+1];
      char s2[] = "12345678901234567890123 4567890";
      strncpy(s1, s2, MAX);
      cout << "String 1 is " << s1
           << "\nString 2 is " << s2;
    ```

```
    return 0;
}
```

5. Because the string in variable s1 is less than that in variable s2, the statement assigns a negative number (-13 to be exact) in variable i.

6. The call to function strcmp compares the substrings "C++" with "Pascal" because the arguments include an offset value. Because "C++" is less than "Pascal", the statement assigns a negative number (-13 again) in variable i.

7. False! Although the basic idea for the function is sound, dimensioning the local variable requires a constant. One solution is to use the same constant, call it MAX_STRING_SIZE, to size up the arguments of parameter s.

```
int hasNoLowerCase(const char* s)
{
  char s2[MAX_STRING_SIZE+1];
  strcpy(s2, s);
  strupr(s2);
  return (strcmp(s, s2) == 0) ? 1 : 0);
}
```

The other solution uses dynamic allocation to create a dynamic local string that stores a copy of the argument of parameter s. This solution works with all arguments of parameter s:

```
int hasNoLowerCase(const char* s)
{
  char *s2 = new char[strlen(s)+1];
  int i;
  strcpy(s2, s);
  strupr(s2);
  // store result in variable i
  i = (strcmp(s, s2) == 0) ? 1 : 0);
  delete [] s2; // first delete local dynamic string
  return i; // then return the result of the function
}
```

Exercises

1. Here is my version of program OUT3.CPP.

```
// C++ program uses the printf function for formatted output

#include <stdio.h>
#include <math.h>

main()
```

```
{
  double x;

  // display table heading
  printf("     X          Sqrt(X)\n");
  printf("----------\n");
  x = 2;
  printf("    %3.0lf         %3.4lf\n", x, sqrt(x));
  x++;
  printf("    %3.0lf         %3.4lf\n", x, sqrt(x));
  x++;
  printf("    %3.0lf         %3.4lf\n", x, sqrt(x));
  x++;
  printf("    %3.0lf         %3.4lf\n", x, sqrt(x));
  x++;
  printf("    %3.0lf         %3.4lf\n", x, sqrt(x));
  x++;
  printf("    %3.0lf         %3.4lf\n", x, sqrt(x));
  x++;
  printf("    %3.0lf         %3.4lf\n", x, sqrt(x));
  x++;
  printf("    %3.0lf         %3.4lf\n", x, sqrt(x));
  x++;
  printf("    %3.0lf         %3.4lf\n", x, sqrt(x));
  return 0;
}
```

2. Here is my version of program OUT4.CPP.

```
// C++ program which displays octal and hexadecimal integers

#include <iostream.h>
#include <stdio.h>

main()
{
  long i;
  cout << "Enter an integer : ";
  cin >> i;

  printf("%ld = %lX (hex) = %lo (octal)\n", i, i, i);
  return 0;
}
```

3. Here is my version of function strlen.

```
int strlen(const char* s)
{
  int i = 0;
  while (s[i] != '\0')
    i++;
  return i;
}
```

4. Here is the other version of function strlen.

```
int strlen(const char* s)
{
  char *p = s;
  while (p++ != '\0')
    /* do nothing */;
  return p - s;
}
```

5. Here is my version of program STRING5.CPP.

```
#include <stdio.h>
#include <string.h>

main()
{
  char str[] = "2*(X+Y)/(X+Z) - (X+10)/(Y-5)";
  char strCopy[41];
  char* tkn[3] = { "+-*/ ()", "( )", "+-*/ " };
  char* ptr;

  strcpy(strCopy, str); // copy str into strCopy
  printf("%s\n", str);
  printf("Using token string %s\n", tkn[0]);
  // the first call
  ptr = strtok(str, tkn[0]);
  printf("String is broken into: ");
  while (ptr) {
    printf(", %s", ptr);
    // must make first argument a NULL character
    ptr = strtok(NULL, tkn[0]);
  }
```

```
      strcpy(str, strCopy); // restore str
      printf("\nUsing token string %s\n", tkn[1]);
      // the first call
      ptr = strtok(str, tkn[1]);
      printf("String is broken into: ");
      while (ptr) {
        printf(", %s", ptr);
        // must make first argument a NULL character
        ptr = strtok(NULL, tkn[1]);
      }

      strcpy(str, strCopy); // restore str
      printf("\nUsing token string %s\n", tkn[2]);
      // the first call
      ptr = strtok(str, tkn[2]);
      printf("String is broken into: ");
      while (ptr) {
        printf(", %s", ptr);
        // must make first argument a NULL character
        ptr = strtok(NULL, tkn[2]);
      }
      printf("\n\n");
      return 0;
  }
```

Answers to Day 8, "Object-Oriented Programming and C++ Classes"

Quiz

1. By default, the members of a class are protected. Therefore, the class declaration has no public member and cannot be used to create instances.

2. The fourth constructor has a default argument, which makes it redundant with respect to the fifth constructor. The C++ compiler detects such an error.

3. True. `String("Hello Turbo C++")` creates a temporary instance of class `String` and then assigns it to the instance s.

4. Yes. The new statements are valid.

Exercise

Here is the implementation of function `main` in my version of program CLASS7.CPP.

```
main()
{
   Complex c[5];
   c[1].assign(3, 5);
   c[2].assign(7, 5);
   c[4].assign(2, 3);

   c[3] = c[1] + c[2];
   cout << c[1] << " + " << c[2] << " = " << c[3] << endl;
   cout << c[3] << " + " << c[4] << " = ";
   c[3] += c[4];
   cout << c[3] << endl;
   return 0;
}
```

Answers to Day 9, "Basic Stream File I/O"

Quiz

1. False. The `read` and `write` functions cannot store and recall the dynamic data, which is accessed by a pointer member of a structure or a class.

2. True.

3. True.

4. False.

Exercise

Here is the code for member function `binSearch` and the updated function `main` in program IO4.CPP. (The output also shows the new global constant `NOT_FOUND` and the updated class declaration.)

```
const unsigned NOT_FOUND = 0xffff;

class VmArray
{
protected:
   fstream f;
   unsigned size;
   double badIndex;

public:
   VmArray(unsigned Size, const char* filename);
   ~VmArray()
      { f.close(); }
   unsigned getSize() const
      { return size; }
```

```
    boolean writeElem(const char* str, unsigned index);
    boolean readElem(char* str, unsigned index);
    void Combsort();
    unsigned binSearch(const char* search);
};

unsigned VmArray::binSearch(const char* search)
{
    unsigned low = 0;
    unsigned high = size - 1;
    unsigned median;
    char str[STR_SIZE+1];
    int result;

    do {
        median = (low + high) / 2;
        readElem(str, median);
        result = strcmp(search, str);
        if (result > 0)
            low = median + 1;
        else
            high = median - 1;
    } while (result != 0 && low <= high);
    return (result == 0) ? median : NOT_FOUND;
}

main()
{
    const unsigned NUM_ELEMS = 10;
    char* data[] = { "Michigan", "California", "Virginia", "Main",
                     "New York", "Florida", "Nevada", "Alaska",
                     "Ohio", "Maryland" };
    VmArray arr(NUM_ELEMS, "arr.dat");
    char str[STR_SIZE+1];
    char c;
    unsigned index;

    // assign values to array arr
    for (unsigned i = 0; i < arr.getSize(); i++) {
        strcpy(str, data[i]);
        arr.writeElem(str, i);
    }
    // display unordered array
    cout << "Unsorted arrays is:\n";
    for (i = 0; i < arr.getSize(); i++) {
        arr.readElem(str, i);
        cout << str << endl;
    }
    // pause
    cout << "\nPress any key and then Return to sort the array...";
    cin >> c;
    // sort the array
    arr.Combsort();
    // display sorted array
    cout << "Sorted arrays is:\n";
    for (i = 0; i < arr.getSize(); i++) {
```

```
        arr.readElem(str, i);
        cout << str << endl
    }
    // pause
    cout << "\nPress any key and then Return to search the array...";
    cin >> c;
    // search for array elements using the pointer data
    for (i = 0; i < NUM_ELEMS; i++) {
        index = arr.binSearch(data[i]);
        if (index != NOT_FOUND)
            cout << "Found " << data[i]
                 << " at index " << index << endl;
        else
            cout << "No match for " << data[i] << endl;
    }
    return 0;
}
```

Answers to Day 10, "The C++ *string* Class, Templates, and the Class Library"

Quiz

1. CSTRING.H must be included to use the C++ string class.

2. A string class variable can be declared either with or without an initial value, such as the following:

   string s1;
   string s2("Initial Value");

3. The string class includes functions for comparing it to a C-style string.

   Operators ==, >, <, >=, <= and d have versions that compare string class variables to C-style strings.

   Another way is to compare the C-style element of the string class variable to the C-string, as in the following:

   result = strcmp(CStyleStr, stringClassVar.c_str());

4. The task performed by the replace member function finds text and substitutes for it in one call.

5. The second character in a string class variable is at index 1. Addressing is the same as with any array, with index 0 being the first item.

6. This can be done with the following declaration:

   string myString("12");

7. Given string s1 = "11"; string s2 = "2112";

    a. The result of s1 + s2 is "112112"

    b. s2.contains(s1); returns 1 because "11" is found in "2112"

    c. s1 > s2 is false

    d. s2.find(s1, 0); returns 1 because "11" is located beginning at index 1 in "2112"

8. False. Templates aren't magic; the compiler still has to be able to figure out how to execute each statement in a template exactly as if it weren't a template. For example, the < comparisons in the Low() template function don't make sense for classes.

```
template <class T> const T& Low(const T& a, const T& b, const T& c)
{
    if (a < b)
        {
        if (a < c)
            return a;
        }
    else if (b < c)
        return b;
    return c;
}
```

What does the < operator mean for a class? There are two solutions.

☐ Write versions of the template that know how to deal with specific classes (which almost defeats the purpose of using templates).

☐ Write operators for those classes. (For example, if you wanted to use Low() with a class of your own, you'd need to provide an operator < function that would figure out what makes one class less than another.)

Exercises

1. C-style string of value "12"
```
char myCStyleString[] = "12";
```

C++ string class item of value "12";

either one of the following:

```
string myString("12");
string myString = "12";
```

2. The following is a function that accepts a C++ string as a calling argument and that writes its value to the computer screen:

```
void ShowString(string& myString)
{
   cout << myString;
}
```

3. The following function writes out each character of the passed string individually and then returns the size of the string:

```
size_t ShowString(string& myString)
{
   size_t index;
   size_t len = myString.length();

   // write each char from the string to the screen
   // one for each pass through the loop

   for (index = 0; index < len; ++index)
      cout << myString[index];

   return len; // return the length of the string
}
```

4. The following shows a way to reverse the characters in a C++ string using the strrev function:

```
strrev(myString.c_str());
```

Answers to Day 11, "Programming Windows with OWL 2.5"

Quiz

1. False. The type's already changed between Windows 3.1 and Windows NT, for example. (WORD, for example, changed from an unsigned int to an unsigned short.) The idea, however, is that if you use the Windows types, you won't have to make any changes to your own code.

2. True. Even though OWL uses C++ classes, OWL itself is still written using the same functions that a C program would. Using OWL, you get to let the Borland programmers do the work for you.

Answers to Day 12, "Basic Windows"

Quiz

1. True.
2. True.
3. False.

Answers to Day 13, "OWL Controls"

Quiz

1. False. Only the text for controls with SS_SIMPLE style are unchangeable.
2. True.
3. True.
4. True.
5. True, because every control is a window.
6. True, but the OWL-prescribed method is to use the EV_BN_CLICKED macro.

Answers to Day 14, "Dialog Boxes"

Quiz

1. False. You don't need the .RES file until after linking the object modules and libraries.
2. False. There does, however, need to be a method by which the user can signal the dialog box to close itself. This is often done with buttons that, though labeled differently, return IDOK and IDCANCEL.
3. True.
4. False. The best examples of nested dialogs are those related to setting up the printer.
5. False. Dialog boxes can be stand-alone windows.

Answers to Day 15, "Grouped Controls"

Quiz

1. False. The check box can replace the two radio buttons only if these buttons offer opposite alternatives.

2. True.

3. True. Each check box can be independently toggled.

4. False.

Answers to Day 16, "List Box Controls"

Quiz

1. True.

2. True.

3. False. LBN_SELCHANGE indicates that a new item is selected.

4. False. LBN_DBLCLICK indicates that a list item is selected with a double mouse click.

5. False. LBS_STANDARD includes the LBS_SORT style and therefore creates sorted list boxes.

Answers to Day 17, "Scroll Bars, Combo Boxes, and VBX Controls"

Quiz

1. True.

2. False. You need to respond to the CBN_EDITUPDATE message.

3. False. The items are sorted, but not unique. You can insert multiple copies of the same string.

4. True. In order to maintain a chronological order, you must prevent automatic sorting.

5. False.

6. True.

7. False.

Answers to Day 18, "MDI Windows"

Quiz

1. False. MDI child windows cannot have their own menus.

2. False. MDI child windows are confined to the frame area of their parent window.

3. False. You cannot nest MDI child windows.

Answers to Day 20, "OLE 2"

Quiz

1. Linking. This ensures that there is one source document only.

2. `TOleWindow`. `TOleView` is derived from `TOleWindow`.

3. The server must be registered.

Index

functions

SAMS
PUBLISHING

Sams
Learning
Center

Listings

SAMS
PUBLISHING

Sams
Learning
Center

Listings

M

programs

SAMS
PUBLISHING

Sams
Learning
Center

Add to Your Sams Library Today with the Best Books for Programming, Operating Systems, and New Technologies

The easiest way to order is to pick up the phone and call

1-800-428-5331

between 9:00 a.m. and 5:00 p.m. EST.
For faster service please have your credit card available.

ISBN	Quantity	Description of Item	Unit Cost	Total Cost
0-672-30441-4		Borland C++ 4 Developer's Guide (book/disk)	$39.95	
0-672-30471-6		Teach Yourself Advanced C in 21 Days (book/disk)	$24.95	
0-672-30177-6		Windows Programmer's Guide to Borland C++ Tools (book/disk)	$39.95	
0-672-30030-3		Windows Programmer's Guide to Serial Communications (book/disk)	$39.95	
0-672-30097-4		Windows Programmer's Guide to Resources (book/disk)	$34.95	
0-672-30226-8		Windows Programmer's Guide to OLE/DDE (book/disk)	$34.95	
0-672-30364-7		Win32 API Desktop Reference (book/CD)	$49.95	
0-672-30236-5		Windows Programmer's Guide to DLLs and Memory Management (book/disk)	$34.95	
0-672-30312-4		Mastering Windows Programming with Borland C++ 4 (book/disk)	$39.95	
0-672-30338-8		Inside Windows File Formats (book/disk)	$29.95	
0-672-30299-3		Uncharted Windows Programming (book/disk)	$44.95	
0-672-30239-X		Windows Developer's Guide to Application Design (book/disk)	$34.95	
❏ 3 ½" Disk		Shipping and Handling: See information below.		
❏ 5 ¼" Disk		TOTAL		

Shipping and Handling: $4.00 for the first book, and $1.75 for each additional book. Floppy disk: add $1.75 for shipping and handling. If you need to have it NOW, we can ship product to you in 24 hours for an additional charge of approximately $18.00, and you will receive your item overnight or in two days. Overseas shipping and handling adds $2.00 per book and $8.00 for up to three disks. Prices subject to change. Call for availability and pricing information on latest editions.

201 W. 103rd Street, Indianapolis, Indiana 46290

1-800-428-5331 — Orders   1-800-835-3202 — FAX   1-800-858-7674 — Customer Service